GUIDE TO THE
HOOVER INSTITUTION ARCHIVES

GUIDE TO THE
HOOVER INSTITUTION ARCHIVES

CHARLES G. PALM
and
DALE REED

Hoover Institution Press
Stanford University • Stanford, California

This work was made possible through grants from the Research Collections
Program of the National Endowment for the Humanities and the Center for
Research in International Studies (Stanford University).

Hoover Bibliographical Series 59

ISBN # 0–8179–2591–0

Library of Congress Catalog Card Number: 79–91030

Printed in the United States of America

To the memory of
Witold S. Sworakowski,
1903–1979

Contents

Foreword

For more than a half century the Hoover Institution has served the international community of scholars by freely offering them original documentation indispensable to their research. In pursuing this mission the Institution has followed the intentions of its founder, Herbert Hoover, when he initiated in 1919 the collecting program that led to establishment of a major archival repository on the campus of Stanford University.

Publication of this comprehensive *Guide to the Hoover Institution Archives* represents another step forward in the Institution's effort to make its holdings better known and more accessible for research purposes. I am particularly pleased that appearance of the guide closely follows completion of the new Herbert Hoover Memorial Building, which now houses the archives. These modern archival facilities enhance our ability to serve present researchers expeditiously and to preserve our collections for future scholars.

On behalf of the Hoover Institution, I wish to express gratitude to the National Endowment for the Humanities for a grant that made preparation of this guide possible. I also wish to thank the Center for Research in International Studies at Stanford University for a grant that helped with the planning and initial phases of the guide project.

It is always gratifying to hear about the excellence of Hoover Institution collections from writers and scholars who use our holdings. In presenting this guide I am reminded in particular of the words of Dr. Frederick H. Burkhardt, at the time chairman of the National Commission of Libraries and Information Science and longtime president of the American Council of Learned Societies, who, endorsing the passage of legislation for the Herbert Hoover Federal Memorial, stated that the Hoover Institution's special collections "will continue to be useful as far into the future as we can now see." We hope that publication of this guide will facilitate that use for many years to come.

W. GLENN CAMPBELL
Director

Hoover Institution

Acknowledgments

The preparation of this guide was made possible by grants from the Research Collections Program of the National Endowment for the Humanities and the Center for Research in International Studies (Stanford University). In addition, the compilers wish to acknowledge the assistance of current staff members and others who worked on the guide project, including Archivist and Senior Fellow Milorad M. Drachkovitch, Ronald Bulatoff, Grace Hawes, Elena Schafer, Linda Bernard, Ema Lasike, Elisabeth Tatarinoff, Anna Boberg, Jane Collin, Shirley VanVranken, and Ed McLaughlin. The advice of Associate Director Richard F. Staar, Curators Agnes F. Peterson, Peter Duignan, Ramon Myers, Joseph Bingaman, and Anna Bourguina, Senior Fellow Rita Ricardo Campbell, Slavic Bibliographer Joseph Dwyer, Deputy Archivist Robert Hessen, and Research Fellow Molly Sturges also has been appreciated.

The compilers are indebted to the many librarians and archivists who over the years helped to produce the catalog card descriptions and other finding aids on which this guide largely is based. Among them were Nina Almond, librarian (1921–1947); Suda L. Bane, archivist of the Herbert Hoover Archives (1937–1952); Philip T. McLean, librarian (1947–1966); Hazel Lyman Nickel, archivist of the Herbert Hoover Archives (1952–1956); Charlotte Cole, special collections librarian (1955–1969); Arline Paul, head of reader services (1955–1977); Thomas T. Thalken, archivist of the Herbert Hoover Archives (1956–1961); Rita Ricardo Campbell, archivist of the Herbert Hoover Archives (1961–1968); Kenneth M. Glazier, librarian (1966–1969); Crone Kernke, assistant archivist (1969–1977); and Franz G. Lassner, archivist (1969–1974). Special thanks go to the late Witold S. Sworakowski, curator of the Polish Collection (1947–1952), curator of the Western European Collection (1949–1953), curator of the Eastern European Collection (1952–1963), associate director in charge of library operations (1965–1969), and consultant to the director (1969–1979), whose dedicated labors sustained and enriched the archives for more than thirty years.

CHARLES G. PALM
Deputy Archivist

DALE REED
Assistant Archivist

Introduction

This guide describes the archival and manuscript holdings of the Hoover Institution on War, Revolution and Peace at Stanford University. Totalling 3,569 accessions and occupying approximately 18,000 linear feet of shelving, they cover the fields of political, economic, social, and military history since the late nineteenth century for most geographical areas, including North America, Eastern Europe and Russia (also USSR), Western Europe, East and Southeast Asia, Latin America, Africa, and the Middle East. There are records of organizations, papers of individuals, special collections, manuscripts accessioned as single units, and audiovisual materials, as well as microfilm and other copies of collections held privately or located at other repositories. In general, they document the causes of war, propaganda, and military history; wartime dislocation and relief; underground resistance movements and governments-in-exile; political ideologies, especially communism, fascism, and nazism; revolutionary movements and liberation groups; colonialism; international organizations, conferences, and diplomacy; peace negotiations and pacifism; education; and political, economic, and social change in numerous countries.

Holdings vary by geographical area, as illustrated below:

HOLDINGS BY AREA (1979)

Area	Percentage by volume	Percentage by number of accessions
North America (primarily U.S.)	55.2	24.4
Eastern Europe and Russia (USSR)	17.2	26.1
Western Europe	13.8	27.1
International	4.9	5.3
East and Southeast Asia	4.4	8.3
Latin America	3.0	1.8
Africa	1.1	5.4
Middle East	.4	1.6

Within the broad geographical areas listed above, certain countries, historical periods, and themes are emphasized. United States materials dominate the North American section. They relate to politics and government since 1919; diplomacy; military involvement in both world wars, Korea, and Vietnam; communism and internal subversion; journalism and public opinion; economic and social problems.

Russian materials are among the most significant of the archival holdings. They document the czarist regime between 1880 and 1917 (especially diplomacy), revolution and counter-revolution, war relief, civil war, émigré movements, and the USSR. Holdings on Poland are also prominent, especially those concerning foreign affairs between the world wars and the World War II government-in-exile (London). Materials on other East European countries, notably Yugoslavia, Romania, Czechoslovakia, Hungary, Bulgaria, and the Baltic states, primarily concern the interwar, World War II, and immediate postwar periods.

In the West European section, holdings are strongest for Germany, France, Belgium, Spain, and Italy. German subjects covered include the 1919 revolution, the rise of nazism, the Third Reich and its leaders, anti-nazi resistance, the Allied occupation after World War II, and the 1968 student revolt. The French collections emphasize interwar diplomacy, the Vichy regime, World War II resistance, trade unionism, the Fifth Republic, the Algerian war, and the 1968 student revolt. Additional subject areas within the West European collection are war propaganda, relief operations in Belgium, the German occupation of Belgium in both world wars, the Spanish civil war, Italian fascism, the rise of the British Labour party, and the Irish revolutionary movement.

Although smaller and less comprehensive, the other geographical area collections provide valuable archival documentation on selected topics. Among international organizations and conferences covered in depth are the 1919 Paris Peace Conference, the League of Nations, reparations commissions, the 1930 London Naval Conference, international military tribunals at Nuremberg and Tokyo, and the founding conference of the United Nations at San Francisco. East and Southeast Asian materials relate primarily to the Japanese occupation of Korea (1894–1910), missionary work in China, the rise of the Kuomintang under Chiang Kai-shek, the Sino-Japanese war, operations in the China-Burma-India theater during World War II, the postwar Allied occupation of Japan, developments in Indonesia from 1958 to the coup of 1965, and the Vietnam war. Latin American holdings focus on boundary disputes, the Panama Canal, the Cuban revolution, and major political events throughout South America for the period 1954–1964. African archival materials relate primarily to tribal customs, colonialism and colonial administration, nationalism, and revolutionary movements. For the Middle East, significant topics represented are the Arabian American Oil Company, the Muslim Brotherhood in Egypt, and Turkey since the first republic.

Research in the archives is strongly supported by the Hoover Institution's specialized library of published sources. The library houses 1.3 million books, 24,000 periodical titles, 6,000 newspapers, and an extensive collection of government documents, pamphlets, leaflets, and other published ephemera. Except for certain microfilms, the library holdings are not described in this guide.

Use of the Guide   The only previously published comprehensive guide to the archives is *Special Collections in the Hoover Library on War, Revolution and Peace* (1940), by Nina Almond and H. H. Fisher. The present guide supersedes that edition, as well as the special collections section of the printed card catalog published in 88 volumes by G. K. Hall (Boston, 1969–1977). It supplements but does not replace various other published guides that serve special purposes. These include subject and area surveys that describe both library and archival materials relating to particular subjects or geographical regions, finding aids to individual accessions, and a biennial checklist of major archival and manuscript collections. A complete list of these publications is appended to this volume.

The present guide covers virtually all archival and manuscript material accessioned at the Hoover Institution through 1978. Each entry sets forth an individual accession—that is, a group of papers or records, a special collection, or a single manuscript. Entries are numbered consecutively and arranged in two alphabetical sections. The first and largest section describes materials maintained in the archives. These accessions contain mostly originals, although some printed matter, photocopies, and microfilms may be present. The second, smaller section describes microfilms of archival and manuscript materials held in private hands or at other repositories. These microfilms are maintained by the Hoover Institution library, which is administered separately from the archives.

Guide entries have been prepared for the most part according to the *Anglo-American Cataloging Rules* (American Library Association, 1967). Elements of the entries are as follows:

a) **Main entry.** When an accession consists of materials written by or addressed to a person, family, government agency, or other corporate body, it is entered under the name of the person or corporate body. This rule also applies to such accessions if they include other material concerned with the person, family, or corporate body. Any other group of papers is entered under the name of the collector or, if this information is not known, under its title.

b) **Title.** If an accession has a name by which it is known, that is used as the title. In other cases, a title is supplied by the cataloger. The most commonly supplied titles are "papers" for personal or family material, "records" for materials created by corporate bodies, and "correspondence" for letters between persons. When evident in the material, inclusive dates are part of the title. For single manuscripts, the type of document (for example, memoirs, history, report), as well as the author's title, are indicated. English translations of foreign-language titles are given in parentheses.

c) **Volume.** This is given in terms of number of physical containers. The most common containers are a manuscript box, which holds approximately five inches of material; a cubic foot box, which holds fifteen inches of letter-size documents or twelve inches of legal-size documents; and a folder or envelope, which holds one inch or less. When unusual containers are present, their volume in terms of linear feet is indicated in parentheses.

d) **Form.** If the manuscripts or any substantial part of them are copies, rather than originals, the location of the originals, if known, is stated in a separate note.

e) **Scope and content.** This paragraph identifies the records creator, the types of documents constituting the accession, and the subjects covered.

f) **Finding aid.** These generally are of two types: register and preliminary inventory. A register is the more descriptive, accurate, and detailed of the two. Prepared in accordance with established archival standards, it contains a biographical or historical note about the records creator, a description of the record series, and a folder-by-folder container list. A preliminary inventory is a descriptive list that does not meet register standards. Preliminary inventories vary widely in their usefulness and include abbreviated descriptions prepared by donors or staff, shipping lists, box notes written during unpacking, and the like.

g) **Restrictions.** When an accession or parts of it are restricted, a statement governing accessibility is given.

h) **Provenance.** The donor or source of the acquisition, unless this information is unknown or confidential, is provided. Generally, there are three types of acquisitions: gift, purchase, and deposit. In the case of a deposit, the depositor retains ownership and sometimes control over access for a specified period of years.

Users should be aware that the amount of entry information is not necessarily in proportion to an accession's research value. Incomplete entries appear because some birth and death dates of authors, names of donors, and dates of gifts are unavailable. Some variation in entry length is present by design. For example, only those aspects of a person's life that are both significant and pertinent to the papers are generally given. In addition, scope and content descriptions are limited to subjects covered in a substantial way; topics covered only incidentally are usually excluded. It is possible, therefore, that a large, important accession dealing primarily with one or two topics may have a shorter entry than a smaller and less important accession with many subjects represented.

The index cites all names, places, and topics mentioned in the entries. Since entry descriptions are not exhaustive analyses of collection content, users should not expect to find in the index all names and subjects represented in collections. Accessions with large correspondence series, for example, may contain hundreds of names of correspondents, which could not be incorporated into the index. Access at this level is provided by more detailed finding aids that can be consulted in the archives reading room.

Subjects in the index conform to the rules and terms prescribed in *Subject Headings Used in Dictionary Catalogs of the Library of Congress* (1975). In principle, the same heading has been consistently assigned to materials on the same subject matter, and the most specific terms available in *Subject Headings* have been chosen. Since the archives' subject card catalog, on which the index is based, has been developed over a number of years by numerous catalogers, users are encouraged to search under related terms for like materials and to take advantage of the numerous cross-references provided.

Because of the international nature of our holdings, particular attention has been paid to geographical indexing. Every accession with materials of geographical significance has been indexed under the appropriate political jurisdiction or region. This has been done either directly (e.g., Russia-History-Revolution, 1917) or indirectly as subdivisions of topical headings (e.g., Agriculture-Russia). Cross-references have been made from all geographical place names indexed indirectly as subdivisions to the topical headings under which they appear (e.g., Russia. *see* Agriculture-Russia).

Use of Materials

Materials may be examined in the Archives Reading Room in the Herbert Hoover Memorial Building (courtyard level) by anyone who presents personal identification, completes a registration form, and adheres to rules regarding use. Reading room hours are 8:15 a.m. to 4:45 p.m., Monday through Friday. Archives are not available through interlibrary loan. A limited number of photocopies may be purchased in accordance with a reproduction price list and policy statement (available on request). Reference service is provided to reading room users, as well as to persons writing for information. For extensive searches involving detailed research, interpretation, or evaluation of materials, the names of qualified persons who work for a fee can be furnished. Inquiries should be addressed to the archivist.

Since it was founded in 1919, the Hoover Institution has grown from a small documentary collection on World War I to a major research center for domestic and international affairs. Serving as a library and archival repository is now only one of its three principal functions. There is a resident staff of some 50 scholars, pursuing basic research in the fields of economics, education, history, international law, political science, and sociology. The National Fellows Program annually awards visiting fellowships to 15 younger scholars. In addition, the Hoover Institution maintains its own press. Since 1919, some 350 volumes have been published, and the press currently publishes more than 20 books each year.

The Hoover Institution owes its beginnings and much of its continued success to its founder, Herbert Hoover, a member of Stanford University's first graduating class and the thirty-first president of the United States. Inspired by two historians—Andrew D. White, Cornell University president, whose study of the French Revolution impressed Hoover with the importance of contemporary documents, and Ephraim D. Adams, a Stanford University history professor, who encouraged him to preserve his 1914–1919 Belgian relief records—Hoover initiated what he called a "historical collection on the Great War." In April 1919, four months after arriving in Paris to supervise European relief operations, he informed Stanford University President Ray Lyman Wilbur of his plan and requested his support. Receiving a favorable response, Hoover donated $50,000, the first of many financial gifts, and asked that Professor Adams be sent to Paris.

Adams arrived in June and recruited several young scholars from American military personnel; with Hoover's help he secured their release from military service. Among them was Ralph H. Lutz, a future director of the Institution. During the remainder of 1919, Adams and his group used Hoover's letters of introduction and logistical support to collect more than 80,000 items of research value and to establish a network of representatives and friends of the Institution.

The Hoover collection was at first housed in the Stanford University library, although it retained an independent identity. In 1941 it was moved into a separate building, the Hoover Tower, which still remains the central structure of the Hoover Institution complex. In 1946, the Stanford University Board of Trustees designated the Institution as a separate division within the university. This status was spelled out in detail in 1959, and the Hoover Institution defined by the trustees as "an independent institution within the frame of Stanford University." New buildings were added in 1967 (the Lou Henry Hoover Building, named in honor of Mrs. Hoover) and 1978 (the Herbert Hoover Memorial Building, which houses the archives and is the sole federal memorial to President Hoover).

Since its foundation, the Institution has had five directors: Ephraim D. Adams, who served as chairman of the directors, 1920–1925; Ralph H. Lutz, chairman, 1925–1944; Harold H. Fisher, chairman, 1944–1952; C. Easton Rothwell, director, 1952–1959; and W. Glenn Campbell, the present director, who assumed the post on January 1, 1960.

Initially, the collecting program focused narrowly on primary source materials relating to World War I. The wide-ranging concerns of the Paris Peace

Conference and the immediate postwar political turmoil, however, compelled Hoover collectors to expand their interests beyond the confines of the war. As a result, the collecting effort of 1919–1920 laid foundations for most of the Institution's present curatorial areas. Only the East Asian Collection originated at a later date, after World War II. By 1933, additional themes, including postwar reconstruction and the rise of fascism, had been adopted. In 1938, the collecting scope was further enlarged to include all aspects of war, revolution, and peace in the twentieth century throughout most of the world.

An emphasis on contemporary documents, fugitive materials, and other primary sources required a collecting methodology that differed substantially from the librarian's traditional reliance on publishers' trade lists and booksellers' catalogs. Frequent trips abroad, honorary curators in various European universities, permanent representatives in residence abroad, traveling students, and cash purchases—all became common features of a collecting strategy designed to save materials that appeared only briefly and in limited numbers. Although published and printed matter were on Hoover want lists more frequently than manuscripts and archives, the strategy was well suited to archival sleuthing, and from the beginning it led the acquisition of archival and manuscript materials.

Since 1919, growth of archival and manuscript holdings has been uneven. Of the 450 most important accessions in the archives, 8 percent were acquired in the first eleven years, 8 percent in the following fifteen years (1930–1944), 11 percent in the five postwar years (1945–1949), 9 percent during the 1950s, 21 percent in the 1960s, and 43 percent since 1970. The rate and nature of growth were influenced by a number of factors: budgets, availability of materials, the interests and energy of the Institution's staff and representatives abroad, varying opportunities relating to Herbert Hoover's public career, and circumstances of history.

Hoover's support, Adams' imaginative collecting program, and the abundance of war documentation accounted for the success of the first years. Topically, archival materials acquired then deal with international relief, for example the archives of the American National Red Cross (2254)* and the Hoover relief organizations (514, 762, 2817, 2818); war propaganda; European politics, represented in part by the papers of presidential adviser George D. Herron (1177), Austrian journalist Heinrich Kanner (1383), and Swiss journalist William Martin (1732); and the Bolshevik revolution and Russian civil war. Particularly significant are the Russian archives, among which are the papers of White Russian generals (1027, 1310, 1533, 1802, 2508, 3013) and diplomatic representatives (1004, 1172), records of imperial and provisional government diplomatic outposts (2365, 2367, 2369, 2372, 2378), and Paris office files of the czarist secret police (2358). Solicitation of Russian materials in the 1920s was the first instance of what became a characteristic concern for archives of dislocated peoples, exiled or defunct governments, and émigré organizations of every variety.

The rate of acquisitions declined during the subsequent fifteen years of economic depression and world war. Nevertheless, important materials were added to most subject areas. Significant collections on Europe are the files of James A. Logan (1629) and Henry M. Robinson (2303) on reparations and reconstruction, a collection on the separatist movement in the Rhineland (683), the cartoon drawings of Louis Raemaekers (2233), miscellaneous papers of

*Numbers in parentheses refer to guide entries.

Rosika Schwimmer (2474), and the diaries and letters of Rosa Luxemburg (1662).

Some important U.S. materials were received during the 1930s and early 1940s. After leaving public office in 1933, President Hoover and Secretary of the Interior Ray Lyman Wilbur deposited their papers (1216 and 3072),* as well as the records of a number of presidential commissions (2183, 2908, and 3063) and public interest organizations (215 and 1850). The archives of the antiwar America First Committee (52) and papers of pacifist Alice Park (2039) also were acquired.

The Russian collecting program continued successfully during the 1930s with the acquisition of personal papers (266, 1000, 1508, 1512, 1773, 1811, 2023, 2111, 2507) and diplomatic archives (2366, 2368, 2376, 2387, 2388), including the Washington, D.C., embassy files of the czarist and provisional governments (2373).

A concerted collecting effort, involving Herbert Hoover's participation, brought in a significant number of important archives between 1945 and 1949. Several international relief organizations in which Hoover had been active, such as the Commission for Polish Relief (513), the second Commission for Relief in Belgium (515), the Finnish Relief Fund (822), and the National Committee on Food for Small Democracies (1892), deposited their archives at the Hoover Institution. As head of the Famine Emergency Relief Committee after the war, Hoover was in a position to help the archival program. When Hoover visited Berlin in 1946, an American military officer presented him with the diaries of Joseph Goebbels (1019). In Japan, Hoover gained General Douglas MacArthur's cooperation in establishing a collecting office in Tokyo in November 1945. This represented the beginning of the East Asian Collection, which soon included materials on the United Nations Relief and Rehabilitation Administration in China (2812), records of the International Military Tribunal Far East (1290), and microfilmed records of the Japanese government in Korea, 1894–1910 (1336).

In the same period, a number of important diplomatic archives of the prewar Polish government were acquired from former Polish Ambassador Jan Ciechanowski (2120, 2121, 2122, 2123, 2136, 2137). The papers of Imperial Russian Gen. Sergei N. Pototskii (2172) and records of the 1918–1922 anti-Bolshevik government in Siberia (1842) were received. West European materials, especially on Nazi Germany (182, 962, 997, 1019, 1213, 1620, 2925), the Nuremberg war crime trials (1289), war propaganda (1589), resistance movements (179, 1951), and the Spanish civil war (254), were well represented in the postwar collecting program, as were materials on the establishment of the United Nations (1403, 1742, 2808). The Burnett Bolloten Collection on the Spanish civil war (254) is particularly noteworthy.

The momentum of the immediate postwar period subsided by 1951, and during the rest of the decade the Institution experienced declining budgets. Nevertheless, a modest acquisition rate was achieved and valuable collections acquired in most of the Institution's curatorial areas. Among them are the papers of U.S. Sen. Ernest Lundeen (1657), Ambassador Hugh Gibson (1003), Gen. Joseph W. Stilwell (2661), and journalist Mark Sullivan (2690), as well as records of the Hoover Commission on Organization of the Executive Branch

---

*When the Herbert Hoover Presidential Library was established at West Branch, Iowa, in 1962, certain of Hoover's papers, including his Department of Commerce and presidential files, were transferred from Stanford to the new library.

of Government (2868) and of the Polish government-in-exile in London (2118). A special attempt was made to solicit papers from Hoover's former associates in war relief organizations, and many responded favorably: William Palmer Fuller II (901), Joseph C. Green (1066), Lewis L. Strauss (2670), and Edward Eyre Hunt (1254), among others. For the West European Collection, the Hoover Institution microfilmed the archives of the Nationalsozialistische Deutsche Arbeiterpartei (3424), photocopied selected documents of the German Foreign Ministry (959), and obtained the René de Chambrun Collection on Vichy France (417).

By far the most productive period of archival acquisitions has been in recent years. Sixty-four percent of the 450 major collections in the archives have been received since 1960. This growth resulted primarily from a steadily improving financial position. A systematic and centralized solicitation program was developed and holdings in all fields strengthened. In addition, several special collecting projects were instituted, including the development of a New Left Collection dealing with radical left-wing groups of the late 1960s and early 1970s; the re-establishment of the Imperial Russian Collection, named after the late Nicolas A. de Basily, with Prince Vasili Romanov as honorary curator; and the creation of the Paul and Jean Hanna Collection on Education, which focuses on the use of education as an instrument for achieving national objectives.

Solicitation efforts since 1960 have brought in a particularly large number of papers of American military officers, diplomats, statesmen, public administrators, educators, and journalists. Among them are the papers of presidential adviser and columnist Raymond Moley (1822); Gov. Ronald Reagan (2250); Cabinet members George P. Shultz (2534), Carla A. Hills (1192), and Caspar W. Weinberger (3046); Ambassadors Stanley K. Hornbeck (1227) and Howard P. Jones (1361); Generals Robert C. Richardson (2286), Claire Lee Chennault (431), and John R. Chaisson (415); and Adm. Charles M. Cooke (543). Also acquired were the papers of Jay Lovestone, onetime leader of the Communist Party of the United States (1645).

Russian holdings were significantly increased with the addition of the Nicolas A. de Basily Collection on Imperial Russia (156), the Boris I. Nicolaevsky Collection (1946), and the Bertram D. Wolfe papers (3111). The papers of Polish Premiers Ignace Jan Paderewski (2018) and Stanislaw Mikolajczyk (1793); Czechoslovak Ambassadors Stefan Osusky (2009) and Juraj Slavik (2550); Romanian Minister of Foreign Affairs Nicolae Titulescu (2755); and Yugoslav Ambassador Konstantin Fotitch (850) and diplomat and statesman Milan Gavrilović (927), enhanced the East European holdings.

West European acquisitions since 1960 include papers of French Ambassador Gaston Bergery (196), French Minister Louis Loucheur (1642), Belgian trade unionist Walter Schevenels (2449), Spanish political activist Joaquin Maurín (1760), Austrian pacifist Karl B. Frank (867), and German journalists Kurt R. Grossmann (1079) and Franz Schoenberner (2457). The African Collection has been enlarged by the acquisition of microfilms of the British Colonial and Foreign Office records, 1870–1922 (3205), and the research files of scholars S. Herbert Frankel (868), Lewis H. Gann (918), René Lemarchand (1583), Keith Middlemas (1788), Frederick Quinn (2218), and Herbert J. Weiss (3357), among others. Important papers on Homer Lea, military adviser to Sun Yat-sen (262, 2176), and of Arthur Young, financial adviser to the Nationalist government of China (3168), strengthened the East Asian Collection. The papers of historian Theodore Draper (689), documenting revolutions in Cuba and the Dominican Republic, and the records of the Institute of Hispanic-American and Luso-Brazilian Studies (2633) have enriched the Latin American holdings.

As a result of recent acquisitions, current research opportunities in the Hoover Institution Archives abound. Moreover, some older accessions never have been extensively researched; and many of the most frequently consulted materials continue to provide documentation for scholars with new approaches. By disseminating information about these holdings, it is hoped that this guide will encourage new studies and enhance research already under way.

Entries / Original Materials

1

Abel, Theodore Fred, 1896–
Papers (in English and German), 1930–1975. 11 ms. boxes.
American sociologist. Diaries, relating to sociological theory and world politics; and autobiographical sketches by members of the Nationalsozialistische Deutsche Arbeiter-Partei, relating to their reasons for becoming national socialists, collected by T. Abel as research material for his book *Why Hitler Came into Power* (1938).
Preliminary inventory.
Gift, T. F. Abel, 1950. Incremental gift, 1978.

2

Abernethy, David B., 1937–
Miscellaneous papers, 1949–1964. 2 ms. boxes.
Professor of Political Science, Stanford University. Notes and pamphlets, relating to political, economic, cultural and social affairs in Nigeria.
Register.
Gift, D. B. Abernethy, 1972.

3

"Accessories to the Crime."
Memorandum, n.d. 1 folder.
Typescript (mimeographed).
Relates to the territorial dispute between Germany and Lithuania regarding Memel.

4

Adair, Fred L., 1877–1972.
Papers, 1918–1942. 8 ms. boxes, 3 envelopes, 2 phonorecords, 38 posters.
American physician; Red Cross relief worker in Belgium, 1918–1919. Correspondence, reports, photographs, notes and printed matter, relating primarily to activities of the American Red Cross in Belgium, 1918–1919, and to the America First Committee, 1940–1942.
Preliminary inventory.
Gift, F. L. Adair, 1950. Incremental gift, Father John F. Adair, 1973.

5

Adam, Wilhelm, 1877–1949.
Memoirs (in German), n.d. 1 reel.
Microfilm of original located at the Institut fuer Zeitgeschichte, Munich.
Colonel General, German Army. Relates to the failure of the German military to oppose Adolf Hitler during the 1930's.
May not be published or copied without permission of the Institut fuer Zeitgeschichte, except for short excerpts.
Purchase, Institut fuer Zeitgeschichte, 1973.

6

Adamich, Zenon V.
History, n.d. "Royal Yugoslav Navy in World War II." 1 folder.
Typescript (photocopy).
Yugoslav naval officer. Includes a register of Yugoslav naval officers on active and inactive service on April 6, 1941.
Gift, Z. V. Adamich, 1972.

7

Adams, Arthur E.
History, 1960. "Bolsheviks in the Ukraine: The Second Campaign, 1918–1919." 2 vols.
Typescript.
Includes bibliography.

8

Adams, Ephraim Douglass, 1865–1930.
Papers, 1908–1927. ½ ms. box, 1 envelope.
Photocopy of correspondence located in Stanford University Archives.
American historian; Director of the Hoover Institution on War, Revolution and Peace, 1919–1925. Correspondence, leaflets, and photograph relating to the administration and finances of Stanford University and to American participation in World War I. Correspondence mostly with Herbert Hoover. Includes a series of leaflets by E. D. Adams, entitled *Why We Are at War with Germany*, 1918; and a photograph of student assistants of E. D. Adams, 1922.
In part, gift, Stanford University Archives, 1976.

9

Adams, Marie, 1891–1976.
Papers, 1887–1946. 4 ms. boxes.
American Red Cross social worker; internee, Santo Tomás concentration camp, Philippine Islands, 1942–1945. Correspondence, propaganda leaflets, memorabilia and printed matter, relating to the Santo Tomás concentration camp and the Japanese occupation of the Philippine Islands during World War II.
Preliminary inventory.
Gift, estate of M. Adams, 1978.

10

Addio Lugano Bella: Antologia della Canzone Anarchica in Italia (Goodbye, Beautiful Lugano: Anthology of Anarchist Songs in Italy).
Songs (in Italian), n.d. 1 phonorecord.

11

Adenauer, Konrad, 1876–1967.

Miscellaneous papers (in German), 1953–1957. 1 folder, 1 envelope.

Chancellor of West Germany, 1949–1963. Transcripts of an interview and a speech, and photographs, relating to West German politics and foreign relations.

Preliminary inventory.

Gift, Jacques de Launay, 1962. Gift, Elmer E. Robinson.

12

Adleman, Robert H., 1919–

Papers, 1940–1972. 17 ms. boxes, 1 envelope, 28 phonotapes.

American journalist and author. Correspondence, questionnaires, transcripts of interviews, drafts of writings, galleys, research notes, phonotapes, photographs and maps, relating primarily to the First Special Service Force (U.S. and Canadian troops) and its operations in Italy and Southern France during World War II. Used as research material for the books of R. H. Adleman, *The Devil's Brigade, Rome Fell Today* and *The Champagne Campaign.*

Preliminary inventory.

Gift, R. H. Adleman, 1972.

13

Adloff, Virginia, *collector.*

Newspaper clippings (in English and French), 1948–1961. 1 ms. box, 1 envelope.

From the *New York Times, Le Monde, Nice Matin* and the *Economist,* relating to the Republic of the Congo.

Gift, Virginia Adloff.

14

Adrian system blueprints (in French), 1915–1918. ½ ms. box.

"Adrian system" designs for army barracks and for dormitories, kitchens and schools for refugees.

15

Aehrenthal, Aloys Leopold Baptist Lexa von, Graf, 1854–1912.

Memoirs (in German), 1895. "Memorie des Freiherrn von Aehrenthal ueber die Beziehungen zwischen Oesterreich-Ungarn und Russland, 1872–1894" (Memoirs of Baron von Aehrenthal on Relations between Austria-Hungary and Russia, 1872–1894). 1 vol.

Typescript.

16

Africa, French—pictorial, n.d. 1 envelope.

Depicts daily life in, and cultural and scenic sites of, former French African countries, including Niger, Mauritania, Ivory Coast, Mali, Senegal, the Central African Republic, Togo, Cameroun, Chad, the Congo, and the Malagasy Republic.

Preliminary inventory.

Gift, Centre d'Étude et de Documentation sur l'Afrique et l'Outre-Mer of France, 1973.

17

Africa—pictorial, n.d. 46 envelopes.

Depicts African scenes, historical sites, daily life, European and African personalities, industries, and art work.

18

Africa, South—propaganda, 1950.

Flyer, relating to the National Day of Protest, June 26, 1950, in Johannesburg, South Africa.

19

African art slides, 1967. 100 slides.

Depicts African art objects exhibited at the Lowie Museum of Anthropology, University of California, Berkeley.

Preliminary inventory.

Permission of African Curator, Hoover Institution, required for use.

Purchase.

20

African drought and famine collection, 1970–1975. 2 ms. boxes.

Newsletters, congressional hearings, studies, bibliography, newspaper issues and journals, relating to the African drought and famine, 1970–1975, and to U.S. and French relief aid and the relief operations of the Economic and Social Council of the United Nations, the League of Red Cross Societies, and others.

21

African revolutionary movements collection, 1962–1972. 5 ms. boxes, 1 envelope, 3 phonorecords.

Pamphlets, newspaper clippings, government publications, leaflets, and other printed matter, relating to the political and military efforts of African revolutionary organizations, including the People's Movement for the Liberation of Angola, Mozambique Liberation Front, and the South West Africa People's Organization.

Register.

22

Agence Télégraphique de Petrograd.

Daily news bulletins (in French), 1915–1916. 5 vols.

Typescript.

Press service. Relates to world military and political events.

Purchase, Phyllis J. Walsh, 1971.

23

Ahlborn, Emil.

Letter, 1917, to Charles F. Dole. 1 folder.

Holograph.

Relates to the origins of World War I, and to American entry into the war.

24

Aid Refugee Chinese Intellectuals.

Records, 1952–1970. 44 ms. boxes, 3 albums, 6 envelopes.

Private U.S. relief organization. Correspondence, reports, minutes of meetings, financial records and photographs, relating to ARCI relief work for Chinese refugees.
Preliminary inventory.
Gift, Aid Refugee Chinese Intellectuals, 1970.

25

Aiguade, Jaime Anton.
Statement (in Catalan), 1937. "Actuacio Del Govern de la Generalitat i Del Seu President Lluis Companys Durant Les Journades de Maig de 1937" (Activities of the Government and its President Lluis Companys During the Days of May 1937). 1 folder.
Typescript.
Relates to the surrender to the Spanish Government of Catalan autonomy by President Lluis Companys.
Gift, Burnett Bolloten, 1974.

26

Aitchison, Bruce.
Study, 1943. "The Administration of Occupied Enemy Territory by the British Army in the Middle East." 1 folder.
Typescript (mimeographed).
Major, U.S. Army, and Staff Judge Advocate, U.S. Army Forces in the Middle East.

27

Akaëmov, Nikolaĭ.
History (in Russian), 1930. "Kaledinskie Miatezhi" (The Kaledin Rebellion). 1 folder.
Holograph.
Relates to the White Russian movement led by Alekseĭ Kaledin during the Russian Civil War.

28

Akerson (George Edward)—photograph, 1931. 1 envelope.
Depicts G. E. Akerson, Secretary to President Herbert Hoover, 1929—1931, at a testimonial dinner by White House correspondents.

29

Akintievskiĭ, Konstantin Konstantinovich, 1884—1962.
Memoirs (in Russian), n.d. ½ ms. box.
Typescript.
General, Imperial Russian Army. Relates to activities of the Imperial Russian Army during World War I and to the White Russian Forces during the Russian Revolution and Civil War, 1914—1921. Includes an English translation.
Gift, Olga P. Zaitzevsky, 1971.

30

Alai, Hussein.
Writings, 1923—1924. 1 folder.
Persian Minister to the U.S. Relates to the financial situation in Persia, the Persian oil industry, and the role of Persia in world affairs. Includes writings by A. C.

Millspaugh, Administrator General of the Finances of Persia.
Preliminary inventory.
Gift, H. Alai, 1924.

31

Albert I (King of the Belgians)—photograph, n.d. 1 envelope.
Depicts King Albert I of Belgium.

32

Albrecht, Frank McAdams, 1901—
Papers, 1928—1960. 4 ms. boxes.
Major General, U.S. Army Corps of Engineers. Orders, reports, correspondence and drafts of speeches, relating to U.S. military engineering in the European Theater during World War II and in the U.S. in the interwar period.
Gift, F. M. Albrecht, 1968.

33

Albrecht, Ralph G., 1896—
Papers, 1926—1961. 2 ms. boxes, 1 album.
American lawyer; Associate Trial Counsel, Nuremberg War Trials, 1945—1946; counsel to German corporations, 1950—1953. Correspondence, memoranda, writings, notes, leaflets, clippings, and photographs, relating to the Nuremberg war crime trials, the Schuman Plan, European Coal and Steel Community, the dismantling of German steel plants, the settlement of German external debts, and the National Government of Georgia (Transcaucasia) in 1926.
Preliminary inventory.
Gift, R. G. Albrecht, 1972.

34

Aldrich, Mildred, 1853—1928.
Letters, 1914—1917, to an American friend. 1 folder.
American author. Relate to conditions in France during World War I, and to activities of Gertrude Stein and other literary figures in France.

35

Aldrovandi Marescotti, Luigi, conte de Viano, b. 1876.
Memoirs, 1938. *Nuovi Ricordi e Frammenti di Diario per far Seguito a Guerra Diplomatica (1914—1919)* (New Recollections and Diary Fragments as a Sequel to *Diplomatic War* [1914—1919]). 1 folder.
Typescript.
Chief of cabinet of the Italian Foreign Ministry during World War I.

36

Alekseev, F.
Painting (photograph), n.d. 1 envelope.
Russian artist. Depicts the Winter Palace and Peter and Paul Fortress in St. Petersburg.

37

Alekseev, Mikhail Vasil'evich, 1857–1918.

Miscellaneous papers (in Russian), 1905–1918. ½ ms. box.

Photocopy.

General, Russian Imperial Army; Commander-in-Chief, Russian Imperial Armies on the Southwestern front, during World War I; Chief of Staff to Tsar Nicholas II, 1915–1917. Correspondence, notes, diaries, and military orders, relating to Russian military activities during World War I, and to the Russian Revolution and Civil War.

Preliminary inventory.

Gift, Vera Alexeyeva de Borel, 1977.

38

"Aleppo News-Letter."

Newsletter, 1920. 1 folder.

Typescript.

Newsletter of Near East Relief workers in Aleppo, Syria. Four issues, June–July 1920, relating to social conditions and relief work in Syria.

39

Alexander II, Emperor of Russia, 1818–1881.

Decree (in Russian), 1859. 1 folder.

Printed.

Emperor of Russia. Relates to the status of Russian 5% bank notes and of investments in Russian banks.

40

Alexandra (Empress Consort of Nicholas II, Emperor of Russia)—photographs, n.d. 1 envelope.

Depicts Empress Alexandra of Russia.

41

Allen, Benjamin Shannon, 1883–1963.

Papers, 1910–1967. 3 ms. boxes, 1 cu. ft. box, 2 oversize boxes (1 l. ft.), 2 envelopes.

American journalist. Correspondence, press releases, clippings, other printed matter, and photographs, relating to activities of the Commission for Relief in Belgium, U.S. Food Administration and U.S. Fuel Administration during World War I, and of the National Committee on Food for the Small Democracies and Finnish Relief Fund during World War II, to political conditions in the U.S., and to Herbert Hoover.

Preliminary inventory.

Gift, B. S. Allen, 1954. Subsequent increments.

42

Allen, Niel R., 1894–1959.

Papers, 1919. 1 ms. box.

Second Lieutenant, U.S. Army; Editor, *Pontanezen Duckboard,* Camp Pontanezen, Brest, France, 1919. Correspondence, account books, contracts, newspaper clippings, and notes.

Gift, Mrs. N. R. Allen, 1959.

43

Allen, Ronald, 1891–1949.

Letter, 1944, to his mother. 1 folder.

Holograph.

U.S. Military Attaché in Russia. Relates to a discussion between R. Allen and Herbert Hoover in the Waldorf Towers on current world affairs.

Gift, Lloyd Allen, 1976.

44

Allen, Theophilus.

Letter, 1926, to Charles D. Marx. 1 folder.

Holograph.

Relates to the prospects for German admission to the League of Nations.

45

Allied and Associated Powers (1914–1920) Inter-Allied Food Council.

Records (in French and English), 1917–1919. 21 ms. boxes.

Minutes of meetings, reports, correspondence and statistics, relating to the coordination of Allied food supply and regulation during World War I.

Preliminary inventory.

46

Allied and Associated Powers (1914–1920)—Treaties, etc., 1918–1920. 13 folders.

Relates to the conclusion of World War I. Countries represented include the United Kingdom of Great Britain and Ireland, Austria, Austria-Hungary, Bulgaria, Germany, Hungary, Rumania, and Turkey.

Preliminary inventory.

47

Allied Forces. Southwest Pacific Area. Allied Geographical Section.

Study, 1945. "Tokyo and Kwanto Plain." 1 vol.

Printed.

Terrain Study No. 132 of the Southwest Pacific Area Allied Geographical Section, relating to the geography of Tokyo and the Kwanto Plain area of Honshu Island.

48

Allied Forces. Supreme Headquarters. Psychological Warfare Division.

Letter (in German), 1944, to Generalleutnant von Schmettow. 1 folder.

Typescript.

Requests Generalleutnant von Schmettow, Commanding General of the German troops on the Channel Islands, to establish telephone communication from the French mainland to Jersey.

Gift, Martin F. Herz, 1978.

49

Almond, Nina, *collector.*

Nina Almond collection on the Treaty of St. Germain, 1919–1920. 1 ms. box.

Typewritten transcripts of bulletins, reports and memoranda, published in *The Treaty of St. Germain: A Documentary History of Its Territorial and Political Clauses, with a Survey of the Documents of the Supreme Council of the Paris Peace Conference*, edited by Nina Almond and Ralph Haswell Lutz (Stanford: Stanford University Press, 1935).

50

Alsberg, Henry G.
Report, 1917. "Food Conditions in the Central Powers." 1 vol.
Typescript.
American journalist. Relates to food supply in Europe and Turkey during World War I.

51

Altrocchi, Rudolph, 1882–1953.
Papers, 1900–1945. 4 ms. boxes, 2 envelopes.
Second Lieutenant, U.S. Army; Director of Oral Propaganda in Italy, American Bureau of Public Information, 1918; U.S. Army Liaison Service officer, France, 1918–1919. Correspondence, an office diary, reports, speeches, military orders, newspaper clippings, postcards, posters, sheet music, and printed matter, relating to U.S. war propaganda work in Italy and Lyons, France, 1918–1919.
Preliminary inventory.
Gift, Julia G. Altrocchi, 1955. Subsequent increments.

52

America First Committee, 1940–1942.
Records, 1940–1942. 338 ms. boxes, 20 photographs, 50 posters, 3 motion pictures.
Private organization to promote U.S. nonintervention in World War II. Correspondence, minutes of meetings, reports, research studies, financial records, press releases, speeches, newsletters, campaign literature, form letters, clippings, mailing lists, films, photographs and posters.
Register.
Gift, America First Committee, 1942. Subsequent increments.

53

American Children's Fund, 1923–1950.
Records, 1923–1950. 55 ms. boxes.
Charitable organization for the promotion of child health and welfare in the U.S. Correspondence, memoranda, reports, minutes of meetings, financial records and printed matter, relating to funding of the Boy Scouts, Girl Scouts, Boys' Clubs of America and other organizations.

54

American Committee for the Encouragement of Democratic Government in Russia.
Records, 1917. 1 folder.
Organization of American civic leaders sympathizing with the Russian Revolution of February 1917. Correspondence and printed matter, relating to American public opinion regarding the February revolution.

55

American Committee on United Europe.
Records (in French, German, English and Dutch), 1949–1959. 5 ms. boxes.
Conference proceedings, newsletters, pamphlets, reports, clippings, and photographs, relating to the European Federalists' Union, the European Movement, the European Youth Campaign and affiliated organizations in promoting European political and economic unity.

56

American Committee to Keep Biafra Alive. St. Louis Chapter, *collector.*
Ephemera, 1967–1970. 4 ms. boxes, 1 envelope, 2 motion picture reels, 2 phonorecords.
Ephemeral publications of private and governmental organizations, including the U.S. Agency for International Development, the Government of the Republic of Biafra, and the Government of Nigeria; press releases from the U.S. Department of State, U.S. Congressmen, and Markpress, Biafran Overseas Press Division; clippings; periodical literature; and audio-visual materials, relating to the Nigerian Civil War of 1967–1970.
Preliminary inventory.
Gift, Eileen L. Mann, 1971.

57

American Emergency Committee for Tibetan Refugees.
Records, 1959–1970. 17 ms. boxes.
Private organization to provide relief for Tibetan refugees in Nepal and India. Correspondence, reports, minutes of meetings and photographs.
Preliminary inventory.
Gift, American Emergency Committee for Tibetan Refugees, 1970.

58

American engineers in Russia collection, 1927–1933. 4 ms. boxes.
Correspondence, writings, articles, and answers to questionnaires, relating to economic conditions, wages, housing, living costs, and relations with Russian administrative personnel, of American engineers in Russia.
Register.

59

American Foundation.
Miscellaneous records, 1930–1935. 1 folder.
Private foundation for promotion of charitable, scientific, literary and educational activities. Correspondence, notes and printed matter, relating to the question of American adherence to the World Court.

60

American individualism collection, 1966–1974. 2 ms. boxes, 7 phonotapes.
Correspondence, reports, essays, financial records,

notes, leaflets, pamphlets, and printed matter, relating to the organization and activities of the Libertarian Party in California, 1970–1974, other libertarian and conservative youth groups, and the First National Convention of the Libertarian Party.
Preliminary inventory.

61

American Law Institute. Committee to Encourage Discussion of Essential Human Rights.
Report, ca. 1944. "Statement of Essential Human Rights." 1 folder.
Typescript (mimeographed).
Relates to the views of legal experts from several Allied countries regarding human rights.

62

American Library Association War Service.
Records, 1917–1923. ½ ms. box, 33 envelopes.
Photographs, postcards, blueprints, insignia, and reports, relating to the work of the American Library Association War Service in providing library buildings, books, and librarians for U.S. military servicemen in the United States and overseas during World War I.
Preliminary inventory.
Gift, Blanche Galloway, 1963.

63

American National Labor Party.
Pamphlet, 1936. "Platform of the American National Labor Party." 1 folder.
Typescript (mimeographed).
American fascist organization.

64

American Revolution Bicentennial collection, 1976. 1 folder.
Addresses, illustrations, proclamations, and other material, issued in commemoration of the Bicentenary of the United States.

65

American Russian Institute, San Francisco, *collector.*
Photographs, 1950–1956. 3 envelopes.
Depicts scenes in Latvia; Latvian and Russian authors, artists and scientists; and a conference in the Soviet Union commemorating the thirtieth anniversary of the death of the American botanist Luther Burbank, 1956. Includes photographs of the Soviet geneticist Trofim D. Lysenko.

66

American Samoa.
Interim legal code, 1946. ½ ms. box.
Typescript (mimeographed).
Gift, U.S. Naval Station, Pago Pago, 1947.

67

American Songs of Peace.
Songs, n.d. 1 phonorecord.
American songs relating to peace, 1767–1940, sung by John Swingle.

68

American Volunteer Motor Ambulance Corps collection, 1915. 1 folder.
Typescript (some mimeographed).
Letters from members of the American Volunteer Motor Ambulance Corps, relating to activities of the corps in France during World War I.

69

America's Town Meeting of the Air.
Radio program, 1945. 2 phonorecords.
Relates to the founding of the United Nations and its prospective role in ensuring world peace.

70

Amerikas Latweetis.
Translations of articles, 1939–1941. ½ ms. box.
Organ of the American Latvian Workers Union (previous title, *Strahneeku Zihna*). Relates to the Soviet occupation of Latvia, 1940–1941, Latvian foreign relations, the Latvian Communist Party, and the Latvian press in the U.S.
Gift, Arvin Soldner, 1943.

71

Amigos de Durruti collection, 1946. 1 folder.
Three handwritten letters and one photostatic copy of typewritten data, relating to the dissident Spanish anarchist organization Los Amigos de Durruti (Friends of Durruti).
Gift, B. Bolloten, 1974.

72

Amis de la Pologne.
Issuances (in French and Polish), 1940–1941. 1 folder.
French charitable organization. Circulars and memoranda, relating to relief work for Polish refugees in France.

73

Amoedo, Julio.
Transcripts of interviews, n.d. 1 folder.
Typescript.
Argentine Ambassador to Cuba. Relates to the Cuban Revolution of 1959. Interviews conducted by Keith Botsford.
May not be used without permission of J. Amoedo, K. Botsford, and Theodore Draper.
Gift, Keith Botsford, 1964.

74

Amperex Electronic Corporation.
Photographs, 1960. 1 envelope.
Depicts Amperex magnetron and radarscope.

75

Amy, Henry J.
Papers, 1917–1945. 1 ms. box.
Colonel, U.S. Army; Commanding Officer, Troop Equipment Division, New York Port of Embarkation,

1945. Reports, memoranda, clippings, and maps, relating to U.S. military activities in World Wars I and II.
Gift, H. J. Amy, 1964.

76

Anders, Władysław, 1892–1970.
Papers (in Polish), 1939–1946. 34 l. feet.
Polish military officer; Commander-in-Chief of the Polish Armed Forces in the U.S.S.R.; Commander-in-Chief of the 2d Polish Corps in Italy. Orders, reports, card files, questionnaires, accounts, Soviet government documents and publications, photographs, microfiche and printed matter, relating to World War II, the Polish Armed Forces in Russia, the Polish 2d Corps in Italy, Polish citizens arrested and deported under German and Soviet occupations, Polish foreign relations, the Polish Government-in-Exile in London, and Polish Jews.
Preliminary inventory.
Deposit, W. Anders, 1946.

77

Anderson, Dillon, 1906–1974.
Papers, 1950–1969. 1 vol.
Special Assistant to the President for National Security Affairs, 1955–1956. Correspondence, memoranda, speeches, oral history interview, and notes, relating to Dwight D. Eisenhower, President of the U.S., 1953–1961, and to American politics during his administration. Includes facsimile copies of President Eisenhower's handwritten notes.
Gift, Mrs. Jerry Van Kyle, 1975.

78

Anderson, Edgar, 1920–
Study, n.d. "The Baltic Area in World Affairs, 1914–1920." 1 ms. box.
Typescript.
American historian. Relates to military and political aspects of Baltic affairs.

79

Anderson, Frederick Lewis, 1905–1969.
Papers, 1942–1945. 50 l. ft.
Major General, U.S. Army; Deputy Commander of Operations, U.S. Strategic Air Forces in Europe, 1944–1945. Correspondence, memoranda, reports, studies, notes, manuals, printed matter, scrapbooks, films, and memorabilia, relating primarily to bombardment strategy, tactics, and operations in Europe during World War II.
Closed pending processing.
Gift, Elizabeth Anderson Campbell, 1975.

80

Anderson, Roy Scott, d. 1925.
Papers, 1920–1922. ½ ms. box.
American advisor to various officials of the Chinese Government, 1903–1925. Letters and reports, relating to the Chinese economy, Chinese foreign relations with Japan, Russia and the U.S., and historical and political events in China.
Gift, N. Peter Rathvon, 1965.

81

Andreev, N. N.
Letters received (in Russian), 1921–1923, from his son. 1 folder.
Photocopy.
Relates to impressions of the Civil War in Russia formed during a trip from the Crimea to Vladivostok.
Gift, Mrs. Constantine Zakhartchenko, 1975.

82

Andrushkevich, Nikolaĭ Aleksandrovich.
Writings (in Russian), 1931–1936. ½ ms. box.
Holograph.
Histories entitled "Posledniaia Rossiia" (The Last Russia), 1931, and "Prokliatyĭ Korabl'" (The Damned Ship), 1936, relating to the Russian Civil War in Vladivostok and the Far East, 1919–1922, and to travels in Eastern Europe, the Near East and Asia.
Gift, N. A. Andrushkevich, 1936.

83

Angola–slides, 1975. 12 color slides.
Depicts cultural and scenic points of interest in Angola.
Preliminary inventory.
Gift, Peter Duignan, 1976.

84

Anichkov, Vladimir Petrovich.
Memoirs (in Russian), n.d. "Vospominaniia" (Reminiscences). 1½ ms. boxes.
Typescript.
Manager of the Volga Kama Bank and head of the Alapaevsk District. Relates to the Russian Revolution and Civil War in Siberia, 1917–1922. Includes a typescript translation (photocopy) by his daughter, Nathalie Nicolai.
Gift, Nathalie Nicolai, 1975. Incremental gift, 1977.

85

Annenkov, Boris Vladimirovich, 1890–1927.
Orders (in Russian), 1920. 1 folder.
Holograph.
Cossack Ataman and White Russian military leader. Orders (in Russian), of the 1st Assault Mounted Battery of the partisan detachment of B. Annenkov, relating to the Russian Civil War.

86

Anti-Nazi movement leaflet (in German), n.d. 1 folder.
Printed.
Relates to the anti-Nazi movement in Germany during World War II.

87

"Anti-Socialist Activities in Great Britain."
Study, ca. 1928. 1 vol.
Typescript.
Relates to socialist, communist, anti-socialist and anti-communist organizations in existence in Great Britain.

88

Antonenko, V. P.
History (in Russian), ca. 1922. "Kratkaîa Istoriîa Smîeny Pravitel'stv vo Vladivostokîe s 31 Îanvariâ 1920 g. do Evakuaîsiî Oktîabriâ 1922 g." (Brief History of the Changeover of Government in Vladivostok from January 31, 1920 until the Evacuation of October 1922). 1 vol.
Typescript (carbon copy).

89

Applegarth, John S., *collector*.
J. S. Applegarth collection on Latin America, 1964–1965. 4 ms. boxes.
Ephemeral publications, propaganda leaflets, newspaper clippings, photographs, placards, and a sound recording, relating to the riots in the Panama Canal Zone in January 1964 and to activities of political parties in Mexico, and Central and South America.
Register.
Purchase, J. S. Applegarth, 1964. Incremental purchase, 1965.

90

Aras, Tevik Rustu.
Memoirs (in French), n.d. "La Tragédie de la Paix" (The Tragedy of the Peace). 2 vols.
Typescript (carbon copy).
Turkish diplomat. Relates to world politics between World Wars I and II.

91

Arbeiter-Zeitung (Vienna).
Newspaper issues (in German), 1927. 1 folder.
Austrian social democratic newspaper. Relates to the 1927 convention of the Sozialdemokratische Partei Deutschoesterreichs.

92

Arévalo, Apolinar F. de.
Commission (in Spanish), 1899. 1 folder.
Holograph and printed.
Commission as lieutenant colonel of territorial militia of the Philippine Islands.
Gift, W. H. Goede, 1942.

93

Argelander, Frank.
Memorandum, n.d. 1 folder.
Typescript.
American teacher and missionary in China, 1919–1931. Relates to the 1927 uprising of the Communist Party in China.

94

Argentine Republic. Consulado General, Berlin.
Records (in Spanish and German), 1929–1944. 1 ms. box.
Correspondence, reports and clippings. Relates to Argentine-German foreign relations, especially trade relations.
Preliminary inventory.

95

Armour, Lester, 1895–1971.
Papers, 1942–1943. 1 ms. box.
Captain, U.S. Navy. Class notes and correspondence, relating to the Naval Air Combat Intelligence Officers School, Quonset Point, Rhode Island, and the Aviation Intelligence Center, Pacific Ocean Areas, during World War II.
Register.
Gift, Mrs. Lester Armour, 1971. Incremental gift, 1977.

96

Arndt, Edward J., *collector*.
Phonorecords (in German), n.d. 11 phonorecords.
Relates primarily to German history. Includes a series of revolutionary songs recorded in East Germany, entitled "Lieder der Zeit" (Songs of the Times).
Gift, E. J. Arndt, 1953.

97

Arnold.
Memoranda (in German), 1944. 1 folder.
Typescript.
Probable pseudonym of unidentified author. Three memoranda, entitled "Neueste Tragoedie" (Latest Tragedy) and "Der Unabhaengige Staat Kroatien" (The Independent Croatian State), and one untitled, relating to political conditions in Croatia and Istria during World War II.

98

Arnold, Julean Herbert, 1876–1946.
Papers, 1905–1946. 14 ms. boxes.
American consular official; Commercial Attaché in China, 1914–1940. Diary, correspondence, speeches and writings, reports, dispatches, instructions, and memoranda, relating to the U.S. Consular Service in China, to economic and political developments in China, and to American commercial and foreign policy interests in the Far East.
Register.
Gift, William M. Leary, Jr., 1973.

99

Arnold, Ralph, b. 1875.
Essay, n.d. "Laying Foundation Stones." 1 folder.
Typescript (photocopy). Original at the Henry E. Huntington Library.
American geologist; chairman of the Hoover National Republican Club, 1920. Relates to the Herbert Hoover-for-President campaigns between 1920 and 1928.
Gift, Wendel Hammon, 1975.

100

Arrowsmith, Robert, 1860–1928.
Miscellany, 1914–1923. 1 folder, 3 envelopes.
Commission for Relief in Belgium relief worker. Clippings, leaflets, and photographs, relating to conditions in Belgium during the German occupation, and to war loan and relief publicity in the U.S. during World War I.

101

Ashford, Douglas E.
   Papers (in English and French), 1955–1972. 25½ ms. boxes.
   American political scientist and author. Writings, correspondence, reports, clippings, notes, interview transcripts, government publications, other printed matter, and teaching aids, relating to the politics, government, education, and agriculture of Morocco, Tunisia, Algeria and other Northern African nations.
   Gift, D. E. Ashford, 1977.

102

Associated News Service.
   Photographs, 1915–1916. 1 oversize box (½ l. ft).
   Depicts world events from June 1915 to June 1916. Distributed by the Associated News Service.
   Gift, Nelson Carter, 1970.

103

Athanassopoulos, G. D.
   Letter (in French), to Carl L. Hubbs, 1940. 1 folder.
   Holograph.
   Greek educator. Relates to the Italian attack on Greece in World War II.

104

Atomic weapons—testing—photographs, n.d. 1 envelope.
   Depicts an atomic bomb test in the Pacific Ocean.

105

Atwood, William G.
   Letter, 1920. 1 folder.
   Holograph.
   Colonel, U.S. Army; and European Technical Adviser to Yugoslavia, 1920. Relates to the resolution of Yugoslav–Italian boundary disputes by the Treaty of Rapallo in 1920.

106

Augusts, Gvido, *collector.*
   Miscellany, 1940–1966. 1 folder.
   Passbooks, permits, orders, certificates, deeds, and inventories, relating to daily life in Latvia under Nazi occupation, to the status under the Nazis of property previously seized in Latvia by the Soviet government, and to post-war Soviet rule.
   Gift, G. Augusts, 1973.

107

Australia—pictorial, n.d. 1 envelope.
   Depicts scenes at Montefiore and Kadlunga Station, Australia.

108

Austria-Hungary—Army—World War I—photographs, 1915–1918. 6 envelopes.
   Depicts Austro-Hungarian military forces, primarily on the Italian front during World War I.
   Purchase, Karl P. Hess, 1971.

109

Austria—posters (in German), 1938. 7 posters and proclamations.
   Relates to the Anschluss of Austria and Germany.

110

Austria—revolt of 1934—collection (in German), 1934. 1 ms. box.
   Broadsides, leaflets, mimeographed articles, and photographs, primarily relating to the Austrian revolt of 1934.
   Gift, Karl Harbauer, 1935.

111

Austria—socialism/communism—leaflets (in German), ca. 1935–1936. 1 folder.
   Four socialist/communist underground leaflets and camouflage covers, published in Austria.
   Exchange, Library of Congress, 1972.

112

Austria—student organizations—collection (in German), 1970–1971. 1 folder.
   Leaflets, periodicals, and a hand-written poster, distributed at the University of Vienna, and relating primarily to the Osterreichische Studentenunion (Austrian Student Union) and university reform.
   Gift, Grete Heinz, 1974.

113

Austrian annexation plebiscite, 1938-ballot (in German), 1938. 1 folder.
   Printed.
   Used in the Austrian plebiscite on union with Germany in 1938.

114

Austrian anti-Nazi pamphlets (in German), n.d. 1 folder.
   Printed.
   Published by the Austrian Socialist and Communist Parties in the 1930's, relating to the anti-Nazi movement in Austria and to the programs of the Austrian Socialist and Communist parties.
   Gift, Karl Harbauer, 1935; Mr. ver Brugge, 1942.

115

Autograph collection, n.d. ½ ms. box.
   Autographs of various famous persons.

116

Axentieff, N.
   Memorandum, n.d. 1 folder.
   Typescript.
   Relates to relief needs of Russian refugees living in exile. Sent to Herbert Hoover during or immediately after the Russian Civil War.

117

Ayres, Leonard Porter, 1879–1946.
Diary, 1924. 1 folder.
Typescript.
Colonel, U.S. Army; economic adviser to the Reparation Commission. Relates to the work of the commission.

118

Ayres, Paulo.
Lecture transcript, 1964. "The Brazilian Revolution."
1 folder.
Typescript.
Brazilian business executive. Lecture delivered at the Center for Strategic Studies, Georgetown University, relating to the 1964 Brazilian revolution.
Gift, Paulo Ayres, 1972.

119

Baade, Fritz, 1893–
Memoranda, 1947. 1 vol.
Typescript (carbon copy).
Relates to letters of appeal from Reinhold Mayer, Minister President of Baden-Wuerttemberg, to Lucius D. Clay, U.S. High Commissioner for Germany, protesting Allied industrial dismantling of Germany.

120

Babb, Nancy, d. 1948.
Papers, 1917–1925. 1 ms. box.
American Relief Administration and American Friends Service Committee relief worker in Russia, 1917–1925. Correspondence, reports and memoranda, relating to American Relief Administration and American Friends Service Committee work in Russia.
Gift, Elizabeth Baker.

121

Babcock, Conrad Stanton, 1876–1950.
Papers, n.d. 1 ms. box, 1 album, 1 envelope.
Brigadier General, U.S. Army. Memoirs and photographs, relating to American military activities during the Philippine insurrection of 1899–1901, and in France during World War I.

122

Bacon, Walter Meredith, 1946–
Dissertation, 1975. "Nicolae Titulescu and Romanian Foreign Policy, 1933–1934." ½ ms. box.
Typescript (photocopy).
American historian. Relates to the career of Nicolas Titulescu, Romanian Minister of Foreign Affairs and Minister of Finance between 1932 and 1936. Includes clippings and photocopies of diplomatic correspondence, 1925–1972, used as research material for the dissertation.
Gift, W. M. Bacon, 1975.

123

Bade, Wilfrid Albert Karl, 1906–
Papers (in German), 1927–1945. 11 ms. boxes, 1 envelope.

Official of the German Reichsministerium fuer Volksaufklaerung und Propaganda during World War II. Manuscripts of writings, correspondence, memoranda, printed matter and photographs, relating to dissemination of German propaganda during World War II. Preliminary inventory.

124

Baeumer, Gertrud, 1873–1951.
Memorandum (in German), 1946. "In Eigener Sache" (My Own Case). 1 folder.
Typescript.
German author, educator and Reichstag deputy. Relates to allegations that G. Baeumer had engaged in pro-Nazi activities.

125

Bagby, Carroll A., b. 1890.
Papers, 1916–1950. 1 folder.
Colonel, U.S. Army. Orders and personnel records, relating to the military career of C. A. Bagby. Includes photocopy of a diary relating to the U.S. intervention in Mexico in 1916.

126

Bagg, Mrs. L. L. S., *collector.*
Miscellany, ca. 1914–1918. 1 ms. box, 1 envelope.
Newspaper and magazine clippings, maps, ration books, currency, photographs, and memorabilia, relating primarily to Italy in World War I.
Gift, Mrs. L. L. S. Bagg.

127

Bail, Hamilton Vaughan.
Study, 1943. "The Military Government of Cuba, 1898–1902." 1 vol.
Typescript (carbon copy).
Prepared in the Historical Section, Army War College. Relates to organizational and operational aspects.

128

Bailey, H. S.
Memorandum, 1918. 1 folder.
Typescript.
Head of the Oil, Fat and Wax Laboratory, Bureau of Chemistry, U.S. Department of Agriculture, and a substitute member of the U.S. Soap Committee. Relates to the meeting of the Soap Committee on July 30, 1918, regarding war-time regulation of the soap industry.

129

Bailey, Harry Lewis, b. 1879.
Etchings and sketches, n.d. 1 portfolio.
American artist. Depicts shipbuilding and dockside scenes.
Gift, Joanna B. and Mary A. Bailey, 1949.

130

Bailey, Thomas A. and Paul B. Ryan, *collectors.*
Bailey-Ryan collection on the *Lusitania,* 1973–1975.
11 ms. boxes, 11 reels of microfilm, 1 phonotape.

Research notes, photocopies of primary and secondary source materials, clippings, microfilms and one sound tape recording, relating to the sinking of the *Lusitania*. Collected by Thomas A. Bailey and Paul B. Ryan, as research material for their book, *The Lusitania Disaster: An Episode in Modern Warfare and Diplomacy*.
Preliminary inventory.
May be used only with permission of T. A. Bailey and P. B. Ryan.
Gift, T. A. Bailey and P. B. Ryan, 1975.

131
Bailey, Thomas Andrew, 1902–
Miscellaneous papers, 1947. 1½ ms. boxes.
American historian. Diaries, correspondence, notebooks, and passport, relating to conditions in Europe during the summer of 1947. Used as research material for the book by T. A. Bailey, *The Marshall Plan Summer* (Stanford: Hoover Institution on War, Revolution and Peace, 1978).
Gift, T. A. Bailey, 1977.

132
Baker, Elizabeth N.
Miscellaneous papers, 1938–1966. ½ ms. box.
Leaflets, bulletins, correspondence, and clippings, relating to U.S. politics and government and conservative, anti-communist, and pacifist political groups in the United States.
Preliminary inventory.
Gift, E. N. Baker, 1966. Incremental gift, 1967.

133
Baker, George Barr, 1870–1948.
Papers, 1919–1932. 14 ms. boxes.
American journalist; a Director of the American Relief Administration. Correspondence, photographs, and printed matter, relating to the American Relief Administration; Commission for Relief in Belgium; Paris Peace Conference; U.S. presidential politics and the 1924, 1928, and 1932 presidential campaigns; Calvin Coolidge; Herbert Hoover; the Republican party; and the foreign language press.
Preliminary inventory.
Gift, Mrs. W. Parmer Fuller, Jr., 1955. Incremental gift, 1959.

134
Baker, O. E.
Study, ca. 1920–1930. "Land Utilization in China." 1 folder.
Typescript (mimeographed).

135
Baker, Wilder DuPuy, 1890–1975.
Papers, 1914–1975. 4½ ms. boxes, 6 albums, 1 framed photograph, 1 framed certificate, 2 cylinders.
Vice Admiral, U.S. Navy; Chief of Staff of Carrier Force Two in the Pacific Fleet, 1944–1945; Commandant of the 11th Naval District, 1949–1952. Orders, clippings, photographs and memorabilia, relating to the naval career of W. D. Baker, naval operations in the Pacific Theater during World War II, and the San Diego Naval Base.
Gift, W. D. Baker, 1975.

136
Baldwin, Norman Lee, 1890–1945.
Diary, 1943–1944. 1 folder.
Holograph.
Colonel, U.S. Army; Signal Officer, 4th Army, 1943–1944. Relates to American military activities and communications in the vicinity of Paestum, Italy. Includes a memoir by J. M. Huddleston, Colonel, U.S. Army, and Surgeon, VI Corps.
Gift, Mrs. J. Allen Davis, 1968.

137
Balk, A.
Memoirs (in Russian), 1929. "Poslíednie Piât'dneĭ TŠarskago Petrograda, 23–28 Fevralîâ 1917 g.; Dnevnik Poslíedniâgo Petrogradskago Gradonachal'nika" (The Last Five Days of Tsarist Petrograd. February 23–28, 1917: The Diary of the Petrograd Mayor). 1 vol.
Typescript (carbon copy).

138
Ballantine, Joseph William, 1888–1973.
Papers, 1909–1970. 3 ms. boxes.
American diplomat; Special Assistant to the Secretary of State, 1945–1947. Memoirs, notes, reports, articles and printed matter, relating to American foreign policy in the Far East, and to the foreign policy views of Owen Lattimore.
Register.
Gift, Lesley Frost Ballantine, 1973.

139
Baltic states—politics—proclamations (in Russian), 1889. 1 folder.
Printed.
Relates to Russian administration of the Baltic states.

140
Balykov, V. P.
Speech (in Russian), 1935. 1 folder.
Typescript.
Representative of the Russkoĭ Fashistŝkoĭ Partiĭ (Russian Fascist Party) in Japan. Calls for patriotic unity among Russians in the struggle against bolshevism in Russia.

141
Banam, A., *collector*.
Treaty (in Persian), 1945. 1 folder.
Printed.
Treaty between the head of the autonomous government of Azerbaijan and the commander-in-chief of the Tabriz garrison, 12 December 1945.
Gift, A. Banam, 1950.

142

Bane, Suda Lorena, 1886–1952.
Documentary history, 1943. *Organization of American Relief in Europe, 1918–1919.* ½ ms. box.
Galley proofs (annotated).
Relates to World War I relief activities of the American Relief Administration and U.S. Food Administration. Edited by S. L. Bane and Ralph Haswell Lutz. Published in Stanford by the Stanford University Press, 1943.

143

Banque de France.
Report (in French), 1939. "Assemblée Générale des Actionnaires de la Banque de France du 28 janvier 1938 . . . : Compte Rendu au Nom du Conseil Général de la Banque et Rapport de MM. les Censeurs" (General Assembly of the Shareholders of the Bank of France, January 28, 1938 . . . : Report in the Name of the General Counsel of the Bank and Report of the Auditors). 1 folder.
Typescript and printed.
Relates to activities of the Bank of France in 1937.

144

Baraka, Imamu, 1934–
Speech, 1968. 1 phonorecord.
American black nationalist poet and playwright. Delivered at a meeting at the University of Cincinnati sponsored by its United Black Association.

145

Barbé, Henri, 1902–
Memoirs (in French), n.d. "Souvenirs de Militant et de Dirigeant Communiste" (Reminiscences of a Militant and Leading Communist). 1 vol.
Typescript (part carbon copy).
Member and leading official in the French Communist Party, 1920–1934, and in the Executive Committee of the Communist International, 1927–1931.

146

Barber, Alvin B.
Papers, 1919–1922. 5 ms. boxes.
American Relief Administration worker; European Technical Adviser for Poland, 1919–1922. Correspondence, reports, and memoranda, relating to Polish railways, coal, oil, and timber resources, Danzig, and Upper Silesia.
Gift, A. B. Barber, 1959.

147

Barbour, George Brown, b. 1890.
Papers, 1911–1934. 1½ ms. boxes, 1 envelope, 1 motion picture.
American geologist; missionary and educator in China, 1920–1932. Correspondence, photographs, post cards, drawings and a motion picture, relating to political and social conditions in China, missionary service in China, and university education in China.
Gift, Ian Barbour, 1973.

148

Bardin, William, Jr., *collector.*
Miscellany, 1860–1934. 1 folder.
An 1865 mourning badge commemorating the death of Abraham Lincoln; an issue of the *American Union,* August 25, 1865; an issue of the *Virginia Free Press,* November 15, 1860; an issue of the *New York Herald,* April 15, 1865; an 1899 soldier's letter from the Philippines; a World War I Liberty Loan poster; and four letters written in 1933–1934 describing the depression.
Gift, W. Bardin, Jr., 1973.

149

Bargatzky, Walter.
Memorandum (in German), 1945. "Persoenliche Erinnerungen an die Aufstandsbewegung des 20. Juli 1944 in Frankreich" (Personal Reminiscences of the Insurrectionary Movement of July 20, 1944 in France). 1 folder.
Typescript.
Relates to the plot to assassinate Adolf Hitler.

150

Barker, Burt Brown.
Papers, 1887–1966. ½ ms. box, 4 phonotapes.
American educator; boyhood friend of Herbert Hoover. Correspondence, phonotapes, and school catalogs, relating to Herbert Hoover's youth, early schooling, and mining career in Australia. Includes correspondence between Herbert Hoover and B. B. Barker.
Gift, B. B. Barker, 1967; KOIN-TV, Portland, Oregon, 1968.

151

Barnhart, Edward N.
Papers, 1942–1959. 7 ms. boxes, 1 oversize box (½ l. ft.).
American historian. Correspondence, reports, writings, and research notes, relating to U.S. Army internal security measures during World War II directed against U.S. citizens of Japanese, Italian, and German extraction. Used as research material for the book by E. N. Barnhart and Jacobus tenBroek, *Prejudice, War and Constitution* (Berkeley, 1955). Includes a photocopy of a typewritten study, entitled "Internal Security in World War II: Military Programs of Civilian Control."
Preliminary inventory.
Gift, E. N. Barnhart, 1978.

152

Barrett, David Dean, 1892–1977.
Papers, 1933–1970. ½ ms. box, 4 envelopes, 2 phonorecords, 1 oversize box (½ l. ft.).
Colonel, U.S. Army; Chief of the U.S. Dixie Mission to Chinese Communist forces, 1944. Manuscripts of writings, correspondence, printed matter, photographs and phonorecords, relating to the Dixie Mission and the military situation in China during World War II.
Preliminary inventory.
Gift, D. D. Barrett, 1948. Subsequent increments.

153

Barrett, William S.
Diary, 1918–1920. "America in Russia, or the Diary of a Russian Wolfhound." 1 folder.
Typescript.
Captain, U.S. Army. Relates to the U.S. intervention in Siberia during the Russian Revolution.

154

Barringer, Thomas C.
Papers, 1922–1925. 2 ms. boxes.
District Supervisor, American Relief Administration in Russia, 1921–1923. Correspondence, reports, memoranda, photographs, and clippings, relating to relief operations of the American Relief Administration in two famine areas in Russia.
Gift, T. C. Barringer, 1956.

155

Basily-Callimaki, Eva de, 1855–1913.
Papers (in French), 1867–1913. 2½ ms. boxes.
Russian art critic and author. Correspondence, writings, notes, clippings, printed matter, photographs, and memorabilia, relating to French and Western European art history, and to Jean Baptiste Isabey, the French miniaturist. Includes a draft of the biography *Isabey* by E. de Basily-Callimaki.
Gift, Mrs. Nicolas A. de Basily, 1965. Increment, 1978.

156

Basily, Nicolas Alexandrovich de, 1883–1963.
Papers (in Russian and French), 1881–1957. 25 ms. boxes, 4 envelopes.
Imperial Russian diplomat; Deputy Director, Chancellery of Foreign Affairs, 1911–1914; Member, Council of Ministry of Foreign Affairs, 1917. Correspondence, memoranda, reports, notes, and photographs, relating to Russian political and foreign affairs, 1900–1917, Russian involvement in World War I, the abdication of Tsar Nicholas II, and the Russian Revolution and Civil War. Includes drafts of N. A. de Basily's book *Russia Under Soviet Rule*.
Register.
Gift, Mrs. N. A. de Basily, 1965. Subsequent increments.

157

Bass, Walter R., *collector*.
Miscellany (in German), 1920–1945. 1 folder.
Member of the American Military Government in Austria, 1945. Relates to the German Nationalsozialistische Deutsche Arbeiterpartei. Includes a weekly menu card for a German heavy anti-aircraft battery (reserve unit), 1945, the program of the Nationalsozialistische Deutsche Arbeiterpartei, 1920, and an autographed photo of Rudolf Hess.

158

Bastin, Catherine Sylvia.
Papers, ca. 1914–1918. 1 folder, 1 envelope.
American Red Cross nurse in Europe during World War I. Correspondence, pamphlets, clippings, medals, badges, and photographs, relating to C. Bastin's Red Cross service.
Gift, Dorothy Bastin, 1962.

159

Bastunov, Vladimir, J., *collector*.
V. J. Bastunov collection on the Russian Imperial Army (in Russian), 1897–1917. 4 ms. boxes.
Imperial orders, military orders, personnel rosters, and casualty reports, relating to the operations of the Russian Imperial Army and its personnel.
Gift, V. J. Bastunov, 1975.

160

Batchelder, George.
Memoirs, 1914. "Why Hurry?" 1 folder.
Typescript.
American tourist in Germany, 1914. Relates to conditions in Germany at the outbreak of World War I.

161

Batîushin, N. S.
History (in Russian), n.d. "V chem byla sila Rasputina" (What Comprised the Strength of Rasputin). 1 vol.
Typescript (carbon copy).
Relates to Grigoriĭ Rasputin, 1871–1916.

162

Batsell, Walter Russell.
Memorandum, 1925. "Memorandum on the Union of Soviet Socialist Republics." 1 folder.
Typescript.
American visitor to European Russia, 1925. Relates to political conditions in the Soviet Union, and to Soviet foreign policy.
Gift, W. R. Batsell, 1926.

163

"Battalion That Would Not Disband: Story of the 317th Field Signal Battalion, 1917–1972."
History, 1972. 1 folder.
Typescript (mimeographed).
Relates to activities of the 317th Field Signal Battalion of the U.S. Army in France during World War I, and to reunions of veterans of the battalion.
Gift, John B. Donovan, 1972.

164

Baudouin, Paul.
Memorandum (in French), n.d. "A Propos de *La Vérité sur l'Armistice*" (Regarding *The Truth about the Armistice*). 1 folder.
Typescript.
Foreign Minister of France, 1940. Relates to the book by Albert Kammerer, *La Vérité sur l'Armistice* (Paris, 1944), on the French surrender in 1940.

165

Bavaria. Politische Polizci. Fuehrerschutzkommando.
Dossiers (in German), 1934. 1 folder.
Typescript.
Miscellaneous dossiers of police suspects.

166

Baxter, Robert I., *collector*.
Map, n.d. 1 folder.
Hand drawn.
Represents the region around Archangel, Russia, indicating the route followed by a military expedition from Tiagra to Archangel, August-September 1918.
Gift, R. I. Baxter.

167

Bayar (Celâl) collection, 1954. 1 folder.
Souvenir pamphlet (printed), prepared by the Turkish Government, and souvenir program (printed), prepared by the Hoover Institution on War, Revolution and Peace, commemorating the visit of Celâl Bayar (1884–), President of Turkey, to the United States and to the Hoover Institution.

168

Bayen, Malaku E.
Letter fragment, 1940, to Mrs. K. Gillett-Gatty. 1 folder.
Typescript.
International First Vice President, Ethiopian World Federation. Relates to the history of Ethiopia. Includes an issue of *The Voice of Ethiopia* (New York), organ of the Ethiopian World Federation, for September 14, 1940.

169

Bayne, Joseph Breckinridge, 1880–1964.
Papers, 1917–1919. 1 folder, 1 envelope.
American physician; surgeon with the Romanian Red Cross, 1916–1918. Photographs and photocopies of letters, clippings, and certificates, relating to military and civilian hospitals in Romania during World War I.
Gift, Olga Ellis Smith, 1967.

170

Bazarevich, General.
Papers (in Russian), 1919–1924. 5 ms. boxes.
Russian Military Attaché in Belgrade, Yugoslavia. Correspondence and orders, relating to White Russian military activities in Gallipoli, Bulgaria, and Yugoslavia.
Preliminary inventory.

171

Bazarov, Major General.
Papers (in Russian), 1904–1906. 1 ms. box.
Major General, Imperial Russian Army. Reports, orders, field maps, correspondence and clippings, relating to the Russo-Japanese War.
Preliminary inventory.

172

Beach, Edward Latimer.
Translations of letters received, 1916. 1 folder.
Typescript.
Captain, U.S. Navy. Two letters, from Sudre Dartiguenave, President of Haiti, and Louis Borno, future President of Haiti, to E. L. Beach, relating to the role of Captain Beach in the U.S. intervention in Haiti in 1915.

173

Beaumont, Henry G., *collector*.
H. G. Beaumont collection on Japanese war crimes trial, 1946–1948. 1 ms. box.
Affidavits, speeches, biographical data, clippings and memorabilia, relating to the trial of Japanese political and military leaders for war crimes in Tokyo, 1946–1948. Includes the opening speech of the prosecution, and affidavits of the defendants Hideki Tojo and Hiroshi Oshima.
Gift, H. G. Beaumont, 1978.

174

Bedford, Hastings William Sackville Russell, 12th Duke of, 1888–1953.
Papers, 1942–1952. ½ ms. box.
British pacifist and author. Pamphlets by the Duke of Bedford, 1942–1952, and correspondence between the Duke of Bedford and Louis Obed Renne, 1948–1952, relating to pacifism and military disarmament.
Gift, Elsie Renne, 1973.

175

Beer, Alice, *collector*.
Miscellany, 1937–1940. 1 folder.
Correspondence and miscellanea, relating to the Spanish Civil War. Includes letters (typescript) from Margaret Palmer, an American visitor in Spain, 1937.
Gift, A. Beer.

176

Bees of America
Miscellaneous records (in English and French), 1917–1921. 1 vol.
Brooklyn children's organization operating under the auspices of the Brooklyn Women's War Relief Committee. Correspondence, photographs and miscellanea, relating to the provision of relief for Belgian children during World War I.

177

Bekeart, Laura Helene.
Study, n.d. "The A.R.A.: Herbert Hoover and Russian Relief." 1 folder.
Typescript.
Gift, L. H. Bekeart, 1965.

178

Belgium. Cour de Cassation.
Letter (in French), 1943, to Alexander von Falkenhausen, General, German Army, and Military Com-

mander for Belgium and Northern France. 1 folder. Typescript.

Relates to Belgians transported to Germany for forced labor during World War II.

179

Belgium—underground movement—collection (in French, Flemish and English), 1939–1945. 1½ ms. boxes.

Leaflets, press releases, manuscripts of writings, clippings and miscellanea, relating to the Belgian resistance movement during World War II.

180

Belgium (Territory under German occupation, 1914–1918).

Issuances (in German, French and Flemish), 1914–1918. 39 ms. boxes.

Printed.

Public proclamations and announcements issued by the German Military Government in Belgium, arranged and numbered as they appear in *Les Avis, Proclamations et Nouvelles de Guerre Allemandes Affichés à Bruxelles pendant l'Occupation* (German Notices, Proclamations and War News Posted in Brussels during the Occupation) (Ixelles-Bruxelles: Les Editions Brian Hill, 1915–1918). Includes some items not identified in this work.

Gift, Grace Davis Booth.

181

Belgium (Territory under German occupation, 1940–1944) Wirtschaftsministerium.

Report (in German), 1941. "Zur Wirtschaftlichen Lage in Belgien" (On the Economic Situation in Belgium). 1 folder.

Typescript.

182

Belgium (Territory under German occupation, 1940–1944) Militaerbefehlshaber in Belgien und in Nordfrankreich. Propaganda-Abteilung Belgien.

Records (in German, French and Flemish), 1939–1944. 7 ms. boxes.

Propaganda Division of the German occupation government in Belgium. Correspondence, memoranda, and photographs, relating to propaganda activities. Includes examples of German and Allied propaganda distributed in Belgium and of clandestine anti-German propaganda produced in Belgium.

Gift, 1947.

183

Bell, James Ford, 1879–1961.

Papers, 1917–1930. 2 ms. boxes.

American business executive; Chairman, Milling Division, U.S. Food Administration, 1917–1918. Correspondence, reports, financial statements, and photographs, relating to the U.S. Food Administration and the 1928 Herbert Hoover political campaign in Minnesota. Correspondents include Herbert Hoover and Rudolph Lee.

Preliminary inventory.

Gift, J. F. Bell, 1957. Subsequent increments.

184

Bell, Johannes.

Translation of a memorandum, n.d. 1 folder. Typescript.

German diplomat. Relates to the participation of the German delegation in the Paris Peace Conference in 1919. Translated by Alma Luckau.

185

Bell, Lillian, *collector*.

Slides, ca. 1914–1918. 1 ms. box.

Depicts miscellaneous scenes from World War I.

Gift, L. Bell, 1959.

186

Belorussian Liberation Front, London.

Publications, 1955–1969. 1 folder.

Anti-communist and nationalist émigré group. Brochures and printed matter, relating to Belorussian history, nationalism, and cartography.

Gift, Jan Budzich-Bunchuk, 1976.

187

"Bemerkungen zur Frage der Gliederung der Deutschen Wirtschaft" (Remarks on the Question of the Formation of the German Economy).

Memorandum (in German), ca. 1936. 1 folder. Typescript.

Relates to economic conditions in Germany and proposals for the creation of a Ministry of Food.

188

Bendetsen, Karl Robin, 1907–

Papers, 1917–1972. ca. 150 l. ft.

American business executive; Assistant and Under Secretary of the Army, 1950–1952; Special U.S. Representative to West Germany, 1956; Special U.S. Ambassador to the Philippine Islands, 1956; Chairman, Advisory Committee to the Secretary of Defense, 1962; President and Chairman of the Board, Champion International Corporation; member, Board of Overseers, Hoover Institution. Correspondence, memoranda, reports, speeches, studies and scrapbooks, primarily relating to American defense policy and to the Champion International Corporation.

Preliminary inventory.

Closed until July 1988.

Gift, K. R. Bendetsen, 1975.

189

Beneš, Eduard, 1884–1948.

Speech (in Russian), 1921. 1 folder. Typescript.

Foreign Minister of Czechoslovakia, 1918–1935; President of Czechoslovakia, 1935–1938 and 1939–1948. Relates to Soviet-Czechoslovakian foreign relations.

190

Benjamin, Alfred.

Thesis, 1950. "The Great Dilemma." 1 ms. box. Typescript.

Relates to the foreign policy of the Russian Provisional Government, March-May 1917. Political science thesis, Columbia University.

191

Bennett, H. C.
Excerpts from a letter, 1935, to H. E. Lutz. 1 folder.
Typescript.
American visitor to Germany. Relates to conditions in Germany under national socialism.

192

Bennett, Paul G.
Miscellaneous papers, 1968. 1 ms. box.
Letters, cartoons, and newspaper clippings, relating to Panama-U.S. relations in 1968.
Gift, P. G. Bennett, 1968.

193

Bennigsen, Emmanuil Pavlovich, Graf, b. 1875.
Translations of papers, 1914–1919. ½ ms. box.
Typescript.
Colonel, Imperial Russian Army. Diary extracts, letters and poems, relating to Russian military activities during World War I, and to activities of the White Army of General Denikin during the Russian Civil War. Includes an account of the February 1917 Revolution by Grafinîa Bennigsen.

194

Berbig, Reinhard.
Memoirs (in German), n.d. 1 folder.
Typescript.
Soldier, German Army. Relates to the Eastern Front during World War II, 1941, and to Russian prisoner of war camps, 1945–1953.
Gift, Charles Burdick, 1976.

195

Bereczky, Dr.
Radio address (in Hungarian), n.d. "Ungarischer Aufruf" (Hungarian Summons). 1 phonorecord.
Denounces Soviet communism.

196

Bergery, Gaston, 1892–1974.
Papers (mainly in French), 1924–1973. 38 ms. boxes.
French attorney, diplomat, author, journalist, and politician; Secretary-General, Inter-Allied Commission for Reparations, 1918–1924; Director of the Cabinet, Ministry of Foreign Affairs, 1924–1925; Ambassador to the Soviet Union, 1941. Correspondence, telegrams, reports, memoranda, lists, speeches and writings, posters, and leaflets, relating to French political events and foreign relations, France during World War II, and the Front Populaire.
Gift, Mrs. G. Bergery, 1977.

197

Bergson, Abram, 1914–
Report, 1950. "Disposition of the Gross National Product of the USSR in 1937, 1940 and 1948." 1 folder.

Typescript (mimeographed).
Relates to the allocation of Soviet economic resources. Written by A. Bergson and Hans Heymann, Jr., under the auspices of the Rand Corporation.

198

"Bericht ueber die Anti-Nationalsozialistische Taetigkeit der Bayerischen Heimatbewegung" (Report on the Anti-National Socialist Activities of the Bavarian Home Land Movement).
Report (in German), n.d. 1 folder.
Typescript.
Relates to the Bavarian separatist movement during World War II.

199

"Bericht ueber die Kirchliche Lage in der Erzdioezese Salzburg seit Maerz 1938" (Report on the Situation of the Church in the Archdiocese of Salzburg since March 1938).
Report (in German), 1945. 1 folder.
Typescript.

200

Berk, Stephen M.
History, n.d. "The Coup d'État of Admiral Kolchak: The Counterrevolution in Siberia and East Russia, 1917–1918." ½ ms. box.
Typescript.
American historian. Relates to activities of anti-Bolshevik forces in Siberia during the period October 1917 to November 1918.
Deposit, S. M. Berk, 1972.

201

Berlin—blockade, 1948–1949—photographs, 1948–1949. 12 envelopes.
Depicts scenes in Berlin during the blockade and airlift of 1948–1949.
Preliminary inventory.
Gift, World Affairs Council of Northern California, 1950.

202

Berlin nach der Revolution collection (in German), 1918–1920. 3 ms. boxes.
Handbills, proclamation, political campaign literature, pamphlets, posters, and newspaper issues, relating to the end of World War I, the Spartacist uprising, the Bavarian communist regime, the Kapp Putsch, elections of 1920, German nationalism, and antisemitism.

203

Berlin. Polizeipraesidium.
Charts (in German), 1939. 1 folder.
Represents communication networks of the Berlin police.

204

Berlin ration cards list (in German), n.d. 1 folder.
Typescript.
Enumerates ration cards issued in Berlin during World War I, 1915–1919.

205

Berlon, Lieutenant Colonel.
Report (in French), 1942. 1 vol.
Typescript (carbon copy).
French Army officer. Relates to conditions at the German prison camp Oflag G.X.B. during World War II.

206

Berman, Ben.
Photographs, 1943–1950. 1 envelope.
Depicts the birthplace in Scotland of John Paul Jones, naval leader in the American Revolution, and Yehudi Menuhin, American violinist, with army officers in England during World War II.

207

Bernardino, Vitaliano.
Papers, 1966–1977. 2 ms. boxes.
Member, Philippine Department of Education; Director, Southeast Asia Ministers of Education Secretariat. Writings and printed matter, relating to education in Southeast Asia.
Gift, V. Bernardino, 1978.

208

Bernatskiĭ, Mikhail Vladimirovich, b. 1876, *collector.*
Miscellany (in Russian, French and English), 1916–1918. 1 folder.
Reports, correspondence, and statistics, relating to the financing of the Russian war effort during World War I.
Preliminary inventory.

209

Berndt, Alfred-Ingemar.
Report (in German), 1944. 1 folder.
Typescript (photocopy).
Official of the German Ministry of Propaganda. Relates to proposals for administration of the World War II German propaganda effort.

210

Bernfeld, Siegfried, d. 1953, *collector.*
Journals (in German), 1903–1919. 2 ms. boxes.
Typescript (mimeographed) and printed.
Literary journals of German and Austrian secondary schools.
Gift, S. Bernfeld.

211

Bernhard Leopold collection (in German), 1936–1937.
1 folder.
Photocopy.
Correspondence (typewritten) of German Nazi Party officials, relating to the resignation from Nazi Party membership of Prince Bernhard of Lippe-Biesterfeld (1911–), subsequently Prince Consort of Queen Juliana of the Netherlands.

212

Berry, Robert Wallace, 1898–
Papers, 1932–1976. 3½ ms. boxes.
Rear Admiral, U.S. Navy; Assistant to the Secretary of Defense, 1947–1949. Memoirs, reports, printed matter and photographs, relating to American naval operations in World Wars I and II, and to the administration of the U.S. Defense Department under Secretary of Defense James Forrestal.
Preliminary inventory.
Gift, R. W. Berry, 1975. Incremental gift, 1977.

213

Berzins, Alfreds, 1899–1977.
Memoirs (in Latvian), n.d. 1 folder.
Typescript (photocopy).
Latvian politician; Deputy Minister of the Interior, 1934–1937; Minister of Public Affairs, 1937–1940. Relates to Latvian politics, 1934–1940.
Gift, Edgar Anderson, 1978.

214

Besedovskiĭ, Grigoriĭ Zinov'evich.
Articles (in French), 1929. 1 vol.
Printed.
Soviet chargé d'affaires in France. Series of articles published in *Le Matin* (Paris), relating to Soviet diplomacy and the Communist International.

215

Better Homes in America, 1923–1935.
Records, 1923–1935. 65 ms. boxes, 14 scrapbooks.
Association to encourage individual and community efforts at home improvement in the United States; organized by Marie M. Meloney with Herbert Hoover as President. Correspondence, press releases, expense statements, clippings, pamphlets, and photographs.
Gift, Better Homes in America, 1933. Subsequent increments.

216

Bevin (Ernest)—photograph, n.d. 1 envelope.
Depicts the British politician E. Bevin.

217

Beyer, Eduard, *collector.*
E. Beyer collection on Austria (in German), 1914–1917. 1 folder, 1 envelope.
Telegrams from the eastern front, relating to the Austrian forces during World War I, 1914; and 30 photographs depicting Emperor Charles of Austria reviewing troops on the eastern front, 1917.
Gift, E. Beyer, 1930.

218

Biafra Students Association in the Americas.
Phonorecord, n.d. *This is Biafra.*
Includes the national anthem and other songs of Biafra, and a speech by Colonel Odumegwu Ojukwu, Head of State of Biafra, in 1967.

219
"Bibliography of the Most Important Works on Polish Law."
Bibliography (in Polish), 1927. 1 folder.
Typescript.
Includes English translation.

220
Bibliothèque Grimmon.
Catalog (in French), n.d. 1 vol.
Typescript.
Lists books, ephemera and maps relating to World War I.

221
Bickler, Frau Hermann, 1909–
Statement (in German), 1947. 1 folder.
Typescript.
Relates to the activities of Frau Bickler and her husband in the movement to return Alsace-Lorraine to Germany before and during World War II.

222
Bidou, Henry, 1873–1943.
History (in French), 1940. "Une Bataille de 45 Jours, 10 Mai-24 Juin: Voici Comment se Sont Déroulés les Événements les plus Dramatiques de Notre Histoire" (A Battle of 45 Days, May 10–June 24: This Is How the Most Dramatic Events of Our History Unfolded). 1 vol.
Typescript.
Relates to the German invasion of France, and French capitulation, 1940.

223
Bielevskiĭ, Lieutenant, *collector*.
Miscellany (in Russian), 1917. 1 folder.
Military reports and memoranda, relating to the abdication of Tsar Nicholas II, and to disintegration of discipline in the Russian Army during the Russian Revolution.
Preliminary inventory.

224
Bienen, Henry.
Papers, 1961–1967. 1 ms. box.
Professor of Political Science, Princeton University. Drafts of an unpublished chapter of a book, minutes of meetings, reports, pamphlets, and newspaper clippings, relating to Tanzania political development.
Register.
Gift, H. Bienen, 1972.

225
Bilderback, William Winch, 1937–
Dissertation, 1973. "The American Communist Party and World War II." ½ ms. box.
Typescript (photocopy).
Relates to the response of the American Communist Party to World War II. Ph.D. dissertation, University of Washington.

May not be quoted without permission of author. Gift, W. W. Bilderback, 1976.

226
Bilmanis, Alfred, 1887–1948, *collector*.
A. Bilmanis collection on Latvia (mostly in Latvian), 1944–1948. 1 ms. box.
Serial issues, mimeographed bulletins and manuscripts of writings, relating to Latvia during World War II and to postwar Latvian refugees in Sweden, West Germany, Argentina and the U.S.
Gift, A. Bilmanis, 1945. Subsequent increments.

227
Binford, Thomas H., 1896–1973.
Papers, 1940–1967. ½ ms. box, 4 envelopes, 2 albums.
Vice Admiral, U.S. Navy; Commanding Officer, Destroyer Division 58, 1941–1942. Addresses, reports, awards, printed matter, and photographs, relating to the Java Sea Campaign and other Pacific campaigns during World War II, Japanese war criminals, and American attempts to prevent hostilities between China and Taiwan.
Gift, Mrs. T. H. Binford, 1974.

228
Bint (Henri Jean)—dossier (in French and German), 1903–1917. 1 folder.
Holograph and typescript (photocopy).
Dossier of the Swiss police relating to H. J. Bint, an agent of the Russian secret police (Okhrana).
Gift, Swiss Federal Archives, 1967.

229
Bisbee, Eleanor.
Papers, 1918–1956. 16 ms. boxes, 4 envelopes, 3 oversize photographs.
Professor, American University, Istanbul. Correspondence, drafts of books and articles, speeches, memoranda, notes, pamphlets,, clippings, and photographs, relating to the history and government of Turkey in the twentieth century. Includes an interview with Mustapha Kemal, 1922, and manuscripts by Eleanor Bisbee, Resat Guntekin, Abdulhak Hisar, Yakub Osmanoglu, Milli Partisi, and Ahmen Yalman.
Gift, estate of E. Bisbee, 1956.

230
Bittson, Anthony John, *collector*.
Anthony John Bittson collection, 1976. "The Franklin Mint History of the United States." 200 sterling silver coins.
Commemorates each year of America's 200-year history. Minted by the Franklin Mint Company, Franklin Center, Pennsylvania.
Gift, A. J. Bittson, 1976.

231
Bizauskas, K.
Memorandum, 1924. 1 folder.
Typescript.

Lithuanian Minister to the U.S. Relates to the political composition of the Lithuanian Government.

232

Blackwelder, Eliot, 1880–1969.
Papers, 1940–1968. 1 ms. box, 1 envelope.
Professor of Geology, Stanford University, 1922–1945. Correspondence, memoranda, research notes, scrapbook of published writings, printed matter, and photographs, relating to international affairs and cooperation, world economics, an Atlantic Union, and Herbert Hoover's opinion poll of the Stanford University faculty on foreign policy of the U.S.
Gift, Martha B. Merk, 1975.

233

Blagoev, Dimitŭr, 1856–1924.
Translations of writings, n.d. ½ ms. box.
Typescript.
Bulgarian communist leader. Unpublished translations by Olga Hess Gankin of two published books by D. Blagoev, *Prinos kum Istoriiata na Sotsializma v Bulgariia* (Contributions to the History of Socialism in Bulgaria), 1906, and *Moi Vospominaniia* (Memoirs), 1928.

234

Bland, Raymond L.
Papers, 1919–1941. 3 ms. boxes, 3 envelopes, 3 medals.
Statistician, American Relief Administration, 1919–1924; member, President's Committee on War Relief Agencies, 1941. Correspondence, reports, memoranda, financial records, and printed matter, relating to the work of the American Relief Administration in Europe and Russia, 1919–1924, and the President's Committee on War Relief Agencies, 1941.
Register.
Gift, R. L. Bland, 1968. Incremental gift, Mrs. R. L. Bland, 1973.

235

Blankenhorn, Heber.
Report, 1946. "Psychological Warfare Reports: Combat Propaganda in Africa, Italy, United Kingdom and France, 1943–1944." 1 vol.
Typescript (carbon copy).
Consultant to U.S. War Department. Revision of a report made to the U.S. Office of Strategic Services, 1945.

236

Blauwvoetbond. Tak Brussel.
Records (in Flemish), 1930–1933. 1 folder.
Brussels branch of a Flemish nationalist organization. Correspondence, memoranda, and notices of meetings, relating to the Flemish nationalist movement in Belgium.

237

Bliss, Tasker Howard, 1853–1930.
Papers, 1918–1919. 1 folder.
General, U.S. Army; Chief of Staff, 1917; U.S. delegate, Paris Peace Conference, 1918–1919. Correspondence and memoranda, relating to the American Commission to Negotiate Peace at the Paris Peace Conference, the military, economic and political situation in Europe following World War I, and European relief and reconstruction. Includes correspondence with Herbert Hoover.
Preliminary inventory.

238

Bloch, Louis.
Report, 1928. "Facts about Mexican Immigration before and since the Quota Restriction Laws." 1 folder.
Typescript (mimeographed).
Statistician, Division of Labor Statistics and Law Enforcement, California Department of Industrial Relations. Distributed by the Division of Labor Statistics and Law Enforcement.

239

Le Blocus de l'Empire Britannique par la Flotte Aérienne Allemande en 1942 (The Blockade of the British Empire by the German Air Fleet in 1942).
Leaflets (in French), ca. 1927. 1 folder.
Printed.
Relates to the projected development of German air power.

240

Blodnieks, Adolfs, 1889–1962.
Memoirs (in Latvian), n.d. "Ministrn Presidenta Amata" (In the Office of Prime Minister). 1 folder.
Holograph.
Prime Minister of Latvia, 1933–1934. Relates to Latvian politics and to the Karlis Ulmanis coup d'état in 1934.
Gift, Edgar Anderson, 1977.

241

Blunk, Paul, b. 1880.
Translation of excerpts from a speech, 1933. "West Prussia and the Corridor." 1 folder.
Typescript (mimeographed).
Governor of East Prussia. Relates to the territorial dispute regarding the Polish Corridor. Speech delivered in Berlin, March 16, 1933.

242

Boardman, Roger Sherman.
Memoirs, n.d. "My Days with the Red Cross, 1918–19." ½ ms. box.
Typescript.
American Red Cross worker in France during World War I.

243

Boatner, Haydon L., 1900–1977.
Papers, 1932–1975. 8 ms. boxes, 2 envelopes.
Major General, U.S. Army; Chief of Staff of the Chinese Army in India, 1942–1945; Commandant of the United Nations Prisoner of War Command in Korea,

1952. Correspondence, memoranda, reports, studies, orders, maps, notes, photographs, and printed matter, relating to military strategy and operations in the China-Burma-India Theater, and to the United Nations prisoner of war camps during the Korean War.
Register.
Gift, H. L. Boatner, 1974. Subsequent increments.

244

Bodson, Victor.
Lecture, 1943. "Luxembourg." 1 folder.
Typewritten transcript.
Luxembourg Minister of Justice. Relates to the history of Luxembourg, and to post-World War II reconstruction tasks in Luxembourg. Delivered at the University of London, November 25, 1943.

245

Boehm, Dr.
Report, 1919. 1 folder.
Typescript (mimeographed).
Relates to mortality and health of the civilian population of Vienna during World War I.

246

Boels, Jean Frédéric Amédée, Baron, b. 1889.
Essay (in French), n.d. "Descartes au Quai d'Orsay" (Descartes at the Quai d'Orsay). 1 vol.
Holograph.
Relates to the French statesman Robert Schuman.

247

Boetticher, Friedrich von, b. 1881.
Translation of excerpts from a speech, 1938. "Count Alfred Schlieffen, his Life and Work." 1 vol.
Typescript (carbon copy).
Translation by Alfred E. Dedicke, Major, U.S. Army. Speech delivered on February 28, 1933, commemorating the one hundredth anniversary of the birth of Alfred Schlieffen, Field Marshal, German Army.

248

Bogdanov, A., b. 1872.
Writings (in Russian), 1923–1930. ½ ms. box.
Holograph.
Relates to travels in Russia, Siberia, and Manchuria, gold-diggers in the Amur Republic of Zheltuga, and the Russian Revolution and Civil War in Siberia.

249

Bogoiavlensky, Nikolai Vasil'evich.
Correspondence (in Russian), 1928–1937. 1 folder.
Russian émigré in the U.S. Relates to foreign relations between the United States and Russia, and to political activities of Russian immigrants in the United States.
Gift, Gleb Bogoiavlensky, 1946.

250

Bohannan, Charles T. R.
Papers (in Vietnamese and English), 1945–1965. 13 ms. boxes.
Lieutenant Colonel, U.S. Army; Rand Corporation consultant; counter-guerrilla expert. Reports, memoranda, and writings, relating to the war in Vietnam, 1961–1965; counter-guerrilla operations in Colombia, 1959–1960, and Southeast Asia, 1961–1965; and Allied military government in Japan, 1945.
Preliminary inventory.
Gift, C. T. R. Bohannan, 1977.

251

Bolander, Louis H.
Bibliography, n.d. "Bibliography of Naval Literature in the United States Naval Academy Library, 1928–1929." 1 ms. box.
Typescript (mimeographed).

252

Boldyrev, Vasiliĭ Georgievich, b. 1875.
Translation of excerpts from memoirs, n.d. *Direktoriı͡a, Kolchak, Interventy: Vospominaniı͡a* (Directory, Kolchak, Intervention: Recollections). ½ ms. box.
Typescript.
General, Imperial Russian Army; White Russian military leader. Relates to the Russian Civil War in the Siberian Far East, activities of anti-Bolshevik forces, and Allied intervention in Siberia.

253

Bolivian National Revolution, 1946–newspaper clippings (in Spanish), 1944–1946. 1 ms. box.
Bolivian newspaper clippings, relating to the government of Gualberto Villarroel López, President of Bolivia, 1944–1946, and to its overthrow.
Preliminary inventory.
Purchase, Bruce Haberkamp, 1969.

254

Bolloten, Burnett, 1909–
Papers (in Spanish, Catalan, French, English, and Italian), 1936–1978. 55½ ms. boxes, 10 scrapbooks (cited in B. Bolloten's *The Grand Camouflage*), 7,264 items on over 60,000 frames of microfilm, 2 crates (4 1. ft.), and 1 portfolio.
American author; newspaper correspondent in Spain for United Press of America, London Bureau, 1936–1938. Manuscripts of writings by participants in the Spanish Civil War; extensive series of day-by-day clippings from the Spanish, French, Italian, and English press on the Spanish Civil War for the period 1936–1946; reports; periodicals; newspapers; and other printed matter; relating to the political, military, and international aspects of the Spanish Civil War and used as research materials for a book, entitled *The Grand Camouflage* (1961), by B. Bolloten. Includes an original manuscript of a published book, entitled *The Spanish Revolution, the Left and the Struggle for Power during the Civil War*, by B. Bolloten, 1978. Collection also includes over 12,000 bound newspapers and 900 books and pamphlets which have been integrated into the general library holdings.
Register.

Crates and portfolio closed during the lifetime of B. Bolloten.

Gift, B. Bolloten, 1946. Restricted deposit, 1953. Incremental restricted deposit, 1962. Incremental restricted gift, 1974. Incremental gift, 1978.

255

Bolshevik Leninist Party of India.
Bulletin, 1947. 1 vol.
Typescript.
Includes draft resolution by the Central Committee of the Bolshevik Leninist Party of India, relating to the political situation in India.

256

Bolshevik posters (in Russian), 1917–1918. 25 posters and proclamations.
Relates to the Russian Revolution.
Preliminary inventory.

257

Bond, Marshall, 1867–1941.
Diary, 1927. 1 ms. box, 1 microfilm reel.
Typescript (mimeographed).
American visitor to Africa. Relates to general description of Africa. Includes microfilm of diary, and addenda entitled "The Economic Conditions and Commercial Possibilities of Africa," by M. Bond; "The Racial Problem in Africa," by Charis Denison; "African Women," by Margaret Davidson; and "The Progress in Africa," by J. H. Denison.
Purchase, M. Bond, Jr., 1978.

258

Bonnet, Henri, b. 1888.
Draft of a pamphlet, 1942. *The United Nations.* 1 folder.
Typescript.
French League of Nations official. Relates to Allied cooperation during World War II and to the prospects for a postwar international organization. Published under the auspices of the World Citizens Association.

259

Bonnet Rouge (Paris).
Articles (in French), 1916. 1 folder.
Printed proof sheets.
Newspaper articles suppressed by French Government censorship, relating to war news and French politics.

260

Bookplates, n.d. 1 ms. box.
Many autographed by famous persons. Includes many autographed American Red Cross bookplates collected by Noble E. Dawson.
Gift, estate of N. E. Dawson, 1965. Incremental gifts, various sources, various dates.

261

Boone, Turin Bradford.
Memoirs, n.d. 2 vols.
Typescript.

Member of the staff of the Treasurer General of Persia, 1911–1912. Relates to conditions in Persia, and to the return journey of T. B. Boone to the United States.

262

Boothe, Charles Beach, 1851–1913.
Papers, 1908–1911. 1 ms. box.
American businessman. Correspondence, memoranda and clippings, relating to the involvement of C. B. Boothe, Homer Lea and other Americans, with Sun Yat-sen and other Chinese, in schemes to overthrow the Chinese Imperial Government.
Inventory.
Gift, Laurence Boothe, 1965.

263

Borden Merit Award Committee.
Records, 1958–1963. 2 ms. boxes.
Correspondence, memoranda and printed matter, relating to the selection of candidates for the Borden Merit Award, presented by the Borden Company Foundation to scholars for excellence in publications based on research at the Hoover Institution on War, Revolution and Peace.
Gift, Borden Merit Award Committee, 1970.

264

Borkowski, Lieutenant Colonel, *collector*.
Borkowski collection on Poland (mainly in Polish), 1939–1944. 1½ ms. boxes.
Correspondence, reports, memoranda, government documents, bulletins, speeches and writings, and maps, relating to Polish-Soviet relations, Polish military personnel and civilians deported to the Soviet Union, conditions in Poland during the German and Soviet occupations in World War II, and Polish military operations under French and British command.
Preliminary inventory.
Deposit, Lieutenant Colonel Borkowski, 1947.

265

Botha (Louis)—clippings, 1935. 1 folder.
Relates to a prayer for world peace written by Louis Botha (1862–1919), Prime Minister of South Africa, 1910–1919, while attending the Paris Peace Conference as a South African delegate in 1919.

266

Botkine, Serge.
Papers (in Russian, German, French and English), 1918–1930. 8 ms. boxes.
Russian refugee in Germany. Memoirs, correspondence, reports, memoranda, and printed matter, relating primarily to Russian émigrés in Berlin, elsewhere in Germany, and in other European countries, after the Russian Revolution.
Preliminary inventory.
Gift, S. Botkine, 1930.

267

Bouhon, Julien.
History (in French), 1945. "Les Combats de Bastogne, 19 Décembre—26 Décembre, 1944" (The Fights of Bastogne, December 19—26, 1944). 1 vol.
Typescript (mimeographed).

268

Bourget, P. A.
Memorandum (in French), 1940. "Note sur les Possibilités de Défense de l'Afrique du Nord Française en Juin 1940" (Note on the Possibilities of Defense of French North Africa in June 1940). 1 vol.
Typescript (carbon copy).

269

Bourguina, Anna.
Study (in Russian), 1938. "Rabochiĭ Vopros pri Arkhangel'skom Pravitel'stve" (The Labor Question in the Archangel Government). 1 vol.
Typescript.
Relates to the period of the Civil War in Russia, 1918—1920.
Gift, Anna Bourguina.

270

Bouritch, V. P.
Memorandum, 1921. "The End of Montenegro as an Independent State." 1 folder.
Typescript.
Relates to the integration of Montenegro into the state of Yugoslavia.

271

Boushall, Thomas C.
Transcript of a speech, 1944. "Stepping Stones of Peace from the Stumbling Blocks of War." 1 folder.
Typescript (mimeographed).
President of the Morris Plan Bank of Virginia. Relates to postwar reconstruction in the U.S. Delivered before the Rotary Club of Roanoke, Virginia, October 26, 1944.

272

Bowen, Charles F.
Papers, 1941—1965. 1 folder.
Major General, U.S. Army. Memorandum (mimeographed), 1965, and photocopies of clippings, 1941, relating to the dedication in Laredo, Texas, of bronze tablets commemorating the service of the 1st New Hampshire Infantry Regiment, U.S. National Guard, on the U.S.-Mexican border, 1916—1917.

273

Bowles, Chester, 1901—
Report, 1952. "The Indo-American Development Program: The Problems and Opportunities." 1 folder.
Typescript (mimeographed).
U.S. Ambassador to India, 1951—1953 and 1963—1969. Relates to Indian economic development needs and U.S. aid to India.

274

Bowman, Alfred Connor, 1905—
Papers, 1946—1950. 1 folder.
Colonel, U.S. Army. Writings, diary, reports, and minutes, relating to the U.S. military occupation of Italy, Trieste, and Venezia Giulia, 1946—1950, and North Korea, 1950.
Gift, A. C. Bowman, 1966.

275

Bowman, Frank Otto, 1896—
Papers, 1939—1959. 1 ms. box, 1 envelope.
Brigadier General, U.S. Army. Correspondence, reports, memoranda, notes, military maps and charts, and photographs, relating to American military activities during World War II and the Korean War. Includes correspondence with General S. D. Sturgis, Chief of Engineers, 1951—1955; photographs and memoranda on bridge reconstruction in Korea by the U.S. Army, 1952—1953; and comments by F. O. Bowman on a manuscript entitled "Fifth Army Engineers in Italy," 1959.
Preliminary inventory.

276

Boyadjieff, Christo, *collector*.
Printed matter (in Bulgarian, French, German, and English), 1953—1961. ½ ms. box.
Bulgarski Osvedomitelen Biuletin/Boletim Informativo Bulgaro (Bulgarian Information Bulletin), July 1953—August 1955, Sao Paulo, Brazil (in Bulgarian and English), and *Bulgarian Review*, January 1961, Rio de Janeiro, Brazil (in English, French and German), relating to political conditions in Bulgaria.
Gift, C. Boyadjieff, 1978.

277

Boyd, Leonard Russell, 1891—
Papers, 1918—1946. 4 ms. boxes.
Brigadier General, U.S. Army; Commanding General, 93rd Infantry Division, during World War II. Diaries, correspondence, unit histories, clippings and memorabilia, relating to the activities of the 93rd Division at the battle of Bougainville and in other operations in the Pacific Theater during World War II.
Preliminary inventory.
Gift, L. R. Boyd, 1969.

278

Boyle, Francis Dennis, 1910—
Papers, 1950—1959. 1 folder.
Rear Admiral, U.S. Navy. Correspondence, memoranda and photographs, relating to the proposed development of submarine guided missiles.
Gift, F. D. Boyle, 1975.

279

Boynton, Charles Luther, b. 1881.
Papers, 1901—1967. 10 ms. boxes.
American Baptist missionary in Shanghai, 1906—1948. Correspondence, diaries, writings, pamphlets, and

photographs, relating to missionary work in Shanghai, the Shanghai American School, and general conditions in China during this period.

280

Bradley (Omar Nelson)—photograph, n.d. 1 envelope.
Depicts General of the Army O. N. Bradley, U.S. Army.

281

Brady, R. F.
Papers, 1933–1941. 1 folder.
American missionary in China. Notes and printed matter, relating to missionary work in China. Includes a University of Nanking Hospital report for 1940; a report entitled, "Ginling College, 1915–1940"; notes and notices of the Nanking Union Church and Community, 1941; and "Sketches of Nanking," 1933.

282

Bramhall, Burle, *collector.*
B. Bramhall collection on the Petrograd Children's Colony (in Russian), 1973–1976. ½ ms. box.
American Red Cross business manager in Siberia, 1919–1920. Reminiscences of several of the 781 Russian children known as the "Petrograd Children's Colony," who were sent by their parents from Moscow and Petrograd in 1918 because of wartime shortages, were stranded in the Ural Mountains, evacuated from the war zones via Vladivostok by the American Red Cross, and restored to their families in 1920 following a global ocean voyage. Includes a description of the reunion of American Red Cross staff members and members of the Petrograd Children's Colony in Leningrad, 1973.
Gift, B. Bramhall, 1977.

283

Branden, Albrecht Paul Maerker, b. 1888.
History, n.d. "Submarines in World War I." 7 vols.
Typescript (carbon copy).
Relates to British, German, Austrian, French, Italian and Russian submarines.

284

Brandt, Karl, 1899–
Writings, 1942–1945. 1 folder.
American economist; Director, Food Research Institute, Stanford University, 1961–1964. Memorandum (typewritten), 1942, relating to recommendations for U.S. regulation of fat and oil products during World War II; and transcript of a speech (mimeographed), entitled "What to Do with Germany?" 1945, relating to postwar reconstruction of Germany.

285

Brandt, Willy, 1913–
Letter (in German), 1936, to the Kommunistische Jugend (Opposition). 1 folder.
Typescript.
Chancellor of West Germany, 1969–1974. Relates to proposed united front activities. Written by W. Brandt on behalf of Sozialdemokratische Jugend Verein Deutschlands.

286

Braun, Otto, 1872–1955.
Papers (in German), 1943–1944. 1 folder.
German politician; Prime Minister of Prussia, 1920–1921, 1922 and 1925–1933. Memoranda and a letter, relating to prospects for post-World War II reconstruction of Germany.

287

Braunschweig—photographs, n.d. 1 envelope.
Depicts the city of Braunschweig, Germany, before and after destruction during World War II. Includes a street map of Braunschweig.
Gift, Andreas L. Brown, 1975.

288

Brazil. Constitution.
Excerpts from the Brazilian constitution and legal code (in Portuguese), 1947. 1 folder.
Typescript.
Measures which the Brazilian Communist Party was accused of violating.

289

Bredow, Kurt von.
Diaries (in German), 1934. "Tagebuch eines Reichswehrgenerals von Weimar ueber Potsdam nach" (Diary of a German Army General from Weimar to Potsdam). 1 folder.
Printed (photocopy).
General, German Army. Relates to political developments in Germany from May 30, 1932 to January 15, 1933. Attributed to K. von Bredow. Published in *Die Wahrheit* (Prague), 1934. Includes Gestapo memoranda (typewritten in German), 1934, relating to the diaries.

290

Breendonck (Concentration camp)—photographs, n.d. 1 envelope.
Depicts the World War II German concentration camp of Breendonck (Antwerp, Belgium). Distributed by the Police Judiciaire, Anvers.
Preliminary inventory.

291

Breese, Alexander, 1889–1976.
Papers, 1915–1944. ½ ms. box.
Russian-American meteorologist; Assistant Meteorologist, Meteorological Physics Section, U.S. Weather Bureau, 1942–1944. Correspondence, passports, certificates, letters of recommendation, and printed matter, relating to meteorology.

292

Breese, Marie Annenkov.
Memoirs, n.d. "Another Look at Russia." 2 folders.
Typescript.
Member of the Russian nobility; émigré in the U.S. after the Russian Revolution. Relates to the history of the

Annenkov family, the Russian Revolution and Civil War, and émigré life in the U.S., 1922–1943.
Gift, Gordon W. Hewes, 1975.

293

Breger, David.
Cartoons, ca. 1943. 1 folder.
Photocopy.
Second Lieutenant, U.S. Army. Depicts U.S. Army life during World War II.

294

Breitigam, Gerald B.
History, 1923. "The Retreat of the Hundred Thousand." 1 folder.
Typescript.
American journalist. Relates to the Russian Revolution and Civil War.

295

Brenan, J. F.
Correspondence, 1926. 1 folder.
Typescript and printed (photocopies).
British Acting Consul General in Canton, China. Dispatches to the British Foreign Office and letters, relating to interviews between J. F. Brenan and Chen Yu-jen (Eugene Chen), Chinese Foreign Minister, regarding Anglo-Chinese relations, the Chinese trade boycott, and the Canton-Kowloon Railway.
Gift, David Klein, 1971.

296

Brendel, Otto J., 1901–1973.
Study, ca. 1943–1944. "The Social Stratification of Germany." ½ ms. box.
Typescript (photocopy).
German-American archeologist and art historian. Relates to social classes in Germany. Prepared for a U.S. Army training program at Indiana University.
Gift, Mrs. O. J. Brendel, 1978.

297

Brennan, Robert.
Transcript of a speech, 1942. "Ireland Today." 1 folder.
Typescript (mimeographed).
Irish Minister to the U.S. Relates to the role of Ireland in World War II. Delivered at the Nassau Club, Princeton, New Jersey, November 4, 1942.

298

Breshko-Breshkovskaiâ, Ekaterina, 1844–1934.
Miscellaneous papers (in Russian and English), 1919–1931. 2 ms. boxes, 5 envelopes.
Russian Socialist Revolutionary Party leader. Writings, correspondence, biographical data and photographs, relating to the life of E. Breshko-Breshkovskaiâ. Includes drafts of the book by E. Breshko-Breshkovskaiâ, *The Hidden Springs of the Russian Revolution* (Stanford University Press, 1931); a biographical sketch of E. Breshko-

Breshkovskaiâ by Aleksandr Kerenskiĭ; and three letters by E. Breshko-Breshkovskaiâ.
Preliminary inventory.

299

Bricard, Jacques.
Report (in French), 1942. 1 vol.
Typescript (carbon copy).
Lieutenant, French Army. Relates to the German prisoner of war camp Oflag G.X.B. Report to General Bridoux, Secretary of State for War of France.

300

Briegleb, *collector*.
Briegleb collection on Germany and Eastern Europe (in German), 1938–1949. 1 ms. box.
Letters, reports, and memoranda, relating to the political and economic situation in Germany and in Eastern Europe, primarily from 1945–1949, the Nuremberg war crime trials, and communism in Germany after World War II.
Preliminary inventory.
Gift, Mr. Briegleb.

301

Briggs, Mitchell Pirie, *collector*.
M. P. Briggs collection on George D. Herron, 1918–1930. 1 folder.
Manuscripts of writings, correspondence, and clippings, relating to the role of George D. Herron, an adviser to Woodrow Wilson, in formulating the World War I peace settlement and to his subsequent views on European politics. Used by M. P. Briggs as research material for his book, *George D. Herron and the European Settlement*.

302

Briggs, Otis Emmons.
Memoirs, 1920. "Uncommon Letters from a Common Soldier, being a Chronical(!) of the Experiences of an Enlisted Man during Sixteen Months with the American Army in France, March 31, 1918—July 22, 1919." 1 vol.
Typescript (carbon copy).
Includes photographs.

303

Brinton, Jasper T., *collector*.
Paintings, n.d. 9 oversize prints.
Printed.
Depicts scenes at the Italian front during World War I.
Gift, J. T. Brinton, 1958.

304

British Army concert programs, 1919. 1 folder.
Printed.
Four programs of British Army concerts in France, 1919.

305

British Library of Information, New York, *collector*.
Newspaper clippings, 1920–1921. 1 ms. box.
Clippings from U.S. newspapers, exhibiting editorial

reactions to the Versailles peace settlement, the Anglo-Japanese alliance, the establishment of the Irish Free State, and the anticolonial movement in India. Many of the clippings are from German- and French-language newspapers in the U.S.

Gift, British Library of Information.

306

British posters—photographs, 1939–1941. 2 envelopes.
Reproductions of all official posters issued by Great Britain between the outbreak of World War II and September 1941.
Purchase, 1942.

307

British Trade Corporation.
Prospectus, 1917. 1 folder.
Printed.
An organization chartered to promote British commerce upon the close of World War I.

308

Brody, General.
Text of a speech (in French), 1920. 1 folder.
Typescript.
Delivered at the École des Francs-Bourgeois in Paris, July 11, 1920, at a ceremony in honor of the memory of former students of the school who had been killed in World War I.

309

Brokensha, David Warwick, 1923– , *collector*.
D. W. Brokensha collection on Africa, 1960–1970. 1 ms. box.
Studies, writings, pamphlets, newsletters, and printed matter, relating primarily to rural development, agriculture, family life, nutrition, education, and various other socio-economic aspects of life in Ghana, South Africa, and eastern African countries.
Register.
Gift, D. W. Brokensha, 1973.

310

Broneer, Oscar.
Radio broadcast (in English and Greek), n.d. "Greece as I Saw It." 2 phonorecords.
American relief worker in Greece. Relates to social conditions and relief operations in Greece at the end of World War II. Recorded by the National Broadcasting Company.

311

Brookings Institution Seminar on Problems of U.S. Foreign Policy, Stanford, 1948.
Records, 1948. 2 ms. boxes.
Mimeographed working memoranda prepared for the seminar, relating to diverse aspects of current U.S. foreign policy throughout the world. Includes a mimeographed report from the Russian Research Center, Harvard University, and a State Department pamphlet.
Gift, C. Easton Rothwell.

312

Brooks, Sidney, 1892–1944.
Papers, 1925–1926. ½ ms. box.
American economist and author; American Relief Administration worker in Europe, 1920–1923. Correspondence, press releases, and clippings, relating to the book by S. Brooks, *America and Germany* (1925), regarding American-German relations after World War I.
Gift, Gwen Brooks Penniman, 1953.

313

Brown, Andreas, *collector*.
Miscellany (in English and French), 1913–1945. 1 folder, 1 envelope.
Includes telegrams from the White House to Governor Hiram Johnson of California, 1913, relating to the Alien Land Tenure Bill; four World War II French cartoons; the first issue of an Orleans, France, newspaper after the liberation of the city at the end of World War II; photographs of President Harry S. Truman and Generals Dwight D. Eisenhower and George S. Patton visiting the war zones, 1944–1945; and a memorandum relating to the Shantung territorial question at the end of World War II.
Gift, A. Brown, 1971.

314

Brown, Edmund Gerald, 1905–
Press conference, 1964. 1 video tape reel.
Governor of California, 1959–1967. Relates to the death of Herbert Hoover. Includes film of the carillon bells of the Hoover Institution on War, Revolution and Peace playing in tribute to Herbert Hoover.

315

Brown, Everett S., 1886–1964.
Papers, 1917–1924. 7 ms. boxes.
U.S. Food Administration staff member, 1917–1920. Memoranda and news summaries prepared daily for Herbert Hoover, Administrator of the U.S. Food Administration; and correspondence and printed matter, relating to the U.S. Food Administration, U.S. politics and government, and Herbert Hoover.
Gift, E. S. Brown, 1950. Subsequent increments.

316

Brown, Forbes H., *collector*.
F. H. Brown collection on the Catholic Church, 1944–1949. ½ ms. box.
Anti-Catholic pamphlets and annotated books, relating to the relationship of the Catholic Church to fascism and the origins of World War II.
Preliminary inventory.
Gift, F. H. Brown, 1950.

317

Brown, Hugh S.
Papers, 1915–1916. 1 folder.
Commission for Relief in Belgium worker, 1915–1916. Transcript of a speech (typewritten), entitled "An American in Belgium," delivered at the University of

Nevada, February 25, 1916; and pamphlets and clippings, relating to Herbert Hoover and Belgian relief.
Gift, Mrs. H. S. Brown.

318

Brown, Walter Lyman.
Papers, 1917–1932. 1 folder, 2 envelopes, 1 album.
European Director, American Relief Administration European Children's Fund (ARAECF); Director, Rotterdam Office, Commission for Relief in Belgium (CRB). Photographs, correspondence and writings, relating to ARAECF and CRB relief work in Europe during and immediately after World War I.
Gift, W. L. Brown.

319

Browne, Louis Edgar, 1891–1951.
Papers, 1917–1956. 2 ms. boxes.
Correspondent of the *Chicago Daily News* in Russia and Turkey, 1917–1919. Dispatches, correspondence, printed matter and photographs, relating to political conditions in Russia during the Russian Revolution, Allied intervention in Russia, and political conditions in Turkey at the end of World War I.
Preliminary inventory.

320

Brownlee, Aleta.
Papers, 1945–1950. 10 ms. boxes.
Director of Child Welfare in Austria for the United Nations Relief and Rehabilitation Administration (UNRRA) and International Refugee Organization (IRO), 1945–1950. Memoirs and office files, relating to UNRRA and IRO relief work for displaced children in Austria at the end of World War II.
Gift, A. Brownlee, 1969.

321

Brumby, Bob.
Radio news broadcast, 1945. 1 phonorecord.
Radio broadcaster. Relates to the reopening of the Burma Road. Broadcast from Chungking, China, and recorded by the Mutual Broadcasting System.

322

Brunelli, Paul.
Memoirs (in Russian), n.d. "Moi͡a Letopis'—Leib Gvardii v Ismailovskom Polku" (My Chronicle—Izmailovsky Guards Regiments). 1 folder.
Typescript (photocopy).
Colonel, Imperial Russian Army. Relates to activities of the regiment during the year 1897.
Gift, M. Lyons, 1971.

323

Brunet, Court Councillor de.
Papers (in French, Russian, Swedish and German), 1809–1814. 1 ms. box.
Russian Consul General in Norway. Correspondence, proclamations and reports, relating to Russian foreign policy and commerce in the Baltic.

324

Bruns, Armin R., *collector*.
Motion picture, 1954. *This Is Worth Remembering*. 1 reel.
Film of the 80th birthday celebration for Herbert Hoover at West Branch, Iowa.
Gift, A. R. Bruns, 1958.

325

Brunton, Delbert.
Dissertation, 1927. "The German National People's Party, 1918–1920." 1 folder.
Typescript.
Submitted to Stanford University.

326

Brussels. Université Libre. Institut de Sociologie Solvay.
Study, 1921. "The German Annuities." 1 folder.
Typescript.
Relates to German reparation payments after World War I.

327

Bruttan, Helene, 1892–
History (in German), n.d. "Deutsche Schicksale im Schatten von Versailles" (German Fate in the Shadow of Versailles). 1 ms. box.
Typescript.
Relates to social and economic conditions in Germany, 1919–1947, especially during and immediately after World War II.
Gift, H. Bruttan, 1969.

328

Bryant (Mitchel C.)—newspaper clippings, 1928. 1 folder.
Relates to the suicide of M. C. Bryant, an American businessman in France and a member of the American Relief Administration during World War I.

329

Bublikov, Aleksandr Aleksandrovich.
Essay (in Russian), 1923. "Likvidat͡sii͡a Likholi͡et'ia" (Liquidation of Troubled Times). 1 vol.
Typescript.
Relates to Russian reconstruction and public finance after the Russian Civil War.

330

Buch, Walter, 1883–1949.
Report (in German), 1945. 1 folder.
Typescript.
Head of the Nazi Party Supreme Party Court of Munich. Relates to the national socialist judicial system in Germany. Report of an interrogation of W. Buch by Allied authorities, July 17, 1945.

331

Buchenwald (Concentration camp)—photographs, 1945–1946. 1 envelope.
Depicts the Buchenwald concentration camp, and the memorial to the 51,000 persons who died there.

332

Bucher, Lloyd M., 1927–
Papers, 1970–1975. 68 ms. boxes, 1 oversize package (1 l. ft.).
Commander, U.S. Navy; Captain of the U.S.S. *Pueblo*. Correspondence, newspaper clippings, reports, copies of court inquiries, photographs, plaques, and memorabilia, relating to the *Pueblo* incident and its aftermath. Includes memoirs (typewritten), entitled "Bucher, My Story."
Gift, L. M. Bucher, 1976.

333

Buckalew, Frank R.
Notes, ca. 1929. 1 folder.
Typescript.
Member of American Near East Relief. Relates to various aspects, mainly statistical, of the Greek population, economy and government.

334

Buckmaster, Elliott, b. 1889.
Photographs, 1942–1948. 1 envelope.
Rear Admiral, U.S. Navy. Depicts E. Buckmaster and other officers, naval vessels, and American naval operations in the Bay of Whales, Antarctica.
Gift, E. Buckmaster, 1974.

335

Budapest—pictorial, n.d. 1 envelope.
Booklet of mounted photographs of buildings, bridges, and monuments in Budapest, Hungary. Captions in Hungarian and German.

336

Budberg, Alekseĭ Pavlovich, Baron, 1869–1945.
Papers (in Russian), 1919–1920. 1 ms. box.
Lieutenant General, Russian Imperial Army. Memoirs and diaries, relating to Russian military activities during World War I, and to White Russian military activities in Siberia during the Russian Civil War.

337

Buddhist silk embroidered portraits, ca. 1736–1795. ½ ms. box.
Chinese silk embroidered portraits of Buddhas, dating from the Chien-lung period of the Ch'ing dynasty.

338

Bulgaria. Armiíà. Gvardeĭski na Negovo Velichestvo Konen Polk.
Brochure (in Bulgarian), 1939. 1 folder.
Printed.
Commemorates the 60th anniversary of the Bulgarian Gvardeĭski na Negovo Velichestvo Cavalry Regiment.

339

Bułhak, Jan.
Photographs, 1925. 1 envelope.
Depicts various locations in Poland, primarily Warsaw, Vilna, Lwow, and Krakow.

340

Bulíùbash, Evgeniĭ Grigor'evich.
Papers (in Russian), 1954–1964. 1 ms. box.
General, Russian Imperial Army. Correspondence, clippings, printed matter, and photographs, relating to Russian Imperial military forces before, during and after the Russian Revolution and Civil War, and to activities of the Russian émigré community in the U.S.
Gift, Russian Historical Archive and Repository, 1974.

341

Bund Neues Deutschland.
Leaflet (in German), n.d. 1 folder.
Printed.
Relates to prerequisites for post-World War II German reconstruction.

342

Bunescu, Alexander D., 1895–
Papers (in Romanian and English), 1949–1971. 1½ ms. boxes.
Romanian industrialist and university lecturer; Assistant Secretary for Public Works and Communications, 1938–1939; Undersecretary for Reconstruction, 1944–1945. Speeches and writings, lecture notes, reports, studies, newsletters, pamphlets, and printed matter, relating to twentieth century Romanian history, politics, government and foreign relations; Radio Free Europe; the Romanian National Committee; and the Assembly of Captive European Nations.
Box 2 is restricted until January 2, 1989.
Gift, A. D. Bunescu, 1978.

343

Bunin, Viktor M., 1896–
Memoirs (in Russian), n.d. "Deviâtyĭ Val: Vospominaniíà Uchastnika Russkoĭ Grazhdanskoĭ Voĭny 1918–1920 g.g." (The Highest Wave: Reminiscences of a Participant in the Russian Civil War, 1918–1920). 1 vol.
Typescript (carbon copy).

344

Bunjević, Dušan, 1928–
Thesis, 1974. "Draža Mihailović and the National Movement in Yugoslavia, 1941–1945." 1 folder.
Typescript (photocopy).
Relates to the resistance movement headed by Draža Mihailović in Yugoslavia during World War II. Master's thesis, University of San Francisco.
Gift, D. Bunjević, 1974.

345

Bunn, John, *collector*.
J. Bunn collection on athletics in the military, 1945. ½ ms. box.
Manuals and memoranda, issued by various U.S. Army agencies, relating to the organization of athletic programs for American soldiers in Europe.
Gift, J. Bunn, 1946.

346

Bunyan, James, 1898–1977.

Papers (in Russian and English), 1917–1963. 2½ ms. boxes.

Russian-American historian. Excerpts from published sources, documents, and notes (primarily in Russian), relating to the Ukrainian government, Russia, Siberia, and the Far Eastern Republic during the Russian Civil War in 1919, used by J. Bunyan as research material for his book, *The Bolshevik Revolution, 1917–1918* (1934); drafts, notes, charts, and printed matter (primarily in English), relating to Soviet economic, administrative, agricultural, and industrial organization and planning, 1917–1963, used by J. Bunyan as research material for his book, *The Origin of Forced Labor in the Soviet State, 1917–1921* (1967); and drafts of the latter book.

Gift, J. Bunyan, 1975. Subsequent increments.

347

Burden, John Alfred.

Papers (in English and Japanese), 1942–1944. 1 ms. box.

Major, U.S. Army; Language Officer, 25th Division, during World War II. Reports, captured documents and translations, correspondence, diary, maps and photographs, relating to military operations on Guadalcanal and other areas of the Solomon Islands, especially to interrogation of captured Japanese soldiers and translation of captured Japanese documents.

Gift, J. A. Burden, 1978.

348

Burdick, Charles Burton, 1927– , *collector*.

C. B. Burdick collection on the Zimmermann telegram, 1917–1919. ½ ms. box.

Professor of History at San Jose State University. Typewritten copies and photocopies of correspondence, memoranda, reports, and transcripts of hearings, relating to the alleged Austrian espionage activities in the U.S. of Heinrich Kolbeck, Olga Visser and others, in connection with the Zimmermann note incident.

349

Burgess, J. Stewart and Stella F.

Papers, 1910–1935. 1 folder.

American missionaries in China. Letters, poems and printed matter, relating to missionary work of the Young Men's Christian Association in China and to revolutionary movements in China.

350

Burhans, Robert D.

Papers, 1942–1945. 25 ms. boxes, 11 envelopes.

Colonel, U.S. Army. Correspondence, field orders, directives, reports, regulations, handbooks, maps, and photographs, relating to the activities of the First Special Service Force ("Devil's Brigade") and the 474th Infantry during World War II. Used as research material for the book by R. D. Burhans, *The First Special Service Force: A War History of the North Americans, 1942–1944.*

Preliminary inventory.

351

Burke, John.

Memorandum, n.d. "An Account of Certain Feasts, Stories, and Customs of the Are-Are, People of Little Mala in the Southern Solomons." 1 folder.

Typescript (mimeographed).

Lieutenant Commander, U.S. Navy.

352

Burland, Elmer Granville.

Report, 1925. "If the United States Should Negotiate a Commercial Treaty with Soviet Russia." 1 folder.

Typescript.

Relates to the prospects for a U.S.-Soviet trade agreement.

353

Burlin, P. G.

Writings (in Russian), 1941. 1 folder.

Typescript.

Imperial Russian Army officer. Study entitled "Kratkaiå Spravka o Russkom Kazachestve" (Brief Note on the Russian Cossacks), and a report entitled "Proiskhozhdenie Kazakov—Doklad" (Cossack Parentage—A Report), relating to Russian Cossack daily life, and class and military structure.

354

Burma Road radio news broadcast, 1944. 1 phonorecord.

Relates to the reopening of the Burma Road.

355

Burnham, Frederick Russell, 1861–1947.

Papers, 1876–1964. 7 ms. boxes, 1 oversize box.

American explorer; Major and Chief of Scouts, British Army, during the Boer War. Correspondence, writings, clippings, other printed matter, photographs and memorabilia, relating to the Matabele Wars of 1893 and 1896 in Rhodesia, the Boer War, exploration expeditions in Africa, and gold mining in Alaska during the Klondike gold rush.

Preliminary inventory.

Gift, Ilo Burnham, 1978.

356

Burr, Myron Carlos, 1884–1977.

Papers, 1927–1938. 1 folder.

American engineer. Correspondence, and printed matter, relating to Herbert Hoover, the Republican National Convention of 1936, and Stanford University. Includes two letters from Herbert Hoover to M. C. Burr.

Gift, Mrs. Jackson Edwards, 1978.

357

Burrill, Harvey D.

Dispatches, 1918–1919. ½ ms. box.

Typescript.

Newspaper correspondent for the *Syracuse Journal* (New York). Relates to conditions in England and France at the end of World War I.

Gift, family of H. D. Burrill, 1969.

358

Burtŝev, Vladimir L'vovich, 1862–1942.
Papers (in Russian), 1906–1935. 1 ms. box.
Russian revolutionist; later anti-Bolshevik. Memoirs, essays, correspondence, and printed matter, relating to the Menshevik and Social Revolutionary movements before 1917, Evno Azef and other Okhrana agents, and counterrevolutionary movements during the Russian Revolution.

359

Busterud, John Armand, 1921–
Papers, 1972–1977. 22 ms. boxes.
U.S. Deputy Assistant Secretary of Defense for Environmental Quality, 1971–1972; Chairman, Council on Environmental Quality, Executive Office of the President, 1972–1977. Correspondence, speeches and writings, memoranda, reports, studies, and printed matter, relating to international and domestic energy and environmental programs.
Gift, J. A. Busterud, 1977.

360

Butler, Charles A.
History, 1950. "Senator, the Door is Closed." 1 vol.
Typescript.
Relates to American reaction to the Versailles Treaty and the Covenant of the League of Nations, 1919.

361

Butler, Charles Terry, b. 1889.
Memoirs, 1975. "A Civilian in Uniform." ½ ms. box.
Typescript (photocopy).
American physician; U.S. Army surgeon during World War I. Relates to activities of the Medical Corps of the American Expeditionary Forces in France during World War I.
Gift, C. T. Butler, 1975.

362

Byelorussian Central Council, New York.
Memorandum, 1954. 1 folder.
Typescript (mimeographed).
Relates to forced labor and national policy of the Soviet Union towards Belorussia. Addressed to the United Nations.

363

Byers, Clovis E., 1899–1973.
Papers, 1917–1961. 40 ms. boxes, 2 envelopes, 7 albums, 6 oversize photographs, 1 motion picture reel, 1 phonotape.
Lieutenant General, U.S. Army; Chief of Staff, 8th Army, 1944–1945, in the Pacific Theater; Commanding General, X Corps, 1951, in Korea. Correspondence, memoranda, diaries, speeches and writings, clippings, personnel records, and audio-visual material, relating to the Pacific Theater during World War II, the Army of Occupation in Japan, the Korean War, and the North Atlantic Treaty Organization (NATO) command in Europe.

Preliminary inventory.
Gift, C. E. Byers, 1964.

364

Bykadorov, I.
Papers (in Russian), 1919–1920. ½ ms. box.
General, Imperial Russian Army. Mandates, orders, and circulars, relating to the Civil War in the south of Russia. Includes a list of the main events in the history of the Don Army prepared by I. Bykadorov.
Purchase, I. Bykadorov.

365

C.R.B. Educational Foundation.
Records, 1921–1956. 7 ms. boxes, 2 envelopes.
Affiliate of the Commission for Relief in Belgium. Reports, minutes of meetings, correspondence, clippings, posters, and photographs, relating to U.S.-Belgian exchange fellowships sponsored by the foundation, the German occupation of Belgium, King Leopold III of Belgium, and the 1950 Belgian plebiscite on the restoration of the monarchy.
Preliminary inventory.
Gift, C.R.B. Educational Foundation, 1946. Subsequent increments.

366

Cadwalader, Bertram L.
Papers, 1918–1929. 1 ms. box.
Major, U.S. Army. Manuscripts of writings, notes, and memoranda, relating to demoralization in the French Army in 1917, the German offensive and Allied counteroffensive of 1918, and the decision to create an independent U.S. Army command on the western front.
Preliminary inventory.

367

Caen, France—photographs, ca. 1944–1947. 1 envelope.
Depicts destruction in Caen, Normandy, in World War II.

368

Caetani, Gelasio Benedetto Anatolio, 1877–1934.
Papers, 1906–1934. 3 ms. boxes, 1 envelope.
Italian mining engineer and diplomat; Ambassador to the U.S., 1922–1925. Correspondence, speeches and writings, reports, photographs, and clippings, relating to Italy in World War I, Italian—U.S. relations, and Herbert Hoover.
Preliminary inventory.
Gift, James Batcheller and Mrs. Albert Burch, 1944.

369

Calder, Alonzo Bland, 1892–
Papers, 1911–1956. 45 ms. boxes.
American consular official stationed in China, 1920–1941 and 1945–1948. Memoranda, reports, correspondence, clippings, photographs, and pamphlets, relating to U.S. foreign and economic relations with China in the interwar period and immediately after World War II,

and to U.S. foreign and trade relations with Russia, Egypt and Malaya.
Gift, Mrs. A. B. Calder, 1975.

370

Caldwell, John Kenneth, b. 1881.
Memoirs, n.d. 1 folder.
Typescript.
American diplomat; Consul General at Tientsin, China, 1935–1942; Ambassador to Ethiopia, 1943–1945. Relates to U.S. foreign relations and commerce with Japan, Russia, Australia, China and Ethiopia, 1906–1945, and to U.S. participation in international narcotics control agencies.
Gift, J. K. Caldwell, 1976.

371

Caldwell, Oliver Johnson, 1904–
Papers, 1938–1977. 7 ms. boxes.
American educator; Assistant Commissioner for International Education, U.S. Office of Education, 1952–1964; Dean of International Services, Southern Illinois University, 1965–1969. Speeches, writings, memoranda, reports and correspondence, relating to international education, U.S. educational policy, conditions in China prior to World War II, and operations of the U.S. Office of Strategic Services in China during World War II.
Preliminary inventory.
Gift, O. J. Caldwell, 1978.

372

California in World War I collection, 1917–1920. 4 ms. boxes.
Press releases, pamphlets, leaflets, photographs, and miscellanea, relating to military recruitment and conscription, institution of the income tax, Liberty Loan drives, government regulation of the economy and miscellaneous war work activities in California during World War I. Includes photographs of the U.S. delegation at the Paris Peace Conference.

373

"Le Camp d'Internes Civils de Giromagny, Territoire de Belfort" (The Civilian Intern Camp of Giromagny, Belfort Territory).
Report (in French), n.d. 1 vol.
Typescript (carbon copy).
Relates to a German prison camp in France during World War II.

374

Campaign for the 48 States.
Television scripts, 1956. 1 folder.
Typescript (mimeographed).
American political lobby. Relates to the Byrd-Bridges bill to limit the size of the federal budget, and the Reed-Dirksen bill to reform the income tax laws.

375

"Campaign in Burma, 1942."
Report, 1942. 1 folder.
Typescript.
Relates to the course of the 1942 campaign against the Japanese in Burma. Prepared by a member of the staff of General Joseph W. Stilwell, Chief of the Allied Staff in the China-Burma-India Theater.
Anonymous gift, 1972.

376

Campbell, C. Douglas.
Study, 1933. "Railway Transportation in Soviet Russia." 1 folder.
Printed page proofs.
By C. Douglas Campbell and M. S. Miller.

377

Campbell, Hannah Brain, b. 1880.
Memoirs, 1945. 1 folder.
Typescript.
American Red Cross worker in Siberia, 1917–1920. Memoir entitled "Adventure in Siberia," as told to Sarah E. Mathews, relating to activities of the American Red Cross in the eastern part of Russia, 1917–1920; and memoir entitled "Children's Ark," relating to the return of Russian children by the American Red Cross to their parents in Russia in 1920.
Gift, S. E. Mathews, 1973.

378

Campbell, Rita Ricardo, 1920–
Papers, 1964–1976. 38 ms. boxes.
American economist and educator; Chairman, Western Interstate Commission for Higher Education, 1970–1971. Correspondence, memoranda, reports and printed matter, relating to the administration and financing of higher education, the Western Interstate Commission for Higher Education, the Mountain States Regional Medical Program, and the National Center for Higher Education Management Systems.
Preliminary inventory.
Gift, R. R. Campbell, 1978.

379

Canan, Howard V., 1894–
Papers, 1927–1955. 4 ms. boxes, 3 envelopes, 1 album.
Colonel, U.S. Army Corps of Engineers. Addresses, reports, awards, printed matter, and photographs, relating to flood control and land utilization in the U.S., redevelopment in the Nashville, Tennessee district, and the work of the U.S. Army Corps of Engineers. Includes an unpublished history, entitled "Civil War Military Intelligence."
Register.
Gift, H. V. Canan, 1974.

380

Canfield, Mrs. David, *collector*.
Mrs. D. Canfield collection of World War II German toy soldiers, n.d. 1 box.
Gift, Mrs. D. Canfield, 1947.

381

Cannon, Robert Milchrist, 1901–1976.
Papers (in English and Turkish), 1931–1974. 3 ms. boxes, 4 oversize boxes (2 l. ft.), 3 envelopes.
Lieutenant General, U.S. Army; Chief of Staff, Northern Combat Area Command, China-Burma-India Theater, 1944–1945; Commanding General, 6th Army, 1959–1961. Orders, correspondence, speeches, clippings, memorabilia, and photographs, relating to the China-Burma-India Theater, and U.S. military relations with Turkey and the Philippines, 1951–1955.
Gift, Mrs. R. M. Cannon, 1977.

382

Cantacuzène, Marie.
Memoirs (in Romanian), n.d. ½ ms. box.
Typescript.
Romanian aristocrat. Relates to political and social conditions in Romania, 1900–1945, and to Queen Marie of Romania.
Gift, George Duca, 1976.

383

Canton Military Government.
Leaflet, 1921. 1 folder.
Printed.
Relates to the Canton government's assumption of power.

384

Capierri, François.
Memoirs (in French), n.d. "Adieu, Berlin! Le Récit d'une Histoire Vécue" (Good Bye, Berlin! The Account of an Experience). 1 folder.
Typescript.
Italian Army officer. Relates to Italian military activities in the Naples-Cassino region, 1943–1945.
Gift, Jacques de Launay, 1976.

385

Caranfil, Nicolae George, 1893–1978.
Papers (in Romanian, English and French), 1914–1970. 8 ms. boxes.
Romanian engineer; Minister of Air and Navy, 1935–1937; President, Romanian Welfare, New York. Correspondence, reports, printed matter, diaries, maps, photographs and memorabilia, relating to Romania in World Wars I and II, and to the work of the Romanian Relief Committee, the Romanian Red Cross, Humanitas, Caroman, Radio Free Europe and the Romanian National Committee.
Preliminary inventory.
Boxes 5–8 closed until January 2, 1993.
Gift, N. G. Caranfil, 1978.

386

Caraway, Forrest, 1909–
Papers, 1926–1960. 2 ms. boxes.
Brigadier General, U.S. Army; U.S. Senior Adviser to the South Korean II Army Corps, 1953. Correspondence, orders and photographs, relating to the Korean War, and to the Bonus March on Washington in 1932.
Preliminary inventory.
Gift, F. Caraway, 1964.

387

Caraway, Paul Wyatt, 1905–
Papers, 1953–1964. 6 ms. boxes.
Lieutenant General, U.S. Army; Chief of Staff, U.S. Forces in Japan, 1957–1958; High Commissioner of the Ryukyu Islands, 1961–1964. Itineraries, schedules, printed matter, memorabilia and photographs, relating to U.S. forces stationed in Japan and the Ryukyus, and to the visit of Vice President Richard M. Nixon to Asia and the Pacific in 1953.
Preliminary inventory.
Gift, P. W. Caraway, 1953. Subsequent increments.

388

Carinthia. Landtag.
Minutes of meetings (in German), 1926–1927. 1 ms. box.
Typescript (mimeographed).
Relates to activities of the Landtag (Carinthia, Austria) at various sessions and to miscellaneous reports of the Finance and Justice Committees of the Landtag.

389

Carl Schurz Memorial Foundation.
Pamphlet, 1940. *A Fifth of a Nation: Symbolizing a People's Appreciation of Liberty.* 1 folder.
Printed.
Relates to contributions of German-Americans to U.S. history and culture.

390

Carleton, Bob.
Song, ca. 1939–1940. *Let's Send a Buck to Finland.* 1 phonorecord.
Appeals for American aid to Finland during the Russo-Finnish War. Words by Cliff Dixon and music by B. Carleton.

391

Carleton, Don E.
Papers, 1943–1960. 2 ms. boxes.
Brigadier General, U.S. Army; Chief of Staff, VI Corps, during World War II. Diary, manuscripts of writings, transcripts of telephone conversations, correspondence, and memoranda, relating to the military campaign in Italy, 1943–1945, and particularly to the activities of the Allied 15th Army Group and of the U.S. VI Corps.
Gift, Ben Harrell, 1975.

392

Carol II (King of Romania)—photographs. n.d. 1 envelope.
Depicts King Carol II of Romania with the British historian Harold Temperley and others.
Gift, Edgar Robinson.

393

Carr, William G.
    Letters, 1947. 1 folder.
    Typescript (mimeographed).
    Adviser to the U.S. delegation to the second general conference of the United Nations Educational, Scientific and Cultural Organization held in Mexico City, 1947. Relates to the proceedings of the conference.

394

Carroll, Philip H., 1885–1941.
    Papers, 1917–1939. 1 ms. box.
    Captain, U.S. Army, 1917–1920; American Relief Administration (A.R.A.) worker in Germany and Russia, 1920–1922. Memoranda, outlines of procedures, organization and personnel charts, preliminary programs, routine charts, and specimen forms, relating to activities of the U.S. 348th Field Artillery in France and Germany, 1917–1920, of the A.R.A. in Hamburg, Germany, 1920–1921, and of the A.R.A. Russian Unit Supply Division in Moscow, 1921–1922. Includes correspondence with Herbert Hoover, 1934–1939, relating to U.S. politics.
    Gift, P. H. Carroll, 1941.

395

Carson, Arthur Leroy, 1895–
    Diary, 1921. 1 folder.
    Typewritten transcript (photocopy).
    American missionary and educator; teacher in China, 1921–1926 and 1931–1938; President, Silliman University, Philippine Islands, 1939–1953. Relates to a journey from Canton to Linchow, China. Includes a memoir by Edith (Mrs. A. L.) Carson, relating to American refugee life in the Japanese-occupied Philippines, 1942–1944.
    Gift, A. L. Carson, 1978.

396

Carter, Gwendolen.
    Summaries of interviews, 1973. 1 folder.
    Typescript.
    Professor of Political Science, Northwestern University. Interviews held by G. Carter with African scholars and leaders, relating to race and political problems in South Africa and to possible establishment of a British Documentation Center for microfilming or acquisition of Southern African archival and library materials.
    Gift, G. Carter, 1973.

397

Carter, Lieutenant.
    Letter, 1919. 1 vol.
    Holograph.
    British Army officer. Relates to British military intervention against the Bolsheviks in Northern Russia. Includes typewritten copy of original.

398

Casement, Sir Roger David, 1864–1916.
    Papers, 1905–1960. 2 ms. boxes.
    Irish nationalist leader. Correspondence, writings, pamphlets, and clippings, relating to the authenticity of the diaries of R. D. Casement, and to the movement for Irish independence. Includes some printed matter collected by James A. Healy.
    Gift, J. A. Healy.

399

Caspari, John, 1899–
    Pamphlet (in German), 1951. *Das Wort des Geschmaehten* (The Word of the Reviled). 1 folder.
    Printed.
    Relates to the attitude of the Swiss clergy and of the journal *Reformierte Schweiz* (Reformed Switzerland) toward national socialism in Germany. Published under the names of René Sonderegger and Severin Reinhard (pseudonyms of John Caspari).

400

Castillo, J. Cicerón.
    Letter, 1922, to Julio A. Vengoechea. 1 folder.
    Typescript.
    Ecuadoran geologist and entrepreneur. Encloses a report (typewritten), entitled "A Report on the Banana Possibilities of Ecuador."
    Gift, Grace R. Wright, 1961.

401

Castro, Juanita, 1933–
    Phonotape of speeches, n.d. 1 phonotape.
    Sister of Fidel Castro, Premier of Cuba; anti-communist émigré in the U.S. Relates to the communist government of Cuba.

402

Cataret, J. G., *collector*.
    Miscellany (in French), 1913–1919. ½ ms. box.
    Miscellanea, including theater-concert programs, advertisements, sketches, sheet music, and watercolors, relating to conditions in France during World War I.

403

Catroux (Georges)—photograph, n.d. 1 envelope.
    Depicts General Catroux, French Ambassador to the Soviet Union, 1945–1948.

404

Center, Mrs. Hugh Stuart, *collector*.
    Model, n.d.
    Miniature clay model of a Chinese wedding procession.

405

Central and Eastern European Planning Board, New York.
    Records, 1942–1943. 1 folder.
    Joint committee of the Polish, Czechoslovakian, Yugoslavian and Greek governments in exile. Reports and minutes of meetings, relating to planning postwar reconstruction.

406

Centralia Publicity Committee.
  Records, 1922–1932. 1 folder.
  Bulletins, leaflets, pamphlets, correspondence and petitions, mostly issued by the Centralia Publicity Committee, relating to the efforts of the committee to secure the release of members of the Industrial Workers of the World imprisoned as a result of the Centralia, Washington, incident of 1919.

407

Centralny Komitet dla Spraw Szkolnych i Oswiatowych.
  Records (in Polish), 1945–1949. ½ ms. box.
  Polish refugee organization for the administration of schools for Polish displaced persons in Germany after World War II. Correspondence, reports and bulletins, relating to Polish refugee education in Germany.
  Gift, S. Zimmer, 1949. Incremental gift, 1950.

408

Cerf, Jay H., 1923–1974.
  Papers, 1940–1974. 4½ ms. boxes.
  Director, Foreign Policy Clearing House, 1957–1961; U.S. Assistant Secretary of Commerce, 1961–1963; Manager, International Group, U.S. Chamber of Commerce, 1963–1969. Correspondence, writings, reports, instructions, and memoranda, relating to U.S. commercial and foreign policy. Includes the Ph.D. dissertation of J. Cerf, "Blue Shirts and Red Banners," 1957, relating to the East German communist youth organization, Freie Deutsche Jugend.
  Gift, Mrs. J. H. Cerf, 1976. Incremental gift, 1978.

409

Česká Družina.
  Records (in English, Czech and Russian), 1918–1920. 1 folder.
  Czechoslovak Legion in Russia. Orders, leaflets and writings, relating to the activities of the Legion during the Russian Civil War. Includes a history of the Legion, entitled "The Operations of the Czechoslovak Army in Russia in the Years 1917–1920."

410

Chacon, Jose A., 1925–
  Papers, 1968–1972. 1 folder.
  American engineer and government administrator; Consultant, President's Committee on Mexican American Affairs, 1968–1969. Writings and speeches, relating to the problems of Mexican Americans.
  Gift, J. A. Chacon, 1978.

411

Chadbourn, Philip H. and William H.
  Papers, 1915–1929. 2 ms. boxes.
  Commission for Relief in Belgium workers during World War I. Letters, reports, pamphlets, photographs, clippings, and memorabilia, relating to the Commission for Relief in Belgium.
  Gift, P. H. Chadbourn, 1963.

412

Chaigneau, Victor-Louis.
  Papers (in French), 1910–1949. 5 ms. boxes.
  French historian. Manuscripts of writings, memoranda, political campaign literature and clippings, relating to social and economic legislation in France, particularly during the Vichy regime, and to French politics. Includes doctoral thesis of V.-L. Chaigneau, "La Charte du Travail: Loi d' Octobre 1941" (The Charter of Labor: Law of October 1941).

413

Chaikovskiĭ (Anastasia Nikolaevna) collection (in Russian and German), 1920–1932. 3 ms. boxes.
  Interviews, correspondence, notes, newspaper clippings and other printed matter, relating to the case of A. N. Chaikovskiĭ, a woman claiming to be Grand Duchess Anastasia, daughter of Tsar Nicholas II of Russia.
  Preliminary inventory.
  Purchase, S. Botkine, 1937.

414

Chaim Weizmann, Israel and the Jewish People.
  Compilation of sound recordings, 1965. 1 phonorecord.
  Excerpts from speeches and interviews, relating to the life of Chaim Weizmann, Zionist leader and President of Israel, and to the foundation of the Israeli state. Narrated by Abba Eban. Produced and directed by Ram Ben Efraim.

415

Chaisson, John R., 1916–1972.
  Papers, 1940–1975. 17 ms. boxes, 9 envelopes, 18 phonotapes.
  Lieutenant General, U.S. Marine Corps; Chief of Staff, U.S. Marine Corps, 1971–1972. Correspondence, diaries, appointment books, speeches and writings, notes, reports, memoranda, oral history transcript, sound recordings, photographs and printed matter, relating to manpower and budgetary requirements of the U.S. Marine Corps, the Vietnamese Conflict, and U.S. Marine Corps activities during World War II, in China during 1948–1949, in Korea during 1953–1954, and in Vietnam during 1966–1968.
  Register.
  Gift, Mrs. J. R. Chaisson, 1973. Incremental gift, 1975.

416

Chalupny, E.
  Essay, 1938. "Twenty Years of Czechoslovakia." 1 folder.
  Typescript (mimeographed).
  Relates to the history of Czechoslovakia as an independent state and to the political situation in Czechoslovakia, 1938.

417

Chambrun, René, Comte de, 1906– , *collector.*
  R. Chambrun collection on Vichy France (in French), 1945–1974. 10 ms. boxes, 6 l. ft.

Depositions, correspondence and printed matter, relating to political conditions in France under the Pétain Government, 1940–1944. Translations of a portion of the collection published in *France during the German Occupation, 1940–1944* (Stanford, 1958).
Preliminary inventory.
Deposit, R. de Chambrun, 1954. Subsequent increments.

418

Chandler, Robert W.
Study, 1976. "War of Ideas." ½ ms. box.
Typescript (photocopy).
Major, U.S. Air Force. Relates to U.S. propaganda in Vietnam, 1965–1972.
Gift, R. W. Chandler, 1977.

419

Chang, Carsun.
Letters, 1947. 1 folder.
Typescript.
Chairman, Democratic Socialist Party of China. Two letters to U.S. Secretary of State George C. Marshall and General Albert C. Wedemeyer respectively, relating to prospects for a coalition government in China.

420

Chang, Hsin-hai, 1900–1972.
Papers (in English and Chinese), 1936–1976. 19 ms. boxes.
Chinese educator and diplomat; Ambassador to Portugal, 1933–1934; Ambassador to Czechoslovakia and Poland, 1934–1937. Correspondence, writings, clippings, and printed matter, relating to Chinese foreign relations with the United States, 1941–1971; Chinese efforts to gain public support in the United States, 1941–1945; Chinese history; and World War II. Includes correspondence of Siang Mei Rosalynde Chang.
Register.
Deposit, Siang Mei Chang, 1977.

421

Chang (Hsueh-liang)—photograph, n.d. 1 envelope.
Depicts the Chinese General Chang Hsueh-liang.

422

Chang, Kia-ngau, b. 1889.
Papers (in Chinese), 1945–1957. 12½ ms. boxes, 2 oversize boxes, 4 panels of calligraphy.
Chinese banker; Governor of Central Bank of China; President of Bank of China; Minister of Railways and Communications, 1935–1942; Chairman, Northeast (Manchuria) Economic Commission, 1945–1947. Diaries, reports, instructions, statistics and printed matter, relating to economic conditions in Manchuria at the end of World War II, Chinese-Soviet negotiations for the return of Manchuria to Chinese control, and daily commodity prices of Chinese products, 1950–1957. Includes some materials collected from Japanese organizations and calligraphy by Liang Ch'i-ch'ao (1873–1929).
Preliminary inventory.
May not be used before August 1, 1984, without written permission of Chang Kia-ngau.
Gift, Chang Kia-ngau, 1974. Incremental gift, 1978.

423

Chanoine, Marie Jacques Henri.
Memoirs (in French), n.d. 1 folder.
Typescript.
General, French Army; Commanding General, 5e Division Légère de Cavalerie, 1940. Relates to the operations of the 5e Division in Belgium and northern France, May 10—June 12, 1940.
Gift, Mme. Chanoine, 1948.

424

Chapin, Leland T.
Papers, 1941–1944. 1 ms. box.
Executive Secretary, Morale Committee on Educational Institutions in Hawaii; Civil Affairs Officer, U.S. Navy, during World War II. Writings, minutes of meetings, radio transcripts, and serial issues, relating to the promotion of patriotism in Hawaiian schools and within the Oriental community in Hawaii, and to military government in the Marshall Islands during World War II.
Preliminary inventory.
Gift, L. T. Chapin, 1969.

425

Chapman, Frank Michler, 1864–1945.
History, 1920. "The American Red Cross in Latin America." 1 vol.
Typescript.
Relates to Red Cross work in Latin America during World War I.

426

Chappell, Church Allen, d. 1976.
Papers, 1925–1953. 1 ms. box.
Captain, U.S. Navy. Diary, correspondence, orders, booklets, photographs, and printed matter, relating to U.S. Naval activities in the Philippines, 1935—1937, and at Pearl Harbor, 1941, and to the U.S. Naval Academy Postgraduate School.
Gift, C. A. Chappell, 1974.

427

Chatfield, Frederick H.
Miscellany, ca. 1915–1918. 3 framed flour sacks, 1 framed lithograph, 1 framed poster, 1 oversize lithograph, 1 photo album, 9 oversize photos, 2 envelopes.
Member, Commission for Relief in Belgium. Photographs and miscellanea, relating to the activities of the Commission for Relief in Belgium.
Gift, Mrs. William H. Chatfield, 1953.

428

Chauvain, André.
History (in French), n.d. "Histoire du Maréchal Wou Pei-fou, L'Honneur de la Chine" (History of Marshal

Wou Pei-fou, the Honor of China). 1 folder.
Typescript (carbon copy).
Relates to Wu Pei-fu, and Chinese history in the period 1874–1949.
Gift, Jacques de Launay, 1971.

429

Chavchavadze, David.
History, 1950. "The Vlassov Movement: Soviet Citizens Who Served on the German Side, 1941–45." ½ ms. box.
Typescript (mimeographed).

430

Ch'en, Tu-hsiu.
Translation of an appeal, 1933. 1 folder.
Holograph.
Chinese communist leader. Protest to the Kiangsu High Court, relating to the arrest of Ch'en Tu-hsiu by the Kuomintang government for treasonable activities in 1932.

431

Chennault, Claire Lee, 1890–1958.
Papers, 1941–1959. 11 ms. boxes.
Lieutenant General, U.S. Army; Commanding General, American Volunteer Group in China during World War II. Correspondence, memoranda, orders, reports, and clippings, relating to Chinese-American military and diplomatic relations during World War II, and to the activities of the American Volunteer Group ("Flying Tigers") in China.
Inventory.
Gift, Mrs. C. L. Chennault, 1967.

432

Cheriachoukin, A. V.
Papers (in Russian), 1918–1919. 1 folder.
Ambassador of the Don Cossack Republic to the Ukraine during the Russian Civil War. Correspondence, reports, and dispatches, relating to the activities of the anti-Bolshevik movements during the Russian Civil War, and relations of the Don Cossack Republic with the Germans and with the Allied representatives in Odessa.
Preliminary inventory.

433

Cherington, Reed B., 1875–1944.
Papers, 1918–1941. 1 ms. box, 3 albums, 1 envelope, 1 folder.
Chaplain, U.S. Army. Photographs, memorabilia, chaplain's manual and prayer books, and miscellaneous American and German military documents, relating to the American Expeditionary Force in France during World War I.
Gift, Mrs. R. B. Cherington, 1945. Incremental gift, 1949.

434

Cherkasskiĭ family.
Papers (in Russian), 1837–1974. 1½ ms. boxes, 1 oversize roll.

Russian Imperial noble family. Diaries, correspondence, books, memorabilia, writings, genealogy, clippings, printed matter, and photographs, relating to the careers, experiences, and genealogy of the Cherkasskiĭ family, the Russian Revolution and Civil War, the Russian Orthodox Church abroad, and the Russian Imperial Army.
Gift, Russian Historical Archive and Repository, 1975.

435

Chernov, Viktor Mikhailovich, 1873–1952.
Writings (in Russian), n.d. ½ ms. box.
Typescript.
Leader of the Russian Partiia Sotsialistov-Revoliutsionerov. Relates to activities of the Partiia Sotsialistov-Revoliutsionerov (Socialist Revolutionary Party) during the Russian Revolution.

436

Chibas, Raul.
Memoirs (in Spanish), 1966. "Memorias de la Revolucion Cubana, 1927–1958" (Recollections of the Cuban Revolution, 1927–1958). 1 folder.
Typescript.
Relates to political conditions in Cuba, especially during the period 1956–1957.
Purchase, R. Chibas, 1966.

437

Chichagov (Lieutenant General)—photographs, 1903. 1 envelope.
Depicts Lieutenant General Chichagov with a group of Russian military officers.

438

Chicherin, Georgiĭ Vasil'evich, 1872–1936.
Letter, 1918, to Allen Wardwell. 1 folder.
Typescript (photocopy).
Soviet Commissar of Foreign Affairs, 1918–1930. Calls for the condemnation of atrocities by anti-Bolshevik forces in Russia.

439

Children's Letter to the U.N.
Cantata, 1952. 1 phonorecord.
Produced by the American Veterans Committee in cooperation with the American Association for the United Nations, for radio broadcast during United Nations Week.

440

Childs, James Rives, 1893–
Memoirs, n.d. ½ ms. box.
Typescript.
American diplomat; American Relief Administration worker in Russia, 1921–1923; Chargé d'Affaires in Morocco, 1941–1945; Ambassador to Saudi Arabia, 1946–1950; Ambassador to Ethiopia, 1951–1953. Relates to relief work and social conditions in Russia, U.S. foreign relations with Balkan and Near Eastern countries,

diplomacy regarding Morocco in World War II, and the role of Iran in world politics, especially in relation to Russia.

441

China border region reports, 1944–1947. 1 folder.
Typescript.
Relates to economic reconstruction and cooperative movements in the Border Region area of China under communist control.

442

China—communist posters and records (in Chinese), ca. 1949–1953. 63 posters, 19 phonorecords.
Propaganda relating to Chinese revolutionary history, mutual aid teams, policy towards minorities and marriage reforms, Sino-Soviet friendship, Mao Tse-tung, and Lu Hsun.
Preliminary inventory.
Purchase, John W. Powell, 1974.

443

China consortium collection, 1918–1921. 1 folder.
Correspondence and memoranda, relating to the formation of a consortium of American, British, French and Japanese banking groups to conduct commercial activities in China.

444

China. Constitution.
Extracts, 1911–1914. 1 folder.
Typescript.
Constitutional provisions and electoral laws enacted by the Republic of China.

445

China—history—revolution, 1911–1912—photographs, 1911. 1 envelope.
Depicts delegates to the Republican Conference at Nanking, at which Sun Yat-sen was elected President of China, and a newspaper account of the election.

446

China—maps, n.d. 1 folder.
Hand-drawn.
Depicts sections of Szechwan and Hopeh Provinces, China. Includes a table of place names in Szechwan Province (in Chinese).

447

China—photographs, n.d. 2 envelopes.
Depicts scenes in Inner Mongolia and elsewhere in China, including a kindergarten and the Great Wall.

448

China—poster, ca. 1938. 1 folder.
Printed.
Proclamation relating to the use of fireworks in Shanghai during the state of emergency. Issued by the Shanghai Municipal Council.
Gift, E. F. Fields.

449

China Research Institute of Land Economics, Taipei.
Interviews (in Chinese), 1949–1953. 15 phonotapes.
Interviews with twenty-one officials who participated in the Taiwan Land Reform Program, conducted by the China Research Institute of Land Economics. Includes transcripts.
Purchase, China Research Institute of Land Economics, 1977.

450

China—views—photographs, 1936–1938. 2 envelopes.
Depicts Peking, and the bombing of Shanghai, 1937.
Gift, W. G. Stafford.

451

China, 12th War Zone.
Proclamation, 1946. 1 folder.
Printed.
Relates to the reoccupation of Kalgan, China, by Nationalist Chinese troops. Issued by the Headquarters of the Commander-in-Chief of the 12th War Zone of China.

452

Chinese National Relief and Rehabilitation Administration.
Photographs, ca. 1945–1947. 4 ms. boxes.
Negatives.
Depicts scenes of daily life in China and activities of the Chinese National Relief and Rehabilitation Administration.
Gift, Chinese National Relief and Rehabilitation Administration, 1948.

453

Chinese propaganda (in Chinese), ca. 1944. 1 folder.
Pro-Allied Chinese propaganda material.

454

Chinese propaganda—Korean War, ca. 1950–1953. 1 folder.
Propaganda leaflets and photocopies of leaflets (printed), issued by the Chinese Government during the Korean War, and aimed at American troops.

455

Chipman, Miner, b. 1882.
Papers, 1946–1952. 3 ms. boxes.
American novelist. Notes, correspondence, transcripts of governmental hearings and other printed matter, relating to the history of the Chinese in the U.S., especially in California, and to a proposed historical novel by M. Chipman on this subject.
Gift, L. A. Garret.

456

Christian, John L.
Papers, 1942–1943. 3½ ms. boxes.
Major, U.S. Army; Chief of the Southern Asia Branch of the Military Intelligence Service during World War II. Reports, memoranda, studies, aerial photographs,

and maps, relating to military operations in the China-Burma-India Theater, the Pacific, and French Indochina during World War II.
Gift, W. L. Christian, 1948.

457

Christian-Moslem Conference, Aaley, Lebanon, 1947.
Proclamation, 1947. 1 folder.
Printed.
Conference of Lebanese and other Arab delegates. Relates to the question of a Jewish state in Palestine and to the foreign policy of the U.S. and Great Britain concerning Palestine.

458

Christian Science War Relief Depot, Le Mans, France.
Miscellaneous records, 1918–1919. 1 folder.
Two visitor's registers, and photographs of war scenes, mostly in France.
Gift, Mrs. Alden Potter, 1961.

459

Christian, Sutton.
Papers (in Chinese and English), 1931–1945. 1 ms. box.
Director, Chengtu and Sian Branches, China Division, U.S. Office of War Information, 1945. Correspondence, writings, reports, and printed matter, relating primarily to U.S. propaganda activities in the communist border areas of China, 1944–1945.
Gift, Nevada Christian, 1978.

460

Christol, Carl Q.
Study, 1974. "Herbert Hoover, the League of Nations and the World Court." 1 folder.
Typescript.
Professor of International Law and Political Science, University of Southern California. Paper presented at the Herbert Hoover Centennial Summer Seminar on the Presidency of Herbert Hoover, West Branch, Iowa, August 8, 1974.
Gift, C. Q. Christol, 1974.

461

"Chronologie des Activités de M. P. van Zeeland" (Chronology of the Activities of Mr. P. van Zeeland).
Chronology (in French), ca. 1953. 1 vol.
Typescript.
Relates to the public life of Paul van Zeeland, Belgian banker, economist and statesman.

462

Chuhnov, Nicholas.
Open letter (in Russian), 1951, to Harry S. Truman, President of the U.S. 1 folder.
Typescript (mimeographed).
Editor of *The Banner of Russia* (New York). Objects to a comparison of Iosif Stalin and Emperor Alexander I made by President Truman. Includes a translation of the letter (printed).

463

Chung Yang Er Pao (Hankow).
Translations of newspaper articles, 1927. 1 folder.
Typescript (some mimeographed).
Relates to political strategy of the Kuomintang Party.

464

Church, Michael P., *collector*.
M. P. Church collection on American youth movements and communism, 1933–1941. 1 ms. box.
Writings, notes, clippings, leaflets, and pamphlets, relating to American youth movements and communist activities in American educational institutions.
Gift, M. P. Church, 1962. Subsequent increments.

465

Church of Brethren. Brethren Service Commission. Civilian Public Service.
Records, 1941–1946. 5 ms. boxes.
Memoranda, bulletins, newsletters, and reports, relating to compulsory non-military public service, conscientious objectors, and the work of the Brethren Civilian Public Service Committee in the U.S. during World War II.

466

Church-state relations in Czechoslovakia—writings (in Czech), n.d. 1 folder.
Typescript.
Relates to the situation of the Catholic Church in Czechoslovakia in 1949.

467

Churchill, Mrs. Lawrence W., *collector*.
Miscellany, 1944–1948. 1 folder.
Correspondence, clippings, memorabilia, and photographs, relating to the Kiichi Saito family, two members of which were killed while serving in the U.S. armed forces during World War II.
Gift, Mrs. L. W. Churchill, 1968.

468

Churchill (Sir Winston Leonard Spencer)—photographs, n.d. 1 envelope.
Depicts W. L. S. Churchill, Prime Minister of Great Britain, 1940–1945 and 1951–1955.

469

Ciano, Galeazzo, 1903–1944.
Diary (in Italian), 1939–1943. 1 ms. box.
Holograph (photocopy).
Foreign Minister of Italy, 1936–1943. Relates to Italian foreign policy during World War II, January 1, 1939—December 23, 1943.
Gift, Hugh Gibson.

470

Cielens, Felix, 1888–1964.
Papers (in Latvian and English), 1913–1945. 2½ ms. boxes.
Minister of Foreign Affairs of Latvia, 1926–1928;

Latvian Minister to France, 1933–1940. Memoirs, writings, correspondence, memoranda and printed matter, relating to Latvian foreign relations and political conditions.

Gift, estate of F. Cielens, 1966. Deposit, Mrs. F. Cielens, 1973.

471

Citizens Committee for a Free Cuba, 1963–1974.
Records, 1962–1974. 58 ms. boxes.
Anti-communist organization founded in the United States to disseminate information about communism in Cuba and other Latin American countries. Clippings, newsletters, press releases, reports, conference papers, speeches, and printed matter, relating primarily to the political, economic, and social effects of communism in Cuba, communist subversion in Latin America, U.S. foreign policy toward Cuba, and activities of the Cuban émigré community.
Gift, Citizens Committee for a Free Cuba, 1973.

472

Citizens Committee for Reorganization of the Executive Branch of the Government, 1949–1958.
Records, 1949–1958. 103 ms. boxes, 1 motion picture.
Private organization for promotion of U.S. governmental administrative reforms. Correspondence, reports, newsletters, press releases, clippings, and printed matter, relating to the recommendations of the two Hoover Commissions on governmental reorganization.
Preliminary inventory.
Gift, Citizens Committee for Reorganization of the Executive Branch of the Government, 1952. Incremental gift, 1958.

473

Clampett, Donald.
Diary, 1916. 1 folder.
Holograph.
Son of an American relief worker in Belgium. Relates to his journey from the U.S. to Europe with his father.

474

Clapp, Frances Benton, b. 1887.
Study, ca. 1958. "Kyoto, Fact and Fancy: A Historical Sketch and Description of its Places, Shrines, Temples, Institutions and Legends." 1 ms. box.
Typescript.
Professor of Music, Doshisha University, Japan, 1918–1957.
Gift, Charlotte B. DeForest, 1969.

475

Claremont Graduate School. Oral History Program.
Transcripts of oral history interviews, 1964–1966. ½ ms. box.
Photocopy.
Relates to persecution of Jews in German-occupied Austria and Poland during World War II. Includes miscellaneous printed matter relating to anti-Semitism.
Preliminary inventory.
Gift, Joseph Rebhun, 1969.

476

Clark, Birge M., 1893–
Papers, n.d. 1 folder, 1 oversize box (½ l. ft.).
American architect; U.S. Army officer during World War I. Memoirs (typewritten), relating to American aerial operations in World War I, and to the construction of the Herbert Hoover home in Stanford, California; and posters relating to the U.S. Food Administration, 1918, and the Great Depression, 1930–1933.
Gift, B. M. Clark, 1960. Incremental gift, 1971.

477

Clark, Erik.
Papers, 1925. 1 folder, 1 envelope.
Memoirs and photographs, relating to the 1925 student riots in China, precipitated by an incident in Shanghai, during which British and Japanese police killed 21 students.
Gift, Molly Clark, 1974.

478

Clark, Fred G.
Study, 1946. "Money Made Easy: A Primer of Production Receipts Sometimes Called Money." 1 vol.
Printed.
By Fred G. Clark and Richard Stanton Rimanoczy. Includes typewritten comments by Eliot Jones, Professor of Economics, Stanford University.

479

Clark, G. N.
History, n.d. "The First Battalion in France." 1 folder.
Typescript.
Relates to the history of the First Battalion of the Eighth London Regiment of the British Army in France and Belgium from 1915 to 1917. Includes issues of newsletters of the Post Office Rifles Association.

480

Clark, Grover.
Report, 1932. "Research Needs and Opportunities in China: Memorandum for the Director of the Program of Research in International Relations of the Social Science Research Council." 1 folder.
Typescript (mimeographed).
Relates to proposed research topics on political, social and economic conditions in China.

481

Clark, Harold A., *collector.*
Miscellany, 1942–1949. 1 folder.
Correspondence, newsletters and printed matter, relating to civilian public service performed by conscientious objectors in the U.S. during World War II.

482

Clark, Mark Wayne, 1896–
Memoirs, 1954. *From the Danube to the Yalu.* 1 vol.
Galley proofs.
General, U.S. Army; Commander, U.N. Forces in Korea, 1952–1953. Relates to the Korean War.

483
Clark, Marmaduke R., d. 1964.
Papers, 1918–1920. 1 ms. box, 9 envelopes.
Senior Secretary, Young Men's Christian Association; with the American Expeditionary Forces in Siberia. Correspondence, memoranda, writings, newspaper clippings, memorabilia, and photographs, relating to Y.M.C.A. activities in Siberia, political developments during the last stages of the Russian Civil War, and the Allied intervention.
Gift, Robert L. Clark, 1976.

484
Clark, Roy Ross.
Papers, 1919. 1 ms. box.
American engineer; member of Young Men's Christian Association Construction Department attached to American Expeditionary Force in France, 1917–1919. Report (typewritten) with blueprints, relating to the construction of huts for U.S. Army enlisted men in France during World War I; and a certificate presented to R. R. Clark for service as an engineer with the Construction Department.
Gift, R. R. Clark.

485
Clarke, Bruce Cooper, 1901–
Papers, 1944–1970. ½ ms. box, 1 envelope.
General, U.S. Army. Correspondence, speeches and writings and printed matter, relating to military engineering and the theory of military science and tactics, command, leadership and training.
Gift, B. C. Clarke, 1970.

486
Clarke, Ione Clement, b. 1889.
Biography, n.d. "One in a Hundred." 1 folder.
Typescript (photocopy).
Relates to Ernest Wilson Clement, an American missionary in Japan, 1887–1891 and 1895–1927, and father of I. C. Clarke.
Gift, I. C. Clarke, 1973.

487
Cleaveland, Norman, *collector*.
Miscellany (in Chinese, English and Malayan), 1950. 1 folder.
Posters, leaflets and correspondence, relating to the independence movement in Malaya.

488
Clendenen, Clarence Clements, 1899–
Papers, 1881–1968. 13½ ms. boxes, 4 card file boxes (⅔ l. ft.), 7 envelopes, 14 phonotapes.
Colonel, U.S. Army; Curator of Special Collections, Hoover Institution on War, Revolution and Peace. Printed matter, biographical notes, interviews, diaries, correspondence, army manuals, research notes, photographs and maps, relating to American military history, especially during World War II and the Vietnamese War, and to the Punitive Expedition in Mexico in 1916.

Preliminary inventory.
Gift, C. C. Clendenen, 1968. Subsequent increments.

489
Cleveland, Maude.
Miscellany, 1700–1921. 1 ms. box.
Chief, Home Communication and Casualty Service, American Red Cross, Paris, during World War I. Distinguished Service Medal with certificate, January 1921; and a map in Dutch of the known world, ca. 1700.
Gift, M. Cleveland, 1951.

490
Cobb, John B.
Letters, 1946–1948. 1 folder.
Typescript.
American missionary in Japan. Relates to efforts of the Foreign Missions Conference of North America to bring relief supplies to Japan. Letters written for distribution by the Methodist Board of Missions.
Gift, J. B. Cobb, 1974.

491
Coblentz, Edmond D.
Biographical sketch, n.d. 1 folder.
Typescript.
Relates to Margherita Grassini Sarfatti, Italian author and fascist leader.

492
Cochet (Gabriel Roger)–photograph, n.d. 1 envelope.
Depicts the French General G. R. Cochet.

493
Code, James A., Jr., 1893–1972.
Papers, 1923–1952. 2 ms. boxes, 1 envelope, 1 medal case.
Major General, U.S. Army; Assistant Chief Signal Officer, 1942–1945. Correspondence, autobiography, reports, memoranda, military orders and citations, and printed matter, relating primarily to the operation of the U.S. Signal Corps, especially during World War II. Includes three Italian Government documents relating to Benito Mussolini.
Preliminary inventory.
Gift, Mrs. J. A. Code, 1972.

494
Cofer, Mrs. Leland E.
Papers, 1915–1945. 6 ms. boxes, 5 envelopes.
American relief work administrator in World Wars I and II. Correspondence, speeches and writings, reports, postcards, photographs, and memorabilia, relating to the administration of relief during and after the two world wars and, in particular, to the activities of the New York Committee for the Fatherless Children of France. Includes some papers of Leland E. Cofer, Health Officer for the Port of New York and Assistant Surgeon General, U.S. Public Health Service.
Gift, Mrs. L. E. Cofer, 1950.

495

Cohan, George Michael, 1878–1942.
Song (in English and French), ca. 1917–1918. *Over There*. 1 phonorecord.
American composer. World War I American patriotic song, sung by Enrico Caruso.

496

Coleman, Arthur Prudden, *collector*.
Miscellany (in English and Polish), 1937–1942. 1 folder.
Correspondence and printed matter, relating to Polish history and literature.

497

Coleman, Frederick W. B., b. 1874.
Diaries, 1909–1938. ½ ms. box.
Holograph.
American diplomat; Minister to Estonia, Latvia, and Lithuania, 1922–1931; Minister to Denmark, 1931–1933. Relates to U.S. military activities during World War I, and to U.S. foreign relations with the Baltic States and Denmark.
Gift, Ruth Dundas, 1977.

498

Collins, Ernest, b. 1887.
Poems, 1942–1955. 1 folder.
Typescript and printed.
Relates primarily to world peace and the United Nations.
Gift, E. Collins, 1956.

499

Collins, James Hiram, b. 1873.
Writings, 1915–1919. 1 folder.
American journalist; staff member, U.S. Food Administration and U.S. Shipping Board during World War I. Leaflets and magazine articles written by J. H. Collins, relating to war production and war loans in the U.S. during World War I.
Gift, J. H. Collins.

500

Colombian censorship–memorandum (in Spanish), 1914. 1 folder.
Typescript.
Relates to censorship of telegrams in Colombia.

501

Colombian election, 1949—campaign literature (in Spanish), 1949. 1 folder.
Printed.
Relates to the general election in Colombia. Mostly issued by the Liberal Party of Colombia.

502

Colonna di Cesarò, Giovanni.
Miscellany (in French and Italian), 1897–1922. 1 folder.
Two memoranda and a letter, relating to international agreements regarding war profits taxes.

503

Colton, Ethan Theodore, b. 1872.
Papers, 1918–1952. 7 ms. boxes.
American relief worker with the European Student Relief and the Young Men's Christian Association in Russia. Correspondence, reports, manuscripts of writings, and clippings, relating to European Student Relief activities in Russia and other European countries, 1920–1925; and to social conditions, the educational system, and the status of religion in Russia in the 1920's and 1930's. Includes the memoirs of E. T. Colton and 13 antireligious Soviet posters.
Gift, E. T. Colton.

504

Columbia Broadcasting System.
Transcripts of broadcasts, 1938. 1 ms. box.
Typescript (mimeographed).
Relates to the international crisis over Czechoslovakia and Munich agreement, September 24–30, 1938.

505

Columbia University. Naval School of Military Government and Administration.
Report, 1943. "The Problem of Timor: Proposed Organization for Military Government." 1 vol.
Typescript (carbon copy).

506

Comitato d'Azione Maltese.
Posters (in Italian), n.d. 1 folder.
Printed.
Relates to the proposed annexation of Malta by Italy.

507

Comitato di Liberazione Nazionale per l'Alta Italia. Corpo Voluntari della Liberta'.
Records (in Italian), 1943–1946. 1½ ms. boxes, 3 reels of microfilm.
Anti-fascist Italian resistance movement during World War II. Bulletins, reports, proclamations, leaflets, and photographs, relating to the Italian resistance movement during World War II.
Preliminary inventory.
Gift, Charles Delzell, 1946.

508

Comitato Siciliano d'Azione.
Printed matter (in Italian), 1945. 1 folder.
Leaflets and pamphlets, issued by the Comitato Siciliano d'Azione and the Movimento per l'Indipendenza della Sicilia, relating to the Sicilian independence movement.

509

Comité Belge pour la Communauté Atlantique, *collector*.
Newspaper clippings (in French and Flemish), 1959. 9 ms. boxes.
Clippings from Belgian newspapers, relating to a decennial evaluation of the North Atlantic Treaty Organization.
Preliminary inventory.

510

Comité de Defensa de la Pequeña Propiedad.
Proclamation (in Spanish), 1936. *El Problema de la Tierra en León* (The Problem of Land in León). 1 folder. Printed.
Relates to land reform in the region around León, Mexico.

511

Commager, Henry Steele, 1902–
Essay, 1943. "The Price of Eire's Neutrality." 1 folder. Printed.
Professor of History, Columbia University. Relates to the role of Ireland in World War II. Published in the *London Evening Standard*, April 21, 1943.

512

Commémorant le 1er Anniversaire de la Victoire du Peuple de Guinée sur l'Impérialisme International. (Commemorating the First Anniversary of the Victory of the People of Guinea over International Imperialism).
Sound recordings (in French and African languages), 1971. 4 phonorecords.
Guinean songs and music, and speeches by President Sékou Touré of Guinea and others, relating to the Portuguese invasion of Guinea in 1970.

513

Commission for Polish Relief, 1939–1949.
Records, 1939–1949. 51 ms. boxes.
Private organization for provision of relief to Poland during World War II. Correspondence, reports, memoranda, financial records and photographs.
Preliminary inventory.
Gift, Commission for Polish Relief, 1948. Subsequent increments.

514

Commission for Relief in Belgium, 1914–1930.
Records, 1914–1924. 265 l. ft.
Private organization for provision of relief to Belgium during World War I. Correspondence, reports, memoranda, accounts, pamphlets, bulletins and photographs, relating to procurement of food and other supplies in the U.S. and their distribution in German-occupied Belgium and northern France during and immediately after World War I.
Gift, Commission for Relief in Belgium, 1922. Subsequent increments.

515

Commission for Relief in Belgium, 1940–1945.
Records (in English, French, German and Flemish), 1940–1947. 19 ms. boxes.
Affiliate of the National Committee on Food for the Small Democracies. Correspondence, memoranda, reports, photographs, and posters, relating to efforts to provide civilian relief to Belgium and Luxemburg during World War II.

516

Commission Interalliée Permanente d'Armistice.
Miscellaneous records (in English and French), 1919–1920. 1 folder.
Organization for the supervision of the armistice at the end of World War I. Memoranda and correspondence, relating to the transfer of coal and railroad equipment from Germany to the Allied Powers.

517

Commission of Inquiry into Forced Labor.
Report, 1950. 1 folder.
Typescript (mimeographed).
Relates to forced labor in the Soviet Union and Eastern Europe. Report made to the United Nations Economic and Social Council.

518

Committee for Free Asia, *collector.*
Committee for Free Asia collection on China and Taiwan (in Chinese), 1951–1953. 9 ms. boxes.
Clippings and press releases, relating to political, social and economic conditions in China and Taiwan. Includes clippings from Chinese, Hong Kong and Chinese-language U.S. newspapers, and press releases issued by Radio Free Asia.

519

Committee for the Return of Confiscated German and Japanese Property, 1954–1962.
Records (in English and German), 1954–1962. 33 ms. boxes.
Private organization founded in the U.S. to promote restitution of private German and Japanese property confiscated by the U.S. Government during and after World War II. Minutes of meetings, reports, correspondence, press releases, position statements, legal briefs, notes, newspaper clippings, and printed matter.
Register.
Gift, Committee for the Return of Confiscated German and Japanese Property, 1963.

520

Committee of One Million.
Speeches, n.d. 3 phonorecords.
Anti-communist American organization. Relates to the proposed admission of communist China to the United Nations.
Preliminary inventory.

521

Committee on Public Information, Washington, D.C.
Photographs, 1917–1918. 8 envelopes, 6 oversize prints, 1 poster.
Depicts activities of the American Expeditionary Forces in the U.S. and France during World War I, including scenes of training, and aerial and naval operations.
Gift, California State Library, 1962.

522

Committee to Defend America by Aiding the Americans.
Propaganda, 1941. 1 folder.
Printed.
Anti-Semitic propaganda cards.

523

Communist International. Executive Committee.
Instructions, 1922. "Concerning the Next Tasks of the CP of A." 1 vol.
Typescript (photocopy).
Relates to the Communist Party, U.S.A. Seized by the U.S. Department of Justice during a raid on a secret convention of the Communist Party, U.S.A., at Bridgman, Michigan, 1922. Includes a cover letter signed by Nikolai Bukharin, Karl Radek and Otto Kuusinen.

524

Communist Party of Great Britain.
Leaflet, ca. 1939. "Dockers! Defend Your Own Interests!" 1 folder.
Printed.
Calls for wage increases for British dock workers and the immediate end of British participation in the war.
Purchase, H. F. Ashbrook, 1977.

525

Communist Party of India.
Study, 1949. "Struggle for People's Democracy and Socialism: Some Questions of Strategy and Tactics." 1 vol.
Typewritten transcript.
Relates to the communist movement in India. Published in *The Communist*, June–July 1949.

526

Communist Party of South Africa.
Issuances (in English and Afrikaans), 1937–1943. ½ ms. box.
Pamphlets and leaflets, relating to political conditions, race relations and the labor movement in South Africa, and to the South African role in World War II. Includes some material issued by other leftist South African organizations.
Preliminary inventory.

527

Communist propaganda (in French, Italian, German and Vietnamese), 1950–1961. 2 ms. boxes.
Posters, leaflets, and election campaign material, consisting of electoral and other communist propaganda from France, Italy, Austria, East Germany, and Vietnam. Includes some electoral propaganda distributed by non-communist parties in France and Italy, anti-militarist propaganda from West Germany, and one anti-American poster from Korea.
Gift, U.S. Library of Congress, 1962.

528

Communist youth movement collection, 1938. 1 folder.
Report and newsletter, relating to the strategy of the communist youth movement in the U.S., especially with regard to the American Youth Congress and the Boy Scouts.

529

Communists—U.S.—portraits, 1930–1960. 2 envelopes.
Depicts alleged members of the Communist Party of the United States. Includes negatives.

530

Conard-Duveneck collection, 1940–1946. 5 ms. boxes.
Pamphlets, reprints, newsletters, clippings, government reports, letters, and notebooks, relating to conditions in the Japanese relocation centers in the U.S. during World War II.
Preliminary inventory.
Gift, Joseph Conard and Mrs. F. S. Duveneck.

531

Conference for Conclusion and Signature of Treaty of Peace with Japan, San Francisco, 1951.
Records, 1951. 1 ms. box.
Conference that formally ended World War II. Bulletins, press releases, minutes of meetings, agenda, rosters of participants, and texts of the treaty, protocols and statements of delegates.
Preliminary inventory.
Gift, Nathan van Patten.

532

Conference for the Limitation of Naval Armament, Geneva, 1927.
Report, 1927. 1 folder.
Typescript (mimeographed).
Verbatim report of the second plenary session, July 14, 1927, with declarations by the U.S. and Japanese delegations.

533

Conference of the Institutions for the Scientific Study of International Affairs, Milan, 1932.
Report, 1932. 1 vol.
Typescript (mimeographed).
Conference held under the auspices of the International Institute of Intellectual Cooperation of the League of Nations. Report of the fifth session.

534

Conference on Experience in International Administration, Washington, 1943.
Proceedings, 1943. 1 vol.
Typescript (mimeographed).
Conference held under the auspices of the Carnegie Endowment for International Peace. Relates to postwar prospects for the League of Nations.

535

Conference on the Discontinuance of Nuclear Weapon Tests, Geneva, 1958–
    Proceedings, 1961. 1 folder.
    Typescript (mimeographed).
    Proceedings of the 274th–276th and 278th–279th sessions, March 21–23 and 27–28, 1961, relating to proposals for a nuclear test ban treaty.
    Gift, U.S. Department of State, 1961.

536

Conference on the Social Sciences in Historical Study, Hoover Institution on War, Revolution and Peace, Stanford University, 1957.
    Proceedings, 1957. 7 phototapes.
    Relates to the interdisciplinary study of the formation of large-scale political communities.

537

Confesor, Tomás, 1891–1951.
    Miscellaneous papers, 1943–1944. ½ ms. box.
    Governor of Panay, Philippine Islands; participant in the anti-Japanese resistance during World War II. Report, entitled "Notes on Proposed Post-War Reconstruction Programs," 1944, and a letter, February 20, 1943, to Fermin Caram, refusing an appeal to surrender to the Japanese occupation authorities.

538

Conklin, Alvah P., 1892–1976.
    Papers, 1917–1919. 2 oversize boxes (1 l. ft.).
    Captain, U.S. Army; Commanding Officer, 67th Company, Coast Artillery Corps, during World War I. Letters, clippings and photographs, relating to activities of the 67th Coast Artillery Company in France.
    Gift, Sybil Conklin, 1977.

539

Conseil National de Libération (Zaire). Commandement des Forces Armées Populaires. État-Major Général.
    Miscellaneous records (in French and Likeleve), 1964. 1 ms. box.
    General Staff of the Popular Armed Forces Command of the National Council of Liberation, a political movement in Zaire. Correspondence, reports, orders, battle plans and lists, relating to military and political aspects of a rebellion in the Kwilu region of Zaire.
    Gift, Herbert Weiss, 1976.

540

Consell Nacional de la Democracia Catalana.
    Poster (in Catalan), 1946. "Un Manifest Patriotic" (A Patriotic Manifesto).
    Printed.
    Commemorates the 11th of September 1714, and appeals to the Catalans to continue fighting for the cause of liberty.

541

Conservative Party (Great Britain).
    Phonorecord, n.d. *The Conservatives: A History of the Party*.
    Relates to the history of the British Conservative Party.

542

Cook, John Douglas.
    History, n.d. 1 folder.
    Typescript.
    Relates to activities of the U.S. 316th Engineer Regiment, 1917–1918.
    Gift, J. D. Cook, 1970.

543

Cooke, Charles Maynard, 1886–1970.
    Papers, 1920–1964. 36 ms. boxes, 2 envelopes.
    Admiral, U.S. Navy; Deputy Chief of Naval Operations, 1944–1945; unofficial advisor to Chiang Kai-shek, 1950–1951. Correspondence, speeches and writings, reports, dispatches, memoranda, and photographs, relating to U.S. naval operations in World War II, inter-Allied diplomacy in World War II, the defenses of Taiwan, and U.S. domestic and foreign policy.
    Register.
    Court martial proceedings, personnel lists, fitness reports, medical reports, performance evaluations, and personnel files of Commerce International China, Special Technician Program to the Republic of China, 1950–1951 (box 36), are restricted until 2025. Six phonotapes of interviews with Admiral C. M. Cooke are restricted until transcriptions have been prepared and edited.
    Gift, Mary Louise Cooke and C. M. Cooke, Jr., 1968.

544

Cooley, John K.
    Papers (in French and English), 1960–1962. ½ ms. box.
    American journalist; *Christian Science Monitor* correspondent in North Africa. Dispatches, radio broadcast transcripts, memoranda, transcripts of interviews, press releases and printed matter, relating to the French military revolt led by the Organisation Armée Secrète in Algiers in 1961, and to the Algerian independence movement.
    Preliminary inventory.
    Gift, J. K. Cooley, 1963.

545

Coolidge (Calvin)—photograph, n.d. 1 envelope.
    Depicts C. Coolidge, President of the U.S., 1923–1929, and an unidentified woman.

546

Cooper, Merian C., 1894–1973.
    Papers, 1917–1958. 1 ms. box.
    Brigadier General, U.S. Air Force; pilot with the Kosciuszko Squadron in Poland, 1919–1921; Chief of Staff, China Air Task Force, 1942. Correspondence,

memoranda, and memorabilia, relating to the American Relief Administration and the U.S. Food Administration in Poland, the Kosciuszko Squadron during the Polish-Russian wars, 1919–1921, General Douglas MacArthur, Lieutenant General Claire Chennault, U.S. defense policy, air power, and communist strategy.
Gift, M. C. Cooper, 1958. Incremental gift, 1964.

547

Corcoran, William Warwick, 1884–1962.
Papers, 1919–1962. 2 ms. boxes, 1 scrapbook, 1 oversize box (½ l. ft.).
American consular official; Consul General, Goteborg, Sweden, 1936–1947. Correspondence, clippings, medals, plaques, awards, citations, decorations, and photographs, relating to the U.S. consular service, U.S.-Swedish relations, Allied diplomacy in Sweden during World War II, and social conditions in Sweden.
Gift, estate of W. W. Corcoran, 1977.

548

Corey, Lewis, 1894–1953.
Letter, 1936, to Harold H. Fisher. 1 folder.
Typescript.
American communist leader; later anti-communist labor leader and educator. Relates to Marxist publications in the U.S.

549

Corlett, Charles Harrison, 1889–1971.
Autobiography, n.d. *Cowboy Pete*. ½ ms. box.
Typescript.
Major General, U.S. Army. Relates to American military activities in World Wars I and II. Also includes printed copy.

550

Cormack, James.
Letter, 1953, to Mr. and Mrs. William Logan. 1 folder.
Typescript.
Relates to the visit of Queen Elizabeth II of Great Britain to Tonga.

551

Corning Glass Works, Corning, N.Y.
Photograph, n.d. 1 envelope.
Depicts a cathode ray tube for use in high speed electronic printing.

552

Cornwell, William M., *collector*.
W. M. Cornwell collection on the Far East, 1909–1924. 1 ms. box.
Clippings, correspondence and memorabilia, relating to political and social conditions in the Far East, especially China. Includes a map of Tsingtao.
Gift, W. M. Cornwell, 1950.

553

Corović, Vladimir, 1885–1941?
Translation of a history, n.d. "Relations between Serbia and Austria-Hungary in the XX Century." 1 vol.
Typescript (carbon copy).
Translation by Stoyan Gavrilović. Original title, "Odnosi Izmedju Srbije i Austro-Ugarske u XX Veku."

554

La Correspondance Politique de l'Europe Centrale (Political Correspondence of Central Europe).
Newspaper issue (in French, English, Italian and Spanish), 1918. 1 framed issue.
German propagandistic newspaper, ostensibly published in Zurich, Switzerland, and distributed in the Allied countries. Issue of October 31, 1918.
Gift, Harry A. Tuckey, 1947.

555

Corrigan, Robert Foster, 1914–
Papers, 1958–1975. 1 folder.
American diplomat; Deputy Chief of Protocol, U.S. Department of State, 1958–1959; Ambassador to Rwanda, 1972–1973; Deputy Assistant Secretary of Defense, 1973–1975. Clippings, notes, reports and a speech, relating to diplomatic terminology, the visit of President Sékou Touré of Guinea to the U.S. in 1959, the Panama Canal, and American investment in Africa.
Gift, R. F. Corrigan, 1978.

556

Corwin, Norman Lewis, 1910–
Radio program, 1945. *On a Note of Triumph*. 6 phonorecords.
Relates to the surrender of Germany in World War II. Broadcast over the Columbia Broadcasting System, May 8, 1945.

557

Costello, Lorenz, *collector*.
Leaflet, ca. 1914–1918. 1 folder.
Printed.
German propaganda leaflet dropped over France during World War I.
Gift, L. Costello.

558

Cotner, Robert A.
Writings, 1959. 1 folder.
Holograph.
American Relief Administration worker. Two essays, entitled "The Nature of Marxian Communism" and "Some Thoughts Regarding Communism and the World Situation."
Gift, R. A. Cotner, 1959.

559

Coudenhove-Kalergi, Richard, 1894–1972.
Miscellaneous papers (in French), 1922–1969. 1 folder.

French journalist and paneuropean publicist; President, Paneuropa Union. Correspondence, clippings, and printed matter, relating to Charles de Gaulle, European politics, and the Paneuropa Union.
Gift, Vittorio Pons, 1977.

560

Covell, William E. R., 1892–
Papers, 1918–1968. 5 ms. boxes.
Major General, U.S. Army; Commanding General, Services of Supply, China-Burma-India Theater, 1943–1945. Correspondence, writings, diaries, photographs, yearbooks, newspaper clippings, and memorabilia, relating primarily to American military operations in the China-Burma-India Theater during World War II.
Gift, W. E. R. Covell, 1968.

561

Cowan, Laian Gray.
Papers, 1952–1970. 11 ms. boxes.
American author and educator. Reports, articles, seminar papers, speeches, minutes and printed matter, relating to political, economic and social conditions, education, nationalism, and foreign aid in newly independent African states.
Gift, L. G. Cowan, 1974.

562

Crandall, Berton W.
Photographs, 1888–1953. 16 ms. boxes.
Depicts Stanford University campus and buildings, 1888–1941, Herbert Hoover, 1888–1953, Lou Henry Hoover, the Hoover family, Leland Stanford, and Mrs. Leland Stanford.
Preliminary inventory.
Gift, B. W. Crandall, 1960.

563

Cranston, Joseph A., 1898–1973.
Papers, 1943–1945. ½ ms. box, 3 envelopes, 1 album.
Brigadier General, U.S. Army; Commanding General, Services of Supply, Intermediate Section, China-Burma-India Theater, 1943–1944. Awards, citations, correspondence, clippings, orders, printed matter, reports, and photographs, relating to American military activities in the China-Burma-India Theater during World War II.
Gift, Mrs. J. A. Cranston, 1974.

564

Crary, Catherine Snell.
Writings, 1934–1938. 1 folder.
Typescript.
Relates to territorial disputes over Danzig and to political and economic conditions in Danzig.

565

Creel, George, 1876–1953, *collector*.
Printed matter, 1917–1919. 2 ms. boxes.
Pamphlets and bulletins, issued by the U.S. Committee on Public Information, relating to the U.S. war effort in World War I.
Register.
Gift, G. Creel, 1948.

566

Cripe, Harry E.
Papers, 1933–1935. 1 ms. box.
Chauffeur of Herbert Hoover. Letters, photographs, clippings, and memorabilia, relating to Herbert Hoover.
Gift, Simon Otten.

567

Crispell, Reuben B.
Papers, 1918–1919. ½ ms. box.
Captain, U.S. Army; Assistant to U.S. Food Administrator Herbert Hoover during World War I. Digests (typewritten) of U.S. diplomatic dispatches, relating to world political and economic conditions from January to March 1919; and a memorandum, December 1918, relating to foodstuffs available for export from Spain.
Gift, Mrs. R. B. Crispell, 1968.

568

Crocker, George N.
Papers, 1950–1973. 7 l. ft.
American journalist and author. Writings, reports, and printed matter, relating to political issues in the United States and international affairs.
Gift, Mrs. G. N. Crocker, 1973.

569

Cronje, Suzanne, 1925–
Miscellaneous papers (mainly in Spanish), 1969–1977. 1 ms. box.
Photocopy.
Author. Clippings, letters, reports, and printed matter, relating to politics and government of Equatorial Guinea. Used as research material for a pamphlet by S. Cronje, entitled *Equatorial Guinea, the Forgotten Dictatorship: Forced Labor and Political Murder in Central Africa* (London: Anti-Slavery Society, 1976).
Gift, S. Cronje, 1978.

570

Cross, Rowland McLean, b. 1888.
Papers, 1921–1963. ½ ms. box.
American missionary in China. Correspondence, reports, and printed matter, relating to political and social conditions in revolutionary and communist China.
Gift, R. M. Cross, 1972.

571

Crouch, Paul, 1903–1955.
Papers, 1925–1958. 16½ ms. boxes.
American communist leader, 1925–1942; later an anti-communist. Writings, transcripts of court testimony, correspondence, and clippings, relating to communism in the U.S., especially in Hawaii, and to the anti-communist movement. Includes unpublished memoirs,

entitled "Broken Chains," relating to P. Crouch's involvement in the U.S. Communist Party.

Preliminary inventory.

Unpublished memoirs (box 17) may not be quoted without permission of Sylvia Crouch.

Purchase, Myers G. Lowman, 1970 (boxes 1–16); deposit, Sylvia Crouch, 1970 (box 17).

572

Crouzot, Henri.

History, n.d. *History of the Cyprus Conflict, 1946–1959.* 1 ms. box.

Typescript.

Gift, Charles Foley, 1974.

573

Crystal, Thomas L., d. 1971.

Papers, 1939–1945. 1 ms. box.

Colonel, U.S. Army. Correspondence, U.S. War Department reports and memoranda, military maps, clippings, and memorabilia, relating to American military activities during World War II.

Gift, T. L. Crystal.

574

Čubelić, Ratomir Josip.

Memoranda (in German), ca. 1931. 1 folder.

Typescript.

Memoranda entitled "Die Murinsel" and "Die Grenzprobleme der Murinsel" (Border Problems of the Murinsel), relating to the history of territorial disputes regarding the Murinsel or Medjumurje region of Croatia.

575

Curran, Edward Lodge.

Speech, ca. 1940–1941. "Catholic Mandate for Peace." 1 phonorecord.

American Roman Catholic priest; President, International Catholic Truth Society. Appeals to American Catholics to oppose U.S. entry into World War II.

576

Currency collection, n.d. 7 ms. boxes.

Coins, paper currency, and bonds from many countries and various periods of time, but largely from Europe during World War I and the interwar period.

Gifts, various sources.

577

Curtis, Charles, 1860–1936.

Papers, 1863–1933. 1 microfilm reel.

Microfilm of originals at the Kansas State Historical Society.

American politician; U.S. Senator from Kansas, 1907–1913 and 1915–1929; Vice President of the U.S., 1929–1933. Correspondence and certificates, relating to U.S. politics.

Purchase, Kansas State Historical Society, 1966.

578

Cutler, LeVern W.

Memorandum, 1946. "Recommendations for the United Nations Organization Library Program." 1 folder.

Typescript.

Chief of the Documentation Division Library of the Office of the U.S. Chief of Counsel at Nuremberg. Relates to the proposed establishment of a United Nations Library.

579

Cutler, Richard L.

Study, 1972. "The Liberal Middle Class: The Maker of Radicals." ½ ms. box.

Typescript.

Professor of Psychology, University of Michigan. Relates to the causes of radicalism among American middle-class youth during the late 1960's and early 1970's.

Gift, R. L. Cutler, 1973.

580

Cvetković, Dragiša, 1893–1969.

Papers (in Serbo-Croatian), 1928–1965. 2 ms. boxes.

Prime Minister of Yugoslavia, 1939–1941. Correspondence, reports, memoranda, and writings, relating to Yugoslav politics and foreign relations; the regency of Prince Paul, 1934–1941; the Cvetković-Maček agreement; Yugoslavia and the signing of the Tripartite pact; the "Našička Affair"; the coup d'état of March 27, 1941; Yugoslavia during World War II; and Yugoslav émigré politics. Includes an unpublished history by D. Cvetković, entitled "Rat ili Pakt: Unutarnja i Spoljna Politika Namesništva" (War or Treaty: Internal and Foreign Policy of the Regency), 1965.

Register.

Unpublished history (box 2) is closed until July 1, 1980. Remaining papers (box 1) are closed until December 23, 1992.

Gift, Mara Cvetković, 1970. Incremental gift, 1977.

581

Czech National Committee.

Statement (in German), 1950. 1 folder.

Typescript (mimeographed).

Relates to Czechoslovak émigré politics. Agreement between the Czech National Committee in London and the Arbeitsgemeinschaft zur Wahrung Sudetendeutscher Interessen in Munich.

582

"Czechoslovak Land Reform."

Study (typewritten), ca. 1930. 1 folder.

583

Czechoslovakia. Armada. 1. Ceskoslovensky Armadni Sbov v SSSR.

Miscellaneous records (in Czech), 1941–1945. 3 ms. boxes, 1 envelope.

First Czechoslovakian Army, an Allied military unit on the Eastern Front in World War II. Correspondence, telegrams, orders, diaries, proclamations, newspapers, periodicals, clippings and photographs, relating to the organization, training and activities of the First Czechoslovakian Army under General Ludvik Svoboda on the Eastern Front, 1941–1945.
Preliminary inventory.
Gift, M. Stepanek, 1971.

584

Czechoslovakia—invasion, August 1968—collection (in Czech and French), 1968. 1 ms. box, 1 microfilm reel, 1 motion picture reel.
Reports, leaflets, newspapers, cartoons, and photographs, relating to the Russian invasion of Czechoslovakia, August 1968.
Gift, Charles F. Park, 1968. Purchase, Jacques de Launay, 1976. Gift, Miroslav Tucek, 1976. Gift, B. J. Balcar, 1977.

585

Czechoslovakian crisis, September 1938—newspaper issues, 1938. 1 folder.
Czechoslovakian, Polish, French, and Lithuanian newspaper issues, September 19–21, 1938, relating to the German ultimatum for autonomy of the Sudeten Germans in Czechoslovakia and Anglo-French efforts to negotiate.
Gift, Jacques de Launay, 1976.

586

Dachau (Concentration camp).
Miscellaneous records (in German), 1943–1945. 1 oversize box (⅓ 1. ft.).
Lists, tables, diagrams and memoranda, relating to names of prisoners, shoes and clothing issued to prisoners, and the plan of buildings in the camp.
Gift, William Houwink, 1952.

587

Dagdeviren, Hidayet, *collector*.
H. Dagdeviren collection on Turkey (in Turkish), 1831–1951. 28 ms. boxes, 22 binders.
Letters, memoranda, reports, proclamations, speeches, clippings, newspaper issues and photographs, relating to political and social conditions in Turkey during the Ottoman Empire and the early years of the Turkish Republic, to Turkish military activities during World War I, to Turkish foreign relations, and to ethnic minorities in Turkey.
Preliminary inventory.
Purchase, Saadet Dagdeviren, 1952.

588

Dalen, Ebba, *collector*.
Miscellany (in Finnish), ca. 1945–1949. 1 folder.
Propaganda leaflets distributed by the Finnish communist party and labor unions in Finland.
Gift, E. Dalen, 1949.

589

Dambītis, Roberts.
Memorandum (in Russian), 1940. 1 vol.
Typescript (carbon copy).
Minister of War of Latvia. Request addressed to Andrei IÂ. Vyshinskiĭ, Deputy Chairman of the Council of People's Commissars of the Soviet Union, that Latvian military units be allowed to remain in Latvia.

590

Damm, Bertram von.
Letter (in German and English), 1914, to Korvettenkapitaen Prieger. 1 folder.
Typescript (photocopy).
German naval intelligence operative and diplomat in Norway, 1914. Relates to a conversation between B. von Damm and Ernest F. Mackie, Lieutenant Colonel, Canadian Army, concerning German and British morale and the prospect of a German victory.
Gift, Paul von Damm, 1975.

591

Daniel, E. G.
Study, n.d. "Some Historical Sources for a Study of the History of the Great War, with Special Reference to its Naval Aspect." 1 folder.
Typescript.
Relates to archival sources on World War I.

592

Daniel-Zdrojewski (Antoine) collection (in French), 1944–1946. 1 folder.
Correspondence and orders relating to A. Daniel-Zdrojewski, Colonel, Polish Army, and Commander-in-Chief, Polish Military Forces in France, and to relations between the French and Polish resistance movements in France during World War II.

593

Danielopol, Dumitru.
Papers (in English, Romanian and French), 1940–1973. 10 ms. boxes, 1 envelope.
Romanian banker; member of Romanian delegation to Paris Peace Conference, 1946. Correspondence, writings, reports, and photographs, relating to the Paris Peace Conference, 1946, the peace settlement with Romania at the end of World War II, and world politics, 1964–1973.
Preliminary inventory.
Papers on the 1946 Peace Conference, a manuscript entitled "An Unjust Peace," and other materials (boxes 8–10) are closed until January 1, 1980.
Gift, D. Danielopol, 1972. Subsequent increments.

594

Daniels, Helen D.
Maps, n.d. 1 folder.
Hand-drawn (photocopy).
Two maps, entitled "Nanking" and "Nanking and Environs," showing the growth of Nanking, China, from antiquity to the twentieth century.

595

Danişman, Basri.
Memoirs, n.d. "Situation Negative!" 1 vol.
Typescript (photocopy).
Relates to activities of the Turkish 3d Brigade in the Korean War.

596

Danquah, Joseph Boakye, 1895–
Studies, 1961–1963. 1 ms. box.
Typescript.
Fellow, Ghana Academy of Learning. Studies, entitled "Revelation of Culture in Ghana," 1961, and "Sacred Days in Ghana," 1963, relating to Ghanaian culture and the development of the Ghanaian calendar.
Gift, Gail Kelley, 1967.

597

Dark, Robert, 1894–1976.
Papers, 1917–1964. 2 ms. boxes, 4 card file boxes (⅔ l. ft.), 6 envelopes, 4 oversize boxes (2 l. ft.).
Colonel, U.S. Army; Commanding Officer, 321st Infantry Regiment, 1942–1946. Orders, correspondence, speeches, clippings and photographs, relating to the U.S. Army in the Philippine Islands, 1931–1932, to the activities of the 321st Infantry Regiment in the Pacific Theater, 1942–1946, and to the invasion of Angaur and Peleliu Island, 1944.
Gift, Mrs. R. Dark, 1977.

598

Darling, Ernest William, 1905–
Papers, 1920–1960. 4 ms. boxes.
British communist leader, 1932–1946. Writings, correspondence, memoranda, reports, leaflets and clippings, relating to the communist movement, political conditions, labor, and housing in Great Britain.
Preliminary inventory.
Purchase, E. W. Darling, 1947.

599

Darling, Jay Norwood, 1876–1962.
Cartoon, n.d. 1 framed cartoon.
American political cartoonist. Depicts the visit of Herbert Hoover to his boyhood home.
Gift, estate of Travers J. Edmonds, 1961.

600

Darling, William Lafayette, 1856–1938.
Diary, 1917. 1 vol.
Typescript.
American civil engineer; member, U.S. Advisory Commission of Railway Experts to Russia, 1917. Relates to the Russian railway system, May–December 1917.
Gift, W. L. Darling, 1926.

601

Darré, Richard Walther, 1895–1953.
Photographs, 1936. 1 album.
Minister of Agriculture of Germany. Depicts peasants of the Main Franconia region in folk costume. Presented to R. W. Darré by a group of Main Franconia farmers.
Purchase, New York University Medical Center, 1973.

602

Davies, E. Alfred.
Diary, 1919. 1 folder.
U.S. Army officer. Relates to the evacuation of the American Expeditionary Forces in Siberia from Omsk to Irkutsk, September 4–October 4, 1919.
Gift, Bessie Eddy Lyon, 1974.

603

Davis, Benjamin B.
Papers, 1919–1920. ½ ms. box, 2 envelopes.
American Red Cross worker in Siberia, 1919–1920. Correspondence, writings, diary, reports, pamphlets, postcards and photographs, relating to American Red Cross activities in Siberia, primarily in Vladivostok.

604

Davis, Elmer Holmes, 1890–1958.
Narration, 1939. *Then Came War: 1939.* 3 phonorecords.
American journalist and author. Relates to the outbreak of World War II. Includes sound recordings of radio addresses by leaders of the belligerent nations.

605

Davis, Henry William Carless, 1874–1928.
Study, 1920. "History of the Blockade." 1 folder.
Printed.
Vice Chairman, British War Trade Intelligence Department. Relates to the British blockade during World War I.
Gift, H. W. C. Davis, 1925.

606

Davis, Joseph Stancliffe, 1885–1975.
Papers, 1918–1972. 6½ ms. boxes.
American economist; Chief Economist, Federal Farm Board, 1929–1931; Director, Food Research Institute, Stanford University, 1921–1952. Writings, reports, memoranda, correspondence, and printed matter, relating to U.S. agricultural policy during the Hoover Administration, the Federal Farm Board, economic conditions in Europe, and the Dawes Commission on German reparations.
Preliminary inventory.
Gift, J. S. Davis, 1941. Incremental gift, 1975.

607

Davis, Loda Mae.
Papers, 1943–1947. 1 ms. box.
United Nations Relief and Rehabilitation Administration official. Writings, reports, correspondence, and memoranda, relating to U.N.R.R.A. relief in Europe at the end of World War II, particularly to food procurement in the U.S. and distribution in Italy, Greece, Yugoslavia, and the Soviet Union.
Gift, L. M. Davis, 1959.

608
Davis, Richard Hallock, 1913–1972.
Miscellaneous papers, 1949–1950. 1 folder, 1 envelope.
American diplomat; student, Russian Institute, Columbia University, 1949–1950; U.S. Deputy Assistant Secretary of State, 1960–1972. Lecture notes relating to Russian history, government, economics and literature, taken at the Russian Institute at Columbia University, course syllabi, and three unidentified photographs.

609
Davis, Robert E.
Reports, 1917–1919. 1 folder.
Typescript.
Major, U.S. Army; American Red Cross worker in Kuban area, Russia. Relates to the work of the American Red Cross, and the political and military situation in South Russia, 1917–1919. Addressed to Colonel Robert E. Olds, American Red Cross Commissioner to Europe.
Gift, Earl Talbot, 1973.

610
Davis, Rosella Amelia, b. 1876, *collector.*
Miscellany, 1942–1944. 1 folder.
Miscellanea, including alien registration certificates, residence certificates, alien registration fee receipts, and passes, used during the Japanese occupation of the Philippine Islands.
Gift, R. A. Davis, 1946.

611
Dawley, Ernest J., 1886–1973.
Papers, 1918–1944. ½ ms. box, 2 envelopes.
Major General, U.S. Army. Correspondence, diaries, awards, maps, photographs, and printed matter, relating to the landing of the U.S. Fifth Army at Salerno, Italy, September 1943, and to the military career of E. J. Dawley.
Gift, Mrs. E. J. Dawley, 1974.

612
Dawson, Warrington.
Report, 1920. 1 folder.
Typescript.
Special Assistant, U.S. Embassy in France. Relates to the principal newspapers of France, and to their political leanings and editorial policies.

613
Day, Donald.
Letter, 1941, to his brother. 1 folder.
Typewritten transcript.
Chicago Tribune correspondent in Helsinki. Relates to the prospective outcome of World War II.

614
Day, George Martin.
Papers, 1922–1937. ½ ms. box.
Professor of Sociology, Occidental College, Los Angeles. Writings, correspondence and questionnaires, relating to social conditions, education and religion in the Soviet Union, and to the adjustment to American society of Russians living in the Los Angeles area in 1930.

615
Day, Thomas J., *collector.*
Photographs, ca. 1935. 1 envelope.
Depicts Adolf Hitler and scenes in Germany.
Gift, T. J. Day, 1969.

616
Daye, Pierre, 1892–1954?
Memoirs (in French). 2 ms. boxes.
Typescript (photocopy).
Belgian politician and journalist. Relates to Belgian and world politics, the Belgian fascist movement, and Belgium and France under German occupation in World War II. Chapters 60 and 61 and conclusion missing.
Purchase, Jacques de Launay, 1976.

617
Debonnet, Maurice G.
Report, 1918. "Camouflage and the Use of Paint in Warfare." 1 folder.
Typescript.
Relates to military camouflage during World War I.

618
Debs, Eugene Victor, 1855–1926.
Letters, 1885–1926, to Frank X. Holl. 1 folder.
Typewritten transcripts.
American socialist leader. Relates to personal matters and the American labor and socialist movements. Includes a few letters from Theodore Debs, brother of E. V. Debs, to F. X. Holl, 1904–1931. Compiled by Sydney Strong.

619
De Caux, E.
Memoirs, n.d. "With the First-Eighth London Regiment T. F.: 'The Post Office Rifles.'" 1 folder.
Typescript.
Relates to the history of the First Battalion of the Eighth London Regiment of the British Army in France and Belgium from 1915 to 1917.

620
Decker, Benton Clark, 1867–1933.
Papers, 1914–1921. 1 ms. box.
Rear Admiral, U.S. Navy; Captain, U.S.S. *Tennessee*; Naval Attaché to Spain. Correspondence, lectures, notes and photographs, relating to activities of the *Tennessee*, Spanish neutrality, and refugees in the Middle East, during World War I.
Register.
Gift, Benton W. Decker, 1974.

621
Decker, Benton W., 1899–
Papers, 1916–1976. 4 ms. boxes, 1 envelope.
Rear Admiral, U.S. Navy; and Commander, Yokosuka

Naval Base, Japan, 1946–1950. Correspondence, speeches and writings, orders, citations, and printed matter, relating to U.S. occupation forces in Japan, and U.S. foreign relations in the Far East.
Register.
Gift, B. W. Decker, 1974. Incremental gift, 1977.

622

"Déclaration Commune sur la Situation Politique" (Common Declaration on the Political Situation).
Declaration (in French), 1944. 1 folder.
Typescript.
Relates to proposed changes in Vichy Government policy following the Allied landings in Normandy. Written by a group of right-wing French political figures.

623

DeForest, Charlotte B., b. 1879.
Papers, 1909–1971. 1 ms. box.
American missionary at Kobe College, Japan, 1903–1940 and 1947–1950. Correspondence, manuscripts of writings and translations, notes, and printed matter, relating to missionary work and education in Japan.
Register.

624

Degras, Jane.
Study, n.d. "Revisiting the Comintern." 1 folder.
Typescript (photocopy).
Relates to the history and organization of the Communist International.

625

Deichmann, Paul.
History (in German), 1952. "Luftlandeaktion Malta" (Malta Airborne Operation). 1 vol.
Typescript (carbon copy).
Relates to the Malta campaign in World War II.

626

De Kay, John Wesley, 1872–1938.
Chart, 1918. "Intellectus et Labor." 1 folder.
American businessman and author. Outlines a plan to establish an international federation of workers and institutions of intellectual and manual work, contributing to the moral and social regeneration of humanity without distinction as to nationality, race, or religion among men.
Gift, Elizabeth De Kay Keplinger, 1975.

627

Delage, Jean.
Papers (in French), 1941–1944. 1 ms. box.
Chief of Information, Chantiers de Jeunesse. Reports, correspondence, memoranda, instructions, programs, and printed matter, relating to the operation and purpose of youth work camps operated by the Vichy Government in France. Includes a chart outlining French social organization, 1941.
Purchase, Thomas D. Walker, 1975.

628

Delavignette, Robert Louis, 1897–1976.
Papers (in French), 1949–1960. ½ ms. box.
French colonial administrator; Director of Political Affairs, Ministère de la France d'Outre-Mer, 1947–1951. Letters, periodicals, reprints of articles, newspaper issues, and newsletters, relating to economic and social conditions in Algeria, independence movements in the African colonies, and French colonial policy.
Gift, William Cohen, 1976.

629

Délégation Irlandaise, Paris.
Issuances (in French), 1923–1924. 1 folder.
Mimeographed bulletins and communiqués, relating to the Irish independence movement.

630

Delmont, Alcide.
Speech (in French), 1945. 1 vol.
Typescript (carbon copy).
French lawyer; defense attorney for Henri Dentz, French High Commissioner for Syria during World War II, tried as a collaborator, 1945. Summation speech for defense at trial of H. Dentz, Haute Cour de Justice, Paris, April 20, 1945.

631

Delmotte, Guy.
Study (in French), n.d. "La Légion" (The Legion). 2 vols.
Typescript (photocopy).
French journalist. Relates to the activities of the Légion Nationale, a Belgian fascist organization, 1922–1945.
Purchase, Jacques de Launay, 1975.

632

Deluc, Emile, *collector*.
E. Deluc collection on the Garde Bourgeoise (in French and Flemish), 1914–1915. 1 folder.
Orders, proclamations, regulations and memorabilia, relating to activities of the Garde Bourgeoise, an auxiliary civilian police force created in German-occupied Brussels during World War I.
Gift, E. Deluc.

633

Delzell, Charles Floyd.
Writings, 1949–1960. 1 ms. box.
Typescript.
Professor of History, Vanderbilt University. Two studies, "Report on Italy, 1949," 1949, relating to political and economic conditions in Italy, and "Mussolini's Enemies: The Italian Anti-Fascist Resistance," 1960.

634

Dempsey (Sir Miles Christopher)—photograph, n.d. 1 envelope.
Depicts the British General M. C. Dempsey.

635

Denikina, Kseniiā.
 Chronology (in Russian), n.d. "Khronologiiā Sòbytiĭ vo Vremiā Grazhdanskoĭ Voĭny v Rossiĭ" (Chronology of Events during the Civil War in Russia).
 Typescript.
 Relates to the southern and western fronts during the Russian Civil War.

636

"Denkschrift aus Deutsch-Oesterreich" (Memorandum from German Austria).
 Pamphlet (in German), 1915. 1 vol.
 Printed.
 Relates to Central European political, economic and military federation.

637

Dentz, Henri Fernand, 1881–1945.
 Memoirs (in French), 1940–1945. "Affaires de Syrie" (Syrian Affairs). 1 vol.
 Typescript.
 General, French Army; High Commissioner for Syria during World War II. Relates to events in Syria during World War II.

638

Desbons, Georges, 1889–1962.
 History (in French), n.d. "Les Origines Historiques et Politiques de l'Attentat de Marseille et le Procès de Aix-en-Provence" (Historical and Political Origins of the Marseille Outrage and the Aix-en-Provence Trial). 1 ms. box.
 Typescript.
 French lawyer; defense attorney for accused assassins of Alexander I, King of Yugoslavia, and Louis Barthou, Foreign Minister of France, 1934. Relates to the assassinations and trial.
 Gift, Jacques de Launay, 1974.

639

De Toledano, Ralph, 1916–
 Papers, 1940–1971. 5 ms. boxes, 1 envelope.
 American journalist and author; National Reports Editor, *Newsweek*, 1948–1960; syndicated columnist, 1960–. Correspondence, memoranda, reports, drafts and published copies of writings, and printed matter, relating to American communism, politics, and journalism. Includes 98 letters from Whittaker Chambers about the Alger Hiss case.
 Register.
 Access to Whittaker Chambers letters requires written permission of R. de Toledano.
 Gift, R. de Toledano, 1971. Incremental gift, 1972.

640

"Die Deutsche Ernaehrungswirtschaft und die Lebensmittelkarten-Verteilung Gross-Berlins in den Kriegsjahren 1914–1918 und in der Uebergangszeit bis Ende Maerz 1922" (German Nutritional Economy and Ration Card Distribution in Greater Berlin during the War Years 1914–1918, and the Transitional Period to the End of March 1922).
 Study (in German), ca. 1922. 1 vol.
 Typescript.

641

Deutsche Forschungsgemeinschaft.
 Correspondence (in German), 1934–1936. 6ms. boxes.
 German Government organization for promotion of academic research. Correspondence relating to grant applications for research projects. Includes correspondence with the Reichsamtsleitung of the Nationalsozialistischer Deutscher Dozentenbund, the Kreisleitungen of the Nationalsozialistische Deutsche Arbeiterpartei, the various police presidents of German cities, the Dozentenschaften of the various German universities and Technische Hochschulen, and private persons.

642

Deutsche Freiheitsliga.
 Leaflets (in German), n.d. 1 folder.
 Printed.
 Anti-communist West German organization. Anti-communist propaganda leaflets, distributed by the Deutsche Freiheitsliga. Also includes other anti-communist leaflets.

643

"Die Deutsche Jugendfuehrung in der Neuordnung" (The German Youth Leadership in the New Order).
 Memorandum (in German), ca. 1945. 1 folder.
 Typescript.
 Relates to the role of the youth movement in post-World War II German reconstruction.

644

Deutsche National-Zeitung (Munich).
 Newspaper issue (in German), 1955. 1 folder.
 Special issue, relating to allegations of secret East German subsidies to certain West German newspapers.

645

Deutsche Union.
 Minutes of meetings (in German), 1949. 1 folder.
 Typescript.
 West German political organization. Relates to meetings of the Board of Directors and Executive Committee, March 19–20, 1949, concerning problems of post-World War II German reconstruction.

646

De Valera, Eamon, 1882–1975.
 Speech transcript, 1945. 1 folder.
 Typescript (mimeographed).
 Prime Minister of Ireland, 1937–1948, 1951–1954 and 1957–1959; President of Ireland, 1959–1973. Relates to the neutrality of Ireland during World War II and to Anglo-Irish relations. Speech delivered May 16, 1945.

647

Deveiké, Joné, 1907–1965.
Papers (in Lithuanian), 1930–1963. 1½ ms. boxes, 1 package.
Lithuanian attorney, historian, and journalist. Correspondence, notes, reports, and memorabilia, relating to social and political conditions of Lithuanians in France and Germany.
Register.
Correspondence between Jonas Dainauskas and J. Deveiké (1 package), is restricted until September 15, 1999.
Deposit, Žibuntas Mikšys, 1974.

648

De Young (M. H.) Memorial Museum, *collector.*
De Young (M. H.) Memorial Museum collection on World War I, 1914–1919. 3 ms. boxes, 1 envelope, 13 posters.
Posters, photographs, maps, proclamations, and printed matter, relating to World War I. Includes U.S. Shipping Board posters, photographs of the American Expeditionary Force in France, battle maps, statistical summaries concerning the American Expeditionary Force, German proclamations in France and Belgium, and a letter from General John J. Pershing to Congressman Julius Kahn.
Preliminary inventory.
Deposit, M. H. de Young Memorial Museum, 1963.

649

Díaz, Adolfo.
Statement, 1927. 1 folder.
Typescript (mimeographed).
President of Nicaragua. Relates to the roles of Mexico and the U.S. in the Nicaraguan revolution of 1926–1929.

650

Diaz, Felix.
Manifesto (in Spanish), 1918. *Manifiesto que Dirigen al Pueblo Mexicano* (Manifesto to the Mexican People). 1 folder.
Printed (photocopy).
General and Commander of the National Reorganized Army of Mexico. Relates to political conditions in Mexico and to the Mexican Constitution of 1917.

651

Dickie, Jean Kellogg.
Portrait, 1916. 1 jeweled pendant.
Portrait of Princess Maria Jose of Belgium, painted on ivory and ornamented with jewels, presented to J. K. Dickie in gratitude for relief activities of her parents, Vernon and Charlotte Kellogg, with the Commission for Relief in Belgium.
Gift, J. K. Dickie, 1956.

652

Dickinson, Dwight, Jr., 1887–1974.
Letters, 1901–1931. ½ ms. box.
Photocopy.
Rear Admiral, U.S. Navy Medical Corps. Relates to activities of the U.S. Marine Corps in France, 1918, and in Nicaragua, 1928–1929.
Gift, John S. Dickinson, 1975.

653

Dickinson, Thomas H.
History, n.d. 7 ms. boxes.
Typescript and printed galleys.
U.S. Food Administration worker, 1917–1918; American Relief Administration worker, 1919–1922. Relates to the American Relief Administration.

654

Dienstaltersliste I des Deutschen Heeres nach dem Stande vom. 1. Mai 1943 (Seniority List I of the German Army as of May 1, 1943).
List (in German), 1943. ½ ms. box.
Printed (photocopy).
List of German Army officers in order of relative rank, with unit to which attached and date of latest promotion indicated for each.

655

Diewerge, Wolfgang.
Report (in German), 1936. "Sachbericht im Mordprozess gegen den Juden David Frankfurter in Chur" (Case Report in the Murder Proceedings against the Jew David Frankfurter in Chur). 1 vol.
Typescript.

656

Dimitrov, Georgi M., 1903–1972.
Writings (in Bulgarian), n.d. 1 ms. box.
Typescript (photocopy).
Bulgarian émigré politician; Secretary-General, International Peasant Union; President, Bulgarian National Committee. Includes memoirs relating to Bulgaria and Bulgarian émigré politics, and unpublished articles, relating to the Bulgarian Agrarian Union between World Wars I and II, world agriculture, and agriculture in the Soviet Union.
Register.
May not be quoted without written permission of Charles A. Moser.
Gift, C. A. Moser, 1977.

657

Disabled Officers Association collection, 1954–1958. 1 ms. box.
American veterans' organization. Correspondence, memoranda, clippings, and national convention proceedings, relating to activities of the Disabled Officers Association in the U.S.
Gift, Jerry B. Riseley, 1965.

658

Disarmament—posters, ca. 1920–1929. 8 posters.
Relates to disarmament.
Gift, James B. Gibson, 1968.

659

Dmitrievskiĭ, Sergeĭ Vasil'evich.
Translation of biographical sketch, ca. 1932. "V. M. Molotov." 1 vol.
Typescript (carbon copy).
Translation by D. M. Krassovsky of an excerpt from *Sovetskie Portrety* (Soviet Portraits) by S. V. Dmitrievskiĭ.

660

Dmowski, Roman, 1864–1939.
Study, 1917. "Central and Eastern Europe." 1 vol.
Typescript (carbon copy).
Relates to Polish and other territorial questions of the World War I peace settlement.

661

Dnieprostroĭ—photographs, 1931–1932. 1 envelope.
Depicts the construction of Dnieprostroĭ water-power electric plant and its opening on October 10, 1932.

662

Dobriansky, Lev Eugene, 1918–
Papers, 1959–1977. 2 ms. boxes.
Ukrainian-American economist and author; Chairman, National Captive Nations Committee. Correspondence, messages, pamphlets, programs, proclamations, reports, resolutions, and clippings, relating to U.S. foreign policy, the National Captive Nations Committee, the Ukrainian Catholic Church, China and Mao Tsê-tung.
Gift, L. E. Dobriansky, 1978.

663

Dobson, Helen Cutter.
Papers, 1918–1919. 1 ms. box.
American Red Cross worker with the American Expeditionary Forces in France, 1918–1919. Photographs, postcards, clippings, and diary, relating to the American Red Cross and American Expeditionary Forces in France.
Gift, H. C. Dobson, 1953.

664

Dodd, Norris E., 1879–1968.
Papers, 1900–1968. 16 ms. boxes, 3 boxes of slides (1 l. ft.), 1 bust, 4 framed citations.
U.S. Under Secretary of Agriculture, 1946–1948; Director-General, United Nations Food and Agricultural Organization, 1948–1954. Diaries, memoranda, reports, speeches and writings, audio-visual material, and memorabilia, relating to American and world agricultural problems.
Gift, Ara M. Dodd, 1975.

665

Dodge, Alice Sinclair, 1876–1965, *collector*.
A. S. Dodge collection on relocation of Japanese Americans, 1942–1946. 1 ms. box.
Correspondence, mainly with Roy Nakata, 1942–1946; scrapbooks, 1942–1944; San Francisco and Palo Alto newspapers and newspaper clippings, 1942–1945; and minutes of meetings of the Japanese American Citizens League and American Friends Service Committee, 1945,

relating to relocation and citizen rights of Japanese Americans in the U.S. during World War II.
Gift, Mrs. O. Yount, 1970.

666

Doeberitz Theater, Gefangenenlager Doeberitz, Germany.
Miscellany, 1915–1917. 1 folder, 1 envelope.
Printed and mimeographed theater programs and postcards, relating to plays performed by British prisoners of war at Doeberitz Theater in the German prison camp at Doeberitz.

667

Doenitz, Karl, 1891–
Translations of writings, 1945–1946. 1 folder.
Admiral, German Navy. Memorandum (typewritten), entitled "Admiral Doenitz re Pastor Niemoeller," July 24, 1945, relating to anti-Nazi activities and imprisonment of Pastor Martin Niemoeller; and an essay (printed), entitled "The Conduct of War at Sea," January 15, 1946, relating to the role of the German Navy in World War II.

668

Dohnanyi (Hans von) collection (in German), 1938–1945. 1 folder.
Photocopy of originals in the U.S. Mission Berlin Document Center.
Reports and personnel records, relating to H. von Dohnanyi (1902–1944), German Abwehr official active in the anti-Nazi movement, and to the relationship between the Abwehr and the Sicherheitsdienstamt.

669

Dolan, John A.
Papers, 1920–1923. 2 ms. boxes.
Coblentz District Executive, American Department, Interallied Rhineland High Commission, 1920–1922. Correspondence, memoranda, reports, and minutes, relating to Allied administration of occupied territories, relief operations, labor relations, enforcement of laws and ordinances, and complaints made against Allied occupation troops in the Rhineland.
Gift, Mrs. J. A. Dolan, 1956.

670

Dolgorouky, Barbara, Princess, b. 1885.
Memoirs (in Russian), n.d. ½ ms. box.
Typescript (photocopy).
Russian aristocrat. Relates to the Romanov family, the Russian Imperial Court, and the Russian Revolution and Civil War, 1885–1919.
Purchase, B. Dolgorouky, 1973.

671

Dollfuss (Engelbert)—leaflet (in German), 1934. 1 folder.
Printed.
Issued in commemoration of E. Dollfuss (1892–1934), Chancellor of Austria, following his assassination.

672

Dom Polskich Dzieci, Oudtshoorn, South Africa.
Records (in Polish), 1942–1947. 3 ms. boxes.
Polish Children's Home, founded in 1943 for the care

of Polish war orphans from Russia. Correspondence, telegrams, notes, memoranda, clippings, accounts, lists, protocols, reports, inventories, and published materials, relating to the evacuation of the war orphans from Russia to Oudtshoorn, the establishment and operation of the Home, and the care and education of the orphans.
Register.
Gift, Tadeusz Kawalec, 1975.

673

Domanenko, General.
Study (in Russian), n.d. "Sluzhba General'nago Shtaba y Divizii i Korpusie" (General Staff Service in the Division and Corps). 1 vol.
Holograph.
Relates to organization of the Imperial Russian Army.

674

Domke, Paul C.
Audio-visual materials, 1936–1945. 8 motion picture reels, 1 envelope.
Teacher, Carleton College-in-China, 1937–1939; member, U.S. Observer Mission to Yenan, 1944–1945. Films and photographs, depicting missionary schools in China, 1936–1937; the effects of Japanese bombing in China, 1939: the transport of a giant panda from China to the St. Louis Zoo, 1939; scenes at Angkor Wat, 1939; the U.S. Observer Mission to Yenan, 1944–1945; U.S. Army headquarters in Chungking, 1945; and various other scenes in China, 1936–1945.
Gift, P. C. Domke, 1978.

675

Don Cossacks, Province of the.
Memorandum (in Russian), 1919. 1 folder.
Printed.
Relates to the Don national question and the World War I peace settlement. Presented by the delegation of the Don Republic to the Paris Peace Conference.

676

Donhauser, Anton.
Study (in German), 1947. "Foederalismus als Deutsches und Europaeisches Problem" (Federalism as a German and European Problem). 1 folder.
Typescript.
Relates to proposals made by A. Donhauser, a leader of the Bavarian Party, for European federation.

677

Donohoe, Christine, *collector*.
Miscellany, 1931–1960. 1 ms. box.
Publications, mostly anti-communist, relating to communism in the U.S. and Spain.

678

Donovan, James Britt, 1916–1970.
Papers, 1940–1970. 106 ms. boxes.
American lawyer and educator; Associate General Counsel, Office of Scientific Research and Development,

1942–1943; General Counsel, Office of Strategic Services, 1943–1945; Assistant to U.S. Chief Prosecutor, Trial of Major German War Criminals, Nuremberg, 1945; negotiator of Abel-Powers spy exchange with U.S.S.R. and of the Cuban prisoners exchange following the Bay of Pigs; President of the New York City Board of Education, 1963–1965. Correspondence, reports, memoranda, studies, drafts of book manuscripts, scrapbooks, notes, photographs, and printed matter, relating to the U.S. Office of Scientific Research and Development and the Office of Strategic Services during World War II, the Nuremberg war crime trials, the Rudolph Abel-Gary Powers spy exchange, the Cuban prisoner exchange following the Bay of Pigs landing, and the New York City Board of Education.
Preliminary inventory.
Access to materials relating to James B. Donovan's relationship with his family and his associates in law and in business requires the written permission of Mary D. O'Connor or John B. Donovan.
Deposit, Mary D. O'Connor, 1972.

679

Dony, Franciscus Lucien Marie, 1902–
Miscellany (in Dutch), 1943–1945. 1 folder.
A civil defense worker in The Hague. Directives, regulations and miscellanea, relating to civil defense and air raid protection work in the Netherlands during World War II.

680

Dooman, Eugene Hoffman, 1890–1969.
Papers, 1918–1973. 2 ms. boxes, 1 envelope.
American diplomat; Counsellor of Embassy to Japan, 1937–1941; Special Assistant to the Assistant Secretary of State for Far Eastern Affairs, 1944–1945. Manuscripts of writings, transcripts of speeches, correspondence, diaries and printed matter, relating to U.S. foreign policy in the Far East, U.S.-Japanese relations, the decision to drop the atomic bomb on Japan, and Allied policy regarding the occupation of Japan.
Register.
Gift, Mrs. E. H. Dooman, 1976.

681

Dorrian, Cecil.
Papers, 1912–1926. 1 ms. box, 6 envelopes.
American journalist; war correspondent, *Newark Evening News,* 1914–1926. Clippings, writings, postcards, and photographs, relating to World War I, postwar reconstruction in Western Europe, the Balkans, and the Near East, and the Russian Revolution and Civil War.

682

Dorsett, Graham C. *collector*.
Photographs, n.d. 33 envelopes.
Depicts India during and after World War II, the Indian Army in East Africa and Italian East Africa, Indian Independence Day, India's Republic Day, and Indian Navy Day, 1954, ceremonies. Includes prints of Mohandas Gandhi, Jawaharlal Nehru, Indira Gandhi, Krishna

Menon, Sukarno, Tito, the Shah of Iran, and Lord and Lady Mountbatten.
Purchase, Dorsett Foundation, 1964.

683

Dorten, Hans Adam, 1880–1963.
Papers (in German and English), 1919–1964. 1 ms. box.
German author. Writings, speeches and correspondence, relating to the occupation of the Rhineland after World War I, and the Rhineland separatist movement.
Gift, H. A. Dorten, 1931. Subsequent increments.

684

Dotsenko, Paul.
Speech transcript, 1954. "The Fight for Freedom in Siberia: Its Successes and Failures." 1 folder.
Typescript (photocopy).
Relates to Siberia during the Russian Revolution. Speech delivered in New York City, June 1954.

685

Douglas, Charles B.
Photographs, 1918–1920. 1 envelope.
Depicts activities of the American Expeditionary Force in France, a meeting of President and Mrs. Woodrow Wilson with General John J. Pershing and Lieutenant General Liggett at Christmas, 1918, and scenes of destruction in France during World War I.
Gift, C. B. Douglas, 1965.

686

Dowd, Patrick.
Papers, 1968–1971. 3 ms. boxes.
California State Chairman, Young Americans for Freedom, 1969. Correspondence, reports, memoranda, circulars, minutes of meetings, and printed matter, relating to political activities on college campuses, and to the Young Americans for Freedom.
Register.
Gift, P. Dowd, 1973.

687

Dozer, Donald Marquand, 1905–
Memoir, 1956. "The State Department Won't Tell You." 1 folder.
Typescript (photocopy).
American historian; Assistant to the Chief, Division of Historical Policy Research, U.S. Department of State, 1951–1956. Relates to government secrecy in the Department of State.
During his lifetime, access requires the written permission of D. M. Dozer.
Gift, D. M. Dozer, 1970.

688

Dragnich, Alex N., 1912–
Papers (in English and Serbo-Croatian), 1934–1949. 4 ms. boxes.
American political scientist; Senior Propaganda Analyst, U.S. Department of Justice, 1942–1944; Research Analyst, U.S. Office of Strategic Services, 1944–1945; Cultural Attaché and Public Affairs Officer, U.S. Embassy in Yugoslavia, 1947–1950. Writings, correspondence, reports, historical studies, memoranda, legal and government documents, diaries, and newspapers, relating to the history, politics and government of Serbia and Yugoslavia, relations between Croatia and Serbia, activities of the Hrvatski Domobran in the U.S., the Communist Party of Yugoslavia, and the trial of Draža Mihailović.
Gift, A. N. Dragnich, 1977. Incremental gift, 1978.

689

Draper, Theodore, 1912–
Papers, 1912–1966. 37 ms. boxes.
American historian and author. Correspondence, clippings, pamphlets, newspaper issues, and congressional hearings, relating to the revolution led by Fidel Castro in Cuba, political, social, and economic conditions in Cuba, the 1965 crisis and U.S. intervention in the Dominican Republic, and the Communist Party of the U.S.
Preliminary inventory.
Boxes 1–22 are open without restriction. Selected files on Cuba (boxes 23–26) and the Dominican Republic (box 27) as well as all files on the U.S. Communist Party (boxes 28–37) may be used only with the permission of Theodore Draper.
Gift, Theodore Draper, 1967. Incremental gift, 1969.

690

Drafsenko, D. P.
Miscellaneous papers (in Russian), 1919–1920. 1 folder.
General, White Russian Army. Military reports, orders, and correspondence, relating to the Russian Civil War in the Caucasus, political and military conditions in Georgia, and British foreign policy in Transcaucasia.
Preliminary inventory.

691

Drayton, William A.
Papers, 1913–1946. 2 ms. boxes, 1 envelope.
American volunteer, Serbian Army; Member, Serbian Delegation, Paris Peace Conference; Inter-Allied Commissioner, Bulgarian Atrocities Commission. Correspondence, reports, memoranda, speeches and writings, and photographs, relating to Serbia during and after World War I.
Register.
Gift, W. Drayton, Jr., 1976.

692

Drenteln (Aleksandr Aleksandrovich) memorandum (in Russian), n.d. 1 folder.
Typescript (photocopy).
Relates to the life of A. A. Drenteln, Major General, Imperial Russian Army, and Adjutant to Tsar Nicolas II.
Gift, M. Lyons, 1971.

693

Dresel, Ellis Loring, 1865–1925.
Papers, 1915–1925. ½ ms. box.
American diplomat; U.S. Commissioner to Germany,

1919; U.S. Chargé d'Affaires in Germany, 1921–1922. Correspondence and memorabilia, relating to U.S.-German relations.
Preliminary inventory.

694

Dresser, Robert B.
Papers, 1941–1967. 1 ms. box.
American lawyer. Correspondence, public addresses, leaflets, and writings, relating to U.S. relations with Vietnam, Cuba, and Panama, the Korean War, communism, tax laws, civil rights, armaments, and the United Nations.
Preliminary inventory.
Gift, R. B. Dresser, 1967.

695

Drewes, Steven, *collector.*
Motion picture films, 1936–1940. 2 reels.
Berlin im Olympiaschmuck (Berlin Decorated for the Olympics), 1936, depicting the celebration of the 11th Olympic games, including scenes of the flags, the bringing of fire, Adolf Hitler and the Brandenburg gate; and *Degeto Weltspiegel* (Degeto World Mirror), 1940, a newsreel depicting the destruction of Rouen in World War II.
Gift, S. Drewes, 1978.

696

Drumright, Everett F., 1906–
Letters, 1950–1951. 1 folder.
Typescript.
American diplomat; Counselor of Mission to Korea, 1948–1950. Relates to early events of the Korean War, 1950–1951. Addressed to John M. Allison, Assistant Secretary of State for Far Eastern Affairs, and General William L. Roberts. The letters to J. M. Allison were written in lieu of official Embassy dispatches because of the dispersal of the American Embassy in Korea at the time.
Gift, E. F. Drumright, 1972.

697

Drums and Chants of Fighting Biafra.
Songs and music (in Ibo), ca. 1967–1970. 1 phonorecord.

698

Drury, Allen Stuart, 1918–
Papers, 1932–1969. 42 ms. boxes, 6 envelopes.
American novelist. Correspondence, drafts of writings, galley proofs, memorabilia, and photographs, relating to the novels of A. S. Drury on twentieth-century U.S. politics.
Preliminary inventory.
Closed until 1981, or until one year after the death of A.S. Drury, whichever is later.
Gift, A. S. Drury, 1963. Subsequent increments.

699

Duca, George I., 1905–
Papers (in Romanian, French and English), 1919–1975. 60 ms. boxes.

Romanian diplomat; Chief of Mission to Sweden, 1944–1947. Diaries, correspondence, speeches and writings, reports, and photographs, relating to Romanian foreign policy and politics in the twentieth century, and to the Romanian royal family.
Register.
Boxes 1–50 closed until 20 years after the death of G. I. Duca. Boxes 51–54 closed until 1995.
Gift, G. I. Duca, 1975.

700

Duca, Ion George, 1879–1933.
Papers (in Romanian), 1914–1926. 3½ ms. boxes.
Romanian politician; Minister of Education, 1914–1918, Agriculture, 1919–1920, Foreign Affairs, 1922–1926, Interior, 1927–1928, and Prime Minister, 1933. Memoirs, correspondence, notes, and memoranda, relating to Romanian politics and foreign policy.
Preliminary inventory.
Access requires the permission of George I. Duca, during his lifetime.
Gift, G. I. Duca, 1966.

701

Duchesne (Jacques)—photograph, n.d. 1 envelope.
Depicts J. Duchesne.

702

Dulles, John Foster, 1888–1959.
Press conference excerpts, 1953. 1 phonotape.
Secretary of State of the U.S., 1953–1959. Relates to U.S. foreign policy.

703

Dumbacher, Joseph.
Papers, 1962–1966. 2 ms. boxes.
Typewritten account by J. Dumbacher of the 1963 SDS national convention, as well as pamphlets, bulletins and reports, relating to Students for a Democratic Society (SDS) and other organizations of the New Left in the U.S.
Preliminary inventory.
Purchase, Myers G. Lowman, 1967.

704

Duncan, William Young.
Papers, 1918–1920. ½ ms. box.
Photocopy.
American clergyman; Young Men's Christian Association chaplain with the Czechoslovakian Legion in Siberia, 1917–1920. Diary and letters, relating to the Russian Revolution and Civil War and the Allied intervention in Siberia, 1918–1920.
Quotations may not be published without permission of Donald G. Duncan, during his lifetime. Any publication using the collection as a source must carry acknowledgement. A copy of any such publication must be provided D. G. Duncan free of charge.
Gift, D. G. Duncan, 1976.

705

Dunford House Cobden Memorial Association.
Circular letters, 1940–1941. 1 folder.
Typescript (mimeographed).
Organization of British liberals. Relates to proposed bases for peace negotiations to end World War II.

706

Dunner, Joseph H., 1908–
Study, n.d. "Germans Under the Hammer and Sickle: The Administration of the Soviet Zone of Germany from 1945 to 1953." ½ ms. box.
Typescript.
American political scientist.
Gift, J. H. Dunner, 1977.

707

Dusart, Albert, *collector.*
A. Dusart collection on occupied Belgium (in Flemish and French), 1940–1941. 1 ms. box.
Printed.
Clippings from the Belgian newspapers *Volk en Staat* and *Le Nouveau Journal,* relating to conditions in Belgium under the German occupation during World War II and to Belgian collaborators with German occupation authorities.
Preliminary inventory.
Gift, A. Dusart, 1946.

708

Du Val, Miles P.
Papers, 1944–1946. 1 folder.
Captain, U.S. Navy; Captain, Attack Transport Ship *Dade,* Pacific Theater, 1944–1946. Typewritten history of the *Dade* by M. P. Du Val, photographs, and mimeographed issues of the ship newspaper "The Invader."

709

Dyer, Susan Louise, 1877–1966.
Papers, 1895–1965. 9 ms. boxes, 1 scrapbook, 10 envelopes, 1 phonotape.
Lifelong friend of Herbert and Lou Henry Hoover; American Red Cross worker in France, 1918–1919. Correspondence, diary, scrapbooks, memorabilia, clippings, photographs, tape recording, and printed matter, relating to Herbert Hoover, Lou Henry Hoover, Stanford University, the Hoover Institution, the Girl Scouts, and the American Red Cross in France during World War I.
Gift, S. L. Dyer, 1960. Subsequent increments.

710

Dyment, Colin B.
Papers, 1918. ½ ms. box, 1 medal.
Soldier, U.S. 91st Division, during World War I. Notebooks (holograph), relating to circumstances of each fatality in the 91st Division during the battle of the Argonne. Includes a medal presented to Bertha S. Dyment in recognition of her relief work in France during World War I.
Gift, B. S. Dyment.

711

EMNID—Institut fuer Meinungsforschung und Sozialforschung.
Records (in German), 1962. 1 folder.
Public opinion research organization in West Germany. Questionnaires (printed), used in a survey to determine West German and West Berlin public opinion regarding the Berlin question, and excerpts (typewritten), from the results of the survey.

712

Eale (Putnam W.)—photograph, 1916, 1 envelope.
Depicts P. W. Eale.

713

East German economic policy—memorandum (in German), 1949. 1 folder.
Typescript.
Relates to the bases of economic reorganization in the Soviet Zone of Germany.

714

Eaton, William W., *collector.*
Magazine clippings, 1939–1953. 6½ boxes.
Bound volumes of *Life* magazine articles, relating to World War II, 1939–1945, and the Korean War, 1950–1953.
Preliminary inventory.
Gift, W. W. Eaton, 1976.

715

Eckart, Dietrich, 1868–1923.
Broadside (in German), 1919. "An Alle Werktaetigen!" (To All Workers). 1 folder.
Printed.
German theorist of national socialism. Relates to economic conditions in Germany.

716

"Economic Conditions in Kuban Black Sea Region."
Translation of study, n.d. 1 folder.
Typescript.
Relates to the topography and economic conditions of the Kuban District, Russia, during the Russian Civil War.

717

Eden (Anthony, Earl of Avon)—photograph, n.d. 1 envelope.
Depicts A. Eden, Prime Minister of Great Britain, 1955–1957.

718

Edison, J.
Photographs, 1918–1921. 5 envelopes.
Depicts demonstrations, military personnel, railways, and scenery in northern China and southeastern Siberia.
Gift, J. Edison, 1957.

719

"Éditions Stéréoscopiques de Guerre."
Slides, ca. 1914–1918. 1 box.
Depicts World War I scenes in France.
Gift, Hamilton and Kirkland Colleges, 1974.

720

Edwards, Gordon.
Memoirs, n.d. "Forgotten War Memories." 1 folder.
Typescript.
American anesthetist. Relates to the introduction of anesthetic innovations in military hospitals during World War I.

721

Eendracht is Macht.
Records (in Flemish), 1925–1928. 1 folder.
Holograph.
Flemish nationalist organization. Letterbook of outgoing correspondence, relating to the Flemish question in Belgium.

722

Egbert, Donald Drew, 1902–1973.
Study, n.d. "Communism, Radicalism and the Arts: American Developments in Relation to the Background in Western Europe and in Russia from the Seventeenth Century to 1959." 2 ms. boxes.
Typescript (photocopy).
American historian. Relates to the effects of Marxism and communism on American art, and the relationships between works of art and the social, economic, and political beliefs of the artists who produced them, 1680–1959. A revised version of this study was published under the title *Socialism and American Art in the Light of European Utopianism, Marxism and Anarchism* (Princeton, 1967).
Gift, Theodore Draper, 1964.

723

Egbert, Edward H., d. 1939.
Papers, 1914–1921. 1 ms. box.
Chief Surgeon, American Red Cross Detachment in Russia, during World War I; Executive Secretary, Catherine Breshkovsky Russian Relief Fund. Correspondence, notes, clippings, printed matter and photographs, relating to the Russian Revolution, relief work in Russia, and Ekaterina Breshko-Breshkovskaîa. Includes correspondence with E. Breshko-Breshkovskaîa and Herbert Hoover.
Preliminary inventory.
Gift, Margaret Durand, 1960.

724

"Egerskiĭ Vestnik" (Eger Herald).
Bulletins (in Russian), 1925–1932. 1 folder.
Typescript (mimeographed).
Relates to the history of the Russian Imperial Army regiment, Leib-Gvardiĭ Egerskiĭ Polk, especially during the Russian Civil War, and to activities of veterans of the regiment. Issued by a regimental veterans association.
Gift, Russian Historical Archive and Repository, 1974.

725

Egypt. Delegation for Negotiations with Great Britain.
Memorandum (in French), 1946. 1 folder.
Typescript (mimeographed).
Relates to Egyptian demands for the withdrawal of British troops from Egypt.

726

Eichelberger (Robert Lawrence)—photographs, n.d. 1 envelope.
Depicts Lieutenant General R. L. Eichelberger, U. S. Army.

727

Eichmann, Adolf, 1906–1962, *defendant*.
Trial excerpts (in Hebrew and German), 1961. 3 phonotapes.
German Nazi official tried in Jerusalem, for extermination of Jews during World War II. Includes excerpts from the testimony of Eichmann and others, and from the closing defense statement.
Preliminary inventory.

728

Einstein, Albert, 1879–1955.
Letter (in German), 1932, to Fraeulein Jezierska. 1 folder.
Typescript.
German physicist. Relates to requests for reprints of articles by A. Einstein.

729

Eisenhower (Dwight David)—photograph, n.d. 1 envelope.
Depicts D. D. Eisenhower, President of the U.S., 1953–1961.

730

"Ekonomicheskoe Polizhenie Sov. Rossiĭ" (The Economic Situation of Soviet Russia).
Memorandum (in Russian), ca. 1923. 1 folder.
Typescript.

731

Ekstrom, Clarence Eugene, 1902–
Papers, 1943–1962. 1 ms. box, 36 envelopes, 12 albums.
Vice Admiral, U.S. Navy; Commander, Naval Air Force, Pacific Fleet, 1959–1962. Photographs and printed matter, relating to American naval operations in the Pacific Ocean and Mediterranean Sea, during and after World War II.
Gift, C. E. Ekstrom, 1975.

732

Elachich, S. A.
Memoirs (in Russian), 1934. "Obryvki Vospominaniĭ" (Scraps of Reminiscences). 1 vol.
Typescript (carbon copy).
White Russian leader. Relates to the Russian Revolution, the Omsk Government of Admiral Aleksandr Kolchak, and the Czechoslovakian Legion in Siberia.

733

"Les Elections et les Partis" (Elections and Parties).
Memorandum (in French), 1922, 1 vol.
Typescript (carbon copy).
Relates to the Hungarian elections of 1922, and to Hungarian political parties. Signed "J. G."

734

Eliashev.
Study (in Russian), 1923. "Dva Puti Sovetskago Zakono-datel'stva" (Two Methods of Soviet Legislation). 1 folder.
Typescript.

735

Eliel, Paul.
Miscellaneous papers, 1938. ½ ms. box.
Director, Division of Industrial Relations, Graduate School of Business, Stanford University. Correspondence, pamphlets, propaganda materials, and newspaper clippings, relating to labor legislation, unionism, and communism in California during 1938.
Gift, Jackson Library, Graduate School of Business, Stanford University, 1972.

736

Elliott, William Yandell, 1896–
Papers, 1930–1970. 173 ms. boxes.
American political scientist; staff director, House Select Committee on Foreign Affairs, 1947–1949; member, planning board, National Security Council, 1953–1957; consultant to the Secretary of State, 1958–1970. Correspondence, writings, speeches, research notes, clippings, and printed matter, relating to U.S. national security and defense, U.S. politics and foreign relations, U.S., military-industrial relations, and U.S. national labor policy.
Personnel files closed until 1997.
Gift, W. Y. Elliott, 1977.

737

Eloesser, Nina Franstead, *collector*.
Miscellany, 1919. 1 folder.
Poem (typewritten), relating to the World War I relief work of Herbert Hoover, and a photocopy of a newspaper clipping relating to Herbert Hoover.
Gift, N. F. Eloesser, 1958.

738

Eltse, Ruth Ricci.
Papers, 1935–1942. 1 ms. box, 7 envelopes, 5 oversize boxes (2 l. ft.).
American volunteer nurse in the Ethiopian-Italian War, 1935–1936; photographer and journalist in North Africa, 1936–1939. Correspondence, writings, and photographs, relating to the Ethiopian-Italian War, to Italian colonization of Libya, and to Italian relations in North and East Africa. Includes an album of photographs of Benito Mussolini.
Gift, Ann K. Snow, 1977.

739

Embree, Edwin R.
Memorandum, n.d. "Family Journal: Trip to Central America, March and April 1927." 1 folder.
Typescript (mimeographed).
American visitor to Central America. Relates to his observations while traveling.

740

Emerson, Edwin.
Letter, 1934, to Kendall Ellingwood. 1 folder.
Typescript.
American journalist in Switzerland, 1914. Relates to Swiss neutrality during World War I.

741

Emerson, George H.
Papers, 1918–1919. ½ ms. box, 1 envelope.
Colonel, U.S. Army; Commanding Officer, Russian Railway Service Corps. Correspondence, reports, maps, photographs, and clippings, relating to the activities of the Russian Railway Service Corps, the political situation in Russia during the Russian Civil War, and the Czechoslovakian Legion in Siberia.

742

Emery, Jacob Adams.
Letters, 1916–1919, to his mother. 1 folder.
Holograph and typescript.
American soldier during World War I. Relates to Allied military activities during World War I.
Gift, Mrs. J. A. Emery, 1970.

743

Emmet, Christopher Temple, Jr., 1900–1974.
Papers, 1935–1974. 124 ms. boxes, 5 cu. ft. boxes, 33 phonorecords, 9 envelopes.
Chairman, American Friends of the Captive Nations; Executive Vice President, American Council on Germany; officer and organizer of other anti-Nazi and anti-communist organizations. Correspondence, memoranda, reports, press releases, writings, recordings of radio broadcasts, and photographs, relating to anti-Nazi and anti-communist movements in the U.S., U.S. foreign policy during the Cold War, and U.S.-German foreign relations.
Register.
Gift, estate of C. T. Emmet, 1974.

744

Emmons, Delos Carleton, 1888–1965.
Papers, 1904–1951. 1 ms. box.
Lieutenant General, U.S. Air Force; Commanding General, Hawaiian Department, 1941–1943; Commanding General, Western Defense Command, 1943–1944. Correspondence, reports and orders, relating to the U.S. military mission to Great Britain in 1940, and to U.S. troops stationed in Hawaii and on the U.S. Pacific coast during World War II.
Preliminary inventory.
Gift, Mrs. D. C. Emmons, 1969.

745

Emparan, Madie Brown.
Papers, 1928–1965. ½ ms. box.
Republican Presidential campaign worker in 1928. Correspondence, writings, clippings, memorabilia and photographs, relating to the 1928 Republican convention and Presidential campaign of Herbert Hoover in California, and to historic landmarks in California.
Gift, M. B. Emparan, 1968.

746

England, Robert.
Report, ca. 1944. "War Veterans in Western Europe and North America, 1918–45(?): Demobilization and Civil Re-establishment." 1 folder.
Typescript (mimeographed).
Relates to rehabilitation and readjustment of World War I veterans, and expected problems of and approaches to rehabilitating and readjusting World War II veterans, especially in Canada.

747

Engleman, Finis Ewing, 1895–1978.
Papers, 1956–1978. 8 ms. boxes, 1 envelope.
American educator; Connecticut Commissioner of Education, 1955; consultant, U.S. Department of State Office of Overseas Schools, 1976. Correspondence, speeches and writings, reports, photographs and printed matter, relating to the administration of higher education and of international schools, the Association for the Advancement of International Education, the U.S. Department of State Office of Overseas Schools, the American Association of School Administrators, and the Near East/South Asia Council of Overseas Schools.
Gift, Frederick W. Lowe, 1978.

748

Epstein, Fritz Theodor, 1898–
Papers (in German), 1914–1948. 1½ ms. boxes.
German-American historian. Writings, clippings, correspondence and orders, relating to Allied intervention in Russia during the Russian Revolution, German military government of Strasbourg during World War I, the trial of Menshevik leaders in Russia in 1931, and the authenticity of the diaries of Joseph Goebbels. Includes an unpublished history, entitled "Russland und die Weltpolitik, 1917–1920: Studien zur Geschichte der Interventionen in Russland" (Russia and World Politics, 1917–1920: Studies on the History of the Interventions in Russia).
Gift, F. T. Epstein, 1941. Subsequent increments.

749

Epstein, Julius, 1901–1975.
Papers, 1939–1972. 180 ms. boxes.
American journalist and author. Correspondence, speeches and writings, clippings, photographs, and printed matter, relating to World War II, communism, forced repatriation of Russian prisoners to the Soviet Union following World War II, the Katyn forest massacre, unreported deaths of Soviet cosmonauts, and the efforts of J. Epstein to obtain restricted government documents on these subjects.
Gift, Mrs. J. Epstein, 1975.

750

Erasmus-Feit family.
Papers (in Russian), 1895–1956. 3 ms. boxes.
Family of Baron Erasmus-Feit, Russian Imperial Army officer. Correspondence, scrapbooks, memorabilia, printed matter, and photographs, relating to the daily lives of Russian émigrés in China and the U.S., and family matters.
Gift, Mr. and Mrs. Ogden Scoville, 1977.

751

Ergushov, P.
History (in Russian), 1938. "Kasaki i Gortsy na Sunzhenskoĭ Linii v 1917" (Cossacks and Mountaineers on the Sunzhenskiĭ Line in 1917). 1 folder.
Typescript.
Colonel, Imperial Russian Army. Relates to White Russian military activities during the Russian Revolution.

752

Erhard, Ludwig, 1897–1977.
Transcript of speech, 1967. "The European Economic Community with View toward the Future." 1 folder.
Typescript (photocopy).
Chancellor of West Germany, 1963–1966. Delivered at Stanford University, July 17, 1967. Includes an autographed photograph of L. Erhard.

753

Ermakov, Petr Zacharovich.
Memoirs, n.d. "The Massacre of the Romanoffs." 1 folder.
Typescript (photocopy).
Participant in the execution of the Russian royal family, 1918. Written by Richard Haliburton, as told by P. Z. Ermakov.
Gift, M. Lyons, 1971.

754

Erman, Irma C.
Papers (in English and German), 1939–1978. ½ ms. box.
German-American author. Correspondence, writings, and printed matter, relating to the history of antisemitism and to Jewish refugees from Nazi persecution. Includes two plays dramatizing the actions of Paul Grueninger, a Swiss police captain, and Mitsugi Shibata, a Japanese official, in saving the lives of Jewish refugees in Austria and China, respectively, during World War II.
Gift, I. C. Erman, 1978.

755

Estonia. Riigi Kohus.
Records (in Estonian), 1936. 1 folder.
Photocopy.
Estonian State Court. Indictment and summary of police interrogation of witnesses, relating to charges made against Andres Larka, Johannes Holland, and

others, accused of involvement in the 1935 attempted coup against the Estonian government by the organization Eesti Vabadussojalaste Liit (the League of Veterans of the War of Independence).

Gift, Rein Marandi, 1976.

756

"Estoniĭa i Pomoshch Golodaĭushchim" (Estonia and Aid to the Starving).

Essay (in Russian), 1921. 1 folder.

Typescript.

Relates to civilian relief in Estonia at the end of World War I.

757

Etchegoyen, Olivier, Comte d', b. 1873.

Translation of study, n.d. "Poland, Poland!" 1 folder.

Holograph.

Translation by Ivor M. V. S. Livingstead of *Pologne, Pologne* by O. d'Etchegoyen (1925), relating to political, social and economic conditions in Poland immediately after World War I.

758

Ethnogeographic Board, Washington, D.C.

Reports, 1945. "Reports on Area Studies in American Universities." 1 folder.

Typescript (mineographed).

Agency of the Smithsonian Institution. Relates to European and Far Eastern area study programs at the University of California, the University of Chicago, Harvard University, Cornell University, the Carnegie Institute of Technology, and Grinnell College. Edited by William N. Felton.

Gift, Harold H. Fisher, 1945.

759

Etter, Maria von.

Papers (in Russian), 1895–1916. 1 folder, 1 album.

Russian aristocrat. Letters of appointment, commendation, and appreciation, certificates, and awards, relating to the charitable volunteer work of M. von Etter. Includes a record book of patients at the Russian Red Cross von Etter Infirmary, 1915–1916, and a memorial album with an engraved sterling silver plaque dedicated to Ivan Sevastianovich von Etter from the Russian Imperial Kiev officers under his command, containing photographs and autographs of the officers.

Gift, Russian Historical Archive and Repository, 1974.

760

Etterg (General)—photograph, ca. 1877–1878. 1 envelope.

Depicts the Russian General Etterg, commandant of Adrianopol' during the Russo-Turkish War.

761

European socialist parties collection (mostly in German), 1923–1946. 5 ms. boxes.

Reports, leaflets, pamphlets, posters, and newspaper issues, relating to the 3rd and 4th Congresses of the Labour and Socialist International, activities of socialist

parties and their social, cultural and labor affiliates in Germany, Austria and Czechoslovakia in the interwar period, and activities of Czech socialists in England during World War II.

Preliminary inventory.

Purchase, A. Rosenthal Co., 1955.

762

European Technical Advisers.

Records, 1919–1923. 72 ms. boxes.

Private American advisory organization created to assist in European reconstruction after World War I. Correspondence, reports, statistics, and financial records, relating to railway operation, fuel production, and other aspects of economic reconstruction in Austria, Poland, Czechoslovakia and Yugoslavia.

Preliminary inventory.

Gift, European Technical Advisers, 1923.

763

European War, 1914–1918—propaganda, 1914–1918. 1 ms. box.

Propaganda leaflets and broadside, issued by the German Government, German left socialists, and the Allied Governments during World War I.

Gift, Robert B. Honeyman, Jr., 1977.

764

European War, 1914–1918—Russia—collection, n.d. 1 folder.

Typescript.

Translations of editorials from Russian newspapers, July-August 1914, relating to the outbreak of World War I, and to the entry of Russia into the war.

765

European War, 1914–1918—U.S.—collection, 1917. 1 folder.

Negative photocopy of the American declaration of war on Germany, April 1917, and lists (typewritten), of U.S. Congressmen voting for and against the declaration of war.

766

Evangelische Kirchen in Deutschland.

Newsletter (in German), 1937. 1 folder.

Typescript (mimeographed).

Relates to the situation of religion in Germany.

767

Evangelische Kirchen in Deutschland. Hilfswerk.

Letters (in German), 1949. 1 folder.

Typescript.

Relates to food relief received from the Church World Service in Soviet-occupied Germany.

768

Evans, Henry S.

Papers, 1942–1970. 2 ms. boxes, 1 scrapbook, 1 envelope.

American publicist; Director, Midwest Bureau, Chinese

News Service; National Director, U.S. People for the United Nations. Memoranda, transcripts and analyses of radio news broadcasts, press releases, and scrapbook, relating to Syngman Rhee, the 1948 Tibetan Mission to the U.S., conditions in China during World War II, and Mme. Chiang Kai-shek's 1943 visit to the U.S.
    Preliminary inventory.
    Gift, H. S. Evans, 1970.

769

Evatt, Herbert Vere, 1894–1965.
    Interview, 1949. 1 phonorecord.
    Australian politician; President, United Nations General Assembly, 1948–1949. Radio interview conducted by Clark M. Eichelberger, Director of the American Association for the United Nations, and broadcast by the National Broadcasting Company, relating to activities of the United Nations.

770

Event of the Week.
    Radio news broadcast, 1948. 1 phonorecord.
    Broadcast over Station KCVN, College of the Pacific, Stockton, California, relating to controversies regarding the city government of Stockton.

771

Everatt, M. W.
    Legal review petition, ca. 1946. 1 folder.
    Typescript.
    Lieutenant Colonel, U.S. Army; member, American Defense Staff, International Military Tribunal, Dachau. Appeals for a review of the conviction of 74 German soldiers for the massacre of Allied prisoners of war and civilians at Malmedy, Belgium, 1944–1945.

772

Ewers, Ernest A.
    Papers, 1942–1953. 2 ms. boxes, 1 envelope.
    Colonel, U. S. Army; Contracting Officer, Radio Division, Philadelphia Headquarters, Signal Depot and Procurement District, U.S. Army Signal Corps, during World War II. Correspondence, reports, orders, commissions, field and specification manuals, personnel records, and notes, relating to Signal Corps activities in World War II.
    Gift, Military Order of the World Wars, 1972.

773

Exploratory Conference on the Experience of the League of Nations Secretariat, New York, 1942.
    Proceedings, 1942. 1 folder.
    Typescript (mimeographed).
    Conference held under the auspices of the Carnegie Endowment for International Peace. Relates to postwar prospects for the League of Nations.

774

"L'Extermination des Juifs Polonais" (The Extermination of the Polish Jews).
    Memoir (in French), 1943. 1 folder.
    Typescript (mimeographed).

Relates to the genocide carried out against Jews in German-occupied Poland during World War II. Written by an unknown Polish Jew.

775

Exton, Frederick.
    Letter, 1959, to Perrin C. Galpin. 1 folder.
    Typescript.
    Member, Commission for Relief in Belgium. Relates to the relief work of the Commission for Relief in Belgium during World War I.
    Gift, P. C. Galpin, 1960.

776

Fabre-Luce, Alfred.
    Memorandum (in French), 1954. 1 folder.
    Typescript.
    Relates to missing archival material regarding the origins of World War I.

777

Fackert, Harold E., *collector.*
    Miscellany, n.d. ½ ms. box.
    Pamphlets, clippings, and miscellanea, relating to pacifism.

778

Fairclough, Henry Rushton.
    Miscellaneous papers, 1914–1920. 1 folder.
    Professor of Latin, Stanford University; Red Cross worker in Switzerland and Montenegro, 1918–1920. Correspondence, clippings and certificates, relating primarily to Red Cross civilian relief work in Montenegro.

779

Fairman, Charles.
    Report, n.d. "Military Government." 1 folder.
    Printed.
    Relates to problems of legal jurisdiction of Allied military governments during World War II.

780

Falk, Karl L., *collector.*
    K. L. Falk collection on Germany (in English and German), 1923–1937. 1 ms. box.
    Writings, correspondence, reprints, newspaper articles, and miscellanea, relating to the sinking of the *Lusitania* in 1915, to the Saar plebiscite in 1935, to the conditions of Germans living in the Sudetenland, Memel, and the Polish Corridor in the interwar period, and to the economic effects on Germany of the Polish Corridor.

781

Fall, John.
    Recording of poem, ca. 1976. "Wisdom of Years." 1 phonorecord.
    Rhodesian Army chaplain. Relates to Rhodesia. Published in *Assegai*, the magazine of the Rhodesian Army, July 1976.

782

Far Eastern Republic collection, 1917–1921. 1 ms. box.
Memoranda and copies of proclamations and correspondence, relating to the creation of the Far Eastern Republic and to Japanese intervention in Siberia. Includes a mimeographed copy of the constitution of the republic and a memorandum from the Far Eastern Republic Special Trade Delegation to the U.S. Government.

783

Far Western Slavic Conference, Stanford University, 1959.
Proceedings, 1959. 7 phonotapes.
Conference of Slavic studies scholars in the Western U.S. Relates to the history, politics, foreign relations, economy, society and literature of the Soviet Union and Eastern Europe.

784

Farish, Linn M.
Circular, 1940. 1 folder.
Typescript (mimeographed).
Reprints extracts from an article by L. M. Farish, entitled "Huge Reserves, Poor Technique Characterize Soviet Oil Industry," published in *Mining and Metallurgy* in June 1940, and letters to the editor prompted by this article, published in *Mining and Metallurgy* in July 1940, relating to a comparison of economic conditions in the U.S. and the Soviet Union.

785

Farmer, Edward M.
Papers, 1942. 1 ms. box.
American civilian camouflage course instructor. Military documents, pamphlets, and correspondence, relating to the second civilian camouflage course given by E. M. Farmer at Fort Belvoir, Virginia, 1942.

786

Farmers' National Weekly.
Newspaper issues, 1933–1936. 1 ms. box.
Organ of the Farmers' National Committee for Action (a communist front organization), published in Washington, D.C., during 1933, and in Chicago, 1934–1936.
Gift, Theodore Draper, 1971.

787

Farquhar, Francis P., *collector*.
Miscellany, 1902–1941. 1 album, 1 folder.
Photographs, 1902–1918, of U.S. warships and merchant vessels and of shipyards in the San Francisco area, mostly taken during World War I; and a list (printed), 1941, of the principal mountains of Greece.
Gift, F. P. Farquhar, 1931. Subsequent increments.

788

Farquhar, Percival, 1864–1953.
Papers, 1922–1928. 4 ms. boxes.
American engineer. Correspondence, memoranda and reports, relating to negotiations between P. Farquhar and associates and the Soviet government concerning the development of Russia's iron ore and steel resources, and

to the work of American engineers in the Soviet Union. Includes reports on the Makeeva Steel Works, the Krivoi Rog Iron Ore District and Ekatrina and Donets Basin railway developments.

789

Farrand, Stephen M.
Papers, 1943–1945. 3 ms. boxes, 1 scrapbook.
Staff member, Alien Enemy Control Unit, U.S. Department of Justice, and Prisoner of War Division, Office of the Provost Marshal General, U.S. Army, 1942–1946. Bulletins, regulations, correspondence, newsletters, clippings, periodical issues, and photographs, relating to prisoner of war camps in the U.S. during World War II.
Gift, S. M. Farrand, 1949.

790

Fath, Hildegard.
Memorandum, 1945. "Memorandum about Rudolf Hess." 1 vol.
Typescript.

791

Faulkner, Nettie Shaffer, *collector*.
Newspaper clippings, ca. 1921–1945. 19 ms. boxes.
Relates to world politics, Presidents of the U.S., 1921–1945, and World War II diplomatic conferences.
Preliminary inventory.
Gift, N. S. Faulkner.

792

Fearnside, W. Ward, *collector*.
Wooden inkstand, ca. 1939–1945.
Carved in the form of a fox and a rabbit by a Czechoslovakian Jehovah's Witness imprisoned at Mauthausen Concentration Camp near Linz, Austria, during World War II.
Gift, W. W. Fearnside, 1946.

793

Fedichkin, Dmitri I.
Papers (in Russian), 1918–1919. ½ ms. box.
Colonel, Imperial Russian Army; Commander-in-Chief, Izhevsk People's Army, 1918. Writings, correspondence, and handbills, relating to the Russian Civil War, and the rebellion of workers and peasants in Izhevsk against the Bolsheviks, 1918.

794

Fedorov, Georgiĭ.
Memoirs (in Russian), n.d. "Iz Vospominaniĭ Zalozhnika v Piâtigorskom Kont͡sentrat͡sionnom Lagere" (From the Recollections of a Prisoner in the Piatigorsk Concentration Camp). 1 vol.
Typescript (carbon copy).
Relates to the Russian Civil War in the Kuban region.

795

Fedorov (Grigoriĭ Fedorovich) collection (in Russian), 1967–1973. 1 folder.
Brochures, pamphlets, newspaper articles, and photo-

graphs, relating to the public life of G. F. Fedorov (1891–   ), Soviet Government official.
Gift, University of Alaska, 1976.

796

Feierabend, Ladislav K., 1891–1969.
Papers (in Czech, Slovak and English), 1922–1975. 20 ms. boxes.
Czechoslovak agricultural economist; Minister of Agriculture, 1938–1940; Minister of Finance, Czechoslovak Government-in-Exile (London), 1941–1945. Correspondence, speeches and writings, memoirs, photographs and printed matter, relating to agricultural administration, Czechoslovakia in World War II, and Czechoslovak foreign relations with Germany and the Soviet Union.
Preliminary inventory.
Personal papers closed until 1998.
Gift, Ivo Feierabend, 1978.

797

Feiler, Arthur, 1897–1942.
Papers (in German), 1911–1941. 1 ms. box.
German economist. Clippings, pamphlets, correspondence, and notes, relating to international economics and to German economics and politics, principally in the 1930's.

798

Feldmans, Jules, 1889–1953.
Papers, 1919–1955. 18 ms. boxes, 1 envelope.
Latvian diplomat. Correspondence, memoranda, and reports, relating to the Russian occupation of the Baltic states in 1940, displaced persons in Germany, immigration, and Latvian émigré organizations after World War II.
Register.
Gift, American Latvian Association in the U.S., 1973.

799

Feliz, Frank E.
Papers, 1941–1948. 13 ms. boxes, 1 scrapbook.
Director of Information, U.S. War Assets Administration, during World War II. Correspondence, memoranda, reports, writings, and printed matter, relating to labor and production allocations in the United States during World War II, postwar recovery, and activities of the War Production Board, War Manpower Commission, U.S. Employment Service, and War Assets Administration.
Gift, F. E. Feliz, 1963.

800

Fellers, Bonner Frank, 1896–1973.
Papers, 1934–1972. 16 ms. boxes.
Brigadier General, U.S. Army; Director, Psychological Warfare Division, U.S. Army, 1943–1945; Chairman, Citizens Foreign Aid Committee, 1959–1969. Research studies, reports, correspondence, memoranda, and operational instructions, relating to U.S. propaganda and military activities during World War II, the U.S. economy and foreign aid, and the Citizens Foreign Aid Committee

and Taxpayers Committee to End Foreign Aid.
Register.
Gift, B. F. Fellers, 1970. Subsequent increments.

801

Fellowship of Reconciliation.
Records, 1942–1946. 20 ms. boxes.
Non-denominational religious pacifist organization in the U.S. Correspondence, reports, and memoranda, relating to pacifist activities and conscientious objectors in the U.S. during World War II.
Preliminary inventory.

802

Felton, Frederick L.
Excerpts from letters, 1945–1946. 1 folder.
Typescript.
U.S. military lawyer; member of the prosecution staff at the Nuremberg War Crime Trials. Relates to the Nuremberg trials.

803

Ferdinand I, Czar of Bulgaria, 1861–1948.
Proclamation (in Bulgarian), 1912. 1 folder.
Printed.
Relates to Bulgarian entry into the First Balkan War.

804

Ferguson, Alan.
Correspondence, 1938–1939, with William Sidney Graves. 1 folder.
Holograph (photocopy).
American soldier; member, 31st Infantry Regiment, in Siberia, 1918–1919. Relates to the history of the American Expeditionary Forces in Siberia.
Gift, A. Ferguson, 1978.

805

Ferriere, Suzanne.
Translation of study, n.d. "The United States in the Relief of Europe, 1918–1923: Hoover's Work in Europe Since the Armistice." 1 folder.
Typescript.
Translation of *Les Etats-Unis au Secours de l'Europe, 1918–1923: L'Oeuvre de Hoover en Europe depuis l'Armistice* (Geneva: Union Internationale de Secours aux Enfants, 1923).

806

Fetter, Klara.
Papers, n.d. 9 l. ft.
Staff member, Hoover Institution on War, Revolution and Peace. Typewritten notes and English translations of published material, relating to the history of the Hungarian Soviet Republic of 1919.

807

Feuilletau de Bruyn, Willem Karel Hendrik, b. 1886.
Study, 1946. "The Aims, Methods, and Means of Soviet Russia in Asia and the Middle East." 1 vol.
Typescript (carbon copy).

808

Field, Charles K.
List, 1946. "Distinguished Soldiers in World War I." 1 folder.
Typescript.
Relates to American war heroes of World War I. Includes correspondence regarding compilation of the list.

809

Field, Herbert Haviland, 1868–1921.
Papers, 1919. 1 vol.
Typewritten transcripts.
Member of U.S. delegation to the Paris Peace Conference, 1919. Diary and reports, relating to political and economic conditions in Bavaria, January—March, 1919.

810

Field, N. H.
Memorandum, 1946. 1 folder.
Typescript.
Unitarian Service Committee relief worker in Germany. Relates to relief work in the Soviet Zone of Germany.

811

Fielitz, Axel von.
Memorandum (in German), 1915. "Ueber die Bedeutung des Haager Werkes" (On the Significance of the Hague Activities). 1 folder.
Holograph.
Relates to a proposal to end World War I through reconvening the Hague International Peace Conferences.

812

Fife, Austin E.
Anthology, 1947. "Anthology of Folk Literature of Soldiers of the Pacific Theater." 1 vol.
Typescript (carbon copy).
Relates to stories and poems of American soldiers in the Pacific Theater during World War II.

813

Fight for Freedom Committee.
Records, 1940–1942. 4½ ms. boxes.
Private organization lobbying for U.S. intervention in World War II. Correspondence, memoranda, press releases, pamphlets, clippings, and printed matter, relating to the interventionist and non-interventionist movements in the U.S. during World War II, the America First Committee, and the activities of Charles Lindbergh and Herbert Hoover in the non-interventionist movement.

814

Finance, Public—France—table, 1924. 1 folder.
Typescript.
Indicates French war reparation expenditures and internal and foreign debt for 1923, and budget for 1924.

815

Finger, Seymour M., 1915–
Dispatches, 1953, to the U.S. Department of State. 1 folder.
Typescript.
American diplomat; Economic Officer, U.S. Legation in Hungary, 1951–1953. Relates to various aspects of the Hungarian economy between 1950 and 1952.
Register.
Gift, S. M. Finger, 1971.

816

Finland—flag, n.d.
Flag of the Grand Duchy of Finland.

817

Finland in the Russian Revolution—reports, 1919–1920. 1 folder.
Typescript.
Relates to political conditions in Finland during the Russian Civil War, Finnish independence, Karelian nationalism, and German intervention in Finland and the Baltic states.

818

Finley, Margaret A.
Letters received, 1942–1943. 1 folder.
Letters and typewritten copies of letters from Japanese–Americans interned at Poston, Arizona, during World War II, relating to conditions in the relocation camp.

819

"Finliandets" (Finnish).
Bulletins (in Russian), 1963–1972. ½ ms. box.
Typescript (mimeographed).
Organ of the Society of the Household Troops of the Finland Regiment, an organization of veterans of this regiment of the Imperial Russian Army. Relates to activities of members.
Gift, Nicholas T. Yakunin, 1974.

820

Finn, Chester E., Jr.
Papers, 1969–1972. 15 ms. boxes.
American educator; Staff Assistant to the President of the U.S., 1969–1970; Special Assistant for Education to the Governor of Massachusetts, 1972. Speeches and writings, memoranda, reports, correspondence and printed matter, relating to U.S. educational policy during the Presidency of Richard M. Nixon.
Preliminary inventory.
Gift, C. E. Finn, Jr., 1978.

821

Finnish independence movement collection (in Finnish and Swedish), 1900–1903. ½ ms. box.
Pamphlets, bulletins and maps, relating to the Russification program in Finland and to the Finnish independence movement.

822

Finnish Relief Fund, 1939–1946.
Records, 1939–1946. 211 ms. boxes, 1 scrapbook.
American charitable organization for provision of relief to Finland during World War II. Correspondence, office files, accounts, press releases, clippings, pamphlets, and photographs, relating to the raising and disbursement of American funds for civilian relief in Finland during World War II.
Preliminary inventory.

823

Finnish war guilt trials, 1945–1946—transcript of proceedings (in Finnish), 1945–1946. 4 ms. boxes.
Trials held in Helsinki, November 16, 1945 to February 21, 1946, of former leaders of the Finnish Government, accused of responsibility for the entry of Finland into World War II in 1941.

824

Finze, Hans Joachim.
Memoir (in German), 1944. "Die Luftangriffe auf Koethen vom 20.7 und 16.8.1944" (The Air Raids on Koethen from July 20 to August 16, 1944). 1 vol.
Holograph.
Secondary school student in Koethen, Germany.

825

First Aid for Hungary, 1956–1957.
Records, 1956–1957. 3 ms. boxes.
American charitable organization for provision of relief to refugees of the Hungarian Revolution. Correspondence, reports, contribution lists, clippings, and printed matter, relating to relief and resettlement of Hungarian refugees.
Preliminary inventory.
Gift, First Aid for Hungary, 1957.

826

Fischer, Eugen, b. 1881.
History (in German), n.d. "Deutsch-Englische Tragoedie 1871–1914" (The German-English Tragedy, 1871–1914). 1 vol.
Typescript (carbon copy).
Relates to Anglo-German relations, 1871–1914.

827

Fischer-Galati, M. T., *collector.*
Photographs, 1940. 1 envelope.
Depicts the Maginot Line. Photographs taken by German intelligence services.
Gift, M. T. Fischer-Galati, 1973.

828

Fischer, George, 1923–
Study, 1950. "Soviet Defection in World War II." ½ ms. box.
Typescript (mimeographed).
American author and historian. Relates to Russian collaborators with Germany during World War II and especially to the Russian Army of Liberation under General Andreĭ Andreevich Vlasov.
May not be quoted or reproduced without permission of G. Fischer.

829

Fisher, Harold Henry, 1890–1975.
Papers, 1917–1974. 32 ms. boxes, 4 card file boxes (⅔ l. ft.), 5 envelopes, 1 album.
American historian; Director, Hoover Institution on War, Revolution and Peace, 1943–1952. Clippings, printed matter, notes, correspondence, pamphlets, articles, microfilm, and photographs, relating to the Soviet Union, the San Francisco Conference organizing the United Nations, the Civil War in Spain, Herbert Hoover and the American Relief Administration, and the history of Finland.
Register.
Gift, H. H. Fisher.

830

Fisk, A. J.
Report (in Polish), 1921. "Kopalnie Wegla i Górnictwo w Polsce" (Coal Mines and Mining in Poland). 1 folder.
Typescript (mimeographed).
American consulting mining engineer in Poland.

831

Fiume. Comando di Fiume d'Italia.
Bulletins (in Italian), 1919–1920. *Bolletino Ufficiale* (Official Bulletin). 1 folder.
Printed.
Relates to the occupation of Fiume by Italian nationalists under Gabriele d'Annunzio, September 1919—September 1920.

832

Fiume question collection (in Italian), 1918–1924. 1 folder.
Photocopy.
Proclamations, newspaper issues and correspondence, relating to the occupation of Fiume by Italian nationalists, and the growth of the Italian fascist movement.

833

Fleming, Harold M., 1900–
Papers, 1922–1923. 1 ms. box.
American Relief Administration worker in Russia. Correspondence, writings, maps and clippings, relating to the American Relief Administration in Russia, economic conditions, and political and social developments in Russia after the revolution.
Gift, H. M. Fleming, 1956.

834

Fleming, Robert John, Jr., 1907–
Interview, 1975. 2 phonotapes, 1 folder.
Major General, U.S. Army; Deputy Chief of Staff, Central Pacific Area, 1941–1943; Governor of the Panama Canal Zone, 1962–1967. Relates to the attack on Pearl Harbor and the administration of the Panama Canal Zone. Interview conducted by Paul B. Ryan,

Captain, U.S. Navy. Includes sound recording and transcript (typewritten).
Gift, R. J. Fleming, Jr., 1975.

835

Flint, Rebecca.
Papers, 1918–1919. 3 ms. boxes.
Young Men's Christian Association relief worker in France, 1918–1919. Memoranda, pamphlets, photographs, memorabilia, and printed matter, relating to Young Men's Christian Association work with the American Expeditionary Force in France.
Gift, Wisconsin State Historical Society, 1959.

836

Floyd, Barry Neil, 1925–
Study, 1958. "Changing Patterns of African Land Use in Southern Rhodesia." 1 vol.
Typescript (carbon copy).
Paper read before the Social Science Research Committee at the University College of Rhodesia and Nyasaland, November 6, 1958.

837

Flug, V. E.
Writings (in Russian), 1926–1933. 2 ms. boxes.
Holograph.
General, Imperial Russian Army. Includes a study entitled "Pekhota" (Infantry), 1926, relating to infantry organization and tactics, and a memorandum, 1933, relating to activities of the Russian 10th Army in September 1914.
Register.
Gift, N. N. Golovin, 1947.

838

Foch, Ferdinand, 1851–1929.
Memorandum (in French), 1918. 1 folder.
Holograph (photocopy).
Relates to projected future needs for U.S. troops in France. Written by F. Foch, Marshal, French Army, and John J. Pershing, General, U.S. Army, June 23, 1918.

839

Fonck, Charles.
Memorandum (in French), 1940. "Rapport sur la Mission d'Evacuation de la Population Civile Belge Confiée à M. Ch. Fonck" (Report on the Mission of Evacuation of the Civilian Belgian Population Entrusted to Mr. Ch. Fonck). 1 folder.
Typescript.
Belgian relief worker. Relates to relief provided by the Belgian government for Belgian refugees displaced by the German invasion in May 1940.
Gift, C. Fonck, 1942.

840

Forced labor in Germany collection (in German), 1936–1945. 2½ ms. boxes.
Reports, memoranda, regulations, and miscellanea, relating to the importation and supervision of foreign workers in Germany, during World War II. Includes some miscellaneous material relating to the structure of the Hitlerjugend and other Nazi organizations, and to Nazi racial ideology and historical and cultural outlook.

841

Forced labor—Netherlands—letters (in Dutch), 1942. 1 folder.
Typescript.
Three letters from Dutch workers transported to Germany for forced labor, relating to working conditions in Germany.

842

Forced labor—Toulouse—collection (in French and German), 1943–1944. 1 folder.
Correspondence and memoranda, relating to transportation of Spanish refugees in the vicinity of Toulouse to Germany for forced labor during World War II.

843

Ford (Henry) leaflet (in Russian), 1927. 1 folder.
Printed.
Reprints correspondence between H. Ford, American industrialist, and Theodor Fritsch, German antisemitic writer, relating to the works of T. Fritsch.

844

Ford, Mrs. Edsall P.
Papers, 1940–1949. 1 ms. box.
Volunteer Red Cross worker, Dibble General Hospital, Menlo Park, California, 1944–1946. Diary, correspondence, photographs, and clippings, relating to Red Cross work and social conditions in the U.S. during World War II.
Gift, Mrs. E. P. Ford, 1949.

845

Foreign Policy Association.
Miscellany, 1956. 1 folder.
Program (printed), and guest list (mimeographed), for a luncheon held by the Foreign Policy Association, in honor of Herbert Hoover, Jr., U.S. Undersecretary of State, 1954–1957.

846

Forgan, James Russell, 1900–1974.
Papers, 1945–1973. 1 ms. box.
Photocopy.
Colonel, U.S. Army; Assistant to the Director of Intelligence, Office of Strategic Services, 1943–1944; Deputy Commanding Officer, European Theater of Operations, Office of Strategic Services, 1944–1945. Correspondence, reports, minutes of meetings, and lists, relating to the operations of the Office of Strategic Services during World War II, the creation of the Central Intelligence Agency, and the activities of the Veterans of OSS.
Register.
Gift, J. R. Forgan, 1973.

847

Fornel de la Laurencie, Benoît Léon, b. 1879.

Memoirs (in French), 1941. "Mémoires du Général de Fornel de la Laurencie: Une Mission de 4 Mois à Paris en Qualité de Délégué Général du Gouvernement Français auprès du Chef de l'Administration Militaire en France" (Memoirs of General de Fornel de la Laurencie: A Mission of Four Months in Paris in the Capacity of Delegate General of the French Government to the Chief of Military Administration in France). 1 vol.

Typescript (carbon copy).

General, French Army. Relates to relations between the Vichy Government and German occupation authorities.

848

Forney, Edward H., d. 1965.

Papers, 1950–1964. 4 ms. boxes, 2 scrapbooks.

Brigadier General, U.S. Marine Corps. Notebooks, writings, orders, and clippings, relating to the Korean and Vietnamese Wars. Includes daily condensations of the South Vietnamese press, August 5, 1961—December 10, 1962.

Gift, Mrs. E. H. Forney, 1965.

849

Foss, F. F.

Papers, 1890–1917. 20 envelopes, 4 albums, 38 oversize prints, 1 oversize package (½ l. ft.).

Engineer in Russia. Photographs and memorabilia, relating to the development of industry in prerevolutionary Russia.

Gift, F. F. Foss, 1936.

850

Fotitch, Konstantin, 1891–1959.

Papers (in Serbo-Croatian and English), 1934–1964. 56 ms. boxes.

Yugoslav diplomat; Minister and Ambassador to the U.S., 1935–1944. Correspondence, speeches and writings, diaries, printed matter and photographs, relating to Yugoslav-American relations, political and military conditions in Yugoslavia during World War II, postwar communism in Yugoslavia, and Yugoslav émigré politics.

Closed until August 14, 1989.

Gift, Tatiana Fotitch, 1969. Incremental gift, 1974.

851

Foto-Willinger collection, 1919–1945. 53 envelopes.

Photographs depicting scenes of daily life in Germany in the interwar period and during World War II, including social, cultural, industrial, and agricultural activities. Also includes scenes of Nazi activities and of military operations during World War II.

852

Fox, Ernest F.

Slides, 1929–1932. 1 ms. box.

American mining engineer. Depicts scenes of Northern Rhodesia. Photographs taken during geological expeditions, and used to illustrate the book by E. F. Fox, *By Compass Alone* (Philadelphia, 1971).

Reproductions of slides must credit E. F. Fox.

Gift, E. F. Fox, 1971.

853

France, 1665–1871—collection (in French), 1665–1871. ½ ms. box.

Correspondence, decrees, maps, drawings and printed matter, relating to miscellaneous aspects of French governmental administration under the Bourbon and Orleanist monarchies and to the Paris Commune of 1871. Includes original decrees issued by Louis XIV, Louis XV, and Louis Philippe.

854

France. Armée. 7. Corps.

General orders (in French), 1916. 1 folder.

Typescript (mimeographed).

Relates to activities of the VII Corps in the Battle of the Somme, September 9–17, 1916.

855

France. Armée. Détachement d'Armée de l'Atlantique. Etat-Major. Troisième Bureau.

Reports (in French), 1945. ½ ms. box.

Typescript and printed.

Relates to French military operations against the German-occupied ports of Lorient, St. Nazaire, La Rochelle and Royan-Grave, 1944–1945. Includes maps.

856

France. Assemblée Nationale.

Petition (in French), 1871. 1 folder.

Holograph (photocopy).

Relates to public examination of an unspecified issue. Signed by members of the French National Assembly, March 18—April 20, 1871.

857

France Combattante. Afrique Française Libre.

Miscellaneous records (in French), 1940–1942. 1 vol.

Typewritten transcripts.

Orders, decrees and memoranda, relating to Free French military activities in French West Africa during World War II.

Gift, A. Sicé, 1947.

858

France. Commissariat Général à la Famille.

Pamphlets (in French), 1941–1943. 1 ms. box.

Agency of the Vichy Government of France. Relates to encouragement of birth rate increase, promotion of the family as a social institution, and discouragement of alcoholism.

859

France in World War II collection (in French and German), 1942–1946. 1 ms. box.

Pamphlets, leaflets, serial issues, and miscellanea, relating to France during World War II. Includes both pro-Vichy and pro-resistance propaganda, blank forms for travel permit requests used in German-occupied France, and a few postwar political items.

860

France—posters (in French), 1951–1974. 38 posters, 5 photographs.

Posters and photographs of the French elections of June 1951 and May 1974, issued by the Paix et Liberté organization and the Parti Communiste Français.
Preliminary inventory.
Gift, Joseph Binns, 1951. Gift, Mireille Meyer, 1974.

861

France—World War I—photographs, ca. 1917–1918. 1 envelope.

Depicts U.S. military activities in France during World War I. Photographs by Harry J. Edwards.
Gift, Amy Edwards, 1972.

862

France (Territory under German occupation, 1940–1944) Militaerbefehlshaber in Frankreich. Biarritz. Feldkommandatur.

Records (in German), 1940–1943. 7 ms. boxes.
German military occupation government in Biarritz, France. Reports, regulations, proclamations, and correspondence, relating to the administration of Biarritz, especially regarding price control and rationing.

863

France (Territory under German occupation, 1940–1944) Militaerbefehlshaber in Frankreich. Metz. Polizeipraesident.

Regulations (in German), 1937–1944. 1 ms. box.
German police occupying Metz, France. Relates mostly to police personnel policies.

864

Franco Bahamonde (Francisco)—photographs, n.d. 2 envelopes.

Depicts F. Franco, Spanish head of state. Includes photographs of F. Franco with President Dwight D. Eisenhower of the U.S.

865

François, Curt von, 1852–1931.

Memoir (in German), 1914. "Erste Erforschung des Togo Hinterlandes, 1888–89" (First Exploration of the Togo Hinterland, 1888–89). 1 folder.
Typescript (photocopy).
Major, German Army. Relates to German exploration of the Togo region in Africa.
Gift, Charles Burdick, 1970.

866

Frank, Colman D.

Miscellaneous papers, 1918–1919. 1 folder, 1 envelope.

Major, U.S. Army, during World War I; member, U.S. Section, Permanent International Armistice Commission. Guide for interrogation of German prisoners;

military map of Germany and route book; memoir (typewritten), entitled "Inside the Armistice Commission"; and photographs of Allied members of the Permanent International Armistice Commission, and of U.S. military activities in World War I.
Gift, Herbert M. Cobe, 1962.

867

Frank, Karl Boromaeus, 1893–1969.

Papers (in German and English), 1937–1961. 10 ms. boxes, 1 envelope, 7 microfilm reels.
German psychologist; socialist and anti-Nazi leader. Writings, correspondence, clippings, printed matter and photographs, relating to the communist, socialist and anti-Nazi movements in Germany, post-World War II reconstruction in Germany, and political psychology.
Register.
Gift, Mrs. K. B. Frank, 1971.

868

Frankel, Sally Herbert, 1903–

Papers, 1925–1975. 54 l. ft.
British economist; economic adviser to South African and Southern Rhodesian Governments, 1941–1958. Writings, correspondence, statistics, reports, memoranda, notes and commission proceedings, relating to economic conditions, finance, agriculture, mining and transportation in South Africa, Rhodesia and East Africa.
Preliminary inventory.
Purchase, S. H. Frankel, 1978.

869

Franz, Rudolf, *collector*.

R. Franz collection on Germany and Austria (in German), 1914–1924. 3 ms. boxes.
Leaflets, proclamations, political campaign literature, war news announcements and pamphlets, relating to events of World War I, the Spartacist revolt, the Kapp Putsch in Germany, German nationalism, anti-semitism, and German and Austrian politics.
Gift, R. Franz, 1931.

870

Fraser, Leon, 1889–1945.

Papers (in English and French), 1924. ½ ms. box.
American banker; Reparations Commission General Counsel for the Dawes Plan. Reports, memoranda and correspondence, relating to the 1924 London Inter-Allied Conference on Reparations and Inter-Allied Debts, and to the adoption of the Dawes Plan.

871

Frederichs, General.

Papers (in Russian and French), 1835–1876. 5 ms. boxes.
Imperial Russian Military Attaché in France. Correspondence, memoranda, notes and printed matter, relating to Franco-Russian relations and Russian military policy.
Preliminary inventory.
Gift, I. A. Holmsen, 1928.

872

Frederick, Robert Tryon, 1907–1970.
Papers, 1928–1967. 8 ms. boxes, 1 album, 2 envelopes, 2 motion picture reels.
Major General, U.S. Army; Commanding General, First Special Service Force, 1942–1944; Head, U.S. Military Mission to Greece, 1951. Correspondence, diaries, writings, memoranda, photographs, and a film, relating to the history of the First Special Service Force in Italy and France during World War II, to the U.S. Military Mission to Greece in 1951, and to the military career of R. T. Frederick.
Preliminary inventory.
History by Martin Blumenson, entitled "From Salerno to Cassino," may not be reproduced without permission of the Office of the Chief of Military History, U.S. Army.
Gift, R. T. Frederick, 1968. Subsequent increments.

873

Frederiksen, O. J.
Letters, 1924. 1 folder.
Typewritten transcripts.
Relief worker in Leningrad, 1924. Relates to the flood in Leningrad and to the dismissal of students from Russian universities.

874

Free, Arthur M., *collector*.
Photographs, 1914–1918. 8 envelopes.
Depicts German troops and war scenes on the Eastern and Western fronts during World War I, and scenes of the negotiation of the Treaty of Brest-Litovsk, 1918. Captions in German.
Gift, A. M. Free, 1933.

875

"Freedom." Executive Committee.
Translation of leaflet, 1939. "Manifesto of Freedom." 1 folder.
Typescript (mimeographed).
Polish resistance group. Relates to the program of the resistance movement in occupied Poland during World War II.

876

Freeman, Roger Adolf, 1904–
Papers, 1950–1974. Ca. 195 l. ft.
American economist; Senior Fellow, Hoover Institution on War, Revolution and Peace, 1962–1975; Special Assistant to the President of the U.S., 1969–1970, and other government positions. Correspondence, memoranda, reports, studies, speeches and writings, and printed matter, relating to governmental problems in the State of Washington, 1950–1955, fiscal problems of Bolivia, 1957, international economic development, taxation (federal, state, and local), intergovernmental relations in the U.S., public and private education from lower schools to university in the U.S. and the Soviet Union, public welfare in the U.S., and the growth of American government.

May not be used without permission of R. A. Freeman, the Director of the Hoover Institution, or the Director of the Domestic Studies Program of the Hoover Institution.
Deposit, R. A. Freeman, 1975.

877

Freemasons (France) collection (in French), 1807–1947. 20 ms. boxes.
Clippings, serial issues, pamphlets, bulletins, and election campaign material, relating to Freemasonry in France, Freemasons in politics, French politics and international relations in the 1920's and 1930's, the Popular Front, rightist movements in France, and occupied France during World War II.
Purchase, G. E. Stechert and Company, 1947.

878

Frejlich, Joseph, *collector*.
J. Frejlich collection on Poland and world affairs, 1894–1968. 54 ms. boxes.
Clippings, correspondence, and writings, relating, to Polish socialism, World War II, the Yalta conference, Poles in the United States and Canada, and the Russian Orthodox Church.
Deposit, J. Frejlich, 1968.

879

French communism—translations of newspaper articles, 1919–1920. 1 folder.
Typescript.
Relates to the development of a French communist party and to its adherence to the Third International. Translations of articles from French and Russian newspapers.

880

French election posters—photographs, 1951. 1 envelope.
Depicts posters issued by various political parties in Paris before the French elections of June 1951. Photographs were taken by the U.S. Economic Cooperation Administration.
Gift, Bill Hornby.

881

French Fifth Republic collection (in French), 1958–1976. 31 ms. boxes, 21 microfilm reels.
Miscellaneous election leaflets, posters, pamphlets, newspapers, magazines, and government documents, relating to political conditions in France under the Fifth Republic.
Preliminary inventory.

882

French leftist press—newspaper articles (in French), 1917–1919. 1 folder.
Typewritten transcripts.
Relates to the movement for a Third International and to the mutiny of French sailors in the Black Sea. Articles from leftist French newspapers.

883

French relief organizations in World War I—leaflets (in French), 1914—1919. ½ ms. box.
Printed.
Relates to relief activities of a number of organizations in France during World War I.

884

French resistance collection (in French), 1940—1945. 6 ms. boxes.
Memoranda, reports, instructions, orders, letters, maps, charts and photographs, distributed by various resistance groups in German-occupied France during World War II.
Preliminary inventory.

885

French student revolt collection (in French), 1968. 5 ms. boxes, 8 phonotapes, 32 posters.
Pamphlets, leaflets, posters, serial issues and phonotapes of interviews, relating to the French student-worker revolt of 1968.
Preliminary inventory.

886

Frenkel, Lawrence.
Memorandum, 1947. "Displaced Persons Camps." 1 folder.
Typescript.
United Nations Relief and Rehabilitation Administration official in Austria at the end of World War II. Relates to the psychological state and political attitudes of inhabitants of Displaced Persons camps.

887

Frente Popular para la Liberacion de Saguia el Hamra y Rio de Oro.
Issuances (in French and Arabic), ca. 1977. 1 folder, 1 envelope.
Popular Front for the Liberation of Saguia el Hamra and Rio de Oro. Photographs and posters, relating to the movement for independence from Mauritania and Morocco of the peoples of the Western Sahara region (the former Spanish Sahara).
Purchase, Association des Amis de la République Arabe Saharaouie Démocratique, 1978.

888

Frey, Cynthia W.
Study, 1973. "Yugoslav Nationalisms and the Doctrine of Limited Sovereignty." 1 folder.
Typescript (mimeographed).
American political scientist. Relates to the suppression of nationalist movements by the Yugoslav Government, 1946—1971.
May not be quoted without permission of C. W. Frey.
Gift, C. W. Frey, 1974.

889

Fried, Alfred Hermann, 1864—1921.
Papers (in German), 1914—1919. 5 ms. boxes.
Austrian pacifist. Diaries, correspondence, clippings, and notes, relating to the international peace movement, particularly during World War I, pacifism, international cooperation, and the World War I guilt question.

890

Friedberg, Jeffreys, 1891—1975.
Letter, 1918, to his brother. 1 folder.
Holograph.
Second Lieutenant, U.S. Army. Relates to activities of the American Expeditionary Force in France during World War I.

891

Friedland, William H., *collector*.
W. H. Friedland collection on Tanzanian trade unions, 1929—1967. 10 ms. boxes, 3 envelopes, 4 microfilm reels.
Reports, articles, minutes of meetings, and clippings.
Preliminary inventory.
Gift, W. H. Friedland, 1969.

892

Friedlander, Ernst.
Memoir (in German), ca. 1920. "Imprisonment in Siberia." 1 vol.
Typescript.
Austrian soldier taken prisoner during World War I. Includes incomplete translation.

893

Friends, Society of. American Friends Service Committee. Civilian Public Service.
Records, 1941—1945. 4 ms. boxes.
American Quaker organization. Memoranda, bulletins, newsletters, and reports, relating to compulsory non-military public service, conscientious objectors in the U.S. during World War II, and alternative service programs conducted by the Friends Civilian Public Service.

894

Friends, Society of. War Victims Relief Committee.
Records, 1914—1923. 2 ms. boxes.
World War I Quaker relief organization. Reports, correspondence, and minutes of meetings, relating to relief work in France during World War I and in Germany, Austria, Hungary and Poland immediately after the war.

895

Frillmann, Paul William, 1911—1972.
Papers, 1941—1969. 3 ms. boxes, 1 album, 3 envelopes, 3 framed certificates.
American missionary in China, 1936—1941; Chaplain, American Volunteer Group ("Flying Tigers"), 1941—1945; U.S. consular official in China and Hong Kong, 1946—1950. Correspondence, memoranda, orders, notes and photographs, relating to activities of the

American Volunteer Group in China during World War II, U.S. foreign relations with China, 1946–1950, and conditions in China during the civil war.
Register.
Gift, Mrs. P. W. Frillmann, 1975.

896

Frontwacht.
Records (in Flemish), 1915–1933. ½ ms. box.
Youth organization of the Vlaamsche Front (Partij der Vlaamsche Nationalisten), a Flemish nationalist party. Correspondence, memoranda and financial records, relating to Flemish nationalism in Belgium in the interwar period.

897

Frumkin, Jacob G.
Statement, 1957. 1 folder.
Typescript.
Notarized statement, relating to a German offer to negotiate a separate peace with Russia in 1917. Includes second statement on same subject by Ilja Trotzky.
Gift, J. G. Frumkin, 1969.

898

Fryling, Jan.
Papers (mainly in Polish), 1939–1977. 6 ms. boxes.
Polish diplomat, lawyer and politician; Counsellor, Polish Embassy in China. Diaries, speeches and writings, notes, clippings, correspondence, and photographs, relating to political events in Poland, Polish foreign relations with China and India, Poland's role in World War II, and activities of Poles in the United States.
Gift, V. Kuharets, 1977.

899

Fuller, Adaline W., b. 1888.
Papers, 1919–1920. 1 folder.
American Relief Administration worker in Poland, 1919–1920. Correspondence and memoranda, relating to work of the American Relief Administration in France, Belgium, Poland, and Russia. Includes letters from Clemens Pirquet and George B. Baker.
Gift, A. W. Fuller, 1972.

900

Fuller, Benjamin Apthorp Gould, b. 1879.
Papers, 1918–1919. 4 ms. boxes, 2 envelopes.
Captain, U.S. Army; Member, American Section, Supreme War Council of the Allied and Associated Powers, during World War I. Memoranda, daily bulletins, and photographs, relating to military developments, especially on the Italian front, and to political conditions in Europe and Russia.
Preliminary inventory.
Gift, B. A. G. Fuller.

901

Fuller, William Parmer, II, 1888–1969.
Papers, 1920–1962. 3 ms. boxes, 5 envelopes, 3 oversize boxes (1½ l. ft.).

Chief of Mission to Poland for European Children's Fund, American Relief Administration, 1919–1921. Correspondence, reports, memoranda, clippings, telegrams, photographs, and memorabilia, relating to American Relief Administration work in Poland at the end of World War I, and to Herbert Hoover. Includes correspondence with Mr. and Mrs. Herbert Hoover.
Gift, Mrs. W. P. Fuller II, 1957. Subsequent increments.

902

Furlong, Charles Wellington, 1874–1967.
Papers, 1917–1963. 9 ms. boxes, 8 envelopes.
Member, U.S. delegation, Paris Peace Conference, 1918–1919; member, Tacna-Arica Commission, 1926. Correspondence, memoranda, reports, writings, clippings, maps, and photographs, relating to Woodrow Wilson, the Paris Peace Conference, military, political and economic conditions in the Balkans (particularly relating to Fiume and Montenegro), the Tacna-Arica dispute between Peru and Chile, and the work of the Tacna-Arica Plebiscitary Commission, 1925–1926.
Register.
Purchase, C. W. Furlong, 1963.

903

Gadsby, Henry Franklin, b. 1868.
Papers, 1897–1950. 18 ms. boxes.
Canadian journalist and political satirist. Writings, correspondence, printed matter and memorabilia, relating to Canadian and British politics, primarily in the interwar period, and to British Empire war efforts during World War I.
Gift, Clarence V. Blake, Sr., 1978.

904

Gaelic calendar (in Gaelic), 1918. 1 folder.
Printed.
Commemorates traditional Franco-Irish friendship. Published in France.

905

Gaertner, Margarete.
Writings, n.d. 1 folder.
Typescript.
Relates to the interwar dispute between Germany and Lithuania over Memel, East Germany under Soviet occupation after World War II, and the Berlin blockade of 1948–1949.
Preliminary inventory.
Gift, M. Gaertner.

906

Gaeth, Arthur.
Radio news broadcast, 1946. 2 phonorecords.
Broadcast from Nuremberg, Germany, over the Mutual Broadcasting System, relating to the execution of leading Nazis convicted of war crimes.

907

Gaffney, Thomas St. John, 1864–1945.
Papers, 1887–1941. 3 ms. boxes.
U.S. Consul General to Dresden and Munich, 1905–

1915. Correspondence, writings, and printed matter, relating to international relations, the World War I war guilt question, reparations, Irish independence, U.S. domestic politics and foreign policy, and the Jewish question. Includes correspondence with Kaiser Wilhelm II in exile, Baron Hermann Speck von Sternburg (German ambassador to the U.S.), and Jules Cambon (French ambassador to Germany).

908

Gahagan, G. William, 1912–
Papers, 1941–1954. 9 ms. boxes, 10 motion picture reels.
Information and Public Relations Officer, Office of War Information, San Francisco, 1942–1945. Photographs, maps, films, and miscellanea, relating to U.S. Office of War Information analysis of Japanese propaganda and preparation of U.S. propaganda during World War II. Includes a few examples of postwar U.S. anti-communist propaganda.
Gift, G. W. Gahagan, 1975.

909

Gaines, Marcus Junius.
Letterbook, 1849–1858. 1 folder.
Holograph.
U.S. Consul in Tripoli. Copies of dispatches to and instructions from the U.S. Department of State, relating to American-Tripolitan relations.

910

Galinski, Adam J., 1894–1973.
Papers (in English and Polish), 1945–1971. 4 ms. boxes.
Polish resistance leader during World War II; German prisoner, 1944; Soviet forced labor camp prisoner, 1956. Correspondence, reports, personal documents, writings, photographs, and printed matter, relating to conditions in Soviet forced labor camps, and to twentieth century Polish history and culture.
Gift, estate of A. J. Galinski, 1978.

911

Gallem (Leopold) report (in German), 1938. 1 folder.
Typescript.
Relates to military judicial action taken against L. Gallem, Sergeant, German Army, for violation of traffic regulations.

912

Gally, Benjamin W.
Miscellany, 1945–1949. 1 folder, 1 map.
Brigadier General, U.S. Marine Corps. Rubber relief map used in planning the invasion of Iwo Jima, 1945; photocopies of an inventory of items released by the U.S. Government to the Chinese National Palace Museum in Peking, 1946; and photocopies of letters from a British consular official in Tientsin, describing the communist occupation of Tientsin, 1949.
Gift, Gertrude Gally Margah, 1964.

913

Galpin, Perrin C., 1889–1973.
Papers, 1914–1955. 5 ms. boxes, 1 folder.
Secretary, Commission for Relief in Belgium, 1914–1915; Secretary, American Relief Administration, 1919–1923; President, Belgian-American Educational Foundation, 1920–1963. Correspondence, reports, photographs, clippings, and printed matter, relating to the Commission for Relief in Belgium, American Relief Administration, Herbert Hoover and U.S. electoral politics, and the 1938 trip to Europe and 1946 food relief activities in Europe of Herbert Hoover.
Gift, P. C. Galpin, 1957. Subsequent increments.

914

Galvin, John A. T., *collector*.
Reproductions of paintings, n.d. 1 envelope.
Depicts scenes from the Franco-Prussian War, the Boxer Rebellion, and the Russo-Japanese War, including the battle of Tsushima Straits. Also includes miscellaneous scenes, mainly of Japan.
Gift, J. A. T. Galvin, 1955.

915

Gamelin (Maurice Gustave) collection (in French), 1934–1942. 1 folder.
Memoranda, notes, directives and declarations, relating to pre-World War II plans for the defense of the northern frontier of France, and to the conduct of General Maurice Gamelin (1872–1958), in commanding French defenses against the German offensive in May 1940.

916

Gamet, Wayne Neal, 1900–
Memoirs, n.d. "Squadron 40–T." 1 folder.
Typescript.
Rear Admiral, U.S. Navy. Relates to U.S. naval operations in European waters, 1918–1920, and activities of Squadron 40-T in European waters, 1939–1940.
Gift, W. N. Gamet, 1976.

917

Gankin, Olga Hess.
History, 1940. 2 ms. boxes.
Typescript and holograph.
Research associate, Hoover Institution on War, Revolution and Peace. Drafts and notes for her book, *The Bolsheviks and the World War: The Origin of the Third International*. Relates to Russian political events and the Russian Army during World War I, Bulgarian political events during World War I, and the Communist International.

918

Gann, Lewis Henry, 1924–
Papers, 1950–1976. 30 ms. boxes.
Author and historian; Senior Fellow, Hoover Institution on War, Revolution and Peace, 1964– . Correspondence, typewritten drafts of writings, galley proofs, transcribed interviews, and other material, relating to

Federation of Rhodesia and Nyasaland, German colonialism in Africa, and Northern and Southern Rhodesia. Includes drafts of and research materials used for the books by L. H. Gann and Peter Duignan, *Huggins of Rhodesia, A History of Northern Rhodesia, Colonialism in Africa*, and *The Birth of a Plural Society*.
Preliminary inventory.
Gift, L. H. Gann, 1972. Subsequent increments.

919

Gardinier, David E., 1932–
Writings, 1972–1978. 1 folder.
Printed.
American historian. Relates to education in the states of Equatorial Africa.
Gift, D. E. Gardinier, 1978.

920

Garrett, Garet, 1878–1954.
Letter, ca. 1941, to Carl Synder. 1 folder.
Typescript.
Editorial writer-in-chief, *Saturday Evening Post*, 1940–1942. Relates to U.S. foreign policy during World War II. Annotated by Robert A. Millikan, physicist.

921

Garvi, Peter A., 1881–1944.
Writings (in Russian), n.d. ½ ms. box.
Typescript.
Russian socialist. "Vospominaniiã Sot͡sialdemokrata" (Memoirs of a Social-Democrat), relating to the Russian Social-Democratic Workers Party, 1906–1917; "Professional'nye So͡iuzy Rossiĭ v Pervye Gody Revoli͡ut͡siĭ" (Trade Unions of Russia in the First Years of the Revolution); and "Rabochai͡a Kooperat͡sii͡a v Pervye Gody Russkoĭ Revoli͡ut͡siĭ, 1917–1921" (Workers Cooperatives in the First Years of the Russian Revolution, 1917–1921).
Gift, Columbia University Research Program on the History of the C.P.S.U., 1956.

922

Gaskill, C. A.
Diary, 1920. 1 folder.
Typescript.
Colonel, U.S. Army; American Relief Administration worker and technical adviser to Poland, 1919–1921. Relates to conditions in the Ukraine during the Russian Civil War, June 1–16, 1920.
Gift, C. A. Gaskill, 1943.

923

Gauld, Charles Anderson, 1911–
Papers (in English, Portuguese and Spanish), 1932–1968. 18 ms. boxes.
American historian and author. Clippings, correspondence, pamphlets, and serial issues, relating to political, social and economic conditions in Latin America, especially Brazil, to Latin America's role in World War II, to the Castro regime in Cuba, and to problems of birth control, food production, communism and religion in Latin America.
Preliminary inventory.
Gift, C. A. Gauld, 1944. Subsequent increments.

924

Gaulle (Charles de)—photograph, n.d. 1 envelope.
Depicts President C. de Gaulle of France.

925

Gautier, Gilbert.
Caricature, n.d. 1 framed cartoon.
French cartoonist. Depicts Georges Clemenceau, French Premier and War Minister during World War I.
Gift, John Douglas Forbes, 1976.

926

Gauze, René.
Papers (in French), 1949–1963. 1 ms. box.
Chief of Police, Brazzaville, Congo. Diary, relating to the 1959 race riots in Brazzaville; and a history, entitled "La République du Congo ex-Français vers son Destin" (The Ex-French Republic of the Congo Towards Its Destiny), published in an abridged English translation.
Gift, R. Gauze, 1972. Incremental gift, 1973.

927

Gavrilović, Milan, 1882–1976.
Papers (in Serbo-Croatian and English), 1939–1976. 55 ms. boxes.
Yugoslav journalist, politician and diplomat; Ambassador to the Soviet Union, 1940–1941; Member, Yugoslav Government-in-Exile, London, 1941–1943. Correspondence, speeches and writings, office files, and printed matter, relating to Yugoslav politics and government, Yugoslavia during World War II, the Yugoslav Government-in-Exile, Draža Mihailović and the Chetnik resistance movement in occupied Yugoslavia, relations between the Kingdom of Yugoslavia and the Soviet Union, and the activities of Serbian émigré groups following World War II.
Preliminary inventory.
Closed until August 21, 1995.
Gift, Milan Gavrilović, 1975.

928

Gay, Edwin Francis, 1867–1946.
Papers, 1917–1927. 6 ms. boxes, 1 roll of charts.
American economist; Director, U.S. Central Bureau of Planning and Statistics, 1918–1919. Correspondence, diary, reports, memoranda, and writings, relating to U.S. economic mobilization and government control of the economy during World War I, to activities of the Central Bureau of Planning and Statistics, War Industries Board, War Trade Board, Shipping Board, and Commercial Economy Board, and to the U.S. delegation at the Paris Peace Conference.
Gift, Mrs. Godfrey Davies.

929
Gay, George Inness, 1886–1964.
Papers, 1915–1929. 2 ms. boxes.
Member, Statistical Division, Commission for Relief in Belgium, during World War I. Correspondence, drafts of writings and galley proofs, relating to relief activities of the Commission for Relief in Belgium and to the publication of *Public Relations of the Commission for Relief in Belgium: Documents* (Stanford, 1929), compiled by G. I. Gay. Includes three paintings on flour sacks.

930
Geary, John R.
Letters, 1923. 1 folder.
Typescript.
General Electric Company representative in Japan. Relates to the Tokyo earthquake of 1923.

931
Geiger, Theodor.
Memoranda (in German), 1949. 1 folder.
Typescript.
Relates to reconstruction of the German educational system after World War II.

932
Gellois (André)—photograph, n.d. 1 envelope.
Depicts A. Gellois.

933
Gelpke, Alhard, *collector*.
A. Gelpke collection on anti-Nazi organizations (in German), 1936–1957. 1 folder.
Writings, leaflets, and correspondence, relating to activities of anti-Nazi organizations in Switzerland during the 1930s and World War II. Includes samples of anti-Nazi propaganda.

934
General Dynamics Corporation.
Photographs, 1961. 1 envelope.
Depicts guided missiles and space vehicles.

935
General Electric Company.
Photographs, 1960. 1 envelope.
Illustrates pictures resulting from use of different television camera tubes.

936
Genkin, E.
Translation of report, 1924. "A Few Words about Mongolia." 1 folder.
Typescript.
Relates to the development of the communist movement in Mongolia. Original report published in *Tretii S'ezd Mongolskoi Narodnoi Partii* (Third Congress of the Mongolian People's Party), 1924.

937
Genoa. Economic and Financial Conference, 1922.
Records (in English, French and Italian), 1922. 2 ms. boxes.
Minutes of meetings, agenda, committee reports, draft proposals, a roster of delegates, and telegrams sent and received by the Italian delegation, relating to European economic reconstruction and to European economic relations with Russia.

938
George Peabody College for Teachers, Nashville, Tenn.
Reports, 1958–1962. 8 microfilm reels.
Typescript (microfilm). Originals located at the George Peabody College for Teachers.
Relates to a project carried out by the George Peabody College for Teachers in cooperation with the Government of South Korea to provide technical assistance in the training of teachers in South Korea.
Preliminary inventory.
Purchase, George Peabody College for Teachers, 1978.

939
George VI (King of Great Britain)—photograph, n.d. 1 envelope.
Depicts King George VI of Great Britain with British officers.

940
Georgevich, Dragoslav.
Thesis, 1967. "Two Days in Yugoslav History: March 25 and 27, 1941." 1 folder.
Typescript (photocopy).
Relates to the adherence of Yugoslavia to the Tripartite Pact, and to the coup against the government of Prince Paul in Yugoslavia. Master's thesis, San Jose State College.
Gift, D. Georgevich.

941
Georgievich, M.
Study (in Russian), n.d. "Vstriechnyĭ Boĭ Divizĭi i Korpusa" (Encounters of Battle Divisions and Corps). 1 folder.
Typescript.
Relates to Russian military organization during World War I.

942
Georgiĭ Mikhailovich, Grand Duke of Russia, d. 1919.
Letters (in Russian), 1914–1918, to his daughter, Princess Kseniîa. 2 ms. boxes.
Holograph.
Russian aristocrat; special military representative of Tsar Nicholas II during World War I. Relates to political and military conditions in Russia during World War I, the Russian Revolution, and family affairs.
Register.
Gift, Nancy Wynkoop, 1976.

943

Gerbode, Martha.
Report, 1948. 1 folder.
Typescript.
Relates to British, Malay and Chinese public opinion regarding the Malayan independence movement, as revealed by an analysis of British press coverage.

944

German-administered justice in the Netherlands collection (in German and Dutch), n.d. 1 folder.
Miscellaneous lists, notes and statistics, relating to the administration of justice by German occupation authorities in the Netherlands during World War II.

945

German American Bund.
Records (in English and German), 1936–1941. ½ ms. box, 1 envelope.
Photocopy. Most originals located in the U.S. National Archives.
Fascist organization in the U.S. Minutes of meetings of the Executive Committee, translations of Fuehrer commands, financial records, propaganda and photographs, relating to activities of the Bund. Collected by Paul Dunne.
Gift, P. Dunne, 1972.

946

German Army—World War I—photographs, ca. 1914–1918. 3 envelopes.
Depicts German troops, battlefields and war equipment, in France, Belgium and Russia during World War I.

947

German civilian morale in World War I—charts, n.d. 1 folder.
Photocopy.
Illustrates the progression of German civilian morale during World War I, 1914–1918. Prepared by the U.S. Army.

948

German communist anti-Nazi propaganda (in German), ca. 1933–1939. 1 folder.
Printed.
Camouflaged anti-Nazi pamphlets, issued by the Kommunistische Partei Deutschlands.

949

German education essays (in German), 1943. 1 folder.
Holograph.
School essays, written by German pupils.

950

German occupation proclamations—Lithuania (in German, Lithuanian, Polish, Russian and Yiddish), 1916–1918. 1 folder.
Printed.

Relates to regulation of the civilian population in Lithuania. Issued by German occupation authorities.

951

German political campaign literature (in German), 1913–1932. 1 ms. box.
Leaflets, posters, pamphlets, and other campaign material, relating to German elections, and issued by various political parties. A few items relate to Austrian and Swiss elections.
Purchase, Otto Harrassowitz, 1931.

952

[German Prisoners of War in Russia.]
Memoir, 1946. 1 vol.
Typescript (photocopy).
Authored by an unidentified German prisoner of war. Relates to conditions of imprisonment of German prisoners of war in Russia during World War II.

953

German referendum, 1934—proclamation (in German), 1934. 1 folder.
Printed.
Relates to the referendum for combining the offices of President and Chancellor in Germany.

954

German refugee reports (in German), 1948. 1 folder.
Typescript.
Relates to social and economic conditions in Silesia and East Prussia under Polish and Soviet rule. Written by refugees from Silesia and East Prussia.

955

German Revolution collection (in German), 1919. 1 folder.
Reports, leaflets, clippings and miscellaneous printed matter, relating to the German Revolution of 1918–1919 and to anti-semitism in Germany.

956

German soldier's diary (in German), 1944. 1 folder.
Holograph.
Diary of an unidentified German soldier, May—September 1944.

957

German student protest collection (in German), 1966–1972. 10 ms. boxes.
Periodicals, pamphlets, leaflets, and proclamations, issued by leftist student groups in West Germany, relating to West German and international political issues, including the West German emergency laws, the publisher Axel Springer, the visit of the Shah of Iran to Berlin in 1967, the invasion of Czechoslovakia in 1968, and the Vietnamese War.
Register.
Gifts and purchases, various sources, 1970–1974.

958

German youth movement collection (in German), 1908–1973. ½ ms. box.

Radio broadcast transcripts and published articles relating to the German youth movement, the "Wandervogel"—Bewegung, 1901–1933, and various youth movements after the end of World War II.

Preliminary inventory.

Purchase, Archiv der Deutschen Jugendbewegung, 1974.

959

Germany. Auswaertiges Amt.

Records (in German), 1923–1945. 1081 binders and pamphlet boxes, 1 folder.

Photocopy of original documents located in German Bundesarchiv, Koblenz. Microfilm copy located in U.S. National Archives, Washington, D.C.

German Foreign Office. Correspondence, memoranda and reports, relating to German foreign relations in the interwar period and during World War II. Most of these documents have been published in *Documents on German Foreign Policy*, series D, vols. 1–13, and series C, vols. 1–4.

Preliminary inventory.

960

Germany. Auswaertiges Amt. Archiv-Kommission.

Press release (in German), ca. 1939–1945. 1 folder.

Typescript (mimeographed).

Announces the publication of *Roosevelts Weg in den Krieg* (Roosevelt's Course in the War) as the first volume of a series to be entitled *Die Entstehung des Krieges von 1939* (The Origins of the War of 1939), consisting of documents from captured Allied archives.

961

Germany. Auswaertiges Amt. Geschaeftstelle fuer die Friedensverhandlungen.

Summary of memoranda (in German), n.d. 1 folder.

Typescript.

Relates to the contents of memoranda of the German Office for Peace Negotiations, 1919, regarding negotiations concerning the eastern boundaries of Germany at the Paris Peace Conference. Summary prepared by Alma Luckau.

962

Germany. Deutsche Kongress-Zentrale.

Records (in German), 1870–1943. 426 ms. boxes.

German Government agency regulating all congresses and conventions of German and international organizations taking place in Germany. Correspondence, memoranda, pamphlets, conference proceedings, clippings, and newspaper issues, relating to conferences of cultural, scientific, social reform, professional, business, educational, and other organizations.

Register.

963

Germany. Deutsche Waffenstillstands-Kommission. Unterkommission fuer die Rueckgabe von Maschinen und Material an Belgien und Frankreich.

Records (in German and French), 1919. 1 folder.

German Armistice Subcommission. Reports, memoranda and statistics, relating to the German surrender of heavy equipment in compliance with armistice agreements at the end of World War I.

964

Germany. Geheime Staatspolizei.

Reports (in German), n.d. 1 folder.

Typescript (some mimeographed).

Relates to agitation activities, particularly anti-militarist activities, of the Kommunistische Partei Deutschlands between the two world wars, and to communist anti-Nazi activities in Germany and German-occupied areas in the latter half of 1941.

965

Germany. Geheime Staatspolizei. Aussendienststelle, Beuthen, Silesia.

Miscellaneous records (in German), 1935–1936. 1 vol.

Photocopy.

German secret police foreign service office in Beuthen, Silesia. Correspondence, memoranda and reports, relating to the secret national socialist movement in Polish Silesia.

966

Germany. Grosses Hauptquartier.

Telegrams received (in French), 1915–1917. 1 ms. box.

Telegrams from Berlin to German Army Headquarters at Charleville, France, mostly addressed to Captain Schnitzer, reporting political and war news gleaned from the foreign press.

967

Germany. Heer. 9. Armeekorps.

Regulations (in German), 1915–1917. 1 vol.

Typescript (mimeographed).

Relates to censorship in Hamburg during World War I.

968

Germany. Heer. Generalstab. Feldpressestelle. Offizier-Kriegsberichterstattung Westfront.

Press releases (in German), 1917–1918. 1 folder.

Typescript.

Relates to war news from the western front.

969

Germany. Heer. Infanterie-Regiment 163.

Photographs, 1914–1918. 1 ms. box.

Depicts officers and men of Infanterie-Regiment 163 of the German Army, and scenes of their activity in campaigns in France and Belgium during World War I.

970

Germany in World War II—extracts from letters, 1940. 1 folder.
 Typescript (mimeographed).
 Relates to conditions in Germany during World War II. Written by an unidentified anti-Nazi German.

971

Germany. Konsulat, San Francisco.
 Press releases (in German and English), 1933. 1 folder.
 Typescript (mimeographed).
 Relates to the national socialist regime in Germany.

972

Germany. Kriegsmarine.
 Photographs, ca. 1930–1939. 2 envelopes.
 Depicts the German Navy.

973

Germany. Oberste Heeresleitung.
 Records (in German), 1914–1918. 2 ms. boxes.
 Intelligence and other reports, leaflets, radio news scripts, clippings, and press releases, relating to political conditions in Russia and the Netherlands, Allied and Bolshevik propaganda, German propaganda, and military positions at the front during World War I.

974

Germany. Reichsernaehrungsministerium.
 Memoranda (in German), ca. 1935. 1 folder.
 Typescript.
 Ministry of Food of Germany. Relates to German food supply in the period 1924–1935.

975

Germany. Reichsfuehrer SS—und Chef der Deutschen Polizei. SS—und Polizeifuehrer im Distrikt Galizien.
 Report (in German), 1943. "Loesung der Judenfrage in Galizien" (Solution of the Jewish Question in Galicia). 1 vol.
 Typescript (photocopy).

976

Germany. Reichskanzlei. Adjutantur des Fuehrers.
 Records (in German), 1934–1944. 3 ms. boxes.
 Office of the Adjutant to the Fuehrer of Germany. Correspondence, memoranda, personnel records, and miscellanea, relating to the German economy, military activities of the Schutzstaffel (SS) Begleitkommando, and miscellaneous administrative matters.

977

Germany. Reichskanzlei. Fuehrerschutzkommando.
 Logbook (in German), 1934–1937. ½ ms. box.
 Holograph.
 Defense Command of the Fuehrer of Germany. Records correspondence sent and received by the Fuehrerschutzkommando.

978

Germany. Reichskommissar beim Prisenhof Hamburg.
 Extracts from records (in German and Latvian), 1939–1944. 1 folder.
 Typewritten transcripts prepared by Heinz von Bassi from originals at the German Military Archives, Freiburg/Br.
 Prize Court of the German Admiralty. Relates to the seizure of Baltic ships on high seas during World War II, and to indemnification questions.
 Gift, Edgar Anderson, 1976.

979

Germany. Reichsluftfahrtministerium.
 Report (in German), 1935. 1 vol.
 Typescript (carbon copy).
 Report and supporting documents, relating to the history of German military aviation, 1919–1927. Prepared by General Wilberg.

980

Germany. Reichsministerium fuer Volksaufklaerung und Propaganda.
 Miscellaneous records (in German), 1939–1943. 4 ms. boxes.
 Political newsletters, radio broadcast transcripts and letters of radio listeners. Includes an abstract of a speech given before the Berlin Association of Foreign Correspondents on October 14, 1941, and a protocol of the Ministry for Eastern European Affairs regarding its session for October 9, 1943.
 Preliminary inventory.

981

Germany. Reichsrat.
 Miscellaneous records (in German), 1928–1929. 1 ms. box.
 Upper legislative chamber of Germany. Petitions, applications, memorials, proposals, and presentations, submitted by various companies, persons, organizations, and local governments, for deliberation and consideration, December 1928—December 1929.

982

Germany. Reichssicherheitshauptamt. Sicherheitsdienst.
 Miscellaneous records (in German), 1935–1944. ½ ms. box.
 Lessons, exercises, and other instructional material, relating to the training of German police officers in the Sicherheitsdienst in both political and criminal police work.

983

Germany. Reichswirtschaftsministerium.
 Memoranda (in German), 1936. 1 folder.
 Typescript.
 Relates to foreign currency cash requirements for German industry, and to liaison between the Ministry of the Economy and the office of the Deputy to the Fuehrer.

984

Germany—social conditions, 1918–1933—slides, 1919–1933. 2 boxes.

Depicts social conditions in Germany during the period of the Weimar Republic and the first months of Nazi rule, including scenes of theater productions, boxing tournaments, and portraits of military and political figures.

985

Germany Speaks.

Writings (in German and English), 1934. 1 folder.
Typescript.
Relates to national socialism in Germany. Written by several Nazi leaders, and originally intended for publication in the U.S. under the title *Germany Speaks.* Includes copy of a foreword by Adolf Hitler.

986

Germany. Statistisches Reichsamt.

Tables (in German), n.d. 1 folder.
Printed.
Relates to changes in the German labor force from May 31, 1939 to May 31, 1940, broken down by industry, sex and region.

987

Germany. Wehrmacht.

Orders (in German), 1940. 1 folder.
Typescript (photocopy of originals at the Belgian Army Archives).
Relates to German plans for attack on Belgium. Captured from a German officer at Mechelen, Belgium, January 10, 1940.
Gift, Jacques de Launay, 1962.

988

Germany. Wehrmacht. Oberkommando. Fuehrerhauptquartier. Stenographischer Dienst.

Transcripts of conferences (in German), 1942–1945. 5 vols.
Typescript (mimeographed).
Stenographic records of conversations of Adolf Hitler, Fuehrer of Germany, with civilian and military aides, relating to German policy during World War II, December 1942–March 1945.

989

Germany. Wehrmacht. Wehrbezirkskommando Berlin V.

Memoranda (in German), n.d. 1 folder.
Typescript.
Relates to the organization and duties of offices for the registration and conscription of civilians for military service.

990

Germany, West—elections, 1976—collection (in German), 1976. 3 ms. boxes, 69 posters.

Pamphlets, leaflets, flyers, posters, newspaper issues, pins and buttons, flags, and a song book, relating to the general elections in the German Federal Republic on October 3, 1976. Includes a transcript of a television discussion among party leaders Helmut Schmidt, Hans Dietrich Genscher, Helmut Kohl, and Franz-Josef Strauss.
Preliminary inventory.

991

Germany—World War I—collection (in German), 1914–1920. 12 ms. boxes.

Pamphlets, posters, leaflets, proclamations, handbills, cartoons, and photographs, relating to the German Army and the German home front during World War I, prisoners of war in Germany, the German revolution of 1918–1919, and the German elections of 1920.
Preliminary inventory.
Purchase, Dietrich Reimer, 1926.

992

Germany—World War II—photographs, 1939–1945. 1 envelope.

Depicts social conditions in Germany and activities of German Nazi Party officials during World War II, especially Gauleiter Fritz Waechtler of Bavaria.
Gift, Carl L. Edwards, 1946.

993

Germany (Territory under Allied occupation, 1945–1955). Bi-Partite Economic Control Group.

Charts, 1947. 1 folder.
Illustrates levels of economic production in the British and U.S. zones of occupation in Germany, as of September 1, 1947, and October 1, 1947.

994

Germany (Territory under Allied occupation, 1945–1955. U.S. Zone) Office of Military Government for Bavaria. Kreis Traunstein.

Records (in English and German), 1945–1948. 10 ms. boxes.
Memoranda, reports, correspondence, and office files, relating to civil administration of Traunstein, including problems of public health and safety, administration of justice, allocation of economic resources, organization of labor, denazification, and disposition of displaced persons. Includes annual administrative reports for other districts in Bavaria.
Gift, William G. Marvin.

995

Gerngros (Aleksandr Alekseevich von)—photograph, 1901. 1 envelope.

Depicts General A. A. von Gerngros, Chief of Russian Railway Guards, Chinese Eastern Railway.

996

Gerth, Edwin P.

Papers, 1917–1918. 1 vol.
American soldier during World War I. Diary and letters, relating to U.S. military activities in France.

997

Gesamtverband Deutscher Antikommunistischer Vereinigungen.
Records (in German), 1935–1944. 172 ms. boxes, 3 pamphlet boxes (1 1. ft.).
Anticommunist propaganda agency of the German Government. Writings, reports and clippings, relating to the international communist movement and to the Jewish question.
Preliminary inventory.

998

Gesellschaft fuer Kulturellen Austausch mit dem Ausland.
Photographs, 1923–1960. 10 envelopes, 1 microfilm reel.
Cultural agency of the East German Government. Depicts social and economic conditions in East Germany, particularly in the district of Cottbus, and events in the life of Wilhelm Pieck, first president of the German Democratic Republic.

999

Gessen, B.
Memorandum (in Russian), n.d. "Transportnyiâ Sredstva i Transportirovanie" (Means of Transport and Transportation). 1 folder.
Typescript.
Relates to transportation systems in Russia during the Russian Civil War.

1000

Gessen, Iosif Vladimirovich, 1866–1943.
Papers (in Russian and English), 1919–1920. 4 ms. boxes.
Russian journalist and Constitutional Democratic Party leader. Reports, letters, and leaflets, relating to the White Army in the Russian Civil War. Includes two translations of I. V. Gessen's memoirs, *V Dvukh Vekakh* (In Two Centuries), one entitled "Reminiscences," translated from the Russian by E. Varneck, and a second entitled "Legality versus Autocracy," edited and annotated by Ladis K. D. Kristof.
Preliminary inventory.
Purchase, I. V. Gessen, 1938.

1001

Getsinger, Joseph W.
Papers, 1918–1919. 1 scrapbook.
Captain, U.S. Army; served in 340th Field Artillery, 1918–1919. Orders, photographs, maps, clippings, and pamphlets, relating to activities of the 340th Field Artillery in France during World War I and as a part of the occupation force in Germany in 1919.
Gift, J. W. Getsinger, 1943.

1002

Ghent. Rijksuniversiteit.
Congratulatory letter (in Flemish), 1936, to Harvard University. 1 folder.
Printed (photocopy).

Relates to the 300th anniversary of the founding of Harvard University.

1003

Gibson, Hugh Simons, 1883–1954.
Papers, 1903–1954. 81 ms. boxes, 11 cu. ft. boxes, 12 1. ft.
American diplomat; Ambassador to Poland, 1919–1924; Ambassador to Switzerland, 1924–1927; Ambassador to Belgium, 1927–1933 and 1937–1938; Ambassador to Brazil, 1933–1937. Diaries, writings, correspondence, reports, minutes of meetings and printed matter, relating to U.S. foreign relations, international disarmament negotiations, the League of Nations, and relief work in Europe during World Wars I and II.
Preliminary inventory.
Gift, Michael Gibson, 1956.

1004

Giers, Mikhail Nikolaevich de, 1856–1924.
Papers (in Russian), 1917–1926. 53 ms. boxes.
White Russian diplomat; chief diplomatic representative of Baron Vrangel' to the Allied Powers, 1920. Correspondence, reports, telegrams, and memoranda, relating to the Russian Civil War, the Paris Peace Conference, and White Russian diplomatic relations. Includes a file on the American Relief Administration in Soviet Russia and dispatches from White Russian diplomats in Austria, the Baltic states, Belgium, Bulgaria, Czechoslovakia, Denmark, Egypt, Finland, Germany, Great Britain, Greece, Hungary, Italy, Japan, the Netherlands, Norway, Palestine, Persia, Poland, Rumania, South America, Spain, Sweden, Switzerland, Turkey, United States, and Yugoslavia.
Preliminary inventory.
Gift, Michel de Giers, 1926.

1005

Giesecke, Erna E.
Letters received (in German), 1923–1926. 1 ms. box.
Holograph.
Letters to E. E. Giesecke, relating to economic and social conditions in southern Germany.
Gift, E. E. Giesecke, 1958.

1006

Gilbert, Horace N.
Report, 1931. "The Russian Industrialization Program." 1 folder.
Typescript.
American visitor to Russia.

1007

Gilbert, John J., II, *collector*.
Painting, n.d.
Depicts two soldiers on guard on the Eastern front during World War II. Found in German Army barracks in 1945.
Gift, Lolly Gilbert, 1977.

1008

Gill, Cecil B., *collector*.
Miscellany (in English and German), 1877–1905. 1 folder.
Deeds of sale and certificates (handwritten originals and photocopies), relating to the ownership of Likiep and other islands in the Marshall Islands group.

1009

Gill, Charles C.
Essay, 1951. "The Tenth Anniversary of Pearl Habor." 1 folder.
Typescript (mimeographed).
Colonel, U.S. Army. Relates to experiences of American veterans of the attack on Pearl Harbor, who were residing in Claremont, California, in 1951.

1010

Gilman, G. W.
Memoranda, 1932–1934. 1 folder.
Typescript.
Bell Telephone Laboratories engineer. Relates to the organization and equipment of an international radio-telephone communications system in Japan.

1011

Giraud, Henri Honoré, 1879–1949.
Translation of report, 1940. 1 vol.
Typescript (carbon copy).
General, French Army. Relates to causes of the French military defeat in 1940. Report to Henri-Philippe Pétain, Chief of State of France.

1012

Girin, Bernard C.
Report, ca. 1964. "The Association of the African States and the Malagasy Republic with the E.E.C.: A Reappraisal." 1 vol.
Typescript (carbon copy).

1013

Gitlow, Benjamin, 1891–1965.
Papers, 1918–1960. 17 ms. boxes.
American communist leader; later anti-communist writer. Writings, correspondence, minutes of meetings, clippings, and printed matter, relating to communism and socialism in the U.S. and Europe.
Preliminary inventory.
Purchase, Myers G. Lowman, 1967.

1014

Glaser, Kurt, *collector*.
K. Glaser collection on Western Europe (in German, English and French), 1949–1970. 1 ms. box.
Bulletins, press releases and correspondence, relating to Allied military governmental structure in Germany after World War II, governmental structure in Switzerland, the Common Market, Sudeten Germans, and the views of Senator William E. Jenner on U.S. foreign policy.
Gift, K. Glaser, 1969. Subsequent increments.

1015

Glassford, William A.
Study, 1930. "Jutland Decisions." 1 vol.
Typescript (mimeographed).
Captain, U.S. Navy. Relates to tactics of the naval battle of Jutland, 1916.

1016

Gniessen, Vladimir F.
Memoirs, n.d. "Through War and Revolution: Memoirs of a Russian Engineer." 1 ms. box.
Typescript.
Engineer and Colonel, Russian Imperial Army. Relates to Russian military activities during World War I, and White Russian military activities, especially in Turkestan, during the Russian Civil War.
Gift, V. F. Gniessen, 1948.

1017

Godard, Yves Jean Antoine Noël, 1911–1975.
Papers (in French), 1929–1974. 14½ ms. boxes, 1 vol., 1 envelope.
Colonel, French Army; Director of Police in Algeria, 1958–1960; organizer of the Organisation Armée Secrète (O.A.S.), 1961–1962. Correspondence, messages, reports, dossiers, maps, photographs, clippings, speeches and writings, relating to military and resistance operations during World War II, military operations during the Indochinese War, and military, police and terrorist activities during the Algerian independence struggle. Includes records of the Armée Secrète de Haute-Savoie (Secret Army of Resistance Fighters of Haute-Savoie).
Register.
Purchase, Mrs. Yves Godard, 1976.

1018

Godson, Roy, 1942–
Study, 1978. " 'Eurocommunism': Implications for East and West." 1 folder.
Typescript (photocopy).
Relates to the Communist parties of Western Europe. Written by R. Godson and Stephen Haseler.
Gift, Sidney Hook, 1978.

1019

Goebbels, Joseph Paul, 1897–1945.
Papers (in German), 1925–1945. 7½ ms. boxes, 20 microfilm reels, 1 phonotape.
Microfilm consists of six reels of a negative copy of the 1942–1943 diaries, six reels of a positive copy of the 1942–1943 diaries, one reel of a negative copy of the 1925–1926 diary, and seven reels of a second negative copy (defective edition) of the 1942–1943 diaries.
German Minister of Propaganda, 1933–1945. Diaries, correspondence, memoranda, taped speech, photograph, and expense accounts, relating to activities of the Nazi Party and of the German Government during World War II, especially military and political affairs. Includes diaries from August 12, 1925 to October 27, 1926, from January 21, 1942 to December 9, 1943 (incom-

plete), and for October 3, 1944, as well as a tape sound recording of a speech, entitled "Discorso Al Campo Di Maggio," September 28, 1937.

Preliminary inventory.

Gift, William Heimlich, 1947. Incremental gifts from various other sources.

1020

Goerdeler, Karl Friedrich, 1884–1945.

Miscellaneous papers (in German), 1938–1945. ½ ms. box.

Mayor of Leipzig, 1930–1937; German Commissioner of Price Control, 1934–1945. Writings and reports, relating to political and economic conditions in Belgium, Canada, Great Britain, France, and the United States as observed on his trip of 1937–1938, to his participation in the July 20, 1944 assassination attempt on Adolf Hitler, and to postwar reconstruction in Germany.

1021

Goering (Hermann) collection (in German and English), 1914–1946. ½ ms. box, 1 envelope.

Reports, correspondence, photographs and miscellanea, relating to H. Goering (1893–1946), Reichsmarschall of Germany, 1940–1945. Includes a U.S. Office of Strategic Services report on art looting by H. Goering, 1945, and the transcript of an interrogation of Hermann Goering, 1946.

1022

Gold, G. Leonard, *collector.*

G. L. Gold collection on the A.E.F. in France (in English and French), 1914–1921. 1 ms. box, 1 envelope, 1 scroll.

Posters, photographs, pamphlets, and miscellanea, relating to World War I and the American Expeditionary Force in France. Includes French war posters.

Gift, G. L. Gold, 1958.

1023

Gold mines and mining—Russia—collection (in English and Russian), n.d. 1 folder.

Studies, maps and mine records, relating to the gold mining industry in the Russian Far East, Transbaikalia and Outer Mongolia.

1024

Golder, Frank Alfred, 1877–1929.

Papers (in English and Russian), 1812–1930. 40 ms. boxes, 1 envelope.

American historian; American Relief Administration worker in Russia. Correspondence, diaries, memoranda, articles, pamphlets, and photographs, relating to Russian history in the late nineteenth and early twentieth centuries, the Russian American Company in Alaska, the Russian Revolution, and American Relief Administration work in Russia.

Preliminary inventory.

Gift, Thomas and Henrietta Eliot and H. M. Hart.

1025

Goldman, Jack, 1895–   , *collector.*

Medals, 1511–1971. 4 cu. ft. boxes.

Medals from 121 countries. Includes the Malayan Order of the Crown (Third Class) issued in 1511, U.S. Congressional Medal of Honor, British Victoria Cross, Spanish decoration for the Recapture of Vigo (1809), Italian Air Force Bravery Medal (World War II), the Ottoman Empire's decoration for the War against Montenegro (1862–1863), U.S. medal commemorating Admiral Dewey's victory at Manila Bay, U.S. Marine Brevet medal, and the Israeli Six-Day War medal.

Gift, J. Goldman, 1976.

1026

Goldsmith, Alan Gustavus, 1892–1961.

Letters, 1924. 1 folder.

Typescript.

Chief, European Division, U.S. Department of Commerce, 1920–1925; Technical Expert to Committee of Experts, Reparations Commission, 1923–1924. Relates to the work of the Committee of Experts of the Reparations Commission in formulating the Dawes Plan.

Preliminary inventory.

Gift, A. G. Goldsmith, 1924.

1027

Golovan, Sergei Alexandrovich.

Papers (in Russian), 1918–1921. 6 ms. boxes.

White Russian Military Attaché to Switzerland. Correspondence, military orders, communiqués, and clippings, relating to the Russian Civil War, and White Russian military relations with Switzerland.

Preliminary inventory.

Gift, N. N. Golovin, 1928.

1028

Golovin, Nikolai N., 1875–1944.

Papers (in Russian), 1912–1943. 16 ms. boxes.

General, Imperial Russian Army. Correspondence, speeches and writings, and printed matter, relating to Russian military activities during World War I, the Russian Civil War, and the Sino-Japanese War.

Register.

Gift, Michael Golovin, 1947.

1029

Golubev.

History (in Russian), 1926. 1 vol.

Typescript.

Relates to White Russian military activities in Mongolia during the Russian Civil War, and particularly to Baron Roman Ungern-Shternberg.

1030

Gómez Gorkin, Julián, 1901–

Translation of play (in French), n.d. "Douze Fantômes Revivent leur Histoire" (Twelve Phantoms Relive Their History). 1 folder.

Typescript.

Relates to conditions in tsarist Russia during the early twentieth century.

1031

Good, Albert I.
   Papers, ca. 1890–1929. 1 folder.
   American missionary in Cameroon. Memoir, entitled "The Church in the Cameroun," relating to missionary activity in the 1920s, and printed matter, relating to missionary activity in Africa, 1890–1908.
   Gift, Edwin M. Good, 1964.

1032

Good, James William, 1866–1929.
   Transcripts of speeches, 1929. 1 ms. box.
   Typescript.
   U.S. Secretary of War, 1929. Relates to the history and activities of the War Department, U.S. waterways, the Republican Party, and Anthony Wayne, American Revolutionary leader.
   Gift, J. W. Good, Jr., 1959.

1033

Goodfellow, Millard Preston, 1892–1973.
   Papers, 1942–1967. 5 ms. boxes, 2 envelopes.
   Colonel, U.S. Army; Deputy Director, Office of Strategic Services, 1942–1946; Political Adviser to the U.S. Commanding General in Korea, 1946. Correspondence, reports, printed matter and phonotapes, relating to Office of Strategic Services operations in North Africa and the Far East during World War II, and to postwar reconstruction in Korea.
   Register.
   Gift, M. P. Goodfellow, 1969.

1034

Goodman, Allan Erwin, 1944–
   Papers, 1947–1975. 126 ms. boxes, 2 card file boxes, 3 binders, 16 notebooks, and 7 envelopes.
   Consultant on Vietnamese Affairs, U.S. Department of State and Rand Corporation, 1967–1971. Writings, reports, correspondence, clippings, notes, interviews, and printed matter, relating to the Vietnamese War, the Paris peace talks of 1968–1973, elections in South Vietnam from 1967–1971, the South Vietnamese legislature, migration to Saigon, urbanization and political and demographic change in Southeast Asia, counterinsurgency, and Soviet-U.S. detente.
   Register.
   Users must sign a statement agreeing not to identify any persons mentioned in unpublished material in the collection (deceased U.S. citizens may be identified after January 2, 1980). Also 2½ ms. boxes and 12 notebooks are closed until 2005.
   Gift, A. E. Goodman, 1975. Subsequent increments.

1035

Goodwin, Hugh H.
   Miscellaneous papers, 1930–1962. 1 folder.
   Vice Admiral, U.S. Navy. Citations, letters of commendation, published writings, and printed matter, re-

lating to naval aviation and the career of H. H. Goodwin.
   Gift, H. H. Goodwin, 1974.

1036

Goodyear, A. Conger.
   Papers, 1919. 3 ms. boxes.
   President, Central European Coal Commission, 1919. Correspondence, memoranda, reports, maps, photographs, clippings, and printed matter, relating to coal production and distribution in Silesia, Bohemia, Galicia, and Serbia, political and economic conditions in Poland, and the partition of Silesia.
   Gift, A. C. Goodyear, 1956. Incremental gift, 1957.

1037

Gordeeff, Woldemar, 1912–
   Essays (in German), ca. 1946. "Unter uns Deutschen: Ein Bilderbuch Deutschen Lebens" (Among Us Germans: A Picture Book of German Life). 1 vol.
   Typescript.
   Relates to conditions in Germany during World War II.

1038

Gordon, Charles George, 1833–1885.
   Extracts from letters, 1874–1875. 1 folder.
   General, British Army; Governor of Equatoria Province, Sudan, 1874–1876. Relates to British administration of Equatoria.

1039

Goremykin (Ivan Logginovich)—photograph, n.d. 1 envelope.
   Depicts I. L. Goremykin, Prime Minister of Russia, 1914–1916.

1040

Gor'kiĭ (Maksim) collection (in Russian and English), 1921. 1 folder.
   Appeal (handwritten in Russian), by M. Gor'kiĭ (1868–1936), Russian novelist, 1921, relating to the need for foreign relief to aid Russian intellectuals; and four essays (typewritten), by Soviet scholars, relating to the literary, political and humanitarian ideas of M. Gor'kiĭ.
   Gift, Edgar Ammende, 1963. Gift, Soviet Embassy to the U.S., 1943.

1041

Gorton, Willard L., b. 1881.
   Papers, 1927–1932. 2 ms. boxes.
   American civil engineer; consultant to the Soviet Government in Turkestan, 1930–1932. Correspondence, reports, clippings and photographs, relating to reclamation and irrigation projects in Turkestan.
   Preliminary inventory.

1042

Gould, Randall Chase, 1898–
   Papers, 1895–1966. 6 ms. boxes, 3 scrapbooks, 1 envelope, 5 albums.
   American journalist in the Far East, 1923–1949;

editor, *Shanghai Evening Post and Mercury,* 1931–1941 and 1945–1949. Correspondence, writings, clippings, and photographs, relating to political and military events in the Far East, especially in China during the Sino-Japanese War of 1937–1945. Includes photographs of the Japanese bombing of Shanghai in 1937.
Register.
Gift, R. C. Gould, 1969. Subsequent increments.

1043

Graff (Clarence)—photograph, n.d. 1 envelope.
Depicts C. Graff.

1044

Graham, Malbone Watson, 1898–1965.
Papers, 1914–1956. 15½ ms. boxes.
American political scientist. Pamphlets, bulletins, writings, memoranda and clippings, relating to the League of Nations, and to political conditions and diplomatic relations in Finland, the Baltic States, and Eastern Europe from the Russian Revolution to World War II.
Preliminary inventory.
Gift, Gladys Graham, 1967.

1045

Gramotin, Aleksandr Aleksandrovich.
Report (in Russian), 1919. 1 folder.
Holograph (photocopy).
Captain, Imperial Russian Army. Relates to activities of the Russian Imperial family during the Russian Revolution.
Gift, Marvin M. Lyons, 1965.

1046

Grant, Donald, b. 1889.
Writings, 1920–1935. 1 folder.
British author and lecturer; Director, European Student Relief, 1920–1925. Notes, diary entries, letter extracts and a pamphlet, relating to social conditions and relief work in Russia and Eastern and Central Europe, 1920–1922, and to the economic and social policy of the socialist municipal government in Vienna, 1919–1934.
Gift, Joseph Jones, 1977. Gift, D. Grant, 1978.

1047

Grattan, C. Hartley.
Report, 1940. 1 folder.
Typescript.
Relates to conditions in Australia and New Zealand during World War II.
May not be quoted without permission of C. H. Grattan.

1048

Graves, William Sidney, 1865–1940.
Papers, 1914–1932. 3 ms. boxes.
Major General, U.S. Army; Commanding General, American Expeditionary Force in Siberia, 1918–1920. Correspondence, reports, monographs, and photo-graphs, relating to the Allied intervention in Siberia, 1918–1919.
Preliminary inventory.
Gift, Mrs. W. R. Orton, 1960.

1049

Gray, H. L.
Study, 1918. "Dalmatia from the Italian Point of View." 1 folder.
Typescript.
Relates to political and economic conditions in Dalmatia, the history of Dalmatia, and conflicting Italian and Slavic claims to the area.

1050

Gray, Marilyn.
Motion picture script, n.d. 1 vol.
Typescript.
Relates to a fictitious Sino-American war.
Gift, M. Gray, 1969.

1051

Grayson, Walter A.
Papers, 1918–1920. ½ ms. box, 3 envelopes.
First Lieutenant, U.S. Army; served with American Expeditionary Force in Siberia, 1918–1920. Military intelligence studies, photographs, clippings and memorabilia, relating to activities of the U.S. 27th Infantry Regiment in Siberia, 1918–1920.
Gift, W. A. Grayson, 1974. Incremental gift, 1977.

1052

Great Britain. Director of Propaganda in Enemy Countries.
Leaflets (in German), 1918. 1 ms. box.
Printed.
British propaganda leaflets, prepared for distribution behind German lines during World War I.

1053

Great Britain. Foreign Office.
Report, 1916. "Britain's Share in the War." 1 folder.
Typescript (mimeographed).
Relates to the British war effort, 1914–1916, including statistics, a summary of British war activities, and statements of British war aims.

1054

Great Britain. Foreign Office. Wellington House.
Issuances, ca. 1914–1918. 36 pamphlet boxes (12 l. ft), 2 ms. boxes.
Printed.
Propaganda section of the British Foreign Office. Books, pamphlets, and reprints, issued as British propaganda during World War I.
Preliminary inventory.

1055

Great Britain in World War II collection, 1939–1945.
9 ms. boxes.
Pamphlets, relating to conditions in Great Britain dur-

ing World War II, war aims, civil defense, the wartime economy, and postwar reconstruction.
Preliminary inventory.

1056

Great Britain. Ministry of Home Security.
Issuances, ca. 1939–1945. 2 cylinders, 2 motion picture reels.
Diagrams of incendiary bombs, and motion pictures illustrating how to safely dig through bomb debris to rescue survivors, prepared for civil defense use during World War II.

1057

Great Britain. Ministry of Information.
Propaganda, 1938–1949. 9 ms. boxes, 2 envelopes.
Pamphlets, posters, serial issues, press releases, photographs, and postcards, distributed by the British Ministry of Information during World War II, in various languages.

1058

Great Britain. Ministry of Information. Library, *collector.*
Printed matter, 1914–1918. 180 pamphlet boxes, 1 ms. box.
Books, pamphlets, and reprints, distributed as propaganda during World War I, in a variety of European languages.
Preliminary inventory.
Gift, British Foreign Office, 1920.

1059

Great Britain. Navy. Grand Fleet.
Transcripts of radio messages, 1918. 1 folder, 1 envelope.
Messages exchanged between the British Grand Fleet and the German High Seas Fleet prior to the surrender of the High Seas Fleet, November 12–29, 1918. Includes photographs of the German ships and miscellaneous newsletters from the U.S.S. *Arkansas,* which intercepted some of the messages.
Gift, R. Bentham Simons, 1957. Gift, Marlin W. Haley, 1972.

1060

Great Britain. Prime Minister.
Declaration, 1938. 1 vol.
Typescript (photocopy).
Joint declaration by Neville Chamberlain, Prime Minister of Great Britain, and Adolf Hitler, Fuehrer of Germany, September 30, 1938, relating to the settlement of the Czechoslovakian crisis reached at the Munich Four-Power Conference.

1061

Great Britain. War Office. Intelligence Division.
Index, ca. 1919. 1 folder.
Printed.
Indexes information summaries by the British War Office Intelligence Division.

1062

Greece. Hypourgeion Anoikodomēsēos.
Charts (in English and Greek), n.d. 1 oversize box.
Printed.
Ministry of Reconstruction of Greece. Illustrates economic losses suffered by Greece during World War II. Includes handwritten annotations and a typewritten synopsis.
Gift, Herbert Hoover.

1063

Greece in World War II collection (in Greek and English), 1941–1946. 1 folder.
Leaflets and pamphlets, relating to the Greek resistance movement during World War II.

1064

Greece—posters (in Greek), 1940–1945. 13 posters.
Printed.
Relates to the Greek resistance movement during World War II. Issued by resistance groups.
Gift, Mr. Adriopulos, 1968.

1065

Greek political opposition collection (in English and French), 1967–1970. 2 ms. boxes.
Correspondence, reports, printed matter and photographs, relating to the Greek junta, to allegations of its use of torture, and to Greek and international political opposition to the junta.
Preliminary inventory.

1066

Green, Joseph Coy, b. 1887.
Papers, 1914–1957. 21 ms. boxes, 2 envelopes.
American diplomat; Chief of Inspection, Commission for Relief in Belgium, 1915–1917; Director for Romania and the Near East, American Relief Administration, 1918–1919. Diary, correspondence, writings, reports, pamphlets, clippings, maps, and printed matter, relating to the Commission for Relief in Belgium, American Relief Administration activities in Romania and Transcaucasia, and the Herbert Hoover-for-President campaign in 1920.
Register.
Gift, J. C. Green, 1956. Subsequent increments.

1067

Greenspan, Bud, 1926–   , *compiler.*
Compilation of sound recordings, 1966. *December 7, 1941.* 1 phonorecord.
Speeches, radio addresses and radio news broadcasts, 1940–1945, relating to the Japanese attack on Pearl Harbor, the events leading up to it, and its aftermath. Includes facsimiles of pages from the *New York Times,* December 6–9, 1941.

1068

Gregory, Thomas T. C., 1878–1933.
Papers, 1918–1932. 3 ms. boxes, 1 album, 2 envelopes.
American lawyer; American Relief Administration Di-

rector for Central Europe, 1919. Correspondence, reports, memoranda, and printed matter, relating to the work of the American Relief Administration in Central Europe, the fall of the 1919 Bela Kun communist regime in Hungary, and the 1928 Presidential campaign of Herbert Hoover.

Register.

Gift, John M. Gregory, 1972.

1069

Grenfell, Elton Watters, 1903–

Papers, 1926–1969. 11½ ms. boxes, 5 binders (1 1. ft.).

Vice Admiral, U.S. Navy; Commander, Submarine Force, Pacific Fleet, 1956–1959; Commander, Submarine Force, Atlantic Fleet, 1960–1964. Correspondence, orders, drafts of speeches and photographs, relating to U.S. submarine operations during World War II and in the postwar period.

Gift, Mrs. E. W. Grenfell, 1976.

1070

Grewe, Wilhelm.

Memorandum (in German), ca. 1947. "Die Stellung des Christen zu den Grundfragen der Kuenftigen Voelkerordnung" (The Relation of Christians to the Fundamental Questions of the Future Order of Peoples). 1 folder.

Typescript (mimeographed).

Professor, University of Freiburg. Relates to the role of Christians in post-World War II reconstruction, especially in Germany.

1071

Griffin, Robert Allen, 1893–

Papers, 1942–1971. 12 ms. boxes, 3 envelopes.

American newspaper publisher; Deputy Chief, U.S. Economic Cooperation Administration Aid Mission to China, 1948–1949; Chief, U.S. Department of State Economic Mission to Southeast Asia, 1950. Correspondence, reports, memoranda, speeches and writings, photographs, and printed matter, relating to American technical and economic assistance missions to China and Southeast Asia.

Register.

Gift, R. A. Griffin, 1975.

1072

Grigorovich (N. I.)—photograph, n.d 1 envelope.

Depicts N. I. Grigorovich.

1073

Grimm, David Davidovich, b. 1864.

Papers (in Russian), 1919–1934. 4 ms. boxes.

Russian educator; Rector, Petersburg University, 1899–1910; Assistant Minister of Education, Russian Provisional Government, 1917. Correspondence, memoranda, press reports, printed and other material, relating to the Russian émigré community in Finland and other parts of Europe, and to the Russian Civil War.

Register.

Purchase, Nikita Struve, 1976.

1074

Grin, J.

Testimonial (in Dutch), 1913. "Proloog Opgedragen aan de Vrede-Vorstin de Hoog Welgeboren Vrouwe Baronesse Bertha von Suttner" (Prologue Dedicated to the Princess of Peace, the High Well-born Lady, Baroness Bertha von Suttner), 1 vol.

Holograph.

Relates to the Austrian pacifist Bertha von Suttner.

1075

Grivas (George) collection, 1955–1964. 1½ ms. boxes.

Writings, public statements and proclamations, pamphlets, leaflets, and correspondence, relating to the revolutionary activities on Cyprus of the Greek underground organization, EOKA, led by G. Grivas, 1955–1959. Includes original manuscript of *EOKA's Struggle* by G. Grivas.

Gift, Charles M. Foley, 1974.

1076

Gronskiĭ, Pavel Pavlovich, 1883–1937.

Study, n.d. "The Effects of the War upon the Central Government Institutions of Russia." 1 vol.

Typescript (carbon copy).

Relates to the political structure of Russia during World War I and the period of the 1917 Provisional Government.

1077

Grose, Ada Morse, b. 1874.

Papers, 1914–1918. 1 ms. box, 1 envelope, 1 album.

American pacifist; secretary to David Starr Jordan, President of Stanford University; participant, Henry Ford Peace Expedition and Neutral Conference for Continuous Mediation, Stockholm, 1916. Correspondence, memoranda, reports, passports, clippings, handwritten notes, certificate of citizen registration, peace badges, and photographs, relating to the peace movement during World War I.

1078

Grosjean, Paul, *collector*.

Newspaper clippings (in French), 1949. 1 folder.

Clippings from Belgian newspapers, relating to the activities of King Leopold III of Belgium during World War II, and to the future of the Belgian monarchy.

1079

Grossmann, Kurt Richard, 1897–1972.

Papers (in German and English), 1926–1973. 53 ms. boxes, 8 scrapbooks.

German-American author and journalist; President, German League for Human Rights, 1926–1933. Writings, correspondence, clippings, and serial issues, relating to Jewish refugees from Nazi Germany, postwar German and Austrian restitution payments to Jewish war victims, German-Israeli relations, the condition of Jews throughout the world, and civil liberties in the U.S. and Germany.

Purchase, Elsa Grossmann, 1975.

1080

Group of English Speaking Communists.
Leaflet, 1919. 1 folder.
Printed.
Bolshevik propaganda leaflet, distributed to American and British soldiers in Russia.

1081

Grubbs, Thomas W.
Letters, 1945–1949. 1 folder.
Typescript (mimeographed).
American Protestant minister. Relates to conditions at the Tule Lake Japanese relocation center, Newell, California, 1945, and to social conditions and the progress of Christianity in Japan, 1948–1949.
Gift, Clara Stoltenberg.

1082

Grzybowski, Kazimierz.
Study, n.d. "Soviet Public International Law Doctrines and Diplomatic Practice." 2 ms. boxes.
Typescript (mimeographed).
Gift, Robert Turner, 1974.

1083

Gubarev, P. D.
Report (in Russian), 1919. "Vremennoe Polozhenie ob Upravlenii Terskim Voĭskom" (Temporary Situation of the Command of the Tersk Forces). 1 folder.
Typescript.
Chairman, Main Circle, Tersk Forces. Relates to the Russian Civil War in the Tersk area.

1084

Guchkov (Aleksandr Ivanovich)—photographs, n.d. 1 envelope.
Depicts the Russian politician A. I. Guchkov.

1085

Guérard, Albert Léon, 1880–1959.
Papers (in French and English), 1942–1948. 5 ms. boxes.
American educator; broadcaster, U.S. Office of War Information, 1942–1945. Radio transcripts, memoranda, reports, correspondence and pamphlets, relating to broadcasts of the French section of the Office of War Information during World War II, and to the activities of the Committee to Frame a World Constitution.
Register.
Gift, A. L. Guérard, 1956.

1086

La Guerre d'Algérie (The War of Algeria).
Compilation of sound recordings (in French), n.d. 4 phonorecords.
Speeches and radio addresses, 1954–1962, relating to the Algerian War, its repercussions in France, the fall of the Fourth Republic and rise of the Fifth, the attempted military coup of 1961, and the Organisation de l'Armée Secrète.

1087

Gugenheim, Alice Aron, 1872–1955.
Papers (in French), 1914–1916. 1 ms. box.
Belgian relief worker during World War I. Diary notes, annotated sketches, postcards, photographs, clippings, memorabilia, and a biographical sketch, relating to the Commission for Relief in Belgium.
Gift, June Sanders, 1961.

1088

Guignebert (Jean Eugène)—photograph, n.d. 1 envelope.
Depicts the French author J. E. Guignebert.

1089

Guins, George C., b. 1887.
Papers (in Russian), 1918–1921. 1 ms. box, 1 envelope.
Russian educator; White Russian political leader during the Russian Civil War. Correspondence, writings, reports, and declarations, relating to the Russian Revolution and Civil War in the Siberian Far East, the activities of the anti-Bolshevik forces in Siberia, and the Japanese intervention.

1090

Gulyga, Ivan Emel'ianovich, b. 1857.
Memoirs (in Russian), 1923. "Vospominaniia Starago Plastuna o Velikoĭ Voĭnê, 1914–1917" (Reminiscences of an Old Scout about the Great War, 1914–1917). 1 vol.
Holograph.
Imperial Russian Army officer; Commanding Officer, Kubansko-Terskiĭ Plastanskiĭ Korpus, during World War I. Includes a biography (typewritten in Russian) of I. E. Gulyga by Karaushin.

1091

Gunn, Rex.
History, n.d. "Dear Enemy: The Story of Tokyo Rose." ½ ms. box.
Typescript (photocopy).
American journalist. Relates to the 1949 U.S. treason trial of Iva Toguri, accused of making "Tokyo Rose" propaganda broadcasts from Japan during World War II.

1092

Gunn, Selskar M.
Report, 1934. "China and the Rockefeller Foundation." 1 folder.
Typescript (mimeographed).
Relates to educational, scientific, technical and cultural assistance activities of the Rockefeller Foundation in China, and to proposals for future activities.

1093

Gurko, Vladimir Iosifovich, 1862–1927.
History (in Russian), n.d. *Cherty i Siluety Proshlago: Pravitel'stvo i Obshchestvennost' v Tsarstvovanie Nikolaiâ II* (Features and Figures of the Past: Government and Opinion in the Reign of Nicholas II). 1 ms. box.
Typescript.

Imperial Russian Government official. Translation published (Stanford, 1939). Russian manuscript includes two chapters omitted from published translation.

1094

Guthrie, Evelyn Stuart Williams.
Papers, 1921–1975. ½ ms. box.
Wife of Rear Admiral Harry A. Guthrie, U.S. Navy. Memoirs, correspondence, citations, memorabilia, clippings and photographs, relating to the naval career of H. A. Guthrie, shore life of Navy wives, conditions in Germany in the 1930s, the attack on Pearl Harbor, and Red Cross work in Hawaii during World War II.
Gift, E. S. W. Guthrie, 1974. Incremental gift, 1978.

1095

Guttmann, Ketty.
Memorandum (in German), n.d. "Los von Moskau! Erlebnisse einer Kommunistin" (Free of Moscow! Experiences of a Communist). 1 folder.
Typescript.
German communist. Relates to the disillusionment of K. Guttmann with Soviet rule in Russia.

1096

Hablan los Partidos (The Parties Speak).
Speeches (in Spanish), 1977. 7 phonorecords.
Campaign speeches by members of various political parties during the general election in Spain, June 1977.

1097

Haenisch, Konrad, 1876–1925.
Papers (in German), 1907–1915. ½ ms. box.
German socialist; Reichstag deputy; journalist. Correspondence and newspaper issues, relating to political conditions and the socialist movement in Germany and to the role of the Sozialdemokratische Partei Deutschlands in World War I.

1098

Hague International Peace Conference photographs, 1899–1907. 2 framed photographs.
Depicts delegates to the first and second Hague Peace Conferences, 1899 and 1907. Includes an identification chart for the second photograph.
Gift, Mrs. Otto Lorenz, 1960.

1099

Haile Selassie I, Emperor of Ethiopia, 1891–1975.
Study, 1936. *The Abyssinian Tragedy*. 1 folder.
Printed proofs.
Relates to the Italo-Ethiopian War.

1100

Haines, H. H.
Intelligence report, 1919. 1 folder.
Typescript.
Major, U.S. Army. Relates to Turkish port facilities on the Black Sea.

1101

Haislip, Wade H., 1889–1971.
Papers, 1941–1972. 2 ms. boxes, 1 envelope, 1 album.
General, U.S. Army; Commanding General, XV Corps, 1943–1945; Vice Chief of Staff of the Army, 1948–1949. Correspondence, reports, orders, awards, citations, photographs, clippings, and printed matter, relating to American military activities in the European Theater during World War II, and to postwar administration of the Army.
Register.
Gift, Mrs. W. H. Haislip, 1974.

1102

Halacsy, Andrew A.
Memoirs, n.d. 1 vol.
Typescript (photocopy).
Hungarian prisoner in Russia during World War II. Relates to conditions in Soviet forced labor camps.
Gift, A. A. Halacsy, 1965.

1103

Halbrook, Stephen P.
Study, 1973. "Anarchism and Marxism in the Twentieth Century Revolution." ½ ms. box.
Typescript.
Relates to the influence of anarchist and Marxist theories on the Russian and Chinese Revolutions, and on revolutionary movements throughout the world.
Gift, S. P. Halbrook, 1974.

1104

Halder, Franz, 1884–1972.
Letters (in German), 1965–1967, to Dennis Bartlett. 1 folder.
Typescript.
Colonel General, German Army; Chief of Staff, 1938-1941. Relates to military science, the German and American Armies, and the Vietnamese War.
Gift, D. Bartlett, 1976.

1105

Halhous, R.
Translation of almanac, 1921. "Almanac of Czechoslovak Army and Gendarmerie, 1921." 1 vol.
Typescript (carbon copy).
Translation of almanac by R. Halhous and K. Dolezal, published by Czechoslovak Ministry of National Defense.

1106

Hall, Charles L.
Papers, 1922–1923. 1 folder, 1 envelope.
Major, U.S. Army; American Relief Administration worker in Russia. Photographs and memorabilia, relating to famine conditions and American Relief Administration work in Orenburg and Samara, Russia.
Gift, C. L. Hall, 1964.

1107

Hall, Luella J., 1891–1973.
Papers, 1925–1971. 103 ms. boxes, 3 cu. ft. boxes.
American historian; Dean of Hartnell College, 1938–1953. Clippings, notes, writings, and correspondence, relating primarily to foreign relations between the U.S. and Morocco, 1776–1956, and to post-World War II political, social and economic conditions in Africa, especially North Africa. Includes correspondence with Kaiser Wilhelm II relating to the World War I war guilt question and a card index bibliography on the history of Morocco.
Gift, L. J. Hall, 1939. Subsequent increments.

1108

Hall, William Chapman.
Papers, 1917. 1 ms. box.
Member, Commission for Relief in Belgium, during World War I. Letters, a notebook and memorabilia, relating to the inspection of foodstuff distributed by the Commission for Relief in Belgium, and to the departure of American members of the commission from Belgium upon the entry of the U.S. into World War I.
Gift, W. C. Hall, 1959.

1109

Haller, Stanislaw, b. 1872.
Translation of report, 1926. "Warsaw Events of May 12 to May 15, 1926." 1 vol.
Typescript (carbon copy).
Relates to the coup of Jozef Pilsudski. Translation of "Wypadki Warszawskie od 12 do 15 Maja 1926 r."

1110

Hallgarten, George Wolfgang Felix, 1901–1975.
Papers (in German and English), 1912–1975. 39 ms. boxes, 2 microfilm reels.
German-American historian. Correspondence, diaries, speeches and writings, photocopies of government documents, propaganda leaflets, and printed matter, relating to European diplomacy, imperialism, psychology of national socialism and totalitarianism, U.S. and German propaganda during World War II, and the arms race, 1870–1970. Includes drafts of a study by G. W. F. Hallgarten, entitled "Imperialismus vor 1914" (Imperialism before 1914).
Register.
Diaries and private correspondence (boxes 30-39) are closed until May 22, 2000.
Gift, Katherine Drew Hallgarten, 1977.

1111

Halonen, George.
Miscellaneous papers, 1918–1922. 1 ms. box.
Karelian Workers' Commune representative in the U.S., 1918–1919. Correspondence, writings, reports, and printed matter, relating to activities of the Finnish Information Bureau in the U.S. in publicizing and seeking U.S. recognition of the Soviet Government of Fin-

land. Includes writings and correspondence of Santeri Nuorteva, head of the Finnish Information Bureau.
Preliminary inventory.
Gift, G. Halonen, 1950.

1112

Halpern, Joel M., *collector*.
Grant applications, 1968–1969. 1 ms. box.
Photocopy.
Grant applications to the Southeast Asia Development Advisory Group of the Asia Society, relating to proposed research projects on Indonesia, the Philippines, Malaya, and other parts of Southeast Asia.
Closed until June 1990.
Gift, J. M. Halpern, 1976.

1113

Halsey, William Frederick, 1882–1959.
Proclamations, 1944. 1 folder.
Typescript (mimeographed).
Allied Military Governor of Dutch Timor and Portuguese Timor. Relates to Allied occupation of Dutch Timor and Portuguese Timor.

1114

Hamilton, Maxwell McGaughey, 1896–1957.
Papers, 1916–1957. 4 ms. boxes.
American diplomat; Chief, Division of Far Eastern Affairs, U.S. Department of State, 1937–1943; Ambassador to Finland, 1945–1947. Reports, memoranda, correspondence, lectures, press releases, and printed matter, relating to U.S. foreign policy toward China, Japan, the Soviet Union and Finland. Includes a report and series of interviews with Japanese, Chinese, and other government officials concerning economic and political conditions in Japan and Manchuria, 1933–1934.
Register.
Gift, Mrs. Maxwell M. Hamilton.

1115

Hamilton, Minard, 1891–1976.
Papers, 1913–1930. 1 ms. box.
Captain, U.S. Army; executive officer, American Relief Administration operations in the Baltic States, 1919. Diary and correspondence, relating to activities of the 313th Machine Gun Battalion in France during World War I, food distribution by the American Relief Administration in the Baltic States, and civil aviation in China, 1929–1930.
Gift, Albert H. Hamilton, 1977.

1116

Hammarskjöld (Dag)—photograph, 1955. 1 envelope.
Depicts D. Hammarskjöld, Secretary-General of the United Nations, 1953–1961.

1117

Hammerstein, Ludwig von, 1919–
Memorandum (in German), 1945. "Bericht ueber meine Teilnahme am 20. Juli 1944" (Report on My Participation on July 20, 1944). 1 folder.
Typescript.
Relates to the plot to assassinate Adolf Hitler.

1118

Hammon, W. P., 1854–1938.
Papers, 1915–1930. 3 ms. boxes.
American businessman; associated with Yuba Manufacturing Company, San Francisco. Correspondence, reports, contracts, shipping lists, specifications for dredging equipment, annotated maps, and photographs, relating to mining operations in China, Siberia, Korea, Malaya, and Poland.
Preliminary inventory.
Gift, W. P. Hammon, Jr., 1972. Subsequent increments.

1119

Hammond, Lansing V., *collector.*
L. V. Hammond collection on World War II, 1900–1945. 2 file boxes (1 l. ft.).
Photographs and drawings, depicting British, Russian, Japanese, German, American and other ships and airplanes from World War II. Includes a section of photographs illustrating the history of aviation.
Gift, L. V. Hammond, 1957.

1120

Hand, E. R., *collector.*
E. R. Hand collection on the Philippine Islands, n.d.
Artifacts from the Philippine Islands, including knives, spears and a gong.
Preliminary inventory.
Gift, Mrs. E. R. Hand, 1973.

1121

Hanford, Edwin T.
Papers, 1917–1918. 1 folder.
Member, American Protective League. Correspondence and printed matter, relating to activities of the American Protective League, a private patriotic organization, relating to subversive activities in the U.S. during World War I.
Gift, Mrs. Wallace D. Cathcart, 1976.

1122

Hankow, China.
Miscellaneous records (in Chinese), 1946–1949. 1 ms. box.
Relates to the confiscation of Japanese properties by the Chinese Nationalist Government, and to administration of Hankow under the Kuomintang during the Chinese Nationalist Government.
Purchase, 1974.

1123

Hanna, Hugh S.
Letter, 1921. 1 folder.
Typewritten transcript.
Encloses a copy (typewritten), of a letter by Ernest Kletsch, Chief of the Division of Files and Information of the U.S. National War Labor Board during World War I, relating to the compilation of minutes of executive sessions of the National War Labor Board, 1918–1919.

1124

Hanna, Paul L.
Correspondence, 1939, with British Government agencies. 1 folder.
Typewritten transcript.
American historian. Relates to the attitude of the British Government toward the creation of a Jewish state in Palestine in 1917.

1125

Hanna, Paul Robert, 1902–
Miscellaneous papers, 1941–1977. 4 ms. boxes.
American educator; Professor of Education, Stanford University, 1935–1967; Director, Stanford International Development Education Center, 1963–1968; Senior Research Fellow, Hoover Institution on War, Revolution and Peace, 1974– . Bibliographies, books, periodical articles, and speeches, relating to international education.
Gift, P. R. Hanna, 1977.

1126

Hanssen, Hans Peter, 1862–1936.
Translation of diaries, 1955. *Diary of a Dying Empire.* 1½ ms. boxes.
Typescript.
Member of the German Reichstag from Northern Schleswig, 1906–1918; Danish Temporary Minister for South Jutland Affairs, 1919–1920. Relates to political conditions in Germany during World War I, 1914–1918. Originally published as *Fra Krigstiden* (Copenhagen, 1925). Translation by Oscar Osburn Winther, edited by Ralph H. Lutz, Mary Schofield and O. O. Winther, published in Bloomington by Indiana University Press, 1955.

1127

Hard, William.
Transcript of radio broadcast, 1929. 1 folder.
Typescript (mimeographed).
American journalist. Relates to the Kellogg-Briand Pact and U.S. intervention in Latin America.

1128

Hardt, Fred B.
Letters (in German), 1914–1915. ½ ms. box.
Typescript (mimeographed).
German Kriegs-Pressebuero official, Munich. Letters to F. B. Hardt from various Italian correspondents, relating to political events and public opinion in Italy during the period of its neutrality in World War I.

1129

Harms, Meint.
Letter (in German), 1950. 1 folder.
Typescript.
Relates to historical and economic theory.

1130

Harriman (W. A.) and Company, New York.
Agreement (in Russian and English), 1925. 1 folder.
Printed.
Agreement between the Tchitouri Manganese Exporting Society (Tchemo) and W. A. Harriman and Company. Relates to mining rights in Georgia (Transcaucasia).
Gift, Boris Stanfield, 1976.

1131

Harris, David, 1900–1975.
Papers, 1929–1967. 3 ms. boxes, 15 card file boxes (5 l. ft.), 4 envelopes, 8 medals.
American historian; Associate Chief, Central European Affairs Division, U.S. Department of State, 1943–1947; Professor of History, Stanford University, 1930–1966. Correspondence, speeches and writings, reports, research notes, newsletters, lists, and printed matter, relating to Emperor Napoleon I of France, the Balkan crisis of 1875–1878, international affairs in Europe during the interwar period, and reconstruction of Germany and Austria following World War II.
Register.
Gift, D. Harris, 1967. Incremental gift, Katherine Pinkham Harris, 1975.

1132

Harris, Ernest Lloyd, 1870–1946.
Papers, 1918–1921. 6 ms. boxes.
American consular official; Consul General, Irkutsk, Siberia, 1918–1921. Reports, memoranda, and correspondence, relating to the Russian Civil War in Siberia, the Czechoslovakian Legion, political and economic conditions in Siberia, and U.S. policy in Siberia.
Register.
Gift, Mrs. E. L. Harris, 1955.

1133

Harris, Gladys, *collector*.
Photographs, 1919. 1 envelope.
Depicts the headquarters of the American Expeditionary Forces in Siberia, and officers of the Japanese and Czechoslovak forces in Vladivostok.
Gift, G. Harris, 1978.

1134

Harris, Herbert.
Reports, 1956. 1 folder.
Typescript (mimeographed).
American public opinion pollster. Relates to the results of a study of American public opinion regarding the United Nations.

1135

Harris, Lee V., 1897–1969.
Papers, 1944–1955. 2 ms. boxes, 8 maps.
Colonel, U.S. Army; member, Marshall Mission to China, 1946–1947; U.S. Senior Military Attaché, Indochina, 1950–1952. Writings, correspondence, photographs, maps and memorabilia, relating to U.S. military operations in China during World War II, to the Chinese Civil War, and to the Indochinese War.
Preliminary inventory.
Gift, Mrs. L. V. Harris, 1969.

1136

Hart, B. R., *collector*.
Photographs, 1929. 1 envelope.
Depicts the square-rigged sailing ship *Star of Alaska*.
Gift, B. R. Hart, 1929.

1137

Hartigan, John Doane, 1890–1959.
Papers (in English and German), 1909–1958. 33 ms. boxes.
American relief worker in Europe, 1919 and 1939–1941; member, Saar Plebiscite Commission, 1934–1935; member, U.S. Military Government in Austria, 1945–1946. Correspondence, reports, memoranda, writings, pamphlets, clippings, photographs, and posters, relating to relief work during the two world wars, the Saar plebiscite of 1934–1935, the Allied military government in Austria after World War II, and the organization of international trade fairs. Includes correspondence with Herbert Hoover.
Preliminary inventory.
Gift, J. D. Hartigan, 1946. Incremental gift, 1959.

1138

Hartley, Livingston.
Essay, 1950. "UN and AU." 1 folder.
Typescript.
Relates to the functions of the United Nations and of a proposed Atlantic Union. Written by L. Hartley and Clarence Streit.

1139

Hartmann, Waldemar.
Letter, 1933, to Alfred Rosenberg. 1 folder.
Typescript.
Relates to German cultural and propaganda work in the U.S.
Gift, Detlev Auvermann, 1973.

1140

Harvard University. Russian Research Center.
Notices (in Russian and Ukrainian), 1950. 1 folder.
Printed.
Requests the cooperation of refugees from the Soviet Union in a refugee interview project undertaken by the Russian Research Center.

1141

Hasl, Franz Joseph.
Miscellaneous papers, 1916–1919. ½ ms. box.
Austrian author. Memorandum, entitled "Universal Peace," 1916; letter to Woodrow Wilson, 1919; and photograph of F. J. Hasl.

1142

Hass, Rudolf.
Papers (in German), 1936–1937. 1 folder.
German citizen living in Venezuela. Correspondence with the German Government, relating to the expropriation by the Venezuelan Government of the plantation of R. Hass, and to his efforts to enlist the aid of the German Government in securing its return.

1143

Hasselblatt, Werner.
Memorandum (in German), 1944. "Verordnung ueber die Schutzangehoerigen des Reiches" (Regulation Regarding Minorities under the Protection of the Reich). 1 folder.
Typescript.
Chairman, Subcommittee for the Right of Minorities in Germany, Akademie fuer Deutsches Recht. Relates to the rights of non-German nationalities in Germany.

1144

Hastings, William, *collector*.
Newspaper clippings, 1942–1943. 4 ms. boxes.
Clippings from Philippine newspapers, relating to conditions in the Philippines under Japanese occupation during World War II.
Gift, W. Hastings, 1970.

1145

Hatfield, Mark Odom, 1922–
Thesis, 1948. "Herbert Hoover and Labor: Policies and Attitudes, 1897–1928." 1 folder.
Typescript (photocopy).
American politician; Governor of Oregon, 1959–1967; U.S. Senator from Oregon, 1967–   . Relates to the views of President Herbert Hoover on the labor movement. Master's thesis, Stanford University.

1146

Havemann, Ingeborg.
Biographical notes (in English and German), n.d. 1 folder.
Typescript and holograph.
Relates to Arvid and Mildred Harnack, members of the anti-Nazi Rote Kapelle resistance group in Germany during World War II.

1147

Hawaii University, *collector*.
Photographs, 1944–1945. 28 envelopes.
Depicts World War II campaigns in France and Germany, activities of U.S. troops, and Allied military and civilian leaders.

1148

Hawkins, Sylvia Kennedy, *collector*.
Letters, 1941–1945. 1 vol.
Typescript (carbon copy).
From American servicemen in the European and Pacific Theaters during World War II, to relatives and friends in the U.S., relating to war experiences.

1149

Haws, R. Calvert.
Papers, 1920–1932. ½ ms. box, 1 oversize package (½ l. ft.).
American journalist; publicity director for Western states, Republican Presidental campaign, 1932. Correspondence, reports, printed matter, memorabilia and photographs, relating to the Presidential campaign of 1932, and to U.S.-Japanese foreign relations.
Preliminary inventory.
Gift, Mrs. R. C. Haws, 1970. Subsequent increments.

1150

Hayama.
Translation of article, 1934. "The Fight for the General Line in the Japanese Communist Party." 1 folder.
Typescript.
Relates to the history of, and current situation in, the Japanese Communist Party. Original article published in *Sovremennaîa ÎAponiîa* (Present Day Japan), edited by P. Mif and G. Voitinsky (Moscow, 1934).

1151

Hayes, Elinor, *collector*.
Memoranda, 1942. 1 ms. box, 1 envelope.
Teletyped.
Sent to the *Santa Barbara (California) News-Press* by the national wire services and the U.S. Office of Censorship, containing instructions to editors for censorship of war stories.
Gift, E. Hayes, 1972.

1152

Hays, Alice Newman.
Papers, 1940–1945. 1 ms. box, 1 scrapbook.
Letters written to A. N. Hays, and printed matter, relating to the internment of Japanese-Americans in relocation centers during World War II.
Preliminary inventory.
Gift, A. N. Hays, 1951.

1153

Head, Sydney Warren.
Papers, 1942–1946. 1 scrapbook.
Technical Sergeant, U.S. Army, during World War II. Photographs and miscellanea, relating to the condition of troops stationed in the U.S. and Hawaii during World War II.
Gift, S. W. Head, 1969.

1154

Healy, James Augustine, 1891–1975, *collector*.
    J. A. Healy collection on Ireland, 1896–1966. 21 ms. boxes, 24 scrapbooks, 1 motion picture film, 1 envelope, 1 framed photograph.
    Clippings, pamphlets, correspondence, and newspaper issues, relating to political and economic conditions in Ireland. Includes a 16 mm film, "The Irish Rising, 1916," produced for television by George Morrison, and correspondence between Herbert Hoover and J. A. Healy.
    Preliminary inventory.
    Gift, J. A. Healy, 1942. Subsequent increments.

1155

Heiden, Dimitri F., Graf.
    Memoirs (in Russian), n.d. ½ ms. box.
    Typescript and holograph.
    Russian aristocrat. Relates to the involvement of Russia in World War I and the Russian Revolution and Civil War.
    Register.
    Gift, Sophie Isakow, 1975.

1156

Heilbron, Louis H., *collector*.
    Louis H. Heilbron collection on national socialism, n.d.
    German national socialist memorabilia, including two daggers, a bayonet sheath, and a hunting knife.
    Gift, L. H. Heilbron, 1976.

1157

Heiler, Friedrich.
    Sermons (in German), 1943–1945. 1 folder.
    Typescript (some mimeographed).
    German theologian active in the anti-Nazi movement. Delivered in Marburg, Germany.

1158

Heimlich, William F.
    Writings, 1974. 1 folder.
    Typescript (photocopy).
    Colonel, U.S. Air Force. Memoir, entitled "The Eagle and the Bear: Berlin, 1945–1950," and a letter to Eleanor Lansing Dulles, both relating to the Allied occupation of Berlin in 1945.
    Gift, Frank E. Mason, 1974. Incremental gift, W. F. Heimlich, 1978.

1159

Heims, Steven P., *collector*.
    Steven P. Heims collection, 1944–1946. 1 folder.
    Orders, instructions, and printed matter, relating to the civil administration and relief of the Philippine Islands, 1944, war crime trials in the Pacific, and the administration of government in Japan following World War II.
    A personnel file closed until 2000.
    Gift, S. P. Heims, 1974.

1160

Helphand, Alexander, 1867–1924.
    Receipt (in German), 1915. 1 folder.
    Holograph (photocopy).
    Russian-German socialist. Receipt for funds from the German Government for furtherance of revolutionary activities in Russia.
    Gift, Witold S. Sworakowski, 1978.

1161

Henderson, Loy Wesley, 1892–
    Memoirs, n.d. 3 ms. boxes.
    Typescript (photocopy).
    American diplomat; Secretary of Embassy to the Soviet Union, 1934–1938; Assistant Chief, Division of European Affairs, U.S. Department of State, 1938–1942; Director, Near Eastern and African Affairs, U.S. Department of State, 1945–1948; and Ambassador to India, 1948–1951. Relates to American Red Cross relief work in Russia and the Baltic States, 1919–1920, and in Germany, 1920–1921, and to U.S. foreign policy and U.S. relations with Ireland and the Soviet Union between the two world wars.
    Closed during the lifetime of L. W. Henderson.
    Gift, L. W. Henderson, 1977.

1162

Henle, Raymond, 1899–1974, *collector*.
    Raymond Henle coin collection, 1896–1924. 5 coins.
    Four silver dollars, dated 1896, 1922, 1923, and 1924; and one coin from the Jamestown Exposition, 1907.
    Gift, estate of R. Henle, 1976.

1163

Henry, Charles Delano.
    Letter, 1898, to F. W. McFarland. 1 folder.
    Holograph.
    Father-in-law of Herbert Hoover.
    Gift, Mrs. Willis H. Rich, 1967.

1164

Henry, John M., *collector*.
    Photographs, 1957. 1 envelope.
    Depicts the blacksmith shop of Jesse Hoover, father of President Herbert Hoover. Governor of Iowa Herschel Loveless is shown looking at blacksmith tools inside the shop.
    Gift, J. M. Henry, 1957.

1165

Herbert, Sidney.
    Letters received, 1926. 1 folder.
    Typescript and holograph.
    Relates to the British general strike of 1926. Written by unidentified individuals in Great Britain.

1166

Herbert Hoover Oral History Program.
    Transcripts of interviews, 1966–1972. 315 interviews.
    Typescript.

Relates to Herbert Hoover, President of the U.S., 1929–1933. Recollections of political leaders, businessmen, military figures, journalists, writers, physicians, secretaries, research aides, friends and associates of Herbert Hoover. Interviews sponsored by the Institute for Social Science Research and the Herbert Hoover Presidential Library Association on behalf of the Herbert Hoover Presidential Library and the Hoover Institution on War, Revolution, and Peace.

Register.

A few transcripts are closed for various periods of time.

1167

Herbert Hoover plaque, n.d.

Commemorates Herbert Hoover, President of the U.S., 1929–1933.

Gift, Mary B. Black, 1973.

1168

Herbert Hoover Presidential Library, West Branch, Iowa.

Bibliography, n.d. 2 ms. boxes.

Typescript (photocopy).

Lists clippings, pamphlets and other ephemeral publications, 1879–1975, by or about Herbert Hoover. Arranged chronologically.

Exchange, Herbert Hoover Presidential Library, 1978.

1169

Herbits, Stephen E., 1942–

Papers, 1966–1974. 52½ ms. boxes, 1 binder.

Special Assistant to the U.S. Assistant Secretary of Defense (Manpower and Reserve Affairs). Correspondence, writings, reports, memoranda, notes, and printed matter, relating to proposals for an all-volunteer armed force, Congressional action on the proposals, and evaluation of the new volunteer system in operation.

Closed until processed.

Gift, S. E. Herbits, 1975.

1170

Herman, Raphael.

Letter, 1918, to Woodrow Wilson. 1 folder.

Typewritten transcript.

Relates to proposals by R. Herman for the basis of a peace settlement to end World War I, especially regarding territorial questions.

1171

Heroys, Alexandre.

Memorandum (in French), 1918. "Situation Politique et Stratégique sur le Front Roumain et en Russie en 1917 et 1918" (Political and Strategic Situation on the Romanian Front and in Russia in 1917 and 1918). 1 folder.

Typescript.

Relates to Russo-Romanian military activities during World War I and to the Russian Revolution.

Gift, A. Heroys.

1172

Heroys, Boris Vladimirovich.

Papers (in Russian), 1917–1920. 8 ms. boxes.

General, Imperial Russian Army; Chief, Special Military Mission to London sent by General Nikolaĭ Ĭudenich, White Russian military commander, during the Russian Civil War. Correspondence, reports, communiqués and printed matter, relating to the Russian Revolution, anti-Bolshevik activities in Northwest Russia, 1919–1920, and liaison between the White Russian forces and the British War Office.

Preliminary inventory.

Gift, B. V. Heroys, 1925.

1173

Herr, Horace H.

Papers, 1924–1925. 1 folder, 3 envelopes.

American journalist. Diary, photographs, and a memoir entitled "Face to Face With the Mohammedan Menace in the Maghreb," relating to social conditions in Morocco, Algeria and Tunisia.

Gift, Douglas Stiehl, 1976.

1174

Herrera, Noe, *collector*.

Miscellany, n.d. 2 albums.

Photographs and magazine illustrations, depicting V. I. Lenin and Iosif Stalin.

Gift, N. Herrera, 1974.

1175

Herrington, Dorothy, *collector*.

Miscellany, 1954–1959. 1 folder.

Brochure (printed), prepared by the Bohemian Club, commemorating the eightieth birthday of Herbert Hoover, 1954; and menu (printed), for a luncheon for Nikita Khrushchev on the Southern Pacific Railroad, 1959.

Gift, D. Herrington, 1974.

1176

Herrmann, Egon, 1899– , *defendant*.

Trial transcript (in German), 1949. 1 binder.

Typescript.

Relates to the trial of Egon Herrmann and six others in Munich for disturbance of the peace and slander, in connection with protests of refugees against the administration of the Bavarian Secretariat of Refugee Affairs.

1177

Herron, George Davis, 1862–1925.

Papers, 1916–1927. 26½ ms. boxes, 16 vols., 4 scrapbooks.

American clergyman and lecturer; unofficial adviser to Woodrow Wilson, President of the U.S. Correspondence, interviews, lectures, essays, notes and clippings, relating to the League of Nations, territorial questions, prisoners of war, and other political and economic issues

at the Paris Peace Conference.
Preliminary inventory.
Gift, G. D. Herron, 1922. Subsequent increments.

1178

Hertmanowicz, Joseph John.
Papers, 1916–1941. ½ ms. box.
Official, Lithuanian Council of Chicago. Writings and speeches, memoranda, and resolutions, relating to the history, economy, and foreign policy of Lithuania and to the movement for Lithuanian independence. Includes appeals from Lithuanian-American organizations to the U.S. government urging recognition of the independence of Lithuania.
Preliminary inventory.
Gift, J. J. Hertmanowicz.

1179

Hervey, Harcourt, 1892–
Papers, 1937–1955. 1 folder.
Photocopy.
Brigadier General, U.S. Army. Personnel records and correspondence (typewritten), relating to the career of H. Hervey in the U.S. Army and in the California National Guard.

1180

Herz, Martin Florian, 1917– , *collector*.
Propaganda leaflets (in English and Vietnamese), 1967–1969. 1½ ms. boxes.
North Vietnamese and Viet Cong propaganda directed at American soldiers in Vietnam.
Inventory.
Gift, M. F. Herz, 1978.

1181

Heydrich (Reinhard)—photographs, 1942. 1 album.
Depicts the funeral of R. Heydrich (1904–1942), Reich Protector for Bohemia and Moravia.
Purchase, New York University Medical Center, 1973.

1182

Heyworth-Dunne, James, d. 1974.
Papers (in Arabic, Persian, Turkish, German, French and English), ca. 1860–1949. 7 ms. boxes.
Senior Lecturer in Arabic, School of Oriental Studies, University of London. Theses, studies, notes, writings and correspondence, relating to the history, philosophy, literature, education and religion of Egypt, the Arab world, and Turkey.
Purchase, J. Heyworth-Dunne, 1949.

1183

Hiestand, John, *collector*.
J. Hiestand collection on psychological warfare, 1942–1945. 1 ms. box, 2 scrapbooks.
Letters, conference proceedings, transcripts of radio broadcasts, propaganda leaflets, and printed matter, relating primarily to the work of the U.S. Office of War Information and the U.S. Army Psychological Warfare Branch in the Southwest Pacific, 1944–1945.
Preliminary inventory.
Gift, J. Hiestand, 1972.

1184

Higgins, Frank Henry, 1890–1973.
Papers, 1917–1959. 2 ms. boxes, 13 scrapbooks, 2 envelopes.
U.S. Assistant Secretary of the Army, 1954–1959. Correspondence, photographs, printed matter and memorabilia, relating to U.S. defense policy.
Preliminary inventory.
Gift, F. H. Higgins, 1969.

1185

High, Stanley, 1895–1961.
Speech transcript, ca. 1944. "The Road to Victory." 1 folder.
Typescript.
Editor, *Reader's Digest*. Relates to the role of the U.S. in post-World War II reconstruction.

1186

Hill, George Alexander, 1892–
Papers, n.d. 1 folder.
British secret service agent. Memoirs (typewritten), entitled "Reminiscences of Four Years with N. K. V. D.," relating to Anglo-Soviet secret service relations during World War II; and radio broadcast transcripts, entitled "Go Spy the Land," relating to British intelligence activities in Russia, Turkey and the Balkans, 1917–1918.
May not be quoted without permission of G. A. Hill.
Gift, G. A. Hill, 1968.

1187

Hill, Jim Dan, 1897–
Correspondence, 1956, with university libraries. 1 folder.
Typescript (photocopy).
Major General, U.S. National Guard; author of *The Minute Man in Peace and War: A History of the National Guard* (Harrisburg, Pa.: Stackpole, 1964). Relates to the existence of unpublished theses on the militia and National Guards of various states.

1188

Hill, Paul Albert, 1896–1968, *collector*.
P. A. Hill collection on Woodrow Wilson, ca. 1919–1959. 18 ms. boxes.
Letters from famous American and foreign statesmen, authors and scholars, relating to their evaluations of the historical significance of Woodrow Wilson, President of the U.S., 1913–1921.
Preliminary inventory.
Gift, Viola Koch, 1969.

1189

Hiller, Stanley
Papers, 1940. 1 oversize box (½ l. ft.).
Chairman, Willkie Workers League, 1940. Correspon-

dence, campaign literature, and memorabilia, relating to the activities of the Willkie Workers League in promoting the campaign of Wendell Willkie in the U.S. Presidential election of 1940.

Gift, estate of S. Hiller, 1971.

1190

Hillhouse, Joseph Newton, *collector*.

Photographs, 1917–1918. 1 album.

Depicts activities of the American Expeditionary Force in France during World War I.

Gift, Mrs. J. N. Hillhouse, 1964.

1191

Hillman, Sidney, 1887–1946.

Letter, 1923, to Mrs. M. S. Alderton. 1 folder.

Typescript.

American labor leader; President, Russian-American Industrial Corporation. Solicits stock purchases in the Russian-American Industrial Corporation, a company investing in Soviet industrialization.

1192

Hills, Carla Anderson, 1934–

Papers, 1970–1977. 141 cu. ft. boxes.

U.S. Assistant Attorney General, 1974–1975; Secretary of Housing and Urban Development, 1975–1977. Correspondence, reports, speeches, and printed matter, relating to community planning and development, the housing industry during the Presidency of Gerald R. Ford, civil law suits involving the Government, and the Richard M. Nixon Presidency.

Consult the archivist for restrictions.

Gift, C. A. Hills, 1977.

1193

Hilton (Edna M.)—photograph, 1918. 1 envelope.

Depicts E. M. Hilton, member of the U.S. Food Administration and American Relief Administration.

1194

Himmler, Heinrich, 1900–1945.

Papers (in German), 1914–1944. 15 ms. boxes, 2 albums, 5 microfilm reels, 24 phonotapes.

Reichsfuehrer SS und Chef der Deutschen Polizei, 1934–1945. Diaries, 1914–1924; photographs; photocopies and microfilm of correspondence, reports and memoranda from the office files of the Personal Staff of H. Himmler, 1942–1944 (originals in the German Bundesarchiv); and recordings of speeches by H. Himmler, 1940–1944; relating to national socialism in Germany, and activities of the German police and Schutzstaffel during World War II.

Preliminary inventory.

Diaries purchased from an anonymous source, 1956. Photocopies and microfilm made from originals at the U.S. Berlin Document Center.

1195

Hindenburg, Paul von, 1847–1934.

Letter (in German), 1925, to Grand Duke von Mecklenburg. 1 folder.

Typescript.

President of Germany, 1925–1934. Relates to the election of P. von Hindenburg as President.

1196

Hines, Walker Downer, 1870–1934.

Papers, 1919–1927. 16 ms. boxes.

American lawyer and railway executive; Inter-Allied Arbitrator of Questions Pertaining to River Shipping, 1920–1921. Correspondence, memoranda, and reports, relating to questions of navigation rights on the Rhine, Danube, Elbe, Oder, and Vistula Rivers, restitution of captured ships, and reparations for war damage to river shipping, after World War I.

Preliminary inventory.

Gift, James A. Logan.

1197

Hinkel, Hans, 1901–

Speeches and writings (in German), 1924–1944. 1 folder.

Typescript.

German national socialist leader; President, Gesellschaft fuer Deutsche Kultur. Relates to national socialism and to German culture.

1198

Hinshaw, David, 1882–1953.

Book draft, 1950. *Herbert Hoover, American Quaker.* 1 folder.

Typescript.

Published by Farrar, Straus (New York, 1950).

1199

Hirsch, Betty, b. 1873.

Memoirs, 1943–1944. 1 folder.

Typescript.

German social worker. Relates to the rehabilitation of German veterans blinded during World War I.

1200

"Historique de la 2me Section du Ministère de la Défense Nationale du 23 Octobre 1942 au 15 Novembre 1943 et de la 2me Direction du Ministère de la Défense Nationale du 16 Novembre 1943 au 10 Septembre 1944" (History of the Second Section of the Ministry of National Defense from October 23, 1942 to November 15, 1943, and of the Second Directory of the Ministry of National Defense from November 16, 1943 to September 10, 1944).

History (in French), 1944. 1 vol.

Typescript (photocopy).

Relates to the Belgian Ministry of National Defense during the German occupation in World War II, and to the Belgian resistance movement.

1201

Hitler, Adolf, 1889–1945.

Miscellaneous papers (in German), 1879–1956. 3 ms. boxes, 2 file boxes, 4 envelopes, 1 appointment book, 1 tile portrait, 5 phonotapes.

German Chancellor and Fuehrer, 1933–1945. Type-

written drafts of two speeches by him, one relating to the shooting of Ernst Roehm and others, 1934, and the other delivered at a Nazi party convention, 1937; his appointment book, March to June 1943; photographs and a ceramic tile portrait of him; lists of books in his library; a copy of his death certificate; recordings of two speeches by him, 1937 and 1941; and miscellaneous office files of the German Imperial Chancellery, 1879–1945.
Preliminary inventory.
Gifts, W. M. de Majo, 1957; Bradley F. Smith, 1973; Hartford, Connecticut Public Library; U.S. Library of Congress.

1202
Hitler, Adolf, 1889–1945—assassination attempt, July 20, 1944—clippings (in German and English), 1946–1965. 1 folder.
Printed.
Relates to the attempted assassination of Adolf Hitler on July 20, 1944.

1203
Hitoon, Serge E.
Memoir, 1936. "From Aral Sea to the Western Turkestan." 1 vol.
Typescript.
White Russian Army officer. Relates to the Russian Civil War in Mongolia.

1204
Hobson, J. W.
Charts, 1948. "The Hulton Readership Survey, 1948." 1 roll.
Printed.
Relates to findings of a poll on newspaper and magazine reading habits of the British public, broken down by region, sex, age, social class, and other characteristics. Compiled by J. W. Hobson and H. Henry.

1205
Hodge (John R.)—photographs, n.d. 1 envelope.
Depicts Lieutenant General J. R. Hodge, U.S. Army.

1206
Hodges, Charles, d. 1964, *collector*.
Photographs, 1939–1945. 53 envelopes.
Depicts World War II scenes in Europe, North Africa, the Far East, Southeast Asia, the Pacific Islands, India, and the Aleutian Islands, diplomatic conferences, including the Potsdam Conference, 1945, and the Casablanca Conference, 1943, civilian and military leaders, and maps illustrating military campaigns.
Preliminary inventory.
Gift, Mrs. C. Hodges, 1964.

1207
Hohenlohe-Waldenburg-Schillingsfuerst, Stephanie, Prinzessin zu, 1896?–1972.
Papers, 1914–1972. 4 ms. boxes.
Confidant and intermediary of Lord Rothermere, owner of the *Daily Mail* (London), and Adolf Hitler.

Correspondence, memoranda, telegrams, clippings, and printed matter, relating to Anglo-German relations in the 1930s, political developments in Hungary, and personal and literary activities of Princess Hohenlohe.
Preliminary inventory.
Purchase, Franz Hohenlohe, 1977.

1208
Holden, Frank Harvey.
Miscellaneous papers, 1916–1923. 1 folder, 1 envelope.
American Relief Administration worker in France and Russia, 1919–1923. Letter written by F. H. Holden in Moscow in 1923, relating to Russian operations of the American Relief Administration; and photographs of the German cruiser *Wolf*, its crew, and ships encountered and sunk by it during its raiding cruise in World War I, 1916–1917.
Gift, F. H. Holden, 1956. Incremental gift, Miriam Miller, 1977.

1209
Holland Shall Rise Again.
Radio program, ca. 1944–1945. 1 phonorecord.
Relates to the anticipated Allied invasion of the Netherlands. Produced by the Netherlands Information Bureau in New York and narrated by Bernard Dudley.

1210
Hollingsworth, Sidney Pierce.
Papers, 1941–1969. 2 ms. boxes.
American writer. Writings, clippings, and miscellanea, relating to historical trends in the twentieth century, public relations and the social order, the League of Nations and World Court, and a variety of other historical themes.
Gift and deposit, S. P. Hollingsworth, 1956. Subsequent increments.

1211
Holman, Emile.
Papers, 1914–1915. 1 folder, 1 envelope.
Member, Commission for Relief in Belgium, 1914–1915. Draft of a speech (typewritten) delivered at Oxford University in 1915, relating to the relief work of the Commission for Relief in Belgium; and photographs of refugees and war damage in Greece, Bulgaria and Turkey at the end of the Balkan Wars of 1912–1913, and of the visit of David Starr Jordan, E. Holman and others to the war site, 1914.
Gift, E. Holman, 1963.

1212
Holsti, Rudolf, 1881–1945.
Papers, 1930–1944. 1 ms. box.
Finnish diplomat; Foreign Minister of Finland, 1919–1922 and 1936–1938. Writings and correspondence, relating to Finnish independence, foreign relations, and political conditions.

1213

Holtzmann, Robert, b. 1883.

Papers (in German), 1919–1943. 6 ms. boxes, 3 microfilm reels, 4 envelopes.

Major, German Army; business manager, Tannenbergbund. Correspondence, writings, pamphlets, leaflets, newspaper issues, clippings, and photographs, relating primarily to the activities of the Tannenbergbund, a right-wing German political organization, active from 1926 to 1933, founded by General Erich Ludendorff. Includes correspondence with E. Ludendorff.

Register.

Gift, R. Holtzmann, 1949.

1214

Honens, W. H., *collector.*

Photographs, 1916–1917. 3 albums.

Depicts activities of the Stanford Unit of the American Ambulance Service during World War I in France and Albania.

Gift, W. H. Honens, 1976.

1215

Hoo, Victor Chi-tsai, 1894–1972.

Papers (in English and French), 1930–1972. 7½ ms. boxes.

Chinese diplomat; Minister to Switzerland, 1932–1942; Vice Minister of Foreign Affairs, 1942–1945; United Nations Assistant Secretary-General, 1946–1972. Diaries, correspondence, clippings, reports, memoranda and photographs, relating to Chinese political events and foreign relations, international diplomatic conferences, Sino-Soviet relations, and the United Nations.

Gift, Mona Eldridge, 1977.

1216

Hoover, Herbert Clark, 1874–1964.

Papers, 1897–1969. 306 ms. boxes, 90 envelopes, 1 album, 1 microfilm reel, 18 motion pictures, 31 phonotapes, 10 phonorecords.

President of the U.S., 1929–1933. Appointment calendars, correspondence, office files, speeches and writings, analyses of newspaper editorials, printed matter, photographs, motion pictures, sound recordings, and other material, relating to the administration of relief during and after the two world wars, Hoover's relationship with Woodrow Wilson, U.S. politics and government, and the philosophy and public service contributions of Herbert Hoover. Includes photocopies of selected files from his Presidential and Commerce Department papers which are located at the Herbert Hoover Presidential Library, West Branch, Iowa.

Register.

Gift, Herbert Hoover, 1962. Subsequent increments.

1217

Hoover Institution on War, Revolution and Peace. Parabel Project.

Records, 1949–1950. 3 ms. boxes.

Project undertaken by the Hoover Institution on War, Revolution and Peace in cooperation with the Operations Research Office, Johns Hopkins University. Writings, translations, notes, and questionnaire responses, relating to a comparative study of underground movements in China, France, Italy, Kurdistan and Poland, 1939–1947.

Preliminary inventory.

1218

Hoover Institution on War, Revolution and Peace. Program on Overseas Development.

Records, 1955–1956. 1½ ms. boxes.

Program conducted by the Hoover Institution under a contract with the U.S. International Cooperation Administration. Reports and reading lists, relating to the instruction of foreign technicians in matters regarding economic development.

1219

Hoover Institution on War, Revolution and Peace. Revolution and the Development of International Relations Project.

Records, 1948–1952. 69½ ms. boxes, 17 card file boxes (3 l. ft.).

Memoranda, correspondence, data sheets, and printed matter, relating to the comparative study of social, political and economic development in various countries during the twentieth century, and especially to the comparative study of political and military elites in various countries.

Preliminary inventory.

1220

Hoover Institution on War, Revolution and Peace. Russian Provisional Government Project.

Translations of documents, 1955–1960. 10 ms. boxes.

Project for publication of a documentary history of the Russian Provisional Government of 1917. Results published as Robert Browder and Alexander Kerensky, ed., *The Russian Provisional Government, 1917* (Stanford: Stanford University Press, 1961).

Preliminary inventory.

1221

Hoover Institution on War, Revolution and Peace. Soviet Treaty Series Project.

Records, 1957–1959. 12 cu. ft. boxes, 2 file drawers (1 l. ft.).

Correspondence, memoranda, notes, bibliographies, and translations of published material, used in the preparation of *A Calendar of Soviet Treaties, 1917–1957,* by Robert M. Slusser and Jan F. Triska (Stanford University Press, 1959; Hoover Institution Document Series #4).

1222

Hoover Institution on War, Revolution and Peace. Supreme Economic Council and American Relief Administration Documents Project.

Records, 1930–1937. 21 ms. boxes, 45 vols.

Project for compilation of selected Supreme Economic Council and American Relief Administration documents. Typed copies of minutes of meetings, reports, correspondence, press releases and clippings, relating to eco-

nomic policies of the Supreme Economic Council and its predecessor, the Supreme Council of Supply and Relief, and to relief activities of the American Relief Administration in Europe and Russia.
Preliminary inventory.

1223
Hoover, John Elwood, 1924–
Thesis, 1955. "The American Congress and the Russian Revolution, March 1917 to February 1918." ½ ms. box.
Typescript (photocopy).
Major General, U.S. Army. Relates to U.S. Congressional opinions and actions regarding the Russian Revolution. M.A. thesis, Georgetown University.
Gift, Stefan T. Possony, 1978.

1224
Hoover, Lou Henry, 1874–1944.
Miscellany, 1913–1933. 1 oversize box.
Wife of Herbert Hoover. Passport, 1913; war zone passes, 1918; a sketch of Lou Henry Hoover, 1931; a portfolio of reproductions of drawings of Spanish missions in California, 1933; and sketches of the White House, Capitol Building, Washington Monument and Mount Vernon.

1225
Hoover, Mildred Crew Brooke, 1872–1940.
Memoirs, 1940. "Reminiscences of Mildred Crew Brooke." 1 folder.
Typescript.
Sister-in-law of Herbert Hoover. Relates to personal matters, the Hoover family, and the engineering career of Theodore J. Hoover, brother of Herbert Hoover and husband of M. C. B. Hoover.

1226
Hoover, Theodore Jesse, 1871–1955.
Memoirs, 1939. "Memoranda: Being a Statement by an Engineer." ½ ms. box, 1 microfilm reel.
Typescript (photocopy).
American mining engineer; brother of Herbert Hoover; Dean of Engineering, Stanford University, 1925–1936. Relates to engineering and to the Hoover family.
Consult Archivist for restrictions.

1227
Hornbeck, Stanley Kuhl, 1883–1966.
Papers, 1900–1966. 532 ms. boxes, 41 envelopes, 8 oversize photographs.
American diplomat; Chief, Division of Far Eastern Affairs, U.S. Department of State, 1928–1937; Adviser on Political Relations, U.S. Department of State, 1937–1944; Ambassador to the Netherlands, 1944–1947. Correspondence, writings, reports, studies, dispatches and instructions, printed matter, memorabilia and photographs, relating to U.S. foreign relations in China, Japan and other areas of the Far East, political conditions in China and Japan, and U.S.-Dutch relations.
Register.
Gift, Mrs. S. K. Hornbeck, 1967.

1228
Horst Wessel Lied (Horst Wessel Song).
Song (in German), n.d. 1 phonorecord.
National socialist German anthem.
Gift, Marton A. Karr, 1977.

1229
Horthy, Miklos, 1868–1957.
Autobiography (in Hungarian), n.d. ½ ms. box.
Handwritten copy by Leo Zsitvay with holograph annotations by M. Horthy.
Regent of Hungary, 1920–1944. Relates to Hungarian politics and foreign relations in the interwar period and during World War II. Includes signed photograph of M. Horthy with dedication to the Hungarian peasantry, 1919.
In part, gift, Ilona Bowden, 1975.

1230
Hoskin, Harry L., b. 1887.
Papers, 1917–1973. ½ ms. box, 7 envelopes.
American officer, Russian Railway Service Corps, 1917–1920. Correspondence, clippings, reports, affidavits, court proceedings, and photographs, relating to activities of the Russian Railway Service Corps in Siberia, and to subsequent legal disputes regarding the military or civilian status of members of the corps.
Gift, H. L. Hoskin, 1976.

1231
Hoskins, Emmett A.
Memoirs, 1970. "In the Service of the United States Navy, May 26, 1917–August 6, 1919." 1 folder.
Typescript.
Sailor, U.S. Navy. Relates to American naval operations in the Far East and Siberia.
Gift, E. A. Hoskins, 1974.

1232
Hossbach, Friedrich, 1894–
Notes (in German), 1937. 1 folder.
Typewritten transcript.
Chief, Central Department, German General Staff, and Wehrmacht Adjutant to Adolf Hitler. Relates to a conference of Adolf Hitler and German military leaders concerning German foreign policy, November 5, 1937.

1233
Howe, Esther B., *collector*.
Miscellany, n.d. 1 folder, 1 envelope.
Designs for the Imperial Chinese decoration of the Order of the Double Dragon; and autographed photographs of Herbert Hoover and Lou Henry Hoover.
Gift, E. B. Howe, 1973.

1234
Howe, Julia Ward, 1819–1910.
Letter, 1900, to Mrs. J. A. Gravett. 1 folder.
Holograph.
American author; writer of *The Battle Hymn of the Republic*. Relates to personal matters and to her literary work.

1235

Hruska, Roman L., 1904–
Speech, 1977. "Herbert Clark Hoover, 1874–1964: An Appreciation." 1 folder.
Typescript (photocopy).
U.S. Senator from Nebraska, 1954–1976. Speech delivered at West Branch, Iowa, August 10, 1977.
Gift, R. L. Hruska, 1977.

1236

Huang, Fu, 1880–1936.
Papers (in Chinese), 1920–1936. 7 ms. boxes.
Chinese Government official; Minister of Foreign Affairs, 1928; Chairman, Peiping Political Affairs Council, 1933–1935. Correspondence, reports, writings and printed matter, relating to Chinese foreign relations, the 1927 incident at Nanking, the Tangku Truce settlement with Japan in 1933, domestic politics in China, Chiang Kai-shek, and the Nationalist Government of China.
Inventory.
Access requires the written permission of Mrs. Hsi-chih Chiu.
Deposit, Mrs. Hsi-chih Chiu, 1972.

1237

Huber, Johann Heinrich.
Music box, 1754.
Owned by J. H. Huber of Oberkulm, Switzerland, earliest known ancestor of Herbert Hoover.
Gift, Patricia Dutra, 1977.

1238

Hudson, Ray M.
Papers, 1922–1957. 6 ms. boxes.
Chief, Division of Simplified Practice, U.S. Department of Commerce, 1926. Letters, pamphlets, clippings, and other printed matter, relating to U.S. industry, simplification of industrial practice, the public life of Herbert Hoover, and the 1928, 1932, and 1936 Presidential campaigns.
Preliminary inventory.
Gift, R. M. Hudson, 1962.

1239

Huenergardt, Mrs. John F., *collector*.
Miscellany (in English and Hungarian), 1919–1920. 1 folder, 1 envelope.
Printed matter and photographs, relating to relief activities in Hungary at the end of World War I.
Gift, Mrs. J. F. Huenergardt, 1957.

1240

Huete, Angel Zuniga.
Letters (in Spanish), 1940–1941, to U.S. Government officials. 1 folder.
Typescript.
Honduran citizen. Relates to U.S.-Honduran relations.

1241

Huffsmith, V. C.
Letter, 1942, to Brigadier General Earl McFarland. 1 folder.
Typewritten transcript.
Major, U.S. Army. Relates to the service of the 701st and 440th Ordnance Companies in the Philippine campaign of 1942.

1242

Huggins, Sir Godfrey Martin, Viscount Malvern, 1883–1971.
Transcripts of interviews, 1968. 1 folder.
Typescript.
Prime Minister of Southern Rhodesia, 1933–1953, and of the Federation of Rhodesia and Nyasaland, 1953–1956. Relates to the political development of Southern Rhodesia. Interviews conducted by Rex Reynolds.
May not be quoted without permission of Robert Blake, Baron of Braydeston, and the Anglo-American Corporation.
Gift, R. Reynolds, 1974.

1243

Hughes Aircraft Company.
Photographs, 1961. 1 envelope.
Depicts space simulators.

1244

Hughes, James Clark.
Papers, 1943–1945. 1 folder, 1 envelope.
Colonel, U.S. Army; prisoner of war during World War II. Diary, notes and photographs, relating to conditions in Japanese prison camps in the Philippines, Formosa and Manchuria.
Gift, Peggy Hughes Ryan, 1973.

1245

Huldermann, Paul F.
Photographs, 1936–1938. 2 envelopes.
Depicts scenes in China, including military operations of the Chinese Army during the Sino-Japanese War. Includes portraits of Chiang Kai-shek and other Chinese political leaders.
Preliminary inventory.
Gift, P. F. Huldermann, 1938.

1246

Hull (Cordell)—photographs, n.d. 1 envelope.
Depicts Secretary of State C. Hull of the U.S.

1247

Hungary. Fegyverszueneti Bizottság (1918–1919).
Correspondence (in Hungarian), 1918–1919, with Allied authorities. 1 vol.
Typescript.
Hungarian Armistice Commission. Relates to execution of provisions of the armistice between Hungary and the Allied Powers at the end of World War I.

1248

Hungary—history—revolution, 1918–1919—collection (in Hungarian), 1919. 1 folder, 1 envelope.

Photographs, postcards, leaflets, and photocopies of posters, relating to the Hungarian revolution of 1918–1919, and depicting scenes from the revolution and leaders of the Hungarian Soviet Republic.

Gifts, Emile W. Juhasz, 1962, and Paul Tabori, 1972.

1249

Hungary—history, 1918–1945—photographs, 1942. 1 folder.

Depicts Hungarian troops on the Russian front during World War II.

Gift, Gwen Brechin, 1973.

1250

Hungary. Igazságuegyminiszterium.

Court judgments (in German), 1919–1920. 1 vol.

Typewritten transcripts.

Hungarian Ministry of Justice. Relates to the trials of Hungarian communists for participation in the Hungarian revolution of 1918–1919.

1251

Hungary. Kueluegyminisztérium.

Miscellaneous records (in Hungarian), 1915–1922. ½ ms. box.

Hungarian Foreign Ministry. Reports, memoranda, and orders, relating to Austro-Hungarian military activities during World War I, domestic opposition to the war, socialist activities, Bolshevik propaganda, problems of minority nationalities during and after the war, postwar land reform, and the formation of soviets in Hungary.

Preliminary inventory.

Gift, Hungarian Foreign Ministry.

1252

Hungary under Soviet rule—studies (in Hungarian and English), 1958. 1 folder.

Typescript (mimeographed).

Relates to Soviet influence in Hungary, forced labor camps in Hungary, and Hungarian minorities in other communist countries. Written by various Hungarian anti-communist émigré organizations in the U.S.

1253

Hunkanrin, Louis, 1887–1964.

Papers (in French), ca. 1920–1939. 1 ms. box.

Photocopy of original papers in possession of Jean Suret-Canale.

Dahomeyan journalist. Correspondence, clippings and printed matter, relating to French colonial administration of Dahomey. Includes statements of protest concerning injustices of French colonial administrators made by L. Hunkanrin at the Pan-African Congress of 1921.

Gift, Jacques Depelchin, 1970.

1254

Hunt, Edward Eyre, 1885–1953.

Papers, 1914–1949. 62 ms. boxes, 1 envelope.

American economist; relief worker in Europe during World War I; Secretary, President's Emergency Committee for Employment, 1930–1931. Reports, memoranda, writings, and printed matter, relating to relief and reconstruction in Europe during and after World Wars I and II (especially in Belgium, France, Germany, Italy, and Poland), the Commission for Relief in Belgium, the American Red Cross, Herbert Hoover and the Presidential campaign of 1920, and U.S. economic questions between the two world wars.

Register.

Gift, Mrs. E. E. Hunt, 1956. Subsequent increments.

1255

Husen, Peter von.

Memorandum (in German), n.d. 1 folder.

Typescript.

Relates to Helmuth von Moltke and Peter Yorck, members of the anti-Nazi Kreisauer Kreis resistance group in Germany during World War II.

1256

Huston, Jay Calvin.

Papers (in English and Russian), 1917–1931. 14 ms. boxes, 2 envelopes.

American consular official in China, 1917–1932. Writings, pamphlets, leaflets, and clippings, relating to cultural, political, and economic conditions in China, and to communism and Soviet influence in China.

Preliminary inventory.

Gift, Payson J. Treat, 1935.

1257

Hutchinson, J. Kent, *collector.*

Slides, n.d. 1 ms. box.

Depicts scenes of daily life and agricultural and other economic activities in Japan and other Asian countries.

1258

Hutchinson, John Raymond.

Papers, 1918–1961. 9 ms. boxes, 2 envelopes, 5 phonorecords.

American educator; educational and pictorial specialist, U.S. Office of War Information, during World War II. Correspondence, film scripts, printed matter, photographs and filmstrips, relating to the production of U.S. propaganda films by the Office of War Information for distribution in China during World War II, and to the history of television in the U.S.

Preliminary inventory.

Gift, J. R. Hutchinson, 1952. Incremental gift, 1969.

1259

Hutchinson, Lincoln.

Papers, 1923–1935. 2 ms. boxes.

American Relief Administration worker. Correspondence, writings, and reports, relating to American Relief

Administration activities, food conditions in Germany following World War I, and technical assistance provided by American engineers in the Soviet Union.
Gift, J. Kent Hutchinson, 1968.

1260

Huxtable, Edward John, Jr., 1913–
Report, n.d. "Composite Squadron Aboard USS *Gambier Bay*: Some Recollections." 1 folder.
Typescript (photocopy).
Captain, U.S. Navy; Commanding Officer, Composite Squadron Ten, 1943–1945. Relates to the Battle of Leyte Gulf, 1944.
Gift, E. J. Huxtable, Jr., 1977.

1261

ÍAkovlev, ÍAkov Arkad'evich, 1896–
Translation of a pamphlet, 1923. *Derevnia Kak Ona Est'* (The Village as It Is). 1 vol.
Typescript (mimeographed).
Relates to social, economic, political and cultural conditions in Russian villages in 1923. Also includes an article by P. Aksenov, entitled "How the Village Lives" (published in *Pravda*, 1923.)

1262

ÍAremenko, A.
Translation of extracts from a memoir, n.d. "Diary of a Communist." 1 vol.
Typescript.
Russian communist. Relates to the Russian Civil War in Siberia, 1918–1920. Translation of "Dnievnik Kommunista," published in *Revoliutsiia na Dalnem Vostoke* (Revolution in the Far East) (Moscow, 1923).

1263

Iceland in World War I collection (in Icelandic), 1914–1916. 1 folder.
Newspaper issues and proclamations, relating to war news and to conditions in Iceland during World War I.

1264

Ickes, Harold Le Claire, 1874–1952.
Report, 1942. "Minerals and Power to Win the War and Develop the West." 1 folder.
Printed.
U.S. Secretary of the Interior, 1933–1946. Relates to development of mining and power plants in relation to the war effort.

1265

Ileana, Princess of Romania, 1909–
Letters, 1967–1977, to Eudoxia, Mother Superior, Couvent des Soeurs, Bussy-en-Othe, France. ½ ms. box.
Romanian princess; Orthodox Mother Superior, Convent of the Transfiguration, Elwood City, Pennsylvania. Relates to personal and religious matters.
Gift, Ileana, Princess of Romania, 1978.

1266

Iliff, John L., *collector*.
Slides, 1936. 1 ms. box.
Depicts the Caucasus region and the reconstruction of Moscow. Used in a Russian seventh grade class.
Gift, J. L. Iliff, 1945.

1267

Ilin, I. S., *collector*.
Newspaper clippings (in Russian), 1931–1932. 1 oversize package (½ l. ft.).
Relates to Japanese military activities in Manchuria. From Russian-language newspapers in China.
Gift, I. S. Ilin.

1268

Iliou, Ph.
Newspaper article (in French), n.d. "Un Danger" (A Danger). 1 folder.
Typewritten transcript.
Relates to philhellenism in France. Published in the Greek newspaper *Embros*.

1269

Imperial War Museum, London.
Photographs, 1915–1919. 32 envelopes, 12 oversize photographs.
Depicts activities of the British Army and Navy during World War I, including scenes of the western front, the Middle East, aerial operations, women workers on the home front, and the army of occupation in Germany. Distributed by the Imperial War Museum.
Gift, California State Library, 1962.

1270

"Importance de la Georgie en tant que Voie de Transit" (The Importance of Georgia as a Route).
Study (in French), n.d. 1 folder.
Typescript (mimeographed).
Relates to the commercial geography of Georgia.

1271

Inchiesta sulla Morte di Mussolini (Inquest into the Death of Mussolini).
Testimony (in Italian), 1962. 1 phonorecord.
Testimony of eyewitnesses to the death of Benito Mussolini in 1945, taken by a group of investigators under the direction of Marcello Bonicoli, and issued by Aletti Editore.
Gift, Jacques de Launay, 1963.

1272

Indian National Congress. Foreign Relations Department.
Photographs, 1950–1952. 1 envelope.
Depicts Jawaharlal Nehru, Eleanor Roosevelt, the Indian Embassy in Washington, D.C., and various dignitaries and representatives of other nations.

1273

Indonesia—information bulletins, 1948–1952. ½ ms. box.
Press releases and newsletters issued by the Dutch and Indonesian Governments, relating to the independence of Indonesia, Indonesian foreign relations, and the government, economy, and culture of Indonesia.

1274

Indonesia. Special Military Tribunal.
Records (in Indonesian), 1965–1967. 22 ms. boxes.
Relates to the trials of Indonesian communists and others implicated in the attempted coup of 1965, including Politbureau member Sudisman, Foreign Minister Subandrio, and Air Force Chief of Staff Omar Dhani.
Gift, Guy J. Pauker, 1975.

1275

Inglis, John.
Papers, 1898–1902. 1 ms. box.
American missionary at An Ting Hospital, Peking, China, 1898–1900. Memoirs, correspondence and clippings, relating to the Boxer Rebellion and the siege of Peking. Includes papers of Theodora Inglis, wife of J. Inglis.
Preliminary inventory.
May not be quoted without permission of Helen Stote.
Gift, H. Stote, 1973.

1276

Inlichtingsdienst der Deli Planters Vereeniging en Algemeene Vereeniging van Rubberplanters ter Oostkust van Sumatra.
Bulletins (in Dutch), 1925–1929. 1 folder.
Typescript (mimeographed).
Information Service of the Deli Planters Union and of the General Union of Rubber Planters of the East Coast of Sumatra. Relates to communist activities in Indonesia and elsewhere in the Far East.

1277

Innis, Harold Adams, 1894–
Memoir, 1946. "Ottawa to Moscow." 1 vol.
Typescript.
Canadian delegate to the 220th anniversary celebration of the founding of the Akademiı̂a Nauk SSSR, Moscow, 1946. Relates to the visit of Western scholars to the celebration.

1278

Institut d'Etudes Européennes de Strasbourg.
Bulletins (in French), 1945–1946. 1 folder.
Typescript (mimeographed).
Relates to post-World War II reconstruction of Germany and to the Alsace-Lorraine question.

1279

Institut zur Studium der Judenfrage, *collector.*
Propaganda (in German), 1883–1939. 1 ms. box.
German antisemitic propaganda, including clippings, leaflets and posters.

1280

Institute of Current World Affairs.
Memorandum, 1926. 1 folder.
Typescript.
Relates to the aims and organization of an Institute of Current World Affairs for the study of international relations.

1281

Institute of Pacific Relations. American Council.
Records, 1925–1960. 21 ms. boxes, 1 album, 1 envelope.
Correspondence, reports, memoranda, study papers, press releases, printed matter and photographs, relating to the study of political, social and economic conditions in the Far East and of U.S. foreign policy in the Far East by the American Council of the Institute of Pacific Relations. From the papers of Ray Lyman Wilbur, president of the American Council of the Institute of Pacific Relations.
Register.
Gift, R. L. Wilbur.

1282

Institute of Pacific Relations. San Francisco Bay Region Division.
Records, 1944–1947. 26 ms. boxes, 1 card file (1/6 1. ft.).
Private organization for the study of the Far East and of U.S. foreign policy in the Far East. Correspondence, reports, memoranda, studies and printed matter, relating to the study of political, social and economic conditions in the Far East and of U.S. foreign policy in the Far East.
Register.
Gift, Mrs. Frank Gerbode, 1955.

1283

Inter-American Conference. 6th, Havana, 1928.
Records, 1928. 1½ ms. boxes.
Sixth International Conference of American States. Reports, memoranda, correspondence, reprints, and clippings, relating to economic, social, legal, educational, scientific, and cultural aspects of Pan-American cooperation, and to U.S. foreign policy in Latin America.

1284

Interessengemeinschaft Farbenindustrie Aktiengesellschaft. Propaganda-Abteilung.
Bulletins (in German), 1932–1942. 1 folder.
Typescript (mimeographed).
Propaganda Division of the I.G. Farben trust. Relates to conditions in the chemical industry in Germany.

1285

Intergovernmental Oceanographic Commission.
Miscellaneous records, 1962–1964. 1 ms. box.
Agency of the United Nations. Reports, bulletins, and minutes of meetings, relating to the promotion of international oceanographic research under auspices of the United Nations Educational, Scientific and Cultural Organization.

1286

International Committee for Immediate Mediation, 1916.
Records (in English, German and Norwegian), 1916. 1 vol.
Organization created by the Henry Ford Peace Expedition and the Neutral Conference for Continuous Mediation. Reports and minutes of meetings, relating to the international peace movement during World War I.

1287

International Defence and Aid Fund for Southern Africa.
Posters, 1978. 1 folder.
British political group in support of black liberation movements. Depicts scenes of racial struggle and guerrilla warfare in Rhodesia.

1288

International Exhibition of Water Technics, Liège, 1939.
Miscellany, 1939. 1 album.
Drawings and reproductions of photographs, prepared for the International Exhibition of Water Technics held at Liège, Belgium, in 1939, depicting scenes in Liège and illustrating the history of the city.

1289

International Military Tribunal.
Records (in English and German), 1945–1949. 395 1. ft.
Typescript (mimeographed).
Testimony and evidence, relating to the trials of alleged German war criminals at Nuremberg.

1290

International Military Tribunal for the Far East.
Records, 1946–1948. 81 1. ft., 1 envelope.
Exhibits, transcripts and summaries of proceedings, summations of counsel, judgments of the tribunal, and indexes, relating to the trials of Japanese officials accused of World War II war crimes.
Miscellaneous indexes.
Gift, Claude A. Buss, 1949. Incremental gift, 1950.

1291

International Political Science Association. 5th World Congress, Paris, 1961.
Conference papers (in English and French), 1961. 1 ms. box.
Typescript (mimeographed).
Relates to political behavior and to political problems regarding civil-military relations, technocracy, nuclear administration, and poly-ethnic states.

1292

International Union of Students.
Posters, n.d. 1 oversize box (1 1. ft.).
Propagates left-wing and revolutionary causes throughout the world, particularly in Latin America, Africa, and Asia.

1293

Ipatieff, Vladimir Nikolaevich, 1867–1952.
Photographs, 1870–1939. 1 envelope.
Depicts the site of the execution of the Imperial Russian family in 1918; and V. N. Ipatieff, relatives and friends.

1294

Irimescu, Radu.
Papers (in Romanian), 1918–1940. 5 ms. boxes, 5 albums, 11 envelopes.
Romanian diplomat and politician; Minister of Air and Navy, 1932–1938; Ambassador to the U.S., 1938–1940. Correspondence, reports, dispatches, memoranda, clippings, and photographs, relating to Romanian politics and foreign policy, and to the development of aviation in Romania.
Register.
Gift, estate of R. Irimescu, 1975.

1295

Irvine, Dallas D.
Memorandum, 1939. "An American Military Institute." 1 folder.
Typescript (mimeographed).
Relates to the founding of the American Military Institute to promote the study of American military history.

1296

Irwin, William Henry, 1873–1948.
Papers, 1890–1942. 6 ms. boxes, 2 vols.
American journalist and author. Correspondence, writings and printed matter, relating to Herbert Hoover, and political and social conditions in the U.S. Includes drafts of fictional and other writings by W. H. Irwin, and correspondence with Herbert Hoover.
Register.
Gifts, Inez Haynes Irwin, 1948, and William Hyde Irwin, 1965.

1297

Isabelle, Reno, *collector*.
Photographs, 1931. 1 envelope.
Depicts the U.S.S. *Arizona* in Boston, and President Herbert Hoover on the *Arizona* during a cruise to Puerto Rico and the Virgin Islands.

1298

Isambard-Owen, Elizabeth Clemence Heulwen.
Memoirs, n.d. "Four Years under the Boot." 1 vol.
Typescript (carbon copy).
Relates to the German occupation of France during World War II.

1299

Israel and the Arabs collection, 1973–1976. 1 folder.
Brochures and printed matter, relating to Middle East refugee problems, Arab and Palestinian nationalism, Palestinian terrorist organizations, and military armament in the Middle East.

1300

Istoricheskaia Komissiia Markovskogo Artilleriĭskogo Diviziona.

History (in Russian), 1931. "Istoriiā Markovskoĭ Artilleriĭskoĭ Brigady" (History of the Markovskiĭ Artillery Brigade). 1 vol.

Typescript (mimeographed).

White Russian military unit. Relates to activities of the Markovskiĭ Artillery Brigade during the Russian Civil War. Edited by Colonel Zholondkovskiĭ, Lieutenant Colonel Shcharinskiĭ and Captain Vinogradov.

1301

Italian Bureau of Information, New York City.

Photographs, 1915–1918. 4 envelopes.

Photographs and postcards, depicting activities of the Italian Army in World War I, including many scenes of mountain warfare; Woodrow Wilson; and children of the Italian royal family.

Gift, Anita Reinhard, 1960.

1302

Italian fascist propaganda (in Italian), 1921–1943. 1 folder.

Miscellaneous Italian fascist propaganda leaflets and proclamations.

1303

Italo-Ethiopian War propaganda, 1935–1936. 1 folder.

Printed.

Leaflets relating to the Italo-Ethiopian War. Distributed by the Italian Government in Great Britain.

1304

Italy—elections, 1976—collection (in Italian), 1976. 2 ms. boxes, 5 posters.

Pamphlets, leaflets, posters, newspapers, party programs, and other printed election materials, relating to the Italian elections of June 20–21, 1976.

Preliminary inventory.

Gift, Alex Battey, 1977.

1305

Italy. Esercito. 44. Reggimento Artiglieria Motorizzato Marmarica.

Brochure (in Italian), 1940. 1 folder.

Printed.

Commemorates the activities of the Italian 44th Artillery Regiment in the Italo-Austrian campaigns during World War I, 1915–1918.

1306

Italy. Ministero degli Affari Esteri.

Records (in Italian and English), 1938–1939. ½ ms. box.

Photocopy.

Italian Ministry of Foreign Affairs. Correspondence and memoranda, relating to the Munich conference, the outbreak of World War II, and Anglo-Italian relations.

1307

Italy. Ministero Interno. Direzione Generale Pubblica Sicurezza.

Records (in Italian), 1902–1934. 25 reels.

Microfilm.

General Directorate of Public Safety of the Ministry of the Interior of Italy. Correspondence and reports, relating to the communist and anarchist movements in Italy.

Preliminary inventory.

No copies may be made.

Joint microfilm project, Hoover Institution on War, Revolution and Peace, and Centro Studi e Ricerche su Problemi Economico-Sociali (CESES), Milan, 1969.

1308

Italy—photographs and postcards, 1917–1919. 1 envelope.

Photographs and postcards, depicting war damage and military operations in Italy during World War I.

Gift, Mrs. David L. Davies.

1309

Italy—propaganda, 1917–1918. 1 folder.

Italian propaganda leaflets, pamphlets and newspaper issues, directed at Czechs, Poles, Hungarians, Romanians and Croats in the Austro-Hungarian Army during World War I.

Preliminary inventory.

Gift, Alfred Lane, 1958.

1310

Iūdenich, Nikolaĭ Nikolaevich, 1862–1933.

Papers (in Russian), 1918–1920. 21 ms. boxes.

General, Russian Imperial Army; Commander, Northwestern White Russian armed forces, 1918–1920. Correspondence, memoranda, telegrams, reports, military documents, proclamations, maps, and printed matter, relating to the campaigns of the Northwestern White Russian armed forces, communism in Russia, relations with the Allied Powers, and activities of White Russian representatives in Europe.

Preliminary inventory.

Gift, N. N. Iūdenich, 1927.

1311

Iūnakov, N. L.

Memoir (in Russian), 1927. "Moĭ Posliědnie Miěsiāt͡sy v Diěĭstvuiūshcheĭ Armiĭ: Vospominaniiā Byvshago Komanduiūshchego Armieĭ, Oktiābr'-Dekabr' 1917 goda" (My Last Months in the Active Army: Reminiscences of a Former Army Commander, October—December 1917). 1 vol.

Holograph.

1312

Iūsupov (Feliks Feliksovich, Kniaz')—photograph, n.d. 1 envelope.

Depicts Prince F. F. Iūsupov of Russia and his wife.

1313

Ivanić, Delfa, 1881–197[?]
Memoirs (in Serbo-Croatian), n.d. ½ ms. box.
Typescript.
Official, Circle of Serbian Sisters; President, Yugoslav National Women's Federation, 1923–1925. Relates to medical and charitable activities in Serbia during the Balkan Wars and World War I.
Gift, Mr. and Mrs. Ivan Subbotich, 1969.

1314

Ivanov, Vsevolod Nikanorovich.
Translation of extracts from study, n.d. "Manchuria and Manchukuo, 1932: Observations and Prognoses." 1 folder.
Typescript.
Relates to the Chinese Eastern Railway, 1898–1930. Translation by Elena Varneck, of excerpts from "Manchuria i Manchugo, 1932: Nabliudeniiâ i Prognozy."

1315

Ivory Coast. Ministère Fonction Publique et Information.
Photographs, 1961. 1 envelope.
Depicts economic activities and other scenes of daily life in the Ivory Coast.
Gift, Ministère Fonction Publique et Information of the Ivory Coast, 1961.

1316

"Iz Vozzvaniiâ k Karel'skomu Naseleniiû Kemskogo Uezda" (From the Appeal to the Karelian Populace of Kemsk Region).
Appeal (in Russian), 1919. 1 folder.
Typescript.
Relates to the Russian Civil War. Written by a group of White Russian leaders.

1317

Izvestiiâ Revoliûtsionnoĭ Nedeli (News of the Revolutionary Week).
Extracts from newspaper articles (in Russian), 1917. 1 folder.
Typescript.
Petrograd newspaper. Relates to the February 1917 Revolution in Petrograd. Includes texts of Russian Government decrees, and appeals and resolutions of Russian political groups.

1318

Jackson, Florence, *collector*.
Miscellany, 1915–1919. 1 ms. box.
Clippings, leaflets, and miscellanea, mostly relating to relief work in World War I.
Gift, F. Jackson, 1934.

1319

Jackson, Richard Harrison, 1866–1971.
Papers, 1917–1930. 2 ms. boxes.
Admiral, U.S. Navy; Naval Attaché to France, 1917–1918; member, General Board, U.S. Department of the Navy, 1921–1930. Speeches, memoranda, reports, orders and printed matter, relating to U.S. naval policy during the 1920s. Includes summaries of intelligence reports received by the U.S. Embassy in France, 1917–1918.
Gift, Charles Busey, 1978.

1320

Jacobs, Fenton Stratton, 1892–1966.
Papers, 1921–1967. 11 ms. boxes, 3 vols., 1 envelope.
Brigadier General, U.S. Army. Correspondence, writings, printed matter, maps, and photographs, relating to cavalry tactics, logistics, and military transportation during and after the two world wars.
Gift, Mrs. F. S. Jacobs, 1966.

1321

Jacobs, John F. de.
Memoir, 1925. "The American Relief Administration and My Crime." 1 vol.
Typescript.
Interpreter for the American Relief Administration in Russia. Relates to the arrest of J. F. de Jacobs by Soviet authorities.

1322

Jacobs, Joseph Earle, 1893–1971.
Papers, 1925–1951. 1½ ms. boxes.
American diplomat; Political Adviser to the U.S. Commanding General in Korea, 1947–1948; Ambassador to Czechoslovakia, 1948–1949; Ambassador to Poland, 1955–1957. Writings, correspondence, reports and printed matter, relating to reconstruction in Korea after World War II, the Italian communist movement, the Philippine independence movement, and the Shanghai riot of May 30, 1925.
Preliminary inventory.
Gift, J. E. Jacobs, 1969.

1323

Jacobs-Pauwels, F. Marguerite.
Papers (in French), 1914–1964. 11 ms. boxes, 1 cu. ft. box, 2 binders.
Director, Foyer des Orphelins (Orphanage), Charleroi, Belgium, 1914–1923. Correspondence, reports, financial records and photographs, relating to relief in Belgium during World War I and to the operations of the Foyer des Orphelins during and after the war.
Gift, F. M. Jacobs-Pauwels, 1965.

1324

Jacun, Konrad.
Study (in Polish), n.d. "Antagonizm Azyi i Europy" (Antagonism between Asia and Europe). 1 folder.
Typescript and printed.
Relates to the Eurasian nature of Russian civilization.

1325

Jadot, Albert Joseph, 1899–1953.
Papers (in French), 1919–1953. ½ ms. box.
Second in command, Hainaut-Namur Section, Armée

Belge des Partisans. Orders, reports, correspondence, and memorabilia, relating to resistance activities of the Armée Belge des Partisans in Belgium during World War II.
Preliminary inventory.
Gift, Mrs. A. J. Jadot, 1969.

1326

Jałowiecki, Mieczysław, b. 1886.
Memoirs (in Polish), 1964. 7½ ms. boxes, 8 oversize boxes.
Typescript.
Polish-Lithuanian agricultural expert, architect and engineer; chairman, Vilnius Agrarian Association. Relates to historical events in Russia and Lithuania before, during and after the Russian Revolution and Civil War; Poles in Lithuania; and agricultural developments in Lithuania, 1881–1939. Includes watercolor drawings and sketches of scenes and manor houses in Lithuania and Poland.

1327

James, Elizabeth L.
Diary, 1941–1945. 1 ms. box.
Typescript.
American in the Philippines during World War II. Relates to conditions in the Philippines under Japanese occupation.
Gift, E. L. James, 1969.

1328

James, Henry, 1879–1947.
Papers, 1918–1920. ½ ms. box.
U.S. representative, Inter-Allied Danube River Commission, 1919. Reports, correspondence, and financial records, relating to the opening of the Danube River to navigation at the end of World War I, and to the political situation in Hungary at the time of the Hungarian Revolution.
Gift, Harvard University Library, 1949.

1329

Janin, Pierre Thiébaut Charles Maurice, b. 1862.
Extracts from a diary (in French), 1918–1920. 1 folder.
Typewritten transcript.
General, French Army; Commander of Czechoslovak and other Allied forces in Siberia, 1918–1920. Relates to Allied intervention in the Russian Civil War. Extracts published in *Le Monde Slave*, 1924–1925.

1330

Janney, J. H.
Report, 1940. "Notes on the Food Situation in Spain." 1 folder.
Typescript (mimeographed).
Rockefeller Foundation staff member. Relates to the need for food relief in Spain.

1331

Janovsky, Karl.
Reports (in German), 1942. 1 folder.
Typescript (some mimeographed).
Reports, entitled "Bericht ueber die im RWM Stattgefundene Aussprache ueber die Bulgarischen Verhandlungsergebnisse" (Report about the Discussion in the Reichswirtschaftsministerium Regarding the Results of the Bulgarian Negotiations), "Lagebericht ueber die Verhaeltnisse in Suedost" (Situation Report about the Conditions in Southeast), and "Lagebericht 1942 ueber die Verhaeltnisse in Ungarn, Rumaenien und Bulgarien" (Situation Report 1942 About Conditions in Hungary, Romania, and Bulgaria), relating to economic conditions in the Balkan States and German commercial agreements with these countries during World War II.

1332

Janssens, Édouard.
Deposition (in French), 1961. 1 vol.
Typewritten transcript.
Lieutenant General, Belgian Army; Commanding General, Force Publique, Belgian Congo. Relates to the activities of Belgian military forces in the Belgian Congo in the period immediately preceding independence, 1959–1960.

1333

Japan—photographs, n.d. 1 album.
Depicts persons, places and scenes of daily life in Japan during the late nineteenth century.
Gift, Evelyn Zwemer, 1977.

1334

Japan—posters (in Japanese), ca. 1939–1945. 14 posters.
Printed.
Japanese propaganda posters from World War II.
Gift, Hillis Lory, 1972.

1335

Japanese coins—chart, n.d.
Depicts representative coins of the Japanese Empire, 706 A.D. to 1915.
Gift, Paul Dietrich, 1955.

1336

Japanese Government in Korea collection (in Japanese and Chinese), 1894–1910. 23 microfilm reels, 7 cu. ft. boxes.
Original records were destroyed by the Japanese in August 1945. Photographic plates, however, were saved. This collection consists of one set of photographic prints produced from the plates in 1948 by the Hoover Institution and the Korean National History Museum and one set of microfilm prints which the Hoover Institution produced in 1957.
Records of the Japanese Legation in Korea, 1894–1905, the Japanese Residency General in Korea, 1906–1910, and the Japanese Government-General in Korea, 1910, including diplomatic correspondence, dispatches and instructions, reports, treaties and agreements, lists, charts, and personal correspondence, relating to Japan-

ese policy and actions in Korea during the fifteen years preceding annexation, international relations in the Far East, and Korean domestic politics.

Published guide. Andrew C. Nahm, comp., *Japanese Penetration of Korea, 1894–1910: A Checklist of Japanese Archives in the Hoover Institution* (Hoover Institution on War, Revolution and Peace, 1959).

1337

Japanese military insignia, n.d. 1 folder.

Insignia for the ranks of major general, colonel, lieutenant colonel and major in the Japanese Army.

1338

Japanese press reports, 1939–1941. ½ ms. box.

Typescript.

Translations of newspaper articles from Japanese newspapers, relating to world political, military, and diplomatic affairs during the first years of World War II.

Gift, Boleslaw B. Szczesniak, 1973.

1339

Jarvis, Charles E.

Papers, 1918–1919. ½ ms. box, 2 envelopes.

American soldier; assigned to Medical Detail, 28th Engineer Regiment, American Expeditionary Force, during World War I. Correspondence, military tactics book, camp newspaper, French currency, postcards, and personal items of identification, relating to activities of the 28th Engineer Regiment in France during World War I.

Gift, Ohio Historical Society, 1960.

1340

Jasiewicz, Jan.

Phonorecord (in Polish), 1965. "Kawalkada Czasu" (Cavalcade of Time).

Compilation of radio broadcasts and commentaries concerning important international, Polish and Polish émigré historical events, 1952–1964. Compiled and produced by J. Jasiewicz and narrated by Tadeusz Nowakowski.

Gift, Jan Nowak, 1967.

1341

Jaulmes, G. L.

Painting (photograph), n.d. "Le Départ des Américains pour la Guerre" (Departure of Americans for the War). 1 envelope.

French painter. Commemorates the U.S. war effort in World War I.

Gift, Amy Edwards, 1976.

1342

Jeftić, Trivun R.

Papers (in Serbo-Croatian and German), 1941–1944. 1 folder.

Serbian collaborator with German occupation authorities in Yugoslavia during World War II. Correspondence and memoranda, relating to German occupation policy in Yugoslavia, and to the Yugoslav resistance movements.

1343

Jenkins, George D.

Papers, 1903–1969. 24 ms. boxes, 1 box of data cards (⅓ 1 ft.), 23 microfilm reels.

American political scientist. Writings, notes, correspondence, minutes of meetings, ordinances, pamphlets, clippings, and data cards, relating to politics in Nigeria and particularly to the government of Ibadan, Nigeria. Includes drafts of a book, *The Price of Liberty* by Kenneth W. J. Post and G. D. Jenkins.

Preliminary inventory.

Obisesan diaries may not be used without permission of G. D. Jenkins.

Deposit, G. D. Jenkins, 1969.

1344

Jennings, Ralph E., 1897–1971.

Papers, 1918–1966. 5 ms. boxes, 9 envelopes, 4 albums.

Vice Admiral, U.S. Navy; Captain, U.S.S. *Copahee* and *Yorktown*, 1943–1944; Chief, Military Assistance Advisory Group to Norway, 1950–1952; Deputy Commander, Eastern Frontier and Atlantic Fleet, 1952–1953. Correspondence, personnel records, memoranda, reports, speeches, logbooks, clippings, printed matter and photographs, relating to U.S. naval operations in World War II, the U.S.S. *Yorktown*, a historic telecast from the U.S.S. *Leyte* in August 1947, and the Military Assistance Advisory Group to Norway.

Register.

Gift, Mrs. R. E. Jennings, 1971.

1345

Jennison, Harry A.

Letter received, 1920. 1 folder.

Relates to conditions in Russia during the Russian Civil War. Written by a White Russian Army colonel.

Gift, John W. Romine, 1973.

1346

Jenny, Arnold E., 1895–1978.

Papers, 1917–1953. 4½ ms. boxes, 2 envelopes.

Young Men's Christian Association worker in Siberia, 1919–1920, and in Germany, 1945–1946. Correspondence, diary, reports, memoranda, and printed matter, relating to relief work in Siberia during the Russian Revolution, and among displaced persons in Germany at the end of World War II.

Register.

Gift, A. E. Jenny, 1973.

1347

Jessey, Joseph.

Photographs, 1923. 1 envelope.

Crew member on the U.S.S *Henderson*. Photographs and postcards, depicting President and Mrs. Warren G. Harding and Secretary of Commerce Herbert Hoover aboard the U.S.S. *Henderson* en route to Alaska.

Gift, Florence Burgess, 1975.

1348

Job, Martha.
Papers, 1920–1941. ½ ms. box, 3 envelopes.
Young Women's Christian Association worker in China, 1919–1929. Diary, maps, posters, photographs, clippings and booklets, relating to the Young Women's Christian Associations in China, flood relief, the University of Peking, and internal problems in China from 1920–1928.
Gift, M. Job, 1974.

1349

John, Otto, 1909–
Study, n.d. "Some Facts and Aspects of the Plot against Hitler." 1 vol.
Typescript.
Relates to the July 20, 1944 assassination attempt upon Adolf Hitler.

1350

Johnson, Benjamin O., b. 1878.
Papers, 1917–1923. 1 ms. box.
Photocopy.
American engineer; Colonel, Russian Railway Service Corps, 1917–1923; President pro tempore, Inter-Allied Technical Board, 1920–1921. Correspondence, reports, memoranda, diplomatic dispatches and instructions, and printed matter, relating to the Russian Railway Service Corps in Siberia, the Inter-Allied Technical Board, and the Trans-Siberian Railroad during World War I and the Russian Civil War.
Preliminary inventory.
Gift, William B. Bishop, 1973.

1351

Johnson, Douglas.
Letter, 1939, to J. Spencer Smith. 1 folder.
Typewritten transcript.
Chief, Division of Boundary Geography, U.S. Delegation to the Paris Peace Conference, 1919. Relates to territorial settlements at the Paris Peace Conference.

1352

Johnson, Lester J., *collector*.
Miscellany (in Norwegian and German), 1940–1947. 1 folder.
Circulars, memoranda, proclamations, clippings and miscellanea, relating to regulation of the civilian population in German-occupied Norway during World War II, war damage insurance in Norway during World War II, and the postwar Soviet-Norwegian dispute over the establishment of military bases on Spitsbergen.

1353

Johnson, Thomas R., *collector*.
Photographs, n.d. 1 envelope.
Depicts trophy cup presented to the Sturmabteilung of the German Nazi party by the German shoemaking industry.

1354

Johnson, William H.
Papers, 1917–1919. 1 folder, 2 envelopes.
American soldier, assigned to 31st Infantry Regiment during World War I. Diary, correspondence, and photographs, relating to activities of the 31st Infantry Regiment in Siberia.
Gift, Margaret C. Johnson, 1974.

1355

Johnston, Verle B.
History, 1967. *Legions of Babel: The International Brigades in the Spanish Civil War.* ½ ms. box.
Typescript.
Published (University Park, Pennsylvania, 1967).
Gift, V. B. Johnston, 1973.

1356

Joint Chinese and British Commission in China.
Photographs, n.d. 1 album.
Depicts scenes along the upper Yangtze River as part of a survey undertaken by the Commission.
Gift, Ray Lyman Wilbur, 1942.

1357

Joint Commission on Rural Reconstruction in China (U.S. and China).
Memorandum, ca. 1950. "Brief Statement on Animal Industry Projects in Taiwan Supported by JCRR." 1 vol.
Typescript (carbon copy).

1358

Joint U.S./British Ministerial Control Party for OKW/OKH/Para-Mil.
Reports, 1945. 1 folder.
Typescript (mimeographed).
Relates to the organization of the German Defense Ministry, Army, and paramilitary organizations, and to the transfer of their administration to Allied control at the end of World War II.

1359

Jonah, T. F.
Newspaper editorial, ca. 1913–1915. "Intervention in Mexico: Its Cost, Its Beneficiaries." 1 folder.
Typewritten transcript.
Relates to proposals for U.S. military intervention in Mexico. Published in the *El Paso Morning Times*.

1360

Jones, Evelyn Trent, 1892–1970.
Papers, 1925–1969. 1 ms. box, 1 envelope.
American journalist; wife of Manabendra Nath Roy, Indian communist leader. Correspondence, notes, pamphlets, clippings and photographs, relating to M. N. Roy and the communist movement in India.
Gift, Diven Meredith, 1971.

1361

Jones, Howard Palfrey, 1899–1973.
Papers, 1934–1973. 98 ms. boxes, 2 card file boxes (⅓ l. ft.), 12 phonotapes, 5 envelopes, 1 motion picture.
Director, Berlin Element for U.S. High Commissioner for Germany, 1950–1951; Chief of Mission, U.S. Economic Aid Mission to Indonesia, 1954–1955; U.S. Deputy Assistant Secretary of State for the Far East, 1955–1958; U.S. Ambassador to Indonesia, 1958–1965. Writings, correspondence, reports, research files, studies, and printed matter, relating to public finance and postwar reconstruction in Germany, 1945–1951, and to U.S. foreign relations with Indonesia and other areas of East Asia.
Register.
Gift, Mrs. H. P. Jones, 1974.

1362

Jones, Jefferson, *collector*.
Miscellany, 1914–1918. ½ ms. box, 4 envelopes.
Photographs, drawings, posters, printed matter and miscellanea, relating to activities of the Japanese Army in China during World War I, especially to the siege of Tsingtao, 1914; to the Russo-Japanese War of 1904–1905; and to the palace of Kaiser Wilhelm II on the island of Corfu.
Gift, J. Jones, 1959.

1363

Jones (Jenkin Lloyd)—photograph, n.d. 1 envelope.
Depicts J. L. Jones, American clergyman and director of the Abraham Lincoln Center, Chicago, 1905–1918.

1364

Jones, Lucius J.
Miscellany, 1931–1952. 1 folder, 1 envelope.
Photograph and a copy of the marriage license of Mary Green Jones, an ex-slave; and a letter written by L. J. Jones, son of Mary Jones, relating to her reminiscenses of slave life in Mississippi.
Gift, L. J. Jones, 1952.

1365

Jones, Samuel G., *collector*.
Flag, 1914.
Combined flag of the Central Powers (Germany, Austria, Hungary and Turkey) during World War I.
Gift, S. G. Jones.

1366

Jones, Warren Arnold, 1924?–1944, *collector*.
Bible, 1932. 1 vol.
Autographed by President Herbert Hoover.
Gift, Mrs. Warren P. Jones, 1965.

1367

Jongere-Telegrafisten Vereeniging.
Records (in Flemish), 1922–1926. 1 folder.
Telegraphic association in Brussels. Minutes of meetings, by-laws, membership lists, and accounts, relating to the promotion of telegraphy in Belgium.

1368

Jonkherr.
Photographs of caricatures, ca. 1914–1918. 3 envelopes.
Belgian cartoonist. Depicts officials of the Comité National de Secours et d'Alimentation, and of the Comité Provincial de Secours et d'Alimentation du Limbourg, Belgian relief organizations during World War I.

1369

Joos, Leopold.
Memorandum, 1947. 1 folder.
Holograph.
Relates to activities of the Belgian Army during the German offensive of May 1940.
Gift, Belgian American Educational Foundation, 1947.

1370

Jordan, David Starr, 1851–1931.
Papers, 1814–1947. 77 ms. boxes, 4 envelopes, 5 scrapbooks, 8 posters.
American educator and pacifist; President, Stanford University, 1891–1913; Chancellor, Stanford University, 1913–1916. Correspondence, writings, pamphlets, leaflets, clippings and photographs, relating to pacifism and the movement for world peace, disarmament, international relations, U.S. neutrality in World War I, U.S. foreign and domestic policy, civil liberties in the U.S., problems of minorities in the U.S., and personal and family matters.
Register.
Boxes 70-77 are closed until processed.
Gift, Jessie Knight Jordan.

1371

Jordan, R. E.
Notarized statement, 1966. 1 folder.
Typescript.
Relates to alleged advance knowledge of the Japanese attack on Pearl Harbor by U.S. intelligence officers.

1372

Jordan, Raymond Bruce, *collector*.
Miscellany, 1943–1945. ½ ms. box, 1 envelope.
Bulletins, photographs, memorabilia, and mimeographed material, relating to U.S. Army activities in the Pacific Theater during World War II.
Gift, R. B. Jordan, 1962. Incremental gift, 1976.

1373

Jovanović, Dragoljub, 1895–1977.
Writings (in Serbo-Croatian), ca. 1932–1965. 1 ms. box, 1 microfilm reel.
Yugoslav politician. Memoirs (typewritten), entitled "Političke Uspomene" (Political Reminiscences), 1965, relating to political developments in Yugoslavia during World War II; and a pamphlet (printed), entitled "Šta nas Košta Svada sa Hrvatima?" (What Is the Cost of Our Argument with Croatians), ca. 1932, relating to the nationalities question in Yugoslavia.
Gift, Alex Dragnich, 1974. Gift, Jozo Tomasevich, 1957.

1374

Joy, Charles Turner, 1895–1956.
Papers, 1951–1954. 1 ms. box, 1 oversize box (⅓ l. ft.), 1 envelope.
Vice Admiral, U.S. Navy; Senior United Nations delegate, Korean Armistice Conference, 1951–1952. Diaries, notes, clippings and photographs, relating to the Panmunjom negotiations to end the Korean War.
Gift, Captain and Mrs. C. T. Joy, Jr., 1974.

1375

Judd, James R.
Slides, ca. 1915–1916. 10 ms. boxes.
Member of American Ambulance Service in France. Depicts medical and relief work in France during World War I.
Gift, J. R. Judd, Jr., 1959.

1376

Juenger, Ernst, 1895–
Essay (in German), 1944. "Der Friede: Ein Wort an die Jugend Europas, Ein Wort an die Jugend der Welt" (Peace: A Word to the Youth of Europe, A Word to the Youth of the World). 1 vol.
Typescript.
Relates to post-World War II reconstruction.

1377

Jugend (Youth).
Newspaper issues (in German), 1947. 1 folder.
Typescript (some mimeographed).
Prison camp newspaper issued by Austrian prisoners of war at Oesterreichische Jugend Lager 603 in Yugoslavia. Relates to camp life and work.

1378

Juras, Francis Michael, 1891–
Papers (mainly in Lithuanian), 1912–1977. ½ ms. box.
Photocopy.
Lithuanian-American Roman Catholic priest and author. Newspaper and magazine clippings, printed matter, writings, photographs and memorabilia, relating to the career of F. M. Juras and to cultural activities of Lithuanians in the United States.
Gift, F. M. Juras, 1977.

1379

Kader, Boris M., *collector*.
B. M. Kader collection on Peresylnaĭâ Tĭurma (in Russian), 1906. 1 folder.
Articles, notes, and poems, written by the prisoners of Peresylnaĭâ Tĭurma in Petrograd for their secret magazine "Tĭurma" (Prison). Includes description of the material by B. M. Kader, editor of "Tĭurma."
Preliminary inventory.
Gift, B. M. Kader, 1957.

1380

Kaiser, Jakob.
Speech transcript (in German), 1947. 1 folder.
Typescript (mimeographed).
Relates to cooperation between the occupation authorities in Berlin and in the Soviet zone of Germany. Delivered at a meeting of the Union der Ostzone und Berlin in Berlin, July 12, 1947.

1381

Kammerer, Albert, b. 1875.
Journal article (in French), 1946. "Pourquoi J'ai Écrit *La Vérité sur l'Armistice*" (Why I wrote *The Truth about the Armistice*). 1 folder.
Typescript.
Relates to the book by A. Kammerer (published in Paris, 1944) on the French surrender in 1940. Article published in *La France Intérieure* (No. 41, February 15, 1946).

1382

Kampanakes, Patroklos.
Letter (in Greek), 1921, to Th. Homolle. 1 folder.
Holograph.
Greek architect. Relates to the royalist-Venizelist division in Greek politics, Greek foreign policy in Turkey, and Franco-Greek relations.

1383

Kanner, Heinrich, b. 1864.
Writings (in German), 1914–1917. 2 ms. boxes.
Typescript.
Austrian journalist; editor, *Die Zeit* (Vienna). Relates to political conditions and public opinion in Germany and Austria during World War I. Includes a partial translation (typewritten), by Robert Hopwood.
Gift, H. Kanner, 1925.

1384

Kapnist, Lieutenant.
Papers (in Russian, French and Czech), 1919–1920. 1 folder.
White Russian Army officer. Orders, telegrams and correspondence, relating to the liaison work of Lieutenant Kapnist with General Pierre Janin, French Army officer and Commander of Czechoslovak and other Allied troops in Siberia during the Russian Civil War.

1385

Kappel' (Vladimir Oskarovich) collection (in Russian), 1920. 1 folder.
Orders, memoranda and correspondence, relating to the "Icy March" campaign of V. Kappel' (1881–1920), White Russian Army General, in Siberia during the Russian Civil War.

1386

Karcz, George F., 1917–1970.
Papers, 1917–1970. 37 ms. boxes, 4 card file boxes (⅔ l. ft.), 1 phonotape.
American agricultural economist; professor, Univer-

sity of California, Santa Barbara. Correspondence, writings, research notes, statistical surveys and reports, and miscellanea, relating to Soviet and East European agriculture and economics.
Register.
Purchase, Irene Karcz, 1971.

1387

Karling (F. Warner) collection, n.d. 1 folder, 1 envelope.
Biographical sketch and portrait of F. Karling, Commander-in-Chief, Veterans of Foreign Wars of the United States, 1918–1920.
Gift, San Mateo County Free Library.

1388

Karski, Jan, 1914–
Papers (in Polish), 1939–1944. 7 ms. boxes, 24 envelopes, 27 microfilm reels.
Liaison officer and courier of the Polish Government-in-Exile (London) to the Polish underground, 1939–1943; author, *Story of a Secret State* (1944). Correspondence, memoranda, government and military documents, bulletins, reports, studies, speeches and writings, printed matter, photographs, clippings, newspapers, periodicals, and microfilms, relating to events and conditions in Poland during World War II, the German and Soviet occupations of Poland, treatment of the Jews in Poland during the German occupation, and operations of the Polish underground movement during World War II.
Preliminary inventory.
Gift, J. Karski, 1946.

1389

Kaslas, Bronis J., 1910–
Papers, 1918–1974. 4 ms. boxes.
Lithuanian historian. Writings and rare printed matter, relating to Eastern European politics, the Russian occupation of Lithuania, Lithuanians in foreign countries, the Baltic States, Poland, and the Paris Peace Conference of 1946.
Preliminary inventory.
Gift, B. J. Kaslas, 1976.

1390

Kasprzycki, Piotr Pawel.
Memorandum (in German), 1915. "Die Nationalitaeten-Frage und der Voelkerkrieg" (The Nationality Question and the Peoples' War). 1 folder.
Typescript (mimeographed).
Relates to the concept of nationality and its role in World War I.

1391

Kasson, John Adam, 1822–1910.
Letters, 1884–1886, from American citizens. 1 folder.
Holograph (photocopy of originals at Iowa State Historical Department).
American diplomat; U.S. Commissioner, Berlin Conference on African affairs, 1884–1885. Relates to decisions of the conference regarding government and trade in the Congo region.

1392

"Katalog der Spielwaren Ausstellung in Titograd" (Catalog of the Toy Exhibition in Titograd).
Catalog (in German), 1946. 1 vol.
Typescript.
Relates to toys made by Austrian prisoners in the Yugoslav prison camp of Titograd.

1393

Katkov, George.
Study, ca. 1968. "Soviet Historical Sources in the Post Stalin Era." 1 folder.
Typescript (photocopy).
Relates to the history, organization and operations of Soviet archival administration and publication policy since 1954.

1394

Kattermann (Heinrich)—photographs, 1916–1941. 2 albums.
Depicts H. Kattermann (d. 1941), German Army officer and national socialist; German troops in World Wars I and II; and national socialist political rallies.
Purchase, New York University Medical Center, 1973.

1395

Katz, Friedrich, *collector*.
F. Katz collection on world affairs (in German), 1919–1945. 173 pamphlet boxes (43 l. ft.).
Clippings, notes, and pamphlets, relating to international relations, international economic conditions, the oil industry, domestic conditions in Croatia, Croatia's role in international relations, the history and condition of Jews throughout the world, and military operations during World War II.
Preliminary inventory.

1396

Kaujewa, Jackson.
Phonorecord, n.d. "One Namibia, One Nation."
Southwest Africa People's Organization freedom songs sung by the SWAPO Singers, arranged by J. Kaujewa, and released by the SWAPO Department of Information and Publicity in London in cooperation with Action Namibia, Holland.
Purchase, 1978.

1397

Kaul'bars, Aleksandr Vasil'evich, b. 1884.
Study (in Russian), n.d. "Vozdushnyîâ Voĭska" (The Air Forces). 1 folder.
Typescript.
Relates to Russian aerial operations during World War I.

1398

Kautsky, Benedikt, 1894–1963.
Biography (in German), ca. 1945. 1 vol.
Typescript (photocopy).
Relates to August Bebel, German socialist leader.

1399

Kautsky, Karl Johann, 1854–1938.
Essay (in German), 1938. "Der Demokratische Marxismus: Zum Vierzigsten Geburtstag der Russischen Sozialdemokratie" (Democratic Marxism: On the Fortieth Anniversary of Russian Social Democracy). 1 folder.
Typescript (photocopy).
German socialist leader. Relates to the history and future prospects of socialism in Russia. Includes postcard photograph of K. J. Kautsky.
Gift, Karl Kautsky, Jr., 1977.

1400

Kayden, Eugene M.
Memorandum, 1918. "A Memorandum on the Political Changes in Russia since the Revolution." 1 folder.
Typescript.
Staff member, Bureau of Research, U.S. War Trade Board.

1401

Kayser, Josef.
Papers (in German), 1943–1945. 1 ms. box.
German Army chaplain; Russian prisoner of war during World War II. Reports, correspondence, a diary, and sermons, relating to German prisoners of war in Russia and to the Working Council on Religious Questions of the National Committee for a Free Germany, an organization of anti-Nazi German Christians concerned with the reconstruction of Germany after World War II.

1402

Kearns, Henry, 1911–
Papers, 1969–1976. 14 ms. boxes, 5 card file boxes.
American international finance and business consultant; President and Chairman, Export-Import Bank of the U.S., 1969–1973. Correspondence, memoranda, reports, studies, office files and printed matter, relating to international trade and finance policy and operations of the Export-Import Bank during the Presidency of Richard M. Nixon.
Preliminary inventory.
Closed until November 28, 1983.
Gift, H. Kearns, 1978.

1403

Kefauver, Grayson Neikirk, 1900–1946.
Papers, 1943–1946. 38 ms. boxes.
American educator; U.S. representative to Preparatory Commission for Establishing the United Nations Educational, Scientific and Cultural Organization. Correspondence, reports, memoranda, speeches and writings, minutes, and printed matter, relating to international educational reconstruction after World War II, and the organization of the United Nations Educational, Scientific and Cultural Organization.
Gift, G. N. Kefauver, 1947.

1404

Keil, Robert H.
Letters, 1963. 1 folder.
Typescript (photocopy).
American soldier; assigned to the U.S. 8th Cavalry Regiment. Relates to U.S. Army and Texas Ranger operations against bandits on the Texas-Mexican border, 1916–1918.

1405

Keith, Gerald.
Miscellany, 1917–1919. ½ ms. box.
Letters, written by G. Keith and Cary Hayward, American sailors, to family members, relating to U.S. Navy operations during World War I; and aerial photographs of the San Mihiel and Meuse-Argonne regions, 1918.

1406

Kelland, Clarence Budington, 1881–1964.
Letters received, 1961–1964. 1 folder, 1 envelope.
American author and journalist. Letters from Herbert Hoover, General A. C. Wedemeyer, and Roy W. Howard, relating to personal matters and U.S. politics. Includes two photographs of Herbert Hoover and Senator Mark Hatfield.
Gift, Thomas Kelland, 1976.

1407

Kelley, Gerard William, 1903–1969.
Papers, 1942–1944. 1 ms. box, 1 album, 1 envelope.
Brigadier General, U.S. Army; Commanding Officer, 165th Infantry Regiment, 1943–1945. Correspondence, diary, orders, memoranda and photographs, relating to U.S. military operations on Saipan, the Marianas, Makin Atoll, and elsewhere in the Pacific Theater during World War II.
Preliminary inventory.
Gift, Mrs. G. W. Kelley, 1970.

1408

Kelley, Paul X.
Letters received, 1965–1968, from Franz von Papen. 1 folder.
Typescript and holograph.
Major General, U.S. Marine Corps; Deputy for Education, Marine Corps Development and Education Command. Relates to von Papen's view of the world situation.
Gift, P. X. Kelley, 1977.

1409

Kelley, William J.
Memorandum, 1924. 1 folder.
Typescript.
Director, Press Department, Polish Legation in the U.S. Relates to political conditions in Poland and to Polish foreign policy.

1410

Kellock, Harold, b. 1879.
  Letter, 1918, to Lincoln Steffens. 1 vol.
  Holograph.
  Publicity Secretary, Finnish Information Bureau in the U.S. Relates to American relations with the revolutionary governments of Finland and Russia.

1411

Kellogg, Charlotte Hoffman, 1874–1960.
  Papers, 1916–1948. ½ ms. box, 2 scrapbooks, 1 oversize certificate.
  American author; relief worker in Europe during World Wars I and II; wife of Vernon Lyman Kellogg. Writings, correspondence, and printed matter, relating to relief work in Belgium during World War I and in Poland during and after World War II, and to Queen Jadwiga of Poland.
  Gift, C. H. Kellogg, 1956.

1412

Kellogg, R. H., *collector*.
  Miscellany, 1914–1915. 1 folder.
  Letter from G. W. Giddings of the Commission for Relief in Belgium, 1915, enclosing a Christmas greeting from the children of Antwerp to the children of the United States, 1914.
  Gift, Annie F. Kellogg, 1951.

1413

Kellogg, Vernon Lyman, 1867–1937.
  Papers, 1914–1921. 1½ ms. boxes, 1 oversize certificate.
  American zoologist; officer in relief organizations in Europe during World War I. Writings, printed matter, photographs, drawings, and certificates, relating to relief work in Belgium during World War I, the relief activities of Herbert Hoover, and the world food problem.
  Gift, Charlotte Hoffman Kellogg, 1956.

1414

Kemnitz, Hans Arthur von.
  Essays (in German and English), 1945–1948. 1 folder.
  Typescript (some mimeographed).
  Relates to the question of German war guilt for World Wars I and II. Written by H. A. von Kemnitz and Friedrich Wilhelm Adolf Guenther.

1415

Kennedy, John Fitzgerald, 1917–1963.
  Speeches, 1963. 1 phonorecord.
  President of the U.S., 1961–1963. Speeches delivered during a visit to Ireland, relating to Irish-American relations.
  Gift, Mr. and Mrs. Joseph P. Kennedy.

1416

Kennedy, Philip B.
  Report, 1931. "Impressions of Europe, June-October, 1931." 1 vol.
  Typescript (carbon copy).
  U.S. Commercial Attaché to Great Britain. Relates to social conditions and public opinion in Western Europe.

1417

Kerenskiĭ, Aleksandr Fedorovich, 1881–1970.
  Miscellaneous papers (in Russian and English), 1945–1965. 1 ms. box.
  Premier, Russian Provisional Government, 1917. Correspondence and writings, relating to the Russian Revolution and personal matters. Includes a history by Kerenskiĭ, entitled "The Genesis of the 'October Revolution' of 1917," and correspondence with Vasiliĭ Maklakov, Michael Karpovich and Anatole G. Mazour.
  Preliminary inventory.
  Gift, A. F. Kerenskiĭ. Gift A. G. Mazour, 1976.

1418

Kernan, Rosemary.
  Correspondence, 1918–1919. 1 ms. box.
  American relief worker in France, 1918–1919. Relates to work of the Knights of Columbus and of the Comité Anglais in France.
  Gift, Silvine Savage, 1971.

1419

Kerr, George H., 1911–
  Papers, 1943–1951. 7 ms. boxes.
  American historian; Vice Consul, Taipei, Formosa, 1945–1947. Reports, notes, press summaries, clippings, and writings, relating to political and economic conditions in Formosa under Japanese rule, transferral of Formosa's sovereignty to China in 1945, Formosan rebellion against Chinese rule in 1947, U.S. foreign policy toward Formosa, and political and economic conditions in Okinawa and the Ryukyus after World War II.
  Gift, G. H. Kerr.

1420

Kerr, Stanley E.
  Memoir, 1921. "The Story of Marash, a City of Cicilia." 1 vol.
  Typescript (carbon copy).
  American in Turkey. Relates to Turkish massacres of Armenians in Maras, Turkey, 1920.

1421

Keskuela, Aleksandr, 1882–1963.
  Papers (in German), 1915–1963. 2 ms. boxes.
  Estonian socialist; reputed intermediary between V. I. Lenin and the German Government during World War I. Correspondence, writings, and memoranda, relating to personal experiences and to international socialist and communist movements.
  Preliminary inventory.
  Purchase, Ingeborg K. Weidmann, 1966.

1422

Ketcham, W.E.
  Photographs, ca. 1909–1910. 1 envelope.
  Depicts the first public flight of a plane in Japan, at

Meguro Race Track, Tokyo, and a later flight at Yokohama.
Gift, W. Egbert Schenck, 1950.

1423

Key, Kerim Kami.
Dissertation, 1950. "The Ottoman Intellectuals and the Young Turk Reformation of 1908." 1 folder.
Typescript.
Relates to the role of intellectuals in the Young Turk movement and the resurgence of Turkish nationalism.

1424

Keynes, John Maynard, 1883–1946.
Essay, 1925. "The Economic Transition in England." 1 folder.
Typescript.
British economist. Relates to economic conditions in Great Britain.

1425

Khorvat, Dmitriĭ Leonidovich, b. 1858.
Memoirs, n.d. 1 vol.
Typescript (carbon copy).
Lieutenant General, Imperial Russian Army. Relates to Imperial Russian administration of the Chinese Eastern Railway, and to White Russian military activities in the Far East during the Russian Civil War.

1426

Kilgroe, Louisa.
Thesis, 1971. "American Far Eastern Policy in the Sino-Japanese Crisis, 1937." 1 folder.
Typescript (photocopy).

1427

Killie, Charles A.
Photographs, 1900. 2 envelopes.
Depicts the siege of Peking during the Boxer Rebellion in China.
Preliminary inventory.

1428

Kimball, Katrine Rushton Fairclough.
Papers, 1917–1919. 1 folder.
Member, British Army Almeric Paget Military Massage Corps. Correspondence, regulations and miscellanea, relating to physical therapy in British military hospitals during World War I.

1429

Kimura, Toshio.
Letters, 1942–1945. 1 folder.
Typescript and holograph.
Japanese American interned at Heart Mountain, Wyoming, Relocation Camp, 1942–1945. Relates to conditions in the relocation camp and prospects for release. Includes letters from Mrs. T. Kimura.
Preliminary inventory.
Gift, Emi K. Fugii, 1973.

1430

King, David Wooster, 1893–
Papers, 1914–1971. ½ ms. box.
American consular official; Office of Strategic Services officer in North Africa during World War II. Diary, orders, correspondence and memorabilia, relating to French and American military operations in World War I, the U.S. consular service in Ethiopia in 1926, and Office of Strategic Services activities in North Africa during World War II.
Preliminary inventory.
Gift, D. W. King, 1972.

1431

King, Joseph Choate.
Papers, 1915–1964. 1 vol.
Colonel, U.S. Army. Diary and memoirs, relating to American military activities in the Philippines, during the Punitive Expedition into Mexico, and in World War I.

1432

King, Norman D.
Papers, 1944–1945. 1 ms. box, 2 envelopes.
Colonel, U.S. Army. Orders, memoranda, intelligence reports, notebook, clippings, maps, and photographs, relating to activities of the XVI Corps in Europe during World War II.
Gift, N. D. King, 1969.

1433

King, Wunsz, 1892–1968.
Papers, 1919–1952. 2 ms. boxes.
Chinese diplomat; Ambassador to the Netherlands, 1933–1944: Ambassador to exiled governments in London, 1941–1945; Ambassador to Norway, 1945–1950. Transcripts of conversations with foreign officials, memoranda, and reports, relating to Chinese foreign relations with the Netherlands, Belgium, Norway, Poland and Czechoslovakia; the Sino-Japanese War; and the Korean National Council to the League of Nations, 1919.
Gift, Mrs. W. King, 1968.

1434

Kirby, Gustavus T.
Papers, 1914–1941. 2 ms. boxes.
Member, Executive Committee, Friends of Belgium. Reports, correspondence, clippings, map, and card file, relating to relief in Belgium during World Wars I and II, exchange of Belgian and American Fellows through the C.R.B. Educational Foundation, and charitable and goodwill efforts of the Friends of Belgium.
Preliminary inventory.
Gift, Mrs. Thomas M. Waller, 1956.

1435

Kirk (Alan Goodrich)—photographs, n.d. 1 envelope.
Depicts Admiral A. G. Kirk, U.S. Navy.

1436

Kirwan, J. W.

Synopsis of memoir, n.d. "Hoover in Western Australia: Some Goldfields Memories." 1 folder.

Typescript.

Relates to activities of Herbert Hoover as a mining engineer in Australia in the 1890s.

Gift, Felix B. Stump, 1957.

1437

Kitagawa, Kay I., *collector*.

K. I. Kitagawa collection on the Japanese Army, 1943–1944. 2 ms. boxes, 2 swords, 1 rifle, 1 bayonet.

Military manuals, syllabi, and exercises, used by the U.S. Military Intelligence Service Language School at Camp Savage, Minnesota, relating to the organization of the Japanese Army and to the study of the Japanese language. Includes four Japanese weapons.

Preliminary inventory.

Gift, K. I. Kitagawa.

1438

Kitchin, George, 1892–1935.

Memoirs (in Russian), n.d. "Zakliŭchennyĭ OGPU" (Prisoner of the OGPU). ½ ms. box.

Typescript (carbon copy).

Russian concentration camp prisoner. Relates to conditions in Soviet concentration camps, 1928–1932. Translation published as *Prisoner of the OGPU* (New York: Longmans, Green, 1935).

Deposit, Boris Kitchin, 1957.

1439

Kititsyn, Captain.

Order (in Russian), 1920. 1 folder.

Typescript (mimeographed).

White Russian Naval officer. Relates to White Russian naval activities at Vladivostok.

1440

Kittredge, George Lyman, 1860–1941, *collector*.

G. L. Kittredge collection on war relief, 1914–1919. 1 ms. box.

Letters, broadsides, and pamphlets, relating to World War I fund raising and relief.

Gift, Harvard University Library, 1959.

1441

Kittredge, Mabel Hyde.

Miscellaneous papers (in French and English), 1915–ca. 1918. 1 folder.

Summary (mimeographed in French) of mortality statistics for Lille, France, during the German occupation in World War I, prepared by Dr. DuCamp; and an offprint of a journal article, entitled "Taking Care of Belgium," by M. H. Kittredge, 1915, relating to relief work of the Commission for Relief in Belgium.

Gift, M. H. Kittredge.

1442

Kittredge, Tracy Barrett, 1891–1957.

Papers, 1910–1957. 51 ms. boxes, 6 envelopes.

Captain, U.S. Navy; member, Commission for Relief in Belgium, 1914–1917. Correspondence, reports, writings, notes, and clippings, relating to the Commission for Relief in Belgium, 1914–1924; Paris Peace Conference, 1919; controversy between Admiral W. S. Sims and Navy Secretary Josephus Daniels, 1919–1920; League of Red Cross Societies, 1920–1931; and U.S. Navy in World War II.

Preliminary inventory.

Gift, Eleanor H. Kittredge, 1960.

1443

Klatt, Werner, *collector*.

Miscellany (in German and English), 1940–1946. 1 folder.

Reports and memoranda, 1940–1944, issued by various German Government agencies, relating to German food supply policy during World War II. Includes a report by W. Klatt, 1946, relating to German food policy.

Gift, W. Klatt, 1978.

1444

Klein, Julius, 1886–1961.

Papers, 1928–1952. 3 ms. boxes.

Director, U.S. Bureau of Foreign and Domestic Commerce, 1921–1929; Assistant Secretary of Commerce, 1929–1933. Transcripts of radio broadcasts, transcripts of speeches, and correspondence, relating to U.S. economic conditions, foreign trade and economic policy during the administration of President Herbert Hoover.

Preliminary inventory.

Gift, J. Klein, 1956.

1445

Klein, Julius, 1895–

Correspondence, 1935, with Herbert Hoover. 1 folder.

Photocopy.

American journalist and public relations executive. Relates to a projected book by J. Klein on the Irish nationalist leader Sir Roger Casement. Includes a clipping and a statement by George Bernard Shaw regarding Sir Roger Casement.

Gift, J. Klein, 1935.

1446

Der Kleingaertner (The Little Gardener).

Serial issue (in German), 1952. 1 folder.

Printed.

Anti-communist propaganda, camouflaged as a serial issue, and distributed in East Germany.

1447

Klemm, V., b. 1861.

Writings (in Russian and English), 1922–1926. 1 folder.

Holograph and typescript.

White Russian political leader during the Russian Civil War. Autobiographical sketch (typewritten), 1926; a his-

tory (handwritten in Russian), entitled "Ocherk Revol-iûŝionnykh Sobytiĭ v Russkoĭ Sredneĭ Aziĭ" (Sketch of the Revolution in Russian Central Asia), 1922; and a translation (typewritten) of the above.
Gift, V. Klemm, 1926.

1448

Kluss, Walter L.
Letter, 1942, to Marshal Fevzi Çakmak, Turkish Army. 1 folder.
Typescript.
Lieutenant Colonel, U.S. Army; U.S. Military Attaché to Turkey. Relates to an American invitation to the Turkish Government to send a military delegation to visit the U.S.

1449

Kneeland, Norman L.
Letters, 1917–1919, to relatives. 1 folder.
Holograph and typescript.
Sergeant, U.S. Army; soldier in the 32d Division in France during World War I. Relates to military training in Texas, service in France during World War I, and impressions of General John J. Pershing.
Gift, Norman Dudley, 1978.

1450

Knezevich, John, d. 1964.
Papers, 1943–1945. 1 album, 1 envelope.
Major, U.S. Air Force; Head of Joint Intelligence in the Middle East, 1943–1945. Photographs and memorabilia, relating to the Yugoslav guerrilla war against German occupation forces during World War II.
Gift, D. N. Ristic, 1972.

1451

Knîazev, N. N.
Translation, n.d. "The Legendary Baron (From Reminiscences about Lieutenant-General Baron Ungern)." 1 vol., 1 negative microfilm reel.
Typescript.
Relates to Baron Roman Ungern-Shternberg, White Russian military leader in Mongolia during the Russian Revolution. Translation of "Legendarnyĭ Baron," published in *Luch Aziĭ,* 1937.

1452

Knight, Francis Putnam, 1894–
Papers, 1918–1919. ½ ms. box, 1 album, 1 envelope.
Captain, U.S. Army; Commanding Officer, Motor Transportation Corps Supply Depot No. 702, 1918–1919. Diary, correspondence, clippings and photographs, relating to activities of Motor Transportation Corps Supply Depot No. 702 in Paris during World War I.
Preliminary inventory.
Gift, Robert R. Park, 1970.

1453

Knochen, Helmut, 1910–
Memoirs (in German), n.d. 1 folder.
Typescript.

Colonel, German Army. Relates to the German occupation of France, 1940–1944.

1454

Knoll, S., *collector.*
Miscellany, ca. 1940. 1 folder.
Photographs and miscellanea, relating to British prisoners of war in German prison camps during World War II.

1455

Knowland, William Fife, 1908–1974.
Miscellaneous papers, 1956, 1 ms. box.
U.S. Senator from California, 1945–1959. Press releases, reports and campaign literature, relating to the Republican Congressional campaign of 1956.
Preliminary inventory.
Gift, W. F. Knowland, 1969.

1456

Knowlton, Lucerne H.
Papers, 1922–1953. ½ ms. box, 1 envelope.
American missionary in China. Letters, typewritten history, and printed matter, relating to missionary work in China, including reports of Hwa Nan College, newsletter from Foochow, and reports on Methodist Women's Work Conferences at Foochow.

1457

Knuth, Hertha.
Miscellany, 1946. 1 folder, 1 envelope.
Translator, interpreter, and court reporter at the International Military Tribunal, Nuremberg. Photographs and press cables, depicting the proceedings of the International Military Tribunal at Nuremberg, and describing the death sentences and deaths of various defendants.
Gift, H. Knuth, 1967.

1458

Kobal, Daniel, *collector.*
Miscellany, 1963. 1 folder.
Memorabilia, issues of Vietnamese and American Armed Forces newspapers, and photographs, relating to the 1963 coup d'état in South Vietnam and the assassination of John Fitzgerald Kennedy.
Gift, Andrew Kobal, 1964.

1459

Koch, Howard, Jr.
Study, 1973. "Permanent War: A Reappraisal of the Arab-Israeli Conflict, 1948–1967." 1 folder.
Typescript.
Gift, H. Koch, Jr., 1973.

1460

Koehl, Franz.
Diary (in German), 1913–1914. 1 folder.
Typewritten transcript (photocopy).
First Lieutenant, German Army; stationed in German East Africa, 1913–1914. Relates to conditions in German East Africa and the Belgian Congo.
Gift, Charles Burdick, 1972.

1461

Koehler, Benno, b. 1886.
Memoir (in German), 1934. "In Eigener Sache" (In My Own Case). 1 vol.
Typescript (photocopy).
German lawyer. Relates to the arrest of B. Koehler for political offenses and to his imprisonment in the Nazi concentration camp of Oranienburg, 1933—1934.

1462

Koehler, Commander.
Letter, 1925, to John Sellards and Ray Lyman Wilbur, Jr. 1 folder.
Typescript.
U.S. Navy officer. Relates to his observations of the Hawaiian Islands.

1463

Koestner, Nicolai.
Miscellaneous papers (in English and French), 1920—1921. 1 folder.
Estonian Consul in New York City. Writings, press summaries, and memoranda, relating to diplomatic recognition of Estonia by the U.S. and other countries, and to the admission of Estonia to the League of Nations.
Gift, N. Koestner, 1921.

1464

Kohlberg, Alfred, 1887—1960.
Papers, 1937—1960. 224 ms. boxes.
American business executive; National Chairman, American Jewish League Against Communism; Chairman, American China Policy Association; and member of the board, Institute of Pacific Relations. Correspondence, newsletters, clippings and printed matter, relating to communist influence in the U.S., China and other parts of Asia, and to anti-communist movements in the U.S.
Preliminary inventory.
Closed until May 1, 1991.
Gift, Ida Jolles Kohlberg, 1961.

1465

Kokovt͡sov, Vladimir Nikolaevich, 1853—1942.
Translation of memoirs, 1935. *Out of My Past: The Memoirs of Count Kokovt͡sov.* 1 ms. box, 1 envelope.
Typescript.
Russian statesman; Minister of Finance, 1904—1914; Chairman of the Council of Ministers, 1911—1914. Relates to Russian political conditions, 1904—1917, and to the Russian Revolution. Translation published (Stanford: Stanford University Press, 1935). Edited by H. H. Fisher and translated by Laura Matveev. Includes photographs used to illustrate the book.

1466

Kolchak, Aleksandr Vasil'evich, 1873—1920.
Correspondence, May 26—June 4, 1919, with heads of government of the Allied and Associated Powers. 1 vol.
Typescript (mimeographed).
White Russian leader during the Russian Civil War.

Relates to conditions for Allied support of the forces of Admiral Kolchak.

1467

Kolmsperger, M.
Study (in German), 1947. "Vom Militarismus in Bayern: Ein Kurzer Rueckblick" (On Militarism in Bavaria: A Short Retrospect). 1 vol.
Typescript (carbon copy).

1468

Kolobov, Mikhail Viktorovich.
Memoirs (in Russian), n.d. "Bor'ba s Bol'shevikami na Dal'nem Vostoki͡e (Khorvat, Kolchak, Semenov, Merkulovy, Diterikhs): Vospominanii͡a Uchastnika" (Struggle with the Bolsheviks in the Far East: Reminiscences of a Participant). 1 vol.
Typescript (carbon copy).
Relates to White Russian military activities in Siberia during the Russian Civil War.

1469

Kologrivov, Constantine Nikolaevich.
Memorandum, 1917. 1 folder.
Typescript (photocopy).
Captain, Imperial Russian Army. Relates to Tsar Nicholas II's Personal Combined Infantry Regiment and 4th Imperial Family Rifle Guards Regiment. Memorandum addressed to Cornet Serge ĭ Vladimirovich Markov of the Crimean Horse Regiment.
Gift, M. Lyons, 1971.

1470

Komitee der Bewegung "Freies Deutschland" fuer den Westen.
Issuances (in German and French), 1943—1945. 1 folder.
Printed and typescript (mimeographed).
Anti-Nazi German organization. Propaganda bulletins and leaflets, distributed on the western front. Includes similar material distributed by the National-Komitee "Freies Deutschland" on the eastern front.

1471

Kommunisticheskai͡a Partii͡a Sovetskogo Sou͡za. T͡Sentral'nyĭ Komitet. Politicheskoe Bi͡uro.
Resolutions (in Russian and German), January 27, 1934—March 14, 1936. 1½ ms. boxes.
Handwritten and typewritten transcripts.
Politburo of the Communist Party of the Soviet Union. Includes some photocopies.
Gift, Office of the Military Government of the United States in Germany.

1472

Kommunisticheskai͡a Partii͡a Sovetskogo Soi͡uza. T͡Sentral'nyĭ Komitet. Politicheskoe Bi͡uro—photograph, n.d. 1 envelope.
Depicts members of the Political Bureau of the Central Committee of the Communist Party of the Soviet Union, including Andreĭ A. Andreev, Lavrentiĭ P. Berii͡a, Lazar

M. Kaganovich, Mikhail I. Kalinin, Nikita S. Khrush-chev, Anastas I. Mikoian, Vi͡acheslav M. Molotov, Nikolaĭ M. Shvernik, Iosif Stalin, Kliment E. Voroshilov and Andreĭ A. Zhdanov.

1473

Kommunistische Partei Deutschlands.
Report (in German), n.d. 1 folder.
Typescript.
Relates to a meeting of members of the German Communist Party held at Frankfurt, June 9, 1949, to consider German political and economic questions.

1474

Komor, Paul.
Extracts from a letter received, 1951, from an unidentified White Russian émigré in Shanghai. 1 folder.
Typescript.
Relates to political and economic conditions in China.

1475

Komunistička Partija Jugoslavije. Centralni Komitet.
Program and statutes (in Serbo-Croatian), 1976. 1 folder.
Typescript (photocopy).
Compiled by a clandestine "Cominformist" and anti-Titoist political organization in Yugoslavia.
Gift, anonymous, 1976.

1476

Kongres Polakow w Niemczech, Berlin, 1938.
Issuances (in Polish), 1938. ½ ms. box.
Polish Minority in Germany Congress held in Berlin, 1938. Leaflets, pamphlets, reports, postcards, printed matter and memorabilia, relating to the Polish population within Germany.
Gift, Witold S. Sworakowski, 1972.

1477

Konokovich, General.
Report (in Russian), n.d. "Opisanie Boia 15 Iulia 1916 Goda pri Der. Trysten, Kol. Kurgan i Der. Voronchin" (An Account of the Battle of July 15, 1916, near Trysten Village, Kurgan Settlement and Voronchin Village). 1 folder.
Typescript.
Major General, Imperial Russian Army.

1478

Konoye, Fumimaro, Prince, 1891–1945.
Translation of memoirs, n.d. "General Reflections." 1 folder.
Holograph.
Prime Minister of Japan, 1937–1939 and 1940–1941. Relates to political conditions in Japan, 1932–1945. Includes a copy of the published Japanese text.

1479

"Konspiracja w Kraju pod Okupacja Sowiecka" (Conspiracy in the Country under Soviet Occupation).
Report (in Polish), n.d. 1 folder.

Typescript.
Relates to resistance to Soviet occupation forces in Poland at the end of World War II.
Gift, Jim Lesniewicz, 1969.

1480

Konstantin Nikolaevich, Grand Duke of Russia, 1827–1892.
Extracts from letters (in Russian), 1881–1882, to State Secretary Aleksandr Golovnin. 1 folder.
Typescript.
Relates to his travels in Western Europe, and the political situation in Russia.

1481

Konstantinov, P. F.
Newspaper article (in Russian), 1947. "Zhizn' i Vstrechi" (Life and Encounters). 1 folder.
Relates to Professor V. P. Ipat'ev's memoir *Zhizn' Odnogo Khimika* (Life of a Chemist), and conditions in Russia before and after the Revolution of 1917.

1482

Konstitut͡sionno-Demokraticheskai͡a Partii͡a.
Miscellaneous records (in Russian and French), 1920–1924. 2 ms. boxes.
Constitutional Democratic Party of Russia. Minutes of meetings, resolutions, reports, and correspondence, relating to the Russian Revolution and to activities of the Konstitut͡sionno-Demokraticheskai͡a Partii͡a in exile.
Preliminary inventory.

1483

Korea (Territory under U.S. occupation, 1945–   ) Military Governor.
Reports, 1945–1946. 1 folder.
Typescript (mimeographed).
Relates to political conditions in Korea under American occupation, October 1945–June 1946.

1484

Korean Broadcasting System.
Transcripts of radio programs (in Korean), 1948. 1 folder.
Typescript (mimeographed).

1485

"Korean Underground Report."
Newsletters, 1965–1968. ½ ms. box.
Typescript (mimeographed).
Compilation of information from various newspapers and other sources, relating to communist subversion in the United States and international affairs, particularly in relation to South Korea and Southeast Asia. Edited by Kilsoo K. Haan.
Gift, K. K. Haan, 1974.

1486

Kornilov, Lavr Georgivich, 1870–1918.
Writings (in Russian and English), 1917. 1 folder.
General and Commander-in-Chief, Russian Army, 1917. Translation (typewritten) of a speech, and copy

(typewritten in Russian) of an order, both relating to conditions of morale and discipline in the Russian Army in 1917.

1487

Korol'kov, M.
Memoir (in Russian), 1928. "Iz Vospominaniĭ Voennago IÛrista" (From the Reminiscences of a Military Lawyer). 1 vol.
Typescript.
Relates to administration of military justice in the Imperial Russian Army, and to military discipline at the time of the Russo-Japanese War.

1488

Korrçë, Albania—appeal, 1913. 1 folder.
Typescript (mimeographed).
Protests the inclusion of Korrçë in Albania as a part of the Balkan War peace settlement. Written by Greeks in the Korrçë district, and addressed to the conference of ambassadors in London.

1489

Korvin-Kroukovsky, Eugénie A.
Diary (in Russian), 1917–1918. 1 folder.
Typescript.
Relates to events in Petrograd during the Revolution of 1917, and to the escape of E. A. Korvin-Kroukovsky to the United States via the Far East, 1918.
Gift, E. A. Korvin-Kroukovsky, 1971.

1490

Koscinska, Marja.
Memorandum, n.d. "The Conditions in Poland." 1 folder.
Typescript.
Relates to the condition of Poles in Germany between the two world wars.

1491

Kosinskiĭ, Vladimir Andreevich, 1866–1938.
Study (in Russian), n.d. "Russkaiͣa Agrarnaiͣa Revoliͣutͣsiiͣa" (Russian Agrarian Revolution). 2 ms. boxes, 1 envelope.
Typescript.
Professor of Political Science and Economics, Moscow University. Relates to agrarian reforms in Russia from 1905 until 1917.
Gift, Sister Seraphim, 1972.

1492

Koszorus, Ferenc, 1899–1974.
Writings (mainly in Hungarian), 1954–1970. ½ ms. box.
Typescript.
Colonel, Hungarian Army. Relates to Hungarian, German, Soviet and international military strategy during World Wars I and II. Includes a letter and notes from F. Koszorus to General Omar Bradley, 1953.
Register.
Gift, Gabriella Koszorus, 1975.

1493

Koussonskii, Pavel Alekseevich.
Papers (in Russian), 1918–1926. 12 ms. boxes.
Lieutenant General, White Russian Army; staff officer under Generals Denikin, Vrangel', and Miller, 1918–1925. Correspondence, reports, telegrams, orders, circulars, proclamations, lists, maps, and charts, relating to the General Headquarters of the Volunteer Army of the Armed Forces in South Russia; to the Caucasian, Crimean, and other campaigns of the Civil War; to the evacuation and resettlement of General Vrangel''s army; and to Russian émigré military and political life in Europe.
Register.
Gift, I. A. Holmsen, 1928.

1494

Kraft, Rose, *collector*.
Miscellany, ca. 1941–1965. 3 envelopes, 1 box of slides.
Photographs depicting military campaigns in the Pacific during World War II; color slides depicting scenic views in mainly European countries; and programs to Russian theater and ballet performances.
Preliminary inventory.
Gift, R. Kraft, 1972. Subsequent increments.

1495

Krajowa Agencja Wydawnicza (Poland).
Posters (in Polish), 1971–1975. 24 posters.
Printed.
National Publishing Agency of Poland. Relates to social and political conditions in Poland.
Purchase, 1976.

1496

Kramatorsk Machine Tool Factory, Kramatorsk, Russia—photographs, n.d. 1 envelope.
Depicts the Kramatorsk Machine Tool Factory, Kramatorsk, Russia.

1497

Kramer, Howard D., 1907–1975.
Papers, 1942–1957. 2 ms. boxes.
Acting Chief, U.S. Office of War Information Psychological Warfare Branch in the Southwest Pacific, 1945; Acting Chief, U.S. Information Service in the Philippines, 1945–1946. Transcripts of radio broadcasts, posters, leaflets, correspondence, printed matter and photographs, relating to U.S. and Japanese propaganda activities in the Philippines during World War II. Includes a photocopy of the Ph.D. dissertation of H. D. Kramer, "History of the Public Health Movement in the U.S., 1850–1900."
Gift, Mrs. H. D. Kramer, 1976.

1498

Kramer, Jack.
Papers, 1968–1969. 1 ms. box.
American journalist in Eritrea. Correspondence, writings, printed matter, photographs and a tape recording, relating to the Eritrean Liberation Front and the movement for Eritrean independence.

1499

Krasnov, Petr Nikolaevich, 1869–1947.
Letter (in Russian), 1937. 1 folder.
Holograph.
General, Imperial Russian Army; and White Russian leader in the Russian Civil War. Relates to personal matters.

1500

Krasnow, Wladislaw Georgievich, 1937–
Dissertation, 1974. "Polyphony of *The First Circle:* A Study in Solzenicyn's Affinity With Dostoevskij." ½ ms. box.
Typescript (photocopy).
Relates to the Russian novelist Aleksandr Solzhenitsyn. Ph.D. dissertation, University of Washington, Seattle.
Gift, W. G. Krasnow, 1976.

1501

Krassovskiĭ, Vitol'd.
Memoirs (in Russian), 1927. 1 folder.
Typescript.
Imperial Russian Army officer. Relates to Russian military activities during World War I, and to White Russian military activities in southwestern Russia during the Russian Civil War.

1502

Kraucs, Eduards, b. 1898.
Papers (in Latvian), 1945–1977. ½ ms. box, 1 envelope, 474 filmstrips, 3 motion picture reels, 1 album.
Latvian-American photographer and television cameraman. Autobiographical sketch, scrapbook, films, and photographs, relating primarily to Latvian refugees in Germany and the United States. Includes translations.
Preliminary inventory.
Gift, Natalija Kraucs, 1978.

1503

Krause, Johannes.
Study (in German), 1947. "Exposé ueber einen Vorschlag zur Erschuetterung des Schwarzen Marktes" (Exposé of a Proposal to Upset the Black Market). 1 folder.
Typescript.
German economist. Relates to the post-World War II German black market.

1504

Kravchinskiĭ, Sergeĭ Mikhailovich, 1852–1895.
Papers (in Russian), 1892–1908. 1 ms. box.
Russian socialist and novelist. Correspondence, writings, and extracts from printed matter, relating to nineteenth century Russian revolutionary movements. Includes material relating to S. M. Kravchinskiĭ.

1505

Krebs, Rudolf, *collector.*
Newspaper clippings (in German), 1918. 1 folder.
Photocopy.
Relates to the causes of Germany's defeat in World War I.

1506

Kreisauer Kreis.
Memoranda (in German), 1942–1945. 1 folder.
Typescript.
Relates to the anti-Nazi movement and to post-World War II reconstruction in Germany. Written by members of the anti-Nazi Kreisauer Kreis resistance movement.

1507

"Krizis Partiĭ" (Party Crisis).
History (in Russian), n.d. 1 folder.
Typescript.
Relates to the history and structure of the Communist Party of the Soviet Union, 1905–1923.

1508

Krîûkov, Boris Aleksandrovich, 1898–
Papers (in Russian), 1917–1923. 4 ms. boxes, 9 envelopes.
White Russian Army and Marine Corps officer. Memoranda, military and naval intelligence reports, civil, naval and military orders, correspondence and photographs, relating to the Russian Revolution and Civil War in the Siberian Far East, especially operations of the Amur Flotilla (Red) and the Siberian Flotilla (White).
Register.
Gift, B. A. Krîûkov, 1934.

1509

Krivoshein (Aleksandr Vasil'evich)—photograph, n.d. 1 envelope.
Depicts the White Russian political leader A. V. Krivoshein.

1510

Krueger, Fr. W., 1894–
Diaries (in German), 1917–1939. ½ ms. box.
Holograph.
German Army officer; SS-Obergruppenfuehrer, 1938–1939. Relates to activities of Infanterie Regiment von Luetzow (in Rheinland) No. 25, 1917–1918, and to activities of the Schutzstaffel, 1938–1939. Includes photographs.
Purchase, New York University Medical Center, 1973.

1511

Krulak, Victor Harold, 1913–
Papers, 1958–1977. 1 ms. box.
Lieutenant General, U.S. Marine Corps; Commanding General, Fleet Marine Force, Pacific, 1964. Writings, speeches, interviews, and clippings, relating to Marine Corps activities in China in the 1930s and during World War II, the Korean War, and the Vietnamese Conflict.
Gift, V. H. Krulak, 1977.

1512

Krupenskiĭ, Aleksandr Nikolaevich.
Papers (in Russian, French and Romanian), 1918–1935. 9 ms. boxes.
Marshal of Bessarabian Nobility; President, Bessarabian Provincial Zemstvo; Bessarabian delegate to the

Paris Peace Conference, 1919–1920. Correspondence, memoranda, lists, extracts, summaries, reports, appeals, protests, protocols, press analyses, maps, forms, notes, drafts, clippings, newspaper issues, journals, bulletins, and pamphlets, relating to the Bessarabian question, to relations between Russia, Romania and Bessarabia, to the occupation and annexation of Bessarabia by Romania, 1918, and to the Paris Peace Conference.
Register.
Consult Archivist for restrictions.
Gift, A. N. Krupenskiĭ, 1936.

1513

Krymskoe Kraevoe Pravitel'stvo.
Miscellaneous records (in Russian), 1918–1919. 2 ms. boxes.
Crimean Regional Government. Files of the President of the Council of Ministers, Minister of Foreign Affairs, Minister of Justice, and Minister of Internal Affairs, relating to the relations of the Crimean Regional Government and the Constitutional Democratic Party with the Russian Volunteer Army and with the Allies.

1514

Krystufek, Zdenek.
Study (in Czech), 1972. "Sovětský Vzor Vlády V Československu" (Soviet Model of Rule in Czechoslovakia). ½ ms. box.
Typescript.
Professor of Political Science, University of Colorado. Relates to Soviet rule in Czechoslovakia between 1946 and 1968.
Gift, Z. Krystufek, 1973.

1515

Krzeczunowicz, Kornel.
Study (in Polish), n.d. "Ostatnia Kampania Konna" (The Last Cavalry Campaign). ½ ms. box.
Typescript.
Relates to Polish cavalry operations in the war against Russia, 1920.

1516

Kugel, Bernard, *collector.*
B. Kugel collection on German-occupied Belgium (in French and Flemish), 1941–1945. ½ ms. box.
Letters, issues of newspapers (including *La Libre Belgique*), leaflets, notes, British propaganda and drawings, relating to political events in Belgium during the German occupation in World War II.
Purchase, B. Kugel, 1978.

1517

Kuhn, Sylvester E.
Papers, 1920–1976. 1 folder.
Private, U.S. Army; soldier in the 31st Infantry Regiment in Siberia, 1918–1920. Correspondence, reminiscences and photocopies of documents, relating to the American Expeditionary Forces in Siberia during the

Russian Revolution, and especially to the Posolskaiâ incident.
Gift, S. E. Kuhn, 1978.

1518

Kung (Hsiang-hsi)—photograph, n.d. 1 envelope.
Depicts H. H. Kung, Vice President of China, 1939–1944. Photograph is autographed.

1519

Kurguz, Peter Nicholas.
Dissertation, 1963. "Historical Investigation of the Church-State Conflict Caused by the Philosophy of Communism in Russia, 1917–1919." 1 vol.
Typescript (carbon copy).
Ph.D. dissertation, Lincoln University.

1520

Kurtzig, Sigismund Samuel, b. 1882.
History (in German), n.d. "Die 'Legalen' Freicorps: Die Freicorps von ihrer Gruendung bis zum Kapp Putsch" (The 'Legal' Volunteer Corps: The Volunteer Corps from their Establishment until the Kapp Putsch). 1 folder.
Typescript.
Relates to the German Freicorps, 1918–1920.
Gift, Mrs. S. S. Kurtzig, 1976.

1521

Kusnierz, Tadeusz, *collector.*
T. Kusnierz collection on Poland (mainly in Polish), 1938–1946. 5½ ms. boxes.
Photocopy.
Government documents, statutes, charts, historical studies, statistical data, clippings, military orders, and photographs, relating to conditions in Poland during World War II; Polish politics and government and activities of the Germans in Poland during the German occupation; and the internal structure, public administration, and general activities of the Polish Government in Exile.
Preliminary inventory.
Deposit, T. Kusnierz, 1947.

1522

Kutzevalov, Boniface Semenovich.
Study (in Russian), n.d. "Ubiĭstvo Generala Romanovskago" (The Assassination of General Romanovskiĭ). 1 folder.
Holograph.
Captain, Imperial Russian Army. Relates to the assassination of the White Russian military leader Ivan Pavlovich Romanovskiĭ in the Russian Embassy in Constantinople, 1920.
Gift, B. S. Kutzevalov, 1932.

1523

Kwangtung Jen min Ch'u Pan She.
Poster (in Chinese), 1977. 1 folder.
Printed.
Chinese publishing agency. Commemorates the publication of the fifth volume of Mao Tse-tung's *Selected*

Works. Caption reads, "Warmly Welcome the Appearance of Volume Five of Mao Tse-tung's *Selected Works*." Gift, Klaus Mehnert, 1977.

1524

Kwiatkowski, Antoni Wincenty, 1890–1970.

Papers (mainly in Polish and Russian), 1917–1969. 45 ms. boxes, 1 album, 4 envelopes.

Polish scholar. Writings, correspondence, reports, memoranda, research and reference notes, clippings, and photographs, relating to Marxism-Leninism, dialectical and historical materialism, communism and religion, and the Communist International. Includes an autobiography and biography.

Register.

Gift, Annemarie Buschman-Brandes, 1971.

1525

Kwiatkowski, Jerzy, 1894–

Papers (in Polish), 1904–1975. 30 ms. boxes, 2 cu. ft. boxes.

Polish Army officer; survivor of the Nazi concentration camp Majdanek. Correspondence, writings, clippings, memorabilia, and printed matter, relating primarily to Majdanek concentration camp, post-World War II Polish refugee emigration to the United States and other countries, and the organizations and activities of Poles in the United States.

Preliminary inventory.

Gift, J. Kwiatkowski, 1975.

1526

Kyriak, Theodore E., *collector*.

T. E. Kyriak collection on the Hungarian Revolution (mainly in Hungarian), 1956–1966. 3 ms. boxes.

Serial issues, clippings, and pamphlets, relating to the Hungarian Revolution of 1956 and to the international reaction to the revolution.

Preliminary inventory.

Purchase, T. E. Kyriak.

1527

Labor and Socialist International. 4th Congress, Vienna, 1931.

Issuances, 1931. ½ ms. box.

Bulletins, reports, pamphlets, and miscellaneous printed matter, relating to and issued by the Fourth Congress of the Labor and Socialist International.

Gift, Witold S. Sworakowski, 1972.

1528

Lademan, Joseph Uhrig, Jr., 1899–

Papers, 1942–1969. ½ ms. box, 2 envelopes.

Captain, U.S. Navy. Memoranda, writings, reports, printed matter, clippings and photographs, relating to the return of the U.S.S. *Milwaukee* (re-named *Murmansk* by the Russians) to the U.S. Navy from the Soviet Union in 1949, and to the atomic bomb testing at Bikini Island, July 1946. Includes a memoir entitled "The *Gold Star* and Guam: War in the Western Pacific, 1941–42," 1961, re-

lating to the freighter U.S.S. *Gold Star,* which supplied Guam during World War II.

Gift, J. U. Lademan, Jr., 1975.

1529

Lager Altengrabow, Germany.

Prison camp newspaper issues (in Russian and German), 1920. 1 folder.

Typescript (mimeographed).

Relates to conditions at Lager Altengrabow, Germany, and to political events in Russia and Germany. Issued by Russian prisoners of war in the camp.

Preliminary inventory.

1530

Lahousen, Erwin.

Diary (in German), 1940. 1 vol.

Typescript (photocopy).

German Abwehr officer. Relates to German sabotage operations during World War II. Includes negative microfilm copy of diary.

1531

Lalevitch, Dushan.

Translation of memoir, 1951. "Here We Shall Break Your Will Power." 1 folder.

Typescript.

Yugoslav prisoner in the German concentration camp at Dachau during World War II. Relates to conditions at Dachau.

1532

Lambrino, Jeanne Marie Valentine (Zizi), 1895?–

Papers (in French), 1916–1956. 2 ms. boxes.

Wife of Prince Carol of Romania, 1918–1919. Memoirs, diaries, letters, notes, clippings, and photographs, relating to the marriage of J. M. V. Lambrino with Prince Carol and its subsequent annulment. Includes a diary of Prince Carol, 1919–1920.

Register.

Purchase, Henry Bristow, 1973.

1533

Lampe, Alekseĭ Aleksandrovich von, 1885–1960.

Papers (mainly in Russian), 1917–1926. 10 ms. boxes.

General, Russian Imperial Army; Russian Military Agent in Germany, 1922–1926; Russian Military Representative to Hungary, 1921–1926. Correspondence, reports, memoranda, orders, newsletters, clippings, leaflets, maps, pamphlets, and printed matter, relating to operations of the offices of the Russian Military Agent in Germany and the Russian Military Representative to Hungary, Russian counterrevolutionary activities, political events in Russia, and activities of Russian civilians and military personnel in Europe. Includes the office files of the delegation of the Russian Society of the Red Cross for Relief to Prisoners of War, 1919–1922.

Register.

Purchase, Nikolai Golovin, 1928.

1534

Lanao (Province), Philippine Islands. Provincial Governor.
Report, 1944–1945. 2 vols.
Typescript (carbon copy).
Relates to administration of Lanao Province, 1942–1945.

1535

Landesen, Arthur C.
Papers (in Russian), 1926–1933. 3 ms. boxes.
White Russian Consular Agent in San Francisco, 1926–1933. Correspondence, memoranda, and miscellanea, relating to White Russian consular activities in San Francisco.
Preliminary inventory.
Gift, A. C. Landesen.

1536

Lange, F. W. T.
Letter, 1921. 1 folder.
Holograph.
British bibliographer. Relates to the collection of literature on World War I.

1537

Lansing, Robert, 1864–1928.
Miscellaneous papers, 1916–1927. 1 folder.
Photocopy of originals at the Library of Congress.
Secretary of State of the U.S., 1915–1920. Diaries, correspondence and memoranda, relating to U.S. foreign policy during World War I and to the Paris Peace Conference in 1919.
Gift, U.S. Library of Congress.

1538

Lansing, Warren.
Diary, 1940. 1 vol.
Typescript (carbon copy).
American in France. Relates to conditions in France at the time of its capitulation in World War II.

1539

Lapel pins collection, n.d. 1 ms. box.
Lapel pins from the U.S., relating to political parties, elections, the World War I war effort, relief activities, and a variety of other topics.
Gift, various sources.

1540

Lapham, Roger Dearborn, 1883–1966.
Papers, 1948–1949. 1 ms. box.
Chief, U.S. Economic Cooperation Administration Mission to China, 1948–1949. Policy papers, memoranda, and estimates, relating to American aid to China.
During his lifetime, may not be quoted without permission of R. D. Lapham, Jr.
Gift, R. D. Lapham, 1963.

1541

Lapteff, Alexis V.
Papers, 1921–1971. 1 folder, 1 envelope.
American Relief Administration worker in the Ufa-

Urals District of Russia, 1921–1923. Memoirs, reports and photographs, relating to relief work in the Ufa-Urals District.
Preliminary inventory.
Gift, A. V. Lapteff, 1971.

1542

Large, Jean Henry.
Miscellaneous papers, 1900–1906. 1 folder.
Photocopy (in part).
Sister of Lou Henry Hoover. Writings, a diary and correspondence, relating to the genealogy of the Henry family and to personal affairs of Jean Henry Large and Lou Henry Hoover.
Gift, Mrs. Delano Henry Large, 1966.

1543

Larminat, Joseph de.
Diary (in French), 1944. 1 vol.
Holograph.
Relates to the imprisonment of J. de Larminat at Mont-Dore, France, by Vichy Government officials.
Gift, J. de Larminat, 1947.

1544

Larsen, E. S., *collector*.
E. S. Larsen collection on the Far East, 1942–1951. 11 ms. boxes.
Clippings, reports, and pamphlets, relating to political events in the Far East.
Preliminary inventory.

1545

Laserson, Maurice, b. 1880.
Papers (in English, French, German and Russian), 1920–1949. 1½ ms. boxes, 1 envelope.
Russian finance, commerce and law expert. Correspondence, writings, reports, government documents, printed matter, and photographs, relating to life in Russia prior to the 1917 Revolution, the persecution of Jews in Russia and their emigration to Germany, 1904–1906, Soviet financial and commercial policy, 1918–1925, the purchase of 600 locomotives by the Soviet Government from Sweden, 1920, and the German socialist Karl Liebknecht.
Gift, M. Laserson, 1948.

1546

"Latvia Before and After the Establishment of an Authoritative Regime."
Memorandum, 1935. 1 folder.
Typescript (mimeographed).
Relates to the abolition of parliamentary democracy in Latvia in 1934.

1547

Latvia. Sūtniecība (Sweden).
Records (mostly in Latvian), 1917–1939. 14 ms. boxes.
Correspondence, memoranda and reports, relating to

Latvian foreign relations and to Latvian-Swedish relations.
Register.
Gift, Ivar Blums, 1972.

1548
Latvian refugee school certificates (in Latvian and English), 1945–1947. 1 folder.
Printed and handwritten.
Certificates of completion of elementary school by students in Latvian refugee schools in Germany.

1549
Latvian social customs—memorandum, n.d. 1 folder.
Typescript (mimeographed).
Relates to baptismal, wedding and burial customs in Latvia.

1550
Latviešu Centrālā Komiteja.
Records (in Latvian), 1918–1948. 122 ms. boxes, 2 motion picture reels.
Latvian émigré organization. Memoranda, reports, correspondence, registration forms, printed matter and motion pictures, relating to conditions in Latvia under Soviet and German occupation, and to Latvian displaced persons during and after World War II.
Preliminary inventory.
Deposit, Latviešu Centrālā Komiteja, 1948.

1551
Lau, Kenneth, *collector*.
Propaganda (in Chinese), 1947. 1 folder.
Nationalist Chinese propaganda distributed at a student demonstration in Peking.

1552
Launay, Jacques de, 1924–
Papers (in French), 1914–1960. 2 ms. boxes, 4 phonotapes.
Belgian historian. Correspondence, writings, taped interviews, printed matter, and clippings, relating to Romania and Belgium during World War II; the Little Entente; the relationship between Adolf Hitler and Lord Rothermere, 1933–1939; the Walloon Legion, 1941–1945; and education in Europe. Includes sound recordings of interviews by J. de Launay with General T. Bor-Komorowski, 1960; A. Francois-Poncet, 1958; G. Bonnet, 1957; and J. Moch, 1959.
Register.
Purchase, J. de Launay, 1975. Incremental purchase, 1978.

1553
Lausanne. Conference, June 16–July 9, 1932.
Final protocol (in French and English), 1932. 1 folder.
Typescript (mimeographed).
Conference on World War I reparations. Autographed by Ramsay Macdonald, Prime Minister of Great Britain, Sir John Simon, Foreign Secretary of Great Britain,

Franz von Papen, Chancellor of Germany, and Dino Grandi, Foreign Minister of Italy.

1554
Lausanne. Conference on Near Eastern Affairs, 1922–1923—photographs, 1922–1923. 1 envelope.
Depicts delegates to the Lausanne Conference on Near Eastern Affairs.

1555
Lauzanne, Stéphane Joseph Vincent, b. 1874.
Papers (in French), 1898–1954. 2 ms. boxes, 18 scrapbooks.
Editor, *Le Matin* (Paris), 1920–1940. Writings, transcripts of radio broadcasts, and clippings, relating to French politics and foreign policy, international relations, and the Vichy regime in France during World War II.
Preliminary inventory.
Purchase, Mme. de Blowitz, 1967.

1556
LaVarre, William, 1898–
Papers, 1957–1978. ca. 12 ms. boxes.
American author and journalist; Chief, American Republics Unit, U.S. Department of Commerce, 1941–1943; editor-in-chief, *American Mercury*, 1957–1958. Memoirs, letters, memoranda, clippings, periodical issues, lists, notes and financial records, relating to political development in Latin America, especially in the 1930s; U.S. relations with Latin America, 1933–1945; *American Mercury*; international communist subversion; and international affairs.
Memoirs on *American Mercury* closed until January 1984.
Gift, W. LaVarre, 1977. Subsequent increments.

1557
Lavrent'ev, K. I.
Memoir (in Russian), 1925. "Urginskiĭa Sobytiĭa 1921 Goda" (Events in Urga in 1921). 1 folder.
Typescript.
White Russian. Relates to White Russian activities in Mongolia during the Russian Revolution.

1558
Lavrov, Sergeĭ.
Memoir (in Russian), 1942. "Sobytiĭa v Mongoliĭ-Khalkhie, 1920–1921 godakh—Voenno-Istoricheskiĭ Ocherk-Vospominaniĭa" (Events in Mongolia-Khalkha, 1920–1921—A Military-Historical Essay—Reminiscences). 1 folder.
Holograph.
Major, Russian Imperial Army. Relates to Baron Roman Ungern-Shternberg and White Russian military activities in Mongolia, 1920–1921.
Deposit, S. Lavrov, 1948.

1559
Lavrov, Sergey.
Study, ca. 1945. "Why Hongkong Fell: An Analysis." 1 vol.

Typescript.
Captain, U.S. Army. Relates to the Japanese capture of Hong Kong during World War II.

1560

Lawrence, Thomas Edward, 1888–1935.
Letters, 1924–1937. ½ ms. box.
Holograph.
Lieutenant Colonel, British Army. Relates to the publication of two books by T. E. Lawrence, *Seven Pillars of Wisdom* (1926), and *Revolt in the Desert* (1927). Includes some printed matter.
Gift, Nathan van Patten, 1944.

1561

Lazič, Branko M.
Memorandum (in French), n.d. "Informations Fournies par Albert Vassart sur la Politique du P.C.F. entre 1934 et 1938" (Information Furnished by Albert Vassart on the Politics of the P.C.F. between 1934 and 1938). 1 vol.
Typescript.
Editor, *Est et Ouest* (Paris). Relates to the views of Albert Vassart on the Parti Communiste Français.

1562

League of Arab States.
Agreement, 1945. Pact of the League of Arab States. 1 folder.
Typescript (mimeographed).
Relates to pan-Arab cooperation. Includes an annex (typewritten), relating to the Palestinian question.

1563

League of Nations. High Commissioner, Free City of Danzig.
Decision, n.d. "High Commissioner's Decision in the Danzig-Gdingen Conflict." 1 folder.
Typescript (mimeographed).
Relates to the dispute between Danzig and Poland regarding the use of the port of Danzig.

1564

League of Nations. Monetary and Economic Conference, London, 1933.
Miscellaneous records, 1933. 1 ms. box.
Proposals, memoranda, and resolutions, relating to international cooperation in commercial and financial policy.
Gift, Lawrence Richey.

1565

League of Nations—slides, n.d. 1 box.
Depicts officials and activities of the League of Nations.
Preliminary inventory.

1566

League of Red Cross Societies.
Miscellaneous records, 1919–1922. 1½ ms. boxes.
International relief organization. Correspondence, telegrams, reports, and minutes of meetings, relating to the founding of the League of Red Cross Societies and to relief operations in Europe.
Preliminary inventory.
Gift, American National Red Cross, 1928.

1567

Leale, Marion W.
Diary, 1914–1915. 6 vols.
Holograph.
American visitor to Guernsey Island. Relates to conditions on Guernsey Island during World War I.

1568

Leavitt, May Hoover.
Letters, 1928–1952. 1 folder.
Photocopy.
Sister of Herbert Hoover. Letters from Mr. and Mrs. Herbert Hoover to M. H. Leavitt, relating to personal and family matters, and undated letters from the grandmother of Herbert Hoover to her grandchildren.
Gift, Herbert Hoover Oral History Program, 1968.

1569

Lebanese political leaflets (in Arabic), 1943–1957. 1 folder.
Printed.
Issued in Lebanon.

1570

Ledebour, Georg, 1850–1947.
Letters (in German), 1936–1939, to "Fanny." 1 folder.
Holograph.
German socialist leader. Relates to the socialist movement.

1571

Lee, Edward Bartlett.
Papers, 1914–1939. 7 ms. boxes.
American business executive; National War Savings Committee publicity worker during World War I. Correspondence, leaflets, pamphlets, posters, clippings, photographs, and postcards, relating to the activities of various relief organizations during and immediately after World War I and to Liberty Loan drives and other aspects of the war effort in the U.S.

1572

Lee, John Clifford Hodges, 1887–1958.
Papers, 1944–1956. ½ ms. box, 2 envelopes.
Lieutenant General, U.S. Army; Commanding General, Communications Zone, and Deputy Commander, European Theater of Operations, during World War II. Memoirs, printed matter and photographs, relating to U.S. military operations in Europe during World Wars I and II.

1573

Leehey, Donald James, 1897–
Letter, 1964. 1 folder.
Typescript (mimeographed).
Colonel, U.S. Army; member of the U.S. Military

Academy class of 1920. Relates to statistical and other information on the careers of members of the class of 1920.

1574

Lefever, Ernest Warren, 1919–
Papers, 1956–1969. 3 ms. boxes, 1 album, 2 envelopes.
American political scientist; Senior Fellow, Brookings Institution. Writings, correspondence, reports, interviews, notes, pamphlets, newspaper clippings, and printed matter, relating to political conditions in Zaire, Ethiopia, and other African nations.
Register.
Gift, E. W. Lefever, 1973.

1575

Lefranc, Georges Eugène Auguste, 1904–
Papers (in French), 1895–1973. 9 ms. boxes.
French social historian; prominent member of French trade union movement. Writings, reports, syllabi, and printed matter, relating to social conditions and to the socialist, syndicalist and labor movements in France.
Preliminary inventory.
Purchase, G. Lefranc, 1968. Subsequent increments.

1576

LeGendre, William C.
Letter, 1925. 1 folder.
Holograph.
American businessman. Relates to proposals in the U.S. for a negotiated end to World War I and Polish independence, 1916–1917. Also includes translations (typewritten), of excerpts from *Prawda Dziejowa, 1914–1917* (The Truth of History, 1914–1917), by Jerzy Jan Sosnowski, Russian diplomatic representative in the U.S. during World War I.

1577

Legrand, François, 1903–
Papers (in French, English and Dutch), 1945–1946. ½ ms. box.
Belgian Roman Catholic priest; missionary in northern China, 1929–1947. Diary and reports, relating to political and social conditions in Siwantzu and elsewhere in the communist zone of north China, and to the situation of Roman Catholic missionaries in the communist zone.
Gift, F. Legrand, 1947.

1578

Leigh-Mallory (Sir Trafford Leigh)—photograph, n.d. 1 envelope.
Depicts Air Chief Marshal T. L. Leigh-Mallory, British Air Force.

1579

Leipzig under Allied occupation collection (in German and English), 1945. 1 folder.
Proclamations and bulletins issued by civilian and military government authorities in Leipzig, relating to the administration of the city under Allied occupation.

1580

Lejiņš, Jānis, 1897–
Papers (in Latvian and English), 1940–1978. 2 ms. boxes, 1 envelope.
Member of the Latvian parliament, 1931–1940; subsequently an émigré in Canada. Correspondence, writings, clippings, other printed matter and photographs, relating to the annexation of Latvia to the Soviet Union, conditions in Latvia under communism, Latvian émigrés in Canada and the U.S., and anti-communist Latvian émigré movements.
One folder closed until January 1, 1980.
Gift, J. Lejiņš, 1974. Incremental gift, 1978.

1581

Leman, J. Howard.
Reports, 1926. 1 folder.
Typescript.
Agent of the firm Paine, Webber and Company. Relates to political and economic conditions in Poland.

1582

Leman, Rudolf, 1897–
Memoirs (in German), n.d. "Geschichte der Goldenen Zwanziger Jahre in Russland" (History of Twenty Golden Years in Russia). ½ ms. box.
Typescript.
German chemist in Russia, 1920–1930. Relates to economic conditions in Russia, especially Siberia, in the interwar period, and to economic policy of the Vysshiĭ Sovet Narodnogo Khoziaĭstva.
Gift, R. Leman, 1974.

1583

Lemarchand, René.
Papers (in French and English), 1920–1972. 3 ms. boxes.
Director, African Studies Center, University of Florida. Government reports, ephemeral publications, interviews, correspondence, notes, and printed matter, relating to the political development of Zaire, Burundi, and Rwanda.
Register.
Purchase, R. Lemarchand, 1972.

1584

Lemkin, Raphael, *compiler*.
Translation of regulations, n.d. "Military Government in Europe." ½ ms. box.
Typescript (mimeographed).
Regulations of German military governments in various occupied countries in Europe, 1940–1941.
Gift, Jan Ciechanowski.

1585

Lenin, Vladimir Il'ich, 1870–1924.
Miscellaneous speeches and writings (in Russian), 1903–1940. 1 folder, 1 phonotape.
Russian Revolutionary leader; Premier of Russia, 1917–1924. Pamphlet (mimeographed), by V. I. Lenin, entitled "K Studenchestvu: Zadachi Revoliutsionnoĭ Mo-

lodezhi" (To the Students: The Tasks of Revolutionary Youth), 1903; leaflet (printed), by V. I. Lenin and V. Bonch-Bruevich, entitled "Usluzhlivyĭ Liberal" (The Obliging Liberal); photocopy of the table of contents (printed), of *Stat'i i Rechi o Sredneĭ Aziĭ i Uzbekistane* (Articles and Speeches about Central Asia and Uzbekistan), by V. I. Lenin and Iosif Stalin, 1940; and recordings of speeches by V. I. Lenin, 1919–1920.

1586

Lenz, Friedrich.
 Biographical sketch (in German), 1948. "Walther Rathenau: Sociologe und Staatsmann" (Walther Rathenau: Sociologist and Statesman). 1 folder.
 Typescript.
 Professor, University of Berlin. Relates to the career of the German statesman Walther Rathenau.

1587

"Leopold III: Der Koenig im Banne des Schicksals: Sein Liebesroman und Leidensweg" (Leopold III: The King in the Spell of Fate: His Romance and Ordeal).
 Biography (in German), n.d. 1 folder.
 Typescript.
 Relates to King Leopold III of Belgium. Incomplete. Includes a clipping.

1588

LeQueux, William, 1864–1927.
 Fictional work, 1917. "Hushed Up at German Headquarters: The Amazing Confessions of Colonel-Lieutenant Otto von Heynitz, 16th Uhlans, Principal Aide-de-Camp to His Imperial Highness the German Crown-Prince in the Field, and Now Detained in Switzerland; Startling Revelations of the Crown-Prince's Shameful Actions." 1 ms. box.
 Holograph.

1589

Lerner, Daniel, *collector.*
 D. Lerner collection on World War II Allied and German propaganda (in English and German), 1943–1949. 71 ms. boxes.
 Reports, correspondence, pamphlets, leaflets, and radio transcripts, relating to Allied propaganda in Europe during World War II, analysis of German propaganda, evaluation of wartime German morale, and German public opinion during the postwar Allied occupation. Includes reports of interrogations of German prisoners of war.
 Gift, D. Lerner, 1946. Subsequent increments.

1590

L'Escaille, Mademoiselle de.
 Letters (in French), 1863–1921. 1 folder.
 Holograph.
 French governess. Letters from individuals connected closely with the Russian Imperial family, relating to personal matters in the lives of the Russian Imperial family. Includes translations of some letters.
 Gift, Russian Historical Archive and Repository, 1974.

1591

Leschander, Walter L., d. 1966, *collector.*
 W. L. Leschander collection, 1938–1965. 9 ms. boxes.
 Writings, diary, correspondence, photographs, maps, clippings, and pamphlets, relating to espionage, military intelligence, prisoners of war, and escape techniques, primarily during World War II.
 Preliminary inventory.
 Box 9 closed until 1985 or until the death of Sigismund Payne Best.
 Gift, W. L. Leschander, 1966.

1592

Lettrich, Joseph, 1905–1969.
 Papers, 1940–1969. 33 ms. boxes.
 Czechoslovakian statesman; President, National Slovak Council and Slovak Democratic Party, 1945–1948; and founder, Council of Free Czechoslovakia (Washington, D.C.). Correspondence, appointment books, speeches and writings, reports, memoranda, clippings, newsletters, printed matter, and photographs, relating to political developments in Czechoslovakia, the anti-Nazi resistance movement in Czechoslovakia during World War II, communism in Czechoslovakia, and anti-communist émigré organizations in the U.S.
 Gift, Irene Lettrich, 1976.

1593

Leuchtenberg, Nikolaĭ Nikolaevich, Herzog von.
 Diary (in Russian), 1918. 1 folder, 1 envelope.
 Holograph (photocopy).
 Relates to activities of White Russian forces under General Krasnov in southern Russia during the Russian Civil War.
 Gift, Marvin Lyons, 1966.

1594

Levi, Paul, 1883–1930.
 Miscellaneous papers (in German), 1919. 1 folder.
 German communist leader. Funeral oration delivered in Berlin, February 2, 1919, in memory of Karl Liebknecht and Rosa Luxemburg, German communist leaders; and catalog of books in the private library of P. Levi.

1595

Levine, Isaac Don, 1892–
 Miscellaneous papers, 1957–1958. 1 folder.
 American journalist and author. Memorandum (mimeographed), 1958, and transcripts of hearings (printed), of the U.S. Senate Internal Security Subcommittee, 1957, both relating to the dispute between I. D. Levine and Martin K. Tytell regarding the authenticity of documents used by I. D. Levine in his book, *Stalin's Great Secret* (New York, 1956), as proof that Iosif Stalin had been a tsarist spy.

1596

LeVine, Victor T., 1928–
 Papers (in English and French), 1954–1961. 2 ms. boxes.

American political scientist. Pamphlets, campaign literature, clippings, and other printed matter, relating to the political development of the Cameroons. Used as research material for the book by V. T. LeVine, *The Cameroons: From Mandate to Independence* (1964).
Preliminary inventory.
Gift, V. T. LeVine, 1972.

1597

Levitsky, Eugene L.
Writings (in Russian), n.d. 1 folder.
Typescript (photocopy).
Imperial Russian Army officer. History, entitled "Ataka" (Attack), relating to the operations of the 2nd Ufim Cavalry Division during the Russian Civil War in May 1919; and memoirs, entitled "Fevral'skie Dni" (February Days), relating to Russian military operations, 1916–1917, and to the Russian Revoluton.
Gift, E. L. Levitsky, 1974.

1598

Lewis, Roger L., d. 1936.
Papers, 1917–1919. ½ ms. box, 1 envelope.
American journalist and Red Cross worker in Russia. Reports, notes, correspondence, printed matter, clippings, photographs, and memorabilia, relating to operations of the American Red Cross in Archangel, Russia.
Preliminary inventory.
Gift, Helen Wells, 1964.

1599

Ley (Robert) report (in German), n.d. 1 folder.
Typescript.
Relates to a proposal by R. Ley, Leader of the German Labor Front, 1933–1945, for an old-age pension in Germany.

1600

Liebknecht, Karl, 1871–1919.
Newspaper article (in German), 1925. "Wie Es zum Losschlagen Kam . . ." (How the Attack Came About).1 folder.
Photocopy.
German revolutionist. Relates to the preparation of the German Revolution in October-November 1918. Article consisted of previously unpublished notes by K. Liebknecht, and was published in the *Neue Zeitung* (Munich), November 10, 1925.

1601

Liepins, Olberts, 1906–
Papers (mainly in Latvian), 1948–1972. 1 ms. box.
Latvian journalist. Correspondence, clippings, writings, and reports, relating to Latvian domestic and foreign affairs, and Latvians in the United States.
Gift, Gvido Augusts, 1975.

1602

Lietuvia Šalpos Draugija Prancūzije.
Correspondence (in Lithuanian), 1947–1950. ½ ms. box.

Lithuanian Relief Association, France. Relates to Lithuanians serving in the French Foreign Legion.
Closed until December 14, 2004.
Gift, Žibuntas Mikšys, 1974.

1603

Likely, Robert D.
Papers, 1917–1918. ½ ms. box, 1 cu. ft. box.
U.S. Army pilot during World War I. Correspondence, reports, pilot's flying logbook, and memorabilia, relating to activities of the U.S. 135th Aero Squadron in France during World War I.
Gift, Elizabeth D. Morrison, 1976.

1604

Linderfels, Baron von.
Essay (in German), n.d. "Die Wahrheit ueber die Schuld am Nationalsozialismus" (The Truth about the Guilt of National Socialism). 1 folder.
Typescript.
Relates to the financing of the German Nazi Party.

1605

Lindsay, Franklin Anthony, 1916–
Papers, 1944–1976. 8 ms. boxes.
Consultant, U.S. House of Representatives Committee on Foreign Aid, 1947–1948; representative to the Executive Committee, Organization for European Economic Cooperation, 1948–1949. Reports, memoranda and correspondence, relating to post-World War II economic reconstruction in western Europe, the Organization for European Economic Cooperation, and U.S. foreign aid to Europe. Includes a memorandum relating to U.S. Office of Strategic Services contacts with Croatian partisans in 1944.
Memorandum by F. A. Lindsay relating to the Office of Strategic Services may be used only by persons agreeing not to identify its source.
Gift, F. A. Lindsay.

1606

Lindsay, Hsiao-li, Baroness Lindsay of Birker.
Memoirs, n.d. 1 reel.
Microfilm.
Chinese teacher; wife of the British historian Michael Lindsay. Relates to Chinese communist leaders during World War II, the U.S. Observer Mission to Yenan, China, 1944–1945, and two visits of U.S. Ambassador Patrick Hurley to Yenan, 1944.

1607

Linvald, Axel.
Translation of biographical sketch, n.d. 1 vol.
Typescript.
Relates to the Danish politician Hans Peter Hanssen.

1608

Lipkowska, Teresa.
Letter (in Polish), 1941, to Stanislaw Mackiewicz. 1 folder.
Typescript (mimeographed).

Polish journalist and author. Relates to conditions in Soviet concentration camps and the success of the Polish Government in securing the release of its citizens from them.

1609

Lithuania—photographs, ca. 1920–1929. 1 envelope.
Depicts various sites in Wilno, Lithuania.

1610

Lithuanian National Council in America.
Miscellaneous records, 1918–1925. ½ ms. box.
Typewritten transcripts.
Organization of Lithuanian-Americans. Correspondence, resolutions and reports, relating to the movements to secure Lithuanian independence and U.S. recognition of Lithuania.
Gift, Malbone T. Graham.

1611

Litoshenko, Lev Nikolaevich, b. 1886.
Study (in Russian), 1927. 5 ms. boxes.
Typescript and holograph.
Study by L. N. Litoshenko and Lincoln Hutchinson, sponsored by the Committee on Russian Research, Hoover War Library, Stanford University, relating to agricultural policy in the Soviet Union. Includes a translation (typewritten), entitled "Agrarian Policy in Soviet Russia."
Register.

1612

Little, William Henry, 1937–
Thesis, n.d. "The Tsarist Secret Police." 1 vol.
Typescript (carbon copy).
M.A. thesis at the University of Texas.

1613

Littlefield, Marion V., *collector*.
Photographs, ca. 1917—1918. 13 envelopes.
Depicts aerial activities on the western front during World War I, captured or destroyed German planes, and bomb damage in France and Germany. Photographs taken by the U.S. Air Service.
Gift, M. V. Littlefield, 1947.

1614

Littlejohn, Robert M.
Memorandum, 1959. "Passing in Review." 1 folder.
Printed.
Major General, U.S. Army; Chief Quartermaster, European Theater of Operations, during World War II. Relates to the provision of food and clothing by the U.S. Army Quartermaster Corps to U.S. troops in the European Theater.

1615

Lîubimov, Dmitriĭ Nikolaevich, b. 1864.
Memoirs (in Russian), n.d. ½ ms. box.
Holograph.

Chief of Staff, Imperial Russian Ministry of the Interior. Relates to political conditions in Russia, 1902–1906.

1616

Livermore, Edith.
Photographs, 1913–1920. 1 envelope.
Depicts activities of the German Army during World War I, military parades and training exercises in Berlin, war damage in France, a 1913 parade in honor of Tsar Nicholas II at Potsdam, and British troops on parade in London.
Gift, E. Livermore, 1940.

1617

Livingstead, Ivor M. V. Z.
History, n.d. "The Downfall of a Dynasty." 1 vol.
Typescript (carbon copy).
Relates to the fall of the House of Romanov in Russia.

1618

Llerena, Mario.
Memoirs, 1966. 1 ms. box.
Typescript.
Cuban revolutionary. Relates to Fidel Castro and to the Movimiento Revolucionario 26 de Julio in Cuba, 1956–1958. Includes photocopies of correspondence, including two letters from Fidel Castro.
May not be quoted without permission of M. Llerena.
Purchase, M. Llerena, 1968.

1619

Lloyd George, David Lloyd George, 1st Earl, 1863–1945.
Essay, 1934. 1 folder.
Typescript.
British statesman. Relates to the Geneva Disarmament Conference and to prospects for world disarmament.

1620

Lochner, Louis Paul, b. 1887, *collector*.
L. P. Lochner collection on Germany (mainly in German), 1934–1946. 9 ms. boxes.
Correspondence, writings, reports, and printed matter, relating to the Nazi Party, domestic conditions in Germany and German foreign policy before and during World War II, postwar occupation of Germany, denazification efforts, and Communist Party activities in Germany. Includes correspondence of Joachim von Ribbentrop.
Preliminary inventory.
Gift, 1946. Subsequent increments.

1621

Lockley, Fred, *collector*.
F. Lockley collection on pacifism, 1931–1936. 1 ms. box.
Letters, notices, clippings, and mimeographed material, relating to pacifism, disarmament, and the American pacifist leader Sydney Strong.

1622

Lockwood, Charles Andrews, Jr., 1890–1967.
Papers, 1924–1963. 1 ms. box.
Vice Admiral, U.S. Navy; Commander, Submarine Force, Pacific Fleet, 1943–1945. Writings and correspondence, relating to the development of the submarine and to U.S. submarine operations in World War II.
Gift, Mrs. C. A. Lockwood, Jr., 1967.

1623

Lodygensky, Georges.
Writings (in French), n.d. ½ ms. box.
Russian physician. Memoirs, entitled "Une Carrière Médicale Mouvementée" (A Turbulent Medical Career), relating to medical practice in Russia during World War I, the Russian Revolution, and Civil War, 1908–1923; and a history, entitled "Face au Communisme-Le Mouvement Anticommuniste Internationale de 1923–1950" (In the Face of Communism—The Anticommunist International from 1923–1950), relating to the operations of the International Anticommunist Entente.
Gift, G. Lodygensky, 1975.

1624

Loesch, Karl Christian von, b. 1880, *collector*.
K. C. von Loesch collection on Germany, Austria and Croatia (in German), 1918–1944. 7½ ms. boxes.
Pamphlets, leaflets, posters, newspaper issues, and writings, relating to politics and elections in Germany and Austria, the German revolution of 1918–1919, the Kapp Putsch, the Hitler Putsch, the Nazi Party, and the independent Croatian state during World War II.
Purchase, K. von Loesch, 1946.

1625

Loewa, Joachim.
Letters (in German and English), 1913–1925, to Raymond Royce Willoughby. 1 folder.
Holograph and typescript.
German student. Relates to social conditions in Germany and to personal matters.

1626

Loewenberg, Peter.
Study, ca. 1969. "Unsuccessful Adolescence of Heinrich Himmler." 1 folder.
Typescript (photocopy).
Professor of History, University of California at Los Angeles. Analyzes the adolescent personality and behavior of Heinrich Himmler, Reichsfuehrer SS and Chef der Deutschen Polizei (Reich Leader of the SS and Chief of the German Police) of the German Third Reich, based on his diaries, 1914–1924.
Gift, P. Loewenberg, 1969.

1627

Loftis, Anne, 1922–
Papers, 1941–1976. 8 ms. boxes, 3 phonotapes.
American journalist and historian. Correspondence, reports, research notes, printed matter and phonotapes, relating to the evacuation and relocation of Japanese-Americans, 1942–1945. Includes oral history interviews of immigrants to California.
Gift, A. Loftis, 1971. Incremental gift, 1978.

1628

Log-book collection, 1913–1914. 1 folder.
Log-book (handwritten), for a voyage of the steamship *Lottie Bennett* from San Francisco to Valparaiso, Chile, 1914; and logbook (blank), for a voyage of the schooner *W. F. Jewett* from San Francisco to Callao, Peru, 1913.

1629

Logan, James Addison, Jr., 1879–1930.
Papers, 1913–1924. 5 ms. boxes, 18 vols.
American banker; Colonel, U.S. Army; U.S. representative, Supreme Economic Council, during World War I; unofficial U.S. representative, Reparations Commission, 1919–1924. Correspondence, reports and memoranda, relating to the U.S. war effort in World War I, conditions of prisoners of war, the Paris Peace Conference, postwar reconstruction in Europe, and war reparations.
Preliminary inventory.
Gift, estate of J. A. Logan, 1930.

1630

London. Naval Conference, 1930.
Miscellaneous records (in French and English), 1930. 1 ms. box.
International conference on naval armament limitations. Minutes of meetings, reports of committees, and rosters of delegates.
Gift, U.S. Department of State, 1930.

1631

Lonergan, Thomas Clement, 1886–1940, *collector*.
T. C. Lonergan collection on the A.E.F., 1918–1930. 7 ms. boxes.
Writings, letters, notes and maps, relating to activities of the American Expeditionary Force in France during World War I. Includes histories of individual divisions and other units in the American Expeditionary Force.
Preliminary inventory.
Purchase, T. C. Lonergan, 1930.

1632

Long, Victor Dismukes, 1904–
Papers, 1925–1959. 1 folder.
Vice Admiral, U. S. Navy. Orders, citations, and photographs, relating to U.S. naval operations before, during and after World War II.
Gift, V. D. Long, 1975.

1633

The Longest Day.
Sound recording, n.d. 1 phonorecord.
Motion picture dramatizing the Allied invasion of Normandy, June 6, 1944. Recording of excerpts.

1634

Longuevan, Joseph B., *collector.*
J. B. Longuevan collection on Siberia, 1918–1920. 1 folder.
Reminiscences, letters, and printed matter, relating to activities of the U.S. 31st Infantry in Siberia, and to the Russian Revolution in Siberia.
Gift, George Masury and J. B. Longuevan, 1974.

1635

Lonzinov, V.
Memorandum, ca. 1930. 1 folder, 1 envelope.
Typescript (mimeographed).
Relates to the emigration of German Russians from Russia to Germany, and to conditions in Russia causing the emigration. Includes a photograph of German Russian children in Kiel, en route to Canada.

1636

Look, Susanne Avery, 1869–1958.
Papers, 1918–1919. 1 ms. box.
American Red Cross worker in France during World War I. Memoirs and photographs, relating to Red Cross work in St. Aignan, France.
Gift, Pauline P. Wells, 1959.

1637

Lopez-Fresquet, Rufo, 1911–
Memoir, 1965. "14 Months with Castro." 1 ms. box, 2 envelopes.
Typescript.
Minister of Finance of Cuba. Relates to political conditions in Cuba, 1959–1960. Includes photographs. Published as *My 14 Months with Castro* (Cleveland, World Publishing Co., 1966).

1638

Lordkipanidze, Zekeriiâ, *defendant.*
Indictment (in Russian), 1937. 1 vol.
Typescript (carbon copy).
Relates to the indictment of Zekeriiâ Lordkipanidze and others in Georgia on charges of treason, counter-revolutionary activity, sabotage and subversion.

1639

Los Angeles. Soldier's and Sailor's Replacement Bureau.
Report, 1920. "Reconstruction in Los Angeles, 1919." 2 vols.
Typescript (carbon copy).
Relates to post-World War I reconstruction in Los Angeles, California.

1640

Losh, William J., 1896–1973.
Papers, 1917–1967. 2 cu. ft. boxes, 1 oversize photograph.
American journalist; member, American Ambulance Service, 1917–1919; Secretary, Polish Legation in the U.S., 1920–1921. Diaries, correspondence, photographs, memorabilia, and printed matter, relating to the American Ambulance Service in France and Albania during World War I; Polish Legation in Washington, D.C., 1920–1921; Polish Ambassador Casimir Lubomirski; the John Scopes trial in Dayton, Tennessee, 1925; and U.S. politics during the Harding and Coolidge administrations.
Preliminary inventory.
Writings of William J. Losh may not be published in whole or part without permission of Mrs. W. J. Losh.
Deposit, Mrs. W. J. Losh, 1975.

1641

Lotocka, Stefania.
Memoir, 1966. "Those Who Obeyed Orders." ½ ms. box.
Typescript.
Political prisoner in the Nazi concentration camp at Ravensbrueck, Germany, 1941–1945. Relates to conditions at Ravensbrueck.
Gift, S. Lotocka, 1971.

1642

Loucheur, Louis, 1872–1931.
Papers (in French), 1916–1931. 12 ms. boxes, 1 envelope.
French industrialist, statesman and diplomat. Correspondence, speeches, notes, reports, and photographs, relating to industry in Russia during World War I, inter-Allied diplomacy during World War I, war reparations, and post-war French and international politics.
Preliminary inventory.
Gift, Loucheur family, 1960. Subsequent increments.

1643

Louvain. Université Catholique. Bibliothèque—collection, 1914–1973. 1 ms. box. 4 scrapbooks.
Clippings, photocopies of newspaper and periodical articles, photographs, and a bibliography, relating to the destruction of the library of the University of Louvain, Belgium, during World War I, and its subsequent reconstruction.
Gift, Whitney Warren family, 1945. Subsequent increments.

1644

Loveland, Ralph Andrus, 1892–
Papers, 1926–1965. 1 folder.
Major General, U.S. Army; Commanding Officer, 346th Engineer General Service Regiment, 1944–1945; Commanding General, Michigan National Guard. Correspondence and photographs, relating to U.S. military operations on the Mexican border, 1916–1917, to military engineering in the European Theater of Operations, and to the Michigan National Guard.

1645

Lovestone, Jay, 1899–
Papers, 1906–1976. 634 ms. boxes.
General Secretary, Communist Party, U.S.A., 1927–1929, and Communist Party (Opposition), 1929–1940; Executive Secretary, Free Trade Union Committee, American Federation of Labor, 1944–1955; Assistant

Director and Director, International Affairs, American Federation of Labor-Congress of Industrial Organizations, 1955–1974. Correspondence, reports, memoranda, bulletins, clippings, serial issues, pamphlets, other printed matter and photographs, relating to the Communist International, the communist movement in the U.S. and elsewhere, communist influence in U.S. and foreign trade unions, and organized labor movements in the U.S. and abroad.

Published materials are opened. All other materials are closed until five years after the death of J. Lovestone.

Donative sale, J. Lovestone, 1975.

1646

Lowdermilk, Walter Clay, 1888–1974.
Papers, 1914–1968. 14 ms. boxes, 3 envelopes.
American agronomist and forester; conservation consultant in China, 1922–1927; Assistant Chief, U.S. Soil Conservation Service, 1939–1947. Correspondence, writings, printed matter and photographs, relating to land use and soil and water conservation, primarily in China and Japan.
Register.
Gift, W. C. Lowdermilk, 1970.

1647

Lowenkopf, Martin, 1928–
Papers, 1952–1973. 2 ms. boxes.
American political scientist and author. Reports, memoranda, notes, press releases and press summaries, relating to U.S. aid to Liberia, Liberian economic conditions and labor relations, and politics and movements for independence in Uganda and Tanganyika during the 1950's.
Gift, M. Lowenkopf, 1974.

1648

Lowman, Myers G.
Papers, 1920–1966. 93 ms. boxes, 3 motion picture reels, 80 phonotapes, 11 envelopes.
Executive Secretary, Circuit Riders, Inc. Correspondence, memoranda, pamphlets, photographs, and clippings, relating to communism and other leftist movements, the civil rights movement, and anti-communism, primarily in the United States.
Register.
Purchase, M. G. Lowman, 1967.

1649

Lubeck, Paul.
Papers, 1957–1969. 4½ ms. boxes.
American sociologist. Writings, reports, clippings, and notes, relating to the trade union movement in Africa, primarily during the 1960s.
Gift, P. Lubeck, 1975.

1650

Lubin, David, 1849–1919.
Papers, 1905–1941. 4 ms. boxes, 2 scrapbooks.
Founder, International Institute of Agriculture, Rome. Correspondence, writings, pamphlets, clippings, and photographs, relating to world agricultural problems, and activities of the International Institute of Agriculture. Includes papers of Laura Lubin Saqui, daughter of D. Lubin.
Preliminary inventory.
Gift, L. L. Saqui, 1944.

1651

Lucas, June Richardson, d. 1944.
Papers, 1917–1942. 4 ms. boxes.
American relief worker and lecturer. Drafts of lectures, notes, clippings, correspondence, and pamphlets, relating to relief work in World War I, international relations in the 1930's, U.S. foreign policy, and British and Irish politics.
Gift, Mrs. Walter Lyman Upson, 1945.

1652

Luck, James Murray, 1899–
Miscellaneous papers, 1941. 1 ms. box.
American nutrition scientist. Report (mimeographed), relating to the food supply in the U.S., Canada and Great Britain during World War II; and photographs of the British home front during World War II.

1653

Ludecke (Kurt G. W.) collection (in German), 1934–1935. 1 folder.
Correspondence, petitions and clippings, relating to efforts of K. Ludecke to secure reinstatement as a member of the German Nazi Party, and to activities of pro-Nazi German-Americans in the United States.

1654

Luettringhausen (Concentration camp).
Pair of horse's spectacles, 1945.
Made in Luettringhausen concentration camp near Remscheid, Germany, by inmates in solitary confinement, during World War II. These spectacles were evidently used by General Rommel's horses in his Sahara offensive.
Gift, H. A. Renssen-Tollemar, 1978.

1655

Lukomskiĭ, Aleksandr Sergeevich, d. 1939.
Papers (in Russian), 1914–1939. 4 ms. boxes, 1 envelope.
General, Russian Imperial Army; White Russian military leader under Generals Kornilov and Denikin, 1917–1919. Correspondence, memoranda, reports, writings, notes, and printed matter, relating to Russian military operations during World War I, and to the Russian Civil War.
Register.
Gift, Sophie Isakow, 1975.

1656

Lule, Arthur B.
Memorandum, 1924. 1 folder.
Typescript.
Latvian Consul, New York City. Relates to the political composition and policies of the Government of Latvia.

1657

Lundeen, Ernest, 1878–1940.
Papers, 1900–1940. 344 ms. boxes, 10 envelopes.
U.S. representative from Minnesota, 1917–1919 and 1933–1937; U.S. Senator from Minnesota, 1937–1940. Correspondence, speeches and writings, clippings, and printed matter, relating to U.S. politics, U.S. neutrality in World Wars I and II, military conscription in the U.S., New Deal social and economic legislation, the "court-packing scheme" of 1937, the Progressive movement in the U.S., and the Minnesota Farmer-Labor Party.
Preliminary inventory.
Gift, Mrs. Rufus C. Holman, 1950.

1658

Lusk, Graham, 1866–1932.
Papers, 1917–1919. 1 ms. box.
American member, Inter-Allied Scientific Food Commission, 1918. Correspondence, reports, memoranda, statistical tables, photographs, and printed matter, relating to food rationing, food production and distribution, and nutrition in Europe during World War I.

1659

Lutz, Hermann, 1881–1965.
Papers (in English and German), 1931–1965. 3 ms. boxes.
German historian. Writings, notes, and correspondence, relating to British foreign policy before World War I, the World War I war guilt question, German foreign policy under Adolf Hitler, prospects for European reconstruction after World War II, the German Army during World War II, and postwar denazification programs.
Gift, H. Lutz, 1965.

1660

Lutz, Hugh Ward.
Letter, 1918, to his aunt. 1 folder.
Typescript.
U.S. Army soldier during World War I. Relates to conditions at the front in France.

1661

Lutz, Ralph Haswell, 1886–1968.
Papers, 1914–1961. 11 ms. boxes, 2 envelopes.
American historian; Chairman, Board of Directors, Hoover War Library, 1925–1943. Writings, correspondence, notes and diaries, relating to the Austrian peace negotiations of 1919, the German collapse and revolution of 1918–1919, Italian politics 1914–1919, and German politics in the 1930's.
Register.
Gift, Ralph H. Lutz. Incremental gift, Charles Burdick.

1662

Luxemburg, Rosa, 1871–1919.
Papers (mainly in German), 1887–1929. 2 ms. boxes.
German-Polish revolutionary leader. Correspondence, memoirs, diaries, and photographs, relating to the German socialist and communist movements, and to the imprisonment of R. Luxemburg during World War I. Includes papers of Mathilde Jacob, personal secretary of R. Luxemburg.
Preliminary inventory.
Gift, M. Jacob, 1939.

1663

Lykes, Gibbes.
Papers, 1919–1923. 2 ms. boxes.
Captain, U.S. Army; supervisor, Ukrainian District, Russian Unit, American Relief Administration. Reports, dispatches, correspondence and photographs, relating to relief work in the Ukraine and to political conditions in Hungary during the Hungarian Revolution.
Gift, William F. G. Lykes, 1957.

1664

Lyle, Annie G.
Papers, 1928–1932. 3 ms. boxes.
American physician; Republican campaign worker. Correspondence, clippings, and campaign literature, relating to Herbert Hoover and the U.S. Presidential elections of 1928 and 1932.

1665

Lynch, Julie G., *collector*.
Miscellany, 1951. 1 folder.
Memorandum (mimeographed), entitled "Holland and the European Army," and a press release (typewritten), relating to Dutch opinion regarding Dutch national defense and its relation to European collective defense.

1666

Lynn, Harold F.
Papers, 1943–1945. 1 ms. box, 5 albums.
Commander, U.S. Navy; Commanding Officer, 93rd Naval Construction Battalion, during World War II. Photographs and memorabilia, relating to the activities of the 93rd U.S. Naval Construction Battalion in the Pacific Theater during World War II. Includes a time studies report on construction operations.
Gift, estate of H. F. Lynn, 1963.

1667

Lyon, Bessie Eddy.
Papers, 1918–1920. 1 folder.
Stenographer, American Red Cross Commission in Siberia, 1918–1920.
Letters and reports, relating to activities of the American Red Cross Commission in Siberia and the political and military conditions in Siberia during the Russian Civil War.
Gift, B. E. Lyon, 1974.

1668

Lyons, Marvin, *interviewer*.
Interview summary, 1965. "Conversation with a Chekist." 1 folder.
Typescript.
Relates to an interview of a former member of the Chrevychaĭnaiâ Komissiiâ po Bor'be s Kontr-revoliûtsieĭ

i Sabotazhem (CHEKA), the Soviet secret police agency, who served as Political Commissar of the 29th CHEKA Brigade in 1919, regarding CHEKA activities, 1917–1922. Includes a photograph.
Gift, M. Lyons, 1971.

1669

Mabee, James Irving, b. 1870.
Papers, 1917–1919. 1 folder.
Colonel, U.S. Army; Sanitary Inspector, 1st Division, 1917–1918; Division Surgeon, 1st Division, 1918–1919. Memoirs and orders, relating to activities of the Medical Department and 1st Sanitary Train of the 1st Division in France during World War I.

1670

MacArthur, Douglas, 1880–1964.
Speech, 1962. 1 phonotape.
General of the Army, U.S. Army. Relates to the role of the soldier in society. Delivered to the graduating class at the U.S. Military Academy, West Point, May 12, 1962.
Gift, Ray Henle, 1972.

1671

McCann, Robert Ezra, 1901–1961.
Papers, 1949–1961. 5 ms. boxes.
American businessman; President, Frazar Federal, Inc. Correspondence and reports, 1949–1961, relating to U.S. business interests in China, and to the arrest of R. E. McCann by Chinese authorities in 1951 on charges of espionage.
Gift, Bob McCann, 1976.

1672

McCarran, Margaret Patricia.
Writings, 1968–1969. 1 ms. box.
Daughter of Patrick A. McCarran, U.S. Senator from Nevada. Photocopy of study (typewritten), entitled "The Fabian Transmission," relating to Fabian socialist societies in Great Britain and the U.S.; and biographical sketches (printed), relating to Senator McCarran.
Gift, M. P. McCarran, 1973.

1673

MacCloskey, Monro, 1902–
Papers, 1943–1946. 1 ms. box.
Brigadier General, U.S. Air Force; member, Joint Planning Staff, Allied Force Headquarters, Mediterranean Theater of Operations, 1943–1944. Reports, memoranda, and minutes of meetings, relating to operational plans in the Mediterranean Theater during World War II, and to the Japanese chemical industry during the war.
Gift, M. MacCloskey, 1973.

1674

McClure, Donald.
Papers, 1944–1948. 2 ms. boxes.
Lieutenant Colonel, U.S. Air Force; Nuremberg war crime trials official. Correspondence, memoranda, and trial transcripts, relating to "The Long March" of the 1st Division, U.S. Infantry, into German occupied areas following World War I; German military operations in the West during World War II; and German war crime trials, especially the Buchenwald Concentration Camp case, 1947–1948. Includes "German Military Operations Report, 1944–45," by W. H. Scheidt, Historian, Oberkommando der Wehrmacht.
Preliminary inventory.
Gift, D. McClure, 1966. Subsequent increments.

1675

McClure, Robert B., 1896–
Miscellaneous papers, 1945–1946. 1 ms. box.
Major General, U.S. Army; Commanding General, Chinese Combat Command, 1945–1946. U.S. Army report on organization of the Chinese Department of National Defense, 1946; text of a speech at the dedication of radio station XMAG, Nanking, China, 1946; and a guest book, 1945–1946.
Gift, Merrill Moore, 1954.

1676

McConnell, Philip C.
Papers, 1937–1963. 3 ms. boxes.
American petroleum engineer; Vice President, Arabian American Oil Company. Diaries, correspondence, notes, reports, brochures, printed matter, maps and photographs, relating to operations of the Arabian American Oil Company in Saudi Arabia and elsewhere in the Middle East, and to Arab customs.
Gift, P. C. McConnell, 1962.

1677

McCormick, Chauncey, 1884–1954.
Papers, 1917–1954. 1 ms. box, 1 roll of posters, 3 phonorecords.
Member, U.S. Food Administration Mission to Poland, 1919. Reports, correspondence, orders, printed matter, phonograph records, photographs and posters, relating to relief work in Poland and political and economic conditions in Poland at the end of World War I.
Gift, Mrs. C. McCormick, 1957.

1678

McCormick, Vance C., 1872–1946.
Diaries, 1917–1919. ½ ms. box.
Printed.
American delegate, Inter-Allied Conference, London and Paris, 1917; adviser to Woodrow Wilson, Paris Peace Conference, 1919. Relates to inter-Allied diplomacy and the Paris Peace Conference.
Gift, Thomas Bailey, 1941.

1679

McDonnell, Geoffrey.
Papers, 1918–1919. 1 scrapbook.
Lieutenant Colonel, Canadian Army. Photographs, correspondence, and memorabilia, relating to the activities of the Canadian and other Allied expeditionary forces in Siberia.
Gift, A. W. Hazelton.

1680

McDowell, Robert Harbold, 1894–
Papers, 1940–1969. 2 ms. boxes.
Colonel, U.S. Army, during World War II; intelligence officer in Yugoslavia, 1944; civilian adviser, U.S. Department of the Army, 1946–1959. Three book manuscripts, intelligence reports and memoranda, relating to Draža Mihailović and Yugoslav resistance movements during World War II, and to world politics, primarily after World War II.
Gift, R. H. McDowell, 1969.

1681

McDuffee, Roy W.
Dissertation, 1953. "The Department of State and the Russian Revolution, March-November, 1917." ½ ms. box. Mimeograph.
Relates to evaluation of the Russian Revolution and formation of American policy toward it by the U.S. Department of State. Ph.D. dissertation, Georgetown University.
Gift, Stefan T. Possony, 1978.

1682

McGarvey, Patrick J.
Study, 1969. "Magnificent Madness: An Interpretation of Vietnamese Communist Political and Military Strategy, 1967–1968." ½ ms. box.
Typescript (photocopy).
Relates to the Communist Lunar New Year Offensive (Tet offensive) in South Vietnam. Includes maps.

1683

McGrew, Tarn.
Study, n.d. "Settlements by Clearing House Payments." 1 folder.
Typescript.
Relates to proposals for international trade reform.

1684

MacLafferty, James Henry, 1871–1937.
Papers, 1922–1933. 1½ ms. boxes, 1 envelope.
American businessman; U.S. Representative from California, 1922–1925; Assistant to the Secretary of Commerce, 1925–1927. Diaries, letters, memoranda, and photographs, relating to Herbert Hoover and to U.S. politics during the Presidency of Herbert Hoover. Includes photocopies of doodles drawn by Herbert Hoover.
Gift, Mrs. J. H. MacLafferty, 1957. Gift, Hanford Thayer, 1968.

1685

McLean, Hulda Brooke Hoover, 1906–
Papers, 1861–1964. 1½ ms. boxes.
Niece of Herbert Hoover. Photocopies of letters from Mr. and Mrs. Herbert Hoover to Theodore Hoover, brother of Herbert Hoover, and Hulda McLean, 1903–1964, and of letters of Hulda Randall Minthorn Hoover, mother of Herbert Hoover, all relating to personal and family matters; typewritten and printed material relating to the genealogy of the Hoover family; and typewritten

quotations from the writings of Herbert Hoover.
Gift, H. B. H. McLean, 1961. Subsequent increments.

1686

McLean, Katherine S.
Papers, 1918–1920. 1 folder, 1 envelope.
Young Women's Christian Association worker, Camp Fremont and Camp Kearny, California, 1918–1919. Memoranda, clippings, photographs and miscellanea, relating to Y.W.C.A. work among American soldiers stationed at Camps Fremont and Kearny, and Czechoslovakian soldiers evacuated to these camps from Siberia.
Gift, K. S. McLean, 1942.

1687

McMeeking, John G.
Miscellaneous papers, 1946–1948. 1 ms. box.
Typescript (mimeographed) and printed.
Official of the United Nations Relief and Rehabilitation Administration. Reports of the United Nations Relief and Rehabilitation Administration, relating to personnel regulations and to surplus property procurement in China and the Philippines.
Gift, J. G. McMeeking.

1688

Macmillan, Harold, 1894–
Phonorecord, 1960. 1 phonorecord.
Prime Minister of Great Britain. Recording of a speech, entitled "Winds of Change," by H. Macmillan, to the Parliament of South Africa, and a reply by Hendrik F. Verwoerdt, Prime Minister of South Africa.
Gift, Kenneth M. Glazier, 1968.

1689

McMullin, Dare Stark, 1896–1974.
Papers, 1932–1964. 1 ms. box, 1 envelope.
Secretary to Herbert Hoover. Writings and correspondence, including two studies entitled "Heirlooms: An Anthology of White House Furniture" and "The Furniture of the White House," and letters from Herbert Hoover.

1690

MacQueeney, Patrick Thomas, 1892–1976.
Papers, 1912–1976. ½ ms. box.
Brigadier General and Quartermaster General, Massachusetts National Guard. Orders, personnel records, correspondence, certificates and photographs, relating to the service of P. T. MacQueeney in the U.S. Army and Massachusetts National Guard, including his service in the Logistics Group of the Operations Division of the War Department General Staff during World War II.
Gift, Vincent P. MacQueeney, 1978.

1691

MacRae, Lillian Mae.
Papers, 1916–1917. 2 folders.
American relief work publicist during World War I. Correspondence and postcards, relating to the collection

of funds in California for relief work in Belgium and northern France.
Register.
Gift, L. M. MacRae, 1958.

1692

McWilliams, Carey, 1905–
Miscellaneous papers, 1941–1945. 2 ms. boxes.
American author and journalist. Writings, correspondence, press releases, and clippings, relating to the evacuation and relocation of Japanese Americans during World War II. Used as research material for the book *Prejudice* by C. McWilliams (1944).
Preliminary inventory.
Gift, Stanford University Library, 1943.

1693

Máday, István.
Miscellaneous papers (in Hungarian), 1945–1948. 1 folder.
Hungarian psychiatrist. Clippings, relating to the trials of Hungarian political leaders accused of war crimes during World War II; and a memorandum, relating to a conversation with László Bárdossy, Prime Minister of Hungary, 1941–1942, on the eve of his execution in 1946.
Gift, Bela C. Máday, 1978.

1694

Madden. Henry, *collector*.
Miscellany (in German and English), 1946. 1 folder.
Memoranda and reports, relating to activities of Hermann Goering and other high Nazi officials in the final days of the Third Reich, and to German refugees from the Sudetenland and other areas separated from Germany at the end of World War II.

1695

Madeira, Dashiell L., 1897–
Miscellaneous papers, 1930–1952. 1 ms. box.
Rear Admiral, U.S. Navy; Director of Training and Training Activities, Bureau of Personnel, Navy Department, 1944; U.S. Naval Commander, Inland Sea, Japan, 1945–1946. Correspondence, reports, and orders, relating to American naval operations in the Atlantic and Pacific prior to and during World War II, and to the Allied occupation of Japan.
Gift, D. L. Madeira, 1978.

1696

Magnus, Saul.
Papers (in English and Italian), 1918. ½ ms. box.
Captain, U.S. Army; Adjutant, 332d Infantry Regiment, 1918. Military orders, memoranda and maps, relating to activities of the U.S. 332d Infantry Regiment and the Italian 31st Division on the Italian front during World War I, October-November 1918.
Preliminary inventory.
Gift, S. Magnus, 1930.

1697

Magruder, Jeb Stuart, 1934–
Papers, 1968–1975. 26 ms. boxes, 2 oversize boxes, 7 phonotapes, 3 microfilm reels, 1 video cassette.
Special Assistant to the President, 1969–1971; Deputy Director of Communications, the White House, 1970–1971; Deputy Director, Committee for the Re-Election of the President, 1971–1972; Executive Director, Inaugural Committee, 1973. Diary, writings, correspondence, office files, memoranda, reports, testimony, sound recordings and printed matter, relating to the political campaigns of 1970 and 1972, the Republican Convention of 1972, and the Watergate hearings. Includes photocopies of papers obtained from J. S. Magruder by the Watergate Special Prosecution Force of the U.S. Department of Justice through a grand jury subpoena and subsequently accessioned in the National Archives. Also includes microfilm of testimony of J. S. Magruder before the U.S. Senate Select Committee on Presidential Campaign Activities.
Preliminary inventory.
Closed until June 14, 2003.
Gift, J. S. Magruder, 1978.

1698

Maillaud (Pierre)—photograph, n.d. 1 envelope.
Depicts the French author P. Maillaud.

1699

Makarov, N.
Study (in Russian), n.d. "Na puti k Krisizmu Sotsial'nago Rationalizma: Sotsial'no-ekonomicheskie Ocherki o Rossii i eia Revoliutsii, 1917–1920" (On the Path to a Crisis of Social Rationalism: Social-economic Essays on Russia and its Revolution, 1917–1920). 1 folder.
Holograph.

1700

Makerere University.
Slides, 1969. 4 boxes.
Illustrates the history of Christianity in East Africa. Prepared by the Department of Religious Studies and the Audio-Visual Aids Center of Makerere University, Kampala, Uganda.
Preliminary inventory.
Purchase, 1972.

1701

Makhno, Nestor Ivanovich, 1889–1935.
Memoirs (in Russian), 1932. *Pechalnye Stranitsy Russkoi Revoliutsii* (Sad Pages of the Russian Revolution). 1 folder.
Printed.
Russian anarchist leader. Relates to the role of the anarchists in the Russian Civil War. Published serially in the Chicago *Rassvet*.

1702

Makhov, Grigorii Grigor'evich, 1886–1952.
Study (in Russian), 1952. "Sel'skoe Khoziaistvo Ukrainy" (Agriculture in the Ukraine). 1 vol.
Typescript (carbon copy).

1703
Makinsky, Alexander.
Diary, 1940. 1 folder.
Typescript (mimeographed).
Staff member, Paris Office, Rockefeller Foundation. Relates to the evacuation of Rockefeller Foundation personnel and other foreigners from Paris and La Baule, France, at the time of the French surrender, June 8—25, 1940.

1704
Maklakov, Vasiliĭ Alekseevich, 1870—1957.
Papers (in Russian and French), 1917—1956. 22 ms. boxes.
Ambassador of the Provisional Government of Russia to France, 1917—1924. Correspondence, reports, diaries, and clippings, relating to Russian foreign relations with France, the Russian Revolution, and Russian émigrés in France after the revolution.
Preliminary inventory.
Gift, V. A. Maklakov, 1957.

1705
Makowiecki, Zygmunt.
Memorandum (in German), 1916. "Nach der Feier" (After the Celebration). 1 folder.
Typescript.
Relates to the Polish national independence movement.

1706
Malayan Chinese Association.
Speech transcript, 1950. 1 folder.
Typescript (mimeographed).
Relates to political conditions in Malaya during the emergency period. Speech delivered by a spokesman of the Kluang branch of the Malayan Chinese Association, in Malacca, September 8, 1950.

1707
Malayan Communist Party.
Propaganda, 1950—1951. ½ ms. box.
Propaganda leaflets and bulletins and translations of propaganda leaflets and bulletins (mimeographed), issued by the Malayan Communist Party, relating to the communist-led independence movement in Singapore.

1708
Man, Henri de, 1885—1953.
Miscellaneous papers (mainly in French), 1923—1963. 1 ms. box.
Belgian social psychologist; Minister of Public Works and Employment, 1935—1936; Minister of Finance, 1936—1938. Letters, writings, and clippings, relating to Marxism, Belgian politics, European socialism, the German occupation of Belgium during World War II, and the conviction of H. de Man for Nazi collaboration. Includes a photocopy of the book by H. de Man, *Réflexions sur la Paix* (Reflections on Peace), 1942.
Gift, Jacques de Launay, 1977. Incremental purchase, 1978.

1709
"Manchurian Manifesto."
Press release, 1946. 1 folder.
Typescript (mimeographed).
Protests Soviet influence in Manchuria. Signed by a number of American anti-communists.

1710
Manila, Philippine Islands, war damage—photographs, 1944. 1 envelope.
Depicts war damage to various buildings in Manila, Philippine Islands.
Preliminary inventory.
Gift, Patricia S. Applegate, 1971.

1711
Mannerheim, Carl Gustav Emil, Friherre, 1867—1951.
Telegram, 1940, to Elsa Durkheimer. 1 folder.
Field Marshal and Commander-in-Chief, Finnish Army, 1939—1944. Relates to the Russo-Finnish War.

1712
Manuila, Sabin, 1894—1964.
Papers (in Romanian and English), 1940—1975. 24 ms. boxes, 1 scrapbook.
Romanian statistician and politician. Correspondence, memoranda, reports, speeches and writings, clippings, printed matter, and other material, relating to political events in Romania, social conditions in communist Romania, and Romanian anti-communist émigré movements.
Box 24 is restricted until August 1, 1988.
Gift, Mrs. S. Manuila, 1976. Incremental gift, 1977.

1713
Mao, Ping-wen, 1891—1972.
Autobiographical sketch, n.d. 1 folder.
Photocopy.
Nationalist Chinese Army General. Relates to the Sino-Japanese War of 1937—1945, and the civil war in China, 1945—1949.
Gift, C. F. Mao, 1973.

1714
Marawske, Max, *collector*.
M. Marawske collection on World War I (in German), 1890—1918. 34 ms. boxes.
Clippings from German newspapers and periodicals, relating to World War I.
Register.

1715
Marburger Hochschulgespraeche, 1946.
Report (in German), 1946. 1 folder.
Typescript.
Summarizes proceedings of the Marburger Hochschulgespraeche, a conference of German and foreign scholars held at Marburg, concerning academic studies in Germany.

1716

Maria, Queen Consort of Ferdinand, King of Romania, 1875–1938.

Letter, 1936, to Baroness Ines Taxis. 1 folder.
Holograph.
Relates to personal matters and international relations.
Purchase, Baroness I. Taxis, 1970.

1717

Maricourt, André. Baron de, b. 1874.

Memoirs (in French), n.d. "Chez le Maréchal Foch" (With Marshal Foch). 1 folder.
Holograph.
Relates to Ferdinand Foch, Marshal of the French Army.

1718

Marie, Queen Consort of Alexander I, King of Yugoslavia, 1900–1961.

Letters (in Serbo-Croatian), 1953–1959, to Momčilo Vuković-Birčanin. 1 folder.
Typescript.
Relates to Serbian émigré politics.
Gift, M. Vuković-Birčanin, 1975.

1719

Mariîa Feodorovna, Empress Consort of Alexander III, Emperor of Russia, 1847–1928.

Letters (in Danish), 1881–1925, to Alexandra, Queen Consort of Edward VII, King of Great Britain. 15 ms. boxes.
Holograph.
Relates to matters of state and family.
Preliminary inventory.
Closed until January 2, 2001 or until publication of the letters by Princess Eugenie of Greece. Thereafter, may be used with written permission of Princess Eugenie, or, after her death, of Prince Vasili Romanov or the Director of the Hoover Institution.
Gift, Princess Eugenie, 1975.

1720

Marin, Patricia J., *collector*.

Miscellany, 1919. 1 folder.
Postcards depicting scenes along the Rhine River; and a program for a carnival in Coblenz held by the U.S. Third Army while serving as an occupation force in Germany.
Gift, P. J. Marin, 1978.

1721

Maritime Province, Siberia. Komissiîa po Obsledovaniîu Obstoîatel'stv Sobytiî 4-6 Aprelîa vo Vladivostoke.

Report (in Russian), ca. 1920. 1 vol.
Typescript (carbon copy).
Commission for Investigation of Circumstance of the Events of April 4–6 in Vladivostok. Relates to activities of Japanese troops in the Maritime Province of Siberia during the Russian Civil War.

1722

Marizus, J.

Memorandum (in French), 1934. "La Révision des Marchés de Guerre" (Revision of War Contracts). 1 folder.
Typescript.
French lawyer. Relates to changes in the French law regarding taxation of profits of defense contractors.

1723

Markov, Anatoliĭ.

Study (in Russian), n.d. "Entsiklopediîa Belago Dvizheniîa: Vozhdi, Partizany, Fronty, Pokhody i Narodnyîa Vozstaniîa Protiv Sovetov v Rossiĭ" (Encyclopedia of the White Movement: Leaders, Partisans, Fronts, Marches and Popular Uprisings against the Soviets in Russia). 4 vols.
Typescript.
Relates to White Russian activities during the Russian Civil War and after, 1917–1958. Includes biographical sketches.

1724

Markov, Walter.

Outline (in German), 1949. "Das Zeitalter des Imperialismus" (The Age of Imperialism). 1 folder.
Typescript (photocopy).
Professor, Universities of Leipzig and Halle. Relates to world history from 1871 to 1945.

1725

Marković, Lazar, 1882–1955.

Writings (in Serbo-Croatian and French), 1955. 1 ms. box.
Typescript (photocopy).
Serbian politician. Memoirs, entitled "Uspomene" (Memoirs), relating to the formation of the Yugoslav state following World War I and Yugoslav political developments, 1919–1925; and a biography, entitled "Nikolas Pachitch (1845–1926): Histoire d'un Olympien que le Petit Peuple des Serbes a Donné au Monde Politique Européen" (Nikola Pašić: History of the Olympian whom the Little Serbian People Gave to the European Political World), relating to the life and political career of Nikola Pašić, Prime Minister of Serbia and Yugoslavia.
Gift, Alex N. Dragnich, 1975.

1726

Marmon, Howard C., 1876–1960.

Papers, ca. 1914–1919. 1 folder, 7 albums, 2 envelopes.
Lieutenant Colonel, U.S. Army Air Corps, during World War I. Writings, maps, and photographs, relating to Allied aviation activities in Italy during World War I.
Gift, Robert F. Morrison, 1960.

1727

Marshall, Herbert.

Study, 1975. "The Fate of the Great Soviet Film Artist, Sergo Paradjanov." 1 folder.
Typescript (photocopy).

Professor, Center for Soviet and East European Studies in the Performing Arts, at Southern Illinois University. Relates to the arrest and imprisonment in the Soviet Union of Sergeĭ Iosipovich Paradi̇ânov, Soviet film director. Includes a petition for the release of S. I. Paradi̇ânov.
Gift, H. Marshall, 1977.

1728

Marshall McDonald and Associates.
Report, 1967. "Angel Island." 1 folder.
Typescript (photocopy).
Relates to the history of Angel Island, California, the architecture of buildings on the island, and recommendations for developing it as a recreational facility and historical site. Report prepared for the California State Division of Beaches and Parks.
Gift, Donald Abenheim, 1978.

1729

Martens, Ludwig Christian Alexander Karl, 1874–1948.
Letter, 1919, to Boris Bakhmetev. 1 folder.
Typescript (photocopy).
Demands that B. Bakhmetev, Ambassador of the Russian Provisional Government to the U.S., hand over all property of the Russian Government in the U.S. Written by L. C. A. K. Martens and Santeri Nuorteva, Soviet diplomatic representatives in the United States.

1730

Martens, R. C.
Letters, 1942–1946. 1 ms. box.
Typescript.
Lithuanian émigré in the U.S. Relates to diplomatic, economic and political events during World War II.
Gift, Leslie W. Hills, 1975.

1731

Martin, David, 1914–
Miscellaneous papers, 1945–1978. ½ ms. box.
American author; U.S. Congressional aide; Secretary, Committee for a Fair Trial for Draja Mihailovich, 1946; organizer, Commission of Inquiry in the Case of General Mihailovich, 1946. Correspondence, reports, press releases and printed matter, relating to the resistance movement led by Draža Mihailović in Yugoslavia during World War II, and to the trial of Draža Mihailović for treason in Yugoslavia in 1946. Includes transcript of the Commission of Inquiry.
Gift, D. Martin, 1978.

1732

Martin, William, 1888–1934.
Notes (in French), 1915–1933. 4½ ms. boxes.
Typescript (some photocopies).
Paris correspondent of the *Journal de Genève*. Summaries of interviews of European diplomats and statesmen, relating to European and world military, political and diplomatic events during and after World War I.

1733

Martinez-Lorenzo, Cesar.
History (in French), n.d. *Les Anarcho-Syndicalistes Espagnols dans la Lutte Politique, 1868–1968* (The Spanish Anarcho-Syndicalists in Political Struggle, 1868–1968). 1 ms. box.
Typescript.
Published in abridged form.
Gift, Burnett Bolloten, 1973.

1734

Martov, İUliĭ Osipovich, 1873–1923.
Writings (in Russian), 1920. "Oborona Revoli̇ut̄sii i Sot̄sial-Demokrati̇â: Sbornik Stateĭ" (Defense of the Revolution and Social-Democracy: Collected Articles). 1 vol.
Typescript.
Russian Menshevik leader. Relates to the Russian Revolution and Civil War.

1735

Martynov, A. P., d. 1951.
Memoir (in Russian), n.d. 1 ms. box.
Holograph.
Director, Moscow Office, Okhrana (Russian Imperial police), 1912–1917. Relates to activities of the Okhrana, 1906–1917.
Purchase, Museum of Russian Culture, San Francisco, 1963.

1736

Martynov, General.
Study (in Russian), 1925. "Soobrazheni̇â ob Ustroistvie, Obuchenii i Upotreblenii Budushcheĭ Russkoĭ Kavaleriĭ" (Considerations on the Organization, Training and Utilization of the Future Russian Cavalry). 1 folder.
Typescript (mimeographed).
Lieutenant General, Russian Imperial Army.

1737

Martynov, Zakhar Nikiforovich.
Papers (in Russian), 1914–1977. 1 ms. box.
Imperial Russian soldier in the Convoy of His Imperial Majesty Emperor Nicholas II. Correspondence, writings, reminiscences, printed matter, clippings and photographs, relating to the Russian Imperial Army, Russia's role in World War I, the Russian Revolution and Civil War, and anti-communist movements in the U.S. Includes a cigarette case from the desk of Tsar Alexander III, a dagger presented to Tsarevich Alekseĭ Nikolaevich when he was made Ataman of the Cossacks, and the St. George's Cross awarded to Z. N. Martynov for his military service.
Gift, Z. N. Martynov, 1977.

1738

Maruki, R.
Photograph, n.d.
Depicts unidentified Chinese delegation posing with Japanese officials in Shiba Garden, Tokyo.
Gift, Mme. LaRue, 1957.

1739

Marvin Liebman Associates, 1958–1969.
    Records, 1950–1969. 108 ms. boxes, 3 envelopes.
    New York public relations firm. Office files, correspondence, printed matter, press releases, campaign material, photographs and reports, relating to lobbying activities of U.S. conservative and anti-communist organizations involved with Asian and African affairs.
    Register.
Gift, Marvin Liebman Associates, 1969.

1740

Marx, Guido Hugo, 1871–1949.
    Speech transcript, 1936. "War and the Conscientious Objector." 1 folder.
    Typescript.
    Professor of Machine Design, Stanford University. Relates to the pacifist movement in the United States.

1741

Masaryk, Tomáš Garrigue, 1850–1937.
    Proclamation (in Czech), 1919. 1 folder.
    Typescript (photocopy).
    President of Czechoslovakia. Issued to the Czechoslovak Army in Siberia.

1742

Masland, John Wesley, Jr., 1912–1968.
    Papers, 1945. 21 ms. boxes, 1 envelope.
    Staff member, International Secretariat, United Nations Conference on International Organization, San Francisco, 1945. Reports, minutes of meetings, directories, notes and printed matter, relating to the U.N. Conference on International Organization at San Francisco and the founding of the United Nations.
    Preliminary inventory.
    Deposit, J. W. Masland, Jr., 1945.

1743

Maslov, Sergeĭ Semenovich.
    Study (in Russian), n.d. "Kolkhoznaià Rossiià: Istoki, Nasazhdenie i Zhizn' Kolkhozov, ikh Priroda, Evoliutsiià i Budushchee Znachenie dlià s. Khoziàĭstva, Krest'iànstva, Gosudarstva" (Collective Farm Russia: Sources, Propagation and Life of Collective Farms, Their Nature, Evolution and Future Meaning for Agriculture, Peasantry, Government). 1 vol.
    Typescript (mimeographed).

1744

Maslovskiĭ, Evgeniĭ Vasil'evich.
    Letters (in Russian), 1945, to Baron Sergeĭ Evgen'evich Ludinkhausen-Wolff. 1 folder.
    Holograph.
    Russian Imperial Army officer. Relates to Russian military activities in northern Persia before World War I, and in the Turkish campaigns of General IUdenich during World War I.
    Gift, Valery Kuharets, 1977.

1745

Mason, Frank Earl, 1893–1979.
    Papers (in English and German), 1915–1975. 4 ms. boxes, 7 envelopes.
    American journalist; Berlin correspondent and President, International News Service. Correspondence, reports, journalistic dispatches, and other material, relating to German and Soviet politics and diplomacy in the interwar period, and to Allied military administration of Germany at the end of World War II. Includes a copy of the logbook of the submarine that sank the *Lusitania*, 1915, and correspondence with Georgiĭ Chicherin and Karl von Wiegand.
    Preliminary inventory.
    Gift, F. E. Mason, 1955. Subsequent increments.

1746

Mason, James B.
    Papers, 1942–1952. 1 folder, 1 envelope.
    Brigadier General, U.S. Army Medical Corps; Liaison Officer, Chief Surgeon's Office, European Theater of Operations, during World War II. Reports and photographs, relating to U.S. military medical activities in the European Theater during World War II.
    Preliminary inventory.
    Gift, J. B. Mason.

1747

Mason, John Brown, 1904–
    Papers, 1935–1945. ½ ms. box.
    American educator and author; Chief, Training Division, U.S. Foreign Economic Administration, 1944–1946. Reports, memoranda, syllabi and organization charts, relating to the training of U.S. Foreign Economic Administration personnel for service in occupied Germany and Austria at the end of World War II, and to living conditions for U.S. consular officials around the world.
    Gift, J. B. Mason, 1945. Subsequent increments.

1748

Mason, Kenneth, J., *collector.*
    Translation of war declaration, 1941. 1 folder.
    Printed.
    Translation of the Japanese declaration of war on the U.S. and Great Britain, December 8, 1941.
    Gift, K. J. Mason, 1946.

1749

Mathews, Forrest David, 1935–
    Speech transcripts, 1975–1976. ½ ms. box.
    Typescript (photocopy).
    U.S. Secretary of Health, Education and Welfare, 1975–1977. Relates to U.S. social welfare policy.
    Gift, F. D. Mathews, 1977.

1750

Mathews, Sarah E., b. 1880.
    Papers, 1918–1920. 1 folder, 1 album, 1 envelope.
    American Red Cross worker in Siberia, 1918–1920.

Memoirs, diary, reports, clippings, and photographs, relating to the disposition of the remains of Tsar Nicholas II and his family, social and political conditions in Siberia, and relief work of the American Red Cross in Siberia during the Russian Civil War.

Gift, S. E. Mathews, 1971. Incremental gift, 1975.

1751

Mathieu, Jules.

Memoir (in French), n.d. "Légion Wallonie: Historique des Unités du Commandant Jules Mathieu" (The Walloon Legion: A History of Major Jules Mathieu's Units). 1 folder.

Typescript (photocopy).

Major, Walloon Legion. Relates to Belgian troops attached to German forces during World War II, 1941–1945.

Gift, Jacques de Launay, 1975.

1752

Matley, Ian, *collector*.

Propaganda (in German, French, Italian and Korean), ca. 1939–1953. 1 folder.

British propaganda from World War II, and propaganda from both sides in the Korean War.

Gift, I. Matley, 1978.

1753

Matthews, Harold S., 1894–

Papers, 1936–1968. 3 ms. boxes.

American missionary in north China, 1922–1942; Secretary, American Board of Commissioners for Foreign Missions, 1944–1953. Writings, correspondence, reports and printed matter, relating to Christian missionary work in China and Japan, and to the communist movement in China.

Register.

Gift, H. S. Matthews, 1970. Subsequent increments.

1754

Matthews, Herbert Lionel, 1900–

Writings, 1961–1964. 1 ms. box.

American journalist and author. Drafts (handwritten and typewritten) of the book, *The Cuban Story*, 1961, and a draft (typewritten) and galley proofs of the article "Return to Cuba," 1964, relating to conditions in Cuba following the 1959 revolution and to Cuban-American relations.

1755

Matthiessen, Hans Heinrich.

Memoirs (in German), 1975–1976. "Meine Dienstzeit auf einem Kanonenboot in Ostasien, 1910–1912" (My Service on a Gunboat in East Asia, 1910–1912). 1 folder.

Typescript.

German sailor. Relates to activities of the German gunboat *Luchs* off the coast of China.

Gift, Charles Burdick, 1976.

1756

Mattox, Elmer L.

Papers, 1905–1966. 2 ms. boxes.

American missionary in Hangchow, China. Correspondence, writings, pamphlets, and photographs, relating to missionary work in Hangchow, to Hangchow Christian College, and to social conditions in China.

1757

Matveev, General.

Study (in Russian), 1939. "Gibel Rigo-Shavel'skago Otriada" (Downfall of the Rigo-Shavel'skiĭ Detachment). 1 vol.

Holograph.

General, Imperial Russian Army. Relates to Russian military operations during World War I.

1758

"Mau Mau Oath Ceremonies."

Memorandum, n.d. 1 folder.

Typescript (photocopy).

Relates to initiation oaths of the Mau Mau movement in Kenya.

1759

Maugeri, Franco, 1898–

Memoir (in Italian), ca. 1945. "Gegen Deutschland! Contro la Germania!" (Against Germany). 1 ms. box.

Typescript (photocopy).

Admiral, Italian Navy; Chief of Italian Naval Intelligence during World War II. Relates to the Italian secret service during World War II. Includes an English translation of, and correspondence relating to, the memoir, and to its publication.

1760

Maurín, Joaquin, 1896–1973.

Papers (mainly in Spanish), 1920–1973. 24 ms. boxes, 1 oversize box (⅓ 1. ft.).

Spanish politician, journalist and author; Secretary-General, Partido Obrero de Unificación Marxista. Correspondence, writings, newspaper and magazine clippings, photographs, and printed matter, relating to communism and socialism in Spain, the Spanish Civil War, and the American Literary Agency.

Various correspondence (box 24) closed until 1980.

Purchase, Jeanne Maurín, 1977.

1761

Maverick, Lewis A.

Papers, 1914–1940. 4 ms. boxes.

American pacifist. Diary, correspondence, memoranda, photographs, and clippings, relating to the Henry Ford Peace Expedition, 1915, and the Neutral Conference for Continuous Mediation and International Committee for Immediate Mediation, 1916.

1762

Maximova-Kulaev, Antonina Alexandrovna.

Memoir, 1932. 1 folder.

Typescript.

Russian physician. Relates to her service as a surgeon in a Red Army hospital in Koslov, Russia, and to the occupation of Koslov by White Russian forces in 1919.

1763

Mayers, Henry, 1894–
Papers, 1930–1966. 7 ms. boxes, 1 scrapbook.
American advertising executive; member, Committee for Freedom for All Peoples; chairman, Cold War Council. Correspondence, speeches and writings, and printed matter, relating primarily to the Cold War Council.

1764

Mayock, Storey, *collector*.
Propaganda leaflets (in Korean), ca. 1950–1953. 1 folder.
Printed.
Distributed by the U.S. armed forces during the Korean War.
Gift, S. Mayock.

1765

Meader, Ann, 1899–
Diary, 1939–1945. 2 ms. boxes.
Typescript.
British author. Relates to conditions of daily life in England during World War II.
May not be published without permission of A. Meader or of her heirs.
Gift, A. Meader, 1974.

1766

Mears, Eliot Grinnell, 1889–1946.
Papers, 1910–1945. 2 ms. boxes.
U.S. Trade Commissioner in Turkey, 1919–1920. Correspondence, reports, and photographs, relating to economic conditions in the Balkans and Near East, to American commerce with Turkey, and to the U.S. war economy during World War II.
Gift, E. G. Mears, 1925. Subsequent increments.

1767

Medals collection, ca. 1914–1974. 20 ms. boxes.
Medals from many countries, relating to the two world wars, to political events in the twentieth century and to miscellaneous subjects.
Preliminary inventory.
Gift, various sources.

1768

Meeting of Three Scandinavian Kings, Malmoe, 1915.
Communiqué (in Swedish), 1915. 1 folder.
Typewritten transcript.
Official communiqué of the meeting of the kings of Sweden, Norway and Denmark at Malmoe, relating to Scandinavian neutrality in World War I.

1769

Mehring, Franz, 1846–1919.
Miscellaneous papers (in German), 1914–1918. 1 folder.

German socialist leader. Writings and correspondence, relating to political conditions in Germany and to the peace movement during World War I.

1770

Mei, I-ch'i, 1889–1962.
Miscellaneous papers (in Chinese), 1949–1956. 1 ms. box.
President, Tsinghua University, 1931–1953; Minister of Education of Taiwan, 1958–1961. Diaries and correspondence, relating to education and political conditions in Taiwan.
Gift, Mrs. Mei I-ch'i, 1972.

1771

Meiendorf, Maria F., Baronessa, 1869–1962.
Memoirs (in Russian), n.d. "Moï Vospominaniiâ" (My Reminiscences). ½ ms. box, 1 scrapbook.
Typescript.
Russian aristocrat. Relates to social conditions in tsarist Russia, the Russian Revolution and Civil War, and Russian émigré life afterwards. Includes a printed copy of the memoirs (clippings from *Russkaiâ Zhizn'* [San Francisco]).
Purchase, Sophie Koulomzin, 1975.

1772

Meisner, Hans.
Memoir (in German), "Auswertung einer Reise nach Amerika" (Assessment of a Trip to America), 1955. 1 folder.
Typescript (mimeographed).
West German visitor to the U.S. Observations about the U.S. based on a trip funded by the U.S. State Department. Meisner accompanied Arnold Ehlers, Senator for the Interior of the Free City of Bremen.
Gift, Bradley F. Smith, 1978.

1773

Mel'gunov, Sergeï Petrovich, 1879–1956.
Papers (in Russian), 1918–1933. 17 ms. boxes.
Russian historian and editor; author of *The Red Terror in Russia*. Clippings, writings, correspondence and reports, relating to the Russian Revolution and Civil War, and the operations of the Soviet secret police.
Preliminary inventory.
Gift, S. P. Mel'gunov, 1938.

1774

Melrose, Paul C.
Papers, 1906–1949. ½ ms. box.
American missionary in China. Reports, newsletters, and notes, relating to missionary work in China, including the Hainan mission newsletter, 1914–1949, and the Hainan mission annual reports, 1906–1948.

1775

"Memorandum on the Present Condition of the Union of the Soviet Socialistic Republics and Its Population."
Memorandum, 1931. 1 folder.
Typescript (mimeographed).
Relates to economic and social conditions in Russia.

1776

Menke, Carl Fred.
Papers, 1943–1953. 3 ms. boxes.
U.S. Army Air Forces flight instructor during World War II. Correspondence and photographs, relating to the World War II activities and postwar readjustment problems of 63 flight cadets of the U.S. Army Air Forces.
Gift, C. F. Menke, 1954.

1777

Mensing family.
Papers (in German), 1872–1964. 2 ms. boxes.
Franz Mensing (1843–1911), Vice-Admiral, German Navy, and his sons, Friedrich Carl (1888–1975), Captain, German Navy, and Franz (1890–1918). Diaries, logbooks, orders, correspondence, and passports, relating primarily to the journey of Franz Mensing as Captain of the S.M.S. *Prinz Adalbert,* to Asia, Africa, and America, 1883–1885, with the German Crown Prince Friedrich Carl von Preussen on board from Genoa to Spain, 1883; and to the participation of Friedrich Carl Mensing as courier for the German Admiralstab of the Marine in World War I German-American negotiations in Switzerland concerning the exchange of prisoners of war. Includes diaries of the Mensings' housekeeper, Anna Schulz, 1899–1906.
Preliminary inventory.
Gift, Charles Burdick, 1971. Gift, Harriet E. Mensing, 1976.

1778

Menzel, Preben M.
Memoirs (in Danish), 1945. "Erindringer fra 'Foreningen af Lojtnanter og Kornetter's Modstandsgruppe" Reminiscences from "Associations of Lieutenants and Cornets" Resistance Group). 1 folder.
Typescript (mimeographed).
Second Lieutenant, Danish Army. Relates to the Danish resistance movement during World War II.

1779

Mercier, Ernest, 1878–1955.
Papers (in French), 1904–1955. 1 ms. box.
French engineer and businessman. Correspondence, writings and notes, relating to French electrical and oil industries, to the "Redressement Français" movement, and to political conditions in France.
Gift, Mme. E. Mercier.

1780

Merritt, Ralph P.
Report, 1919. "Report of the United States Food Administration for California." 1 ms. box.
Typescript (photocopy).
U.S. Food Administration Commissioner for California. Relates to food production and conservation in California during World War I. Report compiled by Edward Krehbiel.
Gift, R. P. Merritt, 1957.

1781

Merritt, Walle W.
Papers, 1911–1915. 2 ms. boxes.
Executive Secretary, Minnesota Committee, Commission for Relief in Belgium. Letters, telegrams, reports, statistical tables, and posters, relating to the fund-raising activities of the Minnesota Committee of the Commission for Relief in Belgium. Includes personal letters, relating to the founding of fraternity organizations.
Gift, Julianna Royal, 1969.

1782

Metcalfe, John C.
Papers, 1935–1949. 13 ms. boxes, 5 envelopes.
American journalist: *Chicago Times* reporter; investigator for the U.S. House of Representatives Un-American Activities Committee. Diary, correspondence, reports, notes, pamphlets, clippings, and printed matter, relating to the infiltration of the German-American Bund by J. C. Metcalfe as an investigative reporter in 1937, and to the activities of fascist organizations in the U.S.
Register.
Gift, J. C. Metcalfe, 1956. Incremental gift, 1972.

1783

Meurich, Willi, 1903–
Papers, 1941–1942. 1 folder.
German Air Force sergeant. Letters, postcards, memorabilia, maps, and photographs, relating to German military life in Belgium and France during World War II.
Gift, Geraldine Garlick, 1976.

1784

Mexican anti-communist pamphlets (in English and Spanish), 1961. 1 folder.
Printed.
Three anti-communist pamphlets published in Mexico.

1785

Meyer, Henry Cord, 1913–
Miscellaneous papers (in German and English), 1916–1950. ½ ms. box.
Photocopy.
American historian. Correspondence and printed matter, relating to the ideas of Paul Rohrbach, German nationalist author, regarding pan-Germanism, German territorial expansion, and the German occupation of the Ukraine in 1918. Includes correspondence of P. Rohrbach.
Preliminary inventory.
Gift, H. C. Meyer, 1969.

1786

Meyer, Robert Eugene, Jr., 1911– , *collector.*
R. E. Meyer collection on U.S. aviation and Italy, 1944–1969. 2 ms. boxes.
Writings, correspondence, printed matter, photographs and miscellanea, relating to the history of air bases in the U.S. and to miscellaneous subjects regarding Italy.
Preliminary inventory.
Gift, R. E. Meyer, Jr., 1971. Subsequent increments.

1787

Michigan. Legislature. Joint Committee on Reorganization of State Government.

Reports, 1950–1953. 3 ms. boxes.

Typescript (mimeographed).

Relates to the reorganization of various state agencies and departments.

Gift, Frank Andrews, 1958.

1788

Middlemas, Robert Keith, 1935– , *collector*.

R. K. Middlemas collection on Portugal and South Africa, 1966–1976. 9 ms. boxes.

Phonotapes of interviews with British, Portuguese and South African diplomats, politicians, economic advisors, journalists, and businessmen; correspondence, and writings, relating to political events in Portugal and Southern Africa, and to British, Portuguese and South African relations.

Preliminary inventory.

Boxes 8 and 9 may be used only with permission of R. K. Middlemas.

Gift, R. K. Middlemas, 1977.

1789

Miessner, Rudolf.

Papers (in German), 1938. 1 folder.

Sudeten German fascist. Correspondence and writings, relating to the fascist movement in Czechoslovakia and to the Sudetendeutsche Partei.

1790

Mihkelson, Johannes, *collector*.

Miscellany, 1949. 1 folder.

Study (typewritten), and leaflet (printed), relating to the communist system in Estonia, and to Estonian and Latvian émigré politics.

1791

Miki (Takeo)—photographs, ca. 1974–1976. 1 envelope.

Photographs of Takeo Miki, Prime Minister of Japan, 1974–1976, with his wife and family; Kiichi Miyazawa, Minister of Foreign Affairs; and Junko Tabei, the first woman to reach the summit of Mount Everest, with the Prime Minister and others.

1792

Miklas, Wilhelm.

Proclamation (in German), 1934. 1 folder.

President of Austria. Thanks Chancellor Engelbert Dollfuss for his role in the suppression of the Austrian Socialist Party.

1793

Mikołajczyk, Stanisław, 1901–1966.

Papers (in Polish and English), 1938–1966. 137 ms. boxes, 19 cu. ft. boxes.

Polish politician; Prime Minister, Government-in-Exile (London), 1943–1944; Second Vice Premier and Minister of Agriculture, 1945–1947; President, International Peasant Union, 1950–1966. Correspondence, speeches and writings, reports, notes, newsletters, clippings, photographs, tape recordings and printed matter, relating to communism in Eastern Europe and Poland, agriculture in Poland, Polish politics, especially during World War II, Polish-Soviet relations, the International Peasant Union, the Polskie Stronnictwo Ludowe, and Polish émigré politics.

Consult archivist for restriction.

Purchase, Marian Mikołajczyk, 1978.

1794

Milanović, Vladimir J., 1896–1972.

Compilation of articles (in Serbo-Croatian), n.d. "Iz Nedavne Prošlosti" (From the Recent Past). ½ ms. box.

Typescript.

Yugoslav Ambassador to Bulgaria, 1940–1941; Chargé d'affaires, Yugoslav embassy in London and assistant to the Foreign Minister, Yugoslav Government-in-Exile, 1941–1944. Relates to Yugoslav relations with Germany and Bulgaria, 1939–1941, prior to the German invasion of Yugoslavia.

Gift, V. J. Milanović, 1970.

1795

Milburn, Josephine F.

Study, 1973. "British Business and Ghanian Independence." 1 folder.

Typescript.

Relates to the role of business in the development of Ghana, 1937–1957.

Gift, J. F. Milburn, 1973.

1796

Miles, Milton Edward, 1900–1961.

Papers, 1923–1958. 9 ms. boxes, 4 envelopes.

Vice Admiral, U.S. Navy; Deputy Director, Sino-American Cooperative Organization, and Commander, U.S. Naval Group, China, 1942–1945; Director, Pan American Affairs and U.S. Naval Missions, 1950–1954. Correspondence, speeches and writings, reports, memoranda, notes, orders, and photographs, relating to the Sino-Japanese conflict, U.S.-Chinese relations during World War II, postwar military defense in Latin America, Canadian-U.S. joint defense policies, and the Indochina and Korean wars.

Register.

Gift, Mrs. M. E. Miles, 1968. Incremental gift, 1969.

1797

Military operations, World War II—photographs, 1944–1945. 3 envelopes.

Depicts U.S. military activities in the South Pacific and the China-Burma-India Theater during World War II, and the Japanese surrender aboard the U.S.S. *Missouri* in Tokyo Bay.

1798

Military Order of the World Wars.

Records, 1919–1978. 160 linear feet.

Patriotic American organization of veteran officers of American wars since World War I. Biographies, histories, photographs, memorabilia and printed matter, relating to American military activities in World War I, World War II, the Korean War and the Vietnamese War.

For access write to historian general, Military Order of the World Wars, Hoover Institution, Stanford, CA 94305.

Deposit, Military Order of the World Wars, 1931; subsequent renewals.

1799

Miliūkov, Pavel Nikolaevich, 1859−1943.
History, n.d. "From Nicholas II to Stalin: Half a Century of Foreign Politics." 1 vol.
Typescript (carbon copy).
Russian historian. Relates to Russian diplomatic history.

1800

Millay, Edna St. Vincent, 1892−1950.
Poem, 1944. "Poem and Prayer for an Invading Army." 1 phonorecord.
Prepared for the Allied invasion of Normandy, and read by Ronald Colman in a broadcast by the National Broadcasting Company, June 6, 1944.

1801

Miller, Bernice.
Papers, 1928−1970. ½ ms. box, 6 scrapbooks.
Personal secretary to Herbert Hoover, 31st President of the U.S. Photographs, letters, pamphlets, and clippings, relating primarily to the political and other public activities of President and Mrs. Herbert Hoover.
Deposit, Mrs. Joseph A. Miller, 1953. Gift, Bernice Miller, 1977.

1802

Miller, Evgeniĭ Karlovich, 1867−1937.
Papers (in Russian), 1917−1924. 12 ms. boxes.
General, Russian Imperial Army; representative of General Vrangel' in Paris during the Russian Civil War. Correspondence, reports, and military orders, relating to White Russian military and diplomatic activities during the Russian Civil War.
Preliminary inventory.
Gift, N. N. Golovin, 1928.

1803

Miller, Iva M., 1880−1951, *collector*.
Photographs, ca. 1910−1930. 1 envelope.
Depicts scenes at the Isabella Fisher Hospital, Tientsin, China.
Gift, Ethel A. Miller, 1972.

1804

Miller, Oliver W.
Papers, 1943−1972. 1 ms. box, 1 scrapbook, 3 maps.
Colonel, U.S. Air Force; communications and electronics specialist. News releases, radio messages, printed matter, photographs, clippings, and maps, relating to the development of radar and its applications in electronic warfare in the U.S. and Canadian air defense forces, to the beginning of the Korean War, 1950, and to

the truce talks at Kaesong, Korea, 1951. Includes first aerial map produced by the radar mosaic method.
Gift, O. W. Miller, 1975. Incremental gift, 1976.

1805

Miller, William P., 1905−1973.
Papers, 1943−1945. 1 ms. box, 15 envelopes, 5 motion picture reels, 3 oversize boxes.
Lieutenant Colonel, U.S. Army Signal Corps. Letter, biographical information, films, and photographs, relating to U.S. Army Signal Corps operations in North Africa, Germany, Italy, and France, 1943−1945.
Gift, Mrs. Garnet Rainey, 1977.

1806

Millis, Walter, 1899−1968.
Study, 1962. "Abolition of War." 1 folder.
Typescript (mimeographed).
Relates to prospects for peace through international disarmament. Written by W. Millis and James Real. Subsequently published.

1807

Mills, Margaret Netherwood.
Papers, ca. 1914−1918. 1 folder.
British Red Cross nurse. Correspondence, diaries, and clippings, relating to nursing work of the British Red Cross during World War I.
Gift, Frederick G. Coley, 1961.

1808

Mings, Stephen Daniel, 1946−
Dissertation, 1975. "Strategies in Conflict: Britain and the Anglo-American Alliance, 1941−1943." ½ ms. box.
Typescript (photocopy).
Ph.D. dissertation, University of Texas.
May not be quoted without permission of S. D. Mings.
Gift, S. D. Mings, 1976.

1809

The Mining Magazine.
Clippings, 1915−1916. 1 folder.
Photocopy.
Editorials and articles, relating to World War I and to the role of engineers in the war. Collected by H. Foster Bain.

1810

Mirkovich, Nicholas, *editor*.
Reports, 1942. "Jugoslav Postwar Reconstruction Papers." 1 folder.
Typescript (mimeographed).
Relates to the economic reconstruction of Yugoslavia after World War II.

1811

Miroliŭbov, Nikander Ivanovich, 1870−1927.
Papers (in Russian), 1918−1927. 1½ ms. boxes, 1 envelope.
White Russian political leader; chairman, Special Committee for the Investigation of the Murder of the

Romanov Family. Correspondence, memoranda, reports, and clippings, relating to the investigation of the deaths of the Romanovs, 1918–1920, the creation of the first Far Eastern Republic, and Russian émigré organizations in the Far East, 1921–1927.
Register.
Gift, anonymous, 1936.

1812
Mirovicz, General.
Papers (in Russian), 1914–1916. 1 folder, 1 envelope.
General, Imperial Russian Army. Reports, orders, maps, and photographs, relating to military operations of the Second and Third Finland Rifle Brigades in four battles on the Riga Front and in the Carpathian Mountains.
Preliminary inventory.
Gift, General Mirovicz.

1813
Mirrielees, Edith R.
History, 1923. "The Stanford Women's Unit for Relief in France." 1 folder.
Typescript.
Relates to the activities of the Stanford Women's Unit in providing relief services for the American Expeditionary Force in France during World War I.

1814
Missiessy, Pierre de, Comtesse.
Biography (in French), n.d. "Claude de Villermont: Biographie d'un Jeune 'Résistant' Belge" (Claude de Villermont: Biography of a Young Belgian Resistance Member). 1 folder.
Typescript.
Relates to the life of an underground fighter in German-occupied Belgium during World War II.

1815
Mitchell, Anna V. S.
Papers, 1920–1944. 6 ms. boxes, 9 envelopes, 4 medals.
American relief worker. Correspondence, memoranda, reports, clippings, memorabilia, and photographs, relating to World War I relief work in France, 1915–1920, and relief work with Russian refugees in Istanbul, 1921–1936.
Register.
Gift, John Davis Hatch, 1967. Incremental gift, 1975.

1816
Mitchell, Richard Paul, 1925– , *collector*.
R. P. Mitchell collection on the Muslim Brotherhood (mainly in Arabic), ca. 1953–1963. 6 ms. boxes, 6 oversize boxes, 10 vols.
Writings, newspapers, magazines, journals, books and other printed matter, relating to the activities of the Muslim Brotherhood, Islamic culture and political movements, and conditions in Islamic countries.
Preliminary inventory.
Gift, R. P. Mitchell, 1977.

1817
Mitkiewicz, Leon, 1896–1972.
Papers (in Polish), 1918–1969. 8½ ms. boxes.
Colonel and Chief of Intelligence, Polish Army; Military Attaché to Lithuania; Polish representative, Allied Combined Chiefs of Staff, 1943–1945. Diary, correspondence, writings and printed matter, relating to Polish foreign relations with Russia, Czechoslovakia, the Baltic States and other countries, 1914–1944; the Warsaw uprising of August 1944; and World War II Allied diplomacy.
Register.
Gift, L. Mitkiewicz, 1965. Incremental gift, 1976.

1818
Mittelman, Joseph B.
Miscellaneous papers, ca. 1941–1945. 1 ms. box, 1 helmet.
First Lieutenant, U.S. Army; Division Historian, 9th Infantry Division. History (typewritten) of 9th Division operations in Germany, September 1944 to May 1945; and memorabilia from the European Theater in World War II, including items from Nazi headquarters at Berchtesgaden, Germany.
Preliminary inventory.
Gift, J. B. Mittelman, 1946.

1819
Mixed Claims Commission (U.S. and Germany). U.S. Agency.
Letter, 1939. 1 folder.
Typescript.
Relates to evidence of German sabotage in the U.S. during the period of American neutrality in World War I. Includes depositions, 1935, to that effect. Letter written by H. H. Martin, Acting U.S. Agent, Mixed Claims Commission.

1820
Moenkemoeller, Fr. P., *collector*.
F. P. Moenkemoeller collection on Germany (in German), 1914–1920. 37 ms. boxes, 44 pamphlet boxes (11 1. ft.), 5 oversize packages (2 1. ft.).
Pamphlets, leaflets, proclamations, orders, memoranda, reports, newspaper issues, maps, photographs, and postcards, relating to German military operations during World War I, political, social and economic conditions in Germany during the war, war relief, war propaganda, prisoners of war, the revolution of 1918–1919, and the elections of 1920 in Germany.
Preliminary inventory.
Purchase, F. P. Moenkemoeller, 1926.

1821
Mohler, Harry A., *collector*.
Medals, 1881–1972. 10 card file boxes, 5 oversize boxes.
Chinese and Thai military and civil medals. Includes medals issued by various Chinese warlords, 1911–1928.
Inventory.
Gift, H. A. Mohler, 1977.

1822

Moley, Raymond, 1886–1975.

Papers, 1912–1969. 246 ms. boxes, 3 envelopes.

American political scientist and journalist; adviser to Franklin D. Roosevelt, 1932–1933; U.S. Assistant Secretary of State, 1933; contributing editor, *Newsweek,* 1937–1968. Correspondence, diaries, reports, memoranda, speeches and writings, notes, and printed matter, relating primarily to politics in the U.S., particularly the Presidential campaign of 1932; the administration of President Franklin D. Roosevelt; and *Today* and *Newsweek* magazines.

Register.

Correspondence with Richard M. Nixon is closed during the lifetime of the latter.

Donative sale, R. Moley, 1968.

1823

Mollenhauer, Tekla Van Norman.

Papers, n.d. 1 folder, 1 envelope.

Polish-American poet. Memoirs, clippings and miscellanea, relating to pre-World War I social conditions in Poland and Polish émigré life. Includes a photograph of Jósef Pilsudski and Ignacy Paderewski.

Gift, T. Mollenhauer, 1978.

1824

Molotov (Viacheslav Mikhailovich)—photographs, 1945. 1 envelope.

Depicts the Soviet political leader V. M. Molotov at an American Russian Institute reception in San Francisco.

1825

Molteno, Robert.

Miscellaneous papers, 1975–1976. 1 folder.

Study, entitled "The Role of Certain North American Academics in the Struggle Against the Liberation of Southern Africa," presented at the United Nations African Institute for Economic Development and Planning, Conference on Socio-Economic Trends and Policies of South Africa, December 1–8, 1975; and correspondence with Thomas Karis relating to politics and race relations in southern Africa.

Gift, R. Molteno, 1976.

1826

Moltke (Helmuth Karl Bernhard, Graf von)—photograph, 1890. 1 envelope.

Depicts Field Marshal H. K. B. von Moltke, German Army.

1827

Monagan, Walter E., Jr.

Papers, 1945–1948. 8 ms. boxes.

Legal advisor, U.S. Military Government in Korea, 1945–1948. Reports, ordinances, proclamations and legal opinions, relating to political, economic and legal aspects of governmental administration in Korea, and to repatriation of Japanese in Korea.

Preliminary inventory.

Gift, W. E. Monagan, Jr., 1972.

1828

Monday (A.J. and Ann) collection on Ireland, 1969–1975. 1 ms. box, 27 posters, 8 phonorecords.

Pamphlets, leaflets, posters, photographs of posters, and phonorecords, relating to the Irish Republican movement in Northern Ireland. Collected by Mark Monday in memory of his parents, A. J. and Ann Monday.

Preliminary inventory.

Gift, M. Monday, 1976.

1829

Monday, Mark.

Papers, 1961–1974. 2 ms. boxes, 2 envelopes, 3 motion-picture reels.

American journalist; *Phoenix American* reporter. Writings, correspondence, booklets, reports, newspaper clippings, photographs, and films, relating to the Minutemen, Secret Army Organization, and other right-wing paramilitary groups, and to the infiltration of the Minutemen by M. Monday.

Preliminary inventory.

Gift, M. Monday, 1974.

1830

Mongolia (Mongolian People's Republic) Velikiĭ Khuraldan, 1st, Ulan-Bator-Khoto, 1924.

Translation of protocols, 1933. "New Mongolia, or, The Protocols of the First Great Assembly of the Mongolian People's Republic." 1 vol.

Typescript (carbon copy).

Translation by J. Attree.

1831

Mongol'skaia Narodno-Revoliutsionnaia Partiia. 3d Congress, Ulan-Bator-Khoto, 1924.

Translation of report, 1933. "The Third Assembly of the Mongolian People's Party, Urga, August 1924." 1 vol.

Typescript (carbon copy).

Translation by J. Attree.

1832

Monod, Noël, 1911–

Papers (in French and German), 1938–1945. 1 ms. box.

French industrialist; United Nations official; resistance member during World War II. Reports and printed matter, relating to the French resistance movement and to the conscription of French workers for forced labor in Germany during World War II. Includes samples of German propaganda.

Gift, N. Monod, 1954.

1833

Montgomery, John Dickey, 1920–

Papers, 1946–1959. 15 ms. boxes.

American political scientist and author. Writings, reports, notes, interview summaries, and printed matter, relating to U.S. aid to South Vietnam and other southeast Asian countries, economic conditions in these countries, Japanese and German public opinion regarding the purge of wartime leaders after World War II, and

political, social, and economic effects of the purge on Japan and Germany.
Gift, J. D. Montgomery, 1975.

1834

Montgomery of Alamein (Bernard Law Montgomery, 1st Viscount)—photographs, n.d. 1 envelope.
Depicts Field Marshal B. L. Montgomery, British Army.

1835

Monti, Antonio.
Study, n.d. "Standards in Cataloguing Bibliographical and Iconographical Material Relating to the War, 1914–1918: Experiences of the War Archives in Milan." 1 vol.
Typescript.

1836

Montrose, Sherman.
Papers, 1942–1947. 1 ms. box, 2 scrapbooks, 2 envelopes.
American war correspondent during World War II. Correspondence, press copy, memoranda, photographs, and clippings, relating to military campaigns in Europe and the Pacific during World War II.

1837

Mood, James R.
Study, 1921. "The Bagdad Railroad: A Brief Review." 1 folder.
Typescript.
Relates to the construction, financing and diplomatic history of the Bagdad Railroad.

1838

Moody, L. B., *collector*.
L. B. Moody collection on communism and China, 1945–1959. 13 ms. boxes.
Reports, memoranda, pamphlets, bulletins, clippings, and other printed matter, relating to communism and China.
Gift, Elizabeth Moody Allen, 1961.

1839

Moore, Franklin.
Papers (in English and French), 1960–1978. 22 ms. boxes.
American educator; representative of the Ford Foundation in Asia; U.S. Agency for International Development official. Reports and memoranda, relating to the study of education in South America, Africa, and Asia.
Gift, F. Moore, 1978.

1840

Moore, William C., 1904–   , *collector*.
Miscellany, 1914–1917. 1 vol.
Photographs, clippings, a pamphlet, cartoons and poems, relating to the outbreak of World War I, military life during the war, and the First Boy Scout International Jamboree in London, 1920.
Gift, W. C. Moore, 1977.

1841

Moran, Hugh Anderson, b. 1881.
Papers, 1916–1933. 2 ms. boxes.
American clergyman; Young Men's Christian Association worker in Siberia and China, 1909–1918. Correspondence, writings, clippings, maps, posters, and photographs, relating to the Russian Civil War, political and economic conditions in Siberia and Manchuria, and relief work in Siberia and Manchuria, especially in the prisoner of war camps, during the Russian Civil War.
Preliminary inventory.

1842

Moravskiĭ, Valerian Ivanovich, 1884–1940.
Papers (in Russian), 1917–1934. 20 ms. boxes.
White Russian political leader in Siberia during the Russian Civil War. Correspondence, reports, proclamations, and photographs, relating to White Russian political activities in the Far East, the first and second anti-Bolshevik Siberian Governments, 1918–1922, and the Council of Plenipotentiary Representatives of Organizations of Autonomous Siberia.
Preliminary inventory.
Purchase, 1948.

1843

Moreland, William Dawson, Jr., 1907–
Papers, 1949–1965. 6 ms. boxes, 8 envelopes.
American diplomat and consular official; U.S. Consul, Dakar, Senegal, 1949–1951. Correspondence, reports, dispatches, newspapers, clippings, other printed matter, and photographs, relating to political, economic and social conditions in West Africa.
Preliminary inventory.
Gift, W. D. Moreland, Jr., 1959. Incremental gift, 1969.

1844

Moreno, Robert.
Photographs, ca. 1943. 1 ms. box.
Depicts military operations in the Pacific Theater during World War II.

1845

Morrison of Lambeth (Herbert Stanley Morrison, Baron)—photograph, n.d. 1 envelope.
Depicts the British politician H. S. Morrison.

1846

Morvan (Yves André Marie)—photograph, n.d. 1 envelope.
Depicts the French author Y. A. M. Morvan.

1847

Moscow, Conference, 1943—photographs. 1 envelope.
Depicts American, British and Soviet delegates to the Tripartite Conference in Moscow in October 1943.

1848

Moseley, George Van Horn, 1874–1960.
Memoirs, 1936–1955. "One Soldier's Journey." 2 ms. boxes.
Typescript.
Major General, U.S. Army; Chief, 4th Section, General Staff, American Expeditionary Forces in France, 1918–1919; Deputy Chief of Staff, 1930–1933. Relates to the organization of supply for the American Expeditionary Forces in France, to U.S. defense policy between the two world wars, and to right-wing political movements in the U.S., 1938–1944.
Gift, G. V. H. Moseley, 1957.

1849

Mosher, Clelia Duel, 1863–1940.
Papers, 1898–1937. 7 ms. boxes.
American physician and educator; Red Cross worker in France, 1917–1919. Correspondence, writings, office files, photographs, and postcards, relating to relief work of the Red Cross in France from 1917 to 1919, and to the promotion of health education for women in the U.S. Includes correspondence with Lou Henry Hoover.

1850

Motion Picture Research Council.
Records, 1927–1941. 78 ms. boxes, 8 vols.
Private American research organization. Correspondence, by-laws, minutes, administrative reports, records, and research and reference materials, relating to the film industry and the effects of films on the community.
Preliminary inventory.
Deposit, Ray Lyman Wilbur.

1851

Mott, George Fox, 1907–
Miscellaneous papers, 1914–1977. 1 ms. box.
Management and international affairs consultant; representative of the Isthmian Timber Company. Report, correspondence, memoranda, court documents, press release, and other printed matter, relating to the divestment of land from the Isthmian Timber Company by the Panamanian government. Includes a legal case study, entitled "The Panama Canal, Today's Decision, Tomorrow's Security: A Case History from 1903 to 1977."
Gift, G. F. Mott, 1977.

1852

Mott, T. Bentley.
Report, 1918. 1 folder.
Typescript.
Lieutenant Colonel, U.S. Army. Relates to the military situation on the Italian front, and to the condition of the Italian Army. Report to the Assistant Chief of Staff, G-2, General Headquarters, American Expeditionary Forces in France, March 19, 1918.

1853

Motter, T. H. Vail, *collector*.
Newsletter, 1941–1942. 1 ms. box.
Typescript (mimeographed).
Newsletters issued aboard the U.S. Army transport ship *Siboney*, December 29, 1941 to February 1, 1942, relating to ship activities and war news. The ship transported the U.S. Military North African Mission, the U.S. Military Mission to Iran, and the U.S. Military Mission to the USSR, from New York to Eritrea and Iraq.
Gift, T. H. V. Motter, 1958.

1854

Mountbatten of Burma (Louis Mountbatten, Earl)—photograph, n.d. 1 envelope.
Depicts Admiral of the Fleet L. Mountbatten, British Navy. Photograph is autographed.

1855

Mowrer, Edgar Ansel, 1892–
Report, 1940. 1 vol.
Typescript (carbon copy).
Relates to post-World War II reconstruction and prospects for an international organization. Report to the World Citizens Association.

1856

Mozambique—photographs, n.d. 12 envelopes.
Depicts scenes of daily life in Mozambique.
Purchase, Castro e Silva, 1975.

1857

Mozny, Josephine.
Song, "The Blessed American Nation." 1 phonorecord.
A tribute to Herbert Hoover.

1858

Mueller (Alfred)—translation of judicial decision, 1939. 1 folder.
Typescript (mimeographed).
Decision by the Argentine Federal Court of Appeals, relating to allegations by Heinrich Juerges that Alfred Mueller, acting as an agent of the German Government, had plotted to bring about the secession of Patagonia from Argentina.

1859

Mueller and Graeff photographic poster collection, ca. 1914–1945. 4 ms. boxes.
Photographs of posters, relating primarily to Germany during World Wars I and II, German political events in the interwar period, and the Spanish Civil War. Includes posters from the Soviet Union, France, and a number of other countries.
Preliminary inventory.

1860

Muench, Aloisius Joseph, Bp. of South Dakota.
Memorandum, 1947. "The Honor of the United States and Denazification." 1 folder.
Typescript.
Roman Catholic Bishop of South Dakota; Apostolic Visitator in Germany. Relates to Allied denazification policy in Germany.

1861

Muhr, Allan H., *collector*.
Photographs, 1917. 1 envelope.
Depicts the U.S. Army Lafayette Flying Corps in France.
Gift, Philip Muhr, 1974.

1862

Muir, Malcolm.
Memorandum, 1957. "Notes to the Staff on My Russian Trip, June, 1957." 1 vol.
Typescript.
American journalist; *Newsweek* correspondent. Relates to social conditions in the Soviet Union.

1863

Mukhanov, Mikhail Georgievich.
Papers (in Russian), 1862–1963. ½ ms. box.
Russian aristocrat. Correspondence, printed matter, reports, and photographs, relating to conditions in Russia before, during and after the Revolution of 1917, and to experiences of various members of the Mukhanov family. Includes letters from the great-uncle of M. G. Mukhanov, Georgii Bakhmeteff, Russian Imperial diplomat; from the great-great-grandfather of M. G. Mukhanov, Marshal Mikhail Kutuzov, to his wife; and from Grand Duke Nikolai Nikolaevich to the father of M. G. Mukhanov, 1924.
Gift, Russian Historical Archive and Repository, 1975.

1864

Muller, Walter J., 1895–1967.
Papers, 1942–1949. 20 ms. boxes, 2 microfilm reels.
Major General, U.S. Army; Military Governor of Bavaria, 1945–1947. Memoranda, orders, maps, reports, charts, photographs, and printed matter, relating to the invasion of French Morocco, Sicily, and southern France, activities of the 3rd and 7th U.S. Armies, and the occupation of Bavaria.
Preliminary inventory.
Gift, Mrs. W. J. Muller, 1968.

1865

Muncis, Janis, 1886–1955.
Miscellaneous papers (in Latvian), 1925–1951. 1 ms. box.
Latvian stage designer and producer. Photographs, certificates, diplomas, sketches, and memorabilia, relating to mass propaganda open air theatrical productions during the Ulmanis regime in Latvia, 1934–1939.
Gift, Gvido Augusts, 1973. Incremental gifts, 1975 and 1978.

1866

Mungai, Njoroge, 1926–
Letter, 1967, to Reverend R. M. Minto. 1 folder.
Minister of Internal Security and Defense of Kenya, 1964–1969. Relates to acquaintances of N. Mungai at Stanford University.
Gift, R. M. Minto, 1973.

1867

Munger, Henry W., b. 1876.
Diary, 1942–1945. 1 vol.
Typescript.
American missionary in the Philippines. Relates to conditions in Japanese prison camps in the Philippines during World War II.

1868

Munich. Universitaet—students—leaflets (in German), 1931. 1 folder.
Printed.
Relates to Allgemeiner Studentenausschuss (AStA) elections and party politics in Germany. Leaflets distributed at the University of Munich.
Gift, Dorothea Swanson, 1977.

1869

Munro, Dana Carleton, 1866–1933.
Papers, 1908–1923. 4 ms. boxes.
U.S. Inquiry investigator, Paris Peace Conference, 1919; Research Assistant, Committee on Public Information, 1917–1918. Reports, correspondence, leaflets, and notes, relating to political and economic conditions in Turkey, Zionism, relief work and the conduct of German occupying forces in Belgium during World War I, U.S. neutrality in World War I, war propaganda, and proposals for world peace.

1870

Munson, Frederick P., 1904–
Papers, 1939–1951. ½ ms. box, 1 envelope.
Brigadier General, U.S. Army. Captured Japanese war documents, correspondence, orders, memoranda, maps, charts, diaries, and photographs, relating to the Solomon Islands battlefields during the Pacific campaigns of World War II.
Gift, F. P. Munson, 1974.

1871

Munters, Vilhelms, 1898–1967.
Miscellaneous papers (in Latvian and German), 1939–1972. 1 folder.
Photocopies.
Minister of Foreign Affairs of Latvia, 1936–1940. Correspondence, memoranda and press releases, relating to Latvian-Soviet relations and to the imprisonment of V. Munters in the Soviet Union, 1941–1954.
Gift, Edgar Anderson, 1973.

1872

Muraveiskiĭ, S.
Translation of pamphlet, n.d. "Data on the History of the Revolutionary Movement in Central Asia: Result of a Brief Study of the Soviet Party Schools and Political Primary Schools." 1 folder.
Typescript.
Translation by Xenia J. Eudin, of *Ocherki po Istorii Revoliùtsionnogo Dvizheniià v Srednei Azii: Opyt Kratkogo Posobiià dlià Sovpartshkol i Shkol Politgramoty*, published in Tashkent in 1926.

1873

Murav'eva, Ekaterina Ivanovna.
Papers (in Russian), 1914–1948. 6 ms. boxes.
Russian refugee in France. Correspondence, memoirs, and notes, relating to the Russian Revolution and political events in Russia and abroad. Correspondents include V. A. Maklakov, P. N. Miliukov, Vera Figner, and other leading Russian political figures.
Preliminary inventory.
Deposit, E. I. Murav'eva, 1949.

1874

Murphy, Merle Farmer.
Memoir, n.d. "Record of a Russian Year, 1921–1922: Daily Life in Soviet Russia." 1 folder.
Typescript.
American Relief Administration worker in Russia, 1921–1922. Relates to social and economic conditions in Russia.

1875

Murphy, Robert Daniel, 1894–1978.
Papers, 1963–1977. 54 ms. boxes, 3 oversize boxes, memorabilia.
American diplomat and business executive; President's personal representative in North Africa, 1942; Political Adviser to Supreme Headquarters, Allied Expeditionary Forces, 1943–1949; Ambassador to Belgium, 1949–1952, and Japan, 1952; Deputy Under Secretary of State, 1953–1959; chairman, Commission on the Organization of the Government for the Conduct of Foreign Policy, 1973–1975. Correspondence, memoranda, speeches and writings, and printed matter, relating to American foreign policy, business enterprises, and humanitarian organizations.
May not be used without written approval of depositors.
Deposit, Mildred Murphy Pond and Rosemary Murphy, 1978.

1876

Murra, Wilbur Fim, 1910–
Papers, 1943–1974. 1 ms. box.
American educator. Correspondence, writings, printed matter and photographs, relating to comparative and international education.
Gift, W. F. Murra, 1978.

1877

Murray, Augustus Taber, b. 1866.
Papers, 1919–1933. 1 folder.
Resident minister, Friends' Meeting House, Washington, D.C. Photocopies of correspondence and clippings, relating to the attendance of President Herbert Hoover at the Friends' Meeting House. Includes some miscellaneous material on Quaker World War I relief and other charitable activities.
Gift, Mrs. Albert H. Huneke, 1967.

1878

Murray, Columbo P., Jr.
Report, 1929. 1 folder.
Typescript.
Relates to political and economic conditions in China.

1879

Murrow, Edward R., d. 1965.
Compilation of radio news broadcasts, n.d. *A Reporter Remembers: Vol. I, The War Years.* 2 phonorecords.
European Director, Columbia Broadcasting System, 1937–1946. Broadcasts from Europe, 1939–1946, relating to military activities in Europe and the home front in Great Britain during World War II.

1880

Mussolini, Benito, 1883–1945.
Memorandum, n.d. "Taking Care of Agriculture." 1 folder.
Typescript.
Premier of Italy, 1922–1943. Relates to agricultural policy in Italy under fascism.

1881

Muzaffar, Jamal.
Writings, 1957. ½ ms. box.
Typescript.
Writings, including "American-Soviet Policy toward Egypt, 1953–1957"; "The Question of Fertile Crescent Unity," relating to pan-Arabism; and "Terror of the Red Fox and Reform of the Grey Wolf," relating to the Turkish revolution of 1918–1923.
Gift, J. Muzaffar, 1957.

1882

Myers, William Starr, 1877–1956.
Documentary history, 1936. *The Hoover Administration: A Documented Narrative.* 3½ ms. boxes.
Drafts and research material, relating to the Presidential administration of Herbert Hoover. Written by W. S. Myers and Walter H. Newton. Published in New York by C. Scribner's Sons, 1936.

1883

Mysels, Karol.
Translations of extracts from letters, 1945–1946. 1 folder.
Typescript.
Letters written to K. Mysels by a relative living in a Polish refugee camp in new Zealand, relating to the experiences of Polish refugees in Russia and elsewhere during World War II.

1884

Naas, Josephine.
Papers, 1919. 1 ms. box.
Young Men's Christian Association worker in France, 1919. Memoirs and miscellanea, relating to Young Men's Christian Association work with the American Expeditionary Forces in France at the end of World War I.

1885

Naczelny Komitet Narodowy.

Miscellaneous records (in Polish), 1915–1916. 1 folder.

Polish National People's committee. Drafts (handwritten) of minutes of meetings in Warsaw, 1915, relating to the Polish question and World War I; and leaflets, 1915–1916, relating to recruitment for the Legiony Polskie in the Austrian Army.

1886

Nagy, K., *collector*.

K. Nagy collection on Hungary (in Hungarian and English), 1942–1962. 2 ms. boxes.

Interview transcripts, reports, clippings, and printed matter, relating to the Hungarian Revolution of 1956, political events in Hungary during World War II, the Sanders espionage trial, 1950–1951, and the Wynne-Penkovskiĭ espionage trial, 1962.

Preliminary inventory.

Gift, K. Nagy, 1976.

1887

"Nakaz Bol'shogo i Malago Voĭskovogo Kruga Voĭska Terskago" (Order of the Large and Small Military Union of the Tersk Unit).

Memorandum (in Russian), 1919. 1 folder.

Typescript.

Relates to the bylaws of a White Russian officers' association.

1888

Natal Indian Congress.

Circular, 1952. 1 folder.

Protests the arrest of Dr. Yusuf Mahomed Dadoo, President of the South African Indian Congress, and D. W. Bopape, Secretary of the African National Congress, under the Suppression of Communism Act.

1889

National Socialistische Beweging in Nederland collection (in Dutch), 1941–1943. ½ ms. box.

Reports, directives, and leaflets, relating to activities of the fascist Dutch National Socialist Movement. Includes indoctrination material for new party members, and materials on party organization in Zaandam, Netherlands.

1890

National Broadcasting Company.

Motion pictures, 1958–1963. 97 reels.

Documentary films, depicting political events in Cuba.

Preliminary inventory.

Private screenings for library use are permitted; public showings are not permitted.

Deposit, National Broadcasting Company, 1964.

1891

National Citizens' Committee for United Nations Day.

Radio Broadcast, 1952. 1 phonotape.

American organization to commemorate United Nations Day. Includes addresses by Dwight D. Eisenhower and Adlai Stevenson, Republican and Democratic candidates for President of the U.S. Broadcast over the Columbia Broadcasting System.

1892

National Committee on Food for the Small Democracies, 1940–1942.

Records, 1939–1945. 124 ms. boxes.

Private American charitable organization. Correspondence, office files, pamphlets, and serial issues, relating to attempts in the U.S. to organize and secure international agreement for a civilian relief program for Norway, Finland, the Netherlands, Belgium, and Poland during World War II.

Preliminary inventory.

1893

National Council for Prevention of War. Western Office, San Francisco, 1921–1954.

Records, 1921–1943. 3½ ms. boxes.

American pacifist organization. Leaflets, pamphlets, press releases, and serial issues, relating to movements for peace, disarmament, preservation of U.S. neutrality during World War II, and opposition to conscription and military training in educational institutions.

Gift, Northern California Service Board for Conscientious Objectors, 1943.

1894

National-Demokratische Partei Deutschlands (Germany, East).

Syllabus (in German), 1949. 1 folder.

Typescript.

Relates to the curriculum of the National Democratic Party School for National Politics in Buckow, East Germany, regarding the study of German history and political and economic conditions.

1895

National Japanese American Student Relocation Council, 1942–1946.

Records, 1942–1946. 20 l.ft.

Private American organization for aid to relocated Japanese American students. Correspondence, questionnaires, student education records, and miscellanea, relating to efforts to place relocated Japanese American students in colleges in the U.S. during World War II.

Preliminary inventory.

Individual students may not be identified.

Gift, National Japanese American Student Relocation Council, 1947.

1896

National Liberation Front (Yemen).

Translations of issuances, 1955–1968. 1 folder.

Reports, minutes of meetings, and resolutions, relating to activities of the National Liberation Front and the Yemen Civil War.

Gift, Christina Harris.

1897

National Planning Association.
Pamphlet, 1945. *China's Relief Needs.* 1 folder.
Printed.
Relates to China's requirements for immediate relief needs and long-range economic reconstruction.

1898

National Polish Committee of America.
Postcards, ca. 1914–1918. 1 envelope.
Depicts scenes of destruction in Poland during World War I, coins of Lithuania and Poland, and Polish-American soldiers in France during World War I.

1899

National Public Radio.
Radio broadcast, 1977. 1 phonotape.
Relates to political development in Cambodia under communism.
Gift, Donald W. Palmer, 1978.

1900

National Republic, 1905–1960.
Records, 1920–1960. 826 ms. boxes.
Anti-communist American magazine. Clippings, printed matter, pamphlets, reports, indices, notes, bulletins, lettergrams, weekly letters, and photographs, relating to pacifist, communist, fascist, and other radical movements, and to political developments in the United States and the Soviet Union.
Register.
Purchase, National Republic Publishing Company, 1960.

1901

National Research Council. Division of Medical Sciences.
Bulletins, 1942. 1 folder.
Typescript (mimeographed).
Relates to plans for the preparation of a medical history of World War II.

1902

National Zeitung. Berliner Schriftleitung.
Miscellaneous records (in German), 1938. 1 folder.
Berlin newspaper edition. Memoranda and summaries of news stories and editorials, relating to international politics.

1903

Nationale Rotterdamsche Courant.
Memoranda (in Dutch), 1941. 1 folder.
Typescript.
Summaries by correspondents of the Dutch newspaper *Nationale Rotterdamsche Courant,* of press conferences held to provide guidelines for Dutch newspaper publication in the German-occupied Netherlands, 1941.

1904

Nationalsozialistische Deutsche Arbeiter-Partei.
Miscellaneous records (in German), 1923–1944. 2½ ms. boxes, 1 phonotape, 2 flags.
National Socialist German Workers Party. Correspondence, memoranda, office files, propaganda, miscellanea, sound recordings and flags, relating to national socialism in Germany. Includes photocopies of documents located at the U.S. Berlin Document center, relating to Nazi party activities and to Heinrich Himmler; recordings of speeches by Adolf Hitler, Joseph Goebbels, Robert Ley and Heinrich Himmler, and of Nazi loyalty oaths and other ceremonies; a propaganda placard series entitled "Wochenspruch der NSDAP" (Weekly Sayings of the NSDAP); miscellaneous party application and registration forms; and World War II Nazi battle flags.
Photocopies in Boxes 1–2 correspond to listing for Reel B in the published guide, Grete Heinz and Agnes F. Peterson, comp., *NSDAP Hauptarchiv: Guide to the Hoover Institution Microfilm Collection* (Stanford: Hoover Institution on War, Revolution and Peace, 1964). Preliminary inventory of phonotape contents.
In part, gifts, Paul D. Plowman, 1959, Robert A. Braund, 1965, Israel Getzler, 1970.

1905

Nationalsozialistische Deutsche Arbeiter-Partei. Aussenpolitisches Amt.
Report (in German), 1937. "Die Weltpresse zum Reichsparteitag 1937" (The World Press on Reich Party Day 1937). 1 folder.
Typescript (mimeographed).
Foreign Political Office of the National Socialist German Workers Party. Relates to foreign press coverage of Nazi Party Day in 1937.

1906

Nationalsozialistische Deutsche Arbeiter-Partei. Gau Berlin.
Miscellaneous records (in German), 1931–1944. 2 ms. boxes.
Berlin Branch of the National Socialist German Workers Party. Correspondence, memoranda, circulars, ordinances and petitions, relating to Nazi activities in Berlin, the defection of Walter Steenes and others from the Sturmabteilung in 1931, party discipline, and petitions for amnesty.
Preliminary inventory.
Gift, Frank E. Mason, 1951.

1907

Nationalsozialistische Deutsche Arbeiter-Partei. Hauptamt fuer Volksgesundheit.
Miscellaneous records (in German), 1934–1936. 1 folder.
Central Health Office of the National Socialist German Workers Party. Reports and correspondence, relating to the administration of the Berlin-Weissensee Hospital and to the political reliability of its personnel.

1908

Nationalsozialistische Deutsche Arbeiter-Partei. Hitlerjugend—memoranda (in German), n.d. 1 folder.
Typescript.
Memoranda entitled "Einfluss der H. J. auf die

Jugend" (Influence of the H. J. on Youth), and "Wie Ich die H. J. Sah und Erlebte" (How I Saw and Experienced the H. J.), by an unknown member of the Hitlerjugend, relating to Hitlerjugend activities in Germany.

1909

Nationalsozialistische Deutsche Arbeiter-Partei. Oberstes Parteigericht.
Dossiers (in German), ca. 1939. 1 ms. box.
Photocopy.
Supreme Party Court of the National Socialist German Workers Party. Relates to personal data on members of the Nazi Party.
Gift, Office of the Military Government of the U.S., 1949.

1910

Nationalsozialistische Deutsche Arbeiter-Partei. Partei-Kanzlei.
Directives (in German), 1941–1942. 1 folder.
Typescript (mimeographed) and printed.
Party Chancellery of the National Socialist German Workers Party. Relates to administration of the armed forces.

1911

Nationalsozialistische Deutsche Arbeiter-Partei. Reichs-organisationsamt.
Issuances (in German), 1936–1943. 2 ms. boxes.
Organization Office of the National Socialist German Workers Party. Directives, notices, and regulations, relating to party administration and personnel matters.

1912

Nationalsozialistische Deutsche Arbeiter-Partei. Reichsor-ganisationsamt. Hauptabteilung Hilfskasse.
Reports (in German), 1933–1934. 1 folder.
Typescript.
Central Relief Fund Division of the National Socialist German Workers Party. Relates to numbers of injuries and fatalities among Nazi party members, including details of the circumstances of each fatality.

1913

Nationalsozialistische Deutsche Arbeiter-Partei. Reichs-schatzmeister.
Correspondence (in German), 1935–1943. 1 folder.
Typescript.
Treasurer of the National Socialist German Workers Party. Relates to the granting of Goldene Ehrenzeichen awards to individuals for distinguished service to the party.

1914

Nationalsozialistische Deutsche Arbeiter-Partei. Stellver-treter des Fuehrers. Stab. Abteilung M.
Miscellaneous records (in German), 1939–1941. ½ ms. box.
Division M of the Office of the Deputy to the Fuehrer of the National Socialist German Workers Party. Directives, memoranda and correspondence, relating to Ger-

man refugees from the Saarland and miscellaneous administrative matters.

1915

Nationalsozialistische Deutsche Arbeiter-Partei. Sturmab-teilung.
Miscellaneous records (in German), 1938–1943. 1 ms. box.
Storm Division of the National Socialist German Workers Party. Regulations, relating to internal admin-istration of the Sturmabteilung, and a visitor's book for Sturmabteilung headquarters in Berlin.

1916

Nationalsozialistische Deutsche Arbeiter-Partei. Waffen-schutzstaffel. 15. Grenadier-Division.
Records (in Latvian and German), 1941–1945. 4 ms. boxes, 86 maps.
Volunteer Latvian Legion in Waffen-SS during World War II. Correspondence, memoranda, military orders, and printed matter, relating to activities of the Latvian Legion Police Battalions and Regiments.
Preliminary inventory.
Access requires the written permission of the Latvian Welfare Association, Inc.
Deposit, Latvian Welfare Association, Inc., 1973.

1917

Nationalsozialistische Deutsche Arbeiter-Partei. Waffen-schutzstaffel. Leibstandarte SS Adolf Hitler. 7. Panzer Division.
Correspondence logbook (in German), 1944–1945. 1 folder.
Holograph.
Log of official letters sent and received.

1918

Nationalsozialistischer Deutscher Frontkaempferbund (Stahlhelm)—photographs, n.d. 1 envelope.
Depicts a parade of the German rightist veterans' or-ganization Stahlhelm, leaders of the Stahlhelm, and the Royal Bavarian Army during its return to Munich, December 1918.

1919

Nauheimer Kreis.
Newsletters (in German), 1950–1951. 1 folder.
Typescript (mimeographed).
West German political organization. Relates to pro-posals for the reunification and neutralization of Ger-many.

1920

Naumov, Aleksandr Nikolaevich, 1868–1950.
Memoirs (in Russian), 1929–1937. "Iz Utsîelievshikh Vospominaniĭ" (From Surviving Memories). 12 vols.
Typescript.
Russian Imperial Minister of Agriculture, 1915–1916. Relates to political conditions in Russia during the reign of Tsar Nicholas II and during the Russian Revolution and Civil War.

1921
Naylor, Robert.
    Correspondence, 1975. 1 folder.
    Typescript (photocopy).
    Chief of Operations, Vietnamese "Orphans' Airlift," San Francisco. Relates to the airlift of Vietnamese children from Vietnam to California. Includes extract of draft and outline for a projected book by James Kolbe on the airlift.
    Gift, R. Naylor, 1975.

1922
Nazi war crime interrogations (in German and English), 1945–1947. 1 folder.
    Typescript.
    Interrogation reports and transcripts of interrogations of former Nazi officials, relating to Nazi war crimes during World War II.

1923
Nederlandsche Artsenkamer.
    Notices (in Dutch), 1941–1943.
    Typescript (mimeographed).
    Relates to regulations concerning physicians in the German-occupied Netherlands during World War II. Issued by the Nederlandsche Artsenkamer and the Nederlandsche Vereeniging van Ziekenfondsartsen, Dutch physicians' associations.

1924
Nederlandsche Kultuurkamer.
    Memoranda (in Dutch), 1941. 1 folder.
    Typescript (some mimeographed).
    Dutch cultural association. Relates to activities of the Nederlandsche Kultuurkamer in the German-occupied Netherlands during World War II.

1925
Needham, Guy E., 1890–1946.
    Papers, 1916–1920. 1 ms. box, 2 envelopes.
    Soldier, U.S. Army, during World War I. Diaries, letters, memorabilia, and photographs, relating to the U.S. Army Ambulance Service in France during World War I.
    Gift, Mrs. William Nankervis, 1973.

1926
Nehrbas, Laura Belle Crandall.
    Memorabilia, n.d. 1 folder.
    American Red Cross worker in France, 1919; member, Women's Overseas Service League. Relates to the Woman's Overseas Service League, an organization of women veterans of World War I war work abroad.

1927
Nehru, Jawaharlal, 1889–1964.
    Speech, 1949. 2 phonorecords.
    Prime Minister of India, 1947–1964. Relates to U.S.-Indian relations. Speech delivered in San Francisco.

1928
Neil, Allan W., 1891–1950.
    Letters, 1918–1919, to his mother. ½ ms. box.
    Holograph.
    Private, U.S. Marine Corps. Relates to conditions in Marine Corps training camps in the U.S. and to Marine activities in France and Germany during and immediately after World War I.
    Gift, Mrs. Earl A. Mosley, 1957.

1929
Nekrasov, Nikolaĭ Vissarionovich.
    Translation of speech, 1917. 1 folder.
    Typescript.
    Minister of Finance, Russian Provisional Government. Relates to the financial situation of the Provisional Government. Speech delivered in Moscow, August 1917.

1930
Nelson, David T., *collector*.
    Miscellany (in French), 1914–1915. ½ ms. box, 1 secretary.
    Reports, relating to civilian relief activities undertaken by various municipal organizations in the town of Ougrée, Belgium, during World War I, and an ornamental secretary commemorating relief activities in Belgium during World War I.

1931
Nelson, Mrs. Albert M., *collector*.
    Photographs, 1953–1954. 2 envelopes.
    Depicts the signing of the Korean War truce by General Mark Clark, 1953, and U.S. naval activities at Yokosuka, Japan, 1954.
    Gift, Mrs. A. M. Nelson, 1972.

1932
Netherlands liberation proclamations (in Dutch), 1945. 1 folder.
    Printed.
    Relates to the entry of Allied troops into the Netherlands at the end of World War II. Issued by Dutch and Allied military authorities.

1933
Netherlands—posters (in Dutch), 1944–1945. 10 posters.
    Printed.
    Relates to the entry of Allied troops into the Netherlands. Issued by the Dutch Government-in-Exile and printed in advance in England.
    Gift, Siegfried Hymans, 1969.

1934
Netherlands under German occupation collection (in Dutch and German), 1940–1945. 1 folder.
    Proclamations, identification cards, registration forms and miscellanea, issued by German occupation authorities in the Netherlands, relating to regulations of the Dutch civilian population during World War II.

1935

Netherlands—World War II—collection (in Dutch), 1942–1945. 1 folder.

Memorabilia, satirical postcards, proclamation, and clippings, relating to the German occupation of the Netherlands, Allied propaganda, Dutch press coverage of the war, and the liberation of Amsterdam on May 5, 1945.

Preliminary inventory.

Gift, Mrs. Willy Kater, 1976.

1936

Netherlands (Territory under German occupation, 1940–1945) Reichskommissar fuer die Besetzten Niederlaendischen Gebiete. Sicherheitsdienst.

Report (in German), 1942. 1 folder.

Typescript (mimeographed).

German secret police office in the Netherlands. Relates to transportation of Dutch workers to Germany for forced labor. Addressed to the Reichssicherheitshauptamt in Germany.

Gift, Netherlands Institute for War Documentation, 1951.

1937

Neuhaeusler, Johann, Bp., b. 1888.

Letters (in German and English), 1948, to General Lucius D. Clay. 1 folder.

Typescript.

Roman Catholic Suffragan Bishop, Munich. Appeals for stays of execution for certain Germans convicted of war crimes at the Nuremberg trials and sentenced to death.

1938

New China News Agency.

Transcripts of radio broadcasts, ca. 1945–1949. 1 folder.

Typescript (mimeographed).

Communist news source, Yenan, China. Relates to the Chinese Civil War.

1939

New Left collection, 1964–1974. 67 ms. boxes, 31 posters, 3 phonorecords, 1 microfilm reel.

Booklets, leaflets, reports, and clippings, relating to the purposes, tactics, and activities of various New Left and right-wing groups, draft resistance, student disorders, and the anti-Vietnam War movement. Collected by Edward J. Bacciocco.

Preliminary inventory.

1940

New South Wales Medical Board.

Memoranda, 1932. 1 folder.

Typescript.

Relates to conditions for foreign or foreign-trained physicians to practice medicine in New South Wales, and specifies the exclusion of Germans and Austrians and of persons trained at German or Austrian schools.

1941

New York (City) Department of Investigation.

Report, 1944. 1 folder.

Typescript (mimeographed).

Relates to causes of, and recommends measures to prevent, antisemitic vandalism and violence in New York City.

1942

News Research Service, Los Angeles.

Report, n.d. "Summary Report on Activities of Nazi Groups and Their Allies in Southern California, 1936–1940." 3 ms. boxes.

Typescript.

Private anti-Nazi organization. Relates to the German-American Bund and similar groups.

Gift, Edward N. Barnhart, 1974.

1943

Newsom, John Fletcher, 1869–1928.

Photographs, 1892–1920. 21 envelopes, 7 albums.

Depicts Stanford University, 1892–1917; persons associated with Stanford University, including Herbert Hoover, John C. Branner and Joseph Swain; and daily life and tin mining operations in Malaya, 1920.

Preliminary inventory.

1944

Nicholas I, Emperor of Russia, 1796–1855.

Order (in Russian), 1828. 1 folder.

Printed.

Illustrates and describes various medals and awards.

Gift, Russian Historical Archive and Repository, 1974.

1945

Nicholas II, Emperor of Russia, 1868–1918.

Miscellaneous papers (in Russian), 1890–1917.   1½ ms. boxes, 1 oversize roll.

Two imperial orders (printed), signed by Tsar Nicholas II, 1905 and 1908; letters (handwritten and typewritten copies) from Nicholas II to Prime Minister P. A. Stolypin, 1906–1911; facsimile of the abdications of Nicholas II and Grand Duke Michael, 1917; Nicholas II's diary (handwritten copy); two religious books belonging to the Romanov family which were found in Ekaterinburg after their murder; and other materials relating to the reign of Nicholas II. Includes a colored reproduction of a painting of Nicholas II.

1946

Nicolaevsky, Boris I., 1887–1966.

B. I. Nicolaevsky collection (in Russian, also partly in German, French and English), 1850–1966. ca. 400 ms. boxes.

Russian Social Democrat, historian, author, publicist, collector of historical material on social and revolutionary movements in Russia as well as abroad. Letters, memoranda, writings, speeches, memoirs, minutes of meetings, underground leaflets, photographs, clippings and other miscellaneous historical documents relating primarily to the Russian revolutionary movements (radicals, populists, anarchists, and, more specifically and extensively, the Russian Social Democratic Party as well as the Socialist Revolutionary Party); the Tsarist government; the 1905 revolution; the Imperial Duma; the February and October Revolutions; the Civil War; Russian émigré politics; the Vlassov movement during World War II; Russian displaced persons after World War II; history and activities of the First, Second, and Third Internationals; and the labor and socialist movements in Europe and the United States. Consists of approximately 300 units of collected materials, including records of organizations, such as the Social Democratic and Socialist Revolutionary Parties, and personal papers of such political figures as A. Herzen, M. Bakunin, P. Lavrov, G. Plekhanov, P. Akselrod, Iu. Martov, I. Tseretelli, V. Chernov, L. Trotsky, among others.

Register prepared by Curator Anna Bourguina.

Purchase, B. I. Nicolaevsky, 1963; several incremental gifts.

1947

Niederpruem, William J.

Papers, 1917–1951. 5 ms. boxes.

Colonel, U.S. Army; staff officer, 32d Division, during World War I. Military orders and reports, maps, pamphlets, clippings, and newspaper and periodical issues, relating to activities of the American Expeditionary Force, particularly of the 32d Division, in France during World War I; military operations during World War II; and the postwar occupation of Japan.

Gift, W. J. Niederpruem, 1966.

1948

Niemeyer, Gerhart, 1907–

Papers (in English and German), 1935–1967. 2 ms. boxes.

German-American political scientist. Correspondence, speeches and writings, clippings, conference proceedings, and printed matter, relating to communism, international organization and world security, and the foreign policy of the U.S. and the U.S.S.R.

Gift, G. Niemeyer, 1978.

1949

Niemoeller, Martin, 1892–

Memorandum (in German and English), 1945. "Die Staatsrechtlichen Grundlagen zum Aufbau der Bekenntnisschule" (Legal Foundations for the Construction of Parochial Schools). 1 folder.

Typescript.

Anti-Nazi German clergyman. Includes a U.S. Army report (printed), 1947, relating to the activities of M. Niemoeller.

1950

Nieuwe Roterdamsche Courant (New Rotterdam Journal).

Newspaper clippings (printed in Dutch), 1912–1943. 17 ms. boxes.

Rotterdam newspaper. Relates primarily to political and military affairs during the two world wars.

1951

Nijhoff, Martinus, 1894– , *collector.*

M. Nijhoff collection on the German occupation of the Netherlands (in Dutch and German), 1940–1945. 16 ms. boxes.

Books, posters, leaflets, bulletins, other printed matter, memoranda and correspondence, relating to the German occupation of the Netherlands, food and travel restrictions, black market activities, sabotage, cultural activities, recruitment of Dutch volunteers in the German armed forces, and underground presses in the Netherlands and France.

Purchase, M. Nijhoff, 1947.

1952

Nikolaieff, Alexander Mikhailovitch, b. 1876.

Series of articles, 1933–1935. "Japan's Conquest of Manchuria and Jehol." 1 folder.

Proof sheets.

Colonel, Imperial Russian Army. Relates to Japanese military activities in Manchuria. Published in the *Canadian Defence Quarterly.*

1953

Nikol'skiĭ, Evgeniĭ Aleksandrovich.

Memoirs (in Russian), 1934. 1 folder.

Typescript.

Russian Imperial Army officer. Memoirs entitled "Sluzhba v Glavnom Shtabie i Glavnom Upravlenii General'nago Shtaba" (Service in the Main Headquarters and Main Directorate of the General Staff) and "Biezhentsy v Velikuiû Voĭnu" (Refugees in the Great War), relating to the Russian General Staff, 1903–1908, and Russian refugees during World War I.

1954

Nilus, E. Kh., *editor.*

History (in Russian), 1923. "Istoricheskiĭ Obzor Kitaĭskoĭ Vostochnoĭ Zhelieznoĭ Dorogi, 1896–1923 g.g." (Historical Survey of the Chinese Eastern Railway, 1896–1923). 4 vols.

Printed and typescript.

Commissioned by the Board of Directors of the Chinese Eastern Railway, Harbin.

1955

Nirod, Feodor Maksimilianovich, Graf, b. 1871.

Memoirs (in Russian), n.d. "Prozhitoe" (What I Have Lived Through). 1 ms. box.

Typescript and holograph.

Russian Imperial Army officer. Relates to Russian military life, 1892–1917, including the Russo-Japanese War, Russian participation in World War I, and the Russian Revolution.

Gift, Dimitri Shvetsoff, 1970.

1956

Nivelle, Robert Georges, 1858–1924.

Orders (in French), 1916. 1 folder.

Typescript and printed.

General, French Army; Commanding General, II Army. Relates to the Battle of Verdun.

1957

Noetinger, Colonel.
Report (in French), 1940. 1 vol.
Typescript (carbon copy).
French Army officer; Chief of Staff, 42d Infantry Division, 1940. Relates to the activities of the French 42d Infantry Division during the German offensive in France, June 9–17, 1940.

1958

North Korean propaganda—Korean War—posters (in Korean), 1950. 1 folder.
Printed.
Propaganda posters, issued by the North Korean Government during the Korean War.

1959

North Star (Ship)—photograph, 1932. 1 envelope.
Depicts the launching of the ship *North Star* at the Berg Shipbuilding Company yards, Seattle, Washington.

1960

Northcliffe (Alfred Charles William Harmsworth, 1st Viscount)—photograph, n.d. 1 envelope.
Depicts Viscount Northcliffe, publisher of the London *Daily Mail* and British Director of Propaganda in Enemy Countries, 1918.

1961

Norton, Elizabeth.
Diary extracts, 1914. 1 folder.
Typescript (photocopy).
Relates to conditions in London at the time of the outbreak of World War I, August 1914.
Gift, E. Norton, 1971.

1962

Norton, Richard, *collector*.
Letters, 1915. 1 folder.
Typewritten transcripts.
Letters by soldiers in the Scots Guards, a unit of the British Expeditionary Force, relating to campaigns on the Western front during World War I.

1963

Norton, Robert, 1896–1974.
Papers, 1935–1948. 3½ ms. boxes.
American lawyer and journalist; editor, *China Today*. Correspondence, speeches and writings, clippings, printed matter, and photographs, relating to U.S. relations with China and Japan, India's independence from Great Britain, Japanese military incursions into China, and United Nations assistance to China.
Gift, Irene Norton, 1977.

1964

Norway—history—photographs, 1945. 1 envelope.
Depicts the homecoming of Prince Olav and of King Haakon VII of Norway, and the surrender of the Norwegian fortress Akershus.

1965

Norwegian World War I bibliography (in Norwegian), n.d. 1 folder.
Typescript.
Bibliography of pamphlets, reports and serials published in Norway between 1914 and 1919 relating to World War I.

1966

Noske, Gustav, 1868–1946.
Memoirs (in German), 1933–1937. "Aus Aufstieg und Niedergang der Sozialdemokratie" (On the Rise and Fall of Social Democracy). 1 ms. box.
Typescript.
German socialist leader; Minister of Defense, 1919–1920; President of Hannover, 1920–1932. Published as *Erlebtes aus Aufstieg und Niedergang einer Demokratie* (1947).
Gift, Ralph H. Lutz, 1959.

1967

Nosovich, Anatoliĭ.
Writings (in Russian), n.d. 1 folder.
Typescript (photocopy).
General, Russian Imperial Army. Histories entitled "Ulany Ego Velichestva, 1876–1926: Imperator Aleksandr II; Imperator Nikolai II" (Uhlans of His Majesty, 1876–1926: Emperor Alexander II and Emperor Nicholas II), and "Leib Gvardiĭ Ulanskiĭ Ego Velichestva Polk v Velikuiu i Grazhdanskuiu Voĭnu: Kratkow Proshloe Polka v Emigratsiĭ" (Uhlan Household Troops of His Majesty's Regiment in the European and Civil Wars: A Brief History of the Regiment in Emigration).
Gift, Marvin Lyons, 1971.

1968

"Note on the Indebtedness and Credit of the Soviet Government."
Memorandum, 1931. 1 folder.
Typescript (mimeographed).
Relates to the financial situation of the Soviet Union.

1969

Notz, Friedrich-Wilhelm von.
Letter (in German), 1975, to John C. Buchanan. 1 folder.
Typescript.
Colonel, German Army. Relates to the unsuccessful attack of the 1st Vlasov Division against the Soviet bridgehead at Erlenhof, Germany, south of Frankfurt a. Oder, April 13, 1945. Includes a translation of the letter.
Gift, J. C. Buchanan, 1975.

1970

Novaîa Zhizn' (New Life) (1917–1918) Leningrad.
Newspaper articles (in Russian), 1917–1918. 1 vol.
Typewritten transcripts.

Leningrad newspaper. Relates to the role of the railroad workers' union, Vserossiĭskiĭ Ispolniteľnyĭ Komitet Zheleznodorozhnogo Soĭuza (Vikzheľ), in the Russian Revolution.

1971

Nowak, Bohdan, 1900–
Portfolio of drawings (with accompanying text in French), ca. 1930s. "Vox Mortuum" (Voice of the Dead). 1 envelope.
Printed.
Polish artist. Depicts the horrors of war.

1972

Nuremberg, Germany—photographs, 1944–1949. 1 envelope.
Depicts bomb damage in Nuremberg, Germany.
Gift, Rose Klein, 1968.

1973

Nuremberg Trial of Major German War Criminals, 1945–1946, collection (in English and German), 1945–1946. 1 folder, 1 envelope.
Miscellanea relating to the Nuremberg Trial of Major German War Criminals, including photocopies of prison records of defendants, messages (handwritten) written by defendants during the trial, and photographs of defendants after their executions.
Gift, Indiana State Library, 1964. Gift, Douglas B. MacMullen, 1965.

1974

Nyman.
Memorandum, ca. 1949. "On Nature of War Against the Soviet Union." 1 folder.
Typescript.
Anticommunist Russian émigré living in the United States. Relates to the prospects for war between the United States and the Soviet Union.

1975

Oberheitmann, Theo.
Deposition (in German), 1947. 1 folder.
Typewritten transcript.
Relates to allegations made at the Nuremberg war crime trials regarding German propaganda activities during World War II.

1976

Oberlaender, Theodor.
Memoranda (in German), 1943. 1 folder.
Typescript (mimeographed).
First Lieutenant, German Army. Two memoranda, entitled "Buendnis oder Ausbeutung?" (Alliance or Exploitation?) and "Deutschland und der Kaukasus" (Germany and the Caucasus), relating to German relations with the occupied territories in Eastern Europe, especially the Caucasus Region.

1977

Oblastnoĭ Komitet Armiĭ, Flota i Rabochikh Finliandiĭ.
Proclamation (in Russian), 1917. "Praviteľstvo Spaseniia Revoliutsiĭ" (Government for the Rescue of the Revolution).
Printed.
Regional Committee of the Army, Navy and Workers of Finland. Supports the Russian revolutionaries.
Gift, Ivan Blums, 1970.

1978

O'Brian, John Lord, 1874–1973.
Papers, 1916–1962. 4 ms. boxes, 3 microfilm reels.
American lawyer; Head of the War Emergency Division, U.S. Department of Justice, 1917–1919. Correspondence, memoranda, affidavits, clippings, printed matter, and speeches and writings, relating to the administration of the War Emergency Division of the Department of Justice, registration of enemy aliens, civil liberties in time of war, and domestic subversion in the United States during World War I.
Register.
One folder closed until 1989.
Gift, J. L. O'Brian, 1970.

1979

O'Brien, Charles A.
Papers, 1918–1923. ½ ms. box, 1 scrapbook.
American Red Cross worker in Siberia, 1919–1920. Diary, notes, photographs, postcards, clippings and memorabilia, relating to American Red Cross activities in Siberia, and the Russian Civil War and Allied intervention in Siberia.
Gift, John McGinty, 1978.

1980

Obshchestva Formirovaniia Boevykh Otriâdov.
Proclamation (in Russian), 1920. 1 folder.
Printed.
Societies of Forming Combat Detachments, a White Russian organization. States regulations of the Obshchestva Formirovaniia Boevykh Otriâdov.

1981

Obshchestva Obedineniia i Vzaimopomoshchi Russkikh Ofitserov i Dobrovoľtsev.
Proclamation (in Russian), 1920. 1 folder.
Printed.
Societies of Unification and Mutual Assistance of Russian Officers and Volunteers, a White Russian organization. States basic regulations of the Obshchestva Obedineniia i Vzaimopomoshchi Russkikh Ofitserov i Dobrovoľtsev.

1982

Odessa—history—posters (in Russian), 1917–1923. 1 folder.
Printed.
Posters, proclamations, and leaflets, relating to po-

litical events in Odessa, during the Russian Revolution and Civil War.
Preliminary inventory.

1983

Odintŝov, Gleb Nikolaevich.
Papers (in Russian), 1928–1973. 3 ms. boxes, 1 oversize framed photograph.
Colonel, Russian Imperial Army. Correspondence, writings, clippings, printed matter, documents, and photographs, relating to the Russian Imperial Army, events in Russia before, during and after the Russian Revolution and Civil war, the Romanov family, and other Russian dignitaries and nobility.
Gift, G. N. Odintŝov, 1975.

1984

O'Donnell, Edward J.
Correspondence, 1969, with Robert G. Neal, Jr., Major, U.S. Marine Corps. 1 folder.
Rear Admiral, U.S. Navy; Commandant, U.S. Naval Base, Guantanamo, Cuba, 1962. Relates to evacuation procedure plans for dependents of U.S. military personnel at Guantanamo during the 1962 Cuban missile crisis.
Gift, E. J. O'Donnell, 1974.

1985

O'Donovan, James.
Photographs, n.d. 2 ms. boxes.
Depicts scenes in Ireland and events in Irish history in the twentieth century.
Purchase, J. O'Donovan, 1969.

1986

Ogden, David Ayres Depue, 1897–
Letter, 1964. 1 folder.
Holograph.
Lieutenant General, U.S. Army. Relates to the career of D. A. D. Ogden as a military engineer, 1918–1957, including service in the Pacific Theater during World War II, and in the Korean War.

1987

Oiderman, M.
History, n.d. "Estonian Independence." ½ ms. box.
Typescript.
Relates to the history of Estonia during the Russian Revolution and to the establishment of an independent Estonian state. Prepared under the auspices of the Estonian Foreign Office.

1988

Okhrana. *see* Russia. Departament Politsii. Zagranichnaia Agentura, Paris (**2358**).

1989

Okinawa invasion, World War II—photographs, 1945. 1 envelope.
Depicts the battle of Okinawa. Includes photographs of Japanese maps.
Gift, Allyn A. Brenner, 1971.

1990

Olchowski, Edward F., *collector*.
Dental records, ca. 1945. 1 folder.
Relates to German Nazi leaders undergoing trial for World War II war crimes. Includes signatures of the Nazi leaders.
Gift, E. F. Olchowski, 1978.

1991

Olds, Charles Burnell, 1872–1971.
Papers, 1895–1964. ½ ms. box.
American missionary in Japan, 1903–1939. Letters, writings and pamphlets, relating to Christianity in Japan.
Gift, Leavitt Olds Wright, 1971.

1992

Olferieff, Theo.
Study, 1932. "Soviet Russia in the Orient." 1 vol.
Typescript.
Relates to military defenses in the Soviet Far East.

1993

Oliphant, David D., Jr., b. 1886.
Papers, 1917–1918. 1 ms. box.
American lawyer; Chairman, Four Minute Men of Alameda County, California, 1917–1918. Correspondence, speakers' schedules, memoranda and printed matter, relating to Four Minute Men speakers at war loan drives in Alameda County during World War I.
Gift, D. D. Oliphant, Jr., 1961.

1994

Oliveira, Sebastiao Mesquita Correia.
Study (in Portuguese), n.d. "Estudo Critico de Campanha do Sul de Angola em 1904" (Critical Study of Campaigns in the South of Angola in 1904). 1 vol.
Holograph and typescript.

1995

Olivereau, Louise, *defendant*.
Trial transcript, 1917. ½ mx. box.
Typescript.
American anarchist. Relates to the trial of L. Olivereau in U.S. District Court, Western District of Washington, Northern Division, on charges of inciting insubordination and obstructing recruitment in the U.S. Army during World War I. Includes text of indictment.

1996

Ollenhauer (Erich)—photograph, n.d. 1 envelope.
Depicts the German politician E. Ollenhauer.

1997

Olney, Warren, III.
Motion pictures, 1936, n.d. 2 reels.
16 mm film without sound track of the ceremonies held in Hindenburg Park in Los Angeles on German Day, 1936; and a 16 mm film with sound of interviews of Dr. Salin, a criminologist, and W. Olney III, U.S. As-

sistant Attorney General, 1953–1957, relating to the incidence of crime in the U.S.
Gift, W. Olney III, 1966.

1998

"Olonetskai︠a︡ Kareliﬁ︠a︡."
Memorandum (in Russian), 1919. 1 folder.
Typescript.
Relates to Russian influence in Karelia during the Russian Civil War.

1999

One Hundred Years of Revolutionary Internationals, Conference, Hoover Institution on War, Revolution and Peace, Stanford University, 1964.
Proceedings, 1964. 1 ms. box, 10 phonotapes.
Sound recordings and conference papers, relating to the history of Marxist doctrine and of the communist movement.

2000

Oppenheimer, Fritz E., 1898–1968.
Papers, 1945–1967. 2 ms. boxes.
Legal adviser to the U.S. Secretary of State, 1947–1948. Minutes of meetings, reports, speech, and printed matter, relating primarily to the meetings of the Council of Foreign Ministers at Moscow, London, and Washington, D.C., 1947. Includes an eye-witness account by F. E. Oppenheimer of the signing of the German surrender to the Allies in Berlin, May 8, 1945.
Gift, Mrs. F. E. Oppenheimer, 1975.

2001

Orbison, Thomas James, 1866–1938.
Papers, 1919–1922. 2 ms. boxes.
Chief, Latvian Mission, American Relief Administration European Children's Fund, 1919–1920. Diaries, writings, photographs and memorabilia, relating to relief work in Latvia at the end of World War I.
Preliminary inventory.

2002

Organisation de l'Armée Secrète.
Leaflet (in French), 1961. 1 folder.
Typewritten transcript.
Secret Army Organization, a right-wing French political movement. Relates to the program of the Organisation de l'Armée Secrète, and to the Algerian independence movement.

2003

Organization for European Economic Cooperation. Intergovernmental Committee on the Establishment of a European Free Trade Area.
Miscellaneous records (in French and English), 1956–1958. ½ ms. box.
Memoranda, resolutions and reports, relating to the initial plans for the European Free Trade Association.
Gift, Reginald Maudling, 1959.

2004

Orgelsdorfer Eulenspiegel.
Newspaper issues (in German), 1918–1919. 1 folder.
Camp newspaper for German prisoners of war at Fort Oglethorpe, Georgia. Relates to camp activities.

2005

Orlowski, A.
Drawing (printed copy), 1819. 1 envelope.
Depicts two riders in a Central Asian setting.

2006

Oruc (Arif)—newspaper clippings (in Turkish), 1931. 1 folder.
Relates to the trial of A. Oruc for communist activities in Turkey. Articles published in the Istanbul newspaper *Cumhuriyet.*

2007

Osswald, R. P.
Study, 1931. "German-Belgian Understanding in Franktireur Question is Possible, Investigation Shows." 1 folder.
Typescript (mimeographed).
Relates to allegations of German war crimes in combating Belgian resistance fighters during World War I.

2008

Ostroukhov, P., *collector.*
Newspaper articles (in Russian), 1918–1920. 1 folder.
Typewritten transcript.
Relates to the Russian Civil War in Siberia. Articles published in Siberian newspapers.

2009

Osusky, Stefan, 1889–1973.
Papers (in English, French, Czech and Slovak), 1910–1965. 42 ms. boxes, 2 card file boxes (⅓ l. ft.), 1 album, 4 envelopes.
Czechoslovakian diplomat; Ambassador to Great Britain, 1918–1920; Ambassador to France, 1920–1940; Minister of State, Czechoslovakian Government-in-Exile, 1940–1943. Correspondence, memoranda, reports, clippings, printed matter, memorabilia, and photographs, relating to Czechoslovakian politics and diplomacy, and European diplomatic relations between the two world wars.
Register.
Gift, Pavla Osusky, 1974.

2010

Otis, Frances L.
Diary, 1943–1944. 1 vol.
Typescript (carbon copy).
American living in Florence, Italy. Relates to conditions in Florence during World War II.

2011

"Oto Zdrada Narodu Radzieckiego" (This Is a Betrayal of the Soviet People).
Translation of newspaper editorial (in Polish), 1963. 1 folder.

Typescript (mimeographed).

Relates to the policies of the Soviet Government under Nikita Khrushchev. Editorial published in the Chinese newspaper *Zenminzipao*.

2012

Otorchi, Ulan.

Memoir (in Russian), 1928. "Ozero Tolbo: Vospominaniiā o Nachalnom Periode Mongol'skoĭ Revoliûtsiĭ" (Recollections from the Initial Period of the Mongolian Revolution). 1 folder.

Typescript.

Mongolian communist. Relates to the communist movement in Mongolia during the Russian Revolution.

2013

Ovchinnikov, Anton Zakharovich.

Memoirs (in Russian), 1932. 1 vol.

Holograph.

Russian Red Army soldier. Relates to guerrilla warfare in the Russian Far East, 1918–1920.

2014

Ozels, Oskars, 1889–1975.

Memoirs (in Latvian), n.d. "Pieredzejumi Riga Bermonta Dienas" (Experiences in Riga During Bermondt's Campaign). 1 folder.

Typescript (photocopy).

Latvian engineer and educator. Relates to the Bermondt-Avalov campaign in Riga, October-November 1919, during the Russian Civil War.

Gift, Edgar Anderson, 1977.

2015

Paap, C. H. N.

Chronology (in Dutch), ca. 1945. "Overzicht Genomen uit *De Residentiebode* over de Oorlog van 10 Mei 1940 tot 9 Mei, 1945" (Synopsis Taken from *De Residentiebode* on the War from May 10, 1940 to May 9, 1945). 1 vol.

Typescript.

Day-by-day summary of war news as reported in the Hague newspaper *De Residentiebode*.

2016

Pacheco, Felix.

Speech transcript, 1923. 1 folder.

Typescript.

Minister of Foreign Affairs of Brazil. Relates to President Warren G. Harding of the U.S. Delivered at a memorial service in Rio de Janeiro after the death of W. G. Harding.

2017

Pacific Island Employees Foundation.

Newsletters, 1942–1947. ½ ms. box.

Typescript (mimeographed).

Relates to the condition of American prisoners of war held in Japanese prison camps during World War II. Includes issues of the Pacific Island Employees Foundation *Bulletin*, 1942–1945, and a few issues of the *PacPOW Bulletin*, 1945–1947.

Gift, Clara Manson, 1954.

2018

Paderewski, Ignacy Jan, 1860–1941.

Papers (in Polish, English and French), 1894–1941. 6½ ms. boxes, 1 envelope, 1 album.

Polish statesman and musician; Premier, 1919. Correspondence, speeches and writings, clippings, printed matter, and photographs, relating primarily to the establishment of an independent Polish State, the Paris Peace Conference, Polish politics in the interwar period, the occupation of Poland during World War II, and the musical career of I. J. Paderewski.

Preliminary inventory.

Personal financial materials in four folders closed until January 1, 1992. No handwritten material may be reproduced.

Gift, Helena Liibke, 1975. Git, Anne Appleton, 1976.

2019

Paderewski Testimonial Fund, 1941–1959.

Records, 1939–1959. 72 ms. boxes, 2 cu. ft. boxes.

Organization for the relief of Polish refugees during and after World War II. Reports, correspondence, press releases, financial records, printed matter and photographs, relating to relief activities carried on by the Fund and by the Paderewski Hospital in Edinburgh, Scotland.

Preliminary inventory.

Gift, Paderewski Testimonial Fund, 1959.

2020

Paets, Konstantin, 1874–1956.

Letters (in Estonian), ca. 1954. 1 folder.

Holograph (photocopy).

President of Estonia, 1921–1924 and 1931–1940. Relates to the imprisonment of K. Paets in the Soviet Union, and appeals to the United Nations to bring about civil rights and independence in the Baltic States. Includes a translation and a press release from the Consulate General of Estonia, New York, 1977, explaining the acquisition and content of the letters.

Gift, Hilja Kukk, 1977.

2021

Page, Charles R.

Papers, 1917–1920. 2 ms. boxes.

Commissioner, U.S. Shipping Board, 1917–1919. Correspondence, memoranda, minutes of meetings, and miscellanea, relating to the work of the U.S. Shipping Board in regulating shipping rates and practices, allocation of ships, recruitment of seamen, and claims for insurance. Includes correspondence with Edward N. Hurley and Joseph Tumulty.

Preliminary inventory.

Gift, C. Page, Jr., 1968.

2022

Page, Frank Copeland, 1887–1950, *collector*.

Newspaper and periodical clippings, 1916. 1 vol.

Relates to the death of Lord Horatio Herbert Kitchener, British General and Secretary of State for War. Clippings from British newspapers and periodicals.

Gift, F. C. Page, 1949.

2023

Paleologue, Sergei Nikolaevich, b. 1887.
Papers (in Russian), 1920–1933. 34 ms. boxes.
Chairman, Board of the Government Plenipotentiary for the Settlement of Russian Refugees in Yugoslavia. Correspondence, reports, and memoranda, relating to the activities of the Board.
Preliminary inventory.
Gift, G. E. Bozhinskii-Bozhko, 1934.

2024

"Palestine Resistance Movement through 30 June 1970."
Study, 1970. ½ ms. box.
Typescript (photocopy).
Relates to the organization and activities of Palestine liberation and resistance movements in the Middle East, 1947–1970.

2025

Paley, Olga Valerianovna, b. 1865.
Memoirs, n.d. *Memories of Russia, 1916–1919.* ½ ms. box.
Holograph and typescript.
Morganatic wife of Grand Duke Pavel Aleksandrovich of Russia. Relates to the Russian Revolution and Civil War. Memoirs published.
Gift, Harper and Row, Publishers, 1964.

2026

Palitŝyn, Fedor Fedorovich, 1851–1923.
Memoirs (in Russian), 1918–1921. 1 ms. box.
Typescript.
General, Russian Imperial Army; Chief of Staff, 1905—1908. Memoirs, entitled "Perezhitoe, 1916–1918" (My Experience, 1916–1918), 1918, and "Zapiski Generala F. Palitŝyna" (Notes of General F. Palitŝyn), 1921, relating to Russian military activities during World War I, and to White Russian military activities during the Russian Civil War.

2027

Pan-African Congress, 6th, Dar es Salaam, Tanzania, 1974.
Miscellaneous records, 1974. ½ ms. box.
Photocopy.
Reports, declarations, resolutions, speeches, and leaflets, relating to the pan-African movement, colonialism, and worldwide problems of black people. Includes printed matter about the congress, collected by Alma Robinson and Charles Ogletree.
Gift, A. Robinson and C. Ogletree, 1975.

2028

Pan-American Union. Special Neutrality Commission.
Miscellaneous records (in English and Spanish), 1914–1915. 1 vol.
World War I neutrality commission of American states. Minutes of meetings, memoranda, declarations and press releases, relating to interruption of South American commerce by belligerents during World War I.

2029

Panunzio, Constantine Maria, 1884–1964.
Papers (in Italian and English), 1921–1945. 17 ms. boxes.
Italian-American sociologist. Writings, letters, clippings, bibliographies, and booklists, relating to Italian politics, fascism, church and state relations, anti-Semitism and racism, and to Benito Mussolini.
Preliminary inventory.

2030

Papen, Franz von, 1879–1969.
Miscellaneous papers (in German), 1933–1945. ½ ms. box, 2 envelopes.
German politician; Chancellor, 1932; Vice Chancellor, 1933–1934. Correspondence, speech transcripts and photographs, relating to German politics, requests of office-seekers, and the last will of President Paul von Hindenburg.
Gift, Office of the Military Government of the U.S. (Berlin), 1949. Gift, Robert J. Smith, 1973.

2031

Paradise, Scott Hurtt, 1891–1959.
Papers, 1914–1915. ½ ms. box.
Member, Commission for Relief in Belgium, 1914–1915. Writings, correspondence, photographs and memorabilia, relating to Commission for Relief in Belgium relief activities and to conditions in Belgium during the German occupation in World War I.
Gift, S. H. Paradise, 1957.

2032

Paramount Pictures.
Photographs, n.d. 7 binders, 1 cu. ft. box.
Motion picture production company. Photographs used in preparation of motion pictures, entitled "Hitler's Gang," depicting the Nazi rise to power in Germany, scenes of party rallies, parades, SS troops, Adolf Hitler and other Nazi leaders at various stages of their careers; and "The Story of Dr. Wassell," depicting scenes from Southeast Asia during World War II.

2033

Pares, Sir Bernard, 1867–1949.
Miscellaneous papers, 1919. ½ ms. box.
British historian. Correspondence, notes, memoranda and diary, relating to political conditions in Western Siberia during the Russian Civil War.

2034

Paris. Congress, 1856.
Miscellaneous records (in French), 1857–1858. ½ ms. box.
Holograph.
Commission established by the Congress of Paris of 1856. Protocols of meetings and report, relating to the reorganization of the Romanian principalities of Wallachia and Moldavia.
Gift, Mrs. Lascelle de Basily, 1964.

2035

Paris Letter.
> Newsletters, 1940. 1 folder.
> Typescript (mimeographed).
> Newsletter issued by Americans in Paris, January-June 1940. Relates to conditions in France during World War II and to American relief work in France.

2036

Paris. Peace Conference, 1919—newspaper clippings (in French and English), 1919–1920. 3 ms. boxes.
> Relates to the Paris Peace Conference. Clippings from various Paris newspapers, including the Paris edition of the *London Daily Mail*, March 14–August 31, 1919. Also includes a *New York Times* clipping, January 4, 1920, recapitulating the chronology of the conference.

2037

Paris. Peace Conference, 1919. U.S. Division of Territorial, Economic and Political Intelligence.
> Miscellaneous records, 1917–1918. 7 ms. boxes, 3 card file boxes (½ l. feet).
> Organization created to prepare background information for the U.S. delegation to the Paris Peace Conference; known as the Inquiry. Memoranda, notes, and reports, relating to political and economic conditions in the Ottoman Empire and Latin America, proposals for new boundaries in Asia Minor, creation of an independent Armenia, and boundary disputes in South America.

2038

"The Paris Resolutions and Free-Trade."
> Leaflet, 1916. 1 folder.
> Printed.
> Appeal for the continuation of a free trade policy in Great Britain after World War I. Written by a private group of British subjects.

2039

Park, Alice, 1861–1961.
> Papers, 1883–1957. 30 ms. boxes, 3 envelopes.
> American pacifist, feminist and socialist; member, Henry Ford Peace Ship Expedition, 1915. Diaries, correspondence, pamphlets, clippings, and leaflets, relating to pacifism and the peace movement, the Ford Peace Ship Expedition, feminism, socialism, the labor movement, prison reform, child labor legislation, civil liberties, and a variety of other reform movements in the U.S.
> Register.
> Gift, A. Park, 1930. Subsequent increments.

2040

Parmelee, Ruth A., 1885–1973.
> Papers, 1922–1945. 5 ms. boxes.
> American physician and relief worker in Turkey, 1914–1917 and 1919–1922, Greece, 1922–1941 and 1945–1947, and Palestine, 1943–1945. Diaries, notes, correspondence, reports, clippings, printed matter and photographs, relating to refugee relief work and medical service in the Near East.
> Gift, Mrs. W. H. Walker, 1974.

2041

Parming, Tönu.
> Study, 1977. "From the Republic of Estonia to the Estonian Soviet Socialist Republic: The Transfer of Rule and Sovereignty, 1939–1940." 1 folder.
> Estonian-American historian. Published as Chapter 1 of *The Estonian S.S.R.: A Case Study of a Soviet Republic* (Boulder: Westview Press, 1977), edited by T. Parming and Elmar Järvesoo.
> Gift, T. Parming, 1978.

2042

Parsons, Charles.
> Memorandum, 1948. "Tyler Kent." 1 folder.
> Typescript (mimeographed).
> Relates to the allegations of Tyler Kent, a code clerk at the U.S. Embassy in London, that President Franklin D. Roosevelt had conspired to bring about the entry of the U.S. into World War II.

2043

Parsons, Marion Randall, *collector.*
> Slides 1918–1919. 1 box.
> Depicts scenes in France during World War I.

2044

"Partial List of Civilian Internees in Manila."
> List, ca. 1944. 1 vol.
> Typescript.
> List of Americans in the Japanese civilian internment camp at Santo Tomás University, Manila. Compiled by Mr. Tsurŭmi, Japanese Consul in Manila, and delivered to Mr. Spiker, American Consul in Shanghai.

2045

Partido Africano de Independencia da Guiné e Cabo Verde.
> Songs, 1974. *Steh auf, Sklave! Lieder der Kaoguiamo (Kulturgruppe der PAIGC)* (Get up, Slave! Songs of the Kaoguiamo [cultural group of the PAIGC]). 1 phonorecord.
> Guinea Bissau and Cape Verde Islands independence movement party. Protest songs of the peoples of Guinea-Bisseau and Cape Verde Islands.
> Purchase, Afrika-Komitee (West Berlin), 1976.

2046

Partido Comunista de México. 7. Congreso Nacional, Mexico, 1939.
> Proceedings (in Spanish), 1939. 1 vol.
> Typescript (carbon copy).

2047

Partiïa Narodnoĭ Voli collection, n.d. 1 folder.
> Typescript.
> Translations of articles and declarations, relating to the Narodnaïa Volïa and other nineteenth century Russian revolutionary parties, including the Partiïa Sotsialistov-Revoliutsionerov.

2048

Partiı̈a Sotsialistov-Revoliutsionerov.
Miscellaneous records (in Russian), 1914–1923.
Russian Socialist Revolutionary Party. Reports and minutes, relating to the activities and views of the party, and to the Russian Revolution.

2049

Partito Nazionale Fascista.
Miscellaneous records (in Italian), 1932–1933. ½ ms. box.
Letters, telegrams and photographs, sent by local organizations of the Italian Fascist Party to Adolf Hitler to congratulate him upon his attainment of power in Germany.
Gift, Riccardo Poli.

2050

Partridge, Stanley N.
Papers, 1918–1945. 1 ms. box.
Colonel, U.S. Army; served with American Expeditionary Force in Siberia. Photographs, postcards, and letters, relating to conditions in Siberia, China and Japan, 1918–1920; and U.S. military facilities in New Guinea and the Philippines, 1943–1945.
Gift, Mrs. S. N. Partridge, 1967.

2051

Pash, Boris T.
Papers, 1918–1976. 1 ms. box, 4 envelopes, 3 albums, 62 reels of film.
Colonel, U.S. Army; military intelligence officer. Correspondence, memoranda, reports, orders, writings, photographs, films, and printed matter, relating to the naval forces of General Nikolaĭ I͡Udenich during the Russian Civil War; the Russian refugee camp in Wuensdorf, Germany, in 1922; U.S. military intelligence service activities, including the Baja Peninsula mission to investigate the possible establishment of a Japanese base in Mexico in 1942, and the Alsos mission to determine the status of German nuclear development in 1944–1945; and to allegations made in 1975 of the involvement of B. T. Pash with Central Intelligence Agency assassination plots.
Gift, B. T. Pash, 1972. Incremental gift, 1976.

2052

Pastuhov, Vladimir D., 1898–1967.
Papers (in English, French, Russian and Chinese), 1927–1938. 58 ms. boxes, 13 albums, 1 envelope, 3 oversize packages (2 l. ft.).
Secretary, League of Nations Commission of Enquiry in Manchuria, 1931–1934. Correspondence, memoranda, reports, interviews, maps, photographs, and printed matter, relating to the investigation of the Manchurian incident of 1931.
Gift, Alexis Pastuhov, 1967. Gift, Serge D. Pastuhov, 1977.

2053

Patouillet, Madame.
Diary (in French), 1916–1918. 1 vol.
Typescript (carbon copy).
Frenchwoman in Russia. Relates to conditions in Petrograd and Moscow during World War I and the Russian Revolution, October 1916—August 1918.

2054

Patrick, Mary Mills, 1850–1940.
Papers, 1875–1924. 1 ms. box.
President, Constantinople Woman's College, 1890–1924. Memoirs, entitled "Transformations," and letters, relating to the history of Constantinople Woman's College during World War I, conditions in Turkey during the war, Turkish society, and the Turkish educational system.

2055

Patterson, David S.
Seminar paper, 1963. "Herbert Hoover and the Concept of America in Foreign Affairs, 1874–1928." 1 folder.
Typescript (mimeographed) (photocopy).
Student, University of California, Berkeley.
Gift, D. S. Patterson, 1963.

2056

Patton, George Smith, 1885–1945.
Speech transcript, n.d. 1 folder.
Typescript (mimeographed).
General, U.S. Army. Speech to the Third Army during World War II.
Gift, William Chenery, 1948.

2057

Pavila, Professor.
Radio broadcast transcript (in German), 1942. "Finnland: Wie Es Ist und Wie Es Wurde" (Finland: How It Is and How It Developed). 1 folder.
Typescript.
Relates to Finnish history. Prepared for German Government broadcast.

2058

Pavlov, Iv.
Memoir (in Russian), n.d. "Zapiski Oppozitsionera: Vospominaniı͡a, Vpechatleniı͡a, i Vstrechi" (Notes of an Oppositionist: Reminiscences, Impressions and Encounters). 1 vol.
Typescript.
Russian member of Trotskyist opposition group, 1924–1928. Relates to the Trotskyist opposition in Russia.

2059

Peabody, Paul E., 1892–
Papers, 1917–1959. 2 ms. boxes, 2 scrapbooks, 1 roll.
Brigadier General, U.S. Army; Military Attaché to Great Britain, 1943–1944, and Mexico, 1948–1950; Chief of Military Intelligence, 1945–1946. Correspon-

dence, orders, citations, and commendations, relating to American military intelligence operations, military liaison with Great Britain and Mexico, and occupation of Japan after World War II.

Gift, P. E. Peabody, 1973.

2060

Peace collection, 1892–1927. 1 folder.

Memoranda, letters and circulars, by various individuals, relating to proposed plans to ensure world peace through disarmament, establishment of a world government, moral regeneration, and other means.

2061

Peace Officers' Association of the State of California. Crime Prevention Committee. Sub-Committee on Subversive Activities.

Report, 1937. "The Communist Situation in California." 1 vol.

Typescript (carbon copy).

Report at the 17th annual convention of the Peace Officers' Association, Oakland, 1937.

2062

Pearl Harbor, Attack on, 1941—Public opinion—interviews, 1941. 1 phonorecord.

Sound recordings of interviews with Americans in various parts of the U.S., December 8, 1941, relating to the Japanese attack on Pearl Harbor. Includes transcript.

2063

Pearson, Grace Nichols.

Papers, 1941–1945. 2 ms. boxes, 1 folder, 1 wooden carving.

Volunteer worker, Northern California Section, American Friends Service Committee. Correspondence, pamphlets, reports, newspaper articles, photographs, and memorabilia, relating to the evacuation and resettlement of Japanese Americans on the West Coast during World War II.

Preliminary inventory.

Gift, G. N. Pearson, 1946. Subsequent increments.

2064

Peck, Willys Ruggles, 1882–1952.

Papers, 1911–1952. 3 ms. boxes, 1 oversize box (½ l. ft.), 1 envelope.

American diplomatic and consular official in China, 1906–1926 and 1931–1940; Minister to Thailand, 1941–1942. Diary, correspondence, memoranda, biography, and clippings, relating to Chinese foreign relations, domestic politics in China, and the Japanese occupation of Bangkok, Thailand, during World War II.

Preliminary inventory.

Gift, Mrs. L. C. Reynolds, 1953. Incremental gift, 1978. Gift, Celia Harris, 1970.

2065

Peirce, George J.

Letters received, 1941. 1 folder.

Holograph and typescript.

Letters from friends in Great Britain, relating to conditions in Great Britain during World War II, January–February 1941.

2066

Pennington, Levi T.

Correspondence, 1928–1962, with Herbert Hoover. 1 folder.

Photocopy.

President, Pacific College, Newberg, Oregon. Relates to Pacific College, disarmament, the National Committee on Food for the Small Democracies, and the Boys' Clubs of America.

Purchase, University of Oregon, 1968.

2067

Perón (Juan) collection (mainly in Spanish), 1943–1955. 2 ms. boxes.

Photographs, clippings, and newspaper issues, 1943–1955, relating to the presidency of Juan Perón (1895–1974) in Argentina and to Eva Perón, especially the death of Eva Perón and the overthrow of Juan Perón.

Gift, John J. Johnson, 1970.

2068

Perry, Charlotte M., *collector*.

Newspaper clippings, ca. 1914–1918. 3 cu. ft. boxes.

Relates to World War I. Clippings from American and foreign newspapers.

2069

Perry, W. L., *collector*.

Miscellany, 1943. 1 folder.

Pamphlets, leaflets, hand-books and miscellanea, issued as guides to American soldiers in North Africa and Italy during World War II.

2070

Perry, Winfred O., 1893?– , *collector*.

W. O. Perry collection on World War I, 1917–1923. 1 ms. box, 1 oversize box.

Printed matter, maps, photographs, glass slides, and battalion flags relating to U.S. troops in France during World War I.

Gift, W. O. Perry, 1978.

2071

Pershin, Dimitriĭ Petrovich.

Papers (in Russian), 1916–1936. 2½ ms. boxes.

White Russian diplomat. Correspondence, diaries, writings, notes and clippings relating to White Russian and Soviet activities in Mongolia during the Russian Revolution, and the Russian émigré population during the Russian Civil War and subsequent years. Includes a memoir (handwritten) entitled "Baron Ungern, Urga i Altan-Bulak: Zapiski Ochevidt͡sa o Smutnom Vremeni vo

Vneshneĭ (Khakhaskoĭ) Mongoliĭ v Pervoĭ Treti XX-go Veka" (Baron Ungern, Urga and Altan-Bulak: An Eye-witness Account of the Troubled Times in Outer (Khalkha) Mongolia during the First Third of the XXth Century), relating to counter-revolutionary events in Mongolia during the Russian Revolution, and a translation (typewritten) by Elena Varneck of the memoir.

2072

Pershing (John Joseph)—photograph, n.d. 1 envelope.
Depicts General J. J. Pershing, U.S. Army, with Bishop Charles H. Brent, Chaplain General of the U.S. Army. Autographed by J. J. Pershing.

2073

Persian revolution, 1908—photographs, 1908. 1 envelope.
Depicts scenes from the Persian revolution of 1908.

2074

Pertŝov, V. A.
Translation of diary extracts, 1919. 1 vol.
Typescript (carbon copy).
White Russian military aviation cadet, 1919. Relates to the evacuation of White Russian military personnel from Kurgan in Western Siberia, to Spassk, near Vladivostok, July—August 1919.

2075

Pertzoff, Constantin A., 1899–
Letter, 1932, to Harold H. Fisher. 1 vol.
Typescript (photocopy).
White Russian soldier in the Russian Civil War. Relates to the question of Allied responsibility for the downfall of Admiral Aleksandr Kolchak during the Russian Civil War.

2076

Peru. Legación (U.S.).
Memorandum (in Spanish), 1915. "Antecedentes de la Internacion del Vapor Aleman *Luxor* por el Gobierno del Peru" (Events Preceding the Internment of the German Steamship *Luxor* by the Government of Peru). 1 folder.
Typescript.
Relates to the seizure of a German ship during World War I for alleged violation of Peruvian neutrality.

2077

Pétain (Henri Philippe Bénoni Omer) collection (in French), 1944–1945. ½ ms. box, 1 oversize folder.
Depositions, statements and photographs, relating to the trial of Henri Philippe Pétain (1856–1951), Marshal and Chief of State of France, for treason, at the conclusion of World War II. Includes statements prepared by H. P. Pétain in anticipation of his arrest by German authorities in 1944.

2078

Peter, Wilhelm.
Essays (in German), 1944–1953. 1 ms. box.
Typescript.
German socialist. Relates to Marxian philosophy, and to the international and German socialist and communist movements.
Gift, W. Peter, 1948. Subsequent increments. Gift, William Beier, 1954. Subsequent increments.

2079

Peter II, King of Yugoslavia, 1923–1970.
Miscellaneous papers (in Serbo-Croatian), 1943–1974. 1 folder.
Photocopy.
Correspondence and announcements, relating to the Yugoslav exile government during World War II, resistance movements in occupied Yugoslavia, politics and government, and Yugoslav émigré politics.
Register.
Gift, Radomir Petrovitch-Kent, 1974. Gift, Momčilo Vukovič-Birčanin, 1974.

2080

Peterkin, Wilbur J., 1904–
Papers, 1944–1945. 1½ ms. boxes, 4 motion picture reels, 1 envelope, memorabilia (1 l. ft.)
Colonel, U.S. Army; Executive Officer and Commanding Officer, Observer Mission to the Chinese Communists, 1944–1945. Diary transcripts, reports, maps, 16 mm films, and memorabilia, relating to Chinese communist forces and the Japanese occupation of China during World War II. Includes a rifle, a bayonet, a pistol, and a hand grenade used by the Chinese communists during the Sino-Japanese conflict.
Gift, W. J. Peterkin, 1976.

2081

Petrenko, Glenn, 1930–
Photographs, 1964–1965. 1 envelope.
Colonel, U.S. Army. Depicts American military activities in Vietnam, including visits to hamlets by General William C. Westmoreland and Congressman Cornelius E. Gallagher.
Gift, G. Petrenko, 1976.

2082

Petri, Pál.
History (in German), ca. 1917. "Geschichte des Ungarischen Kriegsfuersorgewesens" (History of the Hungarian War Relief System). 1 vol.
Typescript (carbon copy).
Relates to World War I relief in Hungary.

2083

Petrov (Arkadiĭ Nikolaevich)—certificates (in Russian), 1918. 1 folder.
Typescript.
Relates to the appointment of A. Petrov to official

positions under the White Russian Omsk Government in Siberia.

2084

Petrushevich, Ivan, 1875–1950.
Papers, 1910–1941. 6 ms. boxes, 5 microfilm reels. Ukrainian journalist. Diaries, correspondence, speeches and writings, memoranda, and clippings, relating to the Ukraine during the Russian Revolution, Ukrainian territorial questions, the cooperative movement in the Ukraine, and Ukrainians in Canada and the U.S.

2085

Pettus, William Bacon, 1880–1959.
Letters, 1939, to Robert Swain. 1 folder.
President, College of Chinese Studies, Peking, 1916–1945. Relates to the Sino-Japanese War and to political conditions in China and Japan. Includes reports by W. B. Pettus, John Leighton Stuart and others.

2086

Pfister, Bernhard, 1900–
Study (in German), 1947. "Die Wirtschaftliche Verarmung Deutschlands: Verarmungsprozess oder Aufbau?" (The Economic Impoverishment of Germany: Process of Impoverishment or Reconstruction?) 1 vol. Typescript (mimeographed).
Relates to Allied economic policy in occupied Germany. Written by B. Pfister and Elisabeth Liefmann-Keil for the Deutscher Caritasverband.

2087

Philby, Harry St. John Bridger, 1885–1960.
Letters, 1933–1960, to Elisabeth Riefstahl. 1 folder. Holograph and typescript.
British explorer; writer on Saudi Arabia; adviser to King Ibn Sa'ud of Saudi Arabia. Relates to world politics, the Middle Eastern political situation, and Saudi Arabia. Includes an essay (typewritten), entitled "Israel and the Arabs," 1956, relating to the Palestinian question.

2088

Philip (Prince Consort of Elizabeth II, Queen of Great Britain)—photograph, n.d. 1 envelope.
Depicts Prince Philip of Great Britain.

2089

Philipp, Werner.
Translation of study, n.d. "The Historical Conditioning of Political Thought in Russia." 1 folder.
Typescript (mimeographed).
Relates to the Russian tradition of political theory. Original study, entitled "Historische Voraussetzungen des Politischen Denkens in Russland," published in *Forschungen zur Osteuropaeischen Geschichte* (Bd. 1, 1954).

2090

Philippine Islands, World War II—photographs, 1944–1945. 2 envelopes.
Depicts the invasion of the Philippine Islands, war damage, military activities, and military assistance to civilians. Photographs taken by the U.S. Army Signal Corps.

2091

Philippines—guerrilla warfare—collection (in English and Chinese), 1944–1969. ½ ms. box.
Photocopy.
Reports, memoranda, letters, and orders, relating to guerrilla warfare of Chinese volunteers in the Philippines against the Japanese during World War II.
Preliminary inventory.
Gift, Theresa Seng Ku, 1973.

2092

Phillips, Ethel G., *collector*.
E. G. Phillips collection on the New Deal, 1933–1941. 32 ms. boxes.
Clippings from U.S. newspapers, relating to U.S. foreign and domestic policy during the New Deal and reflecting conservative criticism of that policy. Includes pamphlets issued by the American Liberty League, 1935–1936, and texts of radio broadcasts on the Ford Sunday Evening Hour, 1936–1940.
Gift, E. G. Phillips, 1939. Subsequent increments.

2093

Phillips, James Holden, 1898–
Papers, 1916–1953. 1 folder, 1 envelope.
Photocopy.
Major General, U.S. Army; Chief of Staff, III Corps, 1943–1946. Correspondence, orders, memoranda, and photographs, relating to the military career of J. H. Phillips, and to activities of the III Corps in the European theater during World War II.

2094

Phillips, William.
Letter, 1916, to the Hamberger-Polhemus Company, San Francisco. 1 folder.
Typewritten copy.
Third Assistant Secretary of State of the U.S. Relates to the attitude of the U.S. State Department regarding British requirements that certain articles exported from Great Britain during World War I not be re-exported.

2095

Philp, William Russell, 1892–1970, *collector*.
W. R. Philp collection on Germany (in English and German), 1934–1952. 7 ms. boxes, 7 envelopes.
Intelligence reports, interrogation reports, and photographs, relating to Adolf Hitler, the German military structure, national socialism, various aspects of German society during and immediately after World War II, various military campaigns of World War II, denazification, and postwar reconstruction in Germany.
Preliminary inventory.
Gift, W. R. Philp, 1968.

2096

Pickering, A. K.
History, 1944. "Diary of the Admiralty Islands Campaign." 1 vol.
Typescript.
Captain, U.S. Army. Relates to the activities of the U.S. 1st Cavalry Division during the Admiralty Islands campaign, February–April 1944. Includes maps.

2097

Pickett, Carrie.
Papers, 1919–1921. ½ ms. box, 1 envelope.
American Red Cross nurse in Siberia and Poland, 1919–1921. Letters, reports, citations, photographs, and memorabilia, relating to the activities of the American Red Cross in Siberia and Poland. Includes an account of various operations of the Czechoslovak Legion in Siberia.
Gift, Grace Bungey, 1973.

2098

Pier, H. W., *collector.*
Miscellany, 1928–1929. 1 folder.
Two issues (printed) of the *Catapult,* the ship's newspaper of the battleship U.S.S. *Maryland,* relating to the cruise of President-elect Herbert Hoover to South America on the *Maryland,* and a gold pen used by President Woodrow Wilson.
Gift, H. W. Pier.

2099

Pierce, Richard A.
Study, 1957. "The Origins of Bolshevism in Russian Central Asia." 1 vol.
Typescript (carbon copy).
Prepared for the Columbia University Research Program on the History of the Communist Party of the Soviet Union.

2100

Pierre, Chanoine.
Memoir (in French), n.d. 1 vol.
Typescript (carbon copy).
French priest; curate of Giromagny, Belfort, France. Relates to the arrest and imprisonment of Canon Pierre by German occupation authorities, 1944–1945.

2101

Piip, Antonius.
Writings (in English and French), 1920–1932. 1 folder.
Typescript (mimeographed).
Prime Minister of Estonia, 1920–1921. Relates to the independence of Latvia, diplomatic recognition of Estonia, Estonian membership in the League of Nations, and relations between Estonia and the Soviet Union.

2102

Pike, M. J. W.
Memoirs, 1915. 1 ms. box.
Typescript.
Lieutenant Colonel, British Army; Commanding Of-
ficer, 5th Service Battalion, Royal Irish Fusiliers. Relates to the Gallipoli campaign of 1915 in World War I. Includes maps and drawings from the campaign.

2103

Pilcher, Joseph Mitchell, 1896–
Obituary, n.d. 1 folder.
Printed.
American clergyman and writer. Relates to Claude M. McCall, U.S. Army officer killed in World War I. Also includes biographical sketch of J. M. Pilcher.

2104

Piłsudski coup photographs, 1926. 1 envelope.
Depicts street fighting in Warsaw at the time of the coup by Józef Piłsudski in May 1926.

2105

Piłsudski, Jósef, 1867–1935.
Memoirs (in German), 1935. *Erinnerungen und Dokumente* (Reminiscences and Documents). 1 folder.
Proof sheets.
Includes annotations (handwritten) to the preface to the German edition by Hermann Goering, German Nazi leader.

2106

Pink, Louis H.
Report, 1945. "Insurance in the Philippines." 1 folder.
Typescript (mimeographed).
Special Insurance Adviser to the President of the Philippines. Relates to the situation of the insurance business in the Philippines.

2107

Pirnie, Malcolm.
Papers, 1917–1918. ½ ms. box, 1 envelope, 1 album.
American Red Cross worker in Russia, 1917. Diary transcripts, correspondence, photographs, clippings and miscellanea, relating to Red Cross relief work in Russia and to conditions in Russia during the Russian Revolution.
Gift, Mrs. M. Pirnie, 1958.

2108

Pius XI.
Encyclical (in German), 1937. 1 folder.
Typescript.
Pope. Relates to the situation of the Roman Catholic Church in Germany.

2109

"Plan du Redressement Français" (Plan for French Reformation).
Memorandum (in French), 1943. 1 vol.
Typescript (carbon copy).
Proposes German intervention to establish a new French Government. Written by five French collaborationists, Joseph Darnand, Georges Guilbaud, Marcel Déat, Jean Luchaire and M. de Tissot, and addressed to German occupation authorities.

2110

Plank, Ewart G.
Papers, 1944–1945. 1 ms. box.
Brigadier General, U.S. Army; Commanding General, Advance Section Communications Zone, European Theater of Operations, 1944–1945. Photographs, military reports, and newspaper issues, relating to activities of the U.S. Army in France, Belgium and Germany during World War II, and particularly to communications operations.

2111

Platonov, Valerian Platonovich, b. 1809?
Papers (in Russian, French and Polish), 1815–1884. 3 ms. boxes.
Russian State Secretary for Polish Affairs, 1864–1866. Correspondence, reports and printed matter, relating to Russian governmental administration in Poland, political, economic and religious conditions in Poland, and the Polish revolution of 1863–1864.
Gift, Ksenia Denikin, 1936.

2112

Platt, Frances Carson, *collector*.
Photographs, 1918. 3 envelopes.
Depicts activities of the American Expeditionary Force in France in World War I. Includes photographic reproductions of drawings and photographs of Charles G. Dawes as a brigadier general.
Gift, F. C. Platt.

2113

Platt, Phillip Skinner, b. 1889.
Papers, 1916–1976. 1 folder, 1 envelope.
American public health official; member of the Commission for Relief in Belgium, American Relief Administration, American Red Cross, and U.S. Army Sanitary Corps in Europe, 1916–1919. Memoirs (printed), 1976, and photographs, 1916, relating to relief work in Europe during World War I.
Gift, P. S. Platt, 1957. Incremental gift, 1976.

2114

Pleve (Viacheslav Konstantinovich)—photograph, n.d. 1 envelope.
Depicts the tsarist Russian Government official V. K. Pleve.

2115

Plotnicov, Leonard.
Key punch cards, n.d. 2 cu. ft. boxes.
Anthropologist. Relates to court cases, tax rolls, welfare, and education in Africa, 1951–1965.
Gift, L. Plotnicov, 1974.

2116

Pogrebetskiĭ, Aleksandr I.
Translation of excerpts from a study, n.d. "Monetary Circulation and Currencies of the Russian Far East during the Revolution and Civil War." 1 folder.
Typescript.

Original study, entitled *Denezhnoe Obrashchenie i Denezhnye Znaki Dalnego Vostoka za Period Voĭny i Revoliutsiĭ*, published in Harbin, 1924. Translation by Elena Varneck.

2117

Pokrovsk, Russia. Kantonnyĭ Ispolnitel'nyĭ Komitet.
Reports (in Russian), 1926–1927. 1 ms. box.
Cantonal Executive Committee in Pokrovsk, capital of the Volga Germans. Relates to the activities of the local soviets, local administration, and economic questions.
Gift, Walter, R. Batsell, 1929.

2118

Poland.
Records (in Polish), 1918–1945. 976 ms. boxes.
Polish Government-in-Exile in London, 1939–1945. Correspondence, memoranda, and reports, relating primarily to foreign relations and other governmental functions of the Polish Government-in-Exile during World War II. Includes some records of the Polish Republic relating to political conditions in Poland and to Polish foreign relations between the two world wars.
Preliminary inventory.
Gift, Alexander Zawisza, 1959.

2119

Poland. Ambasada (China).
Miscellaneous records (in Polish and English), 1942–1945. 1 ms. box.
Polish Embassy in China. Correspondence and memoranda, relating to relations between China and the Polish Government-in-Exile in London.
Gift, Mrs. Alfred Poninski, 1972.

2120

Poland. Ambasada (France).
Records (in Polish), 1919–1940. 10 ms. boxes.
Polish Embassy in France. Correspondence, memoranda, and telegrams, relating to Embassy operations and diplomatic relations between Poland and France.
Deposit, Jan Cicchanowski, 1945.

2121

Poland. Ambasada (Great Britain).
Miscellaneous records (in Polish), 1931–1939. ½ ms. box.
Polish Embassy in Great Britain. Reports, memoranda, financial studies, and clippings, relating to Embassy operations and diplomatic relations between Poland and Great Britain.
Deposit, Jan Ciechanowski, 1945.

2122

Poland. Ambasada (Russia).
Records (in Polish), 1941–1944. 54 ms. boxes.
Polish Embassy in the Soviet Union. Reports, correspondence, accounts, lists, testimonies, questionnaires, certificates, petitions, card files, maps, circulars, graphs, protocols, and clippings, relating to World War II, the

Soviet occupation of Poland, the Polish-Soviet military and diplomatic agreements of 1941, the re-establishment of the Polish Embassy in Moscow, Polish prisoners-of-war in the Soviet Union, deportations of Polish citizens to the Soviet Union, labor camps and settlements, relief work by the Polish Social Welfare Department delegations among the deportees, the Polish Armed Forces formed in the Soviet Union, evacuation of the Polish Embassy to Kuibyshev, evacuation of Polish citizens to the Middle East, the Katyn massacre of Polish officers, and the breakdown of the Polish-Soviet relations in April 1943. Includes material on the Communist Party of the Soviet Union and the Soviet Government, 1928–1929.
Register.
Deposit, Jan Ciechanowski, 1945.

2123

Poland. Ambasada (U.S.).
Records (in Polish), 1918–1956. 118 ms. boxes.
Polish Embassy in the U.S. Reports, correspondence, bulletins, communiqués, memoranda, dispatches and instructions, speeches and writings, and printed matter, relating to the establishment of the Republic of Poland, the Polish-Soviet War of 1920, Polish politics and foreign relations, national minorities in Poland, the territorial questions of Danzig, Memel, the Polish Corridor, and Galicia, the Polish emigration abroad, Poland during World War II, and the Polish Government-in-Exile in London.
Register.
Deposit, Jan Ciechanowski, 1945.

2124

Poland—centennial celebrations—sound recordings (in Polish), 1966. 2 phonorecords.
Celebrations of the Polish millenium in Rome, Paris, London, New York, Chicago, northern France, Munich and other locations.
Closed until August 1987.
Deposit, Jan Nowak, 1967.

2125

Poland—history—coup d'etat, 1926—report, 1926. 1 folder.
Typewritten transcript.
Relates to the coup by Józef Piłsudski in Poland. Written by an unknown U.S. Government official in Warsaw.

2126

Poland—independence movements—posters (in Polish), 1846–1913. 1 folder.
Printed.
Leaflets and proclamations, relating to Polish independence movements.

2127

Poland. Konsulat, Cape Town.
Miscellaneous records (in Polish), 1939–1948. 1 ms. box.
Polish Consulate in Cape Town, South Africa. Correspondence, clippings, photographs, pamphlets, and printed matter, relating to Polish commercial interests, émigré organizations, fund raising for war relief, and consular activity in South Africa.
Register.
Gift, Tadeusz Kawales, 1975.

2128

Poland. Konsulat Generalny, New York.
Records (in Polish), 1940–1948. 7 ms. boxes.
Polish Consulate General in New York City. Correspondence, telegrams, memoranda, reports, agreements, minutes, histories, financial records, lists, press summaries, photographs and printed matter, relating to the German and Soviet occupation of Poland during World War II, activities of the Polish Government-in-Exile (London), and displaced Polish citizens after World War II.
Gift, Anne Appleton, 1976.

2129

Poland. Konsulat Generalny, Pretoria.
Records (in Polish), 1930–1957. 3 ms. boxes.
Polish Consulate General in Pretoria. Correspondence, telegrams, circulars, notes, speeches, clippings, minutes, protocols, and seals, relating to Polish foreign relations with South Africa and Polish émigré organizations, fund-raising for war relief, and consular activity in South Africa.
Register.
Gift, Tadeusz Kawales, 1975.

2130

Poland. Laws, Statutes, Etc.
Translation of laws, 1935. 1 folder.
Typescript.
Polish electoral by-laws for the Diet, adopted July 8, 1935.

2131

Poland. Ministerstwo Prac Kongresowych.
Miscellaneous records (mainly in Polish), 1940–1944. 11½ ms. boxes.
Ministry of Preparatory Work Concerning the Peace Conference, Polish Government-in-Exile (London). Essays, bulletins, reports and studies, relating to Poland's boundary disputes following World Wars I and II, events and conditions in Poland under German and Soviet occupation during World War II, Polish-Soviet relations, communism in Poland, and twentieth century Polish agriculture, economy, foreign relations, history, politics and government.
Preliminary inventory.
Deposit, Otton Laskowski, 1946. Deposit, Polish Research Centre, 1947.

2132

Poland. Ministerstwo Spraw Wewnetrznych.
Issuances (in Polish), 1942–1944. 16 ms. boxes.
Typescript (mimeographed).
Ministry of the Interior of the Polish Government-in-Exile (London). Reports and bulletins, relating to Polish

politics and government, social conditions in Poland, the German and Soviet occupations of Poland, and the Polish underground movement during World War II. Includes reports and studies prepared by the Ministries of National Defense and Military Affairs.

Preliminary inventory.

Deposit, Otton Laskowski, 1946. Deposit, Jozef Kisielewski, 1947.

2133

Poland. Polskie Rzadowe Centrum Informacyjne, New York.

Records (in Polish and English), 1940–1945. ca. 70 ms. boxes.

Polish Information Center, New York. Clippings (primarily from U.S. sources), correspondence, administrative files, press reviews and summaries, bulletins and printed matter, relating to World War II, the German and Soviet occupations of Poland, the persecution of Jews in Poland, and the spread of communism in Eastern Europe.

Deposit, W. Arlet, 1948.

2134

Poland. Polskie Siły Zbrojne.

Miscellaneous records (in Polish), 1940–1945. 10 ms. boxes.

Armed Forces of the Polish Government-in-Exile (London). Correspondence, telegrams, memoranda, bulletins, reports, military orders and instructions, personnel rosters, lists, charts and maps, relating to the Polish Army in the East and in the U.S.S.R., conditions and events in the Soviet Union, Polish civil and military personnel in the Soviet Union, relations of the Polish Army in the U.S.S.R. with the Soviet military command, and operations of various branches of the Polish Armed Forces in Eastern Europe and the Middle East.

Preliminary inventory.

Deposit, Tadeusz Pełczynski, 1946.

2135

Poland. Polskie Siły Zbrojne. Armia Polska na Wschodzie.

Issuances (in Polish), 1940–1946. 20 ms. boxes.

Polish Army in the East. Instructions, training manuals, regulations, studies, maps, charts, bulletins, diagrams and printed matter, relating to the German, British and American armed forces and their military campaigns, equipment, tactics, weaponry and technical intelligence during World War II. Issued as training material for Polish soldiers. Includes material issued by other Polish agencies.

Gift, Jozef Garlinski, 1946.

2136

Poland. Poselstwo (Bulgaria).

Miscellaneous records (in Polish), 1919–1931. 1 ms. box.

Polish Legation in Bulgaria. Correspondence, memoranda, and telegrams, relating to Legation operations and diplomatic relations between Poland and Bulgaria.

Deposit, Jan Ciechanowski, 1945.

2137

Poland. Poselstwo (Finland).

Records (in Polish), 1919–1939. 2 ms. boxes.

Polish Legation in Finland. Correspondence, memoranda, and telegrams, relating to Legation operations and diplomatic relations between Poland and Finland.

Deposit, Jan Ciechanowski, 1945.

2138

Poland. Poselstwo (Portugal).

Records (in Polish), 1919–1950. 29½ ms. boxes.

Polish Legation in Portugal and Consulate in Lisbon. Correspondence, memoranda, and reports, relating to foreign relations between Poland and Portugal between the two world wars, and to foreign relations between Portugal and the Polish Government-in-Exile in London during and after World War II.

Preliminary inventory.

Gift, N. M. G. Leslie, 1965.

2139

Poland. Rada Ministrow.

Reports, 1946. ½ ms. box.

Typescript (mimeographed).

Council of Ministers of the Polish Government-in-Exile in London. Reports, entitled "Facts and Documents Concerning Polish Prisoners of War Captured by the U.S.S.R. during the 1939 Campaign" and "The Mass Murder of Polish Prisoners of War in Katyn," relating to the Katyn Forest massacre.

2140

Poland. Rada Narodowa.

Records (in Polish), 1940–1945. 11 ms. boxes.

Advisory body to the Polish Government-in-Exile (London). Decrees, reports, stenographic records, minutes of meetings, and speeches, relating to political developments in Poland and Eastern Europe and to activities of the Polish Government-in-Exile.

Preliminary inventory.

Deposit, Polish Research Centre, 1947. Gift, Anne Appleton, 1976.

2141

Poland, William B., d. 1950.

Photographs, 1922. 1 album.

Depicts relief work of the American Relief Administration in Poland. Presented by the Polsko-Amerykánski Komitet Pomocy Dzieciom to W. B. Poland in gratitude for his relief activities with the American Relief Administration in Poland.

2142

Poland—World War II—newspaper clippings (in English and Yiddish), 1942–1943. 1 ms. box.

Relates to German atrocities in occupied Poland, persecution and extermination of Jews, activities of Polish émigré groups, and the case of Victor Alter and Henryk Erlich. Clippings from American daily newspapers and from Yiddish newspapers in the U.S., Canada, Mexico, Argentina, Uruguay and South Africa.

2143

Poletika, W. P. von.
> Miscellaneous papers (in German), 1941–1947.
> 1 folder.
> German economist. Reports, studies, bibliographies and proclamations, relating to Soviet agricultural policy, and to German agricultural policy in occupied parts of Russia during the two world wars.

2144

Polish Grey Samaritans.
> Records, 1918–1965. 3 ms. boxes.
> Organization of Polish-American women relief workers. Memoirs, reports, correspondence, printed matter, photographs and memorabilia, relating to relief activities carried on in Poland at the end of World War I, and to conditions in Poland at that time. Includes memoirs by Martha Gedgowd and Amy Pryor Tapping, members of the Polish Grey Samaritans.
> Gift, Martha Gedgowd and Amy Pryor Tapping, 1957. Subsequent increments.

2145

Polish Information Service, New York.
> Memorandum, n.d. 1 folder.
> Typescript.
> Polish Government agency. Relates to the controversy between Germany and Poland between the two world wars regarding the decision of the Polish Government to destroy the bridge at Opalenica, Poznan Province, that had been constructed by the German Government in 1909.

2146

Polish political parties collection (mainly in Polish), 1915–1919. 4 ms. boxes.
> Leaflets, proclamations, appeals, clippings, correspondence, pamphlets, printed matter, periodicals, explanatory notes, transcriptions, and partial card index, relating to the activities of various political parties, organizations, and revolutionary movements in Poland, and Polish politics and government during and after World War I.
> Preliminary inventory.

2147

Polish Socialist Workers.
> Leaflet (in German), 1917. 1 folder.
> Printed.
> Propaganda leaflet directed at German soldiers in Poland.

2148

Politicheskiĭ Ob'edinennyĭ Komitet.
> Miscellany (in Russian), 1921. 1 folder.
> Russian émigré organization. Memorandum (mimeographed), relating to the program of the Politicheskiĭ Ob'edinennyĭ Komitet, and bulletins (typewritten), relating to the Politicheskiĭ Ob'edinennyĭ Komitet and to political developments in Russia.

2149

Das Politische Leben in Russisch-Polen (Political Life in Russian Poland).
> Pamphlet (in German), ca. 1912. 1 folder.
> Printed.
> Gift, Stanford University Library, 1977.

2150

Polk, Bill.
> Scrapbook, 1968. 1 vol.
> U.S. Navy publicist. Photographs and U.S. Army and Navy press releases, relating to the Vietnamese War.
> Gift, B. Polk, 1975.

2151

Polpress.
> Press releases, 1945–1946. 1 folder.
> Typescript.
> The Polish news agency in Moscow. Relates to Polish political and diplomatic events.

2152

Polski Archiw Wojenny.
> Catalog (in Polish), n.d. ½ ms. box.
> Typescript.
> Polish Military Archives. Catalog of pamphlets, leaflets and periodicals at the archives.

2153

"Poltavskiĭa Eparkhial'nyĭa Diela" (Poltava Diocese Affairs).
> Broadside (in Russian), 1917. 1 folder.
> Printed.
> Relates to the situation of religion in Poltava, Ukraine, during the Russian Revolution.

2154

Poninski, Ellen, Graefin.
> Memoir (in German), n.d. "Aufzeichnungen nach Taeglichen Notizen ueber die Jahre in Potsdam, 1945–1949" (Notes from Daily Notations on the Years in Potsdam, 1945–1949). 1 vol.
> Typescript (carbon copy).
> German aristocrat. Relates to conditions in Potsdam under Soviet occupation after World War II.

2155

Pool, Ithiel de Sola, 1917– , *collector*.
> I. S. Pool collection on American Trotskyism, 1905–1948. ½ ms. box.
> Mimeographed letters and circulars, pamphlets and leaflets, relating to American Trotskyism, especially to factional disputes within the U.S. Socialist Workers Party, 1938–1940, and to Trotskyist activities in the antifascist, anti-war labor movements. Includes some radical non-Trotskyist material.
> Gift, I. de S. Pool, 1950.

2156

Poort, Willem Andries, 1918–
    Daily logbook (in Dutch), 1941–1943. 1 folder.
    Holograph.
    Member of the Dutch resistance movement during World War II. Relates to war news, the Allied bombing campaign against Germany, and conditions in the Netherlands under German occupation.

2157

Pope, Henry, *collector*.
    H. Pope collection on William Wirt, 1932–1934. ½ ms. box.
    Writings, transcripts of speeches, and photographs, relating to the views of the educator William Wirt regarding the monetary situation and the economic policy of the New Deal in the U.S.
    Gift, H. Pope, Jr., 1960.

2158

Pope, Hope Cox, 1871–1937.
    Papers, 1915–1919. 1 folder.
    Treasurer, Montevideo, Uruguay, Chapter, American National Red Cross. History (typewritten) of the Montevideo Chapter of the American National Red Cross, 1917–1919; and correspondence, relating to wartime conditions in South America, 1915–1917.
    Gift, Mary Rudd Cochran, 1957. Incremental gift, 1973.

2159

Popescu, Dimitri G., 1908–
    Papers (in Romanian and French), 1940–1946. 6 ms. boxes.
    Romanian diplomat; Private Secretary to the Secretary of State for Foreign Affairs, G. Gafencu. Memoranda, reports, correspondence and dispatches, relating to Romanian foreign relations during World War II, especially Romanian negotiations with the Allies, and to political conditions in Romania during World War II.
    Register.
    During their lifetimes, access requires the written permission of D. G. Popescu or George Duca. In addition, box 6 and a sealed envelope are restricted until January 1, 2001.
    Gift, D. G. Popescu, 1976.

2160

Popović, Žarko, 1896–
    Papers (in Serbo-Croatian), 1940–1974. 2 ms. boxes.
    Colonel, Yugoslav Army; Military Attaché to the Soviet Union, 1939–1941. Correspondence, reports, memoranda and clippings, relating to Yugoslav-Soviet relations, the Yugoslav coup d'état of March 27, 1941, relations of the Yugoslav Government-in-Exile with the U.S. and Great Britain, the "Scandal of Cairo," and Draža Mihailović and the Yugoslav resistance movement during World War II.
    Register.
    Closed until November 1984.
    Gift, Ž. Popović, 1975.

2161

Poppe, Nikolaĭ Nikolaievich, 1897–
    Interview (in Russian), n.d. 17 phonorecords.
    Relates to the Akademiia Nauk SSSR (Soviet Academy of Sciences). Interview conducted by Sergei Yacobson.

2162

"The Port Arthur Diary."
    Translation of table of contents, n.d. 1 folder.
    Typescript.
    Diary of an unknown Russian, relating to the siege of Port Arthur during the Russo-Japanese War, January 1904—April 1905. Translation by Elena Varneck.

2163

Porto Rico Child Health Committee.
    Disbursement vouchers, 1930–1934. 34 ms. boxes.
    Commission for promotion of child welfare in Puerto Rico. Vouchers drawn on accounts of the U.S. Department of Education and the American Relief Administration Children's Fund.
    Preliminary inventory.
    Gift, Ray Lyman Wilbur.

2164

Portuguese Revolution collection (in Portuguese), 1974. 1 folder.
    Posters and ephemera, relating to the revolution in Portugal in April 1974, issued by various political groups.
    Preliminary inventory.
    Purchase, Cornelius Drijver, 1975.

2165

Posolskaia incident collection, 1920. 1 vol.
    Transcripts of testimony, summaries of conferences, declarations, and notes, relating to the capture of the armored train of Ataman Grigoriĭ Semenov, White Russian military leader, by the U.S. 27th Infantry Regiment at Posolskaia, Siberia, and to alleged atrocities committed by the troops of Ataman Semenov.

2166

Possony, Stefan Thomas, 1913–
    Papers (in English and French), 1940–1977. 27 ms. boxes.
    American political scientist; Senior Fellow, Hoover Institution on War, Revolution and Peace. Correspondence, writings, reports, research notes, bibliographic card files, term papers, examination papers, periodical articles and newspaper clippings, relating to military science, technology, national defense, international relations, Soviet foreign policy, revolution in the twentieth century, and communism.
    Gift, S. T. Possony, 1978.

2167

"Post-War Economic Development of India."
    Report, 1944. 1 folder.
    Typewritten transcript.
    Relates to economic development planning for India

after World War II. Report by eight Indian businessmen and economists, published in the *Hindustani Times*, January 29—February 1, 1944.

2168

Post, Wilber E.
History, 1918–1919. 1 vol.
Typescript (carbon copy).
Relates to the Russian Revolution and Civil War in the Caucasus region, Allied intervention in the area, and economic conditions in the Caucasus. Written by W. E. Post and Maurice Wertheim.

2169

Poster collection. ca. 40,000 posters.
Posters from many countries, relating to the two world wars, political conditions in the twentieth century, and various other subjects. Collection includes primarily propaganda posters issued by the French, German, United States, and British governments during World Wars I and II and by the Russian Bolshevik and German Nazi parties. Some Soviet posters are also present.
Gifts and purchases, various sources, various dates.

2170

Postnikova, E.
History (in Russian), 1924. "R.S.F.S.R.". 1 vol.
Typescript.
Relates to the Russian Socialist Federated Soviet Republic during the Russian Civil War, 1919–1921.

2171

"Postulates, Principles, Proposals for the International Law of the Future."
Report, 1943. 1 folder.
Typescript (mimeographed).
Relates to proposals for post-World War II international organizations and international law.

2172

Pototskiĭ, Sergeĭ Nikolaievich, b. 1877.
Papers (mainly in Russian), 1930–1946. 40 ms. boxes, 2 card file boxes (⅓ l. ft.), 1 envelope.
Major General, Russian Imperial Army; Military Attaché to Denmark, 1915. Correspondence, telegrams, reports, protocols, lists, orders, circulars, accounts and receipts, card file, and photographs, relating to Russian Imperial military agencies in Copenhagen and Berlin, the Russian Imperial Passport Control Office in Copenhagen, the Russian prisoner-of-war and refugee camp at Horserød, the Russian Red Cross, military benevolent émigré organizations and activities, and Russian participation in World War I and the Russian Civil War.
Register.
Consult archivist for restriction.
Gift, S. N. Pototskiĭ, 1947.

2173

Potter, Mrs. W. T.
Memoir, n.d. "Oklahomans Meet Hoover in Argentina." 1 folder.

Typescript.
American in Argentina, 1928. Relates to the visit of President-elect Herbert Hoover to Argentina in December 1928.
Gift, Mrs. W. T. Potter, 1957.

2174

Potulicki, Michał, 1897–
Papers (in Polish), 1933–1945. 2½ ms. boxes.
Polish law professor; Principal Legal Adviser, Foreign Ministry, Polish Government-in-Exile (London), 1941–1945; Secretary General, Inter-Allied Research Committee (London). Bulletins, reports, studies, correspondence, notes and clippings, relating to Polish politics and government, German war crimes, Germany during World War II, prisoners of war in Germany, the German invasion of Poland, and Polish relations with Britain, France and the Soviet Union. Includes bulletins, reports, and studies of the Inter-Allied Research Committee (London), relating to German propaganda during World War II, the German mentality, and nazism.
Preliminary inventory.
Deposit, M. Potulicki, 1946.

2175

Powell-Evans, V.
Report, 1952. 1 folder.
Typescript (mimeographed).
Superintending Police Officer, Kluang Circle, Malaya. Relates to terrorist activities during the emergency period in Malaya.

2176

Powers, Joshua B., 1892–   , *collector.*
J. B. Powers collection on Homer Lea, 1876–1962. 6 ms. boxes, 1 album, 5 envelopes.
Correspondence, telegrams, biographies, articles, pamphlets, clippings, writings, photographs, maps, scrapbooks, and memorabilia, relating to Homer Lea, military advisor to Sun Yat-sen and author of *The Valor of Ignorance,* and to the revolutionary movement in China, ca. 1900–1920. Includes writings and correspondence of H. Lea, Ethel Lea and J. B. Powers.
Register.
Gift, J. B. Powers, 1968.

2177

Powers, Philip M., *collector.*
P. M. Powers collection on World War I and the German revolution (in German), 1914–1921. 8 scrapbooks.
Cartoons from the German press, photographs, and miscellanea, relating to World War I and the German revolution of 1918–1919.

2178

Pravda (Truth).
Translation of newspaper article excerpts (in German), 1917. 1 folder.
Typescript.
Bolshevik newspaper. Relates to the social democratic

peace conference in Stockholm, and to the suppression of the Bolsheviks in Russia during the "July Days." Excerpts are dated July–August 1917.

2179

Preparatory Commission of the United Nations.
Records, 1945. 1 reel.
Microfilm.
Commission for work preparatory to the founding of the United Nations.
Gift, Father Graham, 1977.

2180

"The Present State of Latvia's Railways and the Views for the Future."
Report, n.d. 1 folder.
Typescript (mimeographed).

2181

Presidential inaugurations collection, 1953–1973. 1 folder.
Reception and concert invitations, programs, campaign badge, and photographs, relating to the inaugurations of Presidents Dwight D. Eisenhower and Richard M. Nixon.
Gift, Bernice Miller, 1975.

2182

Presidentielle 1965 (1965 Presidential).
Speeches (in French), 1965. 1 phonorecord.
Speeches of candidates for President of France, including speeches by Marcel Barbu, Charles de Gaulle, Jean Lecanuet, Pierre Marcilhacy, François Mitterand and Jean-Louis Tixier-Vignancour.

2183

President's Research Committee on Social Trends, 1929–1932.
Reports, 1932. 10 ms. boxes.
Typescript.
Committee established by President Herbert Hoover to study social conditions in the United States. Relates to demographic, educational, racial, recreational, cultural, religious, medical, legal and governmental aspects of society; urban and rural trends; and the role of the family. Reports published under the title *Recent Social Trends in the United States* (New York: McGraw-Hill, 1935).
Gift, Ray Lyman Wilbur, 1933.

2184

Press—Archangel, Russia—translations of newspaper article extracts, 1918–1919. 1 folder.
Typescript.
Relates to the Russian Civil War, November 1918–July 1919. Translated from Archangel newspapers.

2185

Presses Nationales Associées.
Press releases (in French), 1958. 1 folder.
Typescript (mimeographed).
Press agency in Liège, Belgium. Relates to the Algiers

coup of 1958 and the return to power of General Charles de Gaulle in France.

2186

Preston, Archibald E.
Papers, 1917–1918. ½ ms. box.
Captain, U.S. Army Corps of Engineers. Correspondence, orders, training manuals, and maps, relating to U.S. military engineering activities in the U.S. and France during World War I.

2187

Preysing (Konrad von) collection (in German and English), 1943–1951. 1 folder.
Correspondence, memoranda and serial issues, relating to the career of Konrad Cardinal von Preysing (1880–1950), Roman Catholic Bishop of Berlin, 1935–1950.

2188

Price, Ernest B., 1890–1973.
Papers, 1914–1960. 13 ms. boxes, 1 envelope.
American consular official in China, 1914–1929; President, China Airways, 1929–1930; Standard Vacuum Oil Company representative in China, 1946–1950. Correspondence, diary, dispatches, writings, lecture material, photographs, and printed matter, relating to Japanese military intervention in China and Manchuria, 1931–1945; political and economic development in China, 1914–1950; and U.S. foreign relations with China, 1914–1929.
Register.
Gift, Mrs. Kenneth Carpenter, 1974. Gift, William Leary, 1974.

2189

Price, Harry Bayard.
Memorandum, 1947. "Proposal and Preliminary Outline for a Comprehensive Program of American Aid to China." 1 vol.
Typescript (carbon copy).

2190

Princeton Listening Post.
Transcripts of radio broadcasts, 1939–1941. 12 ms. boxes.
Typescript.
Monitoring station for European radio broadcasts during World War II. Transcripts of news broadcasts from London, Paris, Rome, Berlin and Moscow, relating to war news, December 1939—May 1941.

2191

Prisoners of war, Dutch—summaries of reports (in Dutch), 1942. 1 folder.
Typescript.
Relates to the transportation of 2000 Dutch officers from the Netherlands to a prison camp in Germany in May 1942, and to living conditions in the camp.

2192

Prisoners' Pie.
Serial issues (in English and French), 1916. 1 folder.
Prison camp magazine entitled *Prisoners' Pie/L'Assiette sans Beurre,* published in Crefeld, Germany, for Allied prisoners of war.

2193

Procopé, Hjalmar Johan Fredrik, 1889–1954.
Papers (in Finnish), 1939–1945. 8 microfilm reels. Microfilm.
Finnish diplomat and politician; Minister of Foreign Affairs, 1924–1925 and 1927–1931; Minister to the U.S., 1939–1944. Correspondence, diplomatic dispatches, memoranda and reports, relating to Finnish foreign relations during the Russo-Finnish War and World War II.
Consult Archivist for restriction.
Deposit, H. J. F. Procopé, 1947.

2194

Pronin, Dimitri, 1900–
History, n.d. "Europe in Flames." ½ ms. box.
Typescript (photocopy).
Relates to the Soviet and German occupation of Poland, 1939–1945.
Gift, D. Pronin, 1971.

2195

Propaganda, Communist—Russia—collection (in Russian), 1929–1931. 1 folder.
Printed.
Leaflets and posters, propagating atheism and communism. Issued in the Soviet Union.

2196

Propaganda in South Korea (in Korean and English), 1948. 1 folder.
Propaganda material, including posters, bulletins, and leaflets, issued by the South Korean Government, U.S. occupation authorities, and South Korean communists, for distribution in South Korea.

2197

Propaganda, Russian (in Russian), ca. 1914–1917. 1 ms. box.
Printed.
Postcards and miscellanea, issued as Russian Imperial propaganda during World War I.

2198

Protestant Episcopal Church in the U.S.A collection, 1974–1978. 1 folder.
Clippings and other printed matter, relating to alleged Marxist influence in the Protestant Episcopal Church in the U.S.A. and in the World Council of Churches. Includes an Episcopalian study guide entitled *Struggling with the System: Probing Alternatives* (1976).
Gift, anonymous, 1978.

2199

Protesting Committee Against the U.S. Marines' Violence. Propaganda (in Chinese), 1947. 1 folder.
Anti-American propaganda distributed at the National University of Taiwan in Taipei.

2200

Protocols of the Wise Men of Zion.
Writings (in Russian), n.d. "Sionskie Protokoly" (Protocols of Zion). 1 folder.
Handwritten.
Anti-Semitic propaganda tract.

2201

Pruitt, Ida, b. 1888.
Miscellaneous papers, 1911–1948. 1 folder.
American missionary in China; member, American Committee in Aid of the Chinese Industrial Cooperatives, 1940–1951. Letters, reports, and printed matter, relating to missionary and social work in China, the Sino-Japanese Conflict, and Chinese industrial cooperatives.
Gift, Henry P. Sheng, 1974.

2202

Prussia. Ministerium des Innern. Politische Abteilung.
Miscellaneous records (in German), 1926–1932. 1 folder.
Political Division of the Ministry of the Interior of Prussia. Copies of correspondence, notes, and proclamations, relating to activities of the Nazi party in Prussia.

2203

Prussia. Polizei-Praesidium in Berlin.
Proclamations (in German), 1870–1871. 1 folder.
Printed.
Prussian police agency. Relates to events in the Franco-Prussian War.

2204

Pryor, Roy, *collector.*
Radio broadcasts, 1941–1942. 57 phonorecords.
Relates to American neutrality in World War II, the Japanese attacks on Pearl Harbor and the Philippine Islands, and the first weeks of American participation in the war. Includes speeches by President Franklin D. Roosevelt of the U.S. and Prime Minister Winston Churchill of Great Britain, and newscasts.
Preliminary inventory.

2205

Pstrokónski, Stanisław.
Study (in Polish), 1947. "Likwidacja Polskich Sił Zbrojnych: Ocena i Konsekwencje." (Liquidation of Polish Armed Forces: Evaluation and Consequences). 1 vol.
Typescript.
Relates to the disbanding of Polish armed forces in Great Britain at the end of World War II.

2206

Puchkov, F. A.
Translation of history, n. d. "The Icy March." 1 vol.
Typescript.
Relates to White Russian military activities in Siberia during the Russian Civil War. Original published under the title "Vos'maia Kamskaia Strelkovaia Diviziia v Sibirskom Ledianom Pokhode" in *Vestnik Obshchestva Russkikh Veteranov Velikoĭ Voĭny*. Translated, with commentary, by Elena Varneck.

2207

Purington, Chester Wells.
Report, 1921. 1 folder.
Typewritten transcript.
American mining engineer. Relates to political and economic conditions in eastern Siberia, and to Japanese intervention in that area, during the period 1918–1921. Report submitted to the U.S. State Department and U.S. Army Military Intelligence Division.

2208

Pusta, Kaarel Robert, 1883–1964.
Papers (in Estonian, French and English), 1918–1964. 20 ms. boxes.
Estonian diplomat; Foreign Minister of Estonia, 1924–1925. Correspondence, speeches and writings, memoranda, reports, printed matter and photographs, relating to Estonian politics and diplomacy, Soviet-Baltic State relations, the League of Nations, international law, and Estonian émigré politics.
Preliminary inventory.
Gift, Mrs. K. R. Pusta, 1964.

2209

Putnam, Edward Kirby, 1868–1939.
Correspondence, 1918–1919. 1 ms. box.
American Red Cross relief worker in France, 1918–1919. Relates to civilian relief work in France.

2210

Putnam, John Risley, *collector*.
Consul General and Mrs. J. R. Putnam collection of oriental art, ca. 1500–1900.
A Chinese hanging scroll painting of the late Ming period (16th century), a set of four Tibetan tankas (mid-19th century), a Chinese hanging scroll (late 19th century), a panel Chinese embroidery with gold thread (late 19th century), a Chinese Mandarin embroidered silk jacket with gold thread designs (late 19th century), and a Chinese Mandarin robe (late 19th century).
May be used only with permission of the Archivist, Hoover Institution on War, Revolution and Peace.
Gift, anonymous, 1975.

2211

Putnam, Osgood, *collector*.
Miscellany, 1914–1917. ½ ms. box.
Correspondence, leaflets, pamphlets, and clippings,

relating to the solicitation of funds in the U.S. by a variety of charitable organizations for relief work in Europe during World War I.
Gift, Elizabeth Whitney Putnam, 1959.

2212

Putnam, Ruth.
Papers (in English and French), 1920–1925. ½ ms. box, 3 envelopes.
American visitor to Luxemburg. Correspondence, writings, notes, and photographs, relating to description of Luxemburg and to the role of Luxemburg in World War I.
Register.

2213

Pye, W. S.
Memorandum, 1942. 1 folder.
Typescript (photocopy).
President, U.S. Naval War College. Relates to reports of U.S. naval activities in the Solomon Islands in August 1942.

2214

Pyeng, Do Yi, *collector*.
Photograph, 1883. 1 envelope.
Depicts the first Korean diplomatic mission to the U.S. Caption in Korean and English.
Gift, Pyeng Do Yi, 1958.

2215

Pyle, Ernest Taylor, 1900–1945.
Dispatches, 1943. 1 vol.
Typescript.
American war correspondent in World War II. Relates to U.S. naval activities in the Mediterranean Sea.

2216

Quayle, Ernest H.
Diary, 1917. ½ ms. box.
Holograph.
Private, U.S. Marine Corps. Relates to U.S. Marine Corps life during World War I, in the U.S. and aboard ship in the Caribbean.
No quotations may be published without the consent of E. H. Quayle or his heirs until 2000.
Gift, E. H. Quayle, 1926.

2217

Quidde, L.
Outline (in German), 1915. "Deutschland nach dem Kriege: Ein Programm fuer Dauernden Frieden" (Germany after the War: A Program for Lasting Peace). 1 folder.
Typescript (mimeographed).
Relates to proposals for the settlement of territorial questions and other outstanding issues of World War I.

2218

Quinn, Frederick.
    Papers (in French, English and German), 1822–1974. 16 ms. boxes, 3 microfilm reels, 4 phonotapes, 2 envelopes.
    American anthropologist. Research notes and drafts, lists, writings, interviews, copies of government documents, printed matter, tapes of tribal chants, and photographs, relating to the Beti society of the Cameroun. Used by F. Quinn as research material for his dissertation, "Changes in Beti Society, 1887–1960" (University of California, Los Angeles, 1970).
    Register.
    Purchase, F. Quinn, 1972. Incremental gift, 1975.

2219

Ra'anan, Gavriel.
    Study, 1977. "The Zhdanovshchina, Soviet Factional 'Debates' over International Policies and the Tito 'Affair.'" 1 folder.
    Typescript (photocopy).
    Relates to Soviet foreign policy decision-making in the early post-World War II period, the Stalin-Tito break, the political struggle between A. A. Zhdanov and G. M. Malenkov, and other Soviet internal controversies and debates.
    May not be used without written permission of G. Ra'anan.
    Gift, G. Ra'anan, 1978.

2220

Rabbitt, James Aloysius, 1877–1969.
    Papers, 1895–1969. 38 ms. boxes, 39 vols.
    American mining engineer in the Far East. Correspondence, memoirs, lectures, reports, surveys, patents, clippings, sketches, and photographs, relating to economic, scientific, and technological developments in the mining and metallurgical industries of China, Japan and the Far East, with emphasis on nickel alloys; China labor and dockyard projects; cultivation of rice in Japan; and related governmental policies of China and Japan.
    Preliminary inventory.
    Gift, Mrs. J. A. Rabbitt, 1971.

2221

Rabinoff, Max, b. 1877.
    Autobiography, n.d. "Web of My Life." ½ ms. box.
    Typescript.
    Russian-American impresario. Relates to unofficial diplomatic and commercial relations between the United States and the Soviet Union during the 1920's.
    Gift, Clifford Forster, 1972.

2222

Race, Jeffrey.
    Writings, 1969–1975. ½ ms. box.
    U.S. Army advisor in South Vietnam, 1967. Photocopy of a study (typewritten), entitled "War Comes to Long An," 1969, relating to political events in Phuoc Tuy Province, South Vietnam, 1954–1968; and an essay (printed) entitled "Whither the Philippines?" 1975, relating to contemporary Philippine politics.
    "War Comes to Long An" may not be quoted or reproduced. "Whither the Philippines?" may be used only with permission of Paul R. Hanna.
    Gift, Robert Turner, 1974. Gift, Paul R. Hanna, 1976.

2223

Radbruch, Gustav.
    Newspaper article (in German), 1949. "Des Reichsjustizministeriums Ruhm und Ende: Zum Nuernberger Juristen-Prozess." (Fame and Finish of the Reich Ministry of Justice: To the Nuremberg Trials). 1 folder.
    Typewritten transcript.
    Published in the *Juristische Wochenschrift*.

2224

Radek, Karl, 1885–1939.
    Letter (in German), 1919, to Paul Levi. 1 folder.
    Holograph (photocopy).
    Russian communist leader. Relates to the communist movement in Germany.

2225

Radicalism—Los Angeles—reports, 1924. 1 folder.
    Typescript (mimeographed).
    Relates to activities of the Workers' (Communist) Party, the Industrial Workers of the World, and other leftist organizations in Los Angeles during this period.

2226

Radikalna Stranka (Srpska).
    Minutes of meetings (in Serbo-Croatian), 1904–1909. 1 folder.
    Holograph (photocopy).
    Serbian Radical Party. Minutes of the Klub Radikalnih Poslanika (Caucus of Radical Deputies) of the Radikalna Stranka, relating to Serbian politics and parliamentary strategy.
    Gift, Alex N. Dragnich, 1975.

2227

Radio Free Europe.
    Propaganda (in Czech and English), 1951. 1 ms. box.
    Anti-communist propaganda released by balloon in Czechoslovakia in 1951 by Radio Free Europe. Includes a balloon, leaflets and a press release.
    Gift, Morton B. White, 1951.

2228

Radio Pyongyang.
    Translations of radio broadcasts, 1948. 1 folder.
    Typescript (some mimeographed).
    North Korean radio station. Relates to the Korean reunification question. Broadcasts monitored by U.S. Army Forces in South Korea.

2229

Radio Sociedad Nacional de Agricultura.
    Radio broadcast (in Spanish), 1973. 1 phonotape.
    Taped copy of phonograph album.

Chilean radio station. Relates to the overthrow of the government of Salvador Allende in Chile by the coup of September 11, 1973.

2230
Radisics, Elemer, b. 1884.
Papers (in Hungarian, French and English), 1920–1964. 5 ms. boxes, 1 oversize box (⅓ l. ft.).
Hungarian attorney, statesman, diplomat and journalist; Chief, Historical Department, Ministry of Foreign Affairs; editor, *Budapesti Hirlap*; member, Secretariat, League of Nations, 1931–1940. Correspondence, reports, diplomatic dispatches, military and historical studies, writings, clippings, and printed matter, relating to Hungarian history, politics and government, the Danube Valley, the Hungarian Revolution of 1956, World War II military campaigns, world politics, Palestinian history, and Jewish-Arab relations.
Preliminary inventory.
Correspondence of E. Radisics may not be used—box 5 closed until 1980, box 6 closed until 1990.
Deposit, E. Radisics, 1960.

2231
Radvanyi, Janos, 1922–
Writings (in Hungarian and English), n.d. ½ ms. box.
Hungarian diplomat; official of the Hungarian Embassy to the U.S., 1962–1967. Relates to the Vietnamese War and to the role of Peter Janos, Foreign Minister of Hungary, in negotiations between the U.S. and North Vietnam.
Closed until January 2, 1985.
Gift, J. Radvanyi, 1969.

2232
Radziwill, Ekaterina Rzewuska, Kniagina.
Diary, 1899–1900. 1 folder.
Typescript.
Polish aristocrat. Relates to South African politics and to Cecil Rhodes.
Gift, Herbert Hoover, 1928.

2233
Raemaekers, Louis, 1869–1956.
Papers (in English, French and Dutch), 1903–1939. 12 ms. boxes, 9 drawers (18 l. ft.), 2 albums, 3 envelopes.
Dutch cartoonist. Correspondence, clippings, newspaper issues, photographs, cartoons, sketches, and paintings, relating to art work of L. Raemaekers, especially anti-German cartoons drawn by L. Raemaekers during World War I.
Preliminary inventory.
Gift, L. Raemaekers, 1944.

2234
Ramirez-Montesinos, Vincente, *collector*.
Photographs, 1953–1956. 5 envelopes.
Depicts Francisco Franco, other Spanish political leaders, foreign diplomats and other officials visiting Spain,

and scenes of political, military, cultural, social and religious life in Spain. Captions in Spanish.
Gift, V. Ramirez-Montesinos, 1978.

2235
Ramplee-Smith, Winifred V., *collector*.
W. V. Ramplee-Smith collection on the Russian revolution (in Russian and English), 1915–1917. 1 ms. box, 1 folder, 1 envelope.
Pamphlets, leaflets, clippings, and postcards, relating to the February 1917 Revolution in Russia. Includes fragments of burned records of the tsarist secret police (Okhrana), which W. V. Ramplee-Smith surreptitiously removed from the Okhrana's St. Petersburg office files, then being burned by Bolshevik soldiers.
Preliminary inventory.
Gift, W. V. Ramplee-Smith, 1963. Subsequent increments.

2236
Ramsay (Sir Bertram Home)—photograph, n.d. 1 envelope.
Depicts Admiral B. H. Ramsay, British Navy.

2237
Rand Corporation.
Reports, 1965–1972. 3 ms. boxes.
Printed.
Relates to the organization, operations, motivation, and morale of Viet Cong and North Vietnamese troops, 1964–1968, based on 2400 interviews with Vietnamese.
Preliminary inventory.
Gift, Rand Corporation, 1976.

2238
Rand (George F.) collection, 1919–1950. 1 ms. box.
Clippings and miscellanea, relating to the Bayonet Trench Monument, erected by G. F. Rand in 1919 on the Verdun battlefield in France in honor of French soldiers buried alive by the collapse of a trench during the battle of Verdun in World War I. Includes biographical information on G. F. Rand.
Gift, F. R. Rogers, 1950.

2239
Rankin, Pauline Jordan.
Memorabilia, ca. 1917–1945. ½ ms. box.
American Ambulance Service worker in France and relief worker in Romania and the Near East during World War I. French helmet, German belt buckle, pin, cigarette lighter, and five decorations (medals, ribbons, and citation) given to P. J. Rankin by the French War Ministry in 1917. Includes two U.S. posters from World War II.
Gift, P. J. Rankin, 1970.

2240
Ranzow Engelhardt, Poul, 1898–
Memoir, 1961. 1 vol.
Typescript (carbon copy).
Major, Danish Army; Colonel, Viking Division, Waffen-SS. Relates to the German occupation of Denmark

during World War II and to the formation of the Viking Division of Scandinavian and Dutch volunteers within the Waffen-SS to fight against the Soviet Army.

2241

"Rapport Relatif aux Circonstances dans lesquelles le Colonel Coignerai, 'Doyen' des Officiers Français, Prisonniers à l'Oflag X B, a Eté Changé de Camp le 19 Juin 1942" (Report Relating to the Circumstances in which Colonel Coignerai, 'Dean' of the French Officers, Prisoners in Oflag X B, Was Exchanged from Camp, June 19, 1942).
    Report (in French), 1942. 1 vol.
    Typescript (carbon copy).
    Relates to prisoners of war at the German prison camp Oflag XB, Nienburg-sur-Weser, during World War II.

2242

"Rapport sur l'Activité Politique de la Francmaçonnerie" (Report on the Political Activity of Freemasonry).
    Report (in French), n.d. 2 vols.
    Typescript.
    Relates to the history of Freemasonry in France and the world, and the relationship of Freemasonry to pacifism, communism, the Spanish Civil War and World War II.

2243

Rasputin, Grigoriĭ Efimovich, 1871–1916.
    Note (in Russian), 1916. 1 folder.
    Holograph (photocopy).
    Adviser to Tsar Nicholas II and Tsarina Alexandra of Russia. Includes explanatory letter by Peter S. Soudakoff, March 4, 1966, and an affidavit copy certifying the authenticity of Rasputin's handwriting.

2244

Rathvon, Nathaniel Peter, 1891–1972.
    Letters received, 1923–1947. 1 folder.
    American business executive. Letters, 1923–1945, from William H. Donald, Australian journalist and adviser to Chiang Kai-shek and other Chinese officials, 1903–1942, relating to historical and political events in China, and letters from Earl Albert Selle, 1946–1947, relating to the preparation of his book *Donald of China* (New York, 1948).
    Gift, N. P. Rathvon, 1965.

2245

Ratzenhofer, Emil, b. 1877.
    Study (in German), n.d. 2 ms. boxes.
    Holograph and typescript.
    General, Austro-Hungarian Army. Relates to mobilization, transportation, and concentration of troops in Austria-Hungary in 1914. Includes translation.
    Purchase, E. Ratzenhofer, 1946.

2246

Ray, J. Franklin, Jr.
    Papers, 1946–1947. 1½ ms. boxes.
    Acting Director, China Office, United Nations Relief and Rehabilitation Administration, 1946–1947. Minutes of meetings and reports, relating to relief activities of the United Nations Relief and Rehabilitation Administration in China at the end of World War II.
    Gift, J. F. Ray, Jr., 1976.

2247

Ray, Philip Alexander, 1911–
    Study, 1965. "The Bird and the Snake: Mexico's New Revolution." 1 vol.
    Typescript (mimeographed).
    Relates to political and economic conditions in Mexico, the Mexican communist movement, and prospects for communism in Mexico.

2248

Raymond, John M., 1894–
    Papers, 1944–1949. ½ ms. box.
    Colonel, U.S. Army; Director, Legal Division, Office of Military Government for Germany (U.S.), 1948–1949. Correspondence, memoranda, reports, press releases, and minutes of meetings, relating to administration of justice in the U.S. occupation zone in Germany, and to the Nuremberg war crime trials.
    Gift, J. M. Raymond, 1975.

2249

Rayski, Ludomił, 1892–1976.
    Papers (in Polish and English), 1966–1975. 1 ms. box.
    General, Polish Air Force; Commander of the Air Force, 1926–1939. Photographs, correspondence, and two histories, entitled "Fakty" (Facts) and "Poland's Treason", relating to the Polish Air Force from World War I to World War II.
    Gift, L. Rayski, 1969. Incremental gift, 1977.

2250

Reagan, Ronald, 1911–
    Papers, 1966–1976. 1795 cu. ft. boxes.
    Governor of California, 1967–1975. Correspondence, cabinet proceedings, speeches, notes, legislation, campaign material, press releases, printed matter, video tapes, film and phonotapes, relating to California politics and government, and to the candidacy of R. Reagan for the 1976 Republican Presidential nomination. Includes records of Citizens for Reagan, 1975–1976.
    Preliminary inventory.
    May be used with permission of R. Reagan or one of the trustees of the collection. Material already released publicly is open without restriction.
    Gift, R. Reagan, 1975. Subsequent increments.

2251

Rechtin, Eberhardt, 1926–
    Miscellaneous papers, 1968–1973. ½ ms. box.
    American engineer; Director, Advanced Research Projects Agency, U.S. Department of Defense, 1967–1970; Principal Deputy Director for Defense Research and Engineering, 1970–1971; Assistant Secretary of Defense for Telecommunications, 1972–1973. Writings and speeches, relating to national defense.
    Gift, E. Rechtin, 1978.

2252

Reconstruction Service Committee.
Memorandum, 1942. 1 folder.
Typescript.
Private American organization for the promotion of post-World War II reconstruction. Relates to the establishment of the U.S. Office of Foreign Relief and Rehabilitation Operations.

2253

Red Cross. International Committee, Geneva. Centenary Congress, 1963—collection, 1957–1964. 3 ms. boxes.
Reports, press releases, and printed matter, relating to the Centenary Congress of the International Red Cross at Geneva.
Gift, Sally Hayes, 1967.

2254

Red Cross. U.S. American National Red Cross.
Records, 1917–1921. 217 ms. boxes, 38 vols., 2 scrapbooks.
American charitable organization. Correspondence, memoranda, reports, financial records and photographs, relating to relief work in Europe, the Middle East, China and Siberia during and immediately after World War I.
Preliminary inventory.
Gift, American National Red Cross, 1928. Subsequent increments.

2255

Red Myth.
Motion picture, 1961. 13 reels.
Relates to the history of communism. Produced for television by KQED-TV, San Francisco, in cooperation with the Hoover Institution on War, Revolution and Peace.
Gift, National Educational Television, 1961.

2256

Redlich, Fritz, 1892–
Correspondence (in German), 1928–1958. ½ ms. box, 1 envelope.
German-American economist and historian. Correspondence, primarily with Wilhelm Gehlhoff, German economist, concerning conditions in German universities after World Wars I and II. Includes personal letters received by Annemarie Labes, sister of F. Redlich, 1947–1957.
Gift, F. Redlich.

2257

Reed, Alice C., b. 1890.
Excerpts from letters, 1916–1948. 1 folder.
American missionary in China, 1916–1948. Relates to social conditions and Christian missionary work in China.
May not be quoted without permission of A. C. Reed.
Gift, A. C. Reed, 1967.

2258

Reiche, V. H. E.
Diary, 1944–1945. 1 folder.
Holograph.
Major, South African Army; German prisoner of war, 1944–1945. Relates to conditions in the German prison camp at Hadamar bei Limberg.

2259

Reichsgruppe Handel. Wirtschaftsgruppe Einzelhandel.
Memorandum (in German), 1939. "Sicherstellung der Versorgung in den Neuen Staedten des Fuehrers durch Errichtung und Finanzierung Gewerblicher und Kultureller Betriebe" (Guaranty of Provisions in the New Cities of the Fuehrer through Establishment and Financing of Commercial and Cultural Operations). 1 vol.
Typescript (mimeographed).
Retail trade agency of the German Government.

2260

Reifenberg, Benno, 1900–
History (in German), ca. 1946. "Zur Geschichte der *Frankfurter Zeitung* seit 1933" (On the History of the *Frankfurter Zeitung* since 1933). 1 vol.
Typescript.
Relates to the German newspaper *Frankfurter Zeitung* during the Nazi regime in Germany.

2261

Remer, Charles F., 1889–1972.
Papers, 1915–1967. 43 ms. boxes, 1 album, 7 envelopes, 6 phonorecords.
American economist. Correspondence, writings, notes, studies, speeches, clippings, and printed matter, relating to the political and economic development of the Far East, especially China.
Register.
Gift, Adah Langmaid, 1972.

2262

Rempel, David, *collector.*
Photographs, 1945. 2 envelopes.
Depicts the signing of documents of surrender by German authorities at the end of World War II.
Gift, D. Rempel, 1948.

2263

Renne, Louis Obed.
History, 1954. *Our Day of Empire: War and the Exile of Japanese-Americans.* ½ ms. box.
Typescript.
Relates to the internment of Japanese-Americans during World War II. Published (Glasgow: Strickland Press, 1954).
Gift, Elsie Renne, 1977.

2264

Renner, Karl, Pres. Austria, 1870–1950.
Interview (in French and German), 1947. 1 vol.
Typewritten transcript.

President of Austria. Relates to Austrian politics. Interview conducted by Jacques de Launay.

2265

"Report on Los Baños Internment Camp."
Report, 1943. 1 vol.
Typescript.
Relates to American prisoners in the Japanese prison camp at Los Baños, Philippine Islands. Report prepared by released prisoners for the U.S. State Department.

2266

Representatives of the German Industry.
Broadside, 1914. 1 folder.
Printed.
German propaganda distributed to Americans leaving Berlin at the outbreak of World War I.

2267

Republican Party. National Convention, 25th, Chicago, 1952—memoir, n.d. 1 folder.
Typescript.
Relates to the Republican National Convention of July 1952, Earl Warren, Dwight D. Eisenhower, and Richard M. Nixon. Written by a convention messenger.
May be used only by persons agreeing not to disclose the identity of the author.

2268

Republican Party. National Convention, 30th, Miami, Fla., 1972.
Program, 1972. 1 vol.
Printed.
Gift, George Hart, 1976.

2269

Requa, Mark Lawrence, 1866–1937.
Memoirs, n.d. 1 folder.
Holograph and typescript (photocopy).
Assistant to the U.S. Food Administrator, 1917–1918; Director, Oil Division, U.S. Fuel Administration, 1918–1919. Relates to activities of the Tax Association of Alameda County, California, in 1912, and of the U.S. Food Administration during World War I.
Gift, Amy Requa Russell, 1976.

2270

Réquin, Edouard Jean, 1879–1953.
Papers (in French), 1915–1940. 4 ms. boxes.
General, French Army; liaison officer between French and American General Staffs, 1918; Commanding General, French 4th Army, 1939–1940. Correspondence, military orders, memoranda, and writings, relating to Allied military operations in World War I, particularly Franco-American military cooperation; to proposals for a treaty of mutual assistance under auspices of the League of Nations, 1922–1923; and to operations of the French 4th Army, May–June 1940.

2271

Rerberg, Fedor Petrovich, b. 1868.
Memoirs (in Russian and French), 1922–1925. 1 ms. box.
Holograph and typescript.
Russian Imperial Army officer; Chief of Staff, X Corps, and Chief of Staff, Sevastopol' Fortress, during World War I. Relates to the X Corps, the Sevastopol' Fortress during World War I and the Russian Civil War, and White Russian and Allied military activities in the Crimea during the Russian Civil War.

2272

Rethel, France. Bureau Communal.
Miscellaneous records (in French), 1914–1918. 1 vol.
Town council of Rethel, France. Copies of correspondence with the German occupation authorities and minutes of meetings.

2273

Reutlingen, Germany—photographs, 1951. 1 envelope.
Depicts the city of Reutlingen, Germany, and vicinity.
Gift, city of Reutlingen, 1951.

2274

"Revel'skaia Gavan' i Bol'sheviki" (Revel Harbor and the Bolsheviks).
Report (in Russian), 1921. 1 vol.
Typescript (carbon copy).
Relates to commerce conducted through the port of Tallinn, Estonia, during the Russian Civil War.

2275

"Die Revolution in der Deutschen Erziehung" (The Revolution in German Education).
Memorandum (in German), n.d. 1 folder.
Typescript.
Relates to education in Germany under national socialism during World War II.

2276

Rey, Sir Charles, d. 1968.
Diaries, 1929–1937. 1 ms. box.
Typewritten transcript of original located at the Botswana National Archives.
British colonial administrator; Resident Commissioner, Bechuanaland Protectorate, 1929–1937. Relates to description and administration of Bechuanaland.

2277

Reymershoffer, Charles, b. 1873.
Petition, 1929. 1 folder.
Typescript.
American citizen living in Germany. Relates to the claim of C. Reymershoffer against the German Government for financial losses resulting from the deposit of his savings in German banks and the subsequent loss of value of German currency. Petition addressed to the U.S. Senate.

2278

Reynolds, Elliott H.
    Letters to Helen B. Sutleff, 1918–1919. 1 folder.
    Holograph.
    Private, U.S. Army. Relating to activities of the American Expeditionary Force in Siberia.

2279

Reynolds, Ralph Hubbard, b. 1888.
    Correspondence, 1944–1945. 3 ms. boxes.
    Typescript (mimeographed) and holograph.
    Correspondence with Stanford University alumni in the U.S. Armed Forces, relating to military life and the home front in the U.S. during World War II.

2280

Rhode, Ilse.
    Translation of excerpts from study, n.d. "The Racial Position in West Prussia and Posen at the Time of the Partition of Poland." 1 folder.
    Relates to the national composition of the West Prussian and Posen populations. Original article published in the *Deutsche Wissenschaftliche Zeitschrift fuer Polen*, 1926.

2281

Rhodes, Cecil John, 1853–1902.
    Miscellany, 1886–1930. ½ ms. box, 1 envelope.
    British financier and politician. Copies of letters, clippings, and miscellanea, relating to C. Rhodes, to the Rhodes scholarships, and to the Rhodes Scholar reunion at Oxford University in 1929. Includes a copy of the will of C. Rhodes.

2282

Rhodes, Charles Dudley, 1865–1948.
    Diary extracts, 1885–1911. ½ ms. box.
    Typescript (photocopy).
    Major General, U.S. Army. Relates to the Indian campaign of 1890–1891; the expedition to Santiago de Cuba, 1898; the China Relief Expedition, 1900; Philippine insurgency, 1901–1903; and a secret mission to Mexico, 1911.
    Gift, U.S. Military Academy.

2283

Rîabukhin, N. M.
    Translation of memoir, n.d. "The Story of Baron Ungern-Sternberg." 1 vol.
    Russian staff physician to Baron Roman Ungern-Shternberg. Relates to activities of White Russian military forces under Baron Ungern-Shternberg in Mongolia during the Russian Civil War.

2284

Richardson, Gardner.
    Papers, 1911–1924. ½ ms. box, 2 albums, 2 envelopes, 1 portfolio.
    Official of the Commission for Relief in Belgium and of the American Relief Administration in Austria. Photographs, resolutions, and letters of gratitude, relating to relief work in Styria, Austria, and in Odessa, Russia, and to the University of Vienna Children's Clinic.
    Gift, G. Richardson.

2285

Richardson, Grace, *collector*.
    Miscellany, 1919. 1 folder.
    Printed matter, clippings and badges, relating to the League to Enforce Peace, the American Red Cross, a 1919 reception for President Woodrow Wilson in Omaha, Nebraska, and women's suffrage in Nebraska.
    Preliminary inventory.
    Gift, G. Richardson, 1949.

2286

Richardson, Robert Charlwood, Jr., 1882–1954.
    Papers, 1917–1954. 71 ms. boxes.
    General, U.S. Army; Military Governor of Hawaii and Commanding General, U.S. Army Forces in the Pacific Ocean Areas, 1943–1946. Correspondence, bulletins, directives, maps, and photographs, relating to American military operations in the Pacific Theater during World War II.
    Preliminary inventory.
    Gift, R. C. Richardson III, 1968. Incremental gift, 1970.

2287

Richter, Rudolf.
    Miscellany (in German), 1935. 1 folder.
    Memoranda, correspondence and forms, submitted by R. Richter as part of the required application for membership in the Schutzstaffel of the German Nazi Party, relating to his genealogy.

2288

Ridge, William Sheldon, b. 1875
    Papers, 1905–1939. 14 ms. boxes.
    Editor, *Peking Chronicle*. Clippings and notes, relating to political, social and economic conditions in China and to Chinese history, foreign relations and civilization.
    Purchase, Mrs. W. S. Ridge, 1947.

2289

Riebe, Friedrich, 1901–
    Personnel records (in German), 1944. 1 folder.
    Private, German Army; guard at Sachsenhausen concentration camp.

2290

Riedel, E. G., *collector*.
    Photographs, 1945. 6 envelopes.
    Depicts the surrender of the German Navy at Flensburg, 1945; V-E Day in Paris, May 8, 1945; and war-damaged buildings in various German cities, 1945.

2291

Rieffel, Aristide, 1859–1941.
Papers (in French and English), 1890–1941. 20 l. ft.
French journalist and pacifist. Correspondence, writings, pamphlets, clippings, and photographs, relating primarily to the temperance movement in France and the U.S., pacifism, international arbitration, the Society for Arbitration between Nations, Alfred Nobel and the Nobel Peace Prize.
Gift, Mireille Rieffel Gale, 1976.

2292

Riegger, Fred G.
Memorandum, n.d., "My Theory of Life." 1 folder.
Typescript.
Relates to philosophy.

2293

Rietveld, Harriet.
Papers, 1925–1941. ½ ms. box.
Missionary. Notes, educational material, and printed matter, relating to missionary work of the Young Women's Christian Association in Chefoo, China; to 1931 flood relief in China; and to other missionary activities in China.
Gift, H. Rietveld, 1973.

2294

Riga, Treaty of, 1920.
Translation of preliminary peace treaty and armistice, 1920. 1 folder.
Typescript.
Treaty between Poland and Russia, signed at Riga, October 11, 1920, halting the Russo-Polish War.

2295

Riggs, Ernest Wilson, 1881–1952.
Papers, 1915–1944. ½ ms. box.
President, Euphrates College, Harput, Turkey, 1910–1921; Child Welfare Director, Near East Relief, 1920–1921. Memoirs and correspondence, relating to Turkish atrocities against Armenians in 1915; the expulsion of Americans from Turkey, 1920–1921; Turkish-U.S. relations; and conditions in Greece during World War II.
Gift, E. W. Riggs.

2296

Rijksinstituut voor Oorlogsdocumentatie.
Prospectus (in Dutch, German and English), 1952–1953. 1 folder.
Typescript (mimeographed).
Dutch institution for the study of war history. Notes and summaries for a projected series of publications, relating to the history of the Netherlands during World War II.

2297

Ringland, Arthur C.
Papers, 1921–1960. 1 folder.
American Relief Administration worker in Czechoslovakia, 1921–1922. Memoranda and printed matter, relating to League of Nations cooperation with American Relief Administration activities in Russia, the attitude of Aleksandr Kerenskiĭ in 1921 toward American Relief Administration activities in Russia, and subsequent Soviet attitudes toward American Relief Administration activities in Russia.
Gift, A. C. Ringland, 1959. Subsequent increments.

2298

Ritter, Gerhard, b. 1888.
Writings (in German), 1947. 1 folder.
German historian. Writings, including "Kirche und Internationale Ordnung" (The Church and the International Order), relating to the ecumenical movement and world peace, and "Die Faelschung des Deutschen Geschichtbildes im Hitlerreich" (The Falsification of the German Historical Image in the Hitler Reich).

2299

Robb, Felix C.
Papers, 1955–1965. ½ ms. box.
American educator; Director, Southern Association of Colleges and Schools; member, Korean Project, George Peabody College for Teachers, 1956–1962. Correspondence, writings, photocopies of contracts, and printed matter, relating to a project of the George Peabody College for Teachers to provide technical assistance for the improvement of education in South Korea.
Gift, F. C. Robb, 1978.

2300

Roberts, Frank N.
Papers, 1940–1943. 1 ms. box.
Colonel, U.S. Army. Memoranda, reports, operations journals, rosters, notes, charts, maps, military studies, and intelligence summaries, relating to the operations of the Allied armed forces in Burma, and the Japanese occupation of Burma during World War II.

2301

Robinett, Paul McDonald.
Papers, 1947–1967. ½ ms. box.
Brigadier General, U.S. Army. Writings, copies of correspondence, and a pamphlet, relating to the battle of Kasserine Pass during World War II; to the book by Martin Blumenson, *Kasserine Pass* (Boston, 1967); and to centralization of the U.S. armed forces in 1947. Includes a translation of the book by Charles Dupont, *Le Haut Commandement Allemand en 1914* (The German High Command in 1914) (Paris, 1922).

2302

Robinson, Arthur Granville, 1892–1967.
Papers, 1913–1968. ½ ms. box, 1 envelope.
Vice Admiral, U.S. Navy; Captain, U.S.S. *Marblehead*, 1940–1942; President, Military Commission on War Crimes in the Pacific Area, 1946–1949. Writings and printed matter, relating to American naval operations in World War II, the bombing of the *Marblehead* in 1942, and trials of Japanese accused of war crimes.
Gift, Mrs. Nelson Nowell, 1974.

2303

Robinson, Henry Mauris, 1869–1937.

Papers, 1917–1932. 27 ms. boxes, 1 envelope, 12 medals.

American lawyer and banker; U.S. representative at various international economic conferences. Correspondence, reports, minutes of meetings, memoranda, notes, printed matter, and medals, relating to the U.S. Council of National Defense during World War I, the Paris Peace Conference, the Allied Supreme Economic Council, the Dawes and Young Committees on Reparations, and the International Economic Conference of 1927.

Register.

Gift, Mrs. H. M. Robinson, 1943. Incremental gift, 1947.

2304

Robinson, Jacob, *editor.*

Bibliography, 1958. *Guide to Research in Jewish History, 1933–1945: Its Background and Aftermath.* 1 vol.

Typescript (mimeographed).

Published (New York, 1958). Edited by J. Robinson and Philip Friedman.

2305

Robnett, George Washington, 1890?–1970.

Papers, 1932–1963. ½ ms. box.

American author and lecturer; Executive Director, Church League of America, and National Laymen's Council, 1937–1956. Reports, speeches, and writings, relating to federal control of education, and to socialist and communist movements in America.

Preliminary inventory.

Gift, Mrs. G. W. Robnett, 1974.

2306

Rode, Lucien J.

Photographs, 1918–1919. 6 envelopes.

Second Lieutenant, U.S. Army Signal Corps; official photographer, Headquarters of General John J. Pershing, Chaumont, France, 1918–1919. Depicts General J. J. Pershing, scenes at his headquarters, and activities of U.S. troops elsewhere in France during World War I.

Gift, Mrs. L. J. Rode, 1959.

2307

Rodgers, Marvin.

Thesis, 1966. "Herbert Hoover and American Relief: A Study of the Relationship between Hoover's American Relief Program and Bolshevism in Europe in 1919." 1 folder.

Typescript (photocopy).

M. A. thesis, Fresno State College.

Gift, M. Rodgers, 1966.

2308

Rodichev, Fedor Izmailovich, 1854–1933.

Memoirs (in Russian), 1924. "Vospominaniîa F. I. Rodicheva o 1917 godu" (Reminiscences of F. I. Rodichev about 1917). 1 folder.

Typescript.

Leader of Russian Konstitutŝionno-Demokraticheskaîa Partiîa; member of all Gosudarstvennaîa Dumas; Minister for Finnish Affairs in the Provisional Government, 1917. Relates to events in Russia during the 1917 Revolution. Includes a biographical sketch of F. I. Rodichev by his daughter, Alexandrine Rodichev, 1933.

2309

Roditi, Harold, *collector.*

Miscellany (in French), 1915–1919. 1 folder.

Safe-conducts, passes and identity cards issued for French military zones during World War I.

Gift, H. Roditi, 1970.

2310

Rodkey, Fred Stanley, 1896–

Papers, 1944–1969. 1 folder.

Captain, U.S. Army. Correspondence and diaries, relating to proposals for psychological warfare activities during World War II.

2311

Rodzianko, Mikhail Vladimirovich, 1859–1924.

Papers (in Russian), 1914–1921. ½ ms. box.

President, Gosudarstvennaîa Duma of Russia. Correspondence, writings, and reports, relating to Russian efforts in World War I, the Russian Revolution and Civil War, and the anti-Bolshevik movements. Includes letters and reports to Generals Vrangel′ and Denikin.

Preliminary inventory.

Gift, Nikolai Golovin, 1927.

2312

Rogers, Leighton W.

Memoir, n.d. "An Account of the March Revolution, 1917." 1 folder.

Typescript.

American official, Petrograd branch, National City Bank, 1917. Relates to the Russian Revolution of February 1917.

2313

Rogers, Pleas B., 1895–

Papers, 1918. 1 folder.

Brigadier General, U.S. Army. Field messages, annotated maps, and notes, relating to activities of the U.S. 36th Division in the Meuse-Argonne region during World War I.

Gift, P. B. Rogers, 1973.

2314

Rolland, Romain, 1866–1944.

Miscellaneous papers (in French), 1932–1935. 1 vol.

French communist intellectual. Correspondence and printed matter, relating to the communist and pacifist movements in France, especially the Association Républicaine des Anciens Combattants. Includes correspondence of Henri Barbusse, Guy Jerram and other pro-communist French intellectuals.

Preliminary inventory.

Gift, Branko Lazitch, 1963.

2315

Romanian National Committee, Washington, D.C.
Records (in Romanian and English), 1946–1975. 19½ ms. boxes.
Anti-communist Romanian émigré organization. Correspondence, memoranda, minutes of meetings, reports, financial records, printed matter, press releases, speeches, and writings, relating to communism in Romania, anti-communist émigré activities, the Assembly of Captive European Nations, the National Committee for a Free Europe, and the Free Europe Committee.
Closed until January 1, 1987.
Gift, Constantin Visoianu, 1976. Incremental gift, 1977.

2316

"Romania's Internal Policy since World War I."
Memorandum, n.d. 1 folder.
Typescript.
Relates to political conditions and rural social structure in Romania between the two world wars.

2317

Romer, Tadeusz, 1894–
Papers (in Polish), 1913–1975. 9 reels.
Microfilm of originals at the Public Archives of Canada.
Polish statesman, diplomat and professor; Ambassador to the Soviet Union, 1942–1943; Minister of Foreign Affairs, Polish Government-in-Exile (London), 1943–1944. Correspondence, memoranda, speeches and writings, reports, telegrams, minutes of meetings, clippings and printed matter, relating to political events in Poland, Polish foreign relations, and Polish émigré politics.
Preliminary inventory.
May not be used without the permission of T. Romer or his representative until ten years after the death of T. Romer.
Exchange, Public Archives of Canada, 1977.

2318

Rommel (Erwin)—photograph, n.d. 1 envelope.
Depicts Field Marshal E. Rommel, German Army.

2319

Ronzhin, Sergeĭ Aleksandrovich.
Study (in Russian), 1925. "Zheliezn'yĭa Dorogoĭ v Voennoe Vremia" (Railroads in Wartime). 1 folder.
Typescript.
General, Russian Imperial Army. Relates to the use of railroads in Russia during World War I.

2320

Roosevelt (Eleanor)—photographs, 1942. 1 envelope.
Depicts the visit of E. Roosevelt (1884–1962), writer, and wife of Franklin D. Roosevelt, President of the U.S., to Great Britain, November 1942.

2321

Roosevelt, Franklin Delano, Pres. U.S., 1882–1945.
Speeches, 1933–1945. 12 phonorecords.
President of U.S., 1933–1945. Relates to U.S. domestic politics and foreign policy. Issued by the National Broadcasting Company, 1946.

2322

Rosdolsky, Roman.
Study (in German), n.d. "Fr. Engels und das Problem der 'Geschichtlosen' Voelker: die Nationalitaetenfrage in der Revolution, 1848–1849 im Lichte der *Neuen Rheinischen Zeitung*" (Fr. Engels and the Problem of 'Historyless' Peoples: The Nationality Question in the Revolution of 1848–1849 in the Light of the *Neue Rheinische Zeitung*). 1 vol.
Typescript (mimeographed).

2323

Rose, Ernest D.
Study, 1961. "How the U.S. Heard About Pearl Harbor." 1 folder.
Typescript.
Relates to the dissemination of information to the American public by radio commentators about the Pearl Harbor attack, 1941.

2324

Rosenbaum-Maier collection on the relocation of Japanese Americans, 1935–1944. 1 ms. box.
Clippings and bibliographical materials, relating to the evacuation, detention, and relocation of persons of Japanese ancestry in the U.S. during World War II. Includes a list of state legislation passed concerning Japanese with copies of the legislation. Collected by Crane Rosenbaum and Henry Maier.
Preliminary inventory.

2325

Rosenberg, Alfred, 1893–1946.
Memorandum (in German), 1939. 1 folder.
Typewritten transcript.
German national socialist leader. Relates to a conversation between A. Rosenberg and Lord Kimsley on the subject of Anglo-German relations.

2326

Rosenbluth, Robert.
Reports, 1919. 1 folder.
Typescript.
American Relief Administration worker in Russia, 1919. Reports, entitled "General Resumé, Russian Situation" and "Memorandum on Russian Affairs," relating to political and economic conditions and relief needs in Russia.

2327

Rosenthal, Ernst, *compiler*.
Memorandum (in German), 1944. "Das Recht des Juedischen Siedlungsgebiets Theresienstadt" (The Law of the Jewish Settlement Area Theresienstadt). 1 folder.
Chief, Detective Division, Terezin concentration camp, Bohemia.
Gift, Frederick E. Kahn, 1978.

2328

Ross, Frank Seymoure, 1893–1970.

Papers, 1942–1954. 20 ms. boxes, 3 albums.

Major General, U.S. Army; Chief of Transportation, European Theater of Operations, 1942–1946. Correspondence, minutes of meetings, notes, reports, printed matter, and photographs, relating to activities of the U.S. Army Transportation Corps in Europe during World War II.

Preliminary inventory.

Gift, F. S. Ross, 1960.

2329

Rossiĭskaiā Sotsial-Demokraticheskaiā Rabochaiā Partiiā.

Miscellaneous issuances (in Russian), ca. 1904–1910. 1 folder.

Printed.

Russian Social Democratic Labor Party. Notice of change of address of party headquarters in Geneva, 1904; broadside relating to tsarist agents provocateurs and the trial of socialist deputies of the Duma, 1907; and proclamation by the Vpered Group relating to internal party politics, ca. 1910.

Gift, Antony Sutton, 1970.

2330

Rossiĭsko-Amerikanskaiā Kompaniiā—summaries of laws (in Russian), ca. 1700–1860. 1 folder.

Typescript and printed.

Laws made by the Russian Government to regulate settlements established by the Russian-American Company on the Pacific coast of North America.

2331

Rost van Tonningen, Meinoud Marinus, 1894–1945.

Memorandum (in Dutch), 1940. 1 folder.

Typescript.

Dutch fascist leader. Relates to a conversation with the former chairman of the Dutch Socialist Party, concerning the dissolution of the Dutch Socialist Party in the German-occupied Netherlands.

2332

Rostovtseff, Fedor.

Papers (in Russian), n.d. 2 ms. boxes.

Russian émigré teacher in France. Writings, reports, notes and outlines for lectures, clippings, memorabilia, and syllabi for courses in Russian high schools in Paris, relating to Russian history from 1850 to 1940, French history, and logic.

Gift, F. Rostovtseff.

2333

Rote Fahne (Red Flag).

Translations of newspaper articles, 1919. 1 folder.

Typescript.

German communist newspaper. Relates to the Hungarian Soviet Republic. Translated by Eupemie Emiger.

2334

Rote Kapelle (German resistance movement)—biographical notes, n.d. 1 folder.

Typescript.

Relates to members of the German anti-Nazi resistance movement Rote Kapelle during World War II.

2335

Roter Frontkaempferbund—collection, 1922–1929. 1 envelope.

Postcards and photographs, depicting communist rallies and parades in Germany, held under the auspices of the Roter Frontkaempferbund and other organizations.

2336

Rouček, Joseph Slabey, 1902–

Papers, 1920–1949. 38 ms. boxes, 2 envelopes.

American sociologist and political scientist. Correspondence, writings, clippings, photographs, slides, and miscellanea, relating to Slavs in the U.S., and politics, social conditions, and education in Eastern Europe, especially the Balkan countries.

Register.

Gift, J. S. Rouček, 1949.

2337

Rougier, Louis Auguste Paul, b. 1889.

Tear sheets of journal article (in French), 1946. "Le Réquisitoire de M. Albert Kammerer au Sujet de l'Armistice" (The Indictment of Mr. Albert Kammerer on the Subject of the Armistice). 1 folder.

Relates to the book by Albert Kammerer, *La Vérité sur l'Armistice* (The Truth about the Armistice) (Paris, 1944), on the French surrender in 1940. Article published in *Questions Actuelles* (No. 23, August-September 1946).

2338

Round Table on Possible Psychological Contributions in a National Emergency, Washington, 1939.

Summary of proceedings, 1939. 1 folder.

Typescript (mimeographed).

Conference sponsored by the American Association for Applied Psychology. Relates to prospects for the development of psychological warfare.

2339

Rounds, Leland Lassels, 1891–

Papers, 1917–1954. 1 ms. box.

American aviator, Lafayette Escadrille, during World War I; U.S. Vice Consul, Oran, Algeria, 1941–1943; member, Office of Strategic Services, during World War II. Memoranda, orders, correspondence, and photographs, relating to the Lafayette Escadrille, and to preparation for the Allied landings in North Africa in 1942.

Preliminary inventory.

Gift, Edward de Pianelli, 1971.

2340

Rowan, Andrew Summers, 1857–1943.
Papers, 1891–1940. 9 ms. boxes, 7 scrapbooks.
Major, U.S. Army. Writings, correspondence, military orders, clippings, serial issues, maps, and photographs, relating to the exploit of A. S. Rowan in carrying the "message to Garcia" during the Spanish-American War, and to other U.S. military activities in Cuba and the Philippines during the war and the Philippine insurrection.
Gift, Mrs. A. S. Rowan, 1945.

2341

Rowe, David Nelson, 1905–
Papers (in English and Chinese), 1931–1974. 136 ms. boxes, 1 oversize box.
American political scientist; Special Assistant to the U.S. Ambassador to China, 1941–1942. Correspondence, speeches and writings, notes, reports, printed matter, photographs, slides, phonotapes, microfilm, maps, posters, post cards and memorabilia, relating to Chinese history and foreign relations, Asian area studies, Japanese World War II propaganda, application of the People's Republic of China for admission to the United Nations, and communism in Asia.
May not be used without written permission of D. N. Rowe.
Deposit, D. N. Rowe, 1978.

2342

Rowell, Chester H.
Newspaper article, 1934. "Catalog of the Reds!" 1 folder.
Typewritten transcript.
Relates to the anticommunist movement in the U.S. Published in the *San Francisco Chronicle*, May 14, 1934.

2343

Rowell, Milo E., 1904?–
Papers, 1945–1946. ½ ms. box.
Lieutenant Colonel, U.S. Army; military lawyer, Government Section, General Headquarters, Supreme Commander for the Allied Powers, 1945–1946. Reports, drafts, and memoranda, relating to the writing of the revised Japanese constitution.
Gift, M. E. Rowell, 1975.

2344

Rozenshil'd-Paulin, Anatoliĭ Nikolaevich.
Diary extracts (in Russian), 1915–1916. 1 vol.
Typescript (carbon copy).
General, Russian Imperial Army; Commanding General, 29th Infantry Division. Relates to operations of the 29th Division during World War I and to the imprisonment of A. N. Rozenshil'd-Paulin in a German prison camp.

2345

Rudneff, Ilya Alexeevich, 1892–1969.
Papers (in Russian), 1913–1923. 1 ms. box, 3 envelopes.
Colonel, Russian Imperial Air Forces. Correspondence, photographs, and miscellany, relating to Russian aviation in World War I, and White Russian military activities during the Russian Civil War.
Gift, Bertha Rudneff, 1970.

2346

"Rufe aus dem Felde" (Voices from the Field).
Poems (in German), n.d. 1 folder.
Typescript.
Relates to German war policy during World War I.

2347

Ruhl, Arthur.
Series of articles, 1925. "Russia Revisited." 1 folder.
Typescript.
American visitor to Russia. Relates to social conditions and the situation of industry, education and religion in Russia.

2348

Rukhlov (Sergeĭ Vasil'evich)—photograph, n.d. 1 envelope.
Depicts the tsarist Russian government official S. V. Rukhlov.

2349

Russell, Anna, *collector*.
Letters, 1918. 1 folder.
Letters from American soldiers, relating to their experiences in France during World War I. Some letters were written from military camps in the U.S.
Gift, A. Russell, 1963.

2350

Russell, Bruce.
Cartoon, 1959. 1 envelope.
Hand-drawn.
Relates to the Antarctic Treaty of 1959.
Gift, Mary M. DeWitt, 1960.

2351

Russell, Francis H.
Memoir, 1947. "Around the World in Thirteen Days." 1 folder.
Typescript (mimeographed).
Passenger on the first scheduled commercial round-the-world airplane flight, 1947. Relates to the flight.

2352

Russell, Frank Marion, b. 1886, *collector*.
Memoranda (in English and French), 1923. 1 folder.
Typescript (some mimeographed).
Relates to French administration of the Saar coal mines.

2353

Russell, Mrs. Henry Potter.
Papers, 1946–1958. 25 ms. boxes.
Member, U.S. National Committee for UNESCO. Correspondence, reports, memoranda, position papers, resolutions, and minutes, relating to the activities of the

United Nations Educational, Scientific and Cultural Organization and the U.S. National Commission for UNESCO.
  Gift, Mrs. H. P. Russell, 1954. Incremental gift, 1960.

2354
Russell, Tom, *collector.*
  Campaign literature, 1928. 1 folder.
  Printed.
  Republican campaign literature, relating to Herbert Hoover and the Presidential election of 1928.
  Gift, T. Russell, 1956.

2355
Russia. Armiiâ. Kavkazskaîâ Armiîâ.
  Miscellaneous records (in Russian), 1915–1916. 1 folder.
  Russian Imperial Caucasian Army. Orders, reports and a map, relating to Russian military operations in Transcaucasia during World War I.

2356
Russia. Armiiâ. 10. Korpus.
  War journal (in Russian), 1914. 1 vol.
  Typescript.
  Russian Imperial 10th Army Corps. Relates to activities of the 10th Corps at the outbreak of World War I, August 10–31, 1914.

2357
Russia, Armiiâ. Leib-Gvardiĭ Kirasirskiĭ Ego Velichestva Polk—collection (in Russian), 1916–1974. 7 ms. boxes, 1 album.
  Correspondence, diaries, reports, memoranda, newsletters, books, photographs, and printed matter, relating to the activities of the Imperial Russian Kirasir Household Troops Regiment of His Majesty before and during the Russian Revolution and Civil War and to the activities of surviving members in foreign countries after their emigration from Russia.
  Preliminary inventory.
  Gift, Russian Historical Archive and Repository, 1975.

2358
Russia. Departament Politsiĭ. Zagranichnaîâ Agentura, Paris.
  Records (mainly in Russian), 1883–1917. 203 ms. boxes, 10 vols. of clippings, 163,802 biographical and reference cards, 8 linear feet of photographs.
  Russian Imperial Secret Police (Okhrana), Paris office. Intelligence reports from agents in the field and the Paris office, dispatches, circulars, headquarters studies, correspondence of revolutionaries, and photographs, relating to activities of Russian revolutionists abroad.
  Preliminary inventory.
  Deposit, Vasiliĭ Maklakov, 1926. One item purchased from Jacob Rubin, 1976.

2359
Russia—famines—photographs, 1922–1923. 1 envelope.
  Depicts Russian famine scenes.
  Gift, Fresno State College Library.

2360
Russia, Gosudarstvennaîâ Duma—collection (in Russian and English), 1906–1916. 1 ms. box, 1 envelope.
  Proclamations, speeches, photograph and translation of proceedings of the Russian Duma, relating to activities of the Duma and to political conditions in Russia.

2361
Russia—history—Revolution of 1905—photograph, n.d. 1 envelope.
  Depicts a poster commemorating the Russian Revolution of 1905.

2362
Russia—history—revolution, 1917–1921—collection (in Russian), ca. 1917–1921. 1 ms. box.
  Miscellaneous posters and broadsides, and photocopies of newspaper and periodical articles, relating to the Russian Civil War.

2363
Russia—history—German occupation, 1941–1944—proclamations (in German, Russian and Ukrainian), 1941. 1 folder.
  Printed.
  Relates to regulations imposed upon the civilian population of Russia. Issued by German occupation authorities.

2364
Russia. Kabinet Ego Imperatorskago Velichestva Ispolnitel'naîâ Kommissiîâ po Ustroĭstvu zemel' Glukhoozerskoĭ Fermy.
  Account book (in Russian), 1900. 1 vol.
  Holograph.
  Russian Imperial Cabinet Executive Commission for the Organization of Lands of the Glukhoozerskaîâ Farm. Relates to expenses of digging canals on the Glukhoozerskaîâ Farm, an estate of Nicholas II, Tsar of Russia.

2365
Russia. Konsul'stvo, Breslau.
  Records (in Russian and German), 1860–1914. 10 ms. boxes.
  Russian Consulate in Breslau. Correspondence, intelligence reports, orders, and printed matter, relating to Russian-German relations, especially commercial relations.
  Preliminary inventory.
  Gift, Serge Botkine, 1929.

2366
Russia. Konsul'stvo, Leipzig.
  Records (in Russian and German), 1830–1914. 7 ms. boxes.
  Russian Consulate in Leipzig. Correspondence, re-

ports, and printed matter, relating to Russian-German relations, especially commercial relations.
Preliminary inventory.
Gift, Serge Botkine, 1934.

2367

Russia. Legatsiia (Hesse).
Records (in Russian and German), 1857–1913. 17 ms. boxes.
Russian Legation in Hesse (Hesse-Darmstadt until 1866). Correspondence, reports, circulars, instructions, telegrams and printed matter, relating to Russian-German relations.
Preliminary inventory.
Gift, Serge Botkine, 1929.

2368

Russia. Legatsiia (Saxe-Weimar-Eisenach).
Records (in Russian, French and German), 1902–1908. 2 ms. boxes.
Russian Legation in Saxe-Weimer-Eisenach. Correspondence, orders, reports, and printed matter, relating to Russian-German relations.
Preliminary inventory.
Gift, Serge Botkine, 1934.

2369

Russia. Legatsiia (Wuerttemberg).
Records (in French, Russian and German), 1828–1904. 16 ms. boxes.
Russian Legation in Wuerttemberg. Correspondence, reports, orders, memoranda, and notes, relating to Russian-Wuerttemberg relations.
Preliminary inventory.
Gift, Serge Botkine, 1928.

2370

Russia. Ministerstvo Imperatorskogo Dvora.
Bulletins (in Russian), 1894. 1 folder.
Printed.
Ministry of the Imperial Court of Russia. Relates to the illness and death of Alexander III, Tsar of Russia.

2371

Russia—photographs, 1887–1977. 6 envelopes, 1 album, 20 glass slides.
Photographs and postcards, depicting members of the Romanov family and Imperial Russian nobility, military officers, statesmen, Russian churches, icons, art objects, cities, buildings, and scenes of daily life before 1917. Includes some post-1917 émigré subjects.
Various sources, various dates.

2372

Russia. Posol'stvo (France).
Records (in Russian and French), 1917–1924. 36½ ms. boxes.
Russian Embassy in France. Correspondence, reports, memoranda, and notes, relating to relations between France and the Russian Provisional Government, the Russian Revolution, counter-revolutionary movements,

the Paris Peace Conference, and Russian émigrés after the revolution.
Register.
Gift, Vasilii Maklakov, 1926. Incremental gift, G. de Lastours, 1961.

2373

Russia. Posol'stvo (U.S.).
Records (mainly in Russian), ca. 1914–1933. 260 l. ft.
Russian Imperial and Provisional Government Embassies in the U.S. Correspondence, telegrams, memoranda, reports, agreements, minutes, histories, financial records, lists, and printed matter, relating to Russia's role in World War I, the Russian Revolution and Civil War, activities of the Russian Red Cross, Russian émigrés in foreign countries, and operations of the embassy office. Includes files of the Russian Military Attaché in the U.S., the Russian Financial Agent in the U.S., and numerous Imperial Russian and Provisional Government embassies and legations which closed after the Russian Revolution and Civil War.
Gift, Serge Ughet, 1933.

2374

Russia. Shtab Verkhovnogo Glavnokomanduiushchego.
Miscellaneous records (in Russian), 1914–1917. 1 ms. box.
Supreme Command, Russian Imperial Army. Military orders and directives issued by the Supreme Command, 1914–1915, and clippings collected by the Supreme Command, 1914–1917, relating to World War I military campaigns, principally on the Eastern front.

2375

Russia. Sovet Ministrov.
Miscellany, 1914. 1 folder.
Translation (typewritten) of a summary report of the meeting of the Council of Ministers of Russia, July 11, 1914, relating to the reaction of the Russian Government to Austro-Hungarian demands made against Serbia; and a memorandum (typewritten), by Robert C. Binkley, relating to the significance of this document in assessing war guilt for the outbreak of World War I.

2376

Russia. Voenno-Morskoi Agent (Germany).
Records (in Russian and German), 1873–1912. 3 ms. boxes.
Russian Naval Agent in Germany. Correspondence, reports, orders, and printed matter, relating to Russian-German naval relations, and to Russian purchases of ships, ordnance and naval equipment from German firms.
Preliminary inventory.
Gift, Serge Botkine, 1930.

2377

Russia. Voennoe Ministerstvo.
Report (in Russian), ca. 1916. "Kratkii Otchet o Diela-tel'nosti Voennago Ministerstva za 1916 god." (Brief Re-

port on the Activities of the War Ministry for the Year 1916). 1 vol.

Typescript (carbon copy).

Russian Imperial War Ministry. Relates to Russian military activities in World War I.

2378

Russia. Voennyĭ Agent (Japan).

Records (in Russian), 1906–1921. 16 ms. boxes.

Russian Military Attaché in Japan. Letters, telegrams, contracts, minutes, receipts, memoranda, reports, accounts, declarations, requests, orders, instructions, packing and shipping specifications, invoices, insurance policies, bills of lading, blueprints, tables, diagrams, certificates, and lists, relating to the Japanese Army, political movements in Japan, and the purchase by the Russian Army of military supplies from Japanese firms.

Register.

Gift, Nikolai Golovin, 1928.

2379

Russia—World War I—collection (in Russian), 1916–1922. ½ ms. box.

Photographs, calendars, and paper cut-out caricatures, relating to Russia during World War I. Includes lithographs of Russian troops, and pictorial booklet on Russian wounded, photographs of an unidentified Russian officer and his family, caricatures of the belligerent powers, and Bolshevik calendars.

2380

Russia (1917. Provisional Government).

Photographs, 1917. 1 envelope.

Photographs issued by the Russian Provisional Government, depicting scenes of the Russian Revolution.

2381

Russia (1917. Provisional Government) Vserossiĭskoe Uchreditel'noe Sobranie.

Translation of proceedings, 1918. 1 vol.

Typescript.

All-Russian Constituent Assembly. Relates to the opening session of the assembly, January 5, 1918.

2382

Russia (1917– R.S.F.S.R.) Chrezvychaĭnaĭa Komissĭa po Bor'be s Kontr-Revoliutsieĭ i Sabotazhem—photographs, ca. 1920. 1 envelope.

Depicts atrocities committed by the Soviet secret police against White Russian forces in Kiev.

2383

Russia (1917– R.S.F.S.R.) Sovet Narodnykh Komissarov.

Appeal (in French), 1918. "Aux Masses Laborieuses de France, d'Angleterre, d'Amérique et du Japon" (To the Laboring Masses of France, England, America and Japan). 1 folder.

Printed.

Soviet People's Commission. Calls upon the peoples of these countries to protest Allied intervention in Russia.

2384

Russia (1917– R.S.F.S.R.) TSentral'naĭa Komissĭa Pomoshchi Golodaĭushchim.

Translation of report, 1922. "Totals of the Struggle against Famine in 1921–22: Collection of Articles and Reports." 1 ms. box.

Typescript.

Central Famine Relief Committee of the Soviet Government. Translated by the Russian Unit Historical Division of the American Relief Administration.

2385

Russia (1918–1920) Dobrovol'cheskaĭa Armĭa. Glavnyĭ Kaznacheĭ.

Account books (in Russian), n.d. 1 folder.

Treasury of the White Russian Volunteer Army. Relates to the financial operations for the Russian Volunteer Army.

2386

Russia (1918–1920) Donskaĭa Armĭa.

Orders (in Russian), 1918–1920. 1 ms. box.

White Russian Don Army. Relates to the Russian Civil War in the south of Russia.

2387

Russia (1918–1920) Vooruzhennye Sily IUga Rossiĭ. Nachal'nik Snabzhenĭa.

Records (in Russian), 1916–1926. 6 ms. boxes.

Chief of Supply, White Russian Army. Correspondence, reports, receipts, and accounts, relating to the payment of Russian soldiers in Bulgaria and Yugoslavia, financial subsidies to refugees, administration of refugee camp facilities, and the composition and distribution of units of the First Army Corps and the Don Corps.

Register.

Purchase, Ivan A. Holmsen, 1930.

2388

Russia (1918–1920) Vooruzhennye Sily IUga Rossiĭ. Sudnoe Otdielenie.

Records (in Russian and Bulgarian), 1918–1927. 9 ms. boxes.

Justice Department, White Russian Army. Correspondence, reports, memoranda, orders, and affidavits, relating to administration of military justice in the White Russian Army, Russian émigrés in Bulgaria, the political situation in Bulgaria, and the composition and distribution of the First Army Corps and the Don Corps.

Register.

Purchase, Ivan A. Holmsen, 1930.

2389

Russia (1918–1920) Vremennoe Sibirskoe Pravitel'stvo.

Miscellaneous records (in English and Russian), 1918–1919. 1 folder.

Provisional Government of Autonomous Siberia. Proclamations, memoranda and reports. Includes some issuances of the U.S. Army forces in Siberia, relating to the Provisional Government, and to the Civil War in Siberia.

Gift, Dimitri Panteleev.

2390

Russia (1923– U.S.S.R.) Narodnyĭ Komissariat po Inostrannym Delam.

Diagrams (in Russian), 1927. 1 vol.

Handwritten.

Soviet Commissariat for Foreign Affairs. Illustrates the organization of the commissariat.

2391

Russian Civil War in Georgia—newspaper clippings (in Russian), 1920. 1 folder.

Relates to the Russian Civil War in Georgia and elsewhere in Transcaucasia. Printed in Georgian newspapers.

2392

Russian Commercial, Industrial and Financial Union. Committee for Study of Economic Conditions.

Translation of study, 1931. "Farm 'Collectivization' in Soviet Russia." 1 folder.

Typescript (mimeographed).

Relates to agricultural policy in the Soviet Union.

2393

Russian imperial military documents—World War I (in Russian), 1915–1917. 1 folder.

Reports, orders, and maps, relating to Russian imperial military operations during World War I.

Preliminary inventory.

Gift, N. Eshchenko.

2394

Russian National Committee.

Appeal, 1921. 1 folder.

Printed.

Organization of Russian émigrés. Relates to the policy of the Great Powers toward the communist government of Russia. Addressed to the Washington Naval Conference.

2395

"Russian Public Debt: The Problem of the Distribution."

Translation of study, 1923. 1 folder.

Typescript (mimeographed).

Relates to the financial situation of the Russian Government. Study published in *Agence Economique et Financière* (August 2, 1923). Translated by S. Ughet.

2396

Russian Review.

Records, 1941–1973. 10 ms. boxes. 3 cu. ft. boxes.

Monthly periodical published at the Hoover Institution on War, Revolution and Peace. Correspondence, subscription files, unpublished articles submitted for publication, clippings, and printed matter, relating to Russian and Soviet literature, politics and government,

history, and political and social movements, before and after the Russian Revolution of 1917.

Gift, *Russian Review*, 1973.

2397

Russian revolutionary movements. 19th century posters (in Russian), 1880–1900. 1 folder.

Printed.

Leaflets and proclamations, printed in Paris, relating to Russian revolutionary movements.

2398

Russia's Five Year Plan.

Motion picture, n.d. 2 reels.

Relates to the first Five Year Plan, 1928–1932. Includes sound track.

Gift, William H. Green, 1977.

2399

"Russie: Bulletin des Annés 1917–1922" (Russia: Report on the Years 1917–1922).

Bibliographical essay (in French), ca. 1922 1 folder.

Typescript.

Relates to publications during the period 1917–1922 on the subject of Russian history.

2400

Russiian, Viktor Nikolaevich.

Study, n.d. "The Work of Okhrana Departments in Russia." 1 folder.

Typescript.

Major General, Russian Imperial Army. Relates to the structure and operations of the Russian secret service in Russia before the Revolution of 1917. Includes a draft with corrections and annotations.

2401

Russing, John.

History, n.d. "Petrograd Lancers in Service to their Country." 1 folder.

Typescript.

Relates to activities of a Russian Army regiment during World War I.

Deposit, J. Russing, 1974.

2402

"Russka͡ia Narodna͡ia Armi͡ia" (Russian People's Army).

Leaflet (in Russian), 1919. 1 folder.

Printed.

Relates to White Russian military activities during the Russian Civil War. Issued by White Russian forces in Azov.

2403

Russki͡a Vedomosti (Russian News) (Moscow).

Translation of excerpts from articles, 1918. 1 folder.

Typescript.

Moscow newspaper. Relates to instances of religious persecution of the Russian Orthodox Church in the Soviet Union. Includes accounts of events at the Alexandro-Nevskaia Lavra and the All-Russian Church Congress in Moscow, January–February 1918.

2404

Russkoe Aktsionernoe Obshchestvo dlia Primeneniia Ozona.

Issuances (in Russian), 1911–1912. 1 folder.

Russian Joint Stock Company for the Adaptation of Ozone. Relates to the establishment of a filter-ozonizing station in St. Petersburg.

2405

Russkoe Slovo (Russian Word).

Translation of excerpts from articles, n.d. 1 folder. Typescript.

Russian newspaper. Relates to the activities of Roman Malinovskiĭ, a tsarist agent who infiltrated the Bolshevik Party in Russia.

2406

Russo-Japanese War—newspaper clippings, 1904–1905. 5 ms. boxes.

Clippings, from the U.S. press, principally in San Francisco, relating to the Russo-Japanese War.

Gift, Mrs. Tanaka, 1942.

2407

Russo-Romanian relations—report (in French), 1912. 1 folder.

Typewritten transcript.

Relates to conversations between an unnamed Russian Grand Duke and a number of Romanian political leaders regarding Romanian foreign policy and Russo-Romanian relations. Written by the Grand Duke and addressed to Tsar Nicholas II.

2408

Ryan, John W., *collector*.

J. W. Ryan collection on literacy in Iran (in English and Persian), 1976–1978. 1 folder.

Pamphlets and bibliographies, published by the National Committee for World Literacy Programme and the International Institute for Adult Literacy Methods, relating to literacy in Iran.

Gift, J. W. Ryan, 1978.

2409

Ryan, Katharine E. F., d. 1950.

Commemorative tile, 1948. 1 ms. box.

American relief worker during World War II. Tile awarded by Queen Wilhelmina of the Netherlands in recognition of relief work in aid of the Dutch Red Cross during World War II.

Gift, estate of K. E. F. Ryan, 1950.

2410

Ryan, Paul B., 1913–

Papers, 1968–1976. 5 ms. boxes.

Captain, U.S. Navy; Research Associate, Hoover Institution on War, Revolution and Peace. Reports and research notes, relating to the Panama Canal. Used as re-search material for the book by P. B. Ryan, *The Panama Controversy: U.S. Diplomacy and Defense Interests* (Stanford, California: Hoover Institution Press, 1977).

Gift, P. B. Ryan, 1978.

2411

Ryerson, Knowles, 1892–   , *collector*.

Printed matter, 1918–1919. 1 ms. box.

Pamphlets, newspaper and magazine issues, and other printed matter, illustrating World War I humor through cartoons and caricatures.

Gift, K. Ryerson, 1976.

2412

Ryskulov, T.

Excerpts from a study (in Russian), 1925. *Revoliutsiia i Korennoe Naselenie Turkestana* (Revolution and the Indigenous Population of Turkestan). 1 folder.

Typescript.

Relates to the Russian Revolution in Turkestan, 1917–1919. Study published in Tashkent in 1925.

2413

Sabine, Edward G., *collector*.

Photographs, ca. 1921–1923. ½ ms. box.

Depicts famine victims and American Relief Administration relief activities in the Samara region of Russia.

Gift, John Speaks, 1961.

2414

Sabine, W. H. W., *collector*.

W. H. W. Sabine collection on Great Britain, 1916–1939. 1 ms. box.

Leaflets, posters, form letters, pamphlets, and memorabilia, relating to British war aims and propaganda efforts during World War I, civilian defense, the British Union Party, and Oswald Mosley.

Gift, W. H. W. Sabine, 1958.

2415

Sachs, Johannes.

Speech (in German), 1916. "Die Polnische Frage" (The Polish Question). 1 folder.

Typescript (mimeographed).

Relates to World War I and the question of an independent Polish state. Speech delivered in Frankfurt am Main, April 6, 1916.

2416

Sadoul, Jacques, b. 1881.

Correspondence (in French), 1939–1941. 1 folder.

French socialist leader. Relates to political conditions in France and Europe at the beginning of World War II. Correspondents include Léon Blum, Paul Reynaud and Pierre Laval.

Gift, Theodore Draper, 1966.

2417

Safonov, Ludmila Tschebotariov, 1897–

Memoirs, ca. 1974. "Only My Memories." ½ ms. box.

Typescript (photocopy).

Russian émigré in the U.S. Relates to life in Russia from 1900 until 1919, immigration through the Far East and arrival in the United States, and work with displaced persons in Europe during World War II.
Gift, L. Safonov, 1975.

2418

St. Gabriel's School, Pudu, Kuala Lumpur, Malaya.
Filmstrip, n.d. 1 reel.
Depicts scenes of commercial and industrial activity in Malaya.

2419

Sakharov, Konstantin Viâcheslavovich, b. 1881.
Letter, 1933, to William S. Graves. 1 vol.
Typescript (carbon copy).
Relates to the book by W. S. Graves, *America's Siberian Adventure, 1918–1920*.

2420

Salandra, Antonio, 1853–1931.
Translation of speech, 1914. 1 folder.
Holograph.
Premier of Italy, 1914–1916. Relates to the Italian policy of neutrality during World War I. Speech delivered to the Italian Parliament, December 3, 1914. Translated by Jean Black.

2421

Salisbury, Laurence E., 1891–1976.
Papers, 1916–1973. 4 ms. boxes.
American diplomat; Deputy Assistant Chief, Division of Far Eastern Affairs, U.S. Department of State, 1941–1944; editor, *Far Eastern Survey*, 1944–1948. Correspondence, writings, reports, and memoranda, relating to American foreign relations with China, Japan, and the Philippines, and political developments in the U.S.
Register.
Purchase, estate of L. E. Salisbury, 1977.

2422

Salmon, Brainerd P.
Writings, 1923–1924. 1 folder.
Typescript (mimeographed).
Special Commissioner, Greek Ministry of Public Assistance. Letters and reports, relating to relief work for refugees in Greece.

2423

Salnais, Voldemars, 1886–1948.
Papers (mainly in Latvian), 1918–1945. 1½ ms. boxes, 2 envelopes.
Latvian diplomat; delegate to the League of Nations, 1921–1934; Minister to Sweden, Norway and Denmark, 1937–1940. Correspondence, reports, clippings, printed matter, and photographs, relating to Latvian independence movements, foreign relations, and women's organizations, Latvians in Siberia, the Latvian National Council in Siberia (Vladivostok), and the Office of the

Latvian Representative in the Far East and Siberia. Includes some materials collected by Milda Salnais.
Register.
Gift, Lilija Salnais, 1975.

2424

Samizdat collection (in Russian), 1961–1971. 1 folder.
Photocopy.
Underground Samizdat writings, relating to political conditions, civil liberties, and non-Russian nationalism in the Soviet Union. Includes a protest of Latvian communists against Russian national domination.
Gift, Alliance of Russian Solidarists (N. T. S.), 1970.

2425

Sammis, Frederick M., Jr., *collector*.
Photographs, 1939–1945. 35 envelopes.
Depicts various scenes from the German occupation of Memel; the Polish campaign; the Russo-Finnish war; the German air and rocket offensive against Great Britain; naval warfare in the Atlantic; and the European Theater during 1944–1945, including scenes of Allied forces in combat, effects of the war on lives and property in Britain, France, Belgium, Luxemburg, and Germany, the liberation of German concentration camps and of Allied and German prisoners of war. Includes photographs of various Allied and German military and political leaders.
Gift, Mrs. F. M. Sammis, Jr., 1946.

2426

Samsonow, Michael S., 1900–1973.
Papers (in English and French), 1919–1967. ½ ms. box, 1 envelope.
Hungarian-American historian. Memoirs, writings, and a photograph, relating to Tsar Alexander III of Russia, Russian émigrés in Hungary after the Russian Revolution, and the provisions for a veto in the United Nations Charter.
Gift, M. S. Samsonow, 1970. Subsequent increments.

2427

Sander, William, *collector*.
W. Sander collection on occupied Germany (in German), 1945–1949. 2 ms. boxes.
Writings, correspondence, reports, and photographs, relating to political, social and economic conditions and to repression of civil liberties in the zone of Germany under Soviet occupation. Some items relate to the western zones of occupation and to the condition of German refugees from the area east of the Oder-Neisse line.
Purchase, W. Sander, 1948.

2428

Sanders, Harry, 1901– , *collector*.
Photographs, 1941–1949. 1 envelope.
Depicts the meeting aboard the HMS *Prince of Wales* between Franklin D. Roosevelt, President of the U.S., and Winston S. Churchill, Prime Minister of Great Britain, at Newfoundland, 1941; leading U.S. naval and

political figures; and U.S. Navy oil exploration efforts in Alaska, 1949.
Gift, H. Sanders, 1978.

2429

Santo Tomás (Concentration camp) Internee Executive Committee.
Issuances, 1942–1945. 4 vols.
Typescript (mimeographed).
Administrative committee of American and other civilian internees in the Japanese prison camp of Santo Tomás, Philippine Islands. Memoranda, notices and administrative orders, relating to living conditions in the camp.

2430

"Santo Tomás Internment Camp, January 4, 1942 to September 27, 1943."
Report, 1943. 1 vol.
Typescript.
Relates to living conditions in the Japanese prison camp for American and other civilian internees at Santo Tomás, Philippine Islands. Prepared by released prisoners.

2431

Santos, Paulino, 1890–1945.
Translation of diary excerpts, 1942. 1 folder.
Typescript.
Commanding General, Philippine Constabulary. Relates to the Japanese occupation of the Philippines, January 1 to August 26, 1942.

2432

Santovenia y Echaide, Emeterio S., b. 1889.
Writings (in Spanish and English), 1962–1965. 1 folder.
Printed.
Cuban historian. Relates to the history of Cuba and the U.S. and their leaders. Published in *Diario las Americas* and *Journal of Inter-American Studies*.
Gift, Mrs. E. S. Santovenia, 1975.

2433

Sargent, Clyde.
Extracts from letters, 1941–1947. 1 folder.
Typescript.
Professor, Cheeloo University, Chengtu, China, 1941; member, U.S.-U.S.S.R. Joint Commission in Korea, 1947. Relates to the Sino-Japanese War, social conditions in China in 1941, and conditions in North Korea in 1947.

2434

Sarles, Ruth, 1906–
History, 1942. "A Story of America First." 2 vols.
Typescript (carbon copy).
Relates to the America First Committee, isolationist lobby in the U.S. during World War II.

2435

Satorn, Pinyo, *collector*.
Printed matter (in Thai), 1976–1977. 3 ms. boxes.
Relates to education in Thailand. Published by the Thai Ministry of Education.
Preliminary inventory.
Gift, P. Satorn, 1978.

2436

Savez Zemljoradnika.
Leaflet (in Serbo-Croatian), 1932. 1 folder.
Typescript (mimeographed).
Serbian Peasant Party. Relates to the political program of the party.

2437

Savich, N. V.
Memoir (in Russian), n.d. 1 folder.
Typescript.
Member of the Russian Duma. Relates to the Russian war program for 1917.

2438

Savin, Petr Panteleimonovich.
Papers (in Russian), n.d. ½ ms. box.
Captain, Russian Imperial Army. Photocopy of writing, entitled "Gibel' Generala Millera" (The Demise of General Miller), relating to the death of the White Russian military leader, E. K. Miller; and correspondence and printed matter, relating to the writing and to Russian émigré anti-communist activities, 1917–1968.
Gift, P. P. Savin, 1975.

2439

Savinkov, Boris Viktorovich, 1879–1925.
Writings (in Russian and English), 1920–1924. 1 folder.
Russian Socialist Revolutionary Party leader. Letter (typewritten in Russian), to Baron Petr Vrangel', White Russian military commander, 1920, relating to White Russian military activities; and translation (typewritten) of the testimony of B. Savinkov at his trial for counter-revolutionary activities, 1924.

2440

Savintsev, Lieutenant.
Diary (in Russian), 1920–1921. 1 folder.
Typescript.
White Russian Army officer. Relates to the Russian Civil War in Siberia, August 1920—January 1921.

2441

Sazonov, Sergeĭ Dmitrievich, 1861–1927.
Papers (in English, French, German and Russian), 1915–1927. 4 ms. boxes, 1 envelope.
Russian diplomat; Minister of Foreign Affairs, 1910–1916. Memoirs, clippings, photograph, and correspondence, relating to Imperial Russian foreign policy, and the Russian Revolution and Civil War.
Gift, Lascelle de Basily, 1965.

2442

Scaff, Alvin Hewitt, 1914–
> Papers, 1936–1954. 2 ms. boxes, 4 envelopes.
> American sociologist. Memoranda, reports, diaries, photographs, and printed matter, relating to the communist movement in the Philippines, and to Japanese prison camps in the Philippines during World War II. Used as research material for the book by A. H. Scaff, *The Philippine Answer to Communism* (1955).
> Gift, A. H. Scaff, 1972. Incremental gift, 1977.

2443

Scandinavian Airlines System.
> Passenger list, 1950. 1 folder.
> Typescript (photocopy).
> Passenger list of a flight from Rome to Munich, July 1, 1950, including the names of members of the family of Bruno Pontecorvo, British atomic scientist who defected to the Soviet Union.

2444

Scapini, Georges, 1893–
> Papers (in French), 1928–1963. 15½ ms. boxes, 3 oversize boxes.
> French diplomat and politician; Deputy, National Assembly, 1928–1940; Ambassador to Germany and Chief of the Diplomatic Service for Prisoners of War, 1940–1944. Correspondence, memoranda, reports, writings, legal documents, printed matter and photographs, relating to French politics, French prisoners of war in Germany during World War II, and the trial of Georges Scapini as a Nazi collaborator, 1952.
> Preliminary inventory.
> May not be used until March 1, 1998 without written permission of Lucie Marie Scapini, Jean-Marie Scapini, François-Marie Scapini, Pierre Arnal or J. Chaperon.
> Gift, Lucie Marie Scapini, 1978.

2445

Scarf, Maggie.
> Notes, 1978. 1 folder.
> Holograph (photocopy).
> American journalist. Notes on interviews with Israeli political leaders, including Prime Minister Menahem Begin and former Prime Minister Yitzhak Rabin, relating to prospects for a Middle East peace settlement.
> Gift, M. Scarf, 1978.

2446

Schacht, Hjalmar, 1877–1970.
> Miscellaneous papers (in German), 1932–1970. 1 folder, 1 envelope.
> German financial expert; President, Reichsbank, 1924–1930 and 1933–1939; Acting Minister of National Economy, 1934–1937. Correspondence, autographed book, newsletter, photograph, and clippings, relating to the career and economic views of H. Schacht.
> Gift, Mrs. Hjalmar Hertz, 1973.

2447

Schauman, Georg Carl August, 1870–1930.
> Writings (in Swedish and French), 1920. 1 folder.
> Member of the Parliament of Finland. Study (typewritten in Swedish), entitled "Kampen om Statsskicket i Finland 1918" (Struggles over the Constitution of Finland, 1918), and an untitled memorandum (handwritten and typewritten in French), relating to the Finnish Revolution of 1917–1918 and to political conditions in Finland.

2448

Schenck, Hubert Gregory, 1897–1960.
> Papers, 1943–1959. 21 ms. boxes, 34 envelopes.
> Colonel, U.S. Army; Chief, Natural Resources Section, General Headquarters, Supreme Commander of the Allied Powers, Japan, 1945–1951; Chief, Mutual Security Mission to Taiwan, 1951–1954; Consultant, U.S. Foreign Operations Administration, 1954–1955. Correspondence, diary, mimeographed reports, newspaper and magazine clippings and photographs, relating to the Allied occupation of Japan, relations between Taiwan and the U.S., and economic affairs in Japan and Taiwan.
> Preliminary inventory.
> Diary closed until 1980.
> Gift, H. G. Schenck, 1950. Subsequent increments.

2449

Schevenels, Walter, 1894–1966.
> Papers (in French and English), 1930–1966. 13 ms. boxes.
> Belgian international trade union official; General Secretary, International Federation of Trade Unions, 1930–1945; General Secretary, European Regional Organization, International Confederation of Free Trade Unions, 1951–1966. Correspondence, reports, speeches, writings, telegrams, bulletins, interviews, pamphlets, clippings, and printed matter, relating to European trade unions, labor and laboring classes in Europe, and international labor problems.
> Purchase, Sophie Schevenels, 1977.

2450

Schleswig-Holstein. Landesregierung.
> Issuances (in German), 1949–1950. ½ ms. box.
> Printed.
> Pamphlets and leaflets, relating to economic reconstruction in Schleswig-Holstein and to West German participation in the Marshall Plan.

2451

Schmelzer, Janis.
> History (in French), n.d. "Le Combat de Résistance des Travailleurs Forcés Étrangers dans l'Allemagne Hitlérienne et les Alliés" (The Resistance Struggle of Foreign Forced Laborers in Hitlerian Germany and the Allies). 1 vol.
> Typescript.

2452

Schmidt, Frieda, 1894–
Papers (in German), 1914–1945. 1 ms. box.
German pacifist. Diaries, clippings and miscellanea, relating to pacifism and social conditions in Germany during the Nazi period and World War II.
Gift, Louis Lochner, 1946.

2453

Schmidt, Harry, 1886–1968.
Papers, 1909–1964. 3 ms. boxes.
General, U.S. Marine Corps; Commanding General, 5th Amphibious Corps, 1944–1946. Correspondence, orders, speeches, memoranda, printed matter, and photographs, relating to activities of the U.S. Marine Corps in the Pacific Theater during World War II.
Preliminary inventory.
Gift, Mrs. H. Schmidt, 1968.

2454

Schnabel, Lucy Hooker Clark, b. 1844.
Letters, 1914–1924. 1 folder.
Holograph.
American living in Germany. Relates to personal matters and social conditions in Germany. Addressed to relatives and friends in the U.S.

2455

Schneider, Elizabeth.
Letters, 1977. 1 folder.
Typescript.
American visitor to South Africa. Relates to political and racial unrest at the University of Witwatersrand, Johannesburg, South Africa. One letter is written on the obverse side of a leaflet, possession of which was illegal.
Gift, Jack Schneider, 1977.

2456

Schnetzer, Max.
Report (in German), 1945. "Tagebuch der Abenteuer: Endkampf um Berlin, Reise durch Russland." (Diary of an Adventure: Final Struggle in Berlin, Journey through Russia). 1 vol.
Typescript.
Swiss journalist. Relates to conditions in Berlin and in Russia in the spring of 1945, immediately before the German surrender.

2457

Schoenberner, Franz, 1892–1970.
Papers (in German and English), 1899–1970. 4 ms. boxes, 1 envelope, 1 phonotape.
German journalist and author; editor, *Simplicissimus*, 1929–1933. Writings and correspondence, relating to German literature, national socialism in Germany, and anti-Nazi German émigré life.
Register.
Purchase, Georges Breur, 1972.

2458

Scholly, Nora.
Textbook (in German), 1945. "Lustiges Lesen" (Merry Reading). 1 vol.
Printed.
Austrian elementary school textbook published under supervision of Allied occupation authorities.

2459

Scholtz-Klink, Gertrud, 1902–
Translation of speech, 1935. 1 folder.
Typescript (mimeographed).
German Reich Women's Leader. Relates to the role of women under national socialism in Germany. Includes translation of excerpts from a speech by Adolf Hitler, German Fuehrer. Both speeches delivered at the 7th Congress of the Nazi Party at Nuremberg.

2460

Schowalter, Herbert P., *collector*.
H. P. Schowalter collection on World Wars I and II, 1914–1945. 1 ms. box, 1 certificate, 8 envelopes.
Photographs and miscellanea, relating to American military activities in France and the U.S. during World War I, and Arab life in North Africa during World War II. Includes a German pictorial book on Nazi industrial production, and a certificate for superior achievement awarded to a German factory.
Gift, H. P. Schowalter, 1963.

2461

Schubert, Miroslav G., 1895–
Papers (in Czech and English), 1936–1977. 2 ms. boxes.
Czechoslovak diplomat; Chargé d'Affaires in Brazil, 1921–1925; Chargé d'Affaires in Iran, 1927–1932; Counsellor and Deputy Envoy to Germany, 1934–1938; Consul General in Munich, 1945–1948. Correspondence, speeches and writings, memoranda, reports, clippings and other printed matter, relating to World War II, the Soviet occupation of Czechoslovakia in 1945, international affairs in Europe during the interwar period, the communist movement in Czechoslovakia, and the coup d'état of 1948.
Gift, M. G. Schubert, 1978.

2462

Schuder, Kurt.
Writings (in German), 1948. 1 folder.
Typescript.
Relates to world peace and German-American relations.

2463

Schulte, Eduard, b. 1886.
Study (in German), 1945. "Gutachten Betreffend die Grundlegende Behandlung der Deutschen Wirtschaftlichen Nachkriegsprobleme Einschliesslich Konkreter Vorschlaege zu den Wichtigsten Wirtschafts-Komplexen" (Opinions Concerning the Fundamental Treatment

of German Economic Postwar Problems Including Concrete Proposals for the Most Important Economic Complexes). 1 vol.
Typescript (mimeographed).

2464

Schulz, Robert F., *collector*.
Teleprinter dispatches, 1941. 1 ms. box.
United Press dispatches, December 7, 1941, relating to the attack on Pearl Harbor.
Gift, R. F. Schulz, 1967.

2465

Schulz-Schwekhausen, Emil, b. 1868.
Writings (in German), 1928–1947. 2 ms. boxes.
Typescript.
German physician. Memoirs, entitled "Ein Bewegtes Leben" (A Turbulent Life), ca. 1944, relating to world travel and to German culture and politics; and biographical sketches of Stjepan Radić, Croatian peasant leader, and Carl Muth, German Catholic newspaper publisher.
Gift, H. A. Reinhold, 1947.

2466

Schulze-Gaevernitz, Gero von, 1901–1970.
Papers, 1945. 2 folders.
Photocopy.
Special Assistant to Allen W. Dulles, Chief, Office of Strategic Services Mission in Europe during World War II. Letters, relating to liaison between Allied forces and anti-Nazi groups, and the capitulation of German troops in Italy and southern Austria, and a report relating to a journey to Russia in 1923.
Gift, Margiana Stinnes, 1976. Incremental gift, 1977.

2467

Schulze, Hans Georg, d. 1941.
Diary (in German), 1941. 1 vol.
Holograph.
Soldier, German Army. Relates to campaigns on the Eastern front during World War II.

2468

Schutzbund trial—newspaper clippings (in German), 1932. 1 folder.
Relates to the trial of leaders of the Schutzbund, the defense organization of the Austrian Social Democratic Party. Clippings from Austrian newspapers.

2469

Schuyler, Eugene.
Biography, 1883. "Peter the Great, Emperor of Russia: A Study of Historical Biography." 1 ms. box.
Holograph.

2470

Schwarz, Alexis von, b. 1874.
History (in Russian), n.d. "Opisanie Boevykh Dieĭstviĭ pod Ivangorodom s 8-go po 22-e Iĭuliĭa 1915 goda" (An Account of Combat Operations around Ivangorod from 8 to 22 July, 1915). 1 vol.
Typescript (carbon copy).

2471

Schwarz, Salomon, *collector*.
Newspaper articles (in French), 1936. 1 vol.
Typewritten transcripts.
Relates to the sit-down strikes in France in the summer of 1936. Includes photographs.

2472

Schwerin-Krosigk, Lutz, Graf von, b. 1887.
Memorandum (in German), 1945. 1 folder.
Typescript.
German Minister of Finance, 1932–1945. Relates to the position of the Protestant churches in Germany.

2473

Schwien, Edwin E.
Miscellaneous papers, 1952. 1 folder.
Photocopy.
Brigadier General, U.S. Army; liaison officer with French forces, 1944–1945. Memorandum relating to the warning by E. E. Schwien of the impending German attack in the Battle of the Bulge; and two letters from Major General H. R. Vaughan, Military Aide to the President, and from President Harry Truman.
Gift, Mrs. E. E. Schwien, 1977.

2474

Schwimmer, Rosika, 1877–1948.
Papers, 1914–1937. 2 ms. boxes, 1 envelope.
Hungarian feminist and pacifist. Correspondence, petitions, clippings, printed matter and photographs, relating to the pacifist movement during World War I, the Henry Ford Peace Expedition, the International Congress of Women, and the presentation of the World Peace Prize to R. Schwimmer in 1937.
Preliminary inventory.
Purchase, R. Schwimmer, 1937.

2475

Schwyetz, Otto.
Correspondence (in German), 1914. 1 folder.
Holograph.
Soldier, 142d Regiment, German Army. Relates to personal matters and the outbreak of World War I.

2476

Scigliano, Robert.
Papers, 1953–1967. ½ ms. box.
American political scientist. Correspondence, reports, party regulations, interviews, clippings, election posters, cartoon, and maps, relating to political conditions in Vietnam and U.S.-Vietnamese relations.
Gift, R. Scigliano, 1975.

2477

Scitovsky, Tibor von, b. 1875.

Memoirs (in German), n.d. "Erinnerungen an Schicksalsschwere Zeiten: Die Tragoedie eines Tausendjaehrigen Reiches" (Recollections of Fateful Times: The Tragedy of the Thousand-Year Reich). 1 folder.

Typescript.

Hungarian politician and banker; Minister of Foreign Affairs, 1924–1925. Relates to Central European politics, 1918–1945.

Gift, T. Scitovsky, Jr., 1976.

2478

Scott, Roderick.

Papers, 1916–1958. 2 ms. boxes.

American missionary in China; official, Fukien Christian University, Foochow, China, 1917–1949. Correspondence, reports, newsletters, photographs, writings and textbooks, relating to missionary activity and social conditions in China, and to Fukien Christian University.

Gift, Mrs. R. Scott, 1971.

2479

Screens—photographs, n.d. 1 envelope.

Depicts Oriental screen paintings.

2480

Seabury, Paul.

Papers (in German), 1975–1977. 1½ ms. boxes.

American political scientist. Writings, leaflets, correspondence, notes, clippings, reports, books, and other printed matter, relating to West German university reform, higher education in West Germany, government regulation of West German universities, and the International Council on the Future of the University.

Gift, P. Seabury, 1977.

2481

Sebald, Edith de Becker.

Memoir, 1967. "Burma Interlude: Reminiscences of an Ambassador's Wife." 1 vol.

Typescript.

Wife of William J. Sebald, U.S. Ambassador to Burma, 1952–1954. Relates to social conditions in Burma and Burmese-American relations.

2482

Sebald, William Joseph, 1901–

Diary extracts, 1952–1954. 1 vol.

Typescript (carbon copy).

U.S. Ambassador to Burma, 1952–1954. Relates to Burmese-American relations, Burmese politics and the communist movement in Burma.

2483

"Second Report on Hungary under German Occupation."

Report, 1944. 1 folder.

Typescript (mimeographed).

Relates to conditions in Hungary during World War II as revealed from analysis of the Hungarian press, June-July 1944.

2484

Le Secours Français.

Records, 1940–1945. 2 ms. boxes.

Private American charitable organization for relief in France during World War II. Correspondence, memoranda and financial records, relating to fund-raising and relief distribution activities of the organization.

Gift, Harry Elmer Barnes, 1963.

2485

See, Elizabeth M., *collector*.

Photograph, n.d.

Depicts the U.S.S. *Maryland*, a battleship upon which President-elect Herbert Hoover visited South America in 1928.

Gift, E. M. See, 1978.

2486

Seelos, Gebhard.

Memorandum (in German), 1942. 1 folder.

Typescript.

Member of an anti-Nazi resistance movement in Bavaria. Relates to the anti-Nazi movement and to Bavarian separatism.

2487

Segal, Mandal Robert.

Study, 1943. "Some Legal Problems of Military Government in the Present Conflict." 1 vol.

Typescript.

Relates to problems of legal jurisdiction of Allied military governments during World War II. Written by M. R. Segal and Bert Leon Werner, Privates First Class, U.S. Army.

2488

Segall, Joel.

Papers, 1970–1977. 4 ms. boxes.

U.S. Deputy Under Secretary of Labor for International Affairs, 1970–1977. Correspondence, reports, and memoranda, relating to international labor and U.S. labor policy, 1970–1977.

Deposit, J. Segall, 1978.

2489

Seine (Dept.) Préfecture de Police.

Memoranda (in French), 1933–1936. 1 folder.

Typescript.

Prefecture of Police in Paris. Relates to the presence of members of the family of Lev Trotskiĭ, Russian revolutionary, in France, 1933, and to the theft of papers of Lev Trotskiĭ from the International Institute for Social History in Paris, 1936.

Purchase, Jacques de Launay, 1977.

2490

Sēja, Kärlis-Ludvigs, 1885–1962.

Papers (in Latvian, German and English), 1934–1971. 1 folder, 1 envelope.

Latvian diplomat; Minister to the U.S., Great Britain, and Lithuania. Correspondence, photographs and

memorabilia, relating to the displacement of the Sēja family during World War II, and to the arrest of L. Sēja by Soviet authorities at the end of the war.
Preliminary inventory.
Gift, Gvido Augusts, 1973.

2491

Selden, Elizabeth.
Papers (in English and German), 1946–1948. 2 ms. boxes.
Staff member, Education Branch, U.S. Military Government in Germany, 1946–1948. Clippings, writings and notes, relating to conditions in Germany following World War II, the Berlin blockade, reparations, displaced persons, and denazification.
Gift, E. Selden, 1962.

2492

Selling, Lowell S.
Study, 1941. "The Mental-Hygiene Aspect of the Deferred Draftee." 1 folder.
Printed.
Relates to the psychological condition of men rejected for military service in the U.S. during World War II. Published in the *New York State Journal of Medicine*, Vol. I, No. 13, July 1, 1941.

2493

Selzam, Edwart von.
Deposition (in German), 1948. 1 folder.
Typewritten transcript.
German foreign service official. Relates to the activities of Ernst von Weizsaecker as Secretary of State in the German Foreign Office, 1938–1943, and to the war crime charges brought against Weizsaecker at the Nuremberg trials. Includes translation.

2494

Semenov, Evgeniĭ Petrovich, b. 1861.
Translation of articles, 1921. "German Money to Lenin." 1 folder.
Typescript.
Relates to allegations of German Government subsidies to the Bolsheviks. Written by E. P. Semenov and Pavel Miliûkov. Published in *Poslednie Novosti*, April 1921.

2495

Semenov, Grigoriĭ Mikhailovich, 1890–1945.
Memoirs (in Russian), ca. 1937. "Istoriiă Moeĭ Bor'by s Bol'shevikami" (History of My Struggle with the Bolsheviks). 1 folder.
Typescript (photocopy).
Cossack Ataman; White Russian military leader in Siberia during the Russian Civil War. Includes photocopy of a biographical sketch (typewritten in Russian) of G. Semenov, ca. 1937.

2496

Semler, Johannes.
Translation of speech, 1948. 1 folder.
Typescript.

Director, Economic Department, U.S.-British Bizonal Organization in Germany. Relates to Allied economic policy in Germany. Speech delivered before Christlich Sozial Union members of the Bavarian legislature, at Erlangen, Bavaria, January 4, 1948. Includes commentary (mimeographed in German) by J. Semler written to defend the criticisms of Allied policy made in his speech.

2497

Serebrennikov, Ivan Innokentievich, b. 1882.
Papers (in Russian), 1906–1948. 25 ms. boxes, 29 albums, 11 envelopes.
Russian journalist; official, Siberian Government, Omsk, 1917–1918. Diaries, correspondence, writings, photographs, clippings, and notebooks, relating to the Russian Civil War in Siberia, Russian émigrés in the Far East, and Chinese history and culture.
Register.
Consult archivist for access.
Purchase, I. I. Serebrennikov, 1951.

2498

Seth, Ronald.
History, 1955. "The Undaunted: The Story of Resistance in Western Europe." 1 vol.
Holograph.
Relates to anti-Nazi resistance movements in Western Europe during World War II. Autographed letter from Winston Churchill inserted.

2499

Sevastopoulo, Marc.
Letters received (in French), 1957–1959, from Nicolas A. de Basily. 1 folder.
Holograph.
Relates to the Sevastopoulo family genealogy.
Gift, Elizabeth Stenbock-Fermor, 1977.

2500

Seward, Samuel S., d. 1932.
Reports, 1915–1917. 1 folder.
Typescript.
Member, Commission for Relief in Belgium. Relates to relief work carried out by the Commission for Relief in Belgium during World War I.

2501

Seyss-Inquart, Arthur, 1892–1946.
Memorandum (in German), n.d. 1 folder.
Typescript.
Austrian Nazi leader; Chancellor, 1938. Relates to Austrian politics and economics, 1918–1945. Incomplete.

2502

Shanghai. Municipal Council.
Proclamation, 1932. 1 folder.
Printed.
Relates to emergency measures in Shanghai.
Gift, Hsien-chang Ling, 1976.

2503

Shanghai peace delegation declaration (in Chinese), 1948. 1 folder.

Printed.

Relates to a Shanghai delegation sent to the Nationalist Government at Nanking to urge a peaceful conclusion to the Chinese Civil War. Includes a translation (typewritten).

2504

Shapiro-Lavrova, Nadezhda L.

Memoir (in Russian), n.d. 1 folder.

Typescript.

Resident of Blagoveshchensk, Siberia. Relates to the Russian Civil War in the Blagoveshchensk area, and to the trial of A. N. Alekseevskiĭ, a Socialist Revolutionary, by the Bolsheviks in Blagoveshchensk in 1918. Includes a translation (typewritten) of the memoir by Elena Varneck.

2505

Sharp, Ulysses Simpson Grant, 1906–

Miscellaneous papers, 1968–1972. 1 folder.

Admiral, U.S. Navy; Commander in Chief, Pacific, 1963–1968. Transcript of a lecture delivered at the U.S. Naval War College, entitled "The Strategy of the Vietnam War," 1972; and copy of a letter to Richard M. Nixon, 1968, relating to the Vietnam War and to U.S. foreign policy.

Gift, U.S.G. Sharp, 1976.

2506

Shawa, Izzidine.

Summary of interview, 1946. 1 folder.

Typescript.

Personal adviser to King Ibn Sa'ud of Saudi Arabia. Relates to political conditions in the Middle East. Interview conducted in Los Angeles, August 29, 1946.

Gift, Pamelia S. Finley, 1946.

2507

Shchepikhin, Sergeĭ Afanasevich.

Papers (in Russian), 1919–1920. 1 ms. box.

General and Chief of Staff, White Russian Army, 1919–1920. Diaries and writings, relating to the retreat of the Russian Volunteer Armies toward Siberia, the government of Grigoriĭ Semenov, Japanese intervention in the Siberian Far East, and the military activities of the Ural Cossacks against the Bolsheviks.

Purchase, S. A. Shchepikhin, 1933.

2508

Shcherbachev, Dmitriĭ Grigorevich, 1855–1932.

Papers (in Russian and French), 1914–1920. 8 ms. boxes.

General, Russian Imperial Army. Correspondence, orders, reports, and printed matter, relating to Russian prisoners of war in Germany during World War I, and to counter-revolutionary movements during the Russian Revolution.

Preliminary inventory.

Gift, D. G. Shcherbachev, 1929.

2509

Sheiman, Boris.

Translations, 1936–1939. ½ ms. box.

Typescript.

Soviet statutes and articles published in Soviet journals, 1932–1938, relating to the Soviet judicial and penal systems, labor, social and welfare legislation, and the legal position of the family in Soviet society.

Preliminary inventory.

Gift, University of California Law School.

2510

Shekerjian, Haig, 1886–1966.

Papers, 1905–1966. 4 ms. boxes, 1 envelope.

Brigadier General, U.S. Army. Correspondence, notes, speeches, and medals, relating to American chemical warfare activities during World War II.

Register.

Gift, Helen Shekerjian, 1972.

2511

Shelton, Frederick D., *collector*.

Printed matter, 1928. ½ ms. box.

Campaign literature and clippings, relating to the 1928 campaign for the Republican Presidential nomination.

Gift, F. D. Shelton, 1956.

2512

Sherley, Swagar, 1871–1941.

Summary of interview, n.d. 1 folder.

Typescript.

U.S. Congressman from Kentucky, 1903–1919; Chairman, House Appropriations Committee, 1919. Relates to Congressional passage of a $100,000,000 appropriation for European relief in 1919.

2513

Sherwell, G. Butler, *collector*.

Newspaper clippings (printed in Spanish and Portuguese), 1928. 1 ms. box.

Relates to the visit of President-elect Herbert Hoover to Latin America. Clippings from Argentine and Brazilian newspapers.

Gift, G. B. Sherwell, 1960.

2514

Sherwin, Samuel B., 1917–

Papers, 1975–1976. 2 ms. boxes.

U.S. Deputy Assistant Secretary of Commerce for Domestic Commerce, 1975–1977. Transcripts of speeches and Congressional testimony, studies, and reports, relating to U.S. commercial policy.

Gift, S. B. Sherwin, 1977.

2515

Shevelev, Klavdiĭ Valentinovich, b. 1881.

Papers (in Russian), 1919–1948. 1 folder, 1 envelope.

Photocopy.

Rear Admiral, Russian Imperial Navy. Birth certificate, White Russian Naval Ministry identification document, International Refugee Organization documents, and photographs, relating to the naval career and émigré life of K. V. Shevelev.

Gift, Yelena Andrejeff, 1976.

2516

Shil'nikov, Ivan Fedorovich.

History (in Russian), 1933. "Voevyi͡a Di͡eĭstvii͡a i Zabaikal'skogoĭ Kazach'eĭ Divizii v Velikoĭ Voine 1914−1918 Goda" (Military Operations of the Zabaikal Cossack Division in the Great War of 1914−1918). 1 folder.

Typescript.

Published as *l-ai͡a Zabaikal'skai͡a Kazach'ia Divizii͡a v Velikoĭ Evropeĭskoĭ Voine 1914−1918g* (1st Zabaikal Cossack Division in the Great European War, 1914−1918) (Harbin, 1933).

2517

Shimkin, Demitri B.

Study, 1949. "The Mineral Self-Sufficiency of the Soviet Union." 1 folder.

Typescript (mimeographed).

Relates to the extent and distribution of Soviet mineral resources and production.

2518

Shingarev (Andreĭ Ivanovich)—photograph, n.d. 1 envelope.

Depicts A. I. Shingarev, Minister of Finance in the Russian Provisional Government, 1917.

2519

Shinkarenko, Nikolaĭ Vsevolodovich, 1890−1968.

Memoirs (in Russian), n.d. 7 pamphlet boxes (2 l. ft.). Typescript.

Russian Imperial Army officer; Brigadier General of the Cavalry of the White Russian Army; Spanish Foreign Legion officer. Relates to Russian cavalry operations in World War I, White Russian military operations in the Russian Civil War, Spanish military operations in Africa, and Francoist military operations in the Spanish Civil War. Includes copies of letters and photographs.

One sealed folder closed until January 1, 1985.

Purchase, N. V. Shinkarenko, 1968.

2520

Shinyo Maru (Steamship).

Bulletins, 1914. 1 folder.

Printed.

Japanese steamship. Relates to wireless dispatches reporting the outbreak of World War I. Issued on board the *Shinyo Maru*, August 3−4, 1914.

2521

Shishmanian, John Amar, 1882−1945.

Papers (in English, French and Armenian), 1903−1945. 1 ms. box.

Captain, French Foreign Legion, during World War I. Correspondence, printed matter, photographs, and memorabilia, relating to the Armenian-Turkish conflict

at the end of World War I, and to the Armenian question at the Paris Peace Conference.

Preliminary inventory.

Gift, Georgia Cutler, 1941. Subsequent increments.

2522

Shkurkin, P. V.

Study (in Russian), n.d. "Mozhet-li v Kitae Privit'sia Kommunizm?" (Can Communism Become Acclimated in China?). 1 folder.

Typescript (mimeographed).

Includes translation (typewritten).

2523

Shkuro, Andreĭ Grigor'evich, 1887−1947.

Letter (in Russian), to Grand Duke Andreĭ Vladimirovich, 1932. 1 folder.

Typescript (mimeographed).

General, White Russian Army. Relates to Russian émigré politics.

2524

Shneyeroff, M. M., b. 1880.

Papers (in Russian and English), 1918−1957. 1 ms. box.

Member of the Russian Socialist Revolutionary Party. Memoirs, writings, and photographs relating to the Russian revolutionary movement in the early twentieth century.

Preliminary inventory.

Quotations limited to 500 words consecutively, and to 5000 words from any manuscript.

Gift, M. M. Shneyeroff, 1959.

2525

Shoriki (Matsutaro) collection, 1952−1953. 1 folder.

Memorandum and five pamphlets, relating to M. Shoriki, President of Nippon Television Network Corporation, and to his plans for the development of Japanese and international telecommunications systems. Includes pamphlets by M. Shoriki.

Gift, Ginjiro Fujihara, 1953.

2526

"Short Review of the Development of Latvian Literature."

Memorandum, n.d. 1 folder.

Typescript (mimeographed).

2527

Short, Walter Campbell, 1880−1949.

Defense exhibits, 1942. ½ ms. box.

Lieutenant General, U.S. Army; Commanding General, Hawaiian Department, 1941. Relates to the administration of the Hawaiian Department in the period leading up to the attack on Pearl Harbor. Presented to the Roberts Commission investigation of the attack on Pearl Harbor.

May be used only with permission of Robert F. Fleming, Jr., Walter D. Short, or Walter D. Short, Jr.

Gift, W. D. Short, 1975.

2528

Shotwell, James Thomson, 1874–1965.
Memoir, 1919. "A Visit to the Canadian Battle Fields."
1 folder.
Typescript.
American historian. Describes the site of World War I battles between Canadian and German troops in Belgium in 1918.

2529

Shoup, David Monroe, 1904–
Papers, 1927–1971. 27½ ms. boxes, 2 cu. ft. boxes, 5 oversize boxes (5 1. ft.).
General, U.S. Marine Corps; Commander of Marine forces at Tarawa, 1943; Chief of Staff, 2d Marine Division, 1944; Commandant of the Marine Corps, 1960–1963. Correspondence, memoranda, writings, printed matter, photographs, films and sound recordings, relating to the Tarawa campaign, other World War II campaigns in the Pacific Theater, postwar activities of the Marine Corps, and the Vietnam War.
Gift, D. M. Shoup, 1976. Incremental gift, 1977.

2530

Shoup, Mrs. Jack W.
Letters received, 1942–1945. ½ ms. box.
Holograph and typescript.
Relates to conditions in relocation centers of Japanese-Americans in the U.S. during World War II. Written by interned Japanese-Americans.
Gift, Mrs. J. W. Shoup, 1946.

2531

Shrewsbury, Kenneth O.
Papers, 1919–1922. 1 ms. box.
American volunteer in the Kosciuszko Squadron. Photographs, clippings, and miscellanea, relating to the activities of volunteer American aviators who formed the Kosciuszko Squadron of the Polish Army during the Polish-Russian War, 1919–1921.
Gift, K. O. Shrewsbury, 1960.

2532

Shriver, Harry C., *collector.*
Printed matter, 1941–1945. 1 ms. box.
Relates to U.S. propaganda efforts in World War II. Issued by the U.S. Office of War Information.
Gift, H. C. Shriver, 1978.

2533

Shugg, Roland P.
Papers, 1949–1951. 1 folder.
Brigadier General, U.S. Army; U.S. military adviser to Turkey, 1947–1949. Memoranda and correspondence, relating to U.S. military aid to Turkey, and to U.S. defense policy.
Gift, R. P. Shugg, 1969.

2534

Shultz, George Pratt, 1920–
Papers, 1969–1974. 97 1. ft.
U.S. Secretary of Labor, 1969–1970; Director, Office of Management and Budget, 1970–1972; Secretary of the Treasury, 1972–1974. Correspondence, memoranda, reports, speeches, press releases, notes, and printed matter, relating primarily to the economic policies of Richard M. Nixon's Presidency.
Preliminary inventory.
Closed until processed by archives staff.
Deposit, G. P. Shultz, 1977.

2535

Shutko, Iâkov, *collector.*
Miscellany (in Russian), 1916–1917. 1 folder.
Reports, orders and correspondence, relating to Russian troops stationed at La Courtine, France, during World War I, and to revolutionary movements among the troops.

2536

Shvetzoff, Dimitrii Andreevich, 1902–
Memoir, n.d. "Captivity and Escape of Horseguardsman Dimitrii A. Shvetzoff in 1919–1921." 1 folder.
Typescript (photocopy).
Soldier, Russian Imperial Horse Guards. Relates to the activities of the Russian Imperial Horse Guard Regiment during the Russian Revolution and Civil War.
Gift, D. A. Shvetzoff, 1972.

2537

Siebecke, Horst.
Compilation of sound recordings (in German), n.d. 5 phonorecords.
Speeches and radio broadcasts by prominent German political leaders, 1914–1945, relating to World War I, the Weimar Republic, the Third Reich and World War II, selected and edited by H. Siebecke.
Preliminary inventory.
In part, gift, Matt Lehman, 1960.

2538

Simaite, Ona, 1894–1970.
Papers (in Lithuanian), 1941–1970. 2 ms. boxes, 1 envelope.
Lithuanian librarian and literary critic. Correspondence, notes, memorabilia and photographs, relating to underground aid to the Jewish ghetto inhabitants of Vilnius, Lithuania, during the German occupation, 1941–1944.
Register.
Gift, Žibuntas Mikšys, 1974.

2539

Simmons, Robert Glenmore, 1891–1969.
Papers, 1929–1962. 1 ms. box.
Photocopy of original papers located at the Herbert Hoover Presidential Library.

U.S. Representative from Nebraska, 1923–1933; Chief Justice, Nebraska Supreme Court, 1938–1962. Memoirs, correspondence, and memoranda, relating to U.S. politics, and to the relationship between R. G. Simmons and Herbert Hoover.

Exchange, Herbert Hoover Presidential Library, 1971.

2540

Simonet, Joseph.
Memoir (in French), 1914. "Carnet d'un Brancardier de la 3ème Division d'Armée Belge, 1914" (Notebook of a Stretcher-Bearer of the 3d Division of the Belgian Army, 1914). 1 vol.
Typescript and printed.
Belgian soldier. Relates to Belgian military activities during World War I.

2541

Simoni (Simone)—clippings (in Italian), 1944, 1 folder.
Relates to the execution of S. Simoni, General, Italian Army, by German occupation troops in Italy. Clippings from Italian newspapers.

2542

Simpson, John Lowry, *collector*.
Miscellany, ca. 1914–1918. ½ ms. box.
Photographs, depicting war damage in France during World War I; and French and Belgian municipal currency from World War I.
Gift, J. L. Simpson, 1956. Subsequent increments.

2543

Simpson, Robert Moore, 1915–
Papers, 1942–1963. 1 folder.
Captain, U.S. Army Air Corps. Orders, certificates and miscellanea, relating to American bombing operations in the Pacific and European Theaters during World War II.

2544

Sims (William Sowden)—photograph, n.d. 1 envelope.
Depicts Admiral W. S. Sims, U.S. Navy.

2545

Singapore. Criminal Investigation Department.
Memorandum, 1950. "The Police and the People." 1 folder.
Typescript (mimeographed).
Relates to the work of the Singapore police in combating crime and political terrorism.

2546

Skalskiĭ, Vladimir Evgenievich.
Memoir, n.d. 1 folder.
Typescript (photocopy).
Russian Imperial Army officer. Relates to the escape of V. E. Skalskiĭ from Bolshevik captivity, 1918.
Gift, Dmitriĭ Birkin, 1968.

2547

Slaughter, Moses Stephen.
Papers (in Italian and English), 1918–1921. 1 ms. box.
American Red Cross relief worker in Venice, 1918–1919. Memoirs, correspondence, photographs, memorabilia and printed matter, relating to relief activities of the Red Cross in Italy at the end of World War I and to the occupation of Fiume by the forces of Gabriele d'Annunzio. Includes papers of Gertrude Slaughter, wife of M. S. Slaughter.
Gift, G. Slaughter.

2548

"Slaviane v Amerikie"—(Slavs in America).
Report (in Russian), 1917. 1 folder.
Typescript.
Relates to Czechs, Slovaks, Russians, Ukrainians, Yugoslavs, and Poles in North and South America, their national organizations, and political activities during World War I. Written by a Russian diplomatic agent in the U.S.

2549

Slavik, Jan.
Study (in Czech), 1938. "Pad Prvni Republiky" (The Fall of the First Republic). 1 folder.
Proof sheets.
Relates to Czechoslovakia in the Munich crisis of 1938.
Gift, J. Slavik, 1939.

2550

Slavik, Juraj, 1880–1969.
Papers (in Czech, Slovak and English), 1934–1966. 44 ms. boxes.
Czechoslovakian diplomat and statesman; Ambassador to Poland, 1936–1939; Minister of the Interior, 1940–1945; Minister of Foreign Affairs, 1945–1946; Ambassador to the U.S., 1946–1948. Correspondence, speeches and writings, reports, dispatches, memoranda, telegrams, and clippings, relating to Czechoslovakian relations with Poland and the U.S., political developments in Czechoslovakia, Czechoslovakian emigration and émigrés, and anti-communist movements in the U.S.
Gift, Gita Slavik, 1976.

2551

Šljivar, Vojislav, 1925–
Papers (in Serbo-Croatian), 1960–1977. ½ ms. box.
Serbian émigré in the U.S. Correspondence, reports, pamphlets, clippings, printed matter and photographs, relating to his education in Germany and the U.S., the Serbian monarchy, Serbs in the U.S., the Serbian Orthodox Church in the U.S., and Yugoslav history after World War II.
Closed until December 1992.
Deposit, V. Šljivar, 1977. Incremental deposit, 1978.

2552

Slosson, Preston.
Letter, 1924, to E. D. Adams. 1 folder.
Typescript.

Staff member, U.S. delegation, Paris Peace Conference, 1919. Relates to the existence and location of records of the proceedings of the Paris Peace Conference.

2553

Slovak League of America. Congress, 35th, Cleveland, 1957.

Resolution, 1957. 1 folder.

Relates to the fiftieth anniversary of the founding of the Slovak League of America. Addressed to the President and Secretary of State of the U.S., and the U.S. Ambassador to the United Nations.

2554

Smith, Bruce M.

Papers, 1941–1949. 1 folder.

President, Shanghai American Chamber of Commerce, 1939–1940 and 1946–1947. Correspondence, memoranda, reports, minutes of meetings, and clippings, relating to U.S. commercial relations with China, and to the views of U.S. businessmen in China regarding U.S. foreign policy in China.

Gift, David M. Maynard, 1970.

2555

Smith, Dan Throop, 1907–

Papers, 1970–1973. 10 ms. boxes.

American economist; member, President's Commission on International Trade and Investment Policy, 1970–1971; chairman, Tax Policy Advisory Committee, Council on Environmental Quality, 1970–1972. Minutes of meetings, reports, memoranda, and correspondence, relating to U.S. trade and taxation policy.

Register.

Gift, D. T. Smith, 1973. Incremental gift, 1975.

2556

Smith, Eddie.

Diary extracts, 1963–1964. 1½ ms. boxes.

Typescript.

Peace Corps worker in Ghana, 1963–1964. Relates to the Peace Corps and social conditions in Ghana. Edited by George Jenkins. Revised version published under the title *Where Now Black Man?*

Gift, G. Jenkins, 1972.

2557

Smith, Edward Ellis.

History, 1962. "The Department of Police, 1911–1913: From the Recollections of Nikolai Vladimirovich Veselago." 1 vol.

Typescript (carbon copy).

Relates to the Russian Imperial secret police.

2558

Smith (Gerald Lyman Kenneth) collection, ca. 1940–1949. 1 folder, 1 microfilm reel.

Photocopy and microfilm.

Correspondence of Glen A. Chandler and selected records of the Anti-Defamation League, relating to

G. L. K. Smith (1898–1976), his views on the Jewish population and U.S. entry into World War II, and his relationship with Arthur H. Vandenberg.

Gift, G. A. Chandler, 1973.

2559

Smith, Harold.

Dispatches, 1944. 1 phonorecord.

Chicago Tribune reporter on Leyte, Philippine Islands. Relates to American and Philippine guerrilla military activities on Leyte. Recorded by the Mutual Broadcasting System.

2560

Smith, Henry Bancroft, b. 1884.

Papers, 1919–1928. 28 ms. boxes, 1 cu. ft. box.

U.S. Grain Corporation agent, Technical Adviser to Poland, and Commercial Attaché in Poland, 1919–1923; Special Representative, U.S. Department of Commerce, 1923–1928. Diaries, correspondence, reports, memoranda, financial records, printed matter and photographs, relating to American food relief in Europe, economic reconstruction in Poland, and agricultural market conditions in Europe.

Gift, H. B. Smith, 1957.

2561

Smith-Hutton, Henri Harold, 1901–1977.

Papers, 1944–1975. 1 ms. box, 1 envelope.

Captain, U.S. Navy; Naval Attaché in Japan, 1939–1941. Transcript of an oral interview, memoranda, correspondence, photographs and cartoons, relating to American-Japanese relations immediately before the attack on Pearl Harbor, U.S. naval intelligence during World War II, and post-war activities of Radio Free Europe.

Gift, H. H. Smith-Hutton, 1973. Subsequent increments.

2562

Smith, Jack A.

Study, 1950. "White Russian Emigrants and the Japanese Army in the Far East." 1 folder.

Typescript.

Relates to White Russian military activities and Japanese intervention in Siberia during the Russian Civil War.

Gift, Fritz Epstein, 1970.

2563

Smith, Katherine A. H.

Memoirs, n.d. ½ ms. box.

Wife of Truman Smith, Colonel, U.S. Army, and U.S. Military Attaché to Germany, 1935–1939. Relates to the military career of T. Smith, 1935–1946.

Gift, K. A. H. Smith, 1974.

2564

Smith, Ralph C., 1893–

Papers, 1917–1966. 26 ms. boxes, 2 oversize boxes (1 1. ft.).

Major General, U.S. Army; Commanding General, 27th Division, 1942–1944; Military Attaché to France, 1945–1946. Correspondence, reports, writings, and printed matter, relating to the American Expeditionary Forces in France during World War I, activities of the Command and General Staff School and Army War College in the inter-war period, and American military operations in the Pacific Theater during World War II.
Gift, R. C. Smith, 1978.

2565

Smith, Ralph Elbertson, 1910–
Study, 1977. "Academic Grading: Basic Issues and Recommendations." 1 folder.
Typescript (photocopy).
American economist. Relates to grading systems in American colleges and universities.
Gift, R. E. Smith, 1977.

2566

Smith, Richard Harris, 1946–
Papers, 1942–1971. 2 ms. boxes.
American historian. Correspondence and writings, relating to operations of the U.S. Office of Strategic Services during World War II in the European, African, and Asian theaters of operations. Used as research material for the book by R. H. Smith, *OSS: The Secret History of America's First Central Intelligence Agency* (Berkeley, 1972).
During his lifetime may not be used without written permission of R. H. Smith.
Deposit, R. H. Smith, 1978.

2567

Smith, Robert.
Reports, 1932–1934. ½ ms. box.
Typescript.
American visitor to Manchuria and Mongolia. Relates to political and economic conditions in Manchuria and Mongolia, and to Soviet-Japanese relations.

2568

Smith, Robinson.
Writings, 1917. 1 folder.
Member, Commission for Relief in Belgium. Memoir (typewritten), entitled "Hoover: The Man in Action," relating to the administration of the Commission for Relief in Belgium by Herbert Hoover; and a pamphlet (printed), entitled "Food Values and the Rationing of a Country," relating to Commission for Relief in Belgium food relief.
Gift, R. Smith, 1948.

2569

Smith, Truman, 1893–1970.
Papers, 1922–1970. 2½ ms. boxes.
In part, photocopies of selected papers at the Herbert Hoover Presidential Library (box 3).
Colonel, U.S. Army; U.S. Military Attaché to Germany, 1935–1939. Memoirs, correspondence, and reports, relating to the German Army between World

Wars I and II, national socialism in Germany, and U.S. military intelligence activities during World War II.
Preliminary inventory.
Gift, T. Smith, 1969. Exchange, Herbert Hoover Presidential Library, 1978.

2570

Smith (Walter Bedell)—photograph, n.d. 1 envelope.
Depicts General W. B. Smith, U.S. Army.

2571

Smolin, I. S.
Translation of memoir, n.d. "The Alapaevsk Tragedy: The Murder of the Russian Grand Dukes by the Bolsheviks." 1 folder.
Typescript.
White Russian Army General. Relates to the discovery of the bodies of members of the Russian royal family at Alapaevsk, Russia, in 1918. Translated by W. Yourieff.

2572

Snell, Jane, *collector.*
Miscellany, 1930–1965. ½ ms. box.
Clippings, newspaper issues, letters and memorabilia, relating to public activities of Herbert Hoover, President of the U.S., 1929–1933.
Gift, J. Snell, 1968.

2573

Snigirevskiĭ, Konstantin Vasil'evich, d. 1937.
History (in Russian), 1937. "Aleksandrovskiĭ Komitet o Ranenykh" (Aleksandrovskiĭ Committee for the Wounded). 1 folder.
Holograph.
Major General, Russian Imperial Army. Relates to a Russian organization founded in the nineteenth century for the care of wounded soldiers.

2574

Snook, Mrs. John.
Papers, 1915–1919. ½ ms. box.
President, League for the Protection of American Prisoners in Germany, during World War I. Correspondence, pamphlets, and clippings, relating to the deportation of Belgians to Germany, American prisoners of war in Germany, and relief activities for Belgium during World War I. Includes letters from Herbert Hoover and Queen Elizabeth of Belgium.

2575

Snook, Walter B., *collector.*
W. B. Snook collection on the American invasion of Iwo Jima, 1945. 1 ms. box.
Reports, surrender instructions, and military newspaper issues. Includes a telegram from Admiral Chester W. Nimitz on the capture of Iwo Jima, and a proclamation to the people of the Volcano Islands.
Preliminary inventory.
Gift, W. B. Snook, 1967.

2576

Snyder, Frederic Sylvester, 1868–1956.
Papers, 1896–1919. 1 folder.
Photocopy of original papers located in the Herbert Hoover Presidential Library.
American food company executive; U.S. Food Administration official during World War I. Correspondence and memoranda, relating to the U.S. Food Administration, World War I, and the Snyder family genealogy.
Exchange, Herbert Hoover Presidential Library, 1977.

2577

Socialism in France collection (in French), 1897–1946. 9 ms. boxes.
Clippings, newspaper and periodical issues, bulletins, pamphlets and leaflets, issued by communist, socialist, syndicalist and trade-union organizations in France, relating to the international and French communist, socialist, syndicalist and trade-union movements.

2578

Société Agricole Arménienne.
Report (in French), ca. 1919. "La Situation Agricole en Arménie Occidentale, Années 1913 et 1917–1918: Rapport" (The Agricultural Situation in Western Armenia, for the Years 1913 and 1917–1918: Report). 1 vol.
Typescript (mimeographed).

2579

Société des Amis de l'Espagne.
Reports (in French), 1917. 1 folder.
Typescript.
Society of the Friends of Spain, a private French organization. Relates to political conditions in Spain, Franco-Spanish relations, and Spanish public opinion regarding World War I.

2580

Soïuz Voïnstvuïushchikh Bezbozhnikov. Leningradskiï Oblastnoï Sovet.
Appeal, 1932. "To Our Comrade Atheists in Capitalist Countries." 1 folder.
Typescript.
Leningrad Regional Council of the Union of Militant Atheists. Calls for international struggle against religion.

2581

Sokol, Anthony Eugene, 1897–
Miscellaneous papers, n.d. 10 card file boxes, ½ ms. box.
American political scientist. Slides, depicting landscapes, art objects, architecture, and scenes of daily life and economic activity in Indonesia; and the draft of a published article, relating to naval operations in the Adriatic during World War I.
Preliminary inventory.
Gift, A. E. Sokol, 1958.

2582

Sokolnicki, Michał, b. 1880.
Papers (in Polish, French and English), 1931–1968. 14 ms. boxes.
Polish Ambassador to Turkey. Diaries, correspondence, memoranda, and printed matter, relating to Polish-Turkish relations, and to the Polish Government-in-Exile in London during World War II.
Quotations limited to 250 words consecutively and 2000 words total.
Purchase, Mrs. M. Sokolnicki, 1968. Subsequent increments.

2583

Sokolnikov, Grigoriĭ IAkovlevich, 1888–1939.
Translation of study, 1931. *Soviet Policy in Public Finance, 1917–1928.* ½ ms. box.
Typescript.
Soviet Commissar of Finance, 1922–1926; Deputy Commissar of Foreign Affairs and Ambassador to Great Britain, 1929–1934. Translated by Elena Varneck. Translation published (Stanford, 1931).

2584

Sokolnitskii, V.
Translation of memoir, n.d. "Kaigorodovshchina" (Kaigorodoviana). 1 folder.
Typescript.
Colonel, White Russian Army. Relates to the activities of Aleksandr Petrovich Kaigorodov, Cossack Ataman and White Russian military leader in Mongolia during the Russian Civil War, 1919–1921.

2585

Sokolov, Boris N.
Writings, 1931–1932. ½ ms. box.
Typescript (mimeographed).
Writings, entitled "Soviet Dumping," 1931, and "Industry in the U.S.S.R. in 1931," 1932, relating to Soviet commerce and industry.

2586

Sokolov, Nikolaĭ Alekseevich, 1882–1924.
Report (in Russian), 1919. 2 folders.
Holograph.
White Russian official; Judicial Investigator for Especially Important Cases. Relates to the investigation of the murder of Tsar Nicholas II and his family. Intended as a supplement to the report by Lieutenant General M. K. Dieterichs. Includes translation (typewritten).
Gift, E. L. Harris.

2587

Soldiers of the Press.
Sound recordings of news stories, ca. 1941–1945. 16 phonorecords.
News stories by American war correspondents, relating to Allied military, naval and aerial operations in Europe, North Africa and the Pacific during World War II.
Preliminary inventory.

2588

Soloveĭ, Dmytro.
Memorandum (in Ukrainian), 1944. "Istoriî͡a Ukrains'koĭ Kooperatsiĭ: Korotkyĭ Populiarnyĭ Vyklad" (History of Ukrainian Cooperation: Popular Short Version). 1 folder.
Typescript.
Relates to the history of agrarian cooperatives in the Ukraine.

2589

Solov'ev, Emeliî͡an I., 1898–1945.
Memoirs (in Russian), n.d. 1 folder.
Typescript (photocopy).
Russian forced labor camp prisoner. Relates to conditions in the Solovetski Islands concentration camp in the Soviet Union, 1925–1932.
Gift, Robert B. Samuelson, 1976.

2590

Solow, Herbert, 1903–1964.
Papers, 1924—1976. 12 ms. boxes.
American journalist; editor, *Fortune Magazine*, 1945–1964. Correspondence, speeches and writings, memoranda, depositions, clippings and other printed matter, relating to the communist movement in the U.S., the Non-Partisan Defense League, the Commission of Inquiry into the Charges Made Against Leon Trotsky in the Moscow Trials, Soviet espionage in the U.S., Whittaker Chambers and the Alger Hiss case, Zionism, the Nuremberg Trial of Major German War Criminals, 1945–1946, and post-World War II international business enterprises. Includes some papers of Sylvia Salmi Solow, 1964–1976.
Gift, Cassandra Johnson, 1977.

2591

Solzheniî͡tsyn (Aleksandr Isaevich) collection, 1975–1978. 2 ms. boxes.
Articles, publicity leaflet, photographs, and a sound recording, relating to the visits of the Russian novelist A. I. Solzheniî͡tsyn to the Hoover Institution on War, Revolution and Peace in June 1975 and May 1976; clippings relating to A. I. Solzheniî͡tsyn's literary works; his public statements regarding civil rights in the U.S.S.R.; and the text of his Harvard University commencement address, June 8, 1978, with clippings reflecting U.S. public reaction to it.

2592

"Some Books of Reference on Estonia."
Bibliography, 1933. 1 folder.
Typescript.

2593

Soudakoff, Peter.
Writings (in Russian and English), n.d. 1 vol.
Typescript.
Relates to the Romanov dynasty, Lev Troî͡tskiĭ, and the Russo-Japanese War.

2594

South Africa. Delegation to the United Nations Conference on International Organization, San Francisco, 1945.
Proposal, 1945. 1 folder.
Typescript (mimeographed).
Relates to the future disposition of the mandated territory of Southwest Africa.
Gift, Waldo Chamberlin, 1945.

2595

Southern Africa collection, 1969–1977. 8 ms. boxes. 1 oversize box (1 l. ft.).
Leaflets, newsletters, pamphlets, photographs and ephemera of various political action groups and other organizations, relating to political and economic developments in southern African countries, including Angola, Mozambique, Rhodesia (Zimbabwe), South Africa, and South West Africa (Namibia). Collected by African Curatorship, Hoover Institution on War, Revolution and Peace.
Preliminary inventory.

2596

Souvarine, Boris Konstantinovich, 1895–
Papers (in French and Russian), 1925–1971. 2 ms. boxes.
Russian-born French journalist and author; French communist leader, 1919–1924. Correspondence, writings, clippings, and printed matter and other material, relating to the French Communist Party, the Communist International, Marxism, Soviet agricultural and economic policies, and political events in twentieth-century Russia. Includes correspondence with Ekaterina Kuskova, Sergei Prokopovich, Nikolai V. Volsky and the Marx-Engels Institute (Moscow).
Preliminary inventory.
Purchase, B. Souvarine, 1977. Gift, Stanley Plastrik, 1978.

2597

Sovet Oppozitsiĭ Man'chzhuriĭ i Dal'nî͡ago Vostoka.
Pamphlet (in Russian), 1927. "Rossiî͡a dlî͡a Russkikh!" (Russia for Russians!). 1 folder.
Printed.
Russian fascist émigré organization in the Far East. Relates to the program of the organization.

2598

"Soviet Ruble, Gold Ruble, Tchernovetz and Ruble-Merchandise."
Translation of newspaper article, 1923. 1 folder.
Typescript (mimeographed).
Relates to the circulation of currency in the Soviet Union. Original article published in *Agence Economique et Financière*, July 18, 1923. Translated by S. Ughet.

2599

Soviet Union—emigration list (in Russian), ca. 1975. 1 folder.
Holograph (photocopy).
Relates to the procedures required for a Jewish Soviet

citizen in 1975 to procure a visa to emigrate from the Soviet Union to Israel. Includes a translation, and miscellaneous items pertaining to the problems of emigrating from the Soviet Union.
Gift, 1976.

2600

Sowers, Margaret Cosgrave, *collector.*
Newspaper clippings, 1941–1951. 1 ms. box.
Relates to the internment of Japanese-Americans in relocation centers during World War II. Clippings from California newspapers.
Gift, M. C. Sowers, 1956.

2601

Sozialdemokratische Partei Deutschlands collection (in German), 1929–1949. 1 ms. box.
Reports, pamphlets, and leaflets, relating to the 1929 election campaign of the Social Democratic Party of Germany; clandestine antifascist activities of the party, 1933–1938; and social and economic conditions in Soviet-occupied East Germany in 1949. Includes a few communist pamphlets from the 1930s.
Preliminary inventory.

2602

Sozialistische Arbeiterhilfe.
Leaflet (in German), ca. 1933–1939. 1 folder.
Printed.
Socialist Workers' Aid. Lists rules of conduct for underground anti-fascists in Germany.

2603

Sozialistische Einheitspartei Deutschlands.
Miscellaneous records (in German), 1946–1949. 1 folder.
East German communist party. Miscellaneous memoranda and reports, relating to party administration and to political, economic and cultural activities in various parts of East Germany.

2604

Spaatz (Carl)—photograph, n.d. 1 envelope.
Depicts General C. Spaatz, U.S. Air Force.

2605

Spalding, Merrill Ten Broeck.
Papers (in English, Russian, French and Flemish), 1922–1945. 1½ ms. boxes, 1 card file box, 2 envelopes.
American historian. Correspondence, notes, clippings, and other printed matter, relating to economic conditions and labor in Russia from 1917 to World War II. Includes newspaper and periodical issues published in Belgium immediately after its liberation in 1945, and reproductions of paintings at the Tretyakov State Gallery, Moscow.
Gift, M. T. B. Spalding. Incremental gift, Clara Spalding, 1978.

2606

Spaniards in France collection (in Spanish, French, German, Catalan and Basque), 1943–1946. 1 folder.
Bulletins, leaflets and pamphlets, issued by pro-Republican Spanish refugees in France, relating to the anti-Franco Spanish political emigration and to the anti-German resistance in France.

2607

Speranza, Gino, 1872–1927.
Papers, 1911–1925. 32 ms. boxes.
American military and political attaché in Italy. Writings, diaries, correspondence, reports, pamphlets, notes, photographs, and printed matter, relating to Italian politics and diplomacy during World War I and in the postwar period.
Preliminary inventory.
Gift, Florence Speranza, 1942. Subsequent increments.

2608

Sperr, Ingeborg.
Biographical sketch (in German), 1945. 1 vol.
Typescript.
Assistant to Rudolf Hess, Deputy to Adolf Hitler, Fuehrer of Germany. R. Hess is the subject of the sketch.

2609

Spies, Georg.
Correspondence (in German), 1904–1906. 1 vol.
Director, Steauna Romana, an oil company subsidiary of the Deutsche Bank. Relates to Deutsche Bank efforts to secure oil concessions in Romania, Bulgaria and Turkey. Includes explanatory note by M. Laserson.

2610

Spitzer, Tadeusz B., 1893–
Memorandum, 1943. 1 folder.
Typescript.
Polish economist and engineer. Relates to the post-World War II reconstruction of Europe.

2611

Sprague, Joe S.
Thesis, 1948. "Study in Relief: The Commission for Relief in Belgium, 1914–1919." 1 folder.
Typescript.

2612

"Spravki o Glavnokomanduiûshchikh Frontami, Komandirakh Armiiami, Komandirakh Korpusov i Proch" (List of Commanding Officers of the Russian Imperial Army, Arranged by Units, At the Time of the First World War).
List (in Russian), ca. 1916. 1 vol.
Holograph.

2613

Sprenger, Jakob, 1884–1945.
Letter (in German), 1942. 1 folder.
Holograph.
Reichsstatthalter of Hesse, 1933–1944. Relates to national socialism in Germany.

221

2614

Spring, Agnes Wright, *collector*.
Miscellany, 1917–1920. 1 ms. box.
Letters from U.S. and Belgian soldiers in France during World War I, relating to military life at the front, and photographs of U.S. soldiers in the U.S. during World War I.
Gift, A. W. Spring, 1943.

2615

Sprouse, Philip D., 1906–1977.
Papers, 1945–1964. 2 ms. boxes, 18 envelopes.
American diplomat; member of George C. Marshall and Albert C. Wedemeyer Missions to China, 1945–1947; Ambassador to Cambodia, 1962–1964. Printed matter, clippings, maps, invitations, programs, diplomatic list, and photographs, relating to American relations with China and Cambodia, the Marshall Mission of 1945–1946, and cultural and political conditions in Cambodia.
Gift, P. D. Sprouse, 1974.

2616

Spruance, Raymond Ames, 1886–1969.
Miscellaneous papers, 1937–1963. 1 ms. box.
Admiral, U.S. Navy; Deputy Commander-in-Chief, Pacific Fleet, 1942–1943; Commander, Central Pacific Forces, 1944–1945. Correspondence, addresses, statements, biographical material, and lectures, 1937–1963, relating to American naval operations in World War II. Includes correspondence with Presidents Harry S. Truman and Dwight D. Eisenhower.
Gift, R. A. Spruance, 1967.

2617

Squires, Duane.
Speech, 1933. "British Propaganda at Home and in the United States, 1914–1917." 1 folder.
Typewritten transcript.
Speech, delivered at Urbana, Illinois, December 28, 1933.

2618

Staar, Richard F., 1923–   , *collector*.
Photographs, 1945. 1 envelope.
Depicts Admiral Chester W. Nimitz, U.S. Navy, at the signing of the Japanese surrender on board the U.S.S. *Missouri*, and the signature sheet of the surrender document. Autographed by C. W. Nimitz.
Gift, R. F. Staar, 1972.

2619

Stader, James A., b. 1882.
Papers (in English, German and Polish), 1910–1924. 1 ms. box.
Captain, U.S. Army; American Relief Administration worker in Upper Silesia, 1919–1921. Correspondence, reports, orders, photographs and miscellanea, relating to American Relief Administration activities in Silesia at the end of World War I, the German-Polish territorial dispute over Silesia, and political and economic conditions in the area.
Gift, J. A. Stader.

2620

Stafford, Clayton I.
Memoir, n.d. "Incident in the Crimea, 1920." 1 folder.
Typescript.
Sailor, U.S. Navy. Relates to a U.S. naval visit to the Crimea during the Russian Civil War, 1920.
Gift, C. I. Stafford, 1977.

2621

Stalin (Iosif)—photograph, n.d. 1 envelope.
Depicts the Soviet political leader I. Stalin.

2622

Stamps, n.d. 15 albums, 3 boxes, 4 folders.
Postage stamps from many countries issued at various times.

2623

De Standaard (The Standard).
Newspaper issue (in Flemish), 1976. 1 folder.
Brussels newspaper. Relates to the bankruptcy of *De Standaard* and other periodicals.

2624

Stanfield, Boris, b. 1888.
Interview, 1976. 1 phonotape.
Russian-American journalist; reporter for *Izvestiiâ*, 1917–1920. Relates to the Revolution and Civil War in Russia. Interview conducted by Anatole Mazour at the Hoover Institution on War, Revolution and Peace, November 15–16, 1976.
Gift, B. Stanfield, 1976.

2625

Stanford Communist.
Newspaper issues, 1949. 1 folder.
Typescript (mimeographed).
Organ of the Stanford (University) Club of the Communist Party. Two genuine issues, January-February 1949; and one false issue, actually issued by anti-communists, February 1949.

2626

Stanford, Jane Lathrop, 1825–1905.
Letter, 1895, to Grover Cleveland. 1 folder.
Holograph (photocopy).
Widow of Leland Stanford; co-founder of Stanford University. Relates to the prospects of Stanford University and to a U.S. Government suit against the estate of Leland Stanford.

2627

Stanford Listening Post, 1940–1945.
Records, 1940–1945. 29 ms. boxes, 1 envelope.
Project of the Hoover Institution on War, Revolution and Peace to record and analyze trans-Pacific radio

broadcasts. Correspondence, transcripts of radio broadcasts, study papers, notes, and card indexes, relating to radio broadcasts from East and Southeast Asia.
Register.

2628

Stanford Nisei Alumni Newsletter.
Newsletter issues, 1944–1945. 1 folder.
Typescript (mimeographed).
Newsletter of Japanese-American alumni of Stanford University. Relates to Japanese-American activities during World War II.

2629

Stanford Research Institute. China Project.
Translations of newspaper article extracts, 1953. 2 ms. boxes.
Project for the study of Chinese economic policy. Relates to Chinese economic policy, finance and trade, transportation, communications, agriculture, manufacturing and raw materials. Extracts from Chinese newspapers.

2630

Stanford University collection, 1917–1943. 1 folder.
Certificates, leaflets, programs, and mimeographed lists, relating to participation of Stanford University and of Stanford students in the U.S. war effort during the two world wars. Includes certificates from the Fédération Interalliée des Anciens Combattants, 1933, and from the U.S. Navy Department.

2631

Stanford University. Draft Counseling Office, 1967–1973, *collector.*
Printed matter, 1967–1973. 3 ms. boxes.
Newsletters, handbooks, leaflets, and ephemeral publications of government agencies, legal organizations, and political action groups, relating to military conscription in the United States.
Preliminary inventory.
Gift, Stanford University, 1973.

2632

Stanford University. Food Research Institute.
Miscellaneous records, 1919–1955. 1 ms. box.
Private institute for research on world food problems. Correspondence, reports, and printed matter, relating to the founding and research work of the Institute, and to the production, supply, and marketing of wheat.
Preliminary inventory.

2633

Stanford University. Institute of Hispanic American and Luso-Brazilian Studies, *collector.*
Printed matter (in English, Spanish and Portuguese), 1954–1965. 783 ms. boxes.
Pamphlets, clippings and serial issues, relating to political, social and economic conditions in Latin America, Spain and Portugal.
Register.

Gift, Institute of Hispanic American and Luso-Brazilian Studies, 1965.

2634

Stanton, Charles E.
Speech, 1917. 1 vol.
Handwritten transcript.
Relates to the Franco-American alliance during World War I. Speech delivered at the tomb of the Marquis de Lafayette, Paris, July 4, 1917.

2635

Stark, Herbert S., *collector.*
Photographs, ca. 1899–1902. 2 envelopes.
Depicts gold mining operations in South Africa, and British troops in South Africa at the time of the Boer War.
Gift, Mrs. H. S. Stark, 1973.

2636

Starr, Clarence T.
Papers, 1923–1941. 1 ms. box.
American mining engineer in the Soviet Union, 1928–1931. Correspondence, writings, notes, transcripts of testimony and printed matter, relating to the Soviet coal mining industry, forced labor in the Soviet Union, and efforts to secure an embargo on Soviet imports into the U.S.
Gift, Mrs. Leon Howard, 1960.

2637

Starr, Walter A.
Miscellaneous papers, 1919. 1 folder.
Second Vice President, U.S. Grain Corporation, 1919. Transcript of a speech, correspondence and memorabilia, relating to activities of the U.S. Grain Corporation in regulating distribution of grain in the U.S. for domestic consumption and export during and immediately after World War I.
Gift, W. A. Starr, 1958.

2638

"The State Bank of the Republic of Soviets."
Translation of newspaper article, 1923. 1 folder.
Relates to banking institutions in the Soviet Union. Original article published in *Agence Economique et Financière*, April 25, 1923. Translated by S. Ughet.

2639

"A Statement to the Peace Conference."
Statement, 1919. 1 folder.
Typescript.
Opposes the creation of a Jewish state in Palestine. Presented to the Paris Peace Conference by a group of Jewish Americans, March 4, 1919.

2640

Stauffenberg, Hans Christoph, Freiherr von.
Speech, 1963. 1 folder.
Typewritten transcript (mimeographed).
Cousin of Klaus von Stauffenberg, German anti-Nazi

resistance leader. Relates to the German resistance movement and K. von Stauffenberg. Speech delivered at Stanford University, August 2, 1963.
Gift, Karl Brandt, 1975.

2641

Stavrianos, Leften Stavros, 1913–
Papers (in English and Greek), 1942–1963. 4 ms. boxes.
American historian. Writings, press releases, press translations and digests, reports, memoranda, clippings, and pamphlets, relating to political and military developments in Greece and Cyprus, especially during the Greek civil war period, 1944–1949. Includes material collected by a member of the Allied Mission for Observing Greek Elections of March 31, 1946.
Register.
Gift, L. S. Stavrianos, 1973.

2642

Stearns, Cuthbert P.
Lecture, 1943. "Observations in North Africa." 1 vol.
Typewritten transcript.
Relates to general description of North Africa.

2643

Stefan, Abp. of Sofia—photograph, n.d. 1 envelope.
Depicts Archbishop Stefan of Sofia.

2644

Stegner, Wallace Earle, 1909–
Miscellaneous papers, 1914–1950. 1 ms. box.
American novelist. Correspondence, notes, photographs, and copies of newspaper articles and trial transcripts, relating to the murder trial of labor organizer Joe Hill in 1914–1915. Used as research material for the historical novel by W. E. Stegner, *The Preacher and the Slave* (1950).
Gift, W. E. Stegner, 1952.

2645

Steichen, Edward J., 1879–1973.
Photographs, 1942–1945. 1 envelope.
American photographer. Depicts ships and airplanes of the U.S. Navy in action during World War II, mostly in the Pacific Theater.
Gift, Office of the Chief of Naval Operations, 1945.

2646

Steinberg, Isaac Nachman, b. 1888.
History, n.d. "The Events of July 1918." 1 vol.
Typescript.
Relates to the assassination of Graf Wilhelm von Mirbach-Harff, German Ambassador to Russia, in 1918.

2647

Steiner; Gerald John.
Slides, ca. 1930–1939. 2 ms. boxes.
American diplomat and photographer. Tinted glass slides, depicting scenes in Cambodia, including the temple ruins at Angkor Wat and a rice festival of the Panchen Lama. Coloring done by Lucille Douglass.
Gift, G. J. Steiner, 1971.

2648

Steinfeldt, Eric, *collector*.
Photographs, 1918. 1 envelope.
Depicts scenes at Vladivostok, the Allied intervention, and the Czech Legion.
Gift, E. Steinfeldt.

2649

Stenbock-Fermor, Ivan, *collector*.
Miscellany, ca. 1800–1913. 6 coins, 1 map.
Six Russian Imperial coins and one nineteenth century map of St. Petersburg.
Gift, I. Stenbock-Fermor, 1974.

2650

Stepanov, Afanasiĭ Ivanovich.
Papers (in Russian), 1956–1961. 1½ ms. boxes, 1 envelope.
Soviet engineer. Correspondence, legal documents, memoranda, reports, engineering diagrams, and photographs, relating to proposals for technological innovations in the Minsk Motorcycle Factory, the Soviet judicial system, administrative procedures and trade unions, Soviet factory management operations, and daily life and social conditions in the Soviet Union. Compiled by A. I. Stepanov for use in a memoir to have been entitled "V Poiskakh Spravedlivosti" (In Search of Justice).
Gift, A. I. Stepanov, 1962.

2651

Stepanov, Aleksandr Stepanovich.
Outline of projected memoirs (in Russian), 1932. 1 folder.
Typescript.
White Russian Army officer. Relates to secret military organizations in Siberia, 1918–1920.

2652

Stepanova, Vanda Kazimirovna.
Memoirs (in Russian), ca. 1918. "Zapiski Velikoĭ Voĭny 1914–1918 g." (Notes on the Great War, 1914–1918). 1 vol.
Holograph.
Nurse, Russian Imperial 12th Army. Relates to activities of the 12th Army during World War I.

2653

Stephens, Frederick Dorsey, 1891–
Papers, 1909–1945. 1 ms. box.
American relief worker in World Wars I and II. Correspondence, photographs, printed matter and miscellanea, relating to relief activities of the Commission for Relief in Belgium, 1914–1916, of the American Relief Administration in Russia, 1921–1922, and of the Finnish Relief Fund, 1939–1940.
Gift, F. D. Stephens, 1957.

2654

Stepno-Badzheĭskyĭ Volost (Russia) collection (in Russian), 1919. 1 folder.

Memoranda and reports, relating to the gathering of the harvest which was abandoned by the inhabitants of the Stepno-Badzheĭskyĭ District in Russia in 1919.

2655

Sterling, J. E. Wallace, *collector*.

J. E. W. Sterling collection on world affairs, 1937–1951. 5 ms. boxes.

Communiqués of the belligerent governments printed in the *New York Times*, 1942–1945, relating to military operations during World War II; and reports from diverse sources relating to Japanese foreign policy, 1937–1939, postwar Japanese educational reform, postwar Soviet foreign policy, and the Chinese Revolution of 1949.

2656

Stern, Mrs. Harold, *collector*.

Postcards, ca. 1910–1919. 1 ms. box.

Depicts European cities and scenes from World War I.

Gift, Mrs. H. Stern, 1969.

2657

Stevens, Harley C.

Papers, 1901–1961. 3 ms. boxes.

Vice-President, American Independent Oil Company. Texts of treaties, concessions and agreements between various oil companies and governments of the Middle East, relating to Middle Eastern oil concessions.

Preliminary inventory.

2658

Stevens, John Frank, 1853–1943.

Papers, 1917–1931. ½ ms. box.

American civil engineer; Chairman, U.S. Advisory Commission of Railway Experts to Russia, 1917; President, Technical Board, Inter-Allied Railway Commission for the Supervision of the Siberian and Chinese Eastern Railways, 1919–1922. Memoirs and correspondence, relating to railroads in Siberia and Manchuria during the Russian Revolution, and to Allied intervention in the Russian Revolution.

2659

Stevenson, Harry Clinton.

Miscellaneous papers, 1939–1945. 1 folder, 1 envelope.

Admiral, U.S. Navy. Reports, design manual, lists, graphs and photographs, relating to submarine warfare during World War II. Includes photographs of German naval operations.

Gift, H. C. Stevenson, 1969.

2660

Stilson, Fielding J.

Miscellaneous papers, 1920–1933. 1 folder, 1 envelope.

Correspondence and clippings, relating to Herbert Hoover, President of the U.S., and to the Presidential elections of 1920, 1928 and 1932. Includes correspondence with Herbert Hoover.

2661

Stilwell, Joseph Warren, 1883–1946.

Papers, 1900–1971. 61 ms. boxes, 79 envelopes, 4 albums, 10 scrapbooks, 8 rolls (2 l. ft.), 1 wooden box (1 l. ft.).

General, U.S. Army; Commanding General, U.S. Forces in China-Burma-India Theater, and Commander, Chinese Armies in Burma, 1942–1944. Diaries, correspondence, radiograms, memoranda, reports, military orders, writings, annotated maps, photographs, clippings, and printed matter, relating to the political development of Nationalist China, the Sino-Japanese conflict of 1937–1945, and the China-Burma-India Theater during World War II.

Register.

Gift, Winifred A. Stilwell, 1951; bequest, 1972.

2662

Stinnett, Robert B., 1924–

Photographs, 1944–1945. 17 envelopes.

U.S. Navy photographer. Depicts the aircraft carrier *San Jacinto*, naval personnel, prisoner of war camps, life at sea, scenes of battle, naval artillery, Tokyo, and the Pacific Islands.

Gift, R. B. Stinnett, 1963.

2663

Stockton, Gilchrist Baker, 1890–1973.

Papers, 1911–1959. 11 ms. boxes.

Commission for Relief in Belgium and American Relief Administration worker during World War II; U.S. Minister to Austria, 1930–1933. Correspondence, dispatches, reports, clippings, and photographs, relating to activities of the Commission for Relief in Belgium, 1915–1916, and of the American Relief Administration in Austria, 1919–1920; to U.S. and Florida politics, 1924–1928; to U.S.-Austrian relations, 1930–1933; and to the establishment of the Jacksonville, Florida, Naval Air Base.

Register.

Gift, G. Stockton, Jr., 1975.

2664

Stolypin (Petr Arkad'evich)—photographs, n.d. 1 envelope.

Depicts the tsarist Russian government official P. A. Stolypin.

2665

Stone, George E.

Papers, 1918–1919. 1 ms. box, 3 envelopes.

Captain, U.S. Army Signal Corps. Correspondence, reports, memoranda, photographs, and memorabilia, relating to the Photographic Section of the U.S. Army Signal Corps in France during World War I.

Gift, Karl E. Kneiss.

2666

Story, Russell McCulloch, 1883–1942.

Papers, 1917–1921. ½ ms. box, 1 envelope, 6 boxes of slides (2 l. ft.).

War Work Secretary, Young Men's Christian Association in Russia, 1917–1918. Letters, photographs and glass slides, relating to relief work in Russia, conditions in Moscow and elsewhere in Russia during the Russian Revolution, and the Czech Legion; and depicting scenes in Japan, Russia and western Europe.

Preliminary inventory.

Gift, Gertrude A. Story, 1957. Gift, Katherine S. French, 1972.

2667

Stowell, Ellery Cory, 1875–1958.

Papers, 1909–1920. 1 ms. box.

American legal scholar. Correspondence, writings, printed matter, and clippings, relating to the London Naval Conference of 1909, and various proposals for international limitation of armaments.

2668

Stoyadinovitch, Milan, b. 1888.

Translation of speech, 1923. "The Financial Policy of the Kingdom of the Serbs, Croats and Slovenes." 1 folder.

Typewritten transcript (mimeographed).

Minister of Finance of Yugoslavia. Delivered in the Yugoslav Parliament, June 9, 1923.

2669

Stratton, Richard A., 1931–

Papers, 1967–1974. 14 ms. boxes, 3 scrapbooks.

Captain, U.S. Navy; prisoner of war in North Vietnam, 1967–1973. Phonotapes, video tapes, correspondence, memoranda, photographs, clippings, and printed matter, relating to American prisoners of war and persons missing in action during the Vietnam war and to the treatment and release of prisoners in North Vietnam.

Preliminary inventory.

Until July 26, 1985, access requires the written permission of R. A. Stratton.

Gift, R. A. Stratton, 1975.

2670

Strauss, Lewis Lichtenstein, 1896–1974.

Miscellaneous papers, 1918–1945. 1 ms. box.

Secretary to Herbert Hoover, 1917–1919; Chairman, U.S. Atomic Energy Commission, 1953–1958; Secretary of Commerce, 1958–1959. Diary, 1918, relating to the trip of Herbert Hoover to Europe in 1918; and galley proofs of the Allied conference proceedings at Malta and Yalta, 1945.

Gift, L. L. Strauss, 1956.

2671

Street (Cyrus H.) collection, 1908–1960. 1 folder, 1 envelope.

Clippings, miscellanea and a photograph, relating to C. H. Street, editor of *The United Nations*, a bulletin published in Berkeley, California, 1908–1911, which advocated the establishment of a world government to secure world peace. Includes a copy of the first issue of *The United Nations* (November 1908).

Gift, Mrs. Ranson B. Matthews.

2672

Strench, Mary Minthorn, b. 1887.

Correspondence, 1944–1964, with Herbert Hoover. 1 folder, 1 envelope.

Photocopy.

Cousin of Herbert Hoover, President of the U.S. Relates to personal and family matters. Includes a photograph of Henry John Minthorn, uncle of Herbert Hoover.

Gift, M. M. Strench, 1968.

2673

Stricker, Noémi.

Appeal, 1923. 1 folder.

Typescript.

Appeals for contributions for relief work in Germany and France.

2674

Strong, Agnes L.

Journal, 1915. 1 folder.

Typescript.

American Red Cross worker; wife of Richard P. Strong, physician and American Red Cross worker. Relates to Red Cross work in the Balkans during the typhoid epidemic of 1915.

2675

Strong, Sydney.

Newsletters, 1932–1933. 1 folder.

Typescript (mimeographed).

Observer at the Geneva Disarmament Conference. Relates to the conference and to the world disarmament movement.

2676

Stroop, Juergen, 1895–

Report (in German), 1943. "Es Gibt Keinen Juedischen Wohnbezirk in Warschau Mehr!" (There Is No Longer a Jewish Quarter in Warsaw!). 1 folder.

Typescript (photocopy).

German SS and Police Commander, Warsaw District. Relates to the German suppression of the Warsaw uprising and destruction of the Warsaw Ghetto.

2677

Strunk (Roland) collection (in German), 1937. 1 folder.

Reports, correspondence and depositions, relating to a duel fought near Berlin between Horst Krutschinna, Obergebietsfuehrer in the Hitlerjugend, and Roland Strunk, Hauptsturmfuehrer in the Schutzstaffel, resulting in the death of the latter.

2678

Stuart, Gilbert, 1912–1973.

Memoirs, n.d. 1 ms. box.

Typescript.

Colonel, Chinese Nationalist Army. Relates to guerrilla warfare in southern China and Burma during the Sino-Japanese War, Chinese military cooperation with the U.S. Office of Strategic Services during World War II, and Nationalist Chinese military activities in Manchuria during the Chinese Civil War.

Gift, Virginia R. Stuart, 1974.

2679

Stuart, John Leighton, 1876–1966.

Diary, 1946–1949. 1 folder.

Photocopy made in 1971 from a typewritten copy lent by Philip Fugh.

U.S. Ambassador to China and Taiwan, 1946–1953. Relates to the Chinese Civil War and Sino-American relations, July-December 1946 and January-December 1949.

Restricted until January 2, 1984.

2680

Stubbs, Violet, *collector*.

Christmas card, 1923. 1 folder.

Printed.

Depicts British occupation troops in Germany.

2681

Stultz, Newell.

Miscellaneous papers, 1958–1970. 1 folder, 1 envelope.

American political scientist. Letters, pamphlets, leaflets, statistical summaries, and photographs, relating to the political development of the Transkei in South Africa. Used as research material for the book by N. Stultz, *South Africa's Transkei* (1967).

Gift, N. Stultz, 1974.

2682

Sturgis, Samuel Davis, Jr., 1897–1964.

Letter, 1945, to Mrs. S. D. Sturgis, Jr. 1 folder.

Typescript (photocopy).

Lieutenant General, U.S. Army; Chief Engineer, 6th Army. Relates to the capture of Manila by U.S. troops.

2683

Sturies, Carl Herman, 1902–1978.

Papers, 1924–1966. 19½ ms. boxes, 1 envelope.

Colonel, U.S. Army Signal Corps; Senior Signal Adviser, Korean Military Assistance Group, 1950–1952. Diaries, correspondence, orders, reports, printed matter and photographs, relating to the U.S. Army Signal Corps and to South Korean military activities during the Korean War.

Gift, C. H. Sturies, 1967.

2684

Sturtevant Engineering Company.

Pamphlet, 1915. 1 folder.

Printed.

Relates to the American ambulance service in France.

Gift, University of Arizona Library, 1976.

2685

Stuttgart Weltkriegsbuecherei collection (in German), 1921. 1 folder.

Clippings and transcripts of speeches, relating to the opening of the Stuttgart Weltkriegsbuecherei on May 21, 1921.

2686

Sudan. Wizārat al-I'lām wa-al-Thaqāfah.

Photographs, n.d. 1 envelope.

Sudenese Ministry of Information and Culture. Depicts rural areas, agricultural production, ethnic groups, economic development, and factories in the Sudan.

Gift, Wizārat al-I'lām wa-al-Thaqāfah, 1976.

2687

Suez War propaganda (in Arabic), 1956. 1 folder.

Printed.

Propaganda leaflets distributed by the British government in Egypt at the time of the Suez War, November 1956.

2688

Sukacev, Lev Pavlovich, 1895–1974.

Translation of memoirs, n.d. "Soldier Under Three Flags: The Personal Memoirs of Lev Pavlovich Sukacev." ½ ms. box.

Typescript (photocopy).

Lieutenant, Russian Imperial Army; Major, Albanian Army; Colonel, Italian Army. Relates to Russian military activities during World War I and the Russian Civil War; Albanian military activities, 1924–1939; and Italian military activities during World War II. Original memoirs published in *Novoe Russkoe Slovo*, 1972.

Gift, Natalie Sukacev, 1976.

2689

Sukhomlinov (Vladimir Aleksandrovich)—photograph, n.d. 1 envelope.

Depicts the tsarist Russian government official V. A. Sukhomlinov.

2690

Sullivan, Mark, 1874–1952.

Papers, 1883–1952. 62 ms. boxes, 10 scrapbooks, 3 envelopes.

American journalist; editor, *Collier's Weekly*, 1912–1919; columnist, *New York Herald-Tribune*, 1923–1952. Correspondence, diaries, speeches and writings, memoranda, and printed matter, relating to journalism and social, political, and economic developments in the United States.

Register.

Gift, M. Sullivan, Jr., 1955. Gift, Mrs. L. Metcalfe Walling, 1968, with subsequent increments.

2691

Sullivan, William E.

Photographs, 1920–1922. 2 envelopes.

Lieutenant Commander, U.S. Navy. Depicts daily life in the Philippine Islands, 1920; naval activities at Camp

John Hay, Luzon, Philippine Islands, 1920; cultural sites in China; atrocities resulting from the 1920–1922 uprisings in China; and cultural sites on Guam.
Gift, William A. Sullivan, 1974.

2692

Sumans, Vilis, 1887–1948.
Miscellaneous papers (in Latvian, French and German), 1925–1948. ½ ms. box, 1 envelope.
Latvian diplomat and statesman; Director of Administrative and Political Departments, Ministry of Foreign Affairs, 1919–1924; Delegate to the League of Nations Assemblies, 1922–1930; Minister to Italy, 1924–1926, to France, 1926–1934, and to Spain and Portugal, 1928–1933. Correspondence, memoranda, bulletins, press excerpts, clippings, photographs, memorabilia, and other materials, relating to Latvian foreign relations, 1925–1948.
Gift, Lilija Brante-Parupe, 1970. Subsequent increments.

2693

Suomen Kommunistinen Puolue.
Broadsides (in Finnish), 1929. 1 folder.
Typescript (mimeographed).
Finnish Communist Party. Relates to plans for a demonstration.

2694

Surface, Frank Macy, 1882–1965.
Papers, 1915–1933. 8 ms. boxes, 2 cu.ft. boxes.
American economist and author; Acting Chief, Statistical Division, U.S. Food Administration, 1917–1918; Chief Statistician, American Relief Administration, 1919–1920; Assistant Director, U.S. Bureau of Foreign and Domestic Commerce, 1926–1933. Writings, correspondence, memoranda, reports, printed matter and photographs, relating to regulation of the U.S. economy, especially food products, during World War I; American Relief Administration activities; and postwar marketing of U.S. commodities.
Gift, F. M. Surface.

2695

Survey of Race Relations, 1923–1925.
Records, 1924–1927. 37 ms. boxes.
Anthropological investigative project sponsored by various private organizations. Report, correspondence, interview transcripts, questionnaires, and printed matter, relating to the social and economic status of Chinese, Japanese, other Oriental, Mexican, and other minority residents of the Pacific Coast of the U.S. and Canada, and to race relations on the Pacific Coast.
Preliminary inventory.

2696

Susskind, David Howard, 1920–
Memoir, n.d. "Transport to Hell." 1 folder.
Typescript (mimeographed).
Lieutenant, U.S. Navy; an officer on the transport ship

Melletta during World War II. Relates to the activities of the *Melletta* during the battle of Iwo Jima.

2697

Sveikauskas, Leo.
Study, 1976. "A Synthesis of Marx and Freud." 1 vol.
Typescript (photocopy).
Gift, L. Sveikauskas, 1977.

2698

Sviatopolk-Mirsky, N., *collector*.
Postcards, n.d. 1 envelope.
Patriotic Russian Imperial postcards, three from the collection of Tsarina Alexandra. Includes a photograph of Tsar Nicholas II and Tsarina Alexandra.
Preliminary inventory.
Gift, N. Sviatopolk-Mirsky, 1971.

2699

"Svodki o Politicheskom i Ekonomicheskom Polozheniĭ v Sovetskoĭ Rossiĭ za 1922 god" (Summaries of the Political and Economic Status of Soviet Russia for 1922).
Reports (in Russian), 1922. 1 folder.
Typescript.

2700

Swarts, Clifford.
Letter, 1943, to Charles W. Webb. 1 folder.
Typescript.
Official of the Creole Petroleum Corporation. Relates to conditions in Romania during World War II, 1939–1941.

2701

Sweet, Clytie, *collector*.
Miscellany, 1942–1944. 1 folder.
Correspondence and miscellanea, relating to the radio broadcast of a "Salute to the War Mothers," 1942, and the publication of a pamphlet, *Salute to the Gold Star Mothers*, 1943, by American Legion San Francisco Post No. 1.

2702

Swiadkowie Historii (They Witnessed History).
Compilation of sound recordings (in Polish), 1965. 4 phonorecords.
Original speeches and radio addresses and later reminiscences of leading Polish statesmen, diplomats and military officers, relating to twentieth-century Polish history, especially the Polish-Soviet Wars of 1918–1921 and the World War II period. Recorded by the Polish Broadcasting Department of Radio Free Europe.
Gift, Jan Nowak, 1967.

2703

Swinnerton, C. T.
Letter, 1917. 1 folder.
Typescript.
American visitor to Russia. Relates to events in Petrograd during the Russian Revolution, March 12–27, 1917.
Gift, Arthur Daily.

2704

Sychev, E.
Report (in Russian), n.d. "Vozstanie v. Irkutske" (Uprising in Irkutsk). 1 folder.
Typescript.
General, White Russian Army. Relates to the uprising in Irkutsk, and the liquidation of the rule of Admiral Aleksandr Kolchak in the region of Irkutsk in the period from December 23, 1919 to January 5, 1920.

2705

Syndicat des Editeurs.
Issuances (in French), 1940. 1 folder.
Photocopy.
French association of publishers. Convention on censorship and list of books withdrawn from sale, September-October 1940.

2706

Szamuely (Tibor)—photograph, 1919. 1 envelope.
Depicts the Hungarian communist leader T. Szamuely with the Russian communist Nikolaĭ Podvoĭskiĭ.

2707

Ta Chung Cultural Cooperation Association.
Translation of report, 1947. "Struggle for Peace and Democracy in the Northeast." 1 folder.
Typescript.
Relates to military activities of the Chinese Communist Party in Manchuria against the Japanese during World War II and against the Kuomintang.

2708

Tada, T.
Memorandum, 1946. "A Short Explanation of Japanese Culture." 1 folder.
Typescript (mimeographed).
Colonel, Japanese Army. Relates to Japanese social customs.

2709

Tal', Georgiĭ Aleksandrovich von.
Memoir (in Russian), n.d. "Memuary ob Otrecheniĭ ot Prestola Rossiĭskago Gosudaria Imperatora Nikolaiâ II" (Memoirs on the Abdication of Emperor Nicholas II). 1 folder.
Typescript.
Commandant, Imperial Train of Nicholas II, Tsar of Russia, 1917.

2710

Talamon, Mrs. René.
Memoir, n.d. "Registered by One Who Was There." 1 vol.
Typescript.
American visitor to France. Relates to conditions in France during World War I, 1914–1918.

2711

Talbot, Paul Hopkins, 1897–1974.
Diary, 1941–1942. 1 ms. box.
Holograph (photocopy).

Rear Admiral, U.S. Navy. Relates to the American naval engagement with Japanese forces off Borneo. Includes photographs.
Gift, Mrs. P. H. Talbot, 1976.

2712

Talbot, Phillips, 1915–
Letters, 1939–1950, to Walter S. Rogers. 1 folder.
Typescript (mimeographed).
Associate, Institute of Current World Affairs, 1938–1941 and 1946–1951. Relates to political and social conditions in India and the Indian independence movement.

2713

Tan, Cheng Lock.
Papers, 1949–1950. 1 folder.
Leader, Malayan Chinese Association. Memoranda, speeches and mimeographed copies of correspondence, relating to the organization of the Malayan Chinese Association and to the Malayan independence movement.
Gift, Tan Cheng Lock, 1951.

2714

Tarr, Curtis W., 1924–
Papers, 1963–1977. 12 ms. boxes.
President, Lawrence University, 1963–1969; U.S. Assistant Secretary of the Air Force for Manpower and Reserve Affairs, 1969–1970; Director, Selective Service System, 1970–1972; Under Secretary of State for Security Assistance, 1972–1973; Chairman, Defense Manpower Commission, 1974–1976; Vice President, Deere and Co., 1973– . Diaries, memoir, and printed matter, relating to his experiences as a soldier in World War II, his public and educational careers, American military and foreign policy and military conscription during the administrations of Presidents Richard M. Nixon and Gerald R. Ford, and the operations of Deere and Company, a multinational corporation.
During his lifetime access requires the written permission of C. W. Tarr and, after his death, of his wife.
Deposit, C. W. Tarr, 1974. Subsequent increments.

2715

Tarsaidze, Alexandre Georgievich, 1901–1978.
Papers (in English, Russian, French, German and Georgian), 1648–1978. 33 ms. boxes, 9 oversize boxes, 16 reels of film, 1 box of film fragments.
Georgian-American author and public relations executive. Correspondence, speeches and writings, research notes, printed matter, photographs, engravings, lithographs, and maps, relating to the history of Georgia (Transcaucasia), the Romanov family, Russian-American relations, and the Association of Russian Imperial Naval Officers in America. Includes photocopies of Romanov family letters, photographs of Russia during World War I by Donald C. Thompson, and a documentary film of Nicholas II.
Preliminary inventory.
Bequest, A. G. Tarsaidze, 1978.

2716

Tatistcheff, Alexis B.
History, 1971. "The Family of Princes Obolensky." 1 ms. box.
Typescript (photocopy).
Relates to the Obolenskiĭ family and its rise to prominence in Imperial Russia, 1862–1917.
Gift, A. B. Tatistcheff, 1977.

2717

Taylor, Alonzo E., 1871–1949.
Papers, 1917–1922. 27 ms. boxes, 3 oversize folders (¼ l. ft.), 1 album.
Member, U.S. War Trade Board, 1917–1919; Director, Food Research Institute, Stanford University, 1921–1936. Correspondence, memoranda, reports, studies, statistical data, and maps, relating to economic conditions, food supply, and postwar reconstruction in Europe, and to the War Trade Board, U.S. Food Administration and American Relief Administration.
Gift, A. E. Taylor.

2718

Tchernigovetz, Nikolai.
Essay (in Russian), ca. 1976. "Pisateliŭ Solzhenifsynu ot Immigranta Staroĭ Revoliŭfsiĭ" (To Author Solzhenitsyn From an Immigrant of the Old Revolution). 1 folder.
Typescript.
Russian émigré in the U.S. Criticizes Aleksandr Solzhenifsyn for anti-monarchist views and presents a personal evaluation of events in Russia from 1917 to 1976.
Gift, N. Tchernigovetz, 1976.

2719

Tedder (Arthur William Tedder, Baron)—photograph, n.d. 1 envelope.
Depicts Marshall of the Royal Air Force A. W. Tedder, British Air Force.

2720

Telesco, Lee, *collector*.
L. Telesco collection on the Philippines, 1942–1953. 1 ms. box.
Reports, letters, proclamations, newsletters, and miscellanea, relating to Allied guerrilla and intelligence activities in the Philippines during World War II, especially to activities of the First MacArthur Division. Includes examples of Japanese propaganda and reports of Japanese atrocities in the Philippines.
Preliminary inventory.
Gift, L. Telesco, 1947. Subsequent increments.

2721

Teller, Edward, 1908–
Papers, 1940–1975. 7 ms. boxes, 9 oversize boxes (9 l. ft.), 1 package (1 l. ft.), 1 cu. ft. box.
American physicist and educator. Correspondence, speeches and writings, reports, magazine and newspaper clippings, photographs, motion picture films, awards, and plaques, relating to chemical, molecular and nuclear physics; to quantum theory; and to current research on

development of new energy resources, especially on national energy research planning and related national and international security issues.
Gift, E. Teller, 1976. Incremental gift, 1977.

2722

Temperley, Harold William Vazeille, 1879–1939.
Correspondence, 1936, with Sir Stephen Gaselee. 1 folder.
Typewritten transcript.
British historian. Relates to British relations with the Vatican during World War I.

2723

Le Temps des Doryphores (Time of the Potato Bugs).
Motion picture, n.d. 5 reels.
Depicts aspects of social and political conditions in German-occupied France, 1940–1944, including scenes of leading German political and military figures, German armed forces, and daily life in French towns and villages.
Purchase, Jacques de Launay, 1977.

2724

Terlecki, Tymon.
Translation of article (in German), 1943. " 'Alle Juden Raus!' " ('All Jews Out!'). 1 folder.
Typescript (mimeographed).
Relates to the German destruction of the Warsaw Ghetto in 1943. Original article published in *Wiadomósci Polskie* (London), November 7, 1943.

2725

Terman, Lewis M., 1877–1956.
Miscellaneous papers, 1941–1951. ½ ms. box.
American psychologist; Professor of Psychology, Stanford University, 1922–1942. Correspondence, clippings, and questionnaires, relating to a poll conducted by Herbert Hoover of Stanford University faculty opinion on U.S. foreign policy, 1941.
Closed until April 1, 1987.
Gift, Frederick E. Terman, 1977.

2726

Terramare Office, Berlin.
Issuances (in English and German), 1934–1937. 1 ms. box.
Berlin publishing house. Essays, serial issues, and press releases, distributed as propaganda in Great Britain and the U.S., relating to aspects of the Nazi regime, including foreign policy, economic policy, compulsory labor, social welfare, education, culture, racial policy, and the place of women in German society.
Gift, Indiana University Library, 1965.

2727

Terrorism—Germany, West—collection (in German), 1977. 1 folder.
Printed.
Wanted posters for a group of terrorists, headed by Willy Peter Stoll and Friederike Krabbe, accused of murder; reports relating to the highjacking of a Lufthansa

airplane to Somalia; and a compilation by the Christian Democratic Union of West Germany of citations on terrorism.
Gift, Sara Brown, 1977.

2728

Textile Alliance.
Miscellaneous records, 1915–1927. 1 folder.
Organization of American textile manufacturers. Correspondence, memoranda and certificates, relating to the activities of the Textile Alliance in regulating wool importations and textile exportations during World War I.

2729

Thaelmann (Ernst) collection (in German), 1932. 1 folder.
Leaflets and broadsides relating to the campaign of E. Thaelmann (1886–1944), the communist candidate for President of Germany.

2730

Thane, Mrs. J. E.
Papers, 1911–1936. 1 ms. box.
U.S. Food Administration Woman Director of Food Conservation for Alameda County, California, during World War I. Correspondence, printed matter and miscellanea, relating to food conservation in Alameda County and to European relief work of various organizations during World War I.
Preliminary inventory.
Gift, Laura Thane Whipple, 1958.

2731

Thelander, Hulda Evelyn, 1896–
Papers, 1926–1927. 1 folder.
American pediatrician in China, 1926–1927. Diary and excerpts from letters (typewritten), relating to public health in China, and to general description of conditions in China.
Gift, H. E. Thelander, 1970.

2732

Theobald, Robert A., 1884–1957.
Papers, 1908–1959. 12 ms. boxes.
Rear Admiral, U.S. Navy; Destroyer Commander, Pacific Fleet, 1940–1941; Commander, Northern Pacific Force, 1942–1943. Correspondence, speeches and writings, war diaries, dispatches, operations plans and orders, manuals, service lists, memoranda, reports, and war estimates, relating to naval operations in Alaska, May 1942–January 1943, including the Japanese invasion of the Aleutians, June 1942, and the Japanese attack on Pearl Harbor.
Register.
Gift, Mrs. R. A. Theobald, 1960. Incremental gift, 1977. Gift, Mrs. James L. Brainerd, 1960.

2733

"Theodore Roosevelt on Preparedness: A Bibliography."
Bibliography, n.d. 1 folder.
Typescript.
Lists speeches and writings by Theodore Roosevelt,

U.S. President, 1901–1909, relating to U.S. defense policy.

2734

Thezan, Emmanuel.
Campaign platform, 1930. 1 folder.
Typescript (mimeographed).
Candidate for President of Haiti. Relates to Haitian political conditions and the U.S. occupation of Haiti.

2735

Thimme, Annelise.
Study (in German), n.d. "Flucht in den Mythos: Die Deutschnationale Volkspartei und die Niederlage von 1918" (Escape in Myth: The German National People's Party and the Defeat of 1918). 1 folder.
Typescript.
Gift, A. Thimme, 1969.

2736

Thoennings, Johan.
Memorandum, 1939. "The Golden Book: A Document for the British, French, American and German Nations." 1 folder.
Typescript.
Relates to a plan for the assurance of world peace.

2737

Thomas, Elbert Duncan, 1883–1953.
Transcripts of radio broadcasts, 1942. 1 folder.
Typescript (mimeographed).
U.S. Senator from Utah, 1933–1951. Broadcasts to the Japanese people, relating to the Pacific Theater in World War II.

2738

Thomas, Mrs. Jerome B., *collector*.
Publicity cards, ca. 1915–1919. 1 folder.
Hand-painted.
Cards used to solicit funds in the U.S. for the Commission for Relief in Belgium during World War I.
Gift, Mrs. J. B. Thomas, 1959.

2739

Thompson, Charles T.
Papers, 1898–1917. 2 ms. boxes.
American journalist; correspondent for Associated Press. Correspondence, writings, clippings, photographs, and printed matter, relating to the Algeciras Conference in Morocco, 1906; wedding of Alfonso XIII of Spain and assassination attempt on his life, 1906; and the Salonica front, Greece, Serbia, and Albania during World War I. Includes memoirs, entitled "Through the Adriatic: Its Islands, Cities, and Adjacent Country in Their War Garb."
Gift, Walter Trohan, 1967.

2740

Thompson, Dorothy Louise.
Miscellaneous papers, 1936–1945. 1 ms. box, 3 envelopes.

American historian. Dissertation (typewritten), entitled "France, the Czechs and the Question of Austria, 1867–1885," 1945, relating to French foreign policy regarding the Czech national question in Austria-Hungary; and photographs of scenes in Czechoslovakia and the Mediterranean area, 1936–1937.

2741

Thompson, Harold Keith, 1922–   , *collector.*
H. K. Thompson collection on right-wing politics, 1947–1972. 13 ms. boxes.
Leaflets, newsletters, pamphlets, newspaper and periodical issues, clippings, correspondence, and writings, relating to fascist and other rightist political groups in the U.S. and Europe after World War II. Includes a few leftist publications.
Preliminary inventory.
Gift, H. K. Thompson, 1955. Subsequent increments.

2742

Thompson, Paul J.
Photographs, 1918. 1 envelope.
Depicts Italian prisoners of war held by Austria, taken at the time of their release, September 1918.
Gift, P. J. Thompson, 1934.

2743

Thorez, Maurice, 1900–1964.
Letters (in French), 1929–1964. 1 folder.
Holograph.
Secretary General, Parti Communiste Français, 1930–1964. Letters, 1929–1930, to Guy Jerram, French communist movement and the imprisonment of M. Thorez; and photocopies of letters, 1955–1964, to Roger Garaudy, French communist leader and philosopher, relating to the French communist movement and the writings of R. Garaudy.
Gift, Guy Jerram, 1967. Gift, Branko Lazitch, 1972.

2744

Thurston, E. Coppée.
Papers (in English, French and Flemish), 1914–1920. 2 ms. boxes, 1 roll of certificates (¼ l. ft.).
Member of the Commission for Relief in Belgium. Correspondence, memoranda, reports, pamphlets, maps, medals, and certificates, relating to relief work of the Commission for Relief in Belgium in Belgium and northern France during World War I.
Gift, Lois M. Thurston, 1960.

2745

Tielicke, H.
Sermon (in German), 1947. "Passion ohne Gnade" (Passion without Grace). 1 folder.
Typescript.
German clergyman. Relates to problems of post-World War II German reconstruction. Sermon delivered at Markus Church, Stuttgart, Good Friday, 1947.

2746

Tijtgat, Edgard.
Cartoon sequence (in French), ca. 1914–1918. "Le Retour Inespéré d'un Réfugié Belge" (The Unexpected Return of a Belgian Refugee). 1 folder.
Printed.
Depicts the hardships and eventual homecoming of an imaginary Belgian refugee during World War I. Printed in England.

2747

Tikhon, Patriarch of Moscow and All Russia, 1865–1925.
Letter (in Russian), 1918, to the Soviet Council of People's Commissars. 1 folder.
Typewritten transcript.
Relates to the situation of religion in Russia. Includes a photocopy of a translation (typewritten) of the above by Peter Nicholas Kurguz, 1962.

2748

Tillotson, W. D.
Memorandum, 1951. 1 folder.
Typescript.
U.S. Consul General in Japan. Relates to changes in the Japanese governmental system between 1855 and 1891.

2749

Timofievich, Anatoliĭ Pavlovich, d. 1976.
Papers (in Russian), 1890–1976. 2½ ms. boxes, 1 memorabilia box (½ l. ft.).
Russian physician. Correspondence, clippings, and printed matter, relating to various members of the Romanov family and other Russian dignitaries and nobility, events in Russia before, during and after the Russian Revolution, and the Russian emigration to foreign countries. Includes a towel and cloth napkin with the crest of Tsar Nicholas II from Ekaterinburg, and a hand-made rug presented to the Dowager Empress Mariiâ Fedorovna by the students of the Kievo-Fundukleevskaiâ Zhenskaiâ Gimnaziiâ in Kiev, 1915.
Gift, A. P. Timofievich, 1975.

2750

Tinkler, Charles C.
Papers, 1930. 1 folder.
American engineer working in the Soviet Union in 1930. Correspondence and miscellanea, relating to social conditions in the Soviet Union.

2751

Tinley, James Maddison, 1897–
Papers, 1944–1945. ½ ms. box.
Major, U.S. Army. Writings, drawings, photographs, and reprints, relating to conditions in the Netherlands under German occupation during World War II, and to food relief at the end of the war. Includes a study (typewritten), entitled "Wartime Food Problems of the Netherlands."
Gift, J. M. Tinley, 1961.

2752

Tirpitz, Alfred Peter Friedrich von, 1849–1930.
  Appeal (in German), 1917. 1 folder.
  Metal printing plate.
  Grand Admiral, German Navy; German Secretary of State for the Navy, 1897–1916. Relates to German war policy.

2753

Tiso, Stefan, 1897–1949.
  Diary (in Slovak), 1944–1945. 1 folder.
  Premier of Slovakia, 1944–1945. Relates to political and military conditions in Slovakia in the latter stages of World War II.
  Publication requires permission of the Hoover Institution on War, Revolution and Peace and the heirs of S. Tiso.
  Purchase, Vladimir Kovalik, 1952.

2754

Tittle, Walter.
  Portraits, 1922. 1 oversize box (1 1. ft.).
  Hand-drawn.
  American artist. Depicts American, British, Japanese, French, Italian, Belgian, and Chinese delegates to the Washington Conference on the Limitation of Armaments, 1921–1922. Portraits are autographed by their subjects.

2755

Titulescu, Nicolas, 1883–1941.
  Papers (in French and Romanian), 1923–1938. 15½ ms. boxes.
  Romanian statesman and diplomat; Minister of Finance, 1920–1922; Ambassador to Great Britain and delegate to the League of Nations, 1922–1927; Minister of Foreign Affairs, 1927–1928 and 1932–1936. Diaries, correspondence, memoranda, reports, writings, clippings, and printed matter, relating to Romanian politics and diplomacy, and to Romanian-Soviet negotiations, 1931–1932.
  Register.
  May be used only if name of user and copy of any publication based on collection are made available to Mme M. Y. Antoniade.
  Purchase, G. Anastasiu, 1974.

2756

Todd, Carlos, d. 1977.
  Newspaper articles, 1959–1960. 1 oversize box (½ 1. ft.).
  Printed.
  Newspaper columnist, *The Times of Havana*. Relates to political and social conditions in Cuba.
  Gift, Mrs. C. Todd, 1978.

2757

Todd, Laurence, b. 1882.
  Memoirs, 1954. "Correspondent on the Left." 1 ms. box.
  Typescript (photocopy).
  American journalist; Federated Press labor reporter, 1919–1933; TASS correspondent, 1933–1952. Relates to political, economic and labor developments in the U.S. and Europe.
  Purchase, *National Republic Magazine*, 1960.

2758

Todd, Oliver J., 1880–1974.
  Papers, 1900–1973. 47 1. ft.
  American civil engineer; Chief Engineer and Consulting Engineer, China International Famine Relief Commission, 1923–1938; Adviser, United Nations Relief and Rehabilitation Administration Yellow River Project, 1945–1947. Diaries, correspondence, reports, memoranda, and photographs, relating to engineering, relief work, and social, economic, and political conditions in China, 1919–1949.
  Preliminary inventory.
  Gift, O. J. Todd, 1973. Incremental gift, James P. Todd, 1974.

2759

Tokyo Daigaku.
  Statement, 1957. 1 folder.
  Printed.
  Relates to the dangers from radioactive fallout resulting from nuclear weapon testing. Signed by members of the College of General Education of Tokyo University.

2760

Toller, Ernst, 1893–1939.
  Appeal, 1919. 1 folder.
  Typescript (photocopy of original located in the New York Public Library).
  German writer; leader of the Bavarian Soviet Republic, 1919. Appeal on behalf of the young workers of Germany to the young people of the world, relating to the goals of the German Revolution.

2761

Tolstoĭ, Lev Nikolaevich, 1828–1910.
  Miscellaneous papers (in Russian), 1853–1904. 3½ ms. boxes.
  Handwritten and typewritten transcripts of originals located in the Biblioteka SSSR imeni V. I. Lenina, Moscow.
  Russian novelist. Diaries and writings, relating to the life and works of L. N. Tolstoĭ. Includes drafts of the novels by L. N. Tolstoĭ, *Anna Karenina* and *War and Peace*.
  Preliminary inventory.
  Gift, S. Melgunov, 1932.

2762

Tolstoĭ, M. P.
  Miscellaneous papers (in Russian), 1858–1903. ½ ms. box.
  Russian countess. Memorandum notebook, listing major military and state officials, 1858; and photographs

of the 1903 Russian Imperial Costume Ball in St. Petersburg.
Gift, Russian Historical Archive and Repository, 1974.

2763

Tomilov, P. A.
History (in Russian), n.d. "Sievero-Zapadnyi Front Grazhdanskoĭ Voĭny v Rossiĭ 1919 Goda" (Northwestern Front of the Civil War in Russia, 1919). 1 ms. box.
Typescript.

2764

Torres Quintero, M. Gregorio.
Commission, 1917. 1 folder.
Typescript.
Head, Yucatan Department of Public Education. Commission from the State of Yucatan, charging M. G. Torres Quintero with a study of the educational system of the U.S.

2765

"Tower of Peace."
Radio broadcasts, 1957. 13 phonotapes.
Radio program sponsored by the Hoover Institution on War, Revolution and Peace. Relates to the facilities, history, purpose and activities of the Hoover Institution on War, Revolution and Peace. Includes interviews with Herbert Hoover and with staff members and researchers at the Hoover Institution.

2766

Toynbee, Arnold Joseph, 1889–1975.
Miscellaneous papers, 1921–1950. 1 folder, 7 phonorecords.
British historian. Typewritten copies of letters from A. and Rosalind Toynbee to relatives and friends in England, 1921–1923, relating to their observations of conditions in Greece and Turkey during the Greco-Turkish War; and sound recordings of speeches by A. Toynbee in San Francisco and at Stanford University, 1950, relating to the prospects for Western civilization.
Gift, A. Toynbee, 1925. Subsequent increments.

2767

Traaen, Carl Egeberg.
Sermons (in Norwegian), 1941–1944. 1 folder.
Typescript and holograph.
Norwegian clergyman. Sermons delivered to Norwegian resistance movement members imprisoned in German-occupied Norway during World War II.

2768

Trade unions and labor problems—U.S.—handbills, 1931–1932. 1 ms. box.
Printed.
Advocates unionization and unemployment relief in the U.S., and expresses pro-Soviet sympathies. Some issued by the Communist Party of the U.S.

2769

Trail Smelter Arbitral Tribunal.
Records, 1935–1938. 9 ms. boxes.
Arguments presented to, and reports issued by, an international tribunal for adjudication constituted by the U.S. and Canada, relating to U.S. complaints of damage to crops caused by fumes from a smelter at Trail, British Columbia.
Preliminary inventory.
Gift, Robert E. Swain, 1960.

2770

Trainor, Joseph C.
Papers, 1944–1952. 76 ms. boxes, 1 album, 2 envelopes.
Deputy Chief, Education Division, Civil Information and Education Section, General Headquarters, Supreme Commander for the Allied Powers in Japan, 1945–1951. Writings, memoranda, reports, surveys, handbooks, maps, photographs, and printed matter, relating to educational reform in Japan during the Allied occupation.
Register.
Gift, J. C. Trainor, 1972.

2771

Travis, Joseph William, d. 1965.
Papers (in English and French), 1917–1959. ½ ms. box.
First Lieutenant, U.S. Army; member, volunteer American Field Service attached to the French Army during World War I. Orders, certificates, and printed matter, relating to the American Field Service, and to French and U.S. military transportation during World War I.
Gift, Mrs. J. W. Travis.

2772

Treat, Payson J., 1879–1972.
Papers, 1855–1973. 63 ms. boxes, 1 album, 7 envelopes, 12 maps, 4 scrolls.
American historian. Correspondence, reports, interviews, copies of diplomatic records, speeches, writings, notes, photographs, maps, memorabilia, and printed matter, relating to the diplomatic history of Japan, China, and other countries of the Far East. Includes a pamphlet collection on World War I.
Register.
Gift, P. J. Treat, 1960. Subsequent increments.

2773

Treint, Albert, 1889–1971.
Study (in French), n.d. "L'Infernal Paradis" (Infernal Paradise). 1 vol.
Typescript (photocopy).
French communist leader. Relates to capitalism, international politics, materialism, social classes, and socialism, particularly in communist-dominated countries, 1900–1957.

2774

Trevor-Roper, Hugh Redwald, 1914—
Lecture, 1964. "Hitler's Place in History." 3 phonotapes.
British historian. Relates to Adolf Hitler. Delivered at Memorial Auditorium, Stanford University.

2775

Tribe, Mattie.
Memoir, n.d. "An Evacuation from France." 1 folder. Typescript.
Englishwoman living in France. Relates to the evacuation by sea of British subjects from Cannes, France, to Liverpool, England, after the capitulation of France in June 1940.

2776

Tribunal Arbitral, Hague, 1912.
Issuances (in French), 1912. 1 folder.
Printed.
Arguments of the Russian and Turkish governments and decision of the tribunal, relating to a dispute over reparations owed Russia by Turkey as a result of the Russo-Turkish War of 1877–1878.

2777

"Trinadtsat' Let Oktiābria" (Thirteen Years of October).
Study (in Russian), ca. 1930. 1 folder.
Typescript (mimeographed).
Relates to economic progress in the Soviet Union since the Russian Revolution.

2778

Trotskiĭ (Lev) collection, 1921–1970. 1 folder, 1 envelope, 1 motion picture reel.
Letter (typewritten photocopy) from L. Trotskiĭ (1879–1940), Russian revolutionary leader, to Robert T. Lincoln concerning Soviet-American relations, 1921; excerpts (typewritten copy) from the English translation by Charles Malamuth of the book by L. Trotskiĭ, *Stalin: An Appraisal of the Man and His Influence*; photographs and a motion picture film of L. Trotskiĭ in Coyoacan, Mexico, 1938; and a newspaper article from *La Vanguardia Espanola*, 1970, by Maria Serrallach concerning the family of L. Trotskiĭ in Barcelona before the Spanish Civil War.
Gift, Myna Sowengart, 1950. Gift, Maria Serrallach, 1970. Gift, Ivan C. F. Heisler, 1973. Gift, J. M. Crisman.

2779

Trujillo, Robert, 1903–
Interview, 1975. 2 phonotapes.
Colorado state chairman, Communist Party. Relates to the history of the communist movement in Colorado. Interview conducted by Brad Bohland, May 6, 1975.
Gift, Thomas J. Noel, 1976.

2780

Truth About Cuba Committee.
Printed matter, 1968–1971. 1 folder.
Anti-communist organization in Miami, Florida. Leaflets and brochures, relating to living conditions in Cuba and to anti-communist Cuban activities.

2781

Trynin, Ben.
Correspondence, 1932–1936. 1 folder.
Correspondence with Lincoln Steffens, American journalist and social reformer, 1932–1934, and with Ella Winter, widow of Lincoln Steffens, 1936, relating to leftist political movements in the U.S.

2782

Tschebotarioff, Gregory Porphyriewitch, 1899–
Correspondence (in Russian and English), 1941–1975. 1 folder.
Typescript and holograph.
Lieutenant, Russian Army, 1916–1921; subsequently émigré in the U.S. Relates to the Don Cadet Corps during the Russian Revolution, and to relations between the U.S. and Russia in 1941.
Gift, G. P. Tschebotarioff, 1968. Subsequent increments.

2783

Tseng, Chao-lun.
History, 1946. "The Emergence of the Chinese Democratic League." 1 folder.
Typescript.

2784

Tsing Hua Alumni Association.
Circular, 1927. 1 folder.
Typescript (mimeographed).
Organization of alumni of Tsing Hua University, China. Relates to activities of the organization.

2785

Tsipouras, Mary W.
Memoir, 1923. 1 folder.
Typescript.
Wife of a Greek Army colonel. Relates to the Greek Revolution of 1922 and the overthrow of King Constantine.

2786

TSitlidze, Artem Dmitrievich, *defendant.*
Indictment (in Russian), 1937. 1 vol.
Typescript.
Charges A. D. TSitlidze, Shalva Konstantinovich Alaverdashvili and others with counter-revolutionary activities, including terrorism, subversion and sabotage, in Georgia.

2787

TSurikov, N.
Appeal (in Russian), n.d. "Svoim i Chuzhym: O Tragedii 22 Sentiābria" (To Ours and Others: About the Tragedy of September 22). 1 folder.
Typescript (mimeographed).
Member, Russkiĭ Obshchevoĭnskiĭ Soiūz, a Russian émigré association. Relates to the circumstances sur-

rounding the disappearance of Generals E. K. Miller and N. Skoblin, and calls for anti-Bolshevik unity among Russian émigrés.

2788

Tuck, William Hallam, 1890–1966.
Papers, 1914–1957. 7 ms. boxes.
American relief worker in World Wars I and II. Writings, correspondence, memoranda, reports, printed matter and photographs, relating to World War I relief activities of the Commission for Relief in Belgium and American Relief Administration; World War II relief activities of the Commission for Relief in Belgium, Finnish Relief Fund and National Committee on Food for the Small Democracies; World War II Allied military governments; and the world food survey of the Famine Emergency Committee, 1946.
Gift, Mr. and Mrs. W. H. Tuck, 1962. Subsequent increments.

2789

Tule Lake War Relocation Authority Center (California) collection, 1942–1943. 1 ms. box.
Correspondence and photographs, relating to conditions in the Tule Lake War Relocation Authority Center, a U.S. internment camp for Japanese Americans during World War II.
Gift, John Douglas Cook, 1970.

2790

Tunaya, Tarik Z.
Translation of history, 1958. "The Establishment of the Government of the Turkish Grand National Assembly and its Political Character." 1 folder.
Typescript.
Relates to Turkish political development, 1908–1927. Translated by Kerim K. Key. Edited by Elaine D. Smith.

2791

Turauskas, Eduardas, 1896–1966.
Papers (mainly in Lithuanian), 1934–1958. 9 ms. boxes, 1 envelope.
Lithuanian diplomat and journalist; Ambassador to Czechoslovakia, Yugoslavia and Romania, 1934–1939; Political Director, Ministry of Foreign Affairs, 1939–1940. Correspondence, memoranda, reports, printed matter, clippings, and photographs, relating to the Soviet occupation of Lithuania, 1940–1941, and Lithuanian foreign relations in Europe, 1934–1941.
Register.
Purchase, Mme E. Turauskas, 1975.

2792

Turkish Conference, Hoover Institution on War, Revolution and Peace, 1957.
Proceedings, 1957. 10 phonotapes.
Conference held to assess the Turkish library and archival materials at the Hoover Institution and their potential for research use.

2793

Turkish Wilsonian League.
Letter, 1918, to Woodrow Wilson. 1 folder.
Typescript.
Organization of Turkish civic leaders. Requests American assistance for the modernization of Turkish governmental administration.

2794

Turner, Robert F., 1944–
Papers, 1963–1972. 43 ms. boxes, 1 album, 17 envelopes, 1 phonotape.
Public affairs officer, U.S. Embassy in South Vietnam, 1970–1972. Writings, reports, speeches, press releases, printed matter, clippings, and photographs, relating to political, social and cultural conditions in Vietnam and to the Vietnam War.
Register.
Deposit, R. F. Turner, 1974. Incremental deposits, 1977 and 1978.

2795

Turrou, Leon G.
Memorandum, 1926. "An Unwritten Chapter." 1 folder.
Typescript.
American Relief Administration worker in Russia. Relates to a meeting between L. G. Turrou and Feliks Dzerzhinskiĭ, Soviet Cheka Director and Commissar of Transport, in 1922, regarding transport of American Relief Administration supplies.

2796

"USSR Lend-Lease Program."
History, 1945. 1 vol.
Typescript (carbon copy).
Relates to American military assistance to the Soviet Union during World War II.

2797

U.S.S.R.—photographs, 1950–1964. 7 envelopes.
Depicts cultural sites and events, industrial plants and workers, scenes from daily life, and government leaders in the U.S.S.R.
Purchase, W. P. Hammon, 1973.

2798

U.S.S.R.—posters (in Russian), 1930–1976. 254 posters.
Printed.
Relates to political conditions in the Soviet Union. Issued by the Soviet Government.
Gift, Constance Overton Atkins, 1969. Incremental gift, 1976.

2799

U.S.S.R. propaganda, 1945–1950—photographs, 1945–1950. 1 envelope.
Depicts Soviet achievements in the fields of medicine, agriculture, and industry. Used in a Soviet exhibit. Includes printed slogans.

2800

Ufficio Patrioti della Lombardia.

Report (in Italian), n.d. "L'Attivata dell' Ufficio Patrioti della Lombardia dal 1 Maggio fino al 15 Settembre 1945: Relazione Conclusiva" (The Activity of the Patriots' Office of Lombardy from May 1 to September 15, 1945: Final Report). 1 folder.

Typescript.

Relates to activities of the Italian Partisans in Lombardy at the close of World War II.

2801

Uhlig, Heinrich, *compiler*.

Compilation of sound recordings (in German), 1961. *Aufstand des Gewissens: Dokumentation ueber den Deutschen Widerstand gegen Hitler* (Revolt of Conscience: Documentation on the German Resistance against Hitler). 1 phonorecord.

Recordings of speeches, radio addresses and trial proceedings, 1933–1944, relating to the anti-Nazi movement, and especially to the attempt of July 20, 1944, to assassinate Adolf Hitler.

2802

Ukraine-history-revolution, 1917–1921—posters (in Ukrainian), ca. 1921. 1 folder.

Printed.

Relates to elections in the Ukraine.

2803

"Ulany Ego Velichestva, 1876–1926" (His Majesty's Lancers, 1876–1926).

Commemorative history (in Russian), 1926. 1 folder.

Typescript (mimeographed).

Relates to the history of the Uhlan troops of the Russian Imperial Army.

2804

Ulbricht (Walter)—photographs, ca. 1909–1963. 2 envelopes.

Depicts events in the life of W. Ulbricht (1893–1973), East German communist leader. Distributed by the East German Government to commemorate the 70th birthday of W. Ulbricht, 1963.

2805

Unams, Z.

Memoirs (in Latvian), 1946. "Latviesu Tautas Tragedija" (The Latvian National Tragedy). ½ ms. box.

Typescript.

Latvian citizen. Relates to the Soviet and German occupations of Latvia, 1940–1945.

Deposit, Z. Unams, 1949.

2806

Ungern-Shternberg (Roman Fedorovich, Baron) collection, 1921. 1 folder.

Copy (typewritten) of a pamphlet, entitled "Letters Captured from Baron Ungern in Mongolia," reprinting correspondence of Baron Fedorovich Ungern-Shternberg (1887–1921), White Russian military leader; and

translation (typewritten), by Elena Varneck, of a military order issued by Baron Ungern-Shternberg, relating to White Russian activities in Mongolia during the Russian Revolution.

2807

United Nations Association of the United States of America. San Francisco Chapter.

Records, 1945–1970. 37 ms. boxes, 2 oversize boxes, 74 motion picture reels.

Private American organization for support of the United Nations. Correspondence, memoranda, reports, agreements, minutes, histories, financial records, lists, press summaries, pamphlets, posters, clippings, motion pictures, photographs, and printed matter, relating to the operations of United Nations organizations, world politics, and international human rights.

Gift, Mrs. Robert Digiorgio, 1977.

2808

United Nations. Conference on International Organization, San Francisco, 1945.

Sound recordings of proceedings, 1945. 146 phonorecords.

Founding conference of the United Nations. Recorded by the National Broadcasting Company.

Preliminary inventory.

Gift, National Broadcasting Company, 1947.

2809

United Nations. Conference on International Organization, San Francisco, 1945—pictorial works, 1945. 5 envelopes.

Depicts delegates to, and scenes at, the United Nations Conference on International Organization.

2810

United Nations—pictorial works, 1945–1953. 2 envelopes.

Depicts United Nations activities, including founding ceremonies in San Francisco, and officials, including Eleanor Roosevelt, Dean Acheson, Henry Cabot Lodge, Jr., Sir Gladwyn Jess, Prince Faisal Al-Saud, Dr. Mohamed Fadil al-Jamali, Sir Mohammad Zabrulla Khan, and Dr. J.M.A.H. Luns.

2811

United Nations Relief and Rehabilitation Administration collection, 1943–1948. 4 ms. boxes.

Pamphlets, journals, and printed matter, relating to the relief and reconstruction activities of the United Nations Relief and Rehabilitation Administration, particularly in China.

Gift, Mrs. Edward Arnold, 1959.

2812

United Nations Relief and Rehabilitation Administration. China Office.

Records, 1943–1948. 38 ms. boxes.

International organization for World War II relief and reconstruction. Reports, manuals, bulletins, correspondence, and administrative orders, relating to social and economic conditions in China and to United Nations relief activities in China.

Register.

Gift, Pardee Lowe, 1947.

2813

United Press Associations.

Reports, 1940–1941. 1 folder.

Typescript (some mimeographed).

News wire service. Relates to conditions in Europe and the Far East during World War II, and to the censorship policies of various countries.

2814

United Press Is On the Air.

Radio series, ca. 1942. 3 phonorecords.

Relates to news-gathering activities of the United Press during World War II.

2815

United Restitution Organization.

Miscellaneous records (in German), 1957–1967. 6 ms. boxes.

Organization for furtherance of Jewish restitution claims after World War II. Office files, correspondence, and mimeographed directives, relating to Jewish restitution claims against the West German government. Includes draft of a proposed revision of the German restitution law.

Gift, Helmut Erlanger, 1967.

2816

U.S. Advisory Commission of Railway Experts to Russia—correspondence, 1931–1936. ½ ms. box.

Correspondence of former members of the U.S. Advisory Commission of Railway Experts to Russia, relating to the Russian Revolution and activities of the commission in Siberia, 1917–1923.

2817

U.S. American Relief Administration. European Operations.

Records, 1919–1923. 890 ms. boxes, 1 album.

U.S. Government agency to provide relief after World War I (unofficial agency after June 28, 1919, incorporated May 27, 1921). Correspondence, memoranda, reports, appeals, financial records, lists, and press summaries, relating to post-World War I relief operations, food and public health problems, economic conditions, and political and social developments in Europe.

Register.

Gift, American Relief Administration, 1923.

2818

U.S. American Relief Administration. Russian Operations, 1921–1923.

Records, 1919–1925. 336 ms. boxes.

U.S. Government agency to provide relief in Europe after World War I (unofficial agency after June 28, 1919, incorporated May 27, 1921) and as an unofficial agency to provide relief in Soviet Russia between August 1921 and

June 1923. Correspondence, telegrams, memoranda, reports, agreements, minutes, histories, financial records, lists, press summaries, and photographs, relating to relief operations, food and public health problems, agriculture, economic conditions, transportation and communications, and political and social developments in Soviet Russia.

Register.

Gift, American Relief Administration, 1923.

2819

U.S. Army.

Report, 1964. "Former President Herbert C. Hoover State Funeral, 20–25 October, 1964." 1 folder.

Typescript (photocopy).

Relates to the state funeral of Herbert Hoover, with diagrams of the seating arrangement in the Capitol Rotunda, the line of march of the funeral procession in Washington, D.C., and interment ceremonies in West Branch, Iowa.

Gift, Herbert Hoover Oral History Program.

2820

U.S. Army Air Forces.

Communiqués, August 1945. 1 folder.

Typescript (mimeographed).

Relates to American bombing missions carried out against Japan. Issued from Guam.

2821

U.S. Army Air Forces. 13th Air Force Service Command—collection, 1944–1946. 1 ms. box.

Reports and photographs, relating to activities of the 13th Air Force in the Pacific Theater during World War II. Includes an official history, descriptions and photographs of South Pacific air fields, plans for garrisoning the Philippines, and statistics on bomb and ammunition expenditures.

Gift, Austin E. Fife, 1946. Incremental gift, 1947.

2822

U.S. Army Air Forces. Air Materiel Command.

Reports, 1946. 1 folder.

Typescript (mimeographed).

Lists translations made by the U.S. Air Materiel Command of captured German technical reports relating to aeronautics.

Gift, Air Materiel Command, 1946.

2823

U.S. Army Air Forces. Directorate of Weather.

Reports, 1942–1945. 2 ms. boxes.

Relates to the history of the Weather Service, 1935–1943, and to weather and climatic conditions affecting bombing and other military operations in the European and Pacific Theaters during World War II.

Gift, U.S. Army Air Forces, Directorate of Weather, 1946.

2824

U.S. Army. American Expeditionary Force, 1917–1920—collection, 1918–1919. ½ ms. box, 1 envelope, 1 album.

Memoranda, orders, proclamations, bulletins, lists, photographs, and miscellanea, issued by or relating to activities of the American Expeditionary Force in France during World War I.

2825

U.S. Army. American Expeditionary Force—Siberia—collection, 1918–1920. 2 ms. boxes.

Press releases and a report, relating to the Russian Civil War, and U.S. military activities in Siberia, 1919–1920. Includes a report by Edwin Landon, Colonel, U.S. Army, relating to conditions in western Siberia and eastern Russia, 1918.

2826

U.S. Army. American Forces in Germany, 1918–1923. General Staff, G-2.

Issuances, 1919–1923. 7 ms. boxes.

Intelligence section, U.S. Army forces occupying Germany. Bulletins and reports, relating to military, political, and economic developments in Germany. Includes excerpts from the German and French press, reports on censorship activities of the occupying powers in Germany, and regulations regarding the Upper Silesia plebiscite of 1919.

Gift, H. Hossfeld, 1921. Subsequent increments.

2827

U.S. Army. 2d Armored Division.

History, n.d. "Messages Recollecting the 2nd Armored Division of World War II." 3 phonorecords.

Gift, H. W. Zuehlke, 1967.

2828

U.S. Army. First Army. General Staff.

Miscellaneous records, 1918. 3 ms. boxes.

Reports, memoranda, orders, and maps, relating to military conditions in France, the German railway system, and experiences of German and Allied prisoners of war.

2829

U.S. Army. Second Army.

Miscellaneous records, 1918. ½ ms. box.

Field orders, operational orders, operational reports, and summaries of intelligence, relating to activities of the Second Army in France during World War I, October-November 1918.

2830

U.S. Army. Third Army. General Staff, G-2.

Miscellaneous records, 1918–1919. 2 ms. boxes.

Reports, including an official history of the U.S. Third Army in France and Germany, November 14, 1918 to July 2, 1919; and summaries of Third Army intelligence reports, November 17, 1918 to June 28, 1919.

2831

U.S. Army. Sixth Army.

Newsletter, 1964. *Retired Army Personnel Bulletin.* 1 folder.

Photocopy.

Relates to a joint U.S. Army and Air Force training exercise conducted in California, Arizona and Nevada.

2832

U.S. Army. Board of Inquiry, Camp Lewis, Washington.

Transcripts of hearings, 1918. ½ ms. box.

Typescript.

Relates to appeals of men inducted into the U.S. Army to be granted conscientious objector status.

Gift, J. G. Ragsdale, 1952.

2833

U.S. Army. Construction Division.

Report, 1919. "History of the Construction Division of the Army." 7 ms. boxes.

Typescript (some mimeographed).

Relates to army construction work in the United States and its territories, 1917–1919. Prepared under the direction of R. C. Marshall, Jr., Brigadier General, U.S. Army.

Register.

2834

U.S. Army. Corps of Engineers. 319th Regiment.

Regimental song, ca. 1917. "Marching Song of the 319th Engineers." 1 folder.

Printed.

2835

U.S. Army. I Corps.

Intelligence summary, 1918. 1 folder.

Typescript (mimeographed).

Relates to activities on the I Corps front in France, November 8–9, 1918.

2836

U.S. Army. III Corps.

Intelligence summary, 1918. 1 folder.

Typescript (mimeographed).

Relates to activities on the III Corps front in France, November 9–10, 1918.

2837

U.S. Army. IV Corps.

Miscellaneous records, 1918. 1 ms. box.

Orders, maps, and photographs, relating to the activities of the IV Corps of the U.S. Army during the battle of St. Mihiel, September 1918. Includes IV Corps intelligence summaries for November 9 and 10, 1918.

2838

U.S. Army. V Corps.

Intelligence summary, 1918. 1 folder.

Typescript (mimeographed).

Relates to activities on the V Corps front in France, September 1–2, 1918.

2839

U.S. Army. VIII Corps.

Intelligence summaries, 1918. 1 folder.

Typescript (mimeographed).
Relates to activities on the VIII Corps front in France, 1918.

2840

U.S. Army. 2d Division.
Leaflet, 1919. 1 folder.
Printed.
Commemorates the celebration of July 4, 1919, by the U.S. Army of Occupation in Germany.

2841

U.S. Army. 26th Division.
Intelligence summary, 1918. 1 folder.
Typescript (mimeographed).
Relates to activities on the 26th Division front in France, November 9–10, 1918.

2842

U.S. Army. 30th Division—collection, 1919. 1 folder.
Typescript (mimeographed).
Letter, from General John J. Pershing, Commanding General, American Expeditionary Force, and speech, by Major General Edward M. Lewis, Commanding General, U.S. 30th Division, relating to the service of the 30th Division in France during World War I.

2843

U.S. Army. 81st Division.
Miscellaneous records, 1918–1919. 1 folder.
Orders, memoranda, reports and intelligence summaries, relating to activities of the 81st Division in France, November 1918—January 1919.

2844

U.S. Army. 91st Division—collection, 1918–1919. 1 ms. box.
Reports and photographs, relating to activities of the 91st Division in France and Belgium during World War I. Includes Red Cross casualty reports, and divisional intelligence report summaries.

2845

U.S. Army. 97th Division.
Radio program, 1945, 2 phonorecords.
Christmas program broadcast from Tokyo.

2846

U.S. Army. European Command. Historical Division.
Studies (in German and English), 1945–1954. 101 pamphlet boxes (25 l. ft.).
Typescript (carbon copies of original studies located at the U.S. National Archives and Records Service).
Relates to German military operations in Europe, on the Eastern Front, and in the Mediterranean Theater, during World War II. Studies prepared by former high-ranking German Army officers for the Foreign Military Studies Program of the Historical Division, U.S. Army, Europe.
Published guide, U.S. Army, European Command, Historical Division, *Guide to Foreign Military Studies,*

1945–54: Catalog and Index (1954), and *Supplement* (1959).
Gift, U.S. Department of the Army, Historical Office, 1966.

2847

U.S. Army. European Theater of Operations. Communication Zone. Western Base Section.
History, 1944. "History of the Western Base Section, Army Post Office 515, United States Army." 2 vols.
Typescript (mimeographed).
Relates to U.S. military communications in Europe during World War II. Prepared by Fenton S. Jacobs, Colonel, U.S. Army.

2848

U.S. Army. European Theater of Operations. Information and Education Division.
Pamphlets, 1945. 1 ms. box.
Printed.
Relates to the history of individual combat divisions and supporting units of the U.S. Army in the European Theater during World War II.

2849

U.S. Army. Far East Command. Historical Section.
Report, 1947. "Summary of Activities: Historical Section, FEC-SCAP, 16 April 1947–16 July 1947." 1 folder.
Typescript (mimeographed).
Relates to projects of the Historical Section for preparing histories of World War II Pacific Theater campaigns and of the occupation of Japan.

2850

U.S. Army. Far East Command. Psychological Warfare Branch.
Leaflets (in Chinese and Korean), 1950–1953. 4 ms. boxes.
Printed.
Propaganda aimed at North Korean and Chinese soldiers during the Korean War. Includes translations (mimeographed) of the leaflets.

2851

U.S. Army. Forces in China Theater.
Translations of newspaper articles, 1946–1947. 1 folder.
Typescript.
Relates mostly to allegations of abusive treatment of Chinese civilians by U.S. military personnel in China. Translations by U.S. Army forces of articles in the Chinese press.

2852

U.S. Army. Forces in Korea.
Miscellaneous records, 1947–1948. 1 folder.
Miscellaneous correspondence and dispatches, relating to the U.S. occupation of South Korea.

2853

U.S. Army. Forces in the Pacific. General Headquarters. Civil Affairs Section.

Report, 1945. "Philippine Civil Affairs." 1 folder. Typescript (mimeographed).

Relates to governmental administration of the Philippines by the Civil Affairs Section from October 20, 1944 to August 25, 1945.

2854

U.S. Army. Forces in the Pacific. Psychological Warfare Branch.

Issuances, 1944–1946. 1 ms. box, 1 scrapbook.

Propaganda leaflets (printed) prepared for distribution in the Pacific Theater, 1944–1945; and a report (mimeographed) on psychological warfare against Japan during 1944–1945 in the Pacific Theater, 1946.

2855

U.S. Army. Forces in the Western Pacific. Military Commission, Yamashita, 1945.

Miscellaneous records, 1945–1946. 3 ms. boxes.

Commission for trial of Japanese accused of war crimes, Manila, Philippine Islands. Arraignments, trial transcripts, and exhibits, relating to the trials of Jiro Mizoguchi, Seiichi Ohta, Mariano Uyeki, and Tomoyuki Yamashita.

Preliminary inventory.

2856

U.S. Army Industrial College.

Memoranda, 1944–1945. 1 folder. Typescript (mimeographed).

Relates to plans for the development of an industrial mobilization scheme for use in future wars.

2857

U.S. Army Infantry School, Fort Benning, Ga.

Exercises, 1927–1928. 1 folder. Typescript (mimeographed).

Relates to military tactics to be used in suppressing domestic rebellions.

Gift, C. F. Elwell, 1947.

2858

U.S. Army. 38th Infantry.

News bulletin, 1922. 1 folder. Typescript (mimeographed).

Relates to activities of the 38th Infantry regiment, stationed at Camp Lewis, Washington, February—May 1922.

2859

U.S. Army. 511th Infantry (Parachute) 1st Battalion.

Order, 1945. 1 vol. Typescript (carbon copy).

Relates to the rescue of internees at the Los Baños Internment Camp, Philippine Islands.

2860

U.S. Army—intelligence—World War I—collection, 1916–1919. 1 ms. box.

Reports, bulletins, military orders and instructions, relating to U.S. Army intelligence operations during World War I. Issued by various agencies of the U.S. War Department and U.S. Army.

Preliminary inventory.

2861

U.S. Army Ordnance Proving Grounds, White Sands, New Mexico.

Photographs, 1946. 1 envelope.

Depicts test of a V-2 rocket.

2862

U.S. Army reports—July 20 incident, 1944. 1 ms. box. Typescript (mimeographed).

Relates to the attempted assassination of Adolf Hitler on July 20, 1944. Includes a report of the interrogation of Fregattenkapitaen Franz Maria Liebig, a participant in the incident; and a report based on several interrogations entitled "The Political and Social Background of the 20 July Incident." Prepared by U.S. Army agencies.

Gift, John Brown Mason.

2863

U.S. Army. School for Military Government and Administration, New York. 2d Section. Group V.

History, 1943. "The United States Military Government in the Dominican Republic, 1916 to 1922: A Case History." 1 vol.

Typescript.

2864

U.S. Army Signal Corps.

Photographs, 1917–1919. 1 album, 2 envelopes.

Depicts the American Expeditionary Force in France during World War I. Includes many individual and group portraits of senior officers, and a few photographs of American military activities in England, Germany, and the U.S.

Gift, Mr. and Mrs. Ross Blythe, 1950.

2865

U.S. Army War College. Historical Section, *collector.*

U.S. Army War College collection on the A.E.F., 1917–1930. 1 ms. box.

Copies of miscellaneous orders, reports and memoranda of the American Expeditionary Force in France, 1917–1918, collected by the U.S. Army War College, Historical Section; and an outline of the U.S. World War I military participation, 1926, and a guide for indexing U.S. World War I records, 1930, both prepared by the U.S. Army War College, Historical Section.

2866

U.S. Civil Affairs Training School, Stanford University.

Records, 1942–1945. 51½ ms. boxes, 1 card file box, 3 phonorecords.

School for training civil affairs officers for military government administration during World War II. Correspondence, memoranda, reports, financial and personnel records, handbooks, syllabi and instructional materials, relating to the politics, governments, economies and cultures of Japan, other areas in the Pacific, and various countries in Europe, and intelligence assessments of the war in the Pacific.

2867

U.S. Commercial Company. Pacific Ocean Division.
Memorandum, ca. 1946. "Outline of Proposed Economic Survey of Central Pacific Area (Carolines, Marianas, and Marshalls)." 1 folder.
Typescript (mimeographed).
Relates to the study of economic conditions and prospects in the Pacific Islands.

2868

U.S. Commission on Organization of the Executive Branch of the Government, 1947–1949 and 1953–1955.
Records, 1947–1955. 27 ms. boxes.
Correspondence, reports, minutes, press releases, and printed matter, relating to rationalization of the organization of the executive branch of the U.S. Government.
Preliminary inventory.
Deposit, Herbert Hoover, 1955; subsequently donated, 1962.

2869

U.S. Committee upon the Arbitration of the Boundary between Turkey and Armenia.
Report, ca. 1920. 2 vols.
Typescript (carbon copy).

2870

U.S. Consulate General, Zurich.
Circulars, 1914. 1 folder.
Typescript.
Relates to plans for the evacuation of American citizens to the U.S. upon the outbreak of World War I.

2871

U.S. Consulate, Leningrad.
Dispatches, 1917. 1 vol.
Typescript (carbon copy).
Relates to events in Petrograd during the Russian Revolution, March 20—July 10, 1917.

2872

U.S. Council of National Defense. Hospital Committee.
Map, 1918. 1 folder.
Photocopy.
Indicates the location of U.S. Army hospitals in the United States.

2873

U.S. Department of State.
Reports, 1942–1943. ½ ms. box.
Typescript (mimeographed).
Relates to the imposition of international sanctions against aggressor nations. Includes a report on the definition of aggression, and a report on the effects of League of Nations sanctions against Italy in 1935–1936.
Gift, Waldo Chamberlain, 1944.

2874

U.S. Department of State. International Information Administration, *translator*.
Translations of Soviet documents, 1937–1942. 1 folder.
Typescript (mimeographed).
Relates to sentencing of individuals to forced labor, and to the administration of forced labor camps in the Soviet Union. Translated in 1953.

2875

U.S. Department of State. Office of Foreign Liquidation.
Report, 1945. 1 folder.
Printed.
Relates to U.S. lend-lease aid to the Soviet Union, 1941–1945. Includes text of an agreement between the U.S. and Soviet Governments on disposition of material in inventory or procurement in the U.S. at the end of World War II.
Gift, Antony Sutton, 1970.

2876

U.S. Economic Cooperation Administration.
Report, ca. 1950. "Supervision over Fertilizer Distribution in Taiwan since 1949." 1 vol.
Typescript (carbon copy).

2877

U.S. Embassy (Great Britain).
Series of reports, 1942–1943. "Published Materials Relating to Post-War Economic Planning and Reconstruction." 1 folder.
Typescript (mimeographed).
Lists writings published in Great Britain, 1941–1943, relating to post-World War II reconstruction.

2878

U.S. Embassy (Greece).
Reports, 1947–1948. 1 folder.
Typescript (some mimeographed).
Describes the organization and activities of the Embassy, the U.S. Information Service in Athens, and economic conditions in Greece.

2879

U.S. Federal Security Agency.
Radio broadcast series, 1939. "Americans All: Immigrants All." 24 phonorecords.
Relates to the immigration of various nationalities and ethnic groups to the U.S.
Preliminary inventory.
Gift, F. Curtis May, 1972.

2880

U.S. Food Administration.
Records, 1917–1919. 321 ms. boxes, 32 cu. ft. boxes.

U.S. World War I food regulatory agency (created by an executive order of August 10, 1917 and terminated on June 30, 1919). Correspondence, reports, memoranda, minutes of meetings, press releases, surveys, statistics, and printed matter, relating to the regulation of food supply distribution and consumption in the U.S. during World War I.

Preliminary inventory.

2881

U.S. Foreign Broadcast Intelligence Service, 1941–1945.
Miscellaneous records, ca. 1941–1945. 1 ms. box, 1077 phonorecords.
U.S. Government agency monitoring foreign radio broadcasts during World War II. Sound recordings of foreign radio broadcasts, and translations of transcripts of Chinese communist broadcasts from Yenan, China.
Gift, University of Hawaii, 1958.

2882

U.S. Fuel Administration.
Miscellaneous records, 1916–1919. 3 ms. boxes.
U.S. World War I fuel regulatory agency. Press releases, minutes of meetings, and printed matter, relating to production, distribution and conservation of fuel in the U.S. during World War I.
Preliminary inventory.
Gift, Williams College Library, 1970.

2883

U.S.—history—War of 1898—peace—photograph, 1898. 1 envelope.
Depicts American and Spanish delegates signing the treaty ending the Spanish-American War. Autographed by the delegates.

2884

U.S. Information Agency.
Radio broadcasts (in English and Chinese), 1961–1965. 3 phonotapes.
Sound recordings prepared for broadcast on Voice of America, including a program entitled "Have You Been Told?" 1961, relating to Soviet nuclear test resumption (transcript included); and interviews of W. Glenn Campbell, Director of the Hoover Institution on War, Revolution and Peace, and of Dennis J. Doolin, Eugene Wu and Yuan-li Wu, fellows of the Hoover Institution, 1965, relating to activities of the Hoover Institution in the area of Chinese studies.

2885

U.S. Interdepartmental Committee for the Acquisition of Foreign Publications.
Minutes of meeting, 1942. 1 folder.
Typescript.
Relates to plans for microfilming publications abroad for shipment to the U.S., March 4, 1942.

2886

U.S. Library of Congress Mission.
Photographs, 1946. 1 album.

Depicts the shipment of library and archival material from Germany to various Allied repositories by the U.S. Library of Congress Mission at the end of World War II.
Gift, Walter L. Kluss, 1951.

2887

U.S. Maritime Service.
Photographs, 1941–1945. 5 albums.
Depicts activities of the U.S. Maritime Service during World War II, including training, medical examination, and recreational activities of merchant seamen.

2888

U.S. mediation in China collection (in English and Chinese), 1946–1947. ½ ms. box.
Directives, agreements and press releases, relating to U.S. efforts to mediate between Nationalist and Communist Chinese forces. Includes communist Chinese press releases.

2889

U.S. Military Mission to Armenia.
Photographs, 1919. 1 envelope.
Depicts U.S. Army officers in Armenia, and conditions in Armenia at the end of World War I.
Preliminary inventory.
Gift, Eliot Grinnell Mears.

2890

U.S. National Aeronautics and Space Administration.
Photographs, 1968–1969. 1 envelope.
Depicts the moon. Taken by Space Missions Apollo 8, 1968, and Apollo 10, 1969.

2891

U.S. National Emergency Council.
Report, 1936. ½ ms. box.
Typescript (mimeographed).
Relates to an assessment of federal government programs to promote economic recovery in the U.S. in 1935.

2892

U.S. National Industrial Conference, 1st, Washington, D.C., 1919.
Transcript of proceedings, 1919. 1 ms. box.
Typescript (mimeographed).
U.S. Government-sponsored conference of business and labor representatives. Relates to industrial labor relations.
Gift, Herbert Hoover.

2893

U.S. National Industrial Conference, 2d, Washington, D.C., 1919–1920.
Records, 1919–1920. 14 ms. boxes.
U.S. Government-sponsored conference of business and labor representatives. Correspondence, memoranda, reports, minutes, charts, and printed matter, relating to industrial labor relations.
Preliminary inventory.
Gift, Herbert Hoover.

2894

U.S. National Resources Planning Board. Youth Section.
Study, 1941. "Post-Defense Planning for Children and Youth." 1 folder.
Typescript (mimeographed).
Relates to national planning goals for youth in the areas of employment, health, social services, education, and recreation.

2895

U.S. National Student Association. International Commission.
Records, 1946–1967. 313 ms. boxes, 7 envelopes.
Confederation of student bodies at American colleges and universities. Correspondence, reports, memoranda, minutes of meetings, bulletins, circulars, questionnaires, notes, lists, financial records, printed matter, and photographs, relating to the international activities of the association, including delegation and scholarship exchanges with other nations, American representation at annual International Student Conferences, relations with analogous student organizations abroad, and the effects of world politics on education.
Register.
Gift, U.S. National Student Association, 1968.

2896

U.S. Naval Reserve collection, 1940–1942. 1 folder.
Syllabi and examination questions, used to train U.S. Naval Reserve officers at the U.S. Naval Academy, U.S. Naval Reserve schools, and U.S. Naval Reserve Officers' Training Corps programs at various universities.

2897

U.S. Navy. First Naval District.
Photographs, 1942–1943. 1 envelope.
Depicts the site of the Bethlehem Hingham Shipyards, Hingham, Massachusetts, before and after construction of the shipyard.

2898

U.S. Navy. Pacific Fleet and Pacific Ocean Areas.
Communiqués, 1945. 1 folder.
Typescript (mimeographed).
Relates to World War II naval operations in the Pacific Theater. Issued from Pacific Fleet advance headquarters, Guam, January-August 1945.

2899

U.S. Navy. Submarine Squadron 20.
Study, 1945. "Preliminary Intelligence Report on the Japanese Submarine Force." ½ ms. box.
Printed.
Relates to the submarine force at Yokosuka Naval Base, Yokosuka, Japan, in World War II.
Gift, F. A. Boyle, 1975.

2900

U.S. Office of Civilian Defense.
Issuances, 1941–1943. 1 ms. box.
Typescript (mimeographed) and printed.

Pamphlets, bulletins, and memoranda, relating to civil defense, and particularly to blackout regulations, during World War II.
Gift, Leland H. Brown.

2901

U.S. Office of Defense Transportation.
Reports, 1943–1944. ½ ms. box.
Typescript (mimeographed).
Relates to coordination and direction of transportation in the U.S. to facilitate the U.S. war effort during World War II, January 1942-March 1944.

2902

U.S. Office of Naval Intelligence.
History, 1943–1944. *Solomon Islands Campaign.* ½ ms. box.
Printed.
Relates to American naval operations in the Solomon Islands campaign during World War II, 1942–1943. Includes only Volumes I and IV–IX.
Gift, A. E. Fife, 1946.

2903

U.S. Office of Naval Intelligence. Air Intelligence Group.
Maps, 1944. ½ ms. box.
Printed.
Cloth maps of areas in the Pacific Theater, prepared for Navy survival kits.

2904

U.S. Office of Naval Operations. Survey Staff, Yale University.
Card file, ca. 1942. 2 file cabinets (16 l. ft)
Project to compile anthropological information on peoples of the Pacific Islands and East Asia. Notes, photographs, and extracts from printed sources, relating to the people of the Bonin and Izu Islands, the Carolines, Hokkaido, the Kuriles, the Marianas, the Marshalls, Micronesia, Burma, Siam, Indonesia, Nauru, the Ryukyus, and Formosa. Compiled in preparation for Allied military government administration in these areas.
Preliminary inventory.
Gift, U.S. Department of the Navy, 1955.

2905

U.S. Office of War Information.
Miscellaneous records, 1944–1945. 3½ ms. boxes.
U.S. Government organization for dissemination of war information and propaganda during World War II. Reports, press releases, clippings and photographs, relating to background information on many countries during World War II and to dissemination of U.S. propaganda. Includes a mimeographed "Chronology of Adolf Hitler's Life," 1944, prepared as a reference source for the Office of War Information staff.

2906

U.S. Office of War Information. Psychological Warfare Division.
Propaganda (in German, Italian, French, Chinese,

Japanese, Thai, Burmese, Vietnamese and Korean), 1942–1945. 2 ms. boxes.

U.S. Government organization for dissemination of war information and propaganda during World War II. Distributed in Europe and in the China-Burma-India Theater during World War II. Includes translations of most Asian language material.

2907

U.S. President, 1913–1921 (Wilson).
Issuances, 1914–1918. 1 folder, 1 vol.
Printed.
Executive orders and proclamations, relating to American neutrality, trade with belligerents, declaration of war, and establishment of defensive sea area during World War I.
Register.

2908

U.S. President's Conference on Home Building and Home Ownership, Washington, D.C., 1931.
Records, 1929–1933. 40 ms. boxes, 3 ledgers, 1 oversize report.
U.S. Government conference on housing. Memoranda, reports, correspondence, pamphlets, clippings, press releases and expense statements, relating to housing conditions in the United States, and to proposals for improving them.
Gift, Ray Lyman Wilbur, 1933.

2909

U.S. President's Famine Emergency Committee, 1946–1947.
Records, 1946–1947. 30 ms. boxes, 2 envelopes.
U.S. Government organization for the coordination of international famine relief after World War II. Correspondence, reports, notes and clippings, relating to U.S. food conservation and to famine conditions throughout the world. Includes memoranda and diaries of Herbert Hoover, Honorary Chairman of the Committee.
Preliminary inventory.
Herbert Hoover's notes and diaries and various other materials (boxes 29–30) may be used only with permission of the Trustees of the Hoover Foundation.
Gift, Herbert Hoover, 1962.

2910

U.S. prisoner of war camps collection, 1943–1944. ½ ms. box.
Reports, press releases, lists, and miscellanea, relating to conditions in prisoner of war camps in the U.S. during World War II and to the exchange of U.S. and Axis civilian nationals in captivity.
Gift, John Brown Mason.

2911

U.S. Provost-Marshal-General's Bureau. Military Government Division. Training Branch.
Memorandum, 1945. "Principles, Practices, and Plans for Military Government and Occupation of Japan." 1 folder.
Typescript (mimeographed).

2912

U.S. Reparations Mission to Japan.
Photographs, 1946. 1 album.
Mission headed by Edwin W. Pauley, which investigated the condition of Japanese industries in Manchuria. Depicts Manchurian industrial plants, showing destruction or removal of equipment by Soviet occupation forces.
Gift, Edwin W. Pauley.

2913

U.S. Selective Service System.
Report, 1944. 1 folder.
Typescript (mimeographed).
Relates to U.S. Government policy regarding conscientious objectors and to criticisms of this policy made by the National Committee on Conscientious Objectors.

2914

U.S. Shipping Board.
Agreement, 1918. 1 folder.
Typewritten transcript.
Relates to registry of Norwegian ships entering U.S. waters, freight rates, and other terms of trade. Agreement between the U.S. Shipping Board and the Norwegian Ship Owners' Association.

2915

U.S. Special Mission on Yen Foreign Exchange Policy.
Report, 1948. 1 folder.
Typescript (mimeographed).
Relates to the establishment of a currency exchange rate for Japan.

2916

U.S. Strategic Bombing Survey (Pacific).
Reports of interrogations, 1945. 1 folder.
Typescript (mimeographed).
Relates to a variety of aspects of the Japanese war effort in World War II, and especially to Japanese intelligence operations. Based on interrogations of Japanese political, military and naval leaders.

2917

U.S. Subversive Activities Control Board.
Records, 1950–1972. 70 ms. boxes, 6 cu. ft. boxes.
Quasi-judicial U.S. Government agency. Relates to communist and communist-front activities in the U.S.
Preliminary inventory.
Gift, U.S. Subversive Activities Board, 1971. Subsequent increments.

2918

U.S. Supreme Court.
Printed matter, 1943. ½ ms. box.
Legal briefs and court decisions in the cases of *Gordon K. Hirabayashi v. U.S.* and *Minoru Yasui v. U.S.*, reviewed before the U.S. Supreme Court, relating to the constitutionality of restrictions upon the liberties of Japanese Americans on the West Coast of the U.S. during World War II.
Gift, Nathan van Patten.

2919

U.S. War Department. Committee on Education and Special Training—collection, 1918–1919. 2 ms. boxes.

Correspondence, memoranda, reports, and syllabi, relating to the War Issues Courses conducted at Stanford University and various other colleges in the western U.S. under the auspices of the Committee on Education and Special Training of the U.S. War Department during World War I.

Gift, J. S. P. Tatlock and Minna Stillman.

2920

U.S. War Production Board. Office of Civilian Requirements. Civilian Relations Division.

Report, 1944. "Prices Paid by Consumers for 75 Clothing and Textile Items during January to March, 1944." 1 folder.

Typescript (mimeographed).

2921

U.S. War Shipping Administration. Division of Statistics and Research.

Reports, 1945–1946. 1 ms. box.

Typescript (mimeographed) and printed.

Relates to shipping volume for December 1945; and positions of dry cargo and passenger vessels on February 25, 1946, and of tankers on February 26, 1946.

Gift, U.S. War Shipping Administration, 1946.

2922

U.S. Wartime Civil Control Administration.

Miscellaneous records, 1942–1943. 2 ms. boxes, 1 folio.

Agency of the Western Defense Command of the U.S. Army. Proclamations, orders, memoranda, manuals, and maps, relating to the evacuation and relocation of Japanese-Americans in the U.S. during World War II.

Gift, Hugh T. Fullerton, 1968.

2923

U.S. Weather Bureau.

Photographs, n.d. 1 envelope.

Depicts weather balloon launching and meteorological equipment.

2924

United World Federalists collection, 1954–1955. 3 ms. boxes.

Letters, pamphlets, resolutions, and leaflets, relating to the United World Federalists, their activities in southern California, purposes, policies, meetings, financial status, membership, and fund raising, and opposition to their work. Includes some material on the United Nations.

Gift, Gertrude Suppe, 1967.

2925

Universum-Film-Aktiengesellschaft.

Newsreels (in German and Spanish), 1939–1942. 442 motion picture reels, 3 envelopes.

German motion picture company. Relates to military campaigns and conditions in Germany during World War II. Distributed in Spain. Includes a few photographs.

Preliminary inventory.

Gift, 1948.

2926

Unruh, B. H.

Studies (in German), 1948. 1½ ms. boxes.

Typescript.

German historian. Relates to the emigration of German Mennonites from the Soviet Union, 1921–1933. Includes typewritten copies (in German) of documents relating to the Mennonites in Russia from 1820 until 1870.

Deposit, Margarete Woltner, 1948.

2927

Untersuchungsausschuss Freiheitlicher Juristen.

Leaflets (in German), ca. 1950. 1 folder.

Printed.

Investigating Committee of Free Lawyers, an anti-communist West Berlin organization. Lists the names and addresses of alleged communists living in West Berlin.

2928

Uperov, Vasiliĭ Vasil'evich, 1877–1932.

Papers (in Russian), 1916–1917. 1 ms. box.

Major, Russian Imperial Army; Chief of Staff, 5th Infantry Division, 1915–1917. Reports, orders, maps, and diaries, relating to activities of the 5th Infantry Division on the Western front during World War I.

Gift, Nikolai N. Golovin, 1938.

2929

Upman, Frank, 1905–1976.

Papers, 1930–1974. 2 ms. boxes.

American engineer and government official; official in the National Recovery Administration, Work Projects Administration, War Assets Administration, Commission on Organization of the Executive Branch of the Government and other agencies. Correspondence, memoirs, reports and printed matter, relating to American politics, the growth of government bureaucracy and welfare programs, and communists in government.

Register.

Gift, Lola Upman, 1978.

2930

Upovalov, Ivan.

Translation of memoirs, 1922–1923. "How We Lost Our Liberty." 1 folder.

Typescript.

Russian Menshevik. Relates to the Russian Civil War in the areas of Votkinsk and Izhevsk, Russia, in 1918. Original memoirs, entitled "Kak My Poteriali Svobodu" and "Rabochee Vosstanie Protiv Sovetskoĭ Vlasti," published in *Zaria* (Berlin), 1922–1923. Translated by Elena Varneck.

2931

Upson, William Ford.
Diary, 1918–1919. 1 vol.
Typescript (carbon copy).
American Red Cross worker and U.S. member of the Interallied Trade Commission, 1918–1919. Relates to relief work in Europe and interallied trade during World War I.

2932

Urquhart, Leslie.
Letter, 1917. 1 folder.
Typescript.
American living in Petrograd. Relates to the Russian Revolution and its prospective outcome, as of May 1917.

2933

Usher, George L., b. 1890, *collector*.
Photographs, 1909–1918. 3 envelopes.
Depicts World War I German aircraft, American aircraft in 1909, and scenes of Vera Cruz in 1914. Includes aerial reconnaissance views of World War I military activity in France.
Gift, G. L. Usher, 1969.

2934

Ustriâlov, Nikolaĭ Vasil'evich, b. 1890.
Papers (in Russian), 1920–1934. 1 ms. box.
Russian historian. Correspondence and writings, relating to the Russian Revolution, the White governments in Omsk, 1918–1919, and Eurasianism.

2935

Utley, Freda, 1898–1978.
Papers, 1911–1977. 92 ms. boxes.
British-American author, lecturer and journalist; Director, American-China Policy Association. Correspondence, writings, and printed matter, relating to social and political conditions in Russia, Japan, and China in the interwar period; the Sino-Japanese conflict; World War II; U.S. relations with China; Germany in the post-World War II reconstruction period; social and political developments in the Middle East; and anticommunism in the U.S.
Preliminary inventory.
Gift, Jon B. Utley, 1978.

2936

Utro Petrograda (Petrograd Morning).
Newspaper issues (in Russian), 1918. 1 package (½ l. ft.).
Newspaper of the Petrograd Printing Workers Union. Relates to the Russian Civil War, April 1—July 29, 1918. Annotated with identifications of pseudonyms used in the newspaper.

2937

Vagner, Ekaterina Nikolaevna.
Papers (in Russian), 1876–1936. 2 ms boxes.
Russian Social Revolutionary. Correspondence, writings, diaries, and printed matter, relating to revolutionary movements and events in Russia. Includes the "Reminiscences" of N. N. Dzvonkevich (father of E. N. Vagner), a study of the Strelnikovskiĭ trial in Odessa, and letters from Ekaterina Breshko-Breshkovskaîa.
Preliminary inventory.
Purchase, E. N. Vagner, 1937.

2938

Vail, Edwin H.
Letters, 1922–1924. 1 folder.
Typescript.
Relief worker in Russia. Relates to social and economic conditions in Russia, and to Quaker relief work in Russia.

2939

Vajay, Szabolcs de.
Thesis (in French), 1947. "L'Aspect International des Tentatives de la Restauration Habsbourg en Hongrie, Mars-Octobre 1921" (The International Aspect of the Attempts at Hapsburg Restoration in Hungary, March-October 1921). ½ ms. box.
Typescript.
Thesis at the Institut Universitaire des Hautes Etudes Internationales, Paris.
Gift, S. de Vajay, 1947.

2940

Vajraprahar, Dr.
Manifesto, 1947. "The Indian Magna Charta." 1 folder.
Printed copy.
Relates to the Indian struggle for independence.

2941

Vaksmut, A. P.
Memoir (in Russian), n.d. "Koneťs Kaspiĭskoĭ Flotiliĭ Vremeni Grazhdanskoĭ' Voiny pod Komandoĭ Generala Denikina" (The End of the Caspian Flotilla during the Civil War under the Command of General Denikin). 1 folder.
Holograph.
Captain, White Russian Navy.

2942

Valjavec, Fritz, *collector*.
F. Valjavec collection on Central and Southeastern Europe (in German, French, Czech, Greek and Italian), 1934–1938. 2 ms. boxes.
Clippings and research notes, relating to the diplomatic and trade relations of Nazi Germany with the countries of Central and Southeastern Europe and to the economic and political conditions in those countries.

2943

Valkeapaeae, P. J.
Report (in English and Finnish), 1918–1919. 1 folder.
Printed.
Report, entitled "Selostus Toiminnastaan Elintarpeiden Hankkimiseksi Amerikasta Suomeen Vuosina 1918–1919" (Report on American Food Relief Activities in Finland for the Year 1918–1919), by P. J. Valkea-

paeae, 1919; and first issue of the *Finland Sentinel*, organ of the Finland Constitutional League of America, July 4, 1918, relating to Finnish independence.

2944

Valters, Erika.
Letters (in Latvian), 1946–1948, to Valia Turin. 1 folder.
Typescript.
Member of the Latvian Red Cross. Relates to Latvian Red Cross work in Belgium.
Gift, Gvido Augusts, 1973.

2945

Valters, Mikelis, b. 1874.
Papers (in Latvian), 1923–1940. ½ ms. box.
Photocopy.
Latvian diplomat and statesman; Deputy Premier; Ambassador to Italy, Poland and Belgium. Reports to Janis Balodis, Latvian Deputy Prime Minister and Minister of War, 1938–1940, and minutes of the First and Second Conferences of Latvian Envoys Abroad, at Riga, 1923 and 1935, all relating to Latvian diplomacy.
Gift, Edgar Anderson, 1972.

2946

Vámbéry, Rusztem, 1872–1948.
Papers (in Hungarian and English), 1887–1948. 9 ms. boxes.
Hungarian criminologist, author, educator, lawyer, and politician; Ambassador to the U.S., 1946–1948. Correspondence, speeches and writings, reports, and printed matter, relating to criminology, to Hungarian domestic and foreign affairs, to Hungarian-American relations, and to Hungarian émigrés in the U.S.
Register.
May be used only with permission of the Archivist and the Associate Director for Library Operations, Hoover Institution on War, Revolution and Peace. Applications must include résumé and two letters of reference.
Purchase, Robert R. Vambery, 1975.

2947

Van Antwerp, William M.
Papers, 1943–1945. 1 ms. box.
Colonel, U.S. Army; Assistant Chief of Staff for Intelligence, 27th Division, 1943–1945. Reports, writings, maps, and photographs, relating to the campaigns of Saipan, Makin Atoll, Koubash Atoll, and Okinawa during World War II, especially to attitudes of civilian populations, interrogation of prisoners, terrain, disposition of Japanese troops and battles.
Gift, W. M. Van Antwerp, 1967.

2948

Van Cise, Philip S.
Papers, 1917–1919. 1 ms. box.
Lieutenant Colonel, U.S. Army; Assistant Chief of Staff for Intelligence, 81st Division, 1917–1919. Letters, clippings and miscellanea, relating to activities of the American Expeditionary Force in France during World War I.
Gift, Ethel Van Cise, 1940.

2949

Vanderhoof, Frank E.
Outline, 1943. "Vanderhoof 13-Point Peace Plan to Eliminate Future Wars." 1 folder.
Typescript (mimeographed).
Relates to a plan for the assurance of world peace through the establishment of an international association of states.

2950

Van der Kaar, Helena.
Letters received, 1945–1949. 1 ms. box.
Holograph.
Relates primarily to social and economic conditions in Germany and also to conditions in the Netherlands, Switzerland, and Great Britain, immediately after World War II. Written by friends abroad.
Gift, H. Van der Kaar, 1946. Subsequent increments.

2951

Van Hook, Clifford E., b. 1886.
Papers, 1909–1947. 1 ms. box, 1 envelope.
Rear Admiral, U.S. Navy; Deputy Commander, 7th Fleet, during World War II. Correspondence and reports, relating to American naval operations during World Wars I and II.
Gift, Gordon Van Hook, 1976.

2952

Van Keuren, Alexander Hamilton, 1881–1966.
Papers, 1899–1962. 8 ms. boxes, 2 envelopes.
Rear Admiral, U.S. Navy; technical adviser, London Naval Conference, 1930, and Geneva Disarmament Conference, 1932; Director, Naval Research Laboratory, 1942–1944. Correspondence, memoranda, notes, clippings, photographs and memorabilia, relating to the Naval Research Laboratory, Anacostia Station, Washington, D.C., and to the London Naval Conference and the Geneva Disarmament Conference.
Register.
Gift, Mrs. Harold Pestalozzi, 1974.

2953

Van Patten, Nathan, 1887–1956.
Certificate, 1930. 1 folder.
Printed.
Director, Stanford University Libraries, 1927–1947. Certificate awarded to N. Van Patten by the Disabled American Veterans of the World War.

2954

Vansittart, Sarita Vansittart, Baroness.
Letter, 1964. 1 folder.
Holograph.
Widow of Lord Robert Vansittart, British diplomat. Relates to the private life of Lord Vansittart.

2955

Van Zonnefeld, Helen, 1898–
Memoir, n.d. "A Time to Every Purpose." 1 ms. box.
Typescript.
American living in London. Relates to conditions in Great Britain during World War II.
Quotations limited to 5000 words.
Deposit, H. Van Zonnefeld, 1964.

2956

Varneck, Elena.
Papers, n.d. 5 cu. ft. boxes.
Russian-American historian. Research notes, drafts of writings, and translations, relating to a proposed publication entitled "Revolution and Civil War in Siberia and the Far East," pertaining to events of the Russian Revolution and Civil War in Siberia.

2957

Varska, A. S.
Series of articles (in Russian), 1938. "Krovavye Dni na Amure" (Bloody Days on the Amur). 1 folder.
Printed.
Relates to the Russian Civil War in Blagoveshchensk, 1918. Published in the *Russkoe Obozrenie* (Chicago), March 1938. Written by A. S. Varska under the pseudonym A. Ravich.

2958

Vasil'ev, Dimitriĭ Stepanovich, d. 1915.
Miscellanea (in Russian), 1907–1975. 1 folder.
Russian Imperial Naval Attaché in the U.S. Marriage and death certificates, 1907 and 1915. Includes *Bulletins* of the Russian Imperial Naval Academy, 1973–1975, and a document concerning the Russian Military-Naval Agency in the United States, 1915–1918.
Gift, Constantine Zakhartchenko, 1975.

2959

Vasil'ev, E.
Memoirs (in Russian), n.d. "Zapiski o Plienie" (Notes on Prison). ½ ms. box.
Holograph.
Russian soldier. Relates to the imprisonment of E. Vasil'ev in a German prison camp during World War I.
Gift, E. Vasil'ev, 1925.

2960

Vassart, Cilly, d. 1962.
History (in French), 1962. "Le Front Populaire en France" (The Popular Front in France). 1 vol.
Typescript.
Widow of Albert Vassart.

2961

Vatatŝi, Mariîà Petrovna, b. 1860.
Papers (in Russian), 1917–1934. 1½ ms. boxes.
Wife of a tsarist government official in the Caucasus. Memoirs and correspondence, relating to family affairs, political conditions in Russia, 1904–1917, White Russian activities during the Russian Civil War, and the Kuban Republic.

2962

Vatcher, William Henry, Jr., 1920–
Papers, 1939–1965. 18 ms. boxes, 4 envelopes.
American political scientist; member, United Nations Armistice Negotiations Team in Korea, 1951. Correspondence, writings, pamphlets, leaflets, slides, and photographs, relating to South African political parties; Afrikaner and African nationalism; the Afrikaner Broederbond; U.S., Japanese, and North Korean propaganda and psychological warfare methods during World War II and the Korean War; and the Trans-Siberian Railroad.
Register.
Gift, W. H. Vatcher, Jr., 1953. Subsequent increments.

2963

Verbouwe, A., *collector*.
Miscellany (in French, Flemish and German), 1914–1918. 1 ms. box.
Underground serial issues (mostly mimeographed), issued in German-occupied Belgium, relating to war news and the German occupation; and a few ordinances issued by the occupation authorities.
Gift, A. Verbouwe.

2964

Verheye, Pierre C. T.
Chart, n.d. 1 folder.
Chart of comparative military grades of the armies of the United States, Germany, and central and eastern European countries during World War II. Includes grades of the German Waffen-SS and Ordnungspolizei, and of resistance units and collaborationist groups in Yugoslavia.
Gift, P. C. T. Verheye, 1975.

2965

Vernadsky, George, 1887–1973.
Miscellaneous papers (in English and Russian), 1935. ½ ms. box.
Russian-American historian. Notes (handwritten and typewritten) for a projected social and economic history of Russia during the period 1917–1921; and a copy (typewritten in Russian, with translation) of a letter to A. F. Izîùmov, relating to the views of G. Vernadsky on serfdom in Russia.
Gift, G. Vernadsky, 1935.

2966

Vernadsky, Nina.
Memoirs (in Russian), n.d. ½ ms. box.
Typescript.
Russian teacher. Relates to the Russian Revolution and Civil War. Includes an incomplete translation.

2967

Vernon, Manfred C., *collector.*
Letters, 1946. 1 folder.
Holograph.
Letters from Dutch children to American children, in gratitude for American food relief in the Netherlands at the end of World War II.
Gift, M. C. Vernon.

2968

Verstraete, Maurice, b. 1866.
Memoirs (in French), 1949. "Sur les Routes de Mon Passé" (On the Paths of My Past). 1 ms. box.
Typescript.
French diplomat; Consul in Moscow, 1894–1896; Secretary of Embassy to Russia, 1897–1900; Consul General in St. Petersburg, 1901–1918. Relates to French relations with Russia, and historical and political events in Russia from 1894 until 1918.
Gift, M. Verstraete, 1949.

2969

Veselovzorov, Major General.
Commentary (in Russian), n.d. "Ustav Unutrenneĭ Sluzhby" (Regulations of Routine Garrison Service). 1 folder.
Holograph.
Russian Imperial Army officer. Relates to regulations of the Russian Imperial Army.

2970

Vesinne-Larue, Maître de.
Speech (in French), 1945. 1 vol.
Typewritten transcript.
French lawyer; attorney for Henri Dentz, General, French Army. Closing defense address in the trial of H. Dentz on charges of treason, April 20, 1945.

2971

Vesselago, George M., 1892–
Papers (in Russian), 1904–1970. 8 ms. boxes, 1 envelope.
Lieutenant Commander, Russian Imperial Navy. Correspondence, writings, printed matter, clippings, and photographs, relating to Russian naval operations during World War I and the Russian Revolution and Civil War.
Register.
Gift, Vasilii Romanov, 1975.

2972

Veysey, Victor Vincent, 1915–
Papers, 1960–1977. 121 ms. boxes.
Member, California Legislature, 1963–1970; U.S. Representative from California, 1971–1975; Assistant Secretary of the Army, 1975–1977. Correspondence, speeches and writings, clippings, photographs, memoranda, and printed matter, relating to California and U.S. politics, government and election campaigns, and U.S. environmental and energy programs.
May not be used without permission of V. V. Veysey.
Gift, V. V. Veysey, 1977.

2973

Viazemskiĭ, Sergeĭ Sergeevich, d. 1915.
Correspondence (in Russian), 1915. 1 folder.
Captain, Russian Imperial Navy. Relates to Russian naval operations during World War I, especially the battles in Riga Bay in defense of the Irbenskiĭ Strait.
Gift, Olga Karpova, 1975.

2974

Victor, George.
Memoirs, n.d. "Odyssey from Russia." 1 folder.
Transcript (mimeographed).
Relates to emigration of G. Victor from Russia via Turkey and western Europe to the U.S. around the time of the Russian Civil War.

2975

Viereck, George Sylvester, 1884–1962.
Newspaper clippings, 1903–1942. 32 scrapbooks, 1 folder.
German-American poet, playwright and journalist. Relates to the literary career of G. S. Viereck, his arrest and trial as a pro-German propagandist in the U.S. during World War II, German-American relations, and U.S. foreign policy during World War I. Many of the clippings are articles by G. S. Viereck.

2976

Vietnam War letters, 1972. 1 folder.
Holograph.
Letters from East German elementary school students addressed to Stanford University, opposing United States involvement in the Vietnam War.

2977

Vigh, Albert.
Study (in German), ca. 1917. "Die Ausbildung von Kriegsinvaliden in Ungarn." (The Training of War Cripples in Hungary). 1 vol.
Typescript (carbon copy).
Relates to rehabilitation of disabled World War I veterans in Hungary.

2978

Villa, Simeon A.
Translation of diary, 1899–1901. "Flight and Wanderings of Emilio Aguinaldo." 1 vol.
Typescript.
Aide to Emilio Aguinaldo, Philippine revolutionary leader. Relates to the Philippine insurrection against the U.S., November 1899—March 1901.

2979

Vinaver, Rose Georgievni.
Memoirs (in Russian), 1944. 1 vol.
Typescript.
Wife of Maxim Moiseevich Vinaver, a leader of the Russian Constitutional Democratic Party and Foreign Minister of the Crimean Regional Government, 1918–1919. Relates to political conditions in Russia, the Russian Revolution, and the Crimean Regional Government.

2980

Vincent, George E.
 Papers, 1917–1921. 1 folder.
 Soldier, British Army. Military orders, certificates, and soldier's pay book, relating to British military activities in World War I.
 Gift, Mrs. Tom E. Lapp, 1973.

2981

Vining, Robert E.
 Report, 1943. "Restatement and Review of Situation in Ireland (Eire) and Northern Ireland." 1 folder.
 Typescript.
 Lieutenant Commander, U.S. Navy. Relates to political and economic conditions, Irish attitudes toward U.S. military forces stationed in Northern Ireland, and activities of the Irish Republican Army.

2982

Vinogradov, A. K.
 History, 1922. "The Fortunes of the Roumiantzow Museum." 1 vol.
 Typescript.
 Director, Rumîantŝev Museum, Moscow. Relates to the museum, and especially to its library. Includes photographs.

2983

Violin, IÂ. A.
 Study (in Russian), 1922. "Uzhasy Goloda i Lîudoedstva v Rossiĭ v 1921–22 g.g." (The Horrors of Famine and Cannibalism in Russia in 1921–1922). 1 vol.
 Typescript (carbon copy).

2984

Vishniak, Mark Veniîaminovich, 1883–1976.
 Papers (in Russian and English), ca. 1910–1968. 14 ms. boxes.
 Russian historian; Socialist Revolutionary Party leader. Correspondence, writings, and clippings, relating to Russian and Soviet history, Russian revolutionists, Russian émigrés, and political conditions in the Soviet Union.
 Preliminary inventory.
 Gift, M. V. Vishniak, 1970.

2985

Visoianu, Constantin, 1897–
 Papers (in Romanian, French and English), 1937–1960. 5 ms. boxes.
 Romanian Minister of Foreign Affairs, 1945–1946; President, Romanian National Committee, Washington, D.C. Correspondence, memoranda, reports, speeches, writings, and photographs, relating to Romanian foreign relations, political developments in Romania, and anticommunist émigré activities.
 Register.
 During their lifetimes, access requires the written permission of C. Visoianu or George Duca. In addition, boxes 3–5 are restricted until January 1, 2002.
 Gift, C. Visoianu, 1976. Incremental gift, 1977.

2986

Vitkovskiĭ, Vladimir K.
 Memoir (in Russian), 1933. "Konstantinopol'skiĭ Pokhod: Iz Vospominaniĭ o Gallipoli" (The Constantinople March: From Reminiscences about Gallipoli). 1 folder.
 Typescript (mimeographed).
 Lieutenant General, Russian Imperial Army. Relates to the evacuation of White Russian troops at the end of the Russian Civil War.

2987

Vitte (Sergeĭ IÛl'evich, Graf)—photograph, n.d. 1 envelope.
 Depicts the tsarist Russian government official S. I. Vitte.

2988

Vladimir Kirillovich, Grand Duke of Russia, 1917–
 Appeal, 1952. "An Appeal to the Free World." 1 folder.
 Printed (photocopy).
 Relates to communism in Russia. Published in *Nasha Strana* (Buenos Aires).

2989

Vladimirov, Ivan Alekseevich, 1870–1947.
 Paintings, 1918–1923. 40 paintings.
 Russian artist. Depicts scenes of privation and revolutionary justice in Petrograd and elsewhere in Russia during the Russian Revolution and Civil War.
 Register.
 Purchase, I. A. Vladimirov, 1923.

2990

Voegelin, Eric, 1901–
 Papers, 1930–1974. 26 ms. boxes.
 German-American philosopher and political scientist. Correspondence, speeches and writings, reports, and memoranda, relating to international affairs and political science.
 Gift, E. Voegelin, 1975.

2991

"Voice of Democracy" Committee.
 Sound recordings, 1948. 2 phonorecords.
 Promotional announcements and model radio broadcasts, relating to a contest for high school students for radio broadcast scripts on democracy in the U.S., sponsored by the U.S. Junior Chamber of Commerce, the National Association of Broadcasters and the Radio Manufacturers Associations. Includes posters.
 Gift, Federal Radio Education Committee, 1949.

2992

Voice of Peace.
 Sound recorded message, n.d. 1 phonorecord.
 American religious pacifist organization. Appeals to American women to ensure peace through prayer. Includes a recording of the song "Ave Maria" sung by Wilma Reynolds.
 Gift, Voice of Peace.

2993

Voigt, Rector, *collector.*

Voigt collection on postwar Germany (in German), 1914–1922. 6 ms. boxes, 33 pamphlet boxes (11 l. ft.).

Regulations, proclamations, posters, ration cards, and miscellanea, relating to economic conditions in Germany during and immediately after World War I, especially food rationing, procurement of raw materials, and war loan drives.

Preliminary inventory.

Purchase, Rector Voigt, 1922.

2994

Vokietaitis, Algirdas.

Papers (in Lithuanian, English and German), 1943–1944. 1 folder.

Lithuanian underground representative in Sweden during World War II. Photocopies of clandestine printed matter, and translations of declarations and clandestine radio broadcasts, of Lithuanian resistance groups during World War II, relating to their struggle against German and Soviet occupation.

Gift, A. Vokietaitis, 1978.

2995

Volkhovskiĭ, Feliks Vadimovich, 1846–1914.

Papers (in Russian), 1875–1914. 24 ms. boxes.

Russian revolutionist and journalist; Socialist Revolutionary Party leader; editor, *Free Russia* (London). Correspondence, writings, photographs, periodicals, and clippings, relating to revolutionary movements in Imperial Russia.

Preliminary inventory.

2996

Volkonskiĭ, Vladimir Mikhailovich, 1868–1953.

Memoir, n.d. 1 folder.

Typescript (photocopy).

Relates to the canonization of Saint Serafim of Sarov by the Russian Orthodox Church, 1903.

Gift, Vasilii Romanov, 1977.

2997

Volkov, Boris.

Writings (in Russian), 1921–1931. ½ ms. box.

Typescript.

White Russian Army officer. Relates to the Russian Civil War in Siberia and Mongolia, the career of the White Russian commander, Baron Ungern-Shternberg, the capture of Troiťskosavsk, and the massacre of officers on the Khor River. Includes a translation (typewritten), by Elena Varneck, of one manuscript.

Gift, B. Volkov, 1936.

2998

Volkov, Leon, 1914–1974.

Papers, 1948–1974. 7 ms. boxes.

Lieutenant Colonel, Soviet Air Force, during World War II; editor and journalist for *Newsweek* magazine, 1953–1974; consultant on Soviet affairs to the U.S. Departments of State and Defense. Diaries, correspon-

dence, speeches and writings, reports, clippings, press excerpts, and printed matter, relating to social and political conditions in the Soviet Union, Soviet foreign policy, international politics, and Russian refugee life.

Register.

Deposit, Nicholas Volkov, 1977.

2999

Volksdeutsche Bewegung in Luxemburg.

Reports (in German), 1941–1944. 1 folder.

Typescript.

Pro-German organization in Luxembourg. Relates to political conditions in Luxembourg under German occupation. Reports addressed to agencies of the German Nazi Party.

3000

Volkszeitung Leipzig (Leipzig People's Newspaper).

Telegrams (in German), 1919. 3 ms. boxes.

Dispatches from the Budapest correspondent of the *Volkszeitung Leipzig*, relating to the Hungarian Soviet Republic.

Gift, Ralph H. Lutz, 1960.

3001

Vollbehr, Otto H. F., b. 1872.

Writings, 1931–1934. 1 folder.

German book collector. Reprint of a newspaper interview, 1931, and letter to the editor (typewritten), 1934, relating to world politics and national socialism in Germany.

3002

Vologodskiĭ, Petr Vasil'evich.

Papers (in Russian and English), 1918–1925. ½ ms. box.

Prime Minister, White Russian Omsk Government, 1918–1919. Diaries, resolutions, reports, and translations of diary excerpts, relating to the Omsk Government, the Russian Civil War in Siberia, and economic conditions in Siberia.

3003

Vol'skiĭ, Nikolaĭ Vladislavovich, 1879–1964.

Papers (in Russian and English), 1908–1964. 10 ms. boxes, 1 envelope.

Russian revolutionary and author. Correspondence, writings, clippings, reports, and photographs, relating to Russian revolutionary movements and émigré life, Imperial Russian and Soviet agricultural and economic policies, labor movements, Menshevism, and political events in Russia.

Preliminary inventory.

Purchase, Vera Vol'skiĭ, 1965. Purchase, International Institute of Social History, 1976.

3004

Von Arnold, Antonina R.

Study, 1937. "A Brief Study of the Russian Students in the University of California." 1 folder.

Typescript.

American social worker. Relates to the adjustment of

Russian émigré students at the University of California, Berkeley, to American university life.

3005

Von Blon, Henriette B.
Papers, 1939–1940. 1 ms. box.
Letters received (handwritten), 1942–1944, from Japanese Americans interned at the Heart Mountain, Wyoming, relocation center during World War II, relating to conditions in the camp; and clippings from American newspapers, 1939–1940, relating to French culture and the military defeat of France in 1940.
Gift, H. B. Von Blon, 1952.

3006

Von Mohrenschildt, Dimitri Sergius, 1902–
Papers, 1917–1970. ½ ms. box, 1 envelope.
American historian; editor, *Russian Review.* Correspondence, writings, printed matter and photographs, relating to acquisition of Russian historical materials, and the Russian Orthodox Church in the U.S. Includes letters from Sergei A. Von Mohrenschildt, Russian military historian and father of D. S. Von Mohrenschildt, describing political and economic conditions in Poland under Soviet and Lithuanian occupation, 1939–1940.
Register.
Gift, D. S. Von Mohrenschildt, 1971. Incremental gift, 1976.

3007

Von Wiegand, Karl Henry, 1874–1961.
Papers (in English and German), 1911–1961. 88 ms. boxes, 6 binders (1 l. ft.), 1 stack of oversize mounted clippings (1 l. ft.), 2 swords, 1 shield.
American journalist; Hearst Newspaper foreign correspondent, 1917–1961. Correspondence, dispatches, writings, photographs, clippings, and printed matter, relating to European diplomacy and German politics between the world wars, the Sino-Japanese War, the European Theater in World War II, the Cold War, the postwar Middle Eastern situation, and U.S. foreign policy.
Purchase, estate of K. H. Von Wiegand, 1975.

3008

Vorotovov, Colonel.
Memoirs (in Russian), n.d. 1 folder.
Holograph.
White Russian Army officer. Memoirs, entitled "2-i Orenburgskii Kazachii Polk v 1918–1920 g.g." (The 2d Orenburg Cossack Regiment in 1918–1920) and "V Zabaikal'ie i na Primorskom Frontie v 1920–21 g.g." (In the Zabaikal and on the Maritime Front in 1920–21), relating to the Russian Civil War.

3009

Voskevich, P., *collector.*
Photographs, ca. 1905. 1 envelope.
Depicts Imperial Russian and Imperial Japanese officers during negotiations for settling new boundaries on Sakhalin Island, and the Russian Embassy staff in Tokyo.

3010

Votaw, Homer Cutts, *collector.*
Miscellany, ca. 1942–1945. 1 oversize box (½ l. ft.).
Maps, posters, memoranda, letters, news releases, newspapers, proclamations, and articles, relating to the occupation of the Philippine Islands by the Japanese during World War II.
Gift, H. C. Votaw, 1976.

3011

Voyce, Arthur, d. 1977.
Papers, ca. 1948–1960. 27½ ms. boxes, 2 card file boxes (¼ l. ft.).
American art historian. Correspondence, writings, notes, photographs, slides, clippings and other printed matter, relating to Russian art and architecture from the fifteenth to the twentieth century.
Gift, estate of A. Voyce, 1977.

3012

Vrangel', Mariia D.
Papers (in Russian), 1919–1944. ca. 42 linear feet.
Mother of General P. N. Vrangel', Commander of the White Russian forces in Southern Russia. Correspondence, writings, pamphlets, periodicals, newspapers, photographs, clippings, and printed matter, relating to the life and military career of P. N. Vrangel', the anti-Bolshevik campaigns of the Armed Forces in Southern Russia, the Russian Revolution and Civil War, communism in Russia, and the activities of Russian refugees in foreign countries.
Preliminary inventory.
Deposit, M. D. Vrangel', 1932.

3013

Vrangel', Petr Nikolaevich, Baron, 1878–1928.
Papers (in Russian), 1916–1923. 94½ ms. boxes, 18½ linear feet.
Commander-in-Chief, White Russian Volunteer Army, 1920. Correspondence, memoranda, reports, military orders, dispatches, printed matter and photographs, relating to the Russian Revolution and Civil War, the operations of the Volunteer Army and the Armed Forces of Southern Russia, evacuation of White Russian military personnel and civilians from the Crimea in 1920, and the resettlement of Russian refugees first in Constantinople and subsequently in various European countries.
Preliminary inventory.
Deposit, P. N. Vrangel', 1926. Incremental deposit, 1929.

3014

Vrede en Vrijheid.
Leaflet (in Dutch), 1951. 1 folder.
Printed.
Dutch anticommunist organization. Anticommunist propaganda leaflet.

3015

Vsesoîûznyĭ Mendeleevskiĭ S'ezd po Teoreticheskoĭ i Prikladnoĭ Khimii, St. Petersburg, 1911—photograph, 1911. 1 envelope.

Depicts delegates to the All-Union Mendeleev Congress on Theoretical and Applied Chemistry.

3016

Vukcevich, Bosko S.

Study, n.d. "Petar Petrovich-Njegos: Serbian Poet and Philosopher." 1 folder.

Typescript (photocopy).

3017

Vuksanović, Vladeta, 1900–

Study (in Serbo-Croatian), 1970. "Saznanje Države: Teorija Političkog Saznanja" (Knowledge of the State: Theory of Political Knowledge). 2 vols.

Typescript.

Official of the Royal Yugoslav People's Bank; after 1945, Yugoslav government economist.

Gift, V. Vuksanović, 1970.

3018

Vyrypaev, V. I.

Memoir (in Russian), n.d. "Vladimir Oskarovich Kappel': Vospominaniîâ Uchastnika Beloĭ Bor'by" (Vladimir Oskarovich Kappel': Memoirs of a Participant in the White Struggle). ½ ms. box.

Typescript.

Soldier, White Russian Army. Relates to the Russian Civil War, and the activities of the Volunteer Army detachments under the command of V. O. Kappel'. Includes partial translation.

3019

Wainwright, W. A.

Photographs, 1945. 1 envelope.

An aerial view of Iwo Jima, and a photograph of the dedication of a memorial flagstaff on Iwo Jima by U.S. troops.

3020

Waldau, Otto Hoffmann von, d. 1943.

Diary (in German), 1939–1942. ½ ms. box.

Typescript (photocopy).

Major General, German Army; Chief, Operations Branch, General Staff, Luftwaffe. Relates to German air operations during World War II.

May not be quoted.

Gift, anonymous, 1970.

3021

Wales, Nym, 1907–

Papers, 1931–1954. 37 ms. boxes, 30 envelopes.

American journalist and writer; member, Board of Directors, American Committee in Aid of Chinese Industrial Cooperatives, 1941–1951. Personal and collected correspondence, speeches and writings, news dispatches, interviews, reports, memoranda, organizational records, and photographs, relating to the Chinese communists; the industrial cooperative movement, student movement, and labor movement in China; the Sian incident, 1936; the Sino-Japanese Conflict; and Chinese art and literature.

Register.

May not be used without permission of Helen Foster Snow (Nym Wales).

Purchase, Helen Foster Snow, 1958.

3022

Wallace, Earle S., *collector*.

Miscellany, 1918. 1 ms. box.

Pamphlets, photographs, maps, a poster, and memorabilia, relating to activities of the American Expeditionary Force in France during World War I.

Gift, Janet Pennycock.

3023

Wallen, E. Carl, 1889–1961.

Papers, 1918–1923. 1 ms. box.

American photographer. Photographs depicting relief work in the Caucasus, Turkey, and other areas of the Near East at the end of World War I. Includes a few papers of Mary Jane Steel (Mrs. E. C. Wallen), relating to her service as a Red Cross nurse in the Near East at this time, and a photograph of President Warren G. Harding in 1923.

Gift, Barney Gould, 1975.

3024

Wallgren, Albian A.

Cartoon, 1918. 1 folder.

Hand-drawn.

American cartoonist. Relates to the American Expeditionary Force in France during World War I.

Gift, James K. Senior, 1950.

3025

Walsh, Warren B., *translator*.

Translations, n.d. ½ ms. box.

Transcript (photocopy).

Diary of A. Balk, Prefect of Police of Petrograd, 1917, relating to the Russian Revolution of March 1917, and correspondence between Nicholas II, Tsar of Russia, and P. A. Stolypin, President of the Council of Ministers of Russia, 1906–1911, relating to political conditions in Russia. Includes explanatory notes by W. B. Walsh.

May not be quoted without permission of W. B. Walsh.

Gift, W. B. Walsh, 1975.

3026

Walters, Ray P.

Report, 1949. 1 folder.

Typescript (mimeographed).

American engineer; delegate to the American Institute of Mining and Metallurgical Engineers to the Second International Technical Congress of the World Engineering Conference, Cairo, 1949. Relates to proceedings of the congress, especially to activities of communist delegates.

Gift, R. P. Walters, 1978.

3027

Wanda Roehr Foundation, *collector*.
Motion picture, 1939. 1 reel.
Depicts the effects of the German bombing of Warsaw, September 1939.
Gift, Wanda Roehr Foundation, 1968.

3028

War crime trials—Nuremberg, 1946–1949—collection (in German), 1948. 1 folder.
Correspondence, depositions, and memoranda, relating to the defense of several Germans accused of war crimes at the Nuremberg trials.

3029

Warburg, James Paul, 1896–1969.
Memorandum, 1949. "Renascent Nazi Propaganda in Switzerland: The Myth of 'Sidney Warburg'." 1 folder.
Typescript.
American banker. Relates to allegations that the German Nazi Party had received financial support from U.S. bankers, including one "Sidney Warburg."

3030

Warden, A. A.
Writings, ca. 1924–1929. 1 folder.
Typescript.
British physician and pacifist. Writings, entitled "On the Firing-Line of Thought, 1914–1924," 1924, and "Masters of Medicine and War: A Retrospect," ca. 1929, relating to the pacifist movement and the responsibilities of the medical profession in relation to it.

3031

Wardlaw, Ana.
Papers, 1956–1960. 1 ms. box.
Drafts and research notes for a study, entitled "Key People in Satellite Countries, 1944–1955," relating to the communist leadership in Poland, Romania, Bulgaria, Albania, Czechoslovakia, and Hungary.

3032

Warlimont, Walter, 1894–
Writings (in German), n.d. 1 folder.
Typescript.
General, German Army, during World War II. Relates to the political role of the German officer corps under national socialism, and to allegations by General Alfred Jodl that W. Warlimont was guilty of war crimes.

3033

Washington, D.C. Conference on the Limitation of Armaments, 1921–1922—clippings, 1921. 1 folder.
Relates to events at the conference. Clippings from American newspapers.

3034

Washington, Harold George, 1892–1961?, *collector*.
Miscellany, 1918–1920. 1 ms. box.
Depicts social conditions, railroads and Allied troops in Siberia and Manchuria during the Russian Revolu-

tion. Includes some postcards of buildings and war damage in France.
Gift, estate of H. G. Washington, 1961.

3035

Watkins, James Thomas, IV, 1907–
Papers, 1945–1962. 6 l. ft., 2 microfilm reels, 1 envelope, 1 phonorecord.
American political scientist; Political Affairs Officer, Military Government Headquarters, Okinawa, 1945–1946. Correspondence, reports and maps, relating to the Allied military government in Okinawa following World War II, and to miscellaneous aspects of post-war international relations and U.S. politics.
Preliminary inventory.
Gift, J. T. Watkins, IV, 1971. Subsequent increments.

3036

Watkins, Susan E., *collector*.
Miscellany (in English and French), 1916–1921. ½ ms. box.
Correspondence, postcards, leaflets and miscellanea, relating to civilian relief work in France during and after World War I, and especially to the work of Fatherless Children of France.
Gift, Mr. Watkins, 1967.

3037

Watson, Samuel Newell, 1861–1942.
Papers (in English and French), 1914–1920. ½ ms. box, 12 scrapbooks, 1 package (¼ l. ft.).
Rector, American Church of the Trinity, Paris, France, 1912–1918. Correspondence, clippings, pamphlets, posters, photographs and postcards, relating to relief work in France during World War I, and to the Allied powers during the war.

3038

Wattles, Warren F.
Miscellaneous papers, 1936–1941. ½ ms. box.
American lawyer. Correspondence, memoranda, and clippings, relating to World War I and the Spanish Civil War.

3039

Weakley, Charles Enright, 1906–1972.
Papers, 1945–1972. 4 ms. boxes.
Vice Admiral, U.S. Navy; Commander, Antisubmarine Warfare Force, Atlantic Fleet, 1963–1967; Assistant Administrator for Management Development, National Aeronautics and Space Administration, 1968–1972. Correspondence, orders, drafts of speeches, printed matter, photographs, and sound recordings, relating to post-World War II U.S. antisubmarine force operations and to National Aeronautics and Space Administration activities.
Gift, Mrs. C. E. Weakley, 1976.

3040

Webster, James Benjamin, 1879–1929.
Papers, 1903–1931. 22 ms. boxes, 2 envelopes.
American missionary in China. Diaries, correspon-

dence, notebooks, writings and photographs, relating to theology, and to missionary activities and Christian education in China.

Preliminary inventory.

Gift, family of J. B. Webster, 1970. Incremental gift, 1973.

3041

Weekly Review of Events in Ireland.

Bulletins, 1921. 1 folder.

Typescript (mimeographed).

Relates to the Irish independence movement, April-December 1921. Issued by Irish nationalists.

3042

Weeks, George P.

Memorandum, 1924. 1 folder.

Typescript.

Relates to the role of Venustiano Carranza, President of Mexico, 1917–1920, in the Mexican Revolution.

3043

Wegerer, Alfred von, 1880–1945.

Writings (in English and German), 1941. 1 folder.

German historian. Study (typewritten), entitled "From War to Peace," relating to the causes of World War II and prospects for peace; and photocopy of a memorandum (typewritten in German), relating to the proposed establishment of an Academy on War and Peace in connection with the Hoover Institution on War, Revolution and Peace.

Gift, Ralph Lutz, 1943. Gift, Charles Burdick, 1976.

3044

Weidenbaum, Murray Lew, 1927–

Papers, 1960–1977. 2 ms. boxes.

American economist; Assistant Secretary of the Treasury for Economic Policy, 1969–1971. Speeches and writings, pamphlets and clippings, relating to U.S. federal credit programs, business and inflation, government regulation of business, utility regulation, and military-industrial relations.

Gift, M. L. Weidenbaum, 1977.

3045

Weimar Republic collection (in German), ca. 1914–1933. 17 ms. boxes, 24 oversize packages (8 l. ft.).

Posters, leaflets, broadsides and clippings, relating to conditions in Germany during World War I, and to political and economic conditions in Germany during the interwar period.

Preliminary inventory.

Purchase, Duke University.

3046

Weinberger, Caspar W., 1917–

Papers, 1973–1975. 47 ms. boxes, 1 oversize box (1 l. ft.).

Counsellor to the President of the U.S., 1973; Secretary of Health, Education and Welfare, 1973–1975. Correspondence, reports, and photographs, relating to American politics and to social welfare, health, and edu-

cational policy during the presidential administrations of Richard M. Nixon and Gerald R. Ford.

Preliminary inventory.

Consult the Archivist for restrictions.

Deposit, C. W. Weinberger, 1977.

3047

Welch, Claude Emerson, 1939–   , *collector.*

C. E. Welch collection on West Africa (in French), 1951–1965. 1 ms. box.

Pamphlets, government issuances, transcripts of interviews, and ephemeral publications, relating to the political development of West Africa. Collected by C. E. Welch as research material for his book, *Dream of Unity, Pan-Africanism and Political Unification in West Africa* (1966).

Register.

Gift, C. E. Welch, 1972.

3048

Werner, Max Alexis, 1908–

Memorandum (in German), 1945. "Niederschrift ueber meine Arbeitszeit beim Chef der Sicherheitspolizei und des SD Amt VI F 1–6" (Record of My Work with the Chief of the Security Police and SD Office F 1–6). 1 folder.

Typescript.

Member, German Sicherheitsdienst. Relates to secret service activities of Sicherheitsdienst Office VI F.

3049

West, Ralph E.

Papers, 1969–1977. 7½ ms. boxes.

Lieutenant Colonel, U.S. Marine Corps. Correspondence and clippings, relating to the Vietnam War, the Watergate affair, and U.S. and international politics.

Gift, R. E. West, 1977.

3050

West German election campaign literature (in German), 1949. 1 ms. box.

Posters and leaflets, relating to the West German election of 1949. Includes literature issued by the Christlich-Demokratische Union, Sozialdemokratische Partei Deutschlands, Kommunistische Partei Deutschlands, Volkspartei, and Demokratische Volkspartei.

3051

West Indian Conference. 2d, St. Thomas, Virgin Islands, 1946.

Report, 1946. 1 folder.

Typescript (mimeographed).

Report of the Drafting Committee of the second West Indian Conference. Includes transcript of an interview of Rexford G. Tugwell, Governor of Puerto Rico, relating to discussion at the conference of social and economic conditions in the West Indies.

3052

Westchester Security League.

Records, 1930–1958. 1 ms. box.

Political pressure group in Bronxville, New York. Cor-

respondence, memoranda, leaflets, and clippings, relating to the activities of the league in promoting patriotism and isolationism, and in opposing subversion, socialism, communism, the New Deal, and the income tax.
Gift, Mrs. G. F. Hawkins, 1958.

3053
Western College Congress, 1st, Stanford University, 1947.
Records, 1947. 1 folder.
Congress of college student leaders in the western U.S. Resolutions, agenda and study papers, relating to the international situation and U.S. foreign policy.

3054
Western Regional Conference on the Holocaust, 1st, San Jose, 1977.
Proceedings, 1977. 9 phonotapes.
Conference sponsored by the National Conference of Christians and Jews. Relates to the ancient, medieval, and modern origins of the Holocaust, its meaning for western civilization, and the methodology for teaching about the Holocaust in schools and universities.
Gift, Lillian Silberstein, 1977.

3055
Weygand, Maxime, 1867–1965.
Memorandum (in French), ca. 1940. 1 vol.
Typescript (carbon copy).
General, French Army; Commander-in-Chief, 1940. Relates to the capitulation of France in 1940.

3056
Wheeler (Burton K.)—broadside, 1941. 1 folder.
Reproduces a leaflet (printed), mailed by B. K. Wheeler, U.S. Senator from Montana, urging U.S. neutrality in World War II, and letters (typewritten) in reply, from two soldiers who received copies of the leaflet.

3057
Wheeler, Charles Julian, 1895–
Interview transcript, 1970. ½ ms. box.
Typescript (photocopy).
Rear Admiral, U.S. Navy. Relates to American naval operations in World Wars I and II. Interview conducted by Commander Etta Belle Kitchen for the Oral History Office, U.S. Naval Institute, Annapolis, Maryland. Includes several printed copies of articles by C. J. Wheeler.
Gift, C. J. Wheeler, 1977.

3058
Wheeler, Philip H.
Papers, 1896–1906. 1 folder.
American businessman. Contracts, letters of recommendation and a passport, relating to American commercial transactions in Kobe, Japan and elsewhere.

3059
Wheeler, Raymond Albert, 1885–1974.
Papers, 1899–1974. 46 ms. boxes, 6 oversize boxes, 5 reels of film.
Lieutenant General, U.S. Army; Commanding Gen-

eral, U.S. Forces in India and Burma, 1945; Chief of Engineers, U.S. Army, 1945–1949. Correspondence, speeches and writings, reports, diaries, memoranda, maps, films, phonotapes, and photographs, relating to the construction of the Panama Canal, 1911–1912; World War I; the China-Burma-India Theater, World War II; construction of the Stilwell Road; the surrender of the Japanese forces in Singapore, 1945; clearance and widening of the Suez Canal, 1956–1957; development of the Lower Mekong River Basin; and studies conducted by the World Bank.
Users must sign a statement, agreeing to submit writings for publication based on the papers to Virginia M. Talley for review.
Gift, V. M. Talley, 1978.

3060
White, Charles Henry, 1865–1952.
Papers, 1934–1937. ½ ms. box.
American consulting geologist for mining companies. Correspondence, studies, reports, maps, and notes, relating to mineral resources in Bulgaria, Czechoslovakia, Greece, and Yugoslavia.
Gift, Mr. and Mrs. W. P. Hammon, 1973.

3061
White, Geoffrey.
Papers, 1939–1968. 9½ ms. boxes.
American Trotskyist leader. Correspondence, writings, reports, resolutions, minutes, discussion bulletins and printed matter, relating to American Trotskyist politics, the Socialist Workers Party, and the formation of the Spartacist League. Includes a few items relating to the Communist Party of the U.S. and the Independent Socialist League.
Gift, G. White, 1978.

3062
White, Henry, 1850–1927.
Miscellaneous papers, 1919. 1 folder.
Photocopy of originals in Library of Congress.
American diplomat; member, American delegation, Paris Peace Conference, 1918–1919. Memoranda and resolutions, relating to the work of the Paris Peace Conference.

3063
White House Conference on Child Health and Protection, Washington, D.C., 1930.
Records, 1909–1950. 142 ½ ms. boxes, 5 posters.
Conference established by President Herbert Hoover to investigate child welfare in the U.S. Correspondence, reports, memoranda, expense statements and pamphlets, relating to the physical and social condition of children in the U.S., the status of school health education and health service programs, and proposals for the promotion of child welfare. Includes reports of the American Child Health Association.
Preliminary inventory.
Gift, Ray Lyman Wilbur, 1933.

3064

White, J. Gustav.
    Study, 1930. "Caged Men: Observations in 28 German War Prison Camps." 1 vol.
    Typescript (carbon copy).
    Relates to conditions in German prison camps during World War II.

3065

White, William Lindsay, 1900–1973.
    Study, ca. 1945–1947. "Report on the Krauts." 1 folder.
    Typescript.
    American journalist. Relates to the Allied occupation of Germany at the end of World War II and to German public opinion regarding the occupation, World War II and the Nazi regime. Annotated by Herbert Hoover. Subsequently published under the title, *Report on the Germans* (New York, 1947).
    Gift, W. L. White.

3066

Whitehead, James H., *collector*.
    J. H. Whitehead collection on Siberia, 1918–1920. 2 albums, 1 envelope.
    Depicts activities of members of the American Expeditionary Force in Siberia and the Russian Railway Service Corps, General William S. Graves, Czech and Russian military forces, and the living quarters of Tsar Nicholas II at Ekaterinburg.
    Gift, J. H. Whitehead, 1974.

3067

Whiting, Charles Jonathan, 1906–1973.
    Papers, 1925–1969. 9 ms. boxes, 1 framed photograph.
    Rear Admiral, U.S. Navy; judge advocate, court of inquiry investigating the *Panay* incident, 1937. Orders, report, correspondence, photographs, and film, relating to the sinking of the U.S. gunboat *Panay* in China, 1937; to other activities of the U.S. Navy in China, 1937–1940; and to American naval operations in the Atlantic and Mediterranean during World War II.
    Gift, Mrs. C. J. Whiting, 1974.

3068

Whitlock, Brand, 1869–1934.
    Papers, 1913–1934. 7 ms. boxes, 1 folder.
    American author; U.S. Ambassador to Belgium, 1913–1922. Writings, diaries, printed matter and photographs, relating to U.S.-Belgian relations during World War I, work of the Commission for Relief in Belgium, and fictional writings of B. Whitlock.
    Gift, James L. Brainerd, 1953.

3069

Wiasemsky, Serge, Prince.
    Translations of miscellaneous papers, 1923–1924. 1 folder.
    Typescript.
    Leader of the Russian National Progressive Party in

England. Renunciation by S. Wiasemsky of landholdings in Russia, resolutions of the Russian National Progressive Party, and a memorandum on the dynasties of Russia.

3070

Wieliczka, Zygmunt.
    Translation of history (in German), 1932. "Grosspolen und Preussen in der Zeit des Aufstandes 1918–19" (Great Poland and Prussia at the Time of the Revolution of 1918–19). 1 folder.
    Typescript (mimeographed).
    Relates to German-Polish relations during the German Revolution at the end of World War I. Original history published under the title *Wielkopolska a Prusy w Dobie Powstania 1918–19* (1932).

3071

Wijngaert, Mark van den.
    Dissertation (in Flemish), 1972. "Het Bestuur van de Secretarissen-Generaal in Belgie tijdens de Duitse Bezetting, 1940–1944" (The Administration of the Secretaries-General in Belgium during the German Occupation, 1940–1944). ½ ms. box.
    Typescript (mimeographed).
    Belgian historian. Relates to the occupation and administration of Belgium by the Germans during World War II. Doctoral dissertation, Katholieke Universiteit te Leuven. Published in 1975 by the Royal Academy for Sciences, Literature and Arts of Belgium under the title *Het Beleid van het Comité van de Secretarissen-Generaal in België tijdens de Duitse Bezetting, 1940–1944* (The Policy of the Committee of the Secretaries-General in Belgium during the German Occupation, 1940–1944).
    Gift, M. van den Wijngaert, 1974.

3072

Wilbur, Ray Lyman, 1875–1949.
    Papers, 1908–1949. 121 ms. boxes, 11 posters, 3 albums.
    American educator; U.S. Secretary of the Interior, 1929–1933; President, Stanford University, 1916–1943. Correspondence, memoranda, reports, pamphlets, and miscellanea, relating to U.S. and world politics, development of natural resources in the U.S., and national health and other social problems.
    Preliminary inventory.
    Gift, R. L. Wilbur, 1933. Subsequent increments.

3073

Wilcox, Wendell, 1927–
    Diary, 1944–1945. 1 vol.
    Typescript.
    American prisoner in the Japanese prison camp at Los Baños, Philippine Islands. Relates to conditions in the prison camp.

3074

Wildman, Murray Shipley, 1868–1930.
    Miscellaneous papers, 1917–1919. 1 folder.
    American economist; member, Bureau of Research,

U.S. War Trade Board, during World War I. Correspondence, memoranda, reports and statistics, relating to economic conditions in the U.S. during World War I and to the activities of the War Trade Board.

3075

Wilhelm (Crown Prince of the German Empire and of Prussia)—photograph, ca. 1914. 1 envelope.
Depicts Crown Prince Wilhelm of Germany reviewing troops.

3076

Wilhelm II collection, 1905–1925. ½ ms. box. 2 envelopes, 1 framed photograph.
Photographs and copies of letters, relating to Kaiser Wilhelm II of Germany (1859–1941). Includes copies of letters from Wilhelm II, 1925, relating to European diplomacy before World War I; an autographed portrait of Wilhelm II in 1912; photographs of Wilhelm II in Morocco in 1905, with Theodore Roosevelt in 1910, and with Paul von Hindenburg and Erich Ludendorff during World War I; and curtains from the railroad car of Wilhelm II.

3077

Willcox, Mark, Jr.
Report, 1942. 1 folder.
Typescript.
U.S. Navy officer. Relates to political conditions in Ireland and Northern Ireland during World War II, and to Irish public opinion regarding the stationing of U.S. troops in Northern Ireland.

3078

William, Maurice, 1881–1973.
Miscellaneous papers, 1927–1932. ½ ms. box.
American author; adviser to Sun Yat-sen. Drafts and correspondence, relating to the preparation of the book by M. William, *Sun Yat-Sen versus Communism: New Evidence Establishing China's Right to the Support of Democratic Nations* (Baltimore, 1932).

3079

Williams, Rhona, *collector.*
Vases, ca. 1700–1900. 3 vases.
Nineteenth century Japanese vase; eighteenth century Chinese cloisonné vase; and late nineteenth century Persian brass vase.
Gift, R. Williams, 1975.

3080

Williams, Robert Parvin, 1891–
Papers, 1929–1951. 9 ms. boxes.
Brigadier General, U.S. Army Medical Corps; Theater Surgeon, China-Burma-India Theater, 1942–1945. Diaries, memoirs, correspondence, studies, memoranda, photographs, maps, charts, and printed matter, relating to the U.S. Army Medical Service in the China-Burma-India Theater during World War II, and during the Korean War.

3081

Williams, Thomas, 1871–1946, *collector.*
T. Williams collection on U.S. politics and Herbert Hoover, 1936–1946. 1½ ms. boxes, 2 envelopes.
Pamphlets, political addresses, memorabilia, and printed matter, relating to the 1936 U.S. presidential election and to the views of Herbert Hoover on national and international affairs.
Gift, Rhona Williams, 1974.

3082

Willis, Bailey, 1857–1949.
Papers, 1916–1943. 2 ms. boxes.
American geologist; Chief, Latin American Division, the Inquiry, 1918. Studies, correspondence and photographs, relating to activities of Stanford University and former Stanford students during World War I, the Tacna-Arica boundary dispute, European topography, and submarine warfare logistics during World War II.
Preliminary inventory.
Gift, B. Willis, 1926. Subsequent increments.

3083

Willis, Edward Frederick, 1904–
Writings, n.d. 1 ms. box.
Typescript.
American historian. Writings, entitled "Herbert Hoover and the Russian Prisoners of World War I"; "Herbert Hoover and the Blockade of Germany, 1918–1919"; and "The Genesis of the Bonus Army," relating to the Bonus Expeditionary Force march on Washington, 1932.
Gift, E. F. Willis, 1951. Subsequent increments.

3084

Williston, Agnes L.
Letters received, 1941–1942. 1 folder.
Holograph.
Relates to conditions in Great Britain during World War II. Written by a cousin in Scotland.

3085

Willkie, Wendell Lewis, 1892–1944.
Campaign speeches, 1940. 13 phonorecords.
Republican candidate for President of the U.S. Relates to U.S. foreign and domestic policy. Includes speeches delivered at Los Angeles, September 19, and San Francisco, September 21, and a few radio announcements.

3086

Willoughby, Charles Andrew, 1892–1972.
Papers, 1945–1961. 2 ms. boxes, 1 album, 1 envelope, 1 phonorecord, 1 framed certificate.
Major General, U.S. Army; Chief of Intelligence, U.S. Army Forces in the Far East, 1941–1951. Drafts, reports, correspondence, newsletters, and printed matter, relating to the World War II campaigns of General Douglas MacArthur in the Pacific, the Richard Sorge

espionage case, the anti-communism movement in the U.S., Cold War defense needs of the U.S., and Japanese rearmament.
Preliminary inventory.
Gift, C. A. Willoughby, 1961.

3087
Wills, Tony.
Photographs, 1966. 1 envelope.
Depicts Red Guard posters in Canton during the Cultural Revolution.

3088
Wilson, Carol Green, 1892–
Papers, 1918–1969. 14 ms. boxes.
American journalist and author. Correspondence, writings, clippings, and other printed matter, relating primarily to the life of Herbert Hoover. Includes material used for research for the book by C. G. Wilson, *Herbert Hoover: A Challenge for Today.*
Preliminary inventory.
Gift, C. G. Wilson, 1970.

3089
Wilson, Elmer E., *collector*.
E. E. Wilson collection on World War II, ca. 1939–1945. 3 ms. boxes, 1 survival kit.
Memorabilia, correspondence, clippings, and photographs, relating to World War II. Includes a German Luftwaffe survival kit; German Army, Navy, and Air Force insignia; Nazi party insignia; German flags; and other military equipment.
Preliminary inventory.
Gift, Mrs. E. E. Wilson, 1967. Incremental gift, 1969.

3090
Wilson, Laurence L., *collector*.
L. L. Wilson collection on the Philippines, 1942–1946. 1 ms. box.
Writings, leaflets, posters and proclamations, relating to conditions in the Japanese-occupied Philippines during World War II, and to the return of U.S. troops to the Philippines in 1944–1945.
Gift, L. L. Wilson, 1945. Subsequent increments.

3091
Wilson, Philip Whitwell, 1875–1956.
Writings, 1907–1937. 17 binders (3 l. ft.).
Printed.
British journalist; Member of Parliament, 1906–1910. Newspaper and periodical articles, relating primarily to British politics. Includes daily columns by P. W. Wilson in the *London Daily News*, 1907–1917, relating to activities of the British Parliament.
Gift, Mrs. Henry McCurdy.

3092
Wilson, Richard C., 1902–1972.
Papers, 1941–1972. 3 ms. boxes, 6 card file boxes (¾ l. ft.), 4 envelopes.
American journalist; editor, *The Far Easterner*, 1953–

1972. Correspondence, American Red Cross reports, card files on individuals, club membership lists, and printed matter, relating to the personal experiences of former residents of the Far East, as reported in the monthly newsletter, *The Far Easterner*; and to Japanese internment camps, 1941–1942.
Register.
Gift, Mrs. R. C. Wilson, 1972.

3093
Wilson, Robert.
Extracts from letters, 1937–1938. 1 vol.
Typescript.
American physician in China. Relates to the Japanese capture of Nanking, 1937.

3094
Wilson, Samuel Graham.
Letter to Ella W. Stewart, 1916. 1 folder.
Holograph.
Relief worker in Armenia. Relates to relief work in Armenia during World War I.

3095
Wilson, Walter King, Jr., 1906–
Memoirs, n.d. "Observations Made in Rambling around the World, 1943–1947." 1 folder.
Typescript (mimeographed).
Lieutenant General, U.S. Army. Relates to U.S. military activities in India, Ceylon and elsewhere in the Southeast Asia Command and the India-Burma Theater during World War II.

3096
Wilson (Woodrow)—photographs, 1919. 1 envelope.
Depicts Woodrow Wilson, President of the U.S., 1913–1921, during his trip to Europe at the end of World War I.

3097
Wings for Norway.
Appeal, ca. 1939–1945. 1 folder.
Holograph and typescript.
Organization soliciting support for Norwegian Air Force pilots fighting with Allied forces during World War II. Relates to the German occupation of Norway and to the experiences of Norwegian pilots in exile.

3098
Winslow, Alan F.
Letters, 1918. 1 vol.
Typescript (carbon copy).
Lieutenant, U.S. Army; member, 94th Aero Squadron. Relates to American aerial operations in France and Trier, Germany, at the end of World War I.

3099
Winter, Alice Ames, 1865–1944.
Papers, 1918–1925. 1 ms. box, 1 oversize certificate.
President, Minneapolis Women's Club, 1907–1915; President, General Federation of Women's Clubs, 1920–

1924; member, Advisory Committee, Conference on Limitation of Armaments, 1921–1922. Correspondence, passports, invitations, certificate, and clippings, relating to activities of the American Red Cross in France, 1918, and personal and family matters.
Gift, Thomas Winter Ames, 1977.

3100

Wiren, Nicholas.
Sword, n.d.
Belonged to N. Wiren, Russian émigré who was probably an Imperial Russian military officer.
Gift, David Tennant Bryan, 1976.

3101

"Die Wirtschaftliche und Soziale Entwicklung in der Sowjetischen Besatzungszone Deutschlands, 1945–1949" (Economic and Social Development in the Soviet Occupation Zone of Germany, 1945–1949).
Study (in German), 1949. 1 vol.
Typescript (mimeographed).

3102

Wirtschaftspolitische Gesellschaft.
Memorandum, 1935. "Memellanders on Trial for Treason before the Military Court at Kovno." 1 folder.
Typescript (mimeographed).
Political Economy Society, a German organization. Relates to the trial of German nationalists from Memel in Lithuania.

3103

Wisconsin. State Historical Society, *collector*.
Photographs, ca. 1900–1919. 2 ms. boxes.
Depicts military camps in the U.S. during World War I, miscellaneous World War I scenes in Europe, and scenes from the Boxer Rebellion in China. Includes glass slides.
Preliminary inventory.
Gift, State Historical Society of Wisconsin, 1969.

3104

Wiskowski, Włodzimierz, *collector*.
W. Wiskowski collection on Poland (in Polish), 1914–1919. 5 ms. boxes.
Writings, reports, memoranda, booklets, leaflets, magazines, newspapers, memorials and speeches, relating to political conditions in Poland during World War I, and the development of Polish nationalism.
Register.
Purchase, W. Wiskowski, 1921.

3105

Wisner, Lewis S., 1893–1973, *collector*.
L. S. Wisner collection on the Civil War and World War I, 1864–1919. 1 oversize box, 2 envelopes.
Clippings, photographs, postcards and memorabilia, relating to World War I. Includes a dagger made from shells and casings by German hospital prisoners, and a photograph of a Civil War drawing by L. S. Wisner's grandfather, Spottsylvania, Virginia, May 12, 1864.
Gift, Mrs. L. S. Wisner, 1978.

3106

Wissmann, Hellmuth, b. 1884.
Writings (in German), 1939–1947. 1 folder.
Typescript.
Relates to national socialism in Germany, the role of propaganda, post-World War II German reparations, and plans for world peace.

3107

Withington, Robert.
Letters, 1916. 1 folder.
Relief worker, Commission for Relief in Belgium. Relates to work of the Commission for Relief in Belgium during World War I.

3108

Witkin (Zara) collection, 1933–1937. ½ ms. box.
Writings and correspondence, relating to Z. Witkin, an American construction engineer in Russia, 1932–1934. Includes a memoir by Z. Witkin, and a biographical sketch of him by Eugene Lyons.
Gift, E. Lyons, 1968.

3109

Wittenberg, Jean, *collector*.
Printed matter (in French and Flemish), 1940–1945. 2½ ms. boxes.
Belgian socialist active in the resistance. Pamphlets and serial issues, clandestinely issued in German-occupied Belgium during World War II, relating to the Belgian resistance movement.
Preliminary inventory.
Purchase, J. Wittenberg.

3110

Witzleben, Erwin von, 1881–1944, *defendant*.
Transcript of trial (in German), 1944. 1 folder.
Typescript.
Relates to the trial of E. von Witzleben and seven others in Berlin, August 7 to 8, 1944, for complicity in the plot to assassinate Adolf Hitler on July 20, 1944.

3111

Wolfe, Bertram David, 1896–1977.
Papers, 1903–1977. 150½ ms. boxes, 2 card file boxes, 1 oversize box, 6 microfilm reels, 4 phonotapes, 19 envelopes.
American historian; representative of the Communist Party, U.S.A., to the Communist International, 1928–1929; author of *Three Who Made a Revolution* (1948) and other works on communism. Writings, correspondence, notes, memoranda, clippings, other printed matter, photographs and drawings, relating to Marxist doctrine, the international communist movement, communism in the Soviet Union and in the U.S., literature and art in

the Soviet Union and in Mexico, and the Mexican artist Diego Rivera.
Register.
Gift, estate of B. D. Wolfe, 1977.

3112

Wolfe, Henry Cutler, 1898–1976.
Papers, 1921–1923. 1 folder, 1 envelope.
American Relief Administration worker in Russia. Printed matter, identification card, medals, and photographs, relating to conditions in the Samara Province of Russia and operations of the American Relief Administration.
Gift, Mrs. H. C. Wolfe, 1977.

3113

Wolff, Albert.
Memoir (in German), 1945. "Was Ich Euch Sagen Moechte" (What I Want to Say to You). 1 vol.
Typescript (carbon copy).
German national socialist. Relates to the membership of A. Wolff in the Nationalsozialistische Deutsche Arbeiterpartei and to his subsequent disillusionment with the party.

3114

Wolfram, George, 1907–
Papers (in Russian, German and English), 1943–1954. 1 folder.
Russian member of Vlasov forces during World War II. Letters, clippings, photographs and a diary, relating to the Vlasov movement and to Russian refugee life after World War II.
Gift, Antony Sutton, 1970.

3115

Wollenberg, Erich Julian, 1892–1973.
Memoirs (in German), n.d. 1 ms. box.
Typescript (photocopy).
German communist leader and journalist. Relates to the Bavarian Soviet Republic of 1919, the development of the German communist movement to 1933, activities of the Communist International, and the development of communism in the Soviet Union to 1933.
No more than 500 words may be quoted.
Purchase, Klaus Haetzel, 1978.

3116

Wolters, Maria, 1866–1962.
Papers, 1904–1959. 4 ms. boxes.
American relief worker in Japan. Writings, correspondence, photographs, clippings and memorabilia, relating to famine and earthquake relief and child welfare in Japan.
Gift, M. Wolters, 1941. Subsequent increments.

3117

Women's International League for Peace and Freedom. 1st Congress, The Hague, 1915.
Memorandum, 1915. 1 folder.
Typescript.
Relates to the founding of the International Committee of Women for Permanent Peace (later known as the Women's International League for Peace and Freedom), and to its efforts to secure a negotiated peace to end World War I.

3118

Women's International League for Peace and Freedom. 2d Congress, Zurich, 1919.
Resolutions, 1919. 1 folder.
Typescript (mimeographed).
Relates to the World War I peace settlement, the League of Nations, and the rights of women.

3119

Wood, Casey A., *collector*.
Miscellany (in English and Italian), 1915–1935. 1 ms. box, 1 oversize folio.
Pamphlets, memorabilia, and photographs, relating to conduct of German troops in Belgium, to Great Britain, and to World War I, 1916–1918. Includes photographs of Head House Base Hospital, Camp Sherman, Ohio, 1918, and Italian newspapers, 1915–1935, relating to Italian political and military events.

3120

Wood, Hugh Bernard, 1909–
Papers (in Nepali and English), 1955–1971. 3 ms. boxes.
American educator; educational adviser to the Nepali Government, 1954–1962. Writings and printed matter, relating to education in Nepal and India.
Gift, H. B. Wood, 1978.

3121

Woolf, Paul N., *collector*.
Photographs, 1906. 1 envelope.
Depicts people, scenic views, military parades, and captured weapons, in Japan after the end of the Russo-Japanese War.
Preliminary inventory.
Gift, P. N. Woolf, 1963.

3122

Woolley, Barry Lee, 1947–
History, 1974. "Adherents of Permanent Revolution: A History of the Fourth (Trotskyist) International." ½ ms. box.
Typescript (photocopy).
Relates to the American and international Trotskyist movements.
Closed until January 1, 1980. Thereafter during his lifetime, access requires the written permission of B. L. Woolley.
Purchase, B. L. Woolley, 1977.

3123

Work, Hubert, 1860–1942.
Miscellaneous papers, 1922–1939. 2 ms. boxes.
U.S. Postmaster General, 1922–1923; Secretary of the Interior, 1923–1928; Chairman, Republican National

Committee, 1928–1929. Clippings, correspondence, and typescripts of speeches, relating to American politics, Herbert Hoover and the Republican Party.

Purchase, Harry N. Burgess, 1971. Gift, John W. Kinkade, 1974.

3124

World Black and African Festival of Arts and Culture, 2d, Lagos, 1977.

Issuances, 1977. ½ ms. box.

Reports, newsletters, speeches, and informational material, relating to African art.

3125

World War I cartoons, 1914–1918. 5 ms. boxes.

Printed.

Relates to World War I. Most cartoons are from French newspapers; some are from German, Italian, Dutch, Belgian, Norwegian, Spanish, and Swiss newspapers.

3126

World War I clippings, 1914–1918. 3 ms. boxes, 1 scrapbook.

Relates to World War I. Clippings from U.S., French, and German newspapers. Includes clippings on the 79th Division of the U.S. Army.

Gifts, Mary L. Schofield; F. W. H. Beauchamp, 1970; University of Utah Library, 1971; George F. Tyler.

3127

World War I German military orders (in German), 1917–1918. 1 folder.

Typescript.

Relates to military operations on the Western front. Issued by various units of the German Army.

3128

World War I German proclamations (in French), 1914–1916. 1 folder.

Printed.

German proclamations posted in Belgium and France, relating to German military government in occupied areas during World War I. Includes translations and anti-German commentary on the proclamations.

3129

World War I German propaganda—Far East—leaflets (in Chinese), ca. 1914–1918. 1 folder.

Printed.

Propaganda leaflets distributed in the Far East by the German Government during World War I.

3130

World War I—maps, 1916–1918. 12 maps.

Printed.

British and American military maps of the Western Front during World War I.

Gift, Roland J. McGeein, 1971.

3131

World War I—miscellanea (in English, French, Italian and German), 1914–1920. ½ ms. box.

Patriotic stationery and greeting cards, an American Expeditionary Forces telephone directory, and other miscellanea, relating to World War I.

3132

World War I—pictorial collection, ca. 1914–1918. 75 envelopes, 12 albums, 8 ms. boxes, 12 card file boxes, 1 box of glass plates.

Photographs and postcards depicting a variety of scenes and personalities from World War I.

3133

World War I—poster photographs, 1914–1919. 21 albums, 1 envelope.

Depicts posters, issued by the United States and a number of other countries, relating to the war effort during World War I.

Purchase, Thomas J. White Company, 1921. Gift, Leigh M. Pearsall, 1956.

3134

World War I—posters, ca. 1914–1918. 37 posters.

Gift, M. C. Harris, 1956.

3135

World War II Allied propaganda, 1939–1945. 3½ ms. boxes.

Pamphlets, leaflets, and reports, including propaganda material in a variety of languages, distributed by allied forces in both Western and Eastern Europe and Asia during World War II. Includes a U.S. Psychological Warfare Division report on leaflet operations in western Europe, 1945.

3136

World War II Axis propaganda, 1939–1945. 1 ms. box, 1 envelope.

Printed.

Axis propaganda, mostly German, distributed in Europe and Asia during World War II in various languages.

3137

World War II—Balkans—collection, 1941–1944. 1 ms. box.

Studies, reports, handbooks, maps, photographs, diagrams, and printed matter, relating to the political, economic, social, and military conditions in Albania, Bulgaria, Greece, and Yugoslavia, and to the location of strategic power plants and industries in Yugoslavia. Includes two intelligence reports on the Četnik and Partisan resistance movements in Yugoslavia prepared for Allied Military Headquarters, Balkans.

3138

World War, 1939–1945—civilian relief—Yugoslavia—agreement, 1945.

Typescript (mimeographed).

Relates to the provision of civilian relief in Yugoslavia by the United Nations Relief and Rehabilitation Administration at the end of World War II. Agreement between the Yugoslav Government and the United Nations Relief and Rehabilitation Administration.

3139

World War, 1939–1945—Germany—Berlin—pictorial works, 1945. 6 envelopes.

Depicts war damage in Berlin at the end of World War II.

Gift, Bruno Morelli, 1970.

3140

World War, 1939–1945—peace–surrender instrument, 1945. 1 folder.

Photocopy.

Instrument of surrender of Japan to the Allied Powers, September 2, 1945.

Exchange, U.S. Library of Congress, 1945. Gift, Elmer E. Robinson, 1953.

3141

World War II—pictorial, ca. 1939–1945. 80 envelopes.

Photographs and postcards, depicting a variety of scenes from World War II.

3142

World War II—posters, ca. 1939–1945. 1 ms. box.

Gift, Mrs. Hugh S. Price.

3143

World War, 1939–1945—prisoners and prisons, Japanese—proclamation, 1942. 1 folder.

Typescript (mimeographed).

Relates to regulations for civilian prisoners of war captured at Wake Island and being transported from the island on Japanese naval vessels. Issued by Japanese naval officials.

3144

World War, 1939–1945—underground movements—Belgium—collection (in French, Flemish, and German), 1942–1945. 1 folder, 1 envelope.

Photographs, proclamations and miscellanea, relating to the resistance movement in German-occupied Belgium during World War II, and to the entry of Allied troops into Brussels in September 1944.

3145

World War, 1939–1945—underground movements—Czechoslovakia—collection (in Czech and English), ca. 1944–1945. 1 folder.

Two leaflets (mimeographed in Czech), issued by the resistance movement in German-occupied Czechoslovakia, 1945; and a translation (printed), entitled *Svejk in the Protectorate*, of a clandestine Czech resistance pamphlet, ca. 1944.

3146

World War, 1939–1945—underground movements—Denmark—leaflets (in Danish), ca. 1940–1945.

Printed and typescript (mimeographed).

Relates to the resistance movement in German-occupied Denmark during World War II, and to the postwar reconstruction of Denmark.

3147

World War, 1939–1945—underground movements—Norway—leaflets (in German and Norwegian), ca. 1940–1945. 1 folder.

Printed.

Propaganda leaflets, distributed by the resistance movement in German-occupied Norway during World War II.

3148

World War, 1939–1945—underground movements—Poland—serial issues (in Polish), 1940–1944. ½ ms. box.

Photocopies.

Polish underground publications, relating to events and conditions in Poland during the German occupation and World War II.

Preliminary inventory.

Gift, Jan Karski, 1946.

3149

World War, 1939–1945—U.S.—collection, 1942–1946. ½ ms. box.

Letters to and from American soldiers, and miscellanea, relating to U.S. participation in World War II.

3150

World War II—U.S. Armed Forces pamphlets, 1941–1945. 3 ms. boxes.

Printed matter, including manuals and guide books issued by the U.S. Army and Navy, and pamphlets and guide books relating to the U.S. Armed Forces issued by commercial publishers during World War II. Collected separately by Willis Stork and Margaret Windsor.

Preliminary inventory.

Gift, M. Windsor, 1948. Gift, W. Stork, 1964.

3151

Woronoff, Serge.

Letter, 1958. 1 folder.

Typescript.

Member, Foreign Policy Commission, Parti d'Union de la Gauche Socialiste (France). Relates to the founding of the Union de la Gauche Socialiste and to its political orientation.

3152

Woronzow-Daschkow, Hilarion, Graf, *collector*.

Count H. Woronzow-Daschkow collection on Imperial Russia (in Russian), 1903–1911. 3 oversize boxes (2 l. ft.).

Printed photographs from the "Album of the Masquerade Ball at the Winter Palace in February 1903," depicting members of the Russian nobility; and a book, entitled *Kazanskiĭ Sobor, 1811–1911, v Sanktpeterburge* (The Kazan Cathedral, 1811–1911, in Saint Petersburg). Gift, Count Woronzow-Daschkow, 1976.

3153

Wraga, Richard.
Study, 1959. "Basic Problems of Soviet Foreign Policy: Methods and Means." 1 folder.
Typescript (mimeographed).
Presented at the Eleventh Conference of the Institute for the Study of the USSR, held at Munich in 1959.

3154

Wrede (Mathilda Augusta) collection, 1938–1939. 1 folder.
Translations of book reviews and correspondence, relating to two books by Ester Stahlberg, *Mathilda Wrede* and *Mathilda Wredes Testamente*, biographies of Mathilda A. Wrede (1864–1928), a Finnish social worker, active in work with prisoners.
Gift, Finnish Relief Fund, 1940.

3155

Wreden, William P., *collector*.
W. P. Wreden collection on World War I, 1914–1918. 6 ms. boxes.
Scrapbooks of newspaper clippings from the British press and memorabilia, relating to World War I.
Gift, W. P. Wreden, 1947.

3156

Wright, C. P., *collector*.
C. P. Wright collection on German prison camps, 1944–1945. 1 folder.
Letters, reminiscences, and reports, relating to British soldiers in German prison camps during World War II.
Gift, C. P. Wright, 1970.

3157

Wright, D. E., *collector*.
Photographs, n.d. 1 envelope.
Depicts Mazatlan, Mexico; Guatemala City; and the Panama Canal.

3158

Wright, Gordon, 1912–
Dissertation, 1939. "Raymond Poincaré and the French Presidency." ½ ms. box.
Typescript.
American historian. Relates to the Presidency of Raymond Poincaré, 1913–1920.

3159

Wurm, D.
Sermons (in German), 1942–1945. 1 folder.
Typescript (mimeographed) and printed.
German Protestant bishop. Relates to the situation of the Protestant churches in Germany during World War II.

3160

Wynne, Cyril.
Speech transcript, 1938. "Publications of the Department of State." 1 folder.
Typescript.
Chief, Division of Research and Publications, U.S. Department of State. Speech delivered at the Sixth Conference of Teachers of International Law and Related Subjects, at the Brookings Institute, Washington, D.C., April 27, 1938.

3161

Yabes, Leopoldo Y.
Memorial, 1944. 1 vol.
Typescript (carbon copy).
Philippine guerrilla leader. Relates to the anti-Japanese resistance movement in the Philippines during World War II. Addressed to Sergio Osmeña, President of the Philippines.

3162

Yakoubian, Arsen L.
Abstract of dissertation, 1951. "Western Allied Occupation Policies and Development of German Democracy, 1945–1951." 1 vol.
Typescript (carbon copy).
Doctoral dissertation, New York University. Includes bibliography.

3163

Yates (Oleta O'Connor)—circular, 1952. 1 folder.
Typescript (mimeographed).
Relates to appeals for the defense of Oleta O'Connor Yates, under indictment on charges of violating the Smith Act.

3164

Yeaton, Ivan D., 1906–
Papers, 1919–1976. 1 ms. box, 7 envelopes.
Colonel, U.S. Army; Military Attaché in the Soviet Union, 1939–1941; Commanding Officer, Yenan Observer Group in China, 1945–1946. Memoirs, reports, memoranda, correspondence, orders and citations, charts, and photographs, relating to his military career; Soviet military strength in 1941; U.S.-Soviet relations, 1941–1949; organization of U.S. military intelligence during World War II; lend-lease operations; U.S. relations with the Chinese communists, 1944–1946; and the inspection of U.S. Army procurement contracts, 1952–1953.
Register.
Philip Faymonville file closed until January 1, 1996.
Gift, I. D. Yeaton, 1976.

3165

Yen, Hui-Chíng, 1877–1950.
Memoirs, 1946. "An Autobiography." 1 ms. box.
Typescript.
Chinese diplomat and statesman; Minister of Foreign Affairs, 1920–1922; Premier, 1924 and 1926; Ambassa-

dor to the Soviet Union, 1933–1936. Relates to Chinese politics, diplomacy, finance and famine relief.
Gift, Pao-sheng Yen, 1972.

3166

28–29 (Yirmi-Sekiz-Yirmi Dokuz) Kânanu Sani 1921: Karadeniz Kíyílarínda Parcalanan Mustafa Suphi ve Yoldaslarínín Ikinci yíl Dönümleri (January 28–29, 1921: The Second Anniversary of the Assassination of Mustafa Suphi and His Comrades on the Black Sea Coast).
Translation of excerpts from pamphlet, 1923. 1 folder.
Typescript.
Relates to the Turkish communist leader Mustafa Suphi and the Turkish communist movement. Pamphlet published in Moscow, 1923. Translated by Mithat Esmer.

3167

You Can't Beat the Dutch.
Radio program series, ca. 1941–1945. 12 phonorecords.
Relates to Dutch military, naval and aerial operations and to the resistance in the German-occupied Netherlands. Produced by the Netherlands Information Bureau in New York.
Preliminary inventory.

3168

Young, Arthur N., b. 1890.
Papers, 1918–1961. 116 ms. boxes, 1 folder.
American economist; Economic Adviser, U.S. Department of State, 1922–1928; Financial Adviser, Government of China and Central Bank of China, 1929–1946. Diary, correspondence, reports, studies, statistical summaries, financial statements, press releases, clippings, and ephemeral publications, relating to the European financial crisis following World War I, the work of the Reparations Commission in formulating the Dawes Plan in 1924, and the economic and financial situation in China, 1929–1946.
Register.
Materials are opened to users who sign a statement agreeing to the conditions of use set down by A. N. Young. A few items are closed until January 1, 1980.
Gift, A. N. Young, 1966. Subsequent increments.

3169

Young Communist League of the U.S. collection, 1934–1949. 2 ms. boxes.
Leaflets, pamphlets and mimeographed material, relating to Young Communist League activities in San Francisco, the Communist Party U.S.A., election propaganda, labor relations, trade unions, education, and the Spanish Civil War.
Purchase, L. B. Magee, 1943. Subsequent increments.

3170

Young, Hobart.
Memorandum, 1948. 1 folder.
Typescript.
U.S. Army officer. Relates to press coverage by *Stars and Stripes*, the U.S. Army newspaper, of agitation by American soldiers for speedier demobilization in 1945–1946.

3171

Young Men's Christian Associations.
Miscellaneous records, 1917–1920. 68 ms. boxes, 5 folios, 79 envelopes, 40 albums.
International social and charitable organization. Clippings, printed matter, posters, and photographs, relating to activities of the Young Men's Christian Association in the United States and Europe during World War I.
Register.
Gift, World Alliance of Young Men's Christian Associations, 1933.

3172

Yü-keng.
Certificates (in Chinese), 1895–1899. 1 roll.
Chinese diplomat. Presents the credentials of Yü-keng as Chinese Ambassador to Japan, 1895, and as Chinese Ambassador to France, 1899.
Purchase, Alene von Harringh.

3173

Yugoslavia. Narodna Skupština. Hrvatsko Zastupstvo.
Issuances (in Serbo-Croatian), 1928–1935. 1 folder.
Croatian delegation to the Yugoslav National Assembly. Resolution (typewritten), 1928, and memorandum (mimeographed), 1935, relating to political conditions in Croatia and Yugoslavia.
Gift, Jozo Tomasevich, 1957.

3174

Yugoslavia—photographs, n.d. 1 envelope.
Depicts various locations in Yugoslavia.
Gift, Mr. Sviatopolk-Mirsky.

3175

Yugoslavia—politics and government—press releases, 1921. 1 folder.
Typescript.
Relates to the adoption of the Yugoslav Constitution and to the attempted assassination of Prince Regent Alexander of Yugoslavia in 1921.

3176

Yugoslavia. Poslanstvo (U.S.)
Miscellany, 1976. 1 folder.
Yugoslav Embassy (U.S.). Press statement by Yugoslav Ambassador Dimce Belovski; official statement of the Yugoslav Embassy in the U.S.; initiative by members of the U.S. House of Representatives; and excerpts from the transcript of the U.S. Department of State press, radio and television briefing; relating to the bombing of the Embassy of Yugoslavia in Washington, D.C., June 9, 1976.
Gift, Yugoslav Consulate General, San Francisco, 1976.

3177

Yugoslavia—student protest movement—collection (in Serbo-Croatian), 1968. 1 folder.
Photocopy.
Leaflets, circulars, and resolutions, issued by various student groups, relating to student protest movements at the University of Belgrade against social injustice, inequality in higher education, and poor student living conditions.
Gift, Roland V. Layton, Jr., 1976.

3178

Yurchenko, Ivan.
Writings (in Russian), n.d. 25 ms. boxes.
Holograph.
Russian émigré in the U.S. Relates to various aspects of philosophy, religion, and the sciences.
Preliminary inventory.
Gift, I. Yurchenko, 1972.

3179

Zaĭtŝov, Arseniĭ.
Study, 1931. "Military Aspect of the Five Year Plan of the U.S.S.R." 1 folder.
Typescript (mimeographed).
Relates to Soviet economic and military policy.

3180

Zakhartchenko, Constantine L., 1900–
Papers, 1920–1976. 1 ms. box.
Russian émigré; aeronautical engineering designer; Assistant Chief Engineer, Shiuchow Aircraft Works, Kwantung, China, 1934–1943. Correspondence, certificates, airplane designs, blueprints, technical and financial reports, telegrams, contracts, and photographs, relating to engineering and military aspects of Chinese aviation.
Gift, C. L. Zakhartchenko, 1977.

3181

Zaleski, Jerzy, J.
Circular letter (in Polish), 1948. 1 folder.
Typescript (mimeographed).
Asks Poles to sign a demand to August Zaleski, President of the Polish Republic in Exile, for the reorganization of the Polish Government-in-Exile in order to make it more representative. Written by J. J. Zaleski and Zbigniew Wolynski.

3182

Zâni i Kosovës (Voice of Kossovo).
Periodical (in Albanian), 1962–1966. ½ ms. box.
Typescript.
Albanian émigré periodical issued in Jeddah, Saudi Arabia, relating to Albanian culture, literature and politics.
Gift, Julius P. Barkelay, 1975.

3183

Zavadskiĭ, Sergeĭ Vladislavovich.
Biography (in Russian), 1933–1935. "Zhizn' V. R.

Zavadskago, Razskazannaia Synom" (The Life of V. R. Zavadskiĭ, as Told by His Son). 6 vols.
Typescript.
Relates to Vladislav Romual'dovich Zavadskiĭ, Russian Imperial courtier.

3184

Zavarin, Konstantin Nikolaevich.
History (in Russian), n.d. "Rechnaia Boevaia Flotiliia na reke Kame v 1919 godu" (The Fighting River Flotilla on the Kama in 1919). ½ ms. box.
Typescript.
Relates to the river warfare campaigns and tactics of the White Russian forces on the Kama River in Siberia during the Russian Civil War, 1918–1919. Written by K. N. Zavarin and Mikhail Smirnov.
Purchase, Natalie N. Zavarin, 1977.

3185

Zawodny, Jay K.
Interview transcripts, n.d. 1 folder, 1 microfilm reel.
Typescript.
Interviews, conducted by J. K. Zawodny, of former Soviet factory workers residing in the United States, relating to labor conditions in the Soviet Union, 1919–1951.
Gift, J. K. Zawodny, 1954.

3186

Zebot, Cyril A., *collector.*
C. A. Zebot collection on Frank J. Lausche, 1975. 1 vol.
Photocopy.
Clippings, telegrams, letters and speeches, relating to the testimonial dinner in honor of the eightieth birthday of Frank J. Lausche, U.S. Senator from Ohio, held in Washington, D.C., November 16, 1975.
Gift, Wayne Vucinich, 1976.

3187

Zebrak, Nicholas A.
Papers (in Russian), 1920–1931. 1 ms. box.
Chief of Police, Russian Concession, Tientsin; adviser to the local Chinese administration. Correspondence, clippings, and pamphlets, relating to Russian émigrés, police administration, and welfare and veterans' organizations in China.

3188

Zeitungsdienst Graf Reischach.
Newspaper clippings, 1933–1945. 1 folder.
German news service. Newspaper photographs of prominent Germans in politics, business, art, and the military.

3189

Zenzinov, V.
Translations of excerpts from letters and diaries, 1939–1940. 1 folder.
Typescript.
Letters and diaries of Soviet soldiers during the Russo-Finnish War, relating to conditions at the front, living

conditions in the Soviet Union, and personal matters. Translated and compiled by V. Zenzinov. Includes photocopies of the original letters and diaries (in Russian).
Deposit, V. Zenzinov, 1949.

3190

Zershchikov, K.
Memoir (in Russian), n.d. "Sobstvennyĭ Ego Velichestva Konvoĭ v Dni Revoliûtsiĭ" (His Majesty's Personal Convoy in the Days of the Revolution). 1 folder.
Typescript (photocopy).
Colonel, Russian Imperial Army. Relates to the bodyguard of Tsar Nicholas II in 1917.
Gift, M. Lyons, 1971.

3191

Zetkin, Clara, 1857–1933.
Letters (in German), 1916–1932, to "Fanny." 1 folder.
Holograph.
German communist leader. Relates to the communist and feminist movements in Germany. Includes five original letters and photocopies of ten others.

3192

Zilberman, Bella N.
Papers, 1924–1959. ½ ms. box.
American peace advocate. Writings, letters and printed matter, relating to the plans of B. N. Zilberman to bring about world peace.

3193

Zimmerman, Oliver B.
Photograph, 1914. 1 envelope.
Depicts the entrance of the German Army into Brussels, Belgium, August 1914. Taken from the window of the office of the International Harvester Company.
Gift, Gordon B. Zimmerman, 1975.

3194

Zinkin, Harold, *collector.*
Tabernacle, ca. 1835–1845.
Russian tabernacle, inscribed "Ral'k, Supplier for the Imperial Court."
Gift, H. Zinkin, 1977.

3195

Znamiecki, Alexander.
Memoir, 1954. "Hoover's Aid to Poland." 1 folder.
Typescript.
Member, U.S. Food Administration Mission to Poland. Relates to Herbert Hoover and U.S. Food Administration relief work in Poland at the end of World War I.
Gift, A. Znamiecki, 1957.

3196

Zolin, Fred H., 1894–
Papers, 1919–1958. 1 folder.
Chief Petty Officer, U.S. Navy; telegrapher with the American Relief Administration in Austria and Hun-

gary, 1919. Letters, telegraphic dispatches and an autobiographical sketch, relating to conditions in Hungary in 1919 and to the Romanian intervention in Hungary.
Gift, F. H. Zolin, 1958.

3197

Zon, Julius.
Papers (in Polish), 1939–1943. 1 folder.
Polish inmate of the Auschwitz concentration camp. Correspondence and newspaper issues, relating to the German occupation of Poland and German concentration camps.
Preliminary inventory.
Gift, J. Zon, 1975.

3198

Zorn collection (in French, German, Italian and English), ca. 1900–1930. 12 ms. boxes.
Printed.
Relates to international law, the League of Nations, questions of war and peace, territorial disputes, and reparations.
Preliminary inventory.

3199

Zubeẗs, Vladimir Aleksandrovich.
Memoir (in Russian), 1933. "Na Sluzhbĭe v Kitaĭskoĭ Armii" (Service in the Chinese Army). 1 vol.
Typescript.
Russian émigré in the Chinese Army after the Russian Revolution. Translated by Elena Varneck. Includes photographs.

3200

Zuill, William E. S., *collector.*
W. E. S. Zuill collection on British censorship in Bermuda, 1944–1946. 1 folder.
Report and clippings, relating to the imposition of British censorship in Bermuda during World War II.

3201

Žujović, Mladen J., 1895–1969.
Papers (mainly in Serbo-Croatian), 1915–1969. 6½ ms. boxes.
Serbian officer during World War I; attorney and politician in interwar period; one of main advisers to General Draža Mihailović during World War II; a leader of Serbian emigration after war. Diaries from both world wars, correspondence, reports, memoranda, writings and clippings, relating to Serbian military activities in World War I, Yugoslav resistance movements during World War II, and Serbian émigré politics. Includes his handwritten transcription (in French) of memoirs of Queen Natalija Obrenović of Serbia and the latter's correspondence during 1900.
Until July 1, 1990, access requires the written permission of Cathrine Žujović.
Gift, C. Žujović, 1970.

3202

Zvegint͡sov, Nikolaĭ.
Papers (in Russian), 1920–1922. 1 ms. box.
Russian Imperial Naval officer. Correspondence, writings and memoranda, relating to activities of the White Russian military forces during the Russian Civil War.
Register.
Gift, Vasilii Romanov, 1975.

3203

Zwiazek Patriotow Polskich.
Broadside (in Polish), 1943. "Statut Zwiazku Patriotow Polskich w ZSRR" (Statutes of the Union of Polish Patriots in the U.S.S.R.). 1 folder.
Printed.
Union of Polish Patriots. Relates to pro-Soviet Polish organizations during World War II.

The following archival and manuscript materials on microfilm are maintained and serviced by the Hoover Institution Library. Inquiries should be directed to the Reference Librarian, Hoover Institution, Stanford, California 94305.

3204

Addis Ababa. Haile Selassie I University.
Pamphlets, 1961–1965. 1 reel.

3205

Africa: confidential prints. Records of the British Colonial Office and British Foreign Office, 1870–1922. 144 reels.

3206

African National Congress.
Records, 1914–1957. Includes records of the South African Indian Congress, and the autobiography of R. V. Selope Thema. 1 reel.

3207

Aguirre y Lecube, José Antonio de, 1904–
Report on the Spanish Civil War. On the same reel: M. Irujo y Ollo, "La Guerra Civil en Euzkadi antes del Estatuto," 1938. 1 reel.

3208

Aigner, Johann, 1901–
"Als Ordonanz bei Hochverraetern: Ein Beitrag zur Geschichte der Nationalen Erhebung im November, 1923." On the same reel: Edmund Heines, 1898– *defendant*. Transcript of a trial for political disturbances, Munich, 1923. 1 reel.

3209

Ainsworth papers. Papers of John D. Ainsworth, 1895–1917, relating to Kenya. 2 reels.

3210

Allied and Associated Powers (1914–1920) Supreme War Council.
Records, 1917–1919. 2 reels.

3211

Allied Commission for Austria. Allied Council.
Minutes of meetings, 1945–1955. 8 reels.

3212

Allied Commission for Austria. Executive Committee.
Minutes of meetings, 1945–1955. 15 reels.

3213

Allied Forces. Supreme Headquarters. Psychological Warfare Division.
Leaflets. 1 reel.

3214

Allied Forces. Supreme Headquarters. Psychological Warfare Division.
Letters relating to North African and Italian campaigns, 1943. 3 reels.

3215

Archives Jules Humbert-Droz. Papers of J. Humbert-Droz relating to the Communist International and the Communist parties of Europe, 1919–1929. 1 reel.

3216

Articles on Portuguese Africa, 1955–1963. 1 reel.

3217

Austria. Haus-, Hof- und Staatsarchiv.
Collection relating to Austrian policy in Herzegovina before 1914, the assassination of Archduke Franz Ferdinand, political trials, the occupation of Serbia and Poland, 1914–1917, and the anti-monarchical movement of the South Slav immigrants to the U.S., Chile and New Zealand. 8 reels.

3218

Austria (Territory under Allied Occupation, 1945–1955. U.S. Zone).
Instructions to the Provisional Government of Upper Austria relating to public welfare and displaced persons, 1945–1946. 1 reel.

3219

Austria (Territory under Allied Occupation, 1945–1955. U.S. Zone).
Records, 1945–1947. 1 reel.

3220

Avaro, J. Amboroue.
"Le Bas-Ogowe au Dix-neuvième Siècle," 1969. 1 reel.

3221

Bańczyk, Stanisław.
"Polish Communist Party in the Service of Moscow," 1953. On the same reel: Roman Dębicki, "A History of Polish Foreign Policy," 1953; and Stavro Skendi, "Albania: A Handbook." 1 reel.

3222

Baranov, Kh. K.
Introduction by I. ÎU. Krachkovskiĭ to "Arabic-Russian Dictionary of the Contemporary Literary Language," 1946. Translated by Sidney Glazer. 1 reel.

3223

Baumgarten, A.
Testimony in the trial of the Schweizerischer Israelitischer Gemeindebund and the Israelitische Kultusgemeinde, Bern, plaintiffs, vs. Th. Fischer, Zurich, and others, defendants, Bern, 1935. 1 reel.

3224

Beatle, Charles F.
"Whatever Happened to Liberia? Is There a Role for Military Civic Action?" 1969. 1 reel.

3225

"Bemerkungen zum Schuman-Plan," ca. 1950. 1 reel.

3226

Berlin. Freie Universitaet.
Leaflets, issued by student protest groups, 1955–1968. 4 reels.

3227

Berlin. Freie Universitaet. Allgemeiner Studentenausschuss. Konvent.
Minutes, 1965–1967. 2 reels.

3228

Berlin. Freie Universitaet. Institut fuer Politische Wissenschaft.
Collection on student protest movements, 1952–1970. 7 reels.

3229

Berman, Sanford.
"Spanish Guinea, an Annotated Bibliography," 1957. 1 reel.

3230

Bethouart, Bruno.
"Histoire du M.R.P. dans l'Arrondissement de Lille," 1972. 4 microfiche sheets.

3231

Beveridge, James.
"History of the United States Strategic Bombing Survey (Pacific), 1945–1946," 1946. 1 reel.

3232

Blanc, Louis, 1811–1882.
Letters from G. Garibaldi, A. Gerŝen, W. Mickiewicz and others, 1859–1873. 1 reel.

3233

Blau, Georg.
"Der Weg durch den Sumpf: Denen, Die nach Uns Kommen, Erzaehlt," ca. 1945. 2 reels.

3234

Bobrie, François.
"L'Opinion et les Groupes de Pression Face à la Politique Financière et Monétaire de Poincaré," by F. Bobrie and Pierre Gaston, 1970. 2 microfiche sheets.

3235

Bock, Fedor von, 1880–1945.
Diary, 1941–1942, relating to World War II campaigns on the Eastern front. 1 reel.

3236

Boulinguiez, Yves.
"La Situation Ouvrière à Lille-Roubaix-Turcoing de 1925 à 1929: Conditions de Travail, Salaires, Grèves," 1970. 3 microfiche sheets.

3237

Bowen, Thomas Jefferson, 1814–1875.
Papers relating to missionary work in Nigeria. 1 reel.

3238

Boyden, Roland William, 1863–1931.
Correspondence relating to reparations, 1917–1923. 4 reels.

3239

Britain and Europe since 1945. Collection relating to Great Britain and the Common Market. 375 microfiche sheets.

3240

Brockdorff-Rantzau, Ulrich Karl Christian, Graf, 1869–1928.
Papers relating to German foreign relations, 1914–1928. 8 reels.

3241

Browder, Earl Russell, 1891–1973.
Papers, 1891–1975, relating to American communism. 36 reels.

3242

Bukharin, Nikolaĭ Ivanovich, 1888–1938.
Draft program for the Communist International, 1924. 1 reel.

3243

Burke, Fred G.
"The Development of Local Government in Uganda: A Comparative Approach," 1958. 1 reel.

3244

Burmeister, Alfred, *pseud.*
"Dissolution and Aftermath of the Comintern: Experiences and Observations, 1937–1947," 1955. 1 reel.

3245

Buron, Claude.
"Les Élections Législatives des 5 et 12 Mars 1967 dans le Département de Loire-et-Cher," 1967. 3 microfiche sheets.

3246

Cabourne, Patrick J.
"Can the African Soldier Build a Nation? Military Influence on the Development of Ghana and Tanzania," 1969. 1 reel.

3247

Campaign in southern France, August 15—September 15, 1944. Translations of reports of German officers. 1 reel.

3248

Canal Zone.
"Chronology and Background of Rioting by Residents of Panama in the Canal Zone and in Panama during January, 1964," ca. 1964. 1 reel.

3249

Casement, Sir Roger, 1864–1916.
Papers relating to Ireland and the European War, 1914–1916. 3 reels.

3250

Cazden, Robert Edgar, 1930–
"The Free German and Free Austrian Press and Booktrade in the United States, 1933–1950, in the Context of German-American History," 1965. 1 reel.

3251

Chang, Kuo-t'ao, 1897–
Interview notes, 1950, relating to the Chung-kuo Kung Ch'an Tang and Mao Tsê-tung. Interview conducted by Robert C. North. 1 reel.

3252

Chang, Tao-hsing, 1908–
"Russia, China and the Chinese Eastern Railway," 1972. 1 reel.

3253

Chilcote, Ronald H., *comp.*
Collection on emerging nationalism in Portuguese Africa from its inception through 1966. 15 reels.

3254

Chu, Wen-chang, 1914–
"The Policy of the Manchu Government in the Suppression of the Moslem Rebellion in Shensi, Kansu and Sinkiang from 1862 to 1878," 1955. 1 reel.

3255

Clarke, William H.
Memoirs relating to missionary work in Central Africa, 1854–1858. 1 reel.

3256

Cohen, Michael A.
"Urban Policy and Political Conflict in Africa: A Study of the Ivory Coast," 1971. 1 reel.

3257

Colin, Ronald.
"Mutations Sociales et Méthodes de Développement: Essai sur la Dynamique de Changement et l'Animation en Pays Sahara du Tchad," 1972. 1 reel.

3258

Collection of contemporary German newspaper and periodical accounts of the July 20, 1944 plot against Adolf Hitler. 1 reel.

3259

Collection of the Honourable Louis Arthur Grimes, Chief Justice of Liberia, 1831–1947. 6 reels.

3260

Communist International.
Open letter to the Central Executive Committee of the Communist Party of America relating to Finnish members of the party, 1930. 1 reel.

3261

Communist International. Executive Committee.
Instructions to the Central European Bureau in Berlin, 1921. 1 reel.

3262

Communist International. Executive Committee.
Report on the crisis of the Communist Party of Spain, 1925. 1 reel.

3263

Communist International. Executive Committee.
Report on the Enlarged Executive, 1926. 1 reel.

3264

Communist International. Executive Committee. 7th Plenum, 1926.
Report, 1926. 1 reel.

3265

Congreso Cultural de La Habana, 1968.
Records, 1968. 1 reel.

3266

Cuba. Clippings, 1960–1964. 1 reel.

3267

Cuba. Clippings, 1961–1963. 1 reel.

3268

Cuba. Comisión Coordinadora de la Investigación del Empleo, Sub-Empleo y Desempleo.
"Resultados de la Encuesta sobre Empleo y Desempleo en Cuba: Mayo de 1956 a Abril de 1957," 1958. 1 reel.

3269

Danquah, Joseph Boakye, 1895–
"Revelation of Culture in Ghana: Lectures and Essays

of Discovery in the Search for the Ancient Origins of a Progressive People," 1961. 1 reel.

3270

Democratic Party (Uganda).
Records, 1960–1966. 1 reel.

3271

Denikin, Anton Ivanovich, 1872–1947.
"Naviêt na Bîeloe Dvizhenie." 1 reel.

3272

Denver. Public Library. Bibliographical Center for Research.
"The Spanish Civil War and Its Political, Social, Economic and Ideological Backgrounds: A Bibliography," compiled by Floyd Hardin, 1938. 1 reel.

3273

Deutsch-Ostafrikanische Gesellschaft, Berlin.
Records, 1885–1898. 5 reels.

3274

Deutsche Kolonialgesellschaft, Berlin. Vorstand.
Minutes of meetings, 1889–1916. 2 reels.

3275

Di Zerega, Gus.
Articles from the *Journal-World, Wichita Eagle and Beacon* and *Barber County Index*. 1 reel.

3276

Documents by and about the Native Affairs Committee, Southern Rhodesia, 1906–1923. 1 reel.

3277

Documents concerning Harro Schulze-Boysen and the resistance group known as Rote Kapelle, 1942–1943. 1 reel.

3278

Documents concerning the activities of Carl Moor, a Swiss socialist of Austrian parentage, and his relations in 1917 with the Stockholm socialists. 1 reel.

3279

Documents from the German Naval Archives, 1855–1914. 10 reels.

3280

Documents of the Angolan nationalist movement, 1962–1963. 1 reel.

3281

Documents relating to Angola, 1962–1963. 1 reel.

3282

Documents relating to nationalist movements in Portuguese Africa, mostly in Angola and Portuguese Guinea, 1962–1963. 1 reel.

3283

Documents relating to native affairs of Southern Rhodesia, 1894–1953. 1 reel.

3284

Documents relating to Ruanda-Urundi and Rwanda, 1954–1966. 1 reel.

3285

Documents relating to the German Navy, 1919–1939. 6 reels.

3286

Dominican Republic: documents bearing on the relationship of church and state, 1965. 1 reel.

3287

Dominican Republic: ephemera relating to the 1965 Dominican Revolution, 1965. 1 reel.

3288

Dominican Republic: miscellaneous material consisting mostly of correspondence of Dominican students' associations or religious groups relating to the revolution of 1965, 1965. 1 reel.

3289

Dominican Republic: miscellaneous microfilmed material relating to the revolution in 1965, 1965–1966. 1 reel.

3290

Dorrill, William F.
"Kiangsi Campaigns." 1 reel.

3291

Dundas, Sir Charles Cecil Ferquharson, 1884–1956.
Report on German administration in East Africa, 1919. 1 reel.

3292

Eichmann, Adolf, 1906–1962, *defendant.*
Trial transcript, Jerusalem, 1961. 1 reel.

3293

"Les Élections Législatives dans le Nord en 1936," by P. Chandourie and others, 1969. 5 microfiche sheets.

3294

Ellsworth, William J.
"Political Development of Nigeria: Role of Telecommunication," 1969. 1 reel.

3295

Elsas, D. van.
Diary relating to the German occupation of the Netherlands, 1940–1945. 1 reel.

3296

Elsas, D. van.
   Diary relating to the postwar period in the Netherlands, 1945–1947. 1 reel.

3297

Ethiopia. Pamphlets. 1 reel.

3298

Evanston, Ill. Transportation Center at Northwestern University.
   "Labor Migration and Regional Development in Ghana," by Ralph E. Beals and others, 1966. 1 reel.

3299

Federzoni, Luigi, 1878–1967.
   Diary of the Minister of Colonies of Italy, 1927. 1 reel.

3300

France. Agence Économique des Colonies. Bibliothèque.
   "Côte Française des Somalis et Dépendances," by Roger Janvier and Christian Dupont. 1 reel.

3301

France. Ministère des Affaires Étrangères.
   Records relating to the military occupation of Baranya and Pécs by the Royal Serbian Army, and to the Baranya-Bajai Szerb-Magyar Köztársaság, 1919–1921. 1 reel.

3302

Franklin D. Roosevelt Library, Hyde Park, N.Y.
   Papers of Franklin D. Roosevelt relating to Russian-American relations. 1 reel.

3303

French politics. Pamphlets, 1932–1944. 1 reel.

3304

French weekly journals covering the period May–July, 1968. 3 reels.

3305

Gambia publications, from the David P. Gamble collection, 1933–1969. 6 reels.

3306

Gempp, Fritz Georg, *ed.*
   "Geheimer Nachrichtendienst und Spionage des Heeres." 2 reels.

3307

German East Africa. Records of the Deutsche Kolonialgesellschaft and the Reichskolonialamt, 1884–1894. 7 reels.

3308

German records captured during World War II and subsequently microfilmed at Whaddon Hall, England; U.S. National Archives; and Berlin Document Center. For holdings write Reference Librarian, Hoover Institution on War, Revolution and Peace.

3309

German Southwest Africa.
   Records, 1914–1915. 1 reel.

3310

Germany. Auswaertiges Amt.
   Correspondence with Friedrich von Holstein, 1890–1898. 1 reel.

3311

Germany. Auswaertiges Amt.
   Papers of Freiherr Konstantin von Neurath, 1933–1938. 1 reel.

3312

Germany. Auswaertiges Amt.
   Records, 1867–1920. 9 reels.

3313

Germany. Auswaertiges Amt.
   Records relating to agents and spies in France and the French espionage law, 1886–1911. 5 reels.

3314

Germany. Auswaertiges Amt.
   Records relating to attacks on the German Embassy in France regarding the Dreyfus affair, 1894–1896. 1 reel.

3315

Germany. Auswaertiges Amt.
   Records relating to German relations with Russia, 1914–1920. 4 reels.

3316

Germany. Auswaertiges Amt.
   Records relating to peace negotiations with Russia, 1917–1918. 1 reel.

3317

Germany. Auswaertiges Amt.
   Records relating to possessions in Oceanica, 1885–1918. 11 reels.

3318

Germany. Auswaertiges Amt.
   Records relating to preliminaries to the peace negotiations at Brest-Litovsk, 1915–1918. 1 reel.

3319

Germany. Grosses Hauptquartier.
   Records relating to Italy and neutrality, 1914. 1 reel.

3320

Germany. Grosses Hauptquartier.
   Records relating to military operations in World War I, 1915–1919. 1 reel.

3321

Germany. Grosses Hauptquartier.
   Records relating to the diplomatic history of World War I, 1914–1916. 1 reel.

3322

Germany. Heer. Heeresgruppe A.
    War journal of the Western front, 1939–1940. 1 reel.

3323

Germany. Heer. Heeresgruppe B.
    War journal of the Western front, 1939–1942. 1 reel.

3324

Germany. Kolonialrat.
    Records, 1890–1906. 11 reels.

3325

Germany. Luftwaffe. Luftflottenkommando 2.
    Orders for Luftflotten 2 and 3, 1939–1940. 1 reel.

3326

Germany. Reichsjustizministerium.
    Records relating to revolutionary activities in Germany, 1918–1919. 1 reel.

3327

Germany. Reichskanzlei.
    Records relating to Curt Baake, Prince Max von Baden, Edward Hamm and other members of the Government, 1918–1919. 1 reel.

3328

Germany. Reichskanzlei.
    Records relating to the "German Socialist Republic," Workers and Soldiers Councils and their congresses, 1919. 1 reel.

3329

Germany. Reichskanzlei.
    Records relating to the Kommunistische Partei Deutschlands, Spartakus and Bolshevism, 1919–1932. 5 reels.

3330

Germany. Reichskanzlei.
    Records relating to the Nationalsozialistische Deutsche Arbeiter-Partei, 1922–1933. 2 reels.

3331

Germany. Reichskanzlei.
    Records relating to the Unabhaengige Sozialdemokratische Partei Deutschlands, 1919–1923. 1 reel.

3332

Germany. Reichsluftfahrtministerium.
    Records of the Reichsluftfahrtministerium and the Luftwaffe General Staff, 1943. 1 reel.

3333

Germany. Reichstag. Kommission fuer den Reichshaushalt.
    Minutes, 1895–1914. 9 reels.

3334

Germany. Wehrmacht. Oberkommando.
    Directives, 1939–1945. 1 reel.

3335

Germany. Wehrmacht. Oberkommando.
    Records relating to the occupied territories and the Italian campaign, 1940–1943. 1 reel.

3336

Germany. Wehrmacht. Oberkommando.
    Reports, 1939–1942. 3 reels.

3337

Germany (Territory under Allied Occupation, 1945–1955. U.S. Zone). Office of Military Government. Historical Section.
    Collection, 1947–1949. 3 reels.

3338

Germany (Territory under Allied Occupation, 1945–1955. U.S. Zone). Office of Military Government. Information Control Division. Intelligence Branch.
    Collection of miscellaneous captured German documents, mainly from the Reichspropagandaministerium, 1942–1945. 7 reels.

3339

Germany (Territory under Allied Occupation, 1945–1955. U.S. Zone). Office of Military Government. Information Control Division. Opinion Survey Section.
    Results of public opinion polls of the German public, 1945–1948. 3 reels.

3340

Gonzales, Manuel G.
    "Andrea Costa and the Rise of Socialism in the Romagna, 1871–1892," 1976. 1 reel.

3341

Great Britain. Colonial Office.
    Pamphlets relating to Africa. 24 reels.

3342

Great Britain. Colonial Office.
    Pamphlets relating to East Africa. 14 reels.

3343

Great Britain. Foreign Office.
    Records relating to China, 1848–1922. 32 reels.

3344

Great Britain. Foreign Office. Political Intelligence Department.
    Captured German documents issued for propaganda purposes, partly by the Gestapo and the Reichssicherheitshauptamt, 1939–1944. 2 reels.

3345

Great Britain. Foreign Office. Political Intelligence Department.
    German documents, 1941–1945. 1 reel.

3346

Grenfell, David.
    Notes relating to refugees from Angola, 1962–1968. 1 reel.

3347

Grosser, Philip, 1890–1933, *defendant.*
Trial transcript of a conscientious objector, Boston, 1918. 1 reel.

3348

Gussman, B. W.
"African Life in an Urban Area: A Study of the African Population of Bulawayo," 1952. 1 reel.

3349

Guyonnet, Marguerite.
"La Presse au Sénégal jusqu'à 1939," 1964. 1 reel.

3350

Halleman, F. F.
"The Attitudes of White Mining Employees toward Life and Work on the Copperbelt," 1960. 1 reel.

3351

Harris, Ernest Lloyd.
"The Allies in Siberia," 1921. 1 reel.

3352

Hayit, Baymirza.
"Die Nationalen Regierungen von Kokand (Choqand) und der Alasch Orda," 1950. 1 reel.

3353

Helmreich, Jonathan Ernst, 1936–
"Belgian Diplomatic Style: A Study in Small Power Diplomacy," 1961. 1 reel.

3354

Helsinki. Yliopisto. Bibliotek. Slavic Department.
Card catalog. 18 reels.

3355

Henry Shelton Sanford Memorial Library, Sanford, Fla.
Papers of Henry Shelton Sanford relating to the Congo Free State. 9 reels.

3356

Henry White papers, Library of Congress, 1919, relating to the Paris Peace Conference. 1 reel.

3357

Herbert J. Weiss collection on the Belgian Congo, 1947–1963. 10 reels.

3358

Hertz, Paul, 1888–1961.
Papers, 1920–1961, relating to German socialism. 64 reels.

3359

Himmler, Heinrich, 1900–1945.
Diary, 1910–1913. 1 reel.

3360

Hoisington, William A.
"Tax Payer Revolt in France: The National Taxpayers' Federation, 1928–1939," 1973. 1 reel.

3361

Holtzmann, Robert, b. 1883.
"Ludendorff als Kaempfer fuer 'Freiheit, Wahrheit und Recht': Aufzeichnungen auf Grund Persoenlicher Erlebnisse und Besprechungen mit Ludendorff und Seiner Frau, sowie eines Reichen und Viel Seitigen Schriftwechsels," 1937. 1 reel.

3362

Hussey, Alfred Rodman.
Papers, 1945–1948, relating to the Allied occupation of Japan. 12 reels.

3363

Imbata, Pius.
"Organisation et Fonctionnement des Services Administratifs en Province Orientale sous le Régime Gizenga, 1960–1961," 1971. 1 reel.

3364

Independent Labour Party (Great Britain).
Minute books, 1893–1909. 1 reel.

3365

International Association of the Congo.
Records, 1882–1883. 1 reel.

3366

International Congress of Africanists. 1st, Accra, Ghana, 1962.
Conference papers, 1962. 1 reel.

3367

International Military Tribunal for the Far East.
Studies, 1947. 1 reel.

3368

Iran.
Records relating to treaties with Russia, 1828–1931. Translated by J. Rives Childs. 1 reel.

3369

Irish political and radical newspapers of the twentieth century, 1895–1941. 76 reels.

3370

Italy. Ministero degli Affari Esteri.
Papers of Sidney Sonnino, Foreign Minister of Italy, 1914–1919. 54 reels.

3371

Jodl, Alfred, 1890–1946.
Diary, 1943–1945, relating to World War II military operations. 1 reel.

3372

Jodlbauer, Josef N., 1877–1960.
"13 Jahre in Amerika." 1 reel.

3373

Johns, Sheridan Waite.
"Marxism-Leninism in a Multi-Racial Society: The Origin and Early History of the Communist Party of South Africa, 1914–1933," 1965. 1 reel.

3374

Johnson, George Wesley.
Research notes on French West Africa. 1 reel.

3375

Kane, John Francis, b. 1881.
"War or Man the Master? A Report on the Collective Security Plan," 1953. 1 reel.

3376

Keller, George B.
"Communist Chinese Influence in East Africa," 1969. 1 reel.

3377

Kenya. National Archives.
Annual reports of administrative units of the Kenya Government, 1904–1963. 63 reels.

3378

Kenya. National Archives.
Handing over reports of administrative units of the Kenya Government, 1910–1963. 14 reels.

3379

Kenya. National Archives.
Intelligence reports of administrative units of the Kenya Government, 1921–1951. 12 reels.

3380

Kenya. National Archives.
Miscellaneous correspondence of administrative units of the Kenya Government, 1894–1961. 11 reels.

3381

Kenya. National Archives.
Provincial and district record books of administrative units of the Kenya Government, 1902–1958. 18 reels.

3382

Kido, Koichi, Marquis, b. 1889.
Diary, 1931–1945, relating to Japanese politics. 1 reel.

3383

Kommunisticheskaﬁ Partiﬁ Sovetskogo Soﬁuza. 15th Conference, Moscow, 1926.
Records, 1926. 1 reel.

3384

Kommunisticheskaﬁ Partiﬁ Sovetskogo Soﬁuza. Smolenskiĭ Oblastnoĭ Komitet. Partiĭnyĭ Arkhiv.

Records relating to the Zinoviev opposition and the assassination of S. M. Kirov, 1935. 1 reel.

3385

Kommunisticheskaﬁ Partiﬁ Sovetskogo Soﬁuza. TSentral'nyĭ Komitet. Politicheskoe Bﬁuro.
Resolutions, 1934–1936. 1 reel.

3386

Kommunistische Partei Deutschlands. Pamphlets, 1919–1924. 1 reel.

3387

Konobaloff, Colonel.
"History of Ethiopia." 1 reel.

3388

Kordt, Erich, 1903–
"German Political History in the Far East during the Hitler Regime," 1946. Translated by E. A. Bayne. 1 reel.

3389

Korean conflict. Reports on the Korean War. 9 reels.

3390

Labour Party (Great Britain).
Pamphlets and leaflets, 1900–1926. 124 microfiche sheets.

3391

Labour Party (Great Britain) Executive Committee.
Minutes. 666 microfiche sheets.

3392

Lachaume, Jean François.
"Les Élections Législatives des 23 et 30 Novembre 1958 dans le Département de la Creuse," 1961. 2 microfiche sheets.

3393

Lansing, Robert, 1864–1928.
Diary, 1916–1919, relating to American foreign policy in World War I. 1 reel.

3394

Larkin, Bruce Drummond.
"Chinese African Policy," 1965. 1 reel.

3395

London Trades Council.
Financial and other records, 1860–1953. 1 reel.

3396

London Trades Council.
Minutes and other records, 1860–1953. 9 reels.

3397

London Trades Council.
Reports, 1861–1952. 1 reel.

3398

Loosli, C. A.
Testimony in the trial of the Schweizerischer Israelitischer Gemeindebund and the Israelitische Kultusgemeinde, Bern, plaintiffs, vs. the Bund Nationalsozialistischer Eidgenossen, defendant, Bern, 1935. 1 reel.

3399

McVey, Ruth Thomas.
"The Development of the Indonesian Communist
Party and Its Relations with the Soviet Union and the
Chinese Peoples Republic," 1954. 1 reel.

3400

Mandela, Nelson, 1918– *defendant*.
Transcripts of the trials of the National High Command, N. Mandela, Walter Sisulu and others for alleged
sabotage and communist activities, Johannesburg, South
Africa, 1963–1964. 4 reels.

3401

Mandela, Nelson, 1918– *defendant*.
Trial transcript, Pretoria, South Africa, 1962. 1 reel.

3402

Mandelstam, Jean.
"La Palestine dans la Politique de Gamal Abdel Nasser,
Juillet 1952—Février 1955," 1970. 5 microfiche sheets.

3403

Margairaz, Michel.
"Les Propositions de Politique Économique, Financière
et Monétaire de la SFIO de 1934 à 1936: La Reflation,"
1972. 4 microfiche sheets.

3404

Marty, André Pierre, 1886–1956.
Papers relating to communism in France, 1917–1939.
4 reels.

3405

Material relating to the Congo, Leopoldville, from the collection of Robert E. Bartlett, 1959–1960. 1 reel.

3406

Matlock, Jack F.
"An Index to the Collected Works of J. V. Stalin," 1955.
1 reel.

3407

Matos, Hubert, *defendant*.
Trial transcript, Havana, 1960. 1 reel.

3408

Mauritania: political ephemera, collected by Clement H.
Moore. 1 reel.

3409

Mayo-Mokelo, Justin.
"Instabilité dans les Institutions Communales de la

Ville de Kisangani (ex-Stanleyville), 1958–1968," 1971.
1 reel.

3410

Mayo, Sebastián.
"La Educación Socialista en México: El Asalto de la
Universidad Nacional." 1 reel.

3411

Mboladinga-Katako, Jules-Roger.
"Conflit Ekonda-Eswe au Sankuru de 1960 à 1964,"
1970. 1 reel.

3412

Meeting of Consultation of Ministers of Foreign Affairs of
American States. 10th, New York, 1965.
Records relating to the Dominican crisis, 1965. 1 reel.

3413

Menshevik collection of newspapers, periodicals, pamphlets
and books related to the Menshevik movement. 76 reels.

3414

Miner, W. Lawrence.
"Vulnerability of U.S. Pacific Coast to Atomic Attack,"
1950. 1 reel.

3415

Miscellaneous publications on Ethiopia. 1 reel.

3416

Mitchell, Richard Paul, 1925–
"The Society of the Muslim Brothers," 1959. 1 reel.

3417

Mohun, R. Dorsey.
Papers relating to the Congo, Zanzibar and South
Africa, 1892–1913. 3 reels.

3418

Moles, Gary.
"Ethiopia and the Russian Threat," 1970. 1 reel.

3419

Morelli, Anthony.
"The Role of the U.S. Military Assistance in Ethiopia,"
1970. 1 reel.

3420

Mouvement Républicain Populaire. Congrès National.
Proceedings, 1944–1960. 17 reels.

3421

Muabilay-Tshibola, Ch.
"Rebellion à Kisangani, 1964," 1971. 1 reel.

3422

Mulka, Robert Karl Ludwig, 1895– *defendant*.
Trial transcript, Frankfurt am Main, 1963. 1 reel.

3423

Mulumbati, Adrien.
"Diversité Ethnique et Provincettes au Katanga de 1960 à 1966," 1971. 1 reel.

3424

Nationalsozialistische Deutsche Arbeiter-Partei. Hauptarchiv.
Records of the Nationalsozialistische Deutsche Arbeiter-Partei, including materials by and about Adolf Hitler, Heinrich Himmler and Julius Streicher, 1919–1945. 155 reels.

3425

Nationalsozialistische Deutsche Arbeiter-Partei. Reichspropagandaleitung.
Photographs illustrating German military history. 1 reel.

3426

Nationalsozialistische Deutsche Arbeiter-Partei. Reichspropagandaleitung.
Photographs, including portraits, of Germany's contributions to literature, medicine, technology, and other fields. 1 reel.

3427

Nationalsozialistische Deutsche Arbeiter-Partei. Reichspropagandaleitung.
Photographs, including portraits, of World War II events, relating especially to Germany, 1940–1941. 10 reels.

3428

Nationalsozialistische Deutsche Arbeiter-Partei. Reichspropagandaleitung.
Photographs of Adolf Hitler. 1 reel.

3429

Nationalsozialistische Deutsche Arbeiter-Partei. Reichspropagandaleitung.
Photographs of German antiquities. 1 reel.

3430

Nationalsozialistische Deutsche Arbeiter-Partei. Reichspropagandaleitung.
Photographs of Jews. 3 reels.

3431

Nationalsozialistische Deutsche Arbeiter-Partei. Reichspropagandaleitung.
Photographs of Scandinavian and Sicilian antiquities. 1 reel.

3432

Nationalsozialistische Deutsche Arbeiter-Partei. Reichspropagandaleitung.
Photographs of the activities of German women in World War II. 1 reel.

3433

Nationalsozialistische Deutsche Arbeiter-Partei. Reichspropagandaleitung.
Photographs of the Sudetenland. 1 reel.

3434

Nationalsozialistische Deutsche Arbeiter-Partei. Reichspropagandaleitung.
Photographs of war memorials and other subjects. 1 reel.

3435

Nationalsozialistische Deutsche Arbeiter-Partei. Reichspropagandaleitung.
Photographs, portraits and maps illustrating German history from earliest times to and including World War II. 1 reel.

3436

Nationalsozialistische Deutsche Arbeiter-Partei. Reichspropagandaleitung.
Photographs, portraits and maps of life in the U.S. from earliest times. 1 reel.

3437

Nationalsozialistische Deutsche Arbeiter-Partei. Reichspropagandaleitung.
Pictures of the Volkssturm. 1 reel.

3438

Nationalsozialistische Deutsche Arbeiter-Partei. Reichspropagandaleitung.
Views of Germany and portraits of German personalities. 2 reels.

3439

Naumann, Friedrich, 1860–1919.
"Mitteleuropa und Polen: Denkschrift des Arbeitsausschusses fuer Mitteleuropa, dem Herrn Reichskanzler Ueberreicht am 27. Mai 1917," by F. Naumann, Eugen Schiffer and E. Jaeckh, 1917. On the same reel: R. Winterstetten, "Die Polnische Frage und Mitteleuropa," 1917; and "Mitteleuropa, Polen und die Besetzten Oestlichen Gebiete," 1917. 1 reel.

3440

Nehnevajsa, Jiri, 1925–
"The Cuban Crisis, Meaning and Impact," by J. Nehnevajsa and Morris I. Berkowitz, 1962. 1 reel.

3441

Nicholas J. Kremer Somalia collection, 1969. 1 reel.

3442

Nigeria.
Intelligence reports on southern Nigeria prepared by British colonial officials, 1932–1942. 16 reels.

3443

Nigeria collection of Simon Ottenberg, 1940–1965. 15 reels.

3444

Nigerian pamphlets and other publications, from the collection of Simon Ottenberg, 1940–1965. 14 reels.

3445

Nikitović, Časlav M.
"Komunistička Partija Jugoslavije," 1954. 1 reel.

3446

Noirot, Ernest, 1851–1913.
Papers relating to Guinea and the Fouta Djallon and Senegambia regions of West Africa, 1881–1909. 6 reels.

3447

Northern Ireland political literature. 215 microfiche sheets.

3448

"Occupation of Lithuania by the Soviets from the Military Point of View." 1 reel.

3449

"Ocherki Revoliûtsionnogo Dvizheniîa v Sredneĭ Azii," by Feĭzula Khodzhaev and others, ca. 1923. 1 reel.

3450

Onatschungu, Henri.
"Rebellion au Sankuru, 1964," 1969. 1 reel.

3451

Pamphlets and serials on Ethiopia, Rhodesia and Rhodesia and Nyasaland, collected by Richard Greenfield, 1958–1965. 1 reel.

3452

Pamphlets on the Spanish Civil War, 1936–1939. 2 reels.

3453

Panicacci, Jean Louis.
"Nice pendant la 2ème Guerre Mondiale: De la Declaration de Guerre à l'Occupation Italienne, Septembre 1939 à Novembre 1942," 1967. 2 microfiche sheets.

3454

Pankhurst, Richard Keir Pethick, 1927–
"Some Factors Depressing the Standard of Living of Peasants in Traditional Ethiopia," 1965. 1 reel.

3455

Papers of the Communist Party of South Africa and related organizations, 1933–1948. 3 reels.

3456

Papers relating to Ruanda-Urundi, 1877–1933. 4 reels.

3457

Pappas, Chris C.
"An Issue in Black and White Insurgency and Southern Africa," 1970. 1 reel.

3458

Paris. Peace Conference, 1919. Commission on Rumanian and Yugoslav Affairs.
Proceedings, 1919. 1 reel.

3459

Parker, Mary.
"Political and Social Aspects of the Development of Local Government in Kenya with Special Reference to Nairobi," 1959. 1 reel.

3460

Parti Communiste Français. Congrès National.
Proceedings, 1936–1959. 4 reels.

3461

Partido Comunista Dominicano. Comité Central.
Publications, 1965. 1 reel.

3462

Pelckmann, Horst.
Defense address in trial of SS members, Nuremberg, 1946. On the same reel: Horst Pelckmann, "Die Entwicklung der Allgemeinen und der Waffen-SS und Ihr Verhaeltnis zu Anderen Organisationen in Himmler Machtbereich," 1946. 1 reel.

3463

Peters, Karl, 1856–1918.
Papers, 1881–1903, relating to German East Africa. 1 reel.

3464

Picard, Jean Claude.
"Le Nouveau Parti Socialiste, ou le Diagnostic d'une Certaine Gauche," 1971. 3 microfiche sheets.

3465

Pierce, Richard A.
"Native Judicial Procedure in Russian Central Asia," 1951. 1 reel.

3466

Polish resistance movement in France. Collection, 1942–1945. 1 reel.

3467

Political ephemera of French-speaking West Africa in the Claude E. Welch collection. 4 reels.

3468

Portuguese Africa. Clippings, 1960–1963. 1 reel.

3469

Portuguese Africa. Collection, 1961–1964. 4 reels.

3470

Portuguese Angola. Collection relating to the exile revolutionary movement of Angola, 1961–1963. 1 reel.

3471
Portuguese colonies. Collection. 1 reel.

3472
Postwar problems discussed in Latin America during the Second World War. Collection of Harris Learner Latham. 1 reel.

3473
Publications by and about Marcel Déat, 1919–1938. 1 reel.

3474
RIAS (Radio Station) Berlin (West Berlin).
  Letters received from listeners in East Berlin and the Soviet zone, 1961–1963. 6 reels.

3475
Raymond, Edward A.
  "Foreign Students, the Soviet Educational Weapon," 1973. 1 reel.

3476
Reed, David.
  Interviews with participants (rescuers and rescued) from the 1964 Stanleyville, Congo, Massacre, 1964–1965. 3 reels.

3477
Reichsbund Deutscher Seegeltung.
  Photographs. 1 reel.

3478
Reichsbund Deutscher Seegeltung.
  Photographs of German naval vessels. 1 reel.

3479
Reichskolonialbund, Berlin. Bildstelle.
  Photographs and maps of former German African colonies. 1 reel.

3480
Reid, Alexander J.
  "Mongo Land: History and Culture of the Mongo People, 1450–1970," ca. 1970. 1 reel.

3481
Relations between Serbia and the Austro-Hungarian Monarchy. History. 1 reel.

3482
Reports of village development committees of Tanganyika, 1962. 1 reel.

3483
Reuter, Ernst, 1889–1953.
  Papers relating to activities as Buergermeister of West Berlin, 1917–1953. 39 reels.

3484
Rhodesia, Southern.
  Records relating to the native population, 1906–1952. 1 reel.

3485
Rhodesian documents relating to land tenure and economic conditions of the natives, including reports of the Native Land Board, 1933–1936. 1 reel.

3486
Robert Lansing papers, Library of Congress, relating to the peace settlement, 1918–1919. 1 reel.

3487
Rohden, Hans Detlef Herhudt von, 1899–   , ed.
  "Europaeische Beitraege zur Geschichte des Weltkrieges II, 1939–1945: Luftkrieg." 13 reels.

3488
Rossiĭsko-Amerikanskaia Kompaniia.
  Journal of Adol'f Karlovich Étolin, Governor of Russian colonies in America, 1845. 2 reels.

3489
Russia (1917–   R.S.F.S.R.) Chrezvychaĭnaia Komissiia po Bor'be s Kontr-Revoliutsieĭ i Sabotazhem.
  "Krasnaia Kniga VChK," 1920. 1 reel.

3490
Saint-Martin, Yves.
  "Une Source de l'Histoire Coloniale du Sénégal: Les Rapports de la Situation Politique," 1964. 1 reel.

3491
Saleeby, Robert J.
  "The German Army," 1947. 1 reel.

3492
Sampson, Eldon F.
  "Nigeria: Tribalism Versus Nationalism," 1969. 1 reel.

3493
Schier, Bruno, 1902–
  "Hauslandschaften und Kulturbewegungen im Oestlichen Mitteleuropa," 1932. 1 reel.

3494
Seeckt, Hans von, 1866–1936.
  Papers relating to the German Army. 28 reels.

3495
Selected items from the David R. Francis collection at the Missouri Historical Society, pertaining to the Russian Revolution of 1917, 1916–1918. 2 reels.

3496
Selected material from World War II U.S. unit operations reports, mostly dealing with the campaign of 1944 in southern France, 1944. 2 reels.

3497
Selected Uganda land reports, 1914–1932. 1 reel.

3498

A selection of works by and about Edward W. Blyden, 1857–1908. 1 reel.

3499

Sierra Leone.
  Records. 1 reel.

3500

Sisulu, Walter Max Ulyate, *defendant*.
  Trial transcript, Johannesburg, South Africa, 1962. 1 reel.

3501

Skorzeny, Otto, 1908–
  Memoir relating to the rescue of Benito Mussolini in 1943, by O. Skorzeny and Karl Radl. 1 reel.

3502

Socialist Party of America papers, 1897–1963. 142 reels.

3503

South Africa, a collection of miscellaneous documents, 1902–1963. 15 reels.

3504

South African Institute for Scientific and Industrial Research. National Institute for Personnel Research.
  "The Attitude of White Mining Employees towards Life and Work in the Copperbelt," 1961. 2 reels.

3505

South African Institute for Scientific and Industrial Research. National Institute for Personnel Research.
  "The Attitudes of White Mining Employees towards Life and Work at Broken Hill, Northern Rhodesia," 1961. 2 reels.

3506

South African treason trial of thirty accused persons and their co-conspirators, Pretoria, 1959–1960. Transcript. 26 reels.

3507

Stefanovskiĭ, Stepan.
  "Teoriĭa i Praktika Sovetskoĭ Promyshlennoĭ Raĉsionalizaĉsii," ca. 1956. 1 reel.

3508

Stein, Guenther.
  Diary in Yenan, China, 1945. 1 reel.

3509

Steiner, Rolf, *defendant*.
  Trial transcript, Khartum, Sudan, 1971. 1 reel.

3510

Stieff, Hellmuth, 1901–1944.
  Letters, 1928–1944, primarily relating to the attempted assassination of Adolf Hitler in 1944. 1 reel.

3511

Stropp, R.
  "Aufstellungsverzeichnis der Administrativen Registratur des Ministeriums des Aeussern [of Austria] 1830–1918," 1957. 1 reel.

3512

Stropp, R.
  "Aufstellungsverzeichnis des Politischen Archivs des Ministeriums des Aeussern [of Austria] 1848–1918," 1956. 1 reel.

3513

"Struggle for Peace and Democracy in the Northeast," 1946. 1 reel.

3514

Students for a Democratic Society.
  Records, 1958–1970. 41 reels.

3515

Supreme Commander for the Allied Powers. International Prosecution Section.
  "Decisions of Imperial Conferences, Cabinet Meetings and Other Conferences and Meetings Which Appear in the Prosecution's Evidence," by Joseph F. English, 1947. 1 reel.

3516

Syracuse University. Village Settlement Project (Tanzania).
  Reports, 1965–1967. 1 reel.

3517

Tanganyika.
  Provincial and district books, ca. 1914–1950. 27 reels.

3518

Thompson, Virginia McLean, 1903– *comp.*
  "Who's Who in South East Asia, August 1945—December 1949," compiled by V. M. Thompson and Richard Adloff. 3 reels.

3519

Ticonderoga (Battleship).
  Journal, 1878–1880. 2 reels.

3520

Trades Union Congress, London.
  Minutes, 1888–1921. 5 reels.

3521

Transcript of interrogation of Franz Xavier Schwarz, Reich Treasurer of the NSDAP, Nuremberg, 1946. 1 reel.

3522

Tschebotarioff, Gregory Porphyriewitch, 1899–
  Papers of Valentina Ivanovna Chebotareva relating to members of the Romanov family, 1915–1948. 2 reels.

3523

Uganda People's Congress.
Records, 1962. 1 reel.

3524

Underground newspaper collection from the U.S. 222 reels.

3525

U.S. Advisory Commission of Railway Experts to Russia.
Records of the U.S. Advisory Commission of Railway Experts to Russia, the Russian Railway Service Corps and the Interallied Railway Committee, 1917–1922. 40 reels.

3526

U.S. American Relief Administration. Russian Unit.
Reports, 1921–1923. 1 reel.

3527

U.S. Army. American Forces in Germany, 1918–1923.
"American Military Government of Occupied Germany, 1918–1920," 1920. 1 reel.

3528

U.S. Army. Army, Pacific.
"The Handling of Prisoners of War during the Korean War," 1960. 1 reel.

3529

U.S. Army. European Theater of Operations.
"The French Forces of the Interior: Their Organization and Participation in the Liberation of France, 1944," 1945. 2 reels.

3530

U.S. Army. European Theater of Operations. 6th Information and Historical Service.
"Invasion of Southern France," by First Lieutenant Lenthiel H. Downs, 1944. 1 reel.

3531

U.S. Army. Far East Command. Military Intelligence Section. Historical Division.
Translations of statements of Japanese officials on World War II, 1949–1950. 2 reels.

3532

U.S. Army. Forces in China Theater.
"History of the China Theater," by Fenton Keyes and Charles F. Romanus, 1946. 1 reel.

3533

U.S. Army. Forces in China Theater.
Reports, 1946. 3 reels.

3534

U.S. Bureau of Foreign and Domestic Commerce.
Records relating to mineral oils in Russia, 1922–1930. 1 reel.

3535

U.S. Congress. Senate. Special Committee Investigating the National Defense Program.
Records relating to machine tools in the Soviet Union, 1945. 1 reel.

3536

U.S. Department of State.
Records relating to internal affairs of Russia, 1930–1933. 9 reels.

3537

U.S. Department of State.
Records relating to internal affairs of Russia, 1934–1937. 4 reels.

3538

U.S. Department of State.
"Survey of Published Records and Documents of the Paris Peace Conference, 1919," ca. 1939. 1 reel.

3539

U.S. Department of State. Division of Communications and Records.
"Councils, Committees, Commissions, Field Missions, etc., of the Paris Peace Conference, Including Field Missions of the American Commission to Negotiate Peace," ca. 1919. 1 reel.

3540

U.S. Department of State. Division of Far Eastern Affairs.
Papers of Franklin D. Roosevelt relating to preliminary conversations on China for the World Monetary and Economic Conference, 1933. 1 reel.

3541

U.S. Department of State. Special Interrogation Mission.
Reports of interrogations of German prisoners of war, 1945–1946. 1 reel.

3542

U.S. Department of the Army. Office of Military History.
"Civil Affairs and Military Government in the Mediterranean Theater," by Robert W. Komer, ca. 1948. 1 reel.

3543

U.S. Department of the Army. Office of Military History.
"Displaced Persons," by Marcus W. Floyd, 1947. 1 reel.

3544

U.S. Immigration and Naturalization Service.
Report on deportation hearings of Harry Bridges, 1939. 5 reels.

3545

U.S. Library of Congress.
Newspapers published in German prisoner-of-war camps in the U.S., 1943–1946. 15 reels.

3546
U.S. Military Assistance Command, Vietnam. Office of the Assistant Chief of Staff, J-2.
Collection relating to Viet Cong and North Vietnamese Army tactical studies and doctrine, 1965–1970. 1 reel.

3547
U.S. National Archives.
Collection relating to Spanish possessions in Africa, French possessions in Africa, and Portuguese possessions in Africa and the Atlantic, 1942–1943. 1 reel.

3548
U.S. National Archives.
Collection relating to the Shakhta affair, 1928. 1 reel.

3549
U.S. National Archives.
Microfilm publications, primarily of U.S. Department of State records. Series M. For holdings write Reference Librarian, Hoover Institution on War, Revolution and Peace.

3550
U.S. National Archives.
Microfilm publications, primarily of U.S. Department of State records. Series T. For holdings write Reference Librarian, Hoover Institution on War, Revolution and Peace.

3551
U.S. Navy Department.
Letters from captains, 1835. 1 reel.

3552
U.S. Office of Alien Property Custodian.
Records relating to the German American Bund and related organizations. 1 reel.

3553
U.S. Office of Defense Transportation.
Report on railways of the U.S.S.R., 1930. 1 reel.

3554
U.S. Provost-Marshal-General's Bureau.
"History of Military Government Training," ca. 1945. 3 reels.

3555
Vandewalle, Frédéric J. L. A.
"L'Ommegang, II-III: Le Spicilège," 1964. 2 reels.

3556
Vatican. Biblioteca Vaticana.
"Inventaire Sommaire des Manuscrits et Imprimés Chinois de la Bibliothèque Vaticane," by Paul Pelliot, 1922. 1 reel.

3557
Waggener, James S.
"The Future of French Somaliland," 1969. 1 reel.

3558
Walker, Travis L.
"An Analysis of United States Military Assistance: Nigeria," 1969. 1 reel.

3559
Wallerstein, Immanuel Maurice, 1930–
Collection of political ephemera of the liberation movements of Lusophone Africa and Anglophone Southern Africa, 1958–1975. 12 reels.

3560
Warlimont, Walter, 1895–
Letters and statements, 1952–1955. 1 reel.

3561
Wegerer, Alfred von, b. 1880.
Correspondence, 1936–1937, relating to the World War I war guilt question. 1 reel.

3562
Werblan, Andrzej.
"Referat Zagajający Dyskusję o Linii Politycznej Tygodnika *Nowa Kultura* Wygłoszony na Posiedzeniu Komisji Prasowej KC w dniu 6 Maja 1958 w Gmachu KC PZPR w Warszawie," 1958. 1 reel.

3563
"Who's Who of Prominent Germans in the U.S.S.R.," 1944. 1 reel.

3564
"Women in National Development in Ghana," by Jeanne North and others, 1975. 3 microfiche sheets.

3565
Xuma, Alfred Bitini, 1890–1962.
Papers, 1921–1949, relating to South Africa and Southwest Africa. 10 reels.

3566
Yamashita, Tomoyuki, 1885–1946, *defendant*.
Trial transcript, Manila, 1945–1946. 4 reels.

3567
Yugoslav partisan collection. 1 reel.

3568
Zaire colonial documents: de Ryck collection on general administration, Equateur, Kivu and Ruanda-Urundi, 1885–1953. 5 reels.

3569
"Der Zersetzungsdienst der K.P.D.," ca. 1930. 1 reel.

Appendix
Bibliographic Works Based on Hoover Collections

All works are published by the Hoover Institution unless otherwise noted.

A Catalogue of Paris Peace Conference Delegation Propaganda in the Hoover War Library. 1926, 96 p.

N. Almond and R. H. Lutz, *An Introduction to a Bibliography of the Paris Peace Conference, Collections of Sources, Archive Publications, and Source Books.* 1935, 32 p.

W. Chamberlin, *Industrial Relations in Wartime: Great Britain, 1914–18; Annotated Bibliography of Materials in the Hoover Library on War, Revolution, and Peace.* 1940, 239 p.

———. *Industrial Relations in Germany, 1914–39; Annotated Bibliography of Materials in the Hoover Library on War, Revolution, and Peace, and the Stanford University Library.* 1942, 403 p.

Gerhard L. Weinberg, *Guide to Captured German Documents.* 1952, 90 p.; *Supplement,* 1959, 69 p.

F. W. Mote, *Japanese-Sponsored Governments in China, 1937–1945, An Annotated Bibliography Compiled from Materials in the Chinese Collections of the Hoover Library.* 1954, 68 p.

W. S. Sworakowski, *The Hoover Library Collection on Russia.* 1954; second printing, 1955, 42 p.

H. R. Boeninger, *The Hoover Library Collection on Germany.* 1955; second printing, 1961, 56 p.

E. Wu, *Leaders of Twentieth-Century China, An Annotated Bibliography of Selected Chinese Biographical Works in the Hoover Library.* 1956, 106 p.

N. Ike, *The Hoover Institution Collection on Japan.* 1958, 63 p.

A. C. Nahm, *Japanese Penetration of Korea, 1894–1910, A Checklist of Japanese Archives in the Hoover Institution.* 1959, 103 p.

J. Israel, *The Chinese Student Movement, 1927–1937, A Bibliographical Essay Based on the Resources of the Hoover Institution.* 1959, 29 p.

N. Uchida, *The Overseas Chinese, A Bibliographical Essay Based on the Resources of the Hoover Institution.* 1959, 134 p.

C. Hsüeh, *The Chinese Communist Movement, 1921–1937, An Annotated Bibliography of Selected Materials in the Chinese Collection of the Hoover Institution on War, Revolution, and Peace.* 1960, 131 p.

P. Duignan, *Madagascar (the Malagasy Republic), A List of Materials in the African Collections of Stanford University and the Hoover Institution on War, Revolution, and Peace.* 1962, 25 p.

C. Hsüeh, *The Chinese Communist Movement, 1937–1949, An Annotated Bibliography of Selected Materials in the Chinese Collection of the Hoover Institution on War, Revolution, and Peace.* 1962, 312 p.

Peter Duignan, and Kenneth M. Glazier, *A Checklist of Serials for African Studies Based on the Libraries of the Hoover Institution and Stanford University.* 1963, 104 p.

Grete Heinz and Agnes F. Peterson, *NSDAP Hauptarchiv: Guide to the Hoover Institution Microfilm Collection.* 1964, 175 p.

Karol Maichel, *Soviet and Russian Newspapers at the Hoover Institution.* 1966, 235 p.

Edward E. Smith, *"The Okhrana": The Russian Department of Police.* 1967, 280 p.

Library Catalogs of the Hoover Institution on War, Revolution, and Peace, Stanford University. G. K. Hall & Co., Boston, Massachusetts, 1969. 63 vols. *Serials and Newspapers.* 1969. 3 vols. *First Supplement.* 1972. 5 vols. *Second Supplement.* 1977. 6 vols.

Grete Heinz and Agnes F. Peterson, *Establishment and Consolidation, 1958–1965: An Annotated Bibliography of Hoover Institution Holdings for the French Fifth Republic.* 1970, 170 p.

Agnes F. Peterson, *Western Europe, A Survey of Holdings at the Hoover Institution on War, Revolution and Peace.* 1970, 60 p.

Peter Duignan, George Rentz, Karen Fung, and Michel Nabti, *African and Middle East Collections, A Survey of Holdings at the Hoover Institution on War, Revolution and Peace.* 1971, 37 p.

Kenneth M. Glazier and James R. Hobson, *International and English-Language Collections, A Survey of Holdings at the Hoover Institution on War, Revolution and Peace.* 1971, 20 p.

John T. Ma, *East Asia, A Survey of Holdings at the Hoover Institution on War, Revolution and Peace.* 1971, 24 p.

Joseph W. Bingaman, *Latin America, A Survey of Holdings at the Hoover Institution on War, Revolution and Peace.* 1972, 96 p.

Kathleen Tracey, *Herbert Hoover—A Bibliography, His Writings and Addresses.* 1977, 202 p.

Archival and Manuscript Materials at the Hoover Institution on War, Revolution and Peace, A Checklist of Major Collections. 1978 (biennial), 36 p.

Dale Reed, *Bertram D. Wolfe, A Register of His Papers.* Forthcoming.

Elena Schafer and Charles G. Palm, *Herbert Hoover, A Register of His Papers.* Forthcoming.

Joseph D. Dwyer, *Russia, the Soviet Union, and Eastern Europe, A Survey of Holdings at the Hoover Institution on War, Revolution and Peace.* Forthcoming.

Index

Citations are made to entry numbers, not page numbers. A boldfaced number after an index term refers to an entry, the title of which is identical to the term. For further information about the index, please see the introduction.

Carr, William G. **393**

Carranza, Venustiano, Pres. Mexico, 1859–1920. 3042

Carroll, Philip H., 1885–1941. **394**

Carson, Arthur Leroy, 1895– . **395**

Carson, Edith Scott, d. 1973. 395

Cartels. *see* Trusts, Industrial

Carter, Gwendolen. **396**

Carter, Lieutenant. **397**

Carteret cartoon collection. *see* World War I cartoon collection

Cartoons. *see* Caricatures and cartoons

Caruso, Enrico, 1873–1921. 495

Casement, Sir Roger David, 1864– 1916. **398**, 1154, 1445, **3249**

Caspari, John, 1899– . **399**

Castillo, J. Cicerón. **400**

Castro, Fidel, 1927– . 689, 1618, 1637, 3407

Castro, Juanita, 1933– . **401**

Catalan posters. *see* Posters, Catalan

Catalogs, Library. 3354

Catalonia—History. 254
  Autonomy and independence movements. 25

Cataret, J. G., *collector.* **402**

Catholic Church
  see also World War, 1939–1945— Catholic Church
  Austria. 199
  Czechoslovakia. 466
  Doctrinal and controversial works. 316
  Dominican Republic. 3288
  Germany. 2108, 2187
  Relations (diplomatic) with Great Britain. 2722

Catholics in the U.S. 575

Catholics, Ukrainian. 662

Catledge, Turner. 1166

Catroux, Georges, 1877–1969— Portraits, caricatures, etc. **403**

Cavalry. 1320

Cazden, Robert Edgar, 1930– . 3250

Censorship. 133
  see also European War, 1914– 1918—Censorship; Liberty of the press; World War, 1939– 1945—Censorship
  Colombia. 500

Center, Mrs. Hugh Stuart, *collector.* **404**

Central Africa. *see* Africa, Central

Central Africa Party (Rhodesia, Southern). 21

Central America—Description. 739

Central and Eastern European Planning Board, New York. **405**

Central Europe
  see also names of countries; Danube Valley
  Defenses. 636
  Economic conditions. 636, 2942
  Politics. 636, 660, 2942, 3439

Centralia Publicity Committee. **406**

Centralny Komitet dla Spraw Szkolnych i Oswiatowych. **407**

Cerf, Jay H., 1923–1974. **408**

Česká Družina. 200, **409**, 704, 732, 1329, 1384, 1686, 1741, 2075

Ceylon—World War, 1939–1945. *see* World War, 1939–1945— Ceylon

Chacon, Jose A., 1925– . **410**

Chad
  Economic conditions. 3257
  Social conditions. 3257

Chadbourn, Philip H. and William H. **411**

Chaigneau, Victor-Louis. **412**

Chaikovskiĭ (Anastasia Nikolaevna) collection. **413**

Chaim Weizmann, Israel and the Jewish People. **414**

Chaisson, John R., 1916–1972. **415**

Chalupny, E. **416**

Chamberlain, Neville, 1869–1940. 1060

Chambers, Whittaker, 1901–1961. 639, 2590

Chambrun, René, Comte de, 1906– , *collector.* **417**

Champion International Corporation. 188

Chandler, Loren R. 1166

Chandler, Robert W. **418**

Chandourie, P. 3293

Chang, Carsun. **419**

Chang, Chia-ao. *see* Chang, Kiangau, b. 1889

Chang, Hsin-hai, 1900–1972. **420**

Chang, Hsueh-liang, 1898– . Portraits, caricatures, etc. **421**

Chang, Kia-ngau, b. 1889. **422**

Chang, Kuo-t'ao, 1897– . **3251**

Chang, Tao-hsing, 1908– . **3252**

Change, Social. *see* Social change

Chanoine, Marie Jacques Henri. **423**

Chantiers de la Jeunesse. 627

Chapin, Leland T. **424**

Chapman, Frank Michler, 1864– 1945. **425**

Chapman, John. 1166

Emmet, Christopher Temple, Jr., 1900–1974. **743**

Emmons, Delos Carleton, 1888–1965. **744**

Emparan, Madie Brown. **745**

Employees, Training of. 982

Endowments—China. 1092

Enemy aliens. *see* Aliens

Enemy property. 519

Energy policy—U.S. 359, 2972

Energy resources. *see* Power resources

Engelhardt, Poul Ranzow. *see* Ranzow Engelhardt, Poul, 1898–

Engels, Friedrich, 1820–1895. 2322

Engineering. 1226, 3059
China. 2758
Military. *see* Military engineering
Russia. 58, 788, 849, 2650

Engineers. 3026
Russia. 58, 2636, 3108

England, Robert **746**

Engleman, Finis Ewing, 1895–1978. **747**

English, Joseph F. 3515

English literature. 420

Engravings. 303

Entente Internationale Anticommuniste. *see* International Anticommunist Entente

Entente, Little, 1920–1939. *see* Little Entente, 1920–1939

Environmental policy—U.S. 359

Environmental protection—U.S. 359, 2555, 2972

Episcopal Church. *see* Protestant Episcopal Church in the U.S.A.

Epstein, Fritz Theodor, 1898– . **748**

Epstein, Julius, 1901–1975. **749**

Equateur, Zaire (Province)—History. 3568

Equatorial Guinea
see also Forced labor—Equatorial Guinea
Politics and government. 569

Erasmus-Feit family. **750**

Ergushov, P. **751**

Erhard, Ludwig, 1897–1977. **752**
Portraits, caricatures, etc. 752

Erickson, Jack T. 3241

Eritrea—Nationalism. *see* Nationalism—Eritrea

Eritrean Liberation Front. 1498

Erlich, Henryk. 2142

Ermakov, Petr Zacharovich. **753**

Erman, Irma C. **754**

Erosion control. *see* Soil conservation

Escapes. 1591

Esmer, Mithat. 3166

Espionage. 1591
American—China. 1671
Austrian—U.S. 348
German. 1530, 3306
France. 3313, 3314
Russian. 1886
East (Far East). 3086
U.S. 2590

Essener Nationalzeitung. 1745

Estonia
see also Civil rights—Estonia; Communism—Estonia; European War, 1914–1918—Civilian relief—Estonia; League of Nations—Estonia; Political crimes and offenses—Estonia; Tallinn

Estonia (*continued*)
Bibliography. 2592
Commerce—Russia. 2274
Foreign relations. 1463, 2101, 2208
Latvia. 70
Russia. 1987, 2101
U.S. 1463
History. 1421, 1987
Politics and government. 755, 2041
Riigi Kohus. **755**

Estonian refugees. *see* Refugees, Estonian

"Estoniiâ i Pomoshch Golodaiushchim." **756**

Etchegoyen, Olivier, Comte d', b. 1873. **757**

Ethics, Military. *see* Military ethics

Ethiopia. **3297**, 3415, 3451
see also Droughts—Ethiopia; Nationalism—Eritrea
Foreign relations—Russia. 3418
History. 168, 3387
Periodicals. 3451
Politics and government. 1574, 3297, 3415

Ethiopian-Italian War, 1935–1936. *see* Italo-Ethiopian War, 1935–1936

Ethnikē Organōsis Kypriakon Agōnos. 572, 1075

Ethnogeographic Board, Washington, D.C. **758**

Ethnology
Cameroon. 2218
Germany—Pictorial works. 601
Nigeria. 3442
Ruanda-Urundi. 3456
Zaire—Shaba, Zaire (Province). 3423

Étolin, Adol'f Karlovich. 3488

Etter, Maria von. **759**

Etterg, General—Portraits, caricatures, etc. **760**

Eudin, Xenia Joukoff. 1872

Eudoxia, Mother. 1265

Food relief (*continued*)
  Germany (Territory under Allied occupation, 1945–1955. Russian Zone). 767, 810
  Greece. 2422
  Italy. 1254
  Japan. 490
  Luxemburg. 515
  Netherlands. 1892
  Norway. 1892
  Ougrée, Belgium. 1930
  Poland. 1254, 1892
  Russia. 2384, 2818

Food research. 2632

Food Research Institute. *see* Stanford University, Food Research Institute

Food supply. 45, 664, 1413, 1658, 2632, 2788, 2909
  Africa, West. 20
  Germany. 187, 974, 1259
    Berlin. 640
  Latin America. 923
  Spain. 567, 1330
  U.S. 1780, 2576, 2880

Forced labor
  see also Service, Compulsory non-military; World War, 1939–1945—Conscript labor
  Equatorial Guinea. 569
  Europe, Eastern. 517
  Germany. 2451
  Hungary. 1252
  In Germany collection. **840**
  Netherlands—letters. **841**
  Romania. 1712
  Russia. 76, 346, 517, 910, 1102, 1438, 2636, 2874
  Toulouse—collection. **842**
  White Russia. 362

Ford (Henry) leaflet. **843**

Ford, Mrs. Edsall P. **844**

Ford Peace Expedition. *see* Henry Ford Peace Expedition

Foreign aid program. *see* Economic assistance; Military assistance; Technical assistance

Foreign associations, institutions, etc. *see* Associations, institutions, etc., Foreign

Foreign correspondents, American—Correspondence, reminiscences, etc. 1745, 2757

Foreign enlistment—France. 1430

Foreign Missions Conference of North America. 490

Foreign Policy Association. **845**

Foreign relations. *see* International relations

Foreign trade regulation. 1564

Forgan, James Russell, 1900–1974. **846**

Formosa. *see* Taiwan

Fornel de la Laurencie, Benoît Léon, b. 1879. **847**

Forney, Edward H., d. 1965. **848**

Forrestal, James, 1892–1949. 212

Foss, F. F. **849**

Fotitch, Konstantin, 1891–1959. **850**

Foto-Willinger collection. **851**

Foundations (Endowments). *see* Endowments

Fourth International. 3061, 3122

Fox, Ernest F. **852**

Foyer des Orphelins, Charleroi, Belgium. 1323

Fraina, Louis C. *see* Corey, Lewis

France. 1849, 1864, 1884, 2043
  see also Banks and banking—France; Caricatures and cartoons—France; Charities—France; Communism—France; Elections—France; Electric industries—France; European War, 1914–1918—Alsace; European War, 1914–1918—Campaigns—France; European War, 1914–1918—Censorship—France; European War, 1914–1918—Civilian relief—France; European War, 1914–

France (*continued*)
  1918—Food question—France; European War, 1914—1918—France; European War, 1914–1918—Regimental histories—France; Excess profits tax—France; Family—France; Finance, Public—France; Food relief—France; Foreign enlistment—France; Freemasons. France; Hospitals, Military—France; Industrial laws and legislation—France; Labor and laboring classes—France; Medicine, Military—France; Metz, France; Military attachés, Russian—France; Money—France; Mutiny—France; Paris; Petroleum industry and trade—France; Poles in France; Political parties—France; Price regulation—Biarritz, France; Propaganda, German—France; Radicalism—France; Rationing, Consumer—Biarritz, France; Reconstruction (1914–1939)—France; Rethel, France; Rouen; Russians in France; Service, Compulsory non-military—France; Socialism in France; Soldiers' monuments—France; Spaniards in France; Strikes and lockouts—France; Student movements—France; Syndicalism—France; Trade and professional associations—France; Trade-unions—France; Trials (Treason)—France; War memorials—France; World War, 1939–1945—Campaigns—France; World War, 1939–1945—Campaigns—Normandy; World War, 1939–1945—Campaigns—Southern France; World War, 1939–1945—Censorship—France; World War, 1939–1945—Civilian relief—France; World War, 1939–1945—Collaborationists—France; World War, 1939–1945—France; World War, 1939–1945—Regimental histories—France; World War, 1939–1945—Underground movements—France; World War 1939–1945—War work—France; Youth—France
  1665–1871—collection. **853**
Agence Économique des Colonies. Bibliothèque. **3300**
Archives Nationales. 3446

Maricourt, André, Baron de, b. 1874. **1717**

Marie Jose, Princess of Belgium—Portraits, caricatures, etc. 651

Marie, Queen Consort of Alexander I, King of Yugoslavia, 1900–1961. **1718**

Marie, Queen Consort of Ferdinand, King of Romania. *see* Maria, Queen Consort of Ferdinand, King of Romania, 1875–1938

Marii︠a︡ Feodorovna, Empress Consort of Alexander III, Emperor of Russia, 1847–1928. 1590, **1719**

Marin, Patricia J., *collector.* **1720**

Maritime law. 359
see also Seizure of vessels and cargoes; War, Maritime (International law)
Russia. 1082

Maritime Province, Siberia
see also Japanese in Maritime Province, Siberia
History. 84, 88
Pictorial works. 1051
Komissii︠a︡ po Obsledovanii︠u︡ Obstoi︠a︡tel'stv Sobytii 4-6 Apreli︠a︡ vo Vladivostoke. **1721**
Vremennoe Priamurskoe Pravitel'stvo. 1508
Narodnoe Sobranie. 1508
Osvedomitel'nyi Otdel Sibirskoi Flotilii. 1508
Sibirskai︠a︡ Flotilii︠a︡. 88

Marizus, J. **1722**

Marketing. 2694

Markov, Anatolii. **1723**

Markov, Sergei Leonidovich, 1878–1918. 1300

Markov, Walter. **1724**

Marković, Lazar, 1882–1955. **1725**

Marmon, Howard C., 1876–1960. **1726**

Marshall, George Catlett, 1880–1959. 419

Marshall, Herbert. **1727**

Marshall Islands. 1008
World War, 1939–1945. *see* World War, 1939–1945—Campaigns—Marshall Islands; World War, 1939–1945—Marshall Islands

Marshall Islands (Territory under U.S. occupation, 1944–). 424

Marshall McDonald and Associates. **1728**

Marshall Plan. *see* Economic assistance, American

Martens, Ludwig Christian Alexander Karl, 1874–1948. 1111, **1729**

Martens, R. C. **1730**

Marti, José, 1853–1895. 2432

Martin, David, 1914– . **1731**

Martin, Henri Ursin Clément, 1927– . 3404

Martin, William, 1888–1934. **1732**

Martinez-Lorenzo, Cesar. **1733**

Martov, I︠U︡lii Osipovich, 1873–1923. **1734**

Marty, André Pierre, 1886–1956. **3404**

Martynov, A. P., d. 1951. **1735**

Martynov, General. **1736**

Martynov, Zakhar Nikiforovich. **1737**

Maruki, R. **1738**

Marvin Liebman Associates, 1958–1969. **1739**

Marx, Charles D. 44

Marx, Guido Hugo, 1871–1949. **1740**

Marx, Karl, 1818–1883. 2697, 3111

Marxian sociology. *see* Communism and society

Marxism. *see* Communism; Socialism

Maryland (Battleship). 2098
Pictorial works. 2485

Masaryk, Tomas Garrigue, 1850–1937. **1741**

Masland, John Wesley, Jr., 1912–1968. **1742**

Maslov, Sergei Semenovich. **1743**

Maslovskii, Evgenii Vasil'evich. **1744**

Mason, Frank Earl, 1893– . 1166, **1745**

Mason, James B. **1746**

Mason, John Brown, 1904– . **1747**

Mason, Kenneth J. **1748**

Masons (Secret order). *see* Freemasons

Mass communication. *see* Telecommunication; Communication

Massachusetts
Institute of Technology. Center for International Studies. 3399
National Guard. 1690

Massenburg, Carrie B. 1166

Matabele War, 1893. 355

Matabele War, 1896. 355

Material relating to the Congo, Leopoldville, from the collection of Robert E. Bartlett. **3405**

Materialism. 2773
Dialectical. *see* Dialectical materialism

Mathews, Forrest David, 1935– . **1749**